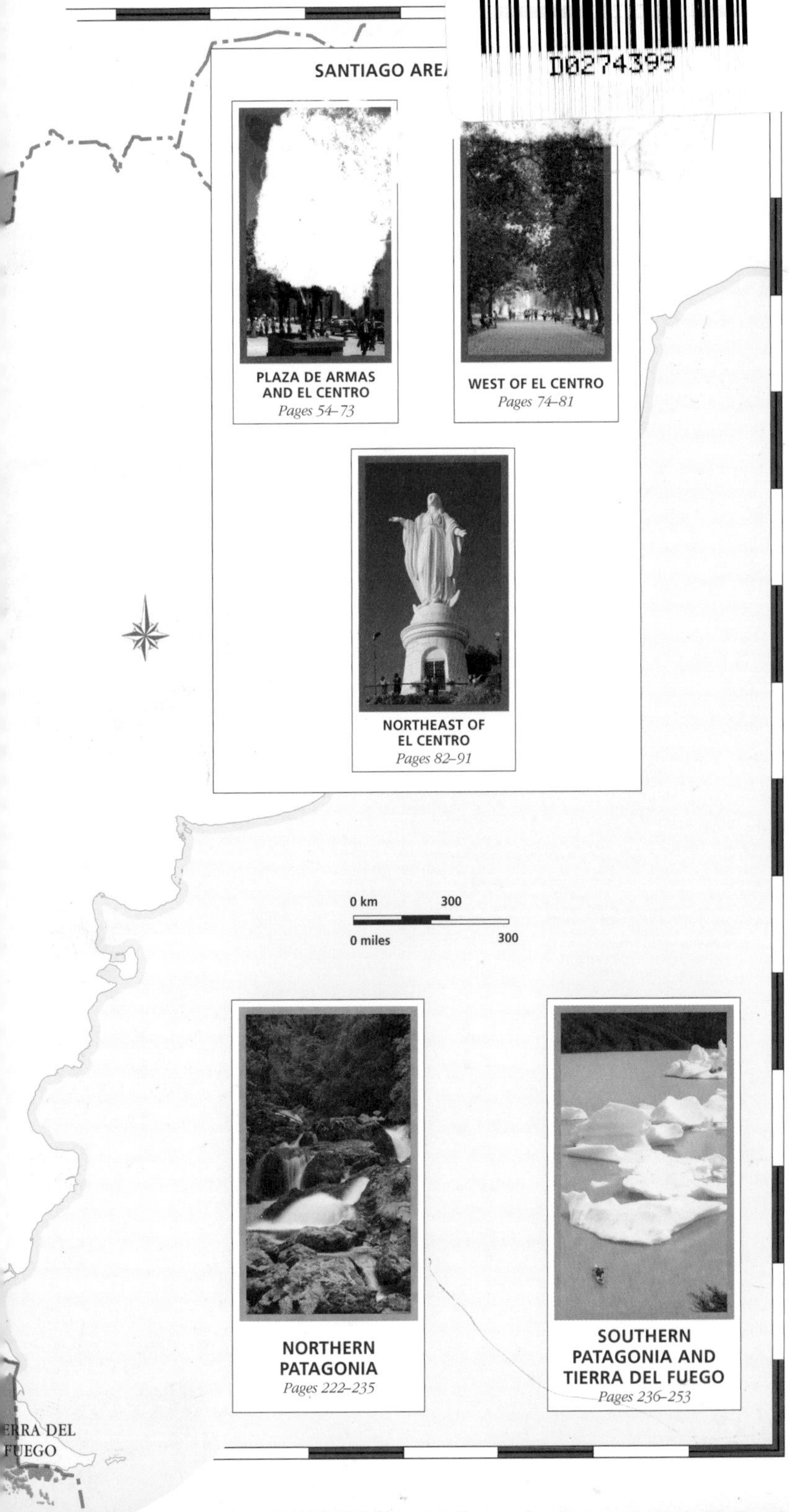
SANTIAGO AREA
PLAZA DE ARMAS AND EL CENTRO
Pages 54–73
WEST OF EL CENTRO
Pages 74–81
NORTHEAST OF EL CENTRO
Pages 82–91
0 km
300
0 miles
300
NORTHERN PATAGONIA
Pages 222–235
SOUTHERN PATAGONIA AND TIERRA DEL FUEGO
Pages 236–253
ERRA DEL
FUEGO

EYEWITNESS TRAVEL

CHILE AND EASTER ISLAND

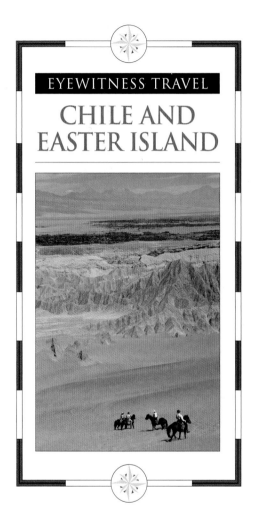

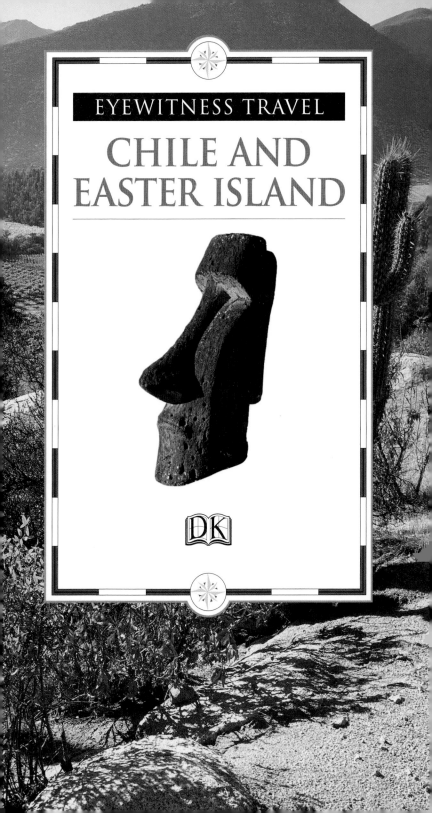

EYEWITNESS TRAVEL

CHILE AND EASTER ISLAND

DK

LONDON, NEW YORK,
MELBOURNE, MUNICH AND DELHI
www.dk.com

MANAGING EDITOR Aruna Ghose
SENIOR EDITORIAL MANAGER Savitha Kumar
SENIOR DESIGN MANAGER Priyanka Thakur
PROJECT EDITOR Sandhya Iyer
PROJECT DESIGNER Stuti Tiwari Bhatia
EDITOR Divya Chowfin
DESIGNER Neha Dhingra
SENIOR CARTOGRAPHIC MANAGER Uma Bhattacharya
CARTOGRAPHER Mohammad Hassan
DTP DESIGNER Azeem Siddiqui

A CIP CATALOGUE RECORD IS AVAILABLE FROM THE BRITISH LIBRARY.

ISBN 978-1-4053-5877-4

FLOORS ARE REFERRED TO THROUGHOUT IN ACCORDANCE WITH AMERICAN USAGE; IE THE "FIRST FLOOR" IS AT GROUND LEVEL.

Front cover main image: Torres del Paine National Park

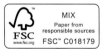

MIX
Paper from responsible sources
FSC www.fsc.org
FSC™ C018179

The information in this DK Eyewitness Travel Guide is checked regularly.

Every effort has been made to ensure that this book is as up-to-date as possible at the time of going to press. Some details, however, such as telephone numbers, opening hours, prices, gallery hanging arrangements and travel information are liable to change. The publishers cannot accept responsibility for any consequences arising from the use of this book, nor for any material on third party websites, and cannot guarantee that any website address in this book will be a suitable source of travel information. We value the views and suggestions of our readers very highly. Please write to Publisher, DK Eyewitness Travel Guides, Dorling Kindersley, 80 Strand, London WC2R 0RL, or to travelguides@uk.dk.com.

Guanacos in Southern Patagonia

CONTENTS

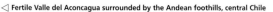

Dancers performing during the Fiestas Patrias celebrations

◁ **Fertile Valle del Aconcagua surrounded by the Andean foothills, central Chile**

Iconic Easter Island *moai*

White-water rafting on Río Futaleufú, Northen Patagonia

The Jesuit Iglesia de Achao, Chiloé

HOW TO USE THIS GUIDE

This guide helps you get the most from your visit to Chile and Easter Island. It provides detailed practical information and expert recommendations. *Introducing Chile and Easter Island* maps the country and its regions, sets it in historical and cultural context, and describes events and festivals through the year. *Chile and Easter Island Region by Region* is the main sightseeing section. It covers all the important sights, with maps, photographs, and illustrations. Information on hotels, restaurants, shops, entertainment, and sports is found in *Travelers' Needs*. The *Survival Guide* has advice on everything from travel to medical services, banks, and communications.

SANTIAGO AREA BY AREA

Chile's capital, dealt with in a separate section, is divided into three sightseeing areas. Each area has its own chapter, which opens with an introduction and a list of the sights described. All sights are plotted on an *Area Map*. The key to the map symbols is on the back flap.

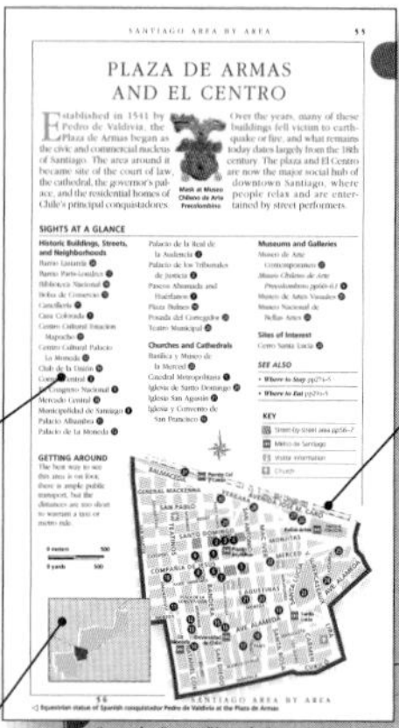

Sights at a Glance lists the chapter's sights by category: Historic Streets and Buildings, Museums and Galleries, Parks and Gardens, and so on.

A locator map shows where the area is in relation to other parts of the city.

1 Area Map

Sights are numbered on a map. Within a chapter, information on each sight follows the numerical order on the map. Sights in each area are also located on the Santiago Street Finder *maps on pages 102–109.*

All pages relating to Santiago have red thumb tabs.

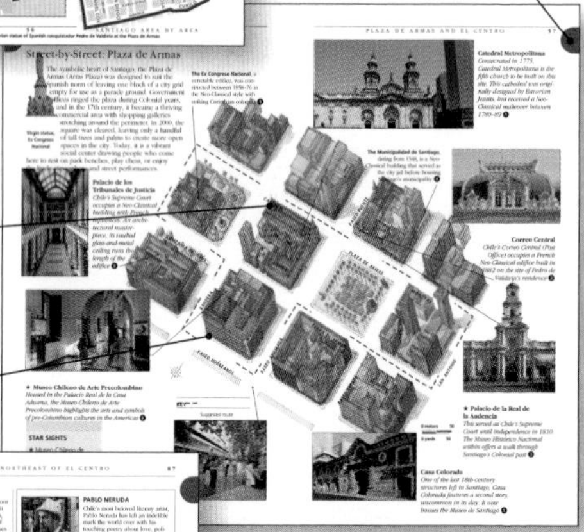

2 Street-by-Street Map

This gives a bird's-eye view of the key area in a chapter.

A suggested route for a walk is shown in red.

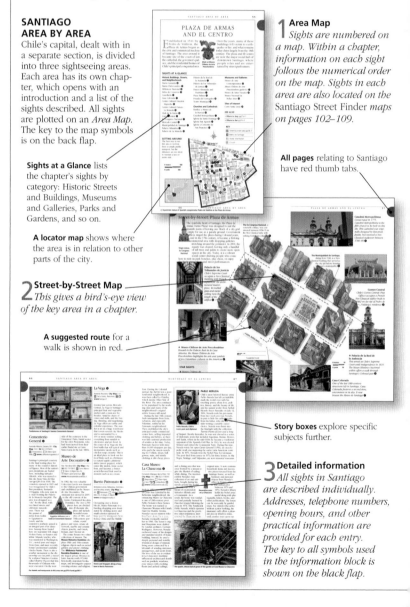

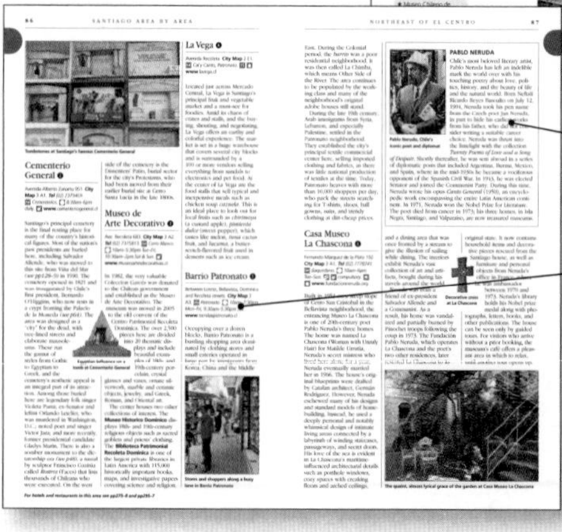

Story boxes explore specific subjects further.

3 Detailed information

All sights in Santiago are described individually. Addresses, telephone numbers, opening hours, and other practical information are provided for each entry. The key to all symbols used in the information block is shown on the black flap.

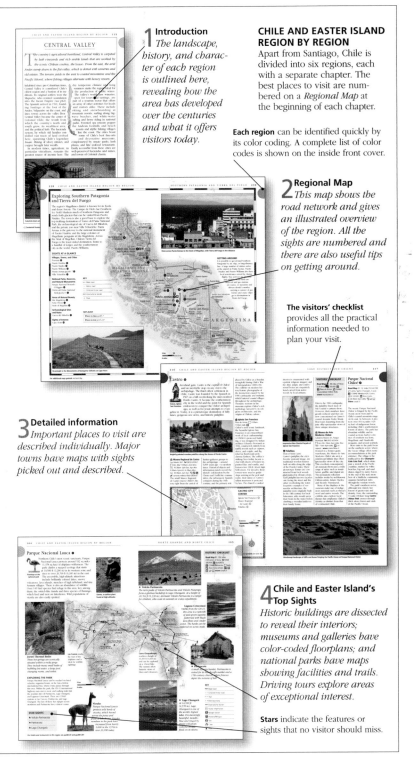

1 Introduction

The landscape, history, and character of each region is outlined here, revealing how the area has developed over the centuries and what it offers visitors today.

CHILE AND EASTER ISLAND REGION BY REGION

Apart from Santiago, Chile is divided into six regions, each with a separate chapter. The best places to visit are numbered on a *Regional Map* at the beginning of each chapter.

Each region can be identified quickly by its color coding. A complete list of color codes is shown on the inside front cover.

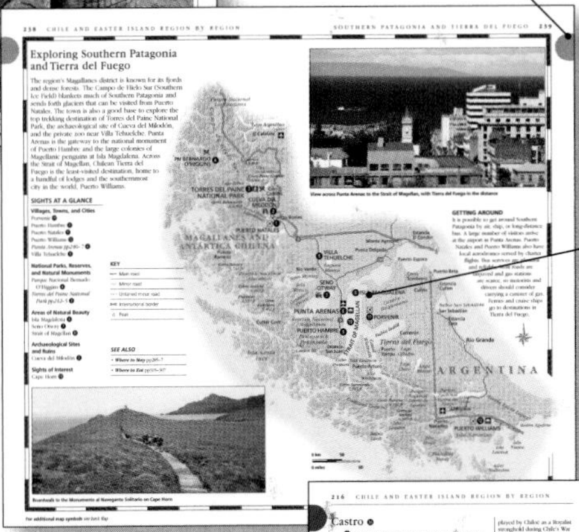

2 Regional Map

This map shows the road network and gives an illustrated overview of the region. All the sights are numbered and there are also useful tips on getting around.

The visitors' checklist provides all the practical information needed to plan your visit.

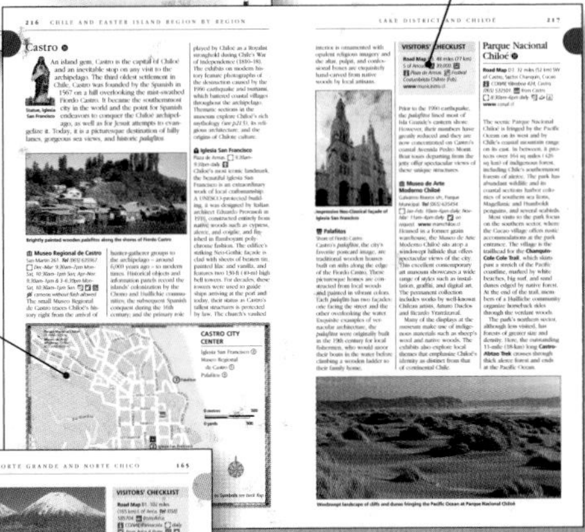

3 Detailed information

Important places to visit are described individually. Major towns have maps with sights picked out and described.

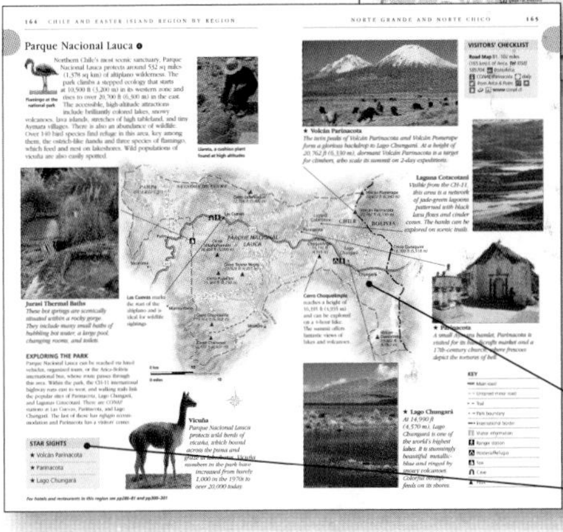

4 Chile and Easter Island's Top Sights

Historic buildings are dissected to reveal their interiors; museums and galleries have color-coded floorplans; and national parks have maps showing facilities and trails. Driving tours explore areas of exceptional interest.

Stars indicate the features or sights that no visitor should miss.

INTRODUCING CHILE AND EASTER ISLAND

DISCOVERING CHILE AND EASTER ISLAND

Visitors to Chile are often surprised by the sheer variety of landscapes that make up this thin country, including arid desert, fertile valleys, lakes and volcanoes, rain forest, beaches, vast prairie, and towering peaks. Given this huge diversity, many consider Chile to be one of South America's key adventure-travel destinations. Patagonia is Chile's most popular stop, but travelers are also discovering the central wine country, the awe-inspiring moonscape of the vast Atacama desert, and the Polynesian culture and archaeological sites of Easter Island. However, domestic air travel is necessary to pack several destinations into one trip.

Ceramic pot, Los Andes

SANTIAGO

- **Architecture in El Centro**
- **Bohemian neighborhoods**
- **Parque Metropolitana de Santiago's sweeping views**

Chile's capital city is best known for its sensational Andean backdrop and its proximity to destinations on the coast and in the Central Valley. Of historic interest in the city is the **Plaza de Armas and El Centro** *(see pp54–73)*, beginning with the central plaza and its Neo-Classical Palacio de la Moneda. The Iglesia San Francisco and Posada del Corregidor are rare examples of Colonial architecture, most buildings of the period having succumbed to earthquakes. Bellavista and **Barrio Lastarría** *(see p70)* exhude bohemia with arts centers, theaters, and cafés, while **Barrio Vitacura** *(see p90)* is best for dining. The green **Parque Metropolitana de Santiago** *(see pp84–5)* on Cerro San Cristobal is dotted with swimming pools, nature trails, funicular rides, and breathtaking views.

Shops and eateries in the Bellavista neighborhood, Santiago

CENTRAL VALLEY

- **Top-notch vineyards**
- **Historic Valparaíso**
- **Andean ski resorts**

The fertile valleys surrounding Santiago hold the remnants of large hacienda-style farms such as **Hacienda Los Lingues** *(see p146)*. The Andes here are home to world-class ski-restorts that draw international visitors each year from June to October. However, Central Valley's biggest attraction is wine. The best-known vineyards are found in **Colchagua Valley** *(see pp148–9)* and **Casablanca Valley** *(see pp138–9)*, both of which offer tours and tastings. On the Central Valley coast is **Valparaíso** *(see pp118–27)*, a UNESCO World Heritage Site. This vibrant city intrigues visitors with a labyrinth of streets, rich history, and madcap architecture.

A herd of vicuña on the altiplano stretch of Parque Nacional Lauca

NORTE GRANDE AND NORTE CHICO

- **Otherworldly terrain of the Atacama desert**
- **Parque Nacional Lauca**
- **Star gazing**

The Atacama, the world's driest desert, and its adobe village **San Pedro de Atacama** *(see p174)* take center stage in this region. Lunar landscapes, purple volcanoes, and high Andean culture make this one of Chile's most popular destinations. The desert's unique flora and fauna are conserved in **Parque Nacional Lauca** *(see pp164–5)*. The clearest skies in the southern hemisphere and some of the world's best observatories are based in the Atacama. These include the **Cerro Paranal Observatory** *(see p177)* and the **Cerro Mamalluca Observatory** *(see p182)*.

◁ Carved depiction of traditional mountain life in Chile

Lago Villarrica, with the eponymous volcano in the background

LAKE DISTRICT AND CHILOÉ

- **Adventure at Pucón**
- **Old towns and forts**
- **Jesuit churches in Chiloé**

Lush panoramas of rain forest and snowcapped peaks draw many visitors to the Lake District, a region also known for adventure activities such rafting, trekking, and back-country skiing. The resort-town **Pucón** *(see p196)* is a popular holiday spot and base for climbs to the top of the smoking volcano in **Parque Nacional Villarrica** *(see pp198–9)*. Abundant geo-thermal activity near Pucón has spawned hot springs that are the ultimate in relaxation. The charming towns **Puerto Varas** *(see p207)* and **Puerto Montt** *(see pp212–13)* feature architecture and cuisine that is heavily influenced by German immigration, while **Valdivia** *(see pp202–203)* and its nearby forts are vivid reminders of the era of Spanish occupation.

South of the Lake District, Chiloé prides itself on its self-sufficiency. Its fascinating culture and folklore make this archipelago truly one-of-a-kind. The capital, **Castro** *(see pp216–17)*, is one of the few sites on Chiloé to retain its *palafitos*, houses on stilts. There are many Jesuit churches in Chiloé *(see pp220–21)*, 16 of which are a UNESCO World Heritage Site.

NORTHERN PATAGONIA

- **Majestic fjordland**
- **Pristine rain forests in national parks**
- **Fly-fishing**

Chile's least visited region, Northern Patagonia could easily be considered the country's best-kept secret. There are no large towns here, except **Coyhaique** *(see p232)*, the regional capital. Road improvements, especially the building of the Carretera Austral, have made this area Chile's definitive road-trip experience. Yet perhaps, the best way to see Northern Patagonia is by cruise or kayak in order to soak in the beauty of the country's emerald fjords. The area's dense forests can be seen in **Parque Pumalín** *(see p226)* and **Parque Nacional de Laguna San Rafael** *(see p233)*. Between November and March, dozens of fly-fishing lodges attract enthusiasts.

SOUTHERN PATAGONIA AND TIERRA DEL FUEGO

- **Torres del Paine**
- **Cruises to Tierra del Fuego**
- **Penguin colonies**

The country's most extreme destination, both for its inclement weather and rugged landscapes, is a magnet for travelers who come to trek, ride, and savor magnificent sanctuaries such as **Torres del Paine National Park** *(see pp242–5)*. Tours and cruises take visitors to penguin colonies off **Seno Otway** *(see p247)* and across the **Strait of Magellan** *(see p250)* to Tierra del Fuego. Those keen to reach **Cape Horn** *(see p251)*, the southern tip of the continent, may have to brave rough seas.

EASTER ISLAND AND ROBINSON CRUSOE

- **Historic sites and *moai***
- **Endemic flora and fauna**

The highlights of Easter Island are the large *moai* statues at sites such as **Rano Raraku** *(see pp262–3)*, but pristine beaches, scuba-diving, and the island's unique Rapa Nui culture are also big draws. Robinson Crusoe Island offers adventures in the wild, with dense forests, scuba-diving, and trekking to sites such as **Mirador Selkirk** *(see p267)*.

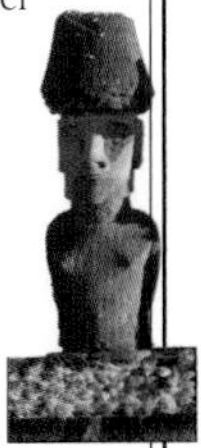
Standing *moai*

Ice floes on Lago Grey, Torres del Paine National Park

Putting Chile and Easter Island on the Map

Chile runs along the western edge of South America and is wedged between the Andes in the east and the Pacific Ocean in the west. It is bordered by the countries of Peru and Bolivia in the north and Argentina in the east. The most striking aspect of Chile is its thin, long shape – spanning some 2,600 miles (4,190 km) from 17° to 56° latitude south, there is no area of Chile that measures more than 115 miles (185 km) in width. The nation is divided into 15 *regiones* (regions) and is occupied by more than 16.3 million inhabitants, of whom nearly 6 million live in Santiago. Chile also claims Easter Island, Robinson Crusoe Island, and a slice of Antarctica as part of its territory. Hanga Roa, the main city on Easter Island, lies about 2,350 miles (3,780 km) west of Santiago.

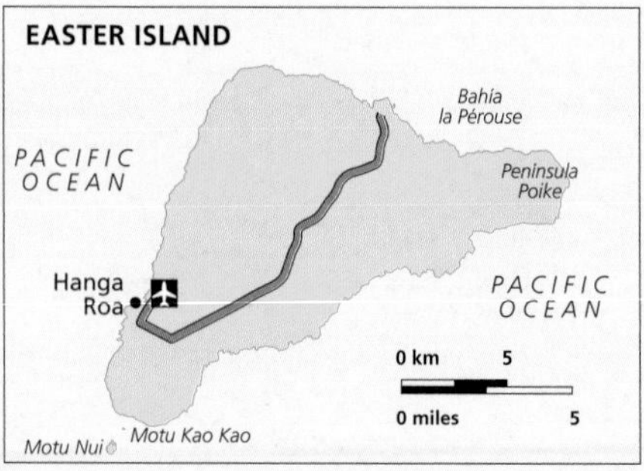

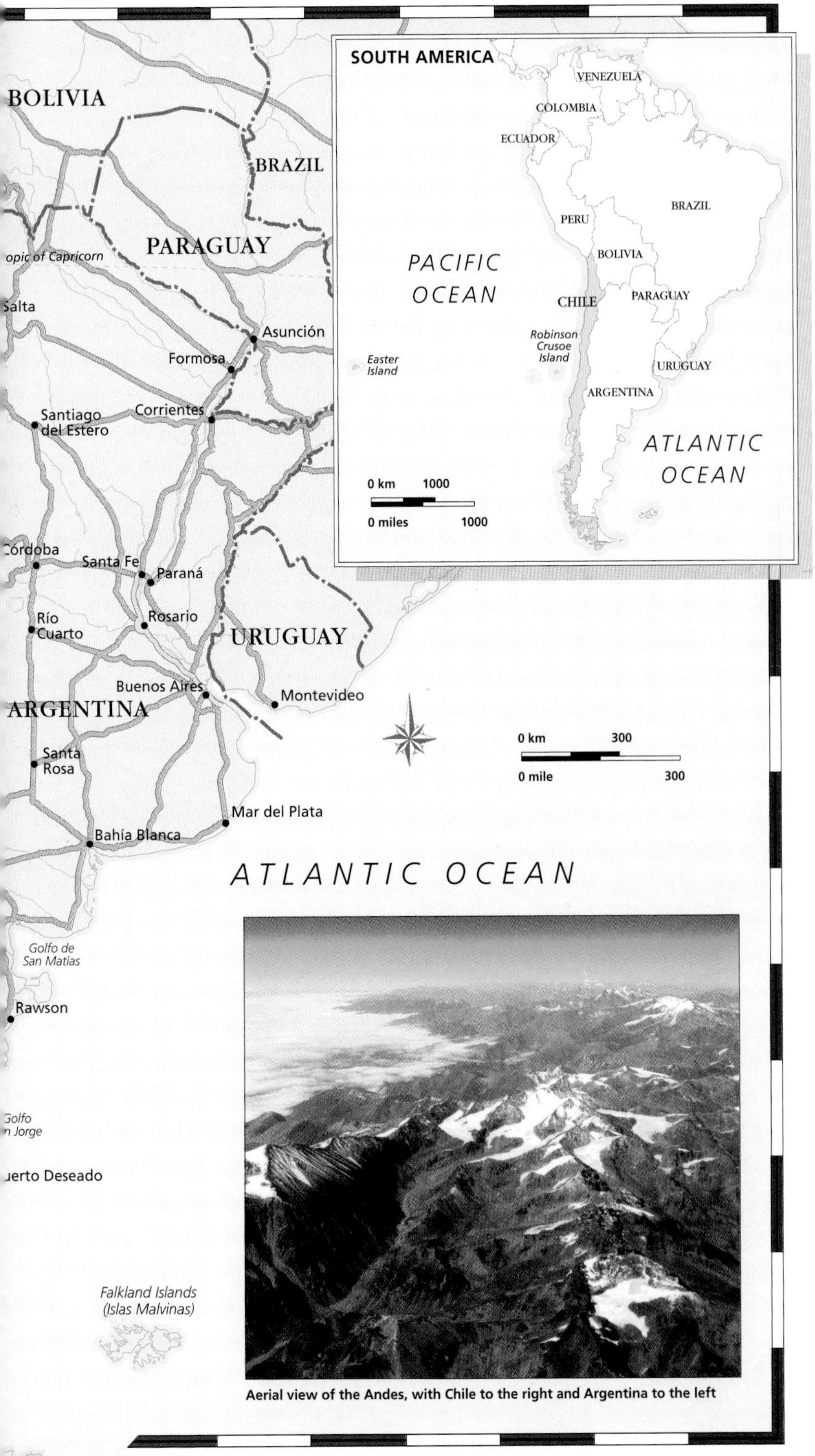

Aerial view of the Andes, with Chile to the right and Argentina to the left

A PORTRAIT OF CHILE AND EASTER ISLAND

A narrow sliver of land on the western edge of South America, Chile is an area of diverse natural beauty, a model of economic prosperity, a politically stable nation, and an emerging paradise for wine connoisseurs. Isolated from the mainland by the Pacific, Easter Island enthralls with its iconic moai *and Polynesian heritage.*

Extending over 39 degrees of latitude, Chile embraces a stunning variety of terrain from the world's driest desert to the ice fields of Patagonia and Antarctica. However, most of this area is unsettled, as the majority of Chile's 16.3 million inhabitants live in the sprawling capital of Santiago and in a handful of other urban centers. A part of Chilean territory, Easter Island is the most remote place on the globe to be populated, with its few thousand inhabitants living in the small capital town of Hanga Roa.

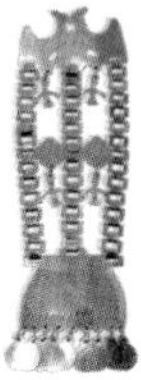

A Mapuche silver necklace

Evidence of human presence in Chile dates from as far back as 13,000 BC and until the 15th century, numerous indigenous groups flourished here. The following centuries saw the Spanish conquest of Chile and the influx of immigrants from Europe. Few ethnic groups have survived these changes and those that have, keep their age-old traditions alive in remote villages and on reservations.

Modern-day Chile has emerged as Latin America's safest country and has excellent tourist facilities. It offers an incredible range of activities, from skiing down volcano slopes and hiking through rain forest to surfing and wildlife-watching. Chile's many vibrant festivals offer an insight into the nation's rich cultural heritage.

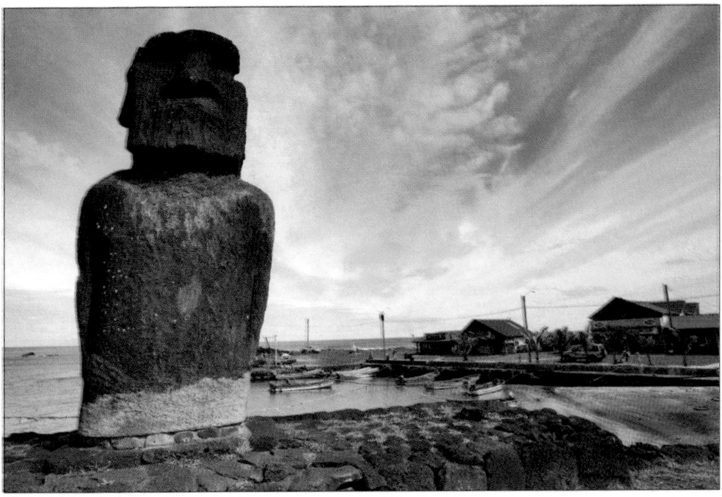

Moai atop the Ahu Tautira platform near Hanga Roa's pier, Easter Island

◁ Chilean *huasos* on horseback at the Fundo Reñihue estate in remote Patagonia

Llamas in the vicinity of Volcán Pomerape and Volcán Parinacota, at Parque Nacional Lauca

LAND AND NATURE

Chile's natural spaces are extensive given the lack of dense human population. The upper third of the country is the dry Atacama desert, known for its otherworldly landscapes. It is bordered on the south by the lush Central Valley, Chile's agricultural belt, and the rain forests, lakes, and snow-capped volcanoes of the Lake District. Farther south, the land breaks to form the many fjords, granite peaks, and awe-inspiring glaciers of Patagonia.

The natural wealth of this land supports the bulk of Chile's economy, with the result that industries such as mining, agriculture, and fishing have, till recently, taken precedence over conservation. On Easter Island, centuries of human intervention has destroyed the island's native forests and palm stands. Growing concern about threats to the ecology has spawned initiatives across Chile. Patagonia Sin Represas, for instance, opposes plans for hydroelectric plants in southern Chile. The Conservation Land Trust, founded by environmentalist Douglas Tompkins, promotes ecotourism and sustainable farming.

ECONOMY

Chile's economy stands out among its South American neighbors for its stability, relative lack of corruption, and overall health. Its foundations, interestingly, were laid during the Pinochet regime which replaced socialist economic policies with plans based on privatization, free market, and stable inflation. By the 1990s, Chile had experienced an economic boom with a seven percent average annual growth. The country faced the 2008 economic slowdown with over US$20 billion in a sovereign wealth fund, averting a major crisis.

A major exporter of minerals, Chile has emerged as the world's top producer of copper, and the state-run Codelco is the largest copper mining agency on the globe. Thriving tourism, along with fishing and subsistence farming, is the backbone of Easter Island's economy.

Economic prosperity has brought about rapid development, reducing poverty. Chile's vast pay inequality, however, is still a problem, along with *pituto*, or nepotism, common even in the most modern corporations.

Fishing boats docked at Hanga Roa, Easter Island

POLITICS AND GOVERNMENT

After years of military dictatorship, Chile has emerged as a strong democratic republic which operates under a constitution. The government comprises the executive, judiciary, and legislative branches, and is led by the president, who is both the head of state and head of government. The country itself is divided into 15 administrative regions and a federal capital.

Chile's Fabian Orellan in a soccer match against Colombia in 2009

Annexed by the Chilean navy in 1888, Easter Island is governed as a province of the Valparaíso region (Región V). Its residents were granted Chilean citizenship only in 1966, and in 2007, the island was recognized as a special territory of Chile.

SPORTS AND ARTS

As in all Latin American countries, *fútbol* (soccer) is a national craze in Chile. Since the last few decades, the country has also made news in the field of tennis with international medal winners such as Nicolás Massú and Fernando González. Golf, skiing, and surfing are popular sports among Chileans. The rodeo remains a much-loved sport in the countryside.

Chile has produced a number of composers and musicians of international renown. While pianist Claudio Arrau remains unparalleled in the arena of classical music, acts such as Congreso and Los Jaivas have brought Chilean folklore into the limelight. Santiago's Teatro Municipal *(see p69)* is the country's foremost cultural institution and hosts world-class opera, symphony, and ballet performances. Chile boasts a rich and long-standing tradition of theater, which is best reflected in the vibrant Festival Internacional Teatro a Mil.

Chile's key contribution, however, is in the field of literature. Chilean writers and poets have enjoyed worldwide acclaim, most notably the Nobel laureates Pablo Neruda and Gabriela Mistral.

PEOPLE AND SOCIETY

There is a staggering contrast between urban and rural lifestyles in Chile. Santiago is known for its cosmopolitan finesse and great cultural and culinary scene. While the new-age residents of this metropolis are fashionable and tech-savvy, people in remote villages still cook over wood-burning stoves and plough their fields with oxen. Spanish is Chile's official language, but indigenous groups speak in their native tongues. Christianity is the predominant religion, though folk religion remains important for many ethnic and rural groups. On Easter Island, religious practices reflect the syncretization of Christian and Polynesian beliefs. Overall, Chilean society is both tolerant and friendly.

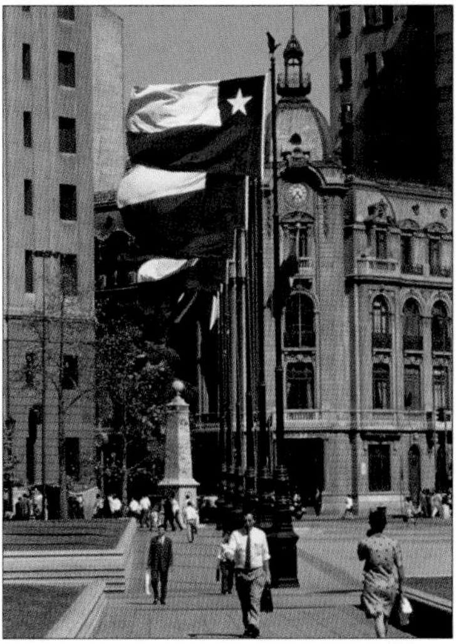

Flags flutter over Plaza de la Constitucíon, Santiago

Landscape and Wildlife

Humboldt penguin

Hemmed in by the towering Andes range in the east, the Pacific Ocean in the west, a vast desert in the north, and thousands of islands and glaciers in the south, Chile incorporates a range of landscapes, from farmlands and forests to immense lakes and ice fields. A part of the geothermally active Pacific Ring of Fire, Chile is also home to a total of 36 live volcanoes and an abundance of thermal hot springs. Owing to its near isolation from the rest of the continent, much of the country's flora and fauna is endemic and is protected in numerous national (as well as some private) parks, reserves, and monuments.

Sparkling waters off the white sands of Playa Anakena, on Easter Island

PLATEAU AND COASTAL DESERT

Chile's desert is the driest in the world. It is composed largely of sand, salt basins, mineral-rich peaks, and volcanoes, interspersed with oases that are fed by aquifers. Near the coast, a Pacific fog known as Camanchaca provides enough moisture for cacti, shrubs, and lichen.

Chilean flamingos *can be seen on the saline altiplano lakes searching for tiny crustaceans, whose carotenoids give the birds their pink color.*

Vicuñas, *smallest of the camelids, graze in groups at high altitudes.*

The vizcacha *is a long-tailed, yellow and brown rodent, part of the chinchilla family. It feeds on vegetation and can frequently be seen at twilight, when it is most active.*

CENTRAL VALLEY

The flat, green valleys of central Chile are divided by the Andes and coastal mountains, and watered by rivers that descend from the Andes. The Mediterranean-like climate here is conducive to agriculture – mostly fruits and vegetables – and to wine production.

The quisco *dominates the lower Andes and is one of the few cacti that can withstand cold and snow.*

The Chilean palm *has a smooth, gray trunk that is rotund in the middle or upper reaches.*

The Andean condor, *Chile's national bird, is one of the world's largest fowls, with a wingspan of over 9 ft (3 m).*

TECTONIC ACTIVITY

The towering Andes mountain range and the hundreds of volcanoes that make up the spine of Chile are the result of plate tectonics: the movement of interlocking plates of the earth's crust that ride on molten material (magma) in the mantle. Along the Chilean coast, the Nazca plate and the South American plate collide and create a subduction zone, whereby the Nazca plate is forced under the South American plate, creating the Peru-Chile Trench. As one of the fastest-moving plates, the Nazca is capable of triggering spectacular earthquakes, such as the 8.8-magnitude quake that affected central Chile in February 2010, and the 9.5-magnitude earthquake in Valdivia in 1960, the strongest recorded in the world.

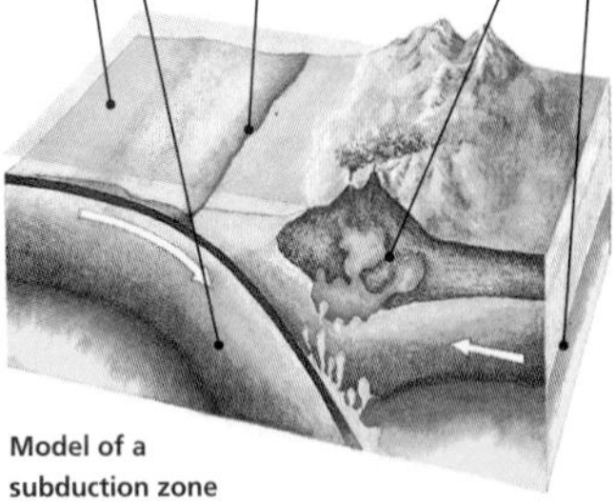

Model of a subduction zone

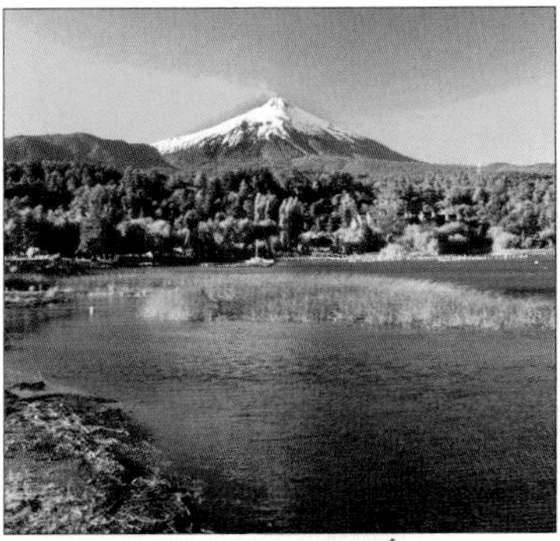

LAKE DISTRICT AND CHILOÉ

The lush Lake District is characterized by snowcapped volcanoes, crystalline lakes and rivers, emerald farmland, and dense Valdivian rain forest. It is home to the alerce, the second-oldest tree on the planet, and the nalca, whose leaves can reach 7 ft (2 m) in diameter.

Copihue, *or the Chilean bellflower, is a waxy red flower which grows in twisted vines around trees and plants. It is Chile's national flower.*

The pudú *is the world's smallest deer, reaching just 33 inches (85 cm) in length. It lives in the dense underbrush of temperate rain forests.*

Monkey-puzzle, *or araucaria, is an evergreen conifer whose branches and razor-sharp leaves take on an umbrella shape.*

PATAGONIA AND TIERRA DEL FUEGO

The windswept pampa grassland of Patagonia forms part of a region packed with granite peaks, glacier fields, fjords, and sheep ranches known as estancias. Adventure-seekers come here for trekking, fly-fishing, and mountain climbing in dramatic, untamed wilderness.

The guanaco, *a camelid, exists in robust populations in the wild and can be spotted throughout Patagonia.*

Pumas *are agile animals with an exceptional leaping ability. These elusive cats can usually only be seen when feeding on a fresh kill.*

The huemul, *or South Andean deer, is an endangered species that is shy, solitary, and stocky, with large ears and short legs.*

The Biodiversity of Chile

A paradise for nature lovers, Chile has a varied landscape which supports a wealth of flora and fauna. The country's rich natural heritage is protected through 33 national parks, 48 national reserves, and 15 national monuments – about 19 percent of the total national territory. Chile is considered a "continental island" because it is isolated from neighboring countries by the Andes mountains, the Pacific Ocean, and the arid Atacama desert. As a result, more than half of its flora is endemic. This is especially true of southern Chile's Valdivian forest, the only temperate rain forest in South America. In regrettable contrast, most of Easter Island's native forests and fauna have disappeared as a result of many centuries of human activity.

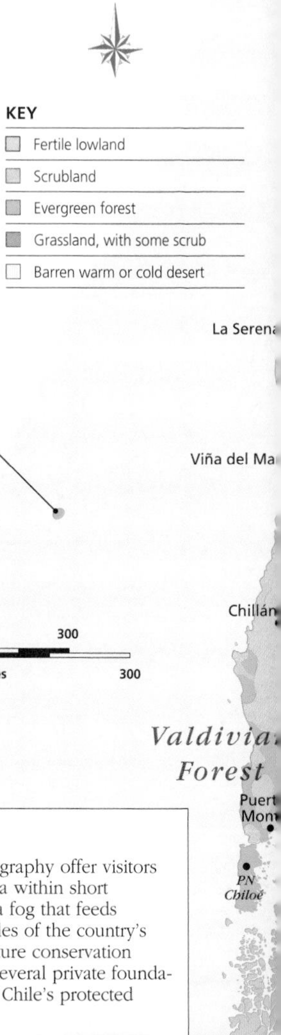

Robinson Crusoe Island (see pp266–7), *through geological isolation, has produced a hothouse of endemic flora that represents two-thirds of the island's vegetation and the highest density of endemic plants in the world. The island has been a UNESCO-designated World Biosphere Reserve since 1997. However, botanists fear that the introduction of alien plant species now threatens the island's ecosystem.*

UNSURPASSED DELIGHTS

Chile's microclimates, geographical isolation, and varying topography offer visitors a chance to experience contrasting landscapes and myriad flora within short distances. Rare phenomena, such as the coastal Camanchaca, a fog that feeds vegetation in the otherwise barren northern desert, are examples of the country's unique biodiversity. In addition, Chile's growing interest in nature conservation has boosted animal populations throughout the country, and several private foundations have established reserves to encourage the expansion of Chile's protected areas and preserve its unique flora and fauna.

The arid Atacama *explodes with wildflowers after an infrequent rain. This phenomenon is known as the Desierto Florido* (see p181).

The firecrown hummingbird, *an endemic and dimorphic species of Robinson Crusoe Island, is one of the rarest birds in the world.*

Parque Nacional Lauca (see pp164–5) *is northern Chile's hotspot for viewing fauna. It has large representations of the country's four camelid species – alpaca, guanaco, llama, and vicuña – over 140 species of birds, and endemic fauna such as the vizcacha.*

Parque Nacional La Campana *(see p135)* is home to the magnificent *Nothofagus oblique*. This tree is the northernmost representation of the 10 *Nothofagus*, or southern beech, species of Chile.

Parque Nacional Alerce Andino (see p213) *harbors large stands of alerce, which date to over 3,500 years. This area is part of the Valdivian rain forest belt, where one-third of the plant species are remnants of the Gondwana supercontinent.*

Isla Magdalena (see p247) *hosts nesting colonies of Magellanic penguins from November to March each year. The largest temperate-climate penguin, members of this species share parental responsibilities equally and can be seen marching comically in single file from their nesting burrows to the sea in the morning and afternoon.*

WHALE CONSERVATION

The waters off Chile's shores are home to over half the world's whale species. Indeed, Herman Melville's masterpiece *Moby Dick* was based on a giant albino sperm whale, Mocha Dick, that harassed ships near Chile's Isla Mocha in the 19th century. Fresh sightings of the humpback, blue, and southern right whales in recent times, signal the comeback of a mammal once nearly hunted into extinction. Several non-profit associations have formed to study whale behavior, and in 2008, the Chilean government designated all national waters a whale sanctuary. Chile is poised to become one of the world's greatest whale-watching destinations, and growing interest has spawned new opportunities to see these magnificent creatures.

A breaching humpback whale

Peoples of Chile and Easter Island

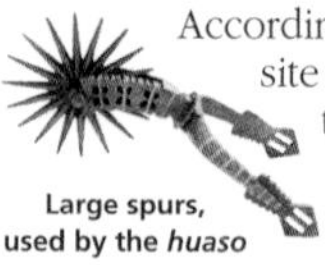
Large spurs, used by the *huaso*

According to studies at the archaeological site of Monte Verde in southern Chile, the first inhabitants of this country arrived around 13,000 years ago. Over the following centuries, these nomadic tribes populated the length of Chile, either as land hunters or seafarers. From the 16th century onward, Chile experienced sporadic immigration at intervals – first the Spanish conquistadores and later German, Swiss, English, Croatian, and Italian arrivals. Today, the majority of the 16.3 million Chileans are mestizo – people of mixed ethnic and European ancestry. Indigenous groups have been reduced to a minority, with a total population of just under one million.

Aymara dancers in bright fiesta clothing in Arica

Mapuche silver jewelry includes a pectoral pendant known as a *pentreor.*

Makuñ is a colorful, finely woven poncho worn by Mapuche men and boys.

The Mapuche *live in the Lake District, many on* reducciones, *or reservations, where they are engaged in a battle to repatriate land taken by settlers or the government over the last centuries.*

INDIGENOUS CHILEANS

Chile was the last country to be conquered by the Spanish, yet what remains of Chile's indigenous groups today represents only five percent of the population. The principal ethnic group is the Mapudungun-speaking Mapuche, with just under 700,000 members, or 87 percent of the total indigenous population. Just nine of Chile's original 14 ethnic groups remain, and several are expected to disappear over the next decade.

The Aymara *is Chile's second-largest ethnic group, with around 48,500 members. They live in Chile's northern desert and depend on the llama and alpaca for meat, wool, and cargo transportation. Their native language is also known as Aymara.*

The Rapa Nui *are descendents of the Polynesians who arrived on Easter Island around AD 1200. Their population declined greatly during the 19th century due to war, famine, and sickness, and they number less than 4,000 today.*

Fuegians *encompass the indigenous groups that existed in Tierra del Fuego and Patagonia. A few, such as the Selk'nam, are now entirely extinct, while others, such as the Yaghan, have been reduced to a handful.*

IMMIGRANTS

While Chile did not witness mass immigration, European settlers did play a major role in shaping the culture, architecture, and cuisine of regions such as the Lake District and Patagonia. Valparaíso, during its heyday in the 1800s, was a cosmopolitan center, with settlers from England, Italy, Ireland, and Germany, each stamping their unique identity in the distinct neighborhoods they created.

Croatians *came to Chile for economic opportunity in the latter part of the 19th century and settled in Patagonia, specifically in modern-day Porvenir and Punta Arenas. Today, one in four residents in the region is of Croatian descent.*

German and Swiss immigrants *arrived in the mid-19th century as part of the Law of Selective Immigration. The law, introduced in 1845, sought to populate the Lake District with people whom the Chilean government considered to be of a high social and cultural status. A sculpture in Puerto Montt commemorates the immigration.*

MESTIZOS AND NON-INDIGENOUS CHILEANS

Although the majority of Chileans are mestizo, each region in Chile displays well-defined cultural styles. These distinct traditions have been heavily influenced by the various immigrant communities that settled throughout the country.

The Roma *community in Chile lives in the Central Valley. This semi-nomadic group, originally from Europe, is recognized by their long, colorful skirts and their tent settlements on the outskirts of towns.*

Boina is a knitted beret that often features a pompon tassle.

Comfortable baggy pants are well-suited for rough outdoor chores.

Tough working boots are sometimes topped with homemade leather gaiters.

Baqueanos *are Patagonian ranch hands who are entrusted to herd sheep and cattle. They are identified by their distinct attire.*

Chilotes, *people of the Chiloé archipelago, consider themselves distinct from their mainland compatriots, and speak with a clear regional accent. Most Chilotes are a mix of the Spanish with Chono and Huilliche groups.*

***Huaso* on horseback rounding up sheep**

HUASO

Residing mainly in the Central Valley, *huasos* are Chilean cowboys who roam the countryside on their horses. The earliest *huasos* lived and worked on large Colonial ranches. Today, members of this community are identifiable by their straw hats and ponchos, and many are adept horsemen. Over the years, *huasos* have become central to Chilean folkloric culture and they play an integral role in most parades and celebrations, particularly Fiestas Patrias, where they perform the *cueca* *(see p24)*. They also sing the *tonada* *(see p25)*, a folk song that is accompanied by a guitar.

Music and Dance

Chile's lively music and dance scene mirrors the diversity of its cultural traditions. International contemporary music appeals to the majority of the urban population, while rural citizens favor folkloric music derived from the Nueva Canción Chilena (New Chilean Song) era, as well as Latin music from Argentina and Mexico. In northern Chile, folk styles such as the *sajuriana* and *cachimbo* are popular. Chile's national dance is the *cueca*, which appeared in the early 1800s. It originated in Spain and is thought to be the evolution of a creole fusion of Spanish, Arab, and African influences.

Fiesta de San Pedro *features performances by dancers donned in traditional bright costumes and colorful head gear.*

DANCE

Chilean dance is conventionally associated with the folkloric *cueca*, which mimics the courtship of the rooster and hen. The dance is generally performed during the Fiestas Patrias celebrations *(see pp32–3)*, when participants turn out in ceremonial dress.

Men appear in striped ponchos, flat-brimmed sombreros, and boots with spurs.

Women wear long, brightly colored skirts with sashes and jackets.

Waving a handkerchief, female dancers respond coyly to their suitors.

The traditional cueca, *danced primarily at Fiestas Patrias, is much loved in rural areas. The* cueca chora *or* bravo *is the urban equivalent, with lyrics that are more associated with city life. The* cueca *in Chiloé* (see pp214–21) *is distinct in that the vocalist has a more important role than the musicians.*

TRADITIONAL MUSIC

Chilean music owes much to its indigenous traditions and folklore. Among this diversity, Andean music is characterized by lyrics that allude to spirits of the earth, nature, and mountains. Also founded on harmony with nature, Mapuche music follows melodic patterns and ancestral rhythms that are transmitted orally. The Rapa Nui people of Easter Island base their music on Polynesian rhythms that have been influenced by Latin sounds and cadences. Chile is also rich in folkloric music, which is derived from indigenous forms that have been heavily influenced by European music.

Rapa Nui music *comprises chanting and singing to instruments such as the* kauaha *(made from the jaw bone of a horse), drums, and accordions. Often, families form a choir and compete in annual contests.*

The *trutruka* is a trumpet used in Mapuche music.

The *kultrun* is designed with symbols representing the cosmic structure.

The Mapuche define rhythms *as* kantun *(instrumental) or* öl *(ceremonial). Their instruments include the* kultrun, *a drum made of wood and leather, and the* trutruka, *a trumpet made of bamboo and a cow horn. Rich and melodious, the sound reflects close contact with nature.*

CONTEMPORARY SOUNDS

In the 1980s, urban music was associated with politics: Los Prisioneros was Chile's most popular band, along with Fiskales Ad Hok and Electrodomésticos. Today, rock, pop, classical, jazz, and hip hop can be heard in all major urban centers.

Classical and jazz *music both have ample audience in Chile, which has produced important composers and conductors. Claudia Acuña is Chile's best-known jazz performer, while Claudio Arrau is one of the 20th century's foremost pianists.*

NUEVA CANCIÓN CHILENA

The nation's most influential contribution to Latin American music is the Nueva Canción Chilena. The genre arose in the early 1960s and is based on Andean rhythms. Its original artists wrote lyrics that focused on social justice for native cultures and those persecuted under the Pinochet dictatorship. Musicians Victor Jara and Violeta Parra were pioneers who disseminated the genre throughout Latin America, and influenced popular Chilean bands such as Inti-Illimani and Los Jaivas.

Musician Victor Jara (1932–73)

Chilean rock band La Ley *have achieved international stardom, as have the rock group Los Tres. Other modern pop and rock bands include Los Bunkers, Lucybell, Chancho en Piedra, and Javiera y Los Imposibles.*

Cumbia, *a music genre that originated in Colombia, has been very popular among the working classes across Latin America. The lyrics often tackle issues such as life, love, and troubles, and its tinny rhythm is popular for dancing at weddings and parties. Well-known bands include Rafaga and La Sonora Palacios.*

Andean music *originated in the high plateau areas of the Andes and is instantly recognizable by the sound of* quena *flutes, pan pipes, and* charango *lutes.*

***Bombo legüero*, an Andean skin drum**

Zampoña, pan pipe made of bamboo

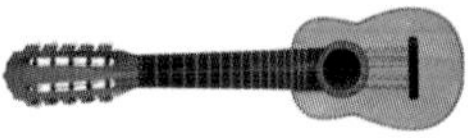

A 10-string charango lute

The melodic tonada *is similar to the* cueca *except that it is not danced. It arose in Spain and shows Arab and Andalucian influences. Popular Chilean groups include the Huasos Quincheros.*

Folklore instruments *such as the pan flute and* quena *(a traditional six-hole bamboo flute) are the essentials of Andean music, and are often combined with the charango lute and violin.*

Literature, Theater, and Cinema

Poet Alonso de Ercilla y Zúñiga

Chile is called a nation of poets, and has been the home of literary giants throughout its history. Among the early writers are such names as Alonso de Ercilla y Zúñiga (1533–94) and Francisco Nuñez de Pineda (1607–82). In the last few centuries, Chile has produced two Nobel laureates and many novelists and playwrights of international renown. Since the end of Pinochet's dictatorship era, artistes in literature, theater, and cinema have delved into subjects that address modern themes and come to terms with the turmoil of Chile's past.

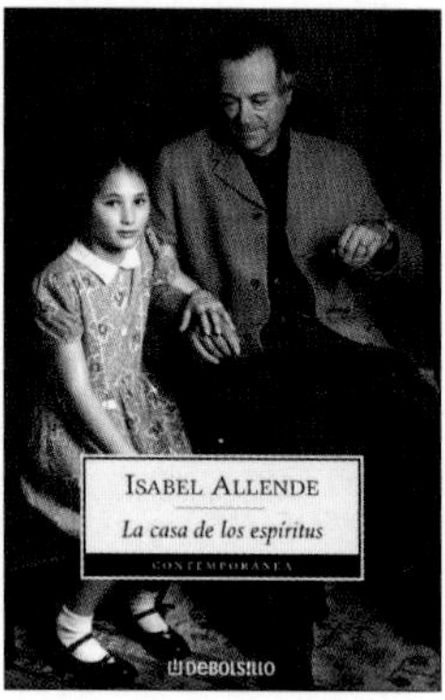

Spanish cover of Isabel Allende's *The House of the Spirits*

LITERATURE

Chile's earliest literary works, dating from the 16th century, mostly relate tales of conquest and colonialism. Prominent in this genre are the Spanish nobleman Alonso de Ercilla y Zúñiga's poem *La Araucana*, describing the Spanish conquest of Chile, and Francisco Núñez de Pineda's *Cautiverio Felíz*, a chronicle of his capture by Mapuches. Such early works tended to romanticize the events they decribed.

Literature in the 19th and 20th century witnessed a turn toward more realistic works. Santiago-born Alberto Blest Gana (1830–1920) is considered the father of the Chilean novel for his authentic portrayal of Chilean history and life in his *Martín Rivas* (1862). In the 20th century, Chile became a major player in the Latin American literary boom, producing influential poets such as Vicente Huidobro (1893–1948), a leading figure in the emergence of avant-garde poetry in the Hispanic world. Huidobro created an experimental verse called Creationism, which sought to bring to life experiences and themes through word play. His 1931 poem "Altazor", was written while he was in Europe, and it became a part of that continent's avant-garde movement. Other prominent 20th-century poets include Nobel laureates Gabriela Mistral and Pablo Neruda *(see p87)*, whose works centered on themes of love and politics respectively. During the second half of the 20th century, the forerunners of

Antonio Skarmeta, Chilean writer exiled during the dictatorship years

Chile's burgeoning literature scene included Nicanor Parra (b.1914), a self-described "anti-poet", who shunned traditional poetic styles and was a major influence on the 1950s' American Beat writers.

The Pinochet dictatorship spawned several major works by exiled writers such as Luís Sepúlveda (b.1949), Antonio Skármeta (b.1940), José Donoso (1924–96), and Isabel Allende (b.1943), many of them writing on themes of exile and loss. A prominent writer of novels such as *The House of the Spirits*, Allende was an exponent of Latin America's Magical Realism movement that blended seemingly normal situations with an element of fantasy.

Magic Realism lost favor in the 1990s with the rise of the Nueva Narrativa Chilena (New Chilean Narrative). The term, coined by writer Jaime Collyer (b.1955), defined the post-dictatorship era and Chile's introduction to consumerism and globalization. This

GABRIELA MISTRAL

Latin America's first Nobel Prize winner, Gabriela Mistral (1889–1957) was a teacher and feminist turned poet, with a unique and lyrical voice that spoke of love and betrayal, life and death, and the Latin American experience in poetical works such as *Ternura* and *Desolation*. Mistral, born Lucila Godoy y Alcayaga, spent much of her adult life outside Chile, as a consul in Spain, France, Italy, and the US, and as a professor in Mexico, and in Vassar College and Barnard University in New York. Mistral was of mixed Amerindian and Basque origin, and celebrated the mestizo race in *Tala*, her second collection of poems that contemplated the blend of Latin American and European culture.

Gabriela Mistral receiving the Nobel Prize in 1945

movement produced writers including Gonzalo Contreras and Alberto Fuguet, whose stories such as "Mas Estrellas Que en el Cielo" dispel the notions of Magic Realism. The current international star is the literary rebel Roberto Bolaño, the posthumous winner of 2009's National Book Critics Circle Award for his epic novel *2666*.

THEATER

Theater appeared in the late 19th century as mostly amateur productions of European plays, and comedies and dramas based on daily Chilean life. However, the founding of the Teatro Experimental in the late 1930s by the Universidad de Chile, established theater as a powerful and socially relevant art form. The subsequent sprouting of theater houses across Chile spawned a boom in productions ranging from folkloric themes to the popular European-origin drama form, the Theater of the Absurd.

By the 1960s and 70s, political radicalization propelled dramatists to bring theater to the masses. A complete censorship of media during the 1970s and 80s led to the emergence of the dramatic arts as society's way of discussing grievances. The Ictus Theater Group, one of the longest-running companies in Chile, played a prominent role in pushing theater's boundaries with plays such as *Andrés of La Victoria* (1985), the plot of which centered around a priest killed by military police. In the late 1980s, the Gran Circo Teatro produced *La Negra Ester*, by Andrés Pérez, that became the most artistically and commercially successful play in Chilean history. The masked performance was based on a popular love tragedy, and signaled a departure from most contemporary drama based on social criticism.

Today, Santiago has dozens of independent and state-sponsored theater houses, including the venerable Teatro Municipal *(see p69)*, the Teatro Nacional, San Ginés, and Universidad Católica, all of which host performances from classical to cutting-edge. Theater takes center stage with the annual Festival Internacional Teatro a Mil *(see p35)*, which features myriad theatrical performances in cultural centers, theaters, and city streets.

Poster of *La Negra Ester* playing at Teatro Oriente, Santiago, in 2009

CINEMA

The Chilean film industry dates from the early 20th century; the first black-and-white movie *Hussar of Death* was released in 1926. Cinema flourished in the 1940s with the founding of the studio Chile Films, but declined until a short revival in the 1960s. During this decade filmmakers combined shades of experimental European cinema and Chilean culture to create art house and national classics. Films of this genre included Patricio Kaulen's *Long Journey* (1967) and Miguel Littín's *The Jackal of Nahueltoro* (1969), which later became the subject of Gabriel García Márquez's book *Clandestine in Chile* (1986). In 1968, the unconventional director Raúl Ruiz produced the cult classic, *Tres Tristes Tigres*, based on Chilean society.

The dictatorship stifled creative filmmaking and exiled cinematic artists, as a result of which just seven films were made in over a decade. The return to democracy led to cinema's comeback with a new wave of Chilean filmmaking.

Today, Chile produces a dozen films a year and receives nominations at international film festivals. In 2005, *Mi Mejor Enemigo* (My Best Enemy) by Alex Bowen entered the competition at the Cannes Film Festival after winning the best Spanish-language film at Spain's Goya awards. Other films to have garnered international publicity include *Machuca* (2002) by Andres Wood, that follows the friendship between two boys during the dictatorship; *Tony Manero* (2008) by Pablo Larraín, a bleak portrayal of marginality during the 1970s; and *The Maid* (2008) by Sebastián Silva, which won the Sundance Festival's World Cinema Jury Prize.

Still from the classic art house film *The Jackal Of Nahueltoro* (1969)

Chilean Art and Architecture

Traditional Mapuche woodwork

Pre-Colonial art in Chile chiefly comprised rock art, of which northern Chile has fine examples. In the Colonial era, both art and architecture were initially influenced by Spanish cultural and ecclesiastical elements. With the influx of immigrants from other European countries in the 19th century, techniques and designs diversified and each region showed trademark styles of the groups that settled there. Today, Chile is among the world's most architecturally prolific countries and has a thriving art scene.

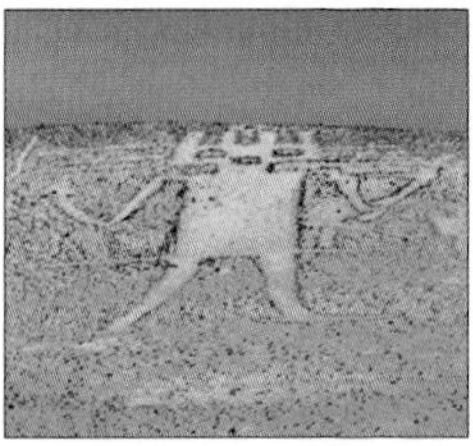
The massive Gigante de Atacama geoglyph in northern Chile

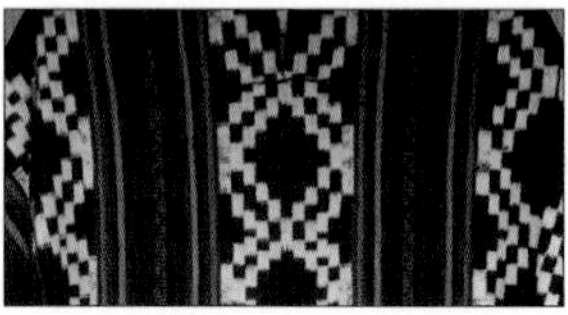
Mapuche textiles woven in traditional geometric patterns

ART

While pre-Hispanic art in Chile reached a level of sophistication, Colonial-era art was limited to portraits and landscapes of criollo life. Today, however, with the integration of immigrant groups into society and the freedom of post-dictatorship Chile, the art world is giving rise to international stars, and Santiago alone is home to dozens of cultural centers and galleries.

INDIGENOUS AND COLONIAL ART

Chile's northern desert and altiplano region has some of the world's largest collections of petroglyphs and geoglyphs, including the 400-ft (121-m) high Gigante de Atacama. Colonial art in Chile did not exhibit complexity, other than the Rococo-style sculptures, paintings, and silverwork produced in the Jesuit workshops of Calera de Tango in the early 1700s.

Ornate silver croziers *and monstrances were among the popular ecclesiatical artifacts crafted by skilled Jesuits in the 16th century.*

Vessel shaped to resemble a bird

Ceramic pottery *in animistic and geometric designs, metalwork, and textile weaving were among the traditional crafts of the Diaguita culture (300 BC – AD 1500) in northern Chile.*

CONTEMPORARY ART

The nation's artistic scene blossomed with the inauguration of Santiago's Museo Nacional de Bellas Artes *(see p71)* in 1880. Renowned artists of that time were Fernando Alvarez de Sotomayor and Arturo Gordon, whose works depicted Chilean life. Among contemporary Chilean artists are Surrealist painter Roberto Matta and Hyperrealist Claudio Bravo.

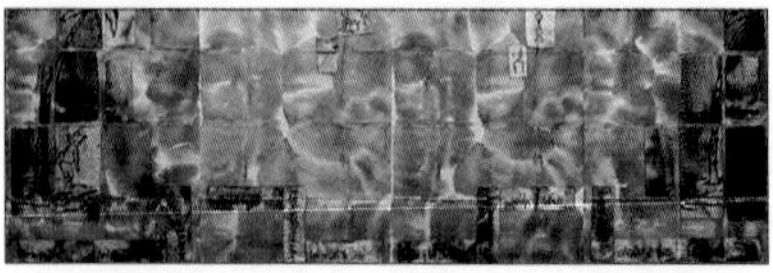
Absent Feet *by Eugenio Dittborn (b.1943) is part of his "Airmail Paintings" series, which could be folded up and sent via post to the location of the exhibition.*

Paisaje Lo Contador *is a well-known canvas by Arturo Gordon, a member of the Generación del Trece group of artists who depicted the lives of the common man, a rare subject in the early 1900s.*

ARCHITECTURE

Chilean architecture is a potpourri of a number of influences. In the early decades of colonization, Chilean towns were modeled after Spanish towns, with a central square surrounded by a cathedral and government buildings with large patios, bare walls, and wrought-iron gates. In the 20th century, Santiago's nouveau riche built their houses to resemble European Neo-Classical mansions. Modern Chileans have adapted North American bungalows, skyscrapers, and malls that reflect the country's economic boom over the past 20 years.

Colonnaded passageway bordering the yard at Convento de San Francisco *(see p68)*, Santiago

COLONIAL

Much of the country's Colonial architecture has succumbed to earthquakes, with the exception of a few 17th-century churches in the desert north and a handful of haciendas in the Central Valley.

The Iglesia de San Francisco de Chiu-Chiu (see p170) *is Chile's oldest church. Its twin bell towers, chañar-wood ceilings, and whitewashed walls are characteristic of 17th-century adobe churches in the Atacama.*

The Casa Colorada (see p59), *named for its rose-tinted walls, is built of brick and stone around a central patio.*

NEO-CLASSICAL

Triangular pediments, hefty columns, and domed roofs are quintessential elements of government buildings in Santiago, and are evidence of the city's preference for Neo-Classical architecture during the 19th century.

Palacio de La Moneda (see p64) *is the best example of 19th-century Neo-Classical structures found in the capital, although it was considered too grandiose when inagurated.*

VERNACULAR

Over the centuries, Chileans have designed and constructed their buildings with locally available resources, and according to cultural and climatic needs. In some cases, the influence of European immigrants is also visible.

Estancias *in Patagonia are low-slung ranches encircled with poplar trees that provide protection against the region's howling winds.*

Wooden shingles *dominate the German-styled homes in the Lake District and prevent the rain from seeping in.*

Chiloé's *palafitos* (see p217), *built during a wave of strong commercial expansion in the 19th century, enabled fishermen to live closer to the sea.*

Sports in Chile

Conventional sports such as soccer, tennis, and rodeo are Chile's favorite pastimes. However, extreme sports are quickly gaining popularity given the country's wealth of destinations suited to such activities. Chile's numerous rivers are formidable challenges for white-water rafting and kayaking, while well-designed trails and challenging peaks draw trekkers to national parks, and the desert regions attract a growing number of mountain-bikers. Hang gliding and helicopter skiing are other adrenaline-fuelled activities on offer.

Getting up close to glaciers using crampons and ropes

Colo-Colo *is the only Chilean soccer team to have won the prestigious South American competition Copa Liberatores de América (in 1991). The team is named for a fierce Mapuche chief who fought against Spanish conquistadores.*

SOCCER

The nation's most popular sport, soccer is played by Chileans of all ages and social classes. The sport was introduced in Valparaíso by British immigrants who established the Federación de Fútbol de Chile in 1895.

Marcelo Salas, *one of Chile's greatest soccer stars, was nicknamed El Matador (The Killer) for his ability to score spectacular goals, as seen during the 1998 FIFA World Cup.*

The FIFA World Cup *returned to South America after a 12-year interval, when it was held in Chile in 1962. The Chilean team, in official red, blue, and white, finished in third place.*

TENNIS

Generally an upper-class sport, tennis is most often played at private clubs. However, Chile's most recent sports stars have come from this field. In 2004, Nicolás Massú and Fernando Gonzalez gave the country its first gold medal at the Olympics in the doubles competition.

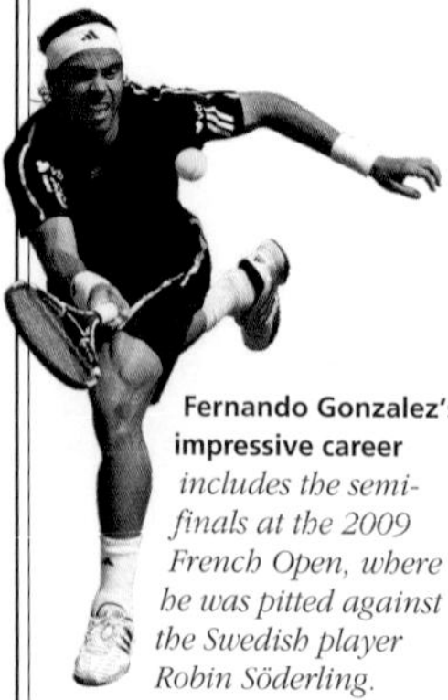

Fernando Gonzalez's impressive career *includes the semi-finals at the 2009 French Open, where he was pitted against the Swedish player Robin Söderling.*

Marcelo Ríos *was the first Latin American tennis player to rank No.1 in the world, in the year 1998.*

RODEO

Chile's national sport, the rodeo, arose in the 16th century when cattle from haciendas were gathered together and branded as a means of identification. The stars of the rodeo are the *huasos* (cowboys), who skilfully steer their horses around a *medialuna*, or half-moon arena, and attempt to corral and pin a cow against the wall. The occasion calls for formal garb, which includes a poncho, wide-brimmed hat, leather leg protectors and pinwheel-sized spurs. *Huasos* compete in a number of annual rodeo events, the largest being the Campeonato Nacional de Rodeo, or National Championship of Chilean Rodeo, held in Rancagua *(see p142)*.

Huasos *use a number of deft maneuvers in their efforts to win the rodeo. This includes such moves as the sliding stop, which involves galloping sideways.*

A collera, *or two-man team, work to nudge a calf against a padded arena wall. The* collera *gains top points for pinning the rear of the calf.*

SURFING

Despite the cold waters of the Humboldt current that runs along Chile's southern and central coast, surfing is popular with both residents and visitors thanks to consistent waves and a myriad of empty beaches. Pichilemu *(see p146)*, Iquique *(see pp166–7)*, and Arica *(see pp160–61)*, are three of the hot surf spots.

US champion Tyler Fox *was one of many big names to attend the 2008 Chile World Tow-In at Punta de Lobos surf break in Pichilemu. This week-long surf festival was one of the most extreme events ever held in the country.*

SKIING AND SNOWBOARDING

From mid-June to early October, skiers and snowboarders head to the Andes for world-class terrain, a relaxed ambience, and relatively few lift lines. The principal resorts are found in Chile's Central Valley *(see pp114–55)*.

Nevados de Chillán *(see p152), Valle Nevado, and Ski Portillo, Chile's top ski resorts, host many North American and European ski teams who come to train in summer.*

The slopes of Volcán Villarrica *(see p198), an active, smoking volcano, is popular with numerous professional snowboarders, notably Markku Koski from Finland.*

Fiestas Patrias

The most important holiday of the year, Fiestas Patrias (Patriotic Festivals) celebrates Chile's Independence Day, informally called the Dieciocho, on September 18, and Armed Forces Day on September 19. Chile's true independence came on February 12, 1818, but the formally recognized date honors the nation's first attempt at secession from Spain, on September 18, 1810. In the weeks leading up to the festival, the country comes together to celebrate all things Chilean, including regional culture, traditional food, and dance. Armed Forces Day is marked by a grand military parade in Santiago. Chileans decorate their town streets and fasten flags on vehicles in a show of nationalist pride, and it is common to see children dressed in traditional dresses and *huaso* suits.

Ex-president Michelle Bachelet, Armed Forces Day parade, 2006

The fonda or ramada *is a temporary structure, erected as a party hall, which is made of either wooden poles and a thatched roof, or a circus-like tent. Nearly every town in Chile has its own* fonda, *featuring a stage for live bands, a dance area with just a dirt or sawdust floor, and beverage and food stands surrounded by tables and chairs.*

MILITARY PARADE

The Armed Forces Day, also known as the Día de las Glorias del Ejército (Day of the Glories of the Military) was designated a holiday in 1915 to celebrate freedoms gained and victories won by Chile's military since the country's inception.

TRADITIONAL FOOD AND DRINK

The barbecue reigns during the patriotic holidays, often carrying on for days and shared among friends and family. Other emblematic foods define the holidays, most having arisen from the countryside.

Chicha *is an alcoholic drink made from fermented fruit, most commonly apples or grapes, and produced toward the end of the summer. However,* chicha *is not commonly drunk outside of the Fiestas Patrias. Mapuches make a regional* chicha *using corn called* muday.

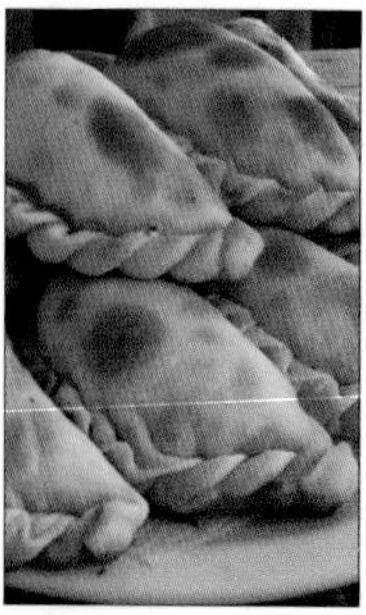

Empanada *is a kind of turnover made with pastry dough and stuffed with* pino, *a mixture of beef, onions, half a boiled egg, raisins, and olives. The dish is then baked in a clay oven.*

The cueca (see p24), *Chile's national dance, is a common sight during Fiestas Patrias. Women dress in flouncy, floral cotton dresses and men in black pants, spurs and boots, a wide-brimmed* huaso *hat, and a white jacket or poncho.*

Over half a million spectators attend the parade, which is often accompanied by displays of the military's latest acquisitions in planes, war vehicles, and technological gadgetry.

The parade, held in Parque Bernardo O'Higgins *(see p81)* in Santiago, includes the army, navy, air force, and the police marching Prussian-style along a gigantic cement esplanade in the middle of the park. More than 7,000 troops participate.

Rodeo contests *take place throughout rural villages up and down the country during Fiestas Patrias. Chile's national sport, the rodeo attracts hordes of enthusiastic spectators to the* medialuna, *where such events are held.*

Kite-flying *is a hugely popular activity, especially as spring breezes rise over the festive weeks.*

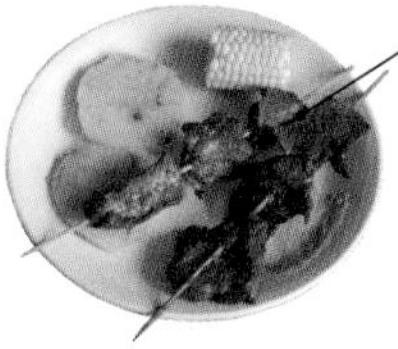

Anticucho, a dish of marinated and skewered meat

Asados, or barbecues, *are synonymous with Fiestas Patrias. Popular items include the* anticucho, *or shish kabob, which dates back to the Incan empire. The barbecue usually starts off with a* choripan, *a sausage sandwiched in a piece of crusty bread and topped with* pebre, *a tomato and cilantro salsa.*

Piscola, *along with the pisco sour, is the popular cocktail of the day. A simple concoction of* pisco, *cola, and ice, it is a major party starter during Fiestas Patrias.*

CHILE AND EASTER ISLAND THROUGH THE YEAR

Festivals are colorful, joyous events in Chile, often carrying on for days if they fall close to a weekend. The northern desert region is home to the country's most vibrant festivals, featuring bright costumes and lively parades. Although most festivals commemorate religious events or venerate saints, there is also a strong influence of pre-Christian and pre-Colonial tradition. While New Year's Eve is celebrated with fireworks and family reunions, Christmas is a relatively brief event with little fanfare. February is the country's official summer break, when most Chileans go on holiday. Across Chile, a variety of *costumbrista* festivals showcase the country's diverse local arts and crafts, foods, and industry.

Moai **displayed at the Tapati festival**

Children dancing during the Fiestas Patrias celebrations

SPRING

Central Chile has temperate weather conditions during the spring months. In the desert north, temperatures are moderate – the days are not too hot, nor are the evenings frigid. Farther south, the Lake District experiences intermittent rainfall. In Patagonia, however, flowers bloom, and birds return to nest. With off-season rates, pleasant weather, and lack of summertime crowds, spring is generally considered the best time to visit Chile.

SEPTEMBER

Fiestas Patrias *(Sep 18 and 19)*, throughout Chile. The country's Independence Day and Armed Forces Day are celebrated with much revelry *(see pp 32–3)*. People spill on to the streets and music reverberates through the air.

OCTOBER

Festival de los Mil Tambores *(1st weekend of Oct)*, Valparaíso. The arrival of spring is celebrated with the Thousand Drums Festival. The streets come alive with the sound of rhythmic drumbeats, outdoor theater, and dance performances.

Día de la Raza *(Oct 12)*, throughout Chile. This festival was originally held to commemorate the discovery of the Americas by Columbus. Today, it celebrates the diverse indigenous groups of Chile. In Santiago, Mapuche Indians parade through the streets, dressed in costumes and playing music on traditional instruments.

Día de las Iglesias Evangélicas y Protestantes *(Oct 31)*, throughout Chile. This relatively new national holiday marks the date that German theologian Martin Luther challenged the Catholic Church.

NOVEMBER

El Ensayo *(early Nov)*, Santiago. Club Hípico *(see p81)* plays host to Chile's premier horse-racing derby and the oldest stakes race in South America.

Feria del Libro *(early Nov)*, Santiago. This annual book festival, displaying the works of Latin American authors, is held at the Centro Cultural Estación Mapocho *(see p73)*.

Festival de Colonias Extranjeras *(Nov)*, Antofagasta. Immigrants and their descendents from around the world celebrate their varied heritage with food, music, and dance.

Festival de Cine Internacional *(Nov)*, Viña del Mar. This film festival showcases contemporary Latin American films. It is also attended by filmmakers hoping to win the PAOA, the prize for excellence.

Performer in vibrant mask at the Festival de Colonias Extranjeras

Traditional dances at the Fiesta Grande de la Virgen de Rosario

SUMMER

A number of Chile's major festivals, especially music events, take place during the summer months. December through February is the best time to visit the beaches, the Lake District, and Northern Patagonia. During January and February, sizable vacationing crowds are drawn to the beaches and resort-towns. In southern Chile, strong gales are common, while temperatures in the northern desert climb high.

DECEMBER

Fiesta Inmaculado Concepción *(Dec 8)*, throughout Chile. This religious festival is celebrated in a variety of venues across the country, with the most extraordinary event held at the Santuario de la Virgen de lo Vasquez, on the road to Valparaíso. Up to 100,000 devotees make an arduous pilgrimage to this sanctuary, often barefoot or on their knees.

Fiesta Grande de la Virgen de Rosario *(late Dec)*, Andacollo. This festival draws up to 150,000 pilgrims, who come to worship the patron saint of mining at the village of Andacollo in northern Chile. It features costumed and masked performers, feasting, and sports such as horse racing and cockfighting.

Noche Buena *(Dec 24)*, throughout Chile. On Christmas Eve, most Chileans meet their extended families, enjoy a late dinner, and attend midnight mass. Children receive gifts from the Viejo Pasquero (Old Man Christmas), while adults enjoy cola de mono, or monkey's tail, a traditional Chilean drink made of coffee and aguardiente.

Santa distributing gifts at Christmas

Navidad *(Dec 25)*, throughout Chile. Nearly all businesses are closed and the streets are quiet as Chileans rest in their homes.

Carnaval Cultural de Valparaíso *(Dec 25–31)*, Valparaíso. The city's yearly cultural carnival runs through the week leading up to New Year's Eve. It features street performances of theater and dance, music shows, art exhibitions, cinematic events, food stalls, and much more.

Fin de Año *(Dec 31)*, throughout Chile. One of Chile's liveliest festivals is best celebrated in Santiago or on the coast, especially in Valparaíso, where revelers pour into the city for street parties and firework displays. The celebration in Valparaíso is regarded as the largest fireworks event in the world.

JANUARY

Año Nuevo *(Jan 1)*, throughout Chile. Quiet streets and closed businesses are the norm on this day, as Chileans recover from the previous evening's heavy *carrete* (party).

Festival Internacional Teatro a Mil *(Jan–early Feb)*, Santiago. The city's top cultural event. Dozens of theater and dance productions by national as well as international artistes are presented. Large-scale street shows draw thousands of onlookers. Alongside performances of established actors, emerging talent is also showcased.

Semana Musical de Frutillar *(late Jan–early Feb)*, Frutillar. Set against a spectacular volcanic backdrop, Frutillar's concert hall plays host to a music festival each year. A series of virtuoso performances of different genres that range from jazz and ballet to chamber music and symphony keep the audiences enthralled.

Giant puppet parading during Santiago's Festival Internacional Teatro a Mil

FEBRUARY

Tapati Rapa Nui *(early Feb)*, Easter Island. Residents of the island celebrate their Polynesian heritage during this 2-week festival *(see p259)*. One of the best and most popular events in Chile, it boasts sophisticated productions of local dance, chant, and song. A variety of competitions such as horse racing, woodcarving, fishing, body decoration, and making *kai kai* (string figures) are also held.
Derby de Viña del Mar *(1st Sun of Feb)*, Viña del Mar. A major equestrian event, this annual derby draws thousands of racing enthusiasts to the Sporting Club track.
Encuentro Folklórico *(early Feb)*, Ancud. This festival promotes folkloric music, traditional dance, distinct cuisine, and the arts and crafts of the verdant archipelago of Chiloé.
Festival Costumbrista Chilote *(early Feb)*, Chiloé. Spread over a weekend, this fascinating cultural festival celebrates the unique culture, folklore, and gastronomy of Chiloé. Visitors can sample over 50 kinds of local dishes and beverages, learn about traditional tools and their use, and buy arts and crafts.
Noche Valdiviana *(3rd Sat of Feb)*, Valdivia. A popular night-long celebration, when lighted boats fill the Río Valdivia and the skies light up with dazzling fireworks.

Residents of Easter Island performing at the Tapati Rapa Nui celebrations

Festival Internacional de la Canción de Viña del Mar *(last week of Feb)*, Viña del Mar. A 5-day music festival that features competitions between rock, pop, and folkloric music by Chilean as well as popular international bands. The winners are decided by the roaring approval of the crowd.
Carnaval de Putre *(end Feb)*, Putre. The pocket-sized village of Putre in the Andean highlands hosts a big party for its carnival. Aymara Indians from the region are drawn to the celebration. The music, costumed events, as well as the food represent the village's Andean heritage.

AUTUMN

By March, the summer vacations are over, but many Chileans continue to head to the beach and other outdoor destinations in search of sunny skies during the last of the warm days. Semana Santa, or Easter week, is a popular time for a quick escape to resort towns or neighboring countries. In the Central Valley, the autumn harvest of ripened grapes brings on the yearly wine festivals.

MARCH

Festival de Vendimia *(Mar)*, Chilean wine valleys. The annual grape harvest is celebrated with events that feature food stands, exhibitions, wine tastings, grape-crushing, and more. Festivals generally begin in early March in northern wine valleys such as Limaní, and continue through late March in the southern Bío Bío.

APRIL

Viernes Santo *(Fri before Easter)*, throughout Chile. Some commemorate Good Friday with re-enactments of Christ's death on the cross, while others flock to fishmongers in order to abide by the religious edict of avoiding meat on this day.
Fiesta del Cuasimodo *(1st Sun after Easter)*, throughout Chile. Priests visit the sick and disabled who were unable to attend church on Easter. They are accompanied by *huasos* (cowboys) in a grand parade. Historically, *huasos* protected the priests from bandits. This is followed by a feast.

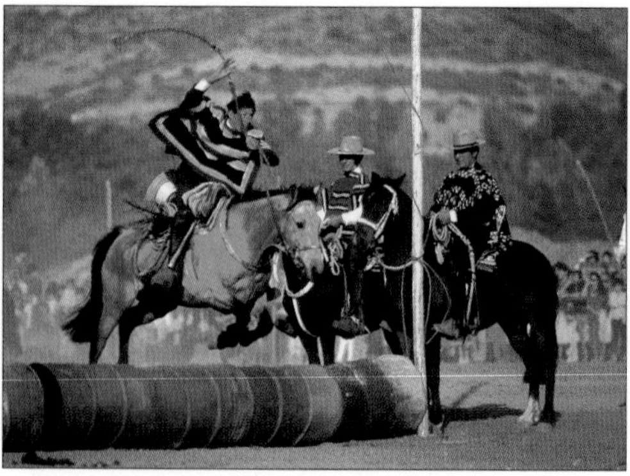
Huasos **watched by crowds at the Fiesta de Cuasimodo**

MAY

Glorias Navales *(May 21)*, throughout Chile. This event commemorates the 1879 Battle of Iquique during the War of the Pacific *(see p45)*. Military ceremonies are held in Santiago, Valparaíso, and Iquique. Traditionally, the president also presents his State of the Union address.

WINTER

Winter months bring chilly temperatures to Patagonia and wet conditions to the Lake District. The northern desert region hosts some of the country's largest festivals during this time. The ski season starts in the south, with many events and competitions at ski resorts.

JUNE

Fiesta de San Pedro *(Jun 29)*, throughout Chile. People on the coast honor St. Peter, the patron saint of fishermen, by carrying his statue out to a harbor and wishing for fortune, good weather, and large catches. Inland, especially at San Pedro de Atacama in northern Chile, residents celebrate St. Peter as the patron saint of the Catholic church with mass and costumed processions.

Spirited dancing by costumed young men at the Festival La Tirana

JULY

Festival de La Tirana *(Jul 12–18)*, La Tirana. This 5-day event *(see p169)* fuses pre-Colombian traditions with Catholic ceremony. Up to 80,000 people visit the village of La Tirana to honor the Virgen de la Carmen with dances. Performers wear costumes and dragon masks.
Fiesta de la Virgen del Carmen *(Jul 16)*, Santiago. This celebration honors Chile's armed forces, the fight for independence, and the Virgen de la Carmen, patron saint of the nation.
Carnaval de Invierno *(3rd weekend of Jul)*, Punta Arenas. This event seeks to cheer up the dark days of winter with nighttime parades, folkloric dances, and fireworks.

PUBLIC HOLIDAYS

Año Nuevo (Jan 1)
Viernes Santo (Mar/Apr)
Día del Trabajo (Labor Day, May 1)
Glorias Navales (May 21)
Corpus Christi (Jun)
St. Peter and St. Paul Day (Jun 29)
Asuncion de la Virgen (Assumption of Mary, Aug 15)
Fiestas Patrias (Sep 18 & 19)
Día de la Raza (Oct 12)
Día de las Iglesias Evangélicas y Protestantes (Oct 31)
Día de Todos los Santos (All Saints' Day, Nov 1)
Fiesta Inmaculado Concepción (Dec 8)
Navidad (Dec 25)

Masked Chileans parading down a narrow street in San Pedro de Atacama during the Fiesta de San Pedro

Climate of Chile

Covering a distance of some 2,600 miles (4,190 km) from north to south, Chile experiences a wide range of weather conditions. The northern section is an arid desert that sees rain once a year, if at all, usually during January or February. The Central Valley enjoys a mild climate, with typically sunny days year round and quick storms. Torrential downpours can last weeks during winter in the Lake District and fjord lands, especially in Chiloé, while Patagonia's legendary weather can change in a matter of hours from sunshine to gale-force winds or rain. Isolated from the mainland, Easter Island is influenced largely by the Pacific Ocean, but despite the exposure to cooling oceanic winds, it faces occasional droughts as well as rainstorms.

Road going through snowy landscape in southern Chile

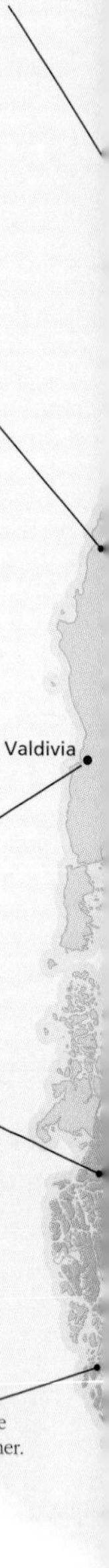

Norte Grande and Norte Chico are arid, with little or no rainfall. The high desert days are warm, but frigid at night.

The Central Valley climate is also called Mediterranean due to warm, dry summers, and mild winters with moderate rainfall.

Northern Patagonia experiences winter precipitation in the form of rain and light snow. Strong winds affect open areas in summers.

Southern Patagonia has highly changeable weather during summer. The winters are cold with mild snowfall.

ROBINSON CRUSOE ISLAND

Month	Apr	Jul	Oct	Jan
°C/F (max)	20/68	15/59	16/61	22/72
°C/F (min)	13/55	10/50	10/50	15/59
Sunshine	11 hrs	10 hrs	13 hrs	14 hrs
Rainfall	100 mm	160 mm	60 mm	20 mm

VALDIVIA

Month	Apr	Jul	Oct	Jan
°C/F (max)	17/63	11/52	17/63	23/73
°C/F (min)	8/46	5/41	7/45	11/52
Sunshine	11 hrs	09 hrs	10 hrs	10 hrs
Rainfall	234 mm	394 mm	127 mm	66 mm

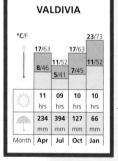

EASTER ISLAND

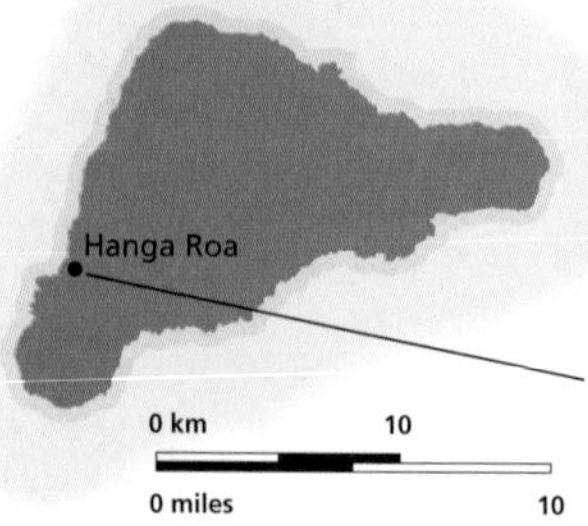

HANGA ROA

Month	Apr	Jul	Oct	Jan
°C/F (max)	24/75	20/68	22/72	26/79
°C/F (min)	18/64	15/59	15/59	19/66
Sunshine	12 hrs	11 hrs	13 hrs	14 hrs
Rainfall	118 mm	94 mm	73 mm	92 mm

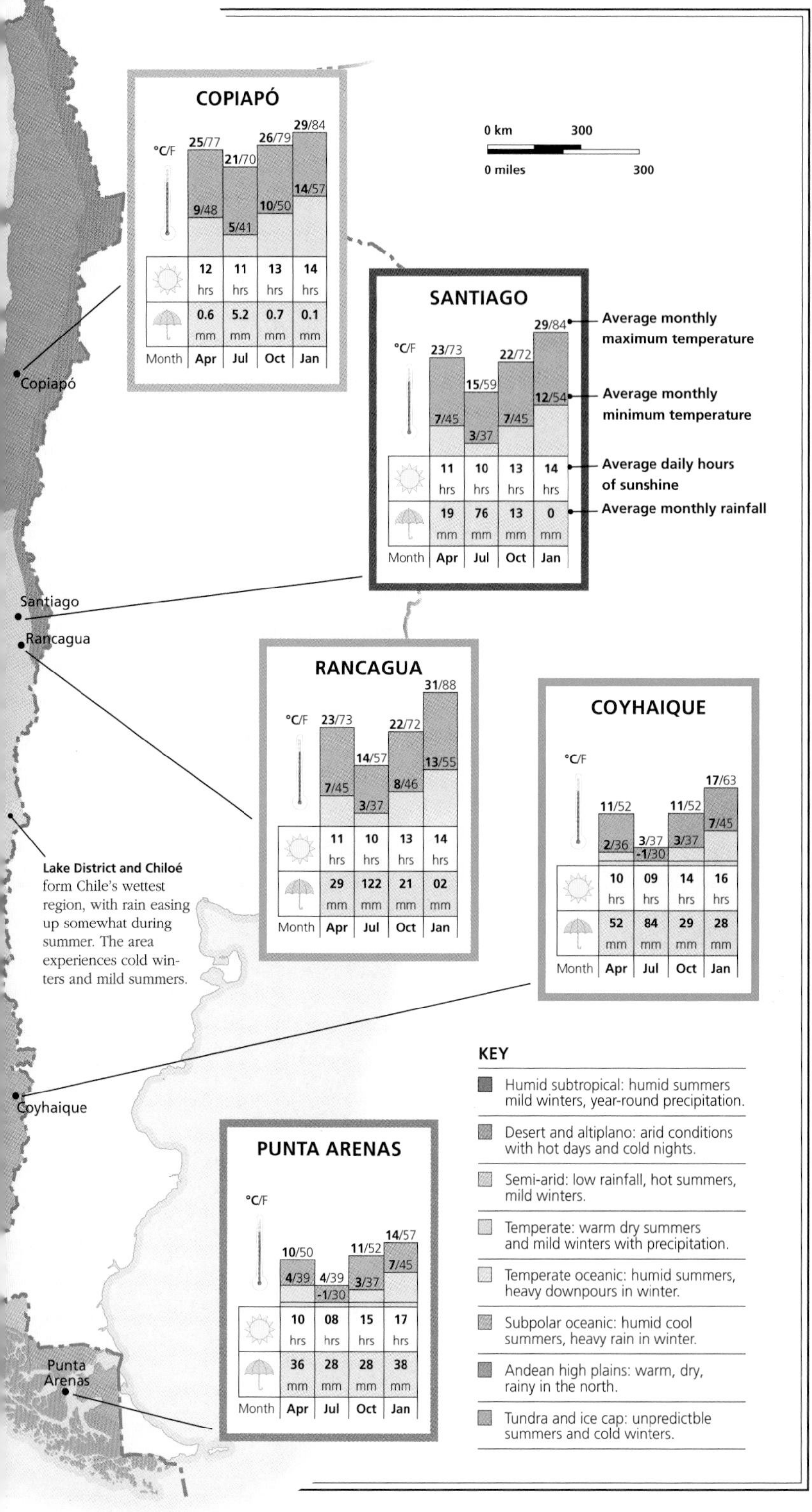

Lake District and Chiloé form Chile's wettest region, with rain easing up somewhat during summer. The area experiences cold winters and mild summers.

COPIAPÓ

Month	Apr	Jul	Oct	Jan
Max °C/F	25/77	21/70	26/79	29/84
Min °C/F	9/48	5/41	10/50	14/57
Sunshine	12 hrs	11 hrs	13 hrs	14 hrs
Rainfall	0.6 mm	5.2 mm	0.7 mm	0.1 mm

SANTIAGO

Month	Apr	Jul	Oct	Jan
Max °C/F	23/73	15/59	22/72	29/84
Min °C/F	7/45	3/37	7/45	12/54
Sunshine	11 hrs	10 hrs	13 hrs	14 hrs
Rainfall	19 mm	76 mm	13 mm	0 mm

RANCAGUA

Month	Apr	Jul	Oct	Jan
Max °C/F	23/73	14/57	22/72	31/88
Min °C/F	7/45	3/37	8/46	13/55
Sunshine	11 hrs	10 hrs	13 hrs	14 hrs
Rainfall	29 mm	122 mm	21 mm	02 mm

COYHAIQUE

Month	Apr	Jul	Oct	Jan
Max °C/F	11/52	3/37	11/52	17/63
Min °C/F	2/36	-1/30	3/37	7/45
Sunshine	10 hrs	09 hrs	14 hrs	16 hrs
Rainfall	52 mm	84 mm	29 mm	28 mm

PUNTA ARENAS

Month	Apr	Jul	Oct	Jan
Max °C/F	10/50	4/39	11/52	14/57
Min °C/F	4/39	-1/30	3/37	7/45
Sunshine	10 hrs	08 hrs	15 hrs	17 hrs
Rainfall	36 mm	28 mm	28 mm	38 mm

KEY

- Humid subtropical: humid summers mild winters, year-round precipitation.
- Desert and altiplano: arid conditions with hot days and cold nights.
- Semi-arid: low rainfall, hot summers, mild winters.
- Temperate: warm dry summers and mild winters with precipitation.
- Temperate oceanic: humid summers, heavy downpours in winter.
- Subpolar oceanic: humid cool summers, heavy rain in winter.
- Andean high plains: warm, dry, rainy in the north.
- Tundra and ice cap: unpredictble summers and cold winters.

THE HISTORY OF CHILE AND EASTER ISLAND

Despite Chile's isolation, its history is an epic one involving ancient settlements and empires. The country also played a role in the European age of exploration and colonization and created its own rich independence period. Equally complex is the history of Easter Island, which, owing largely to its seclusion in the remote South Pacific, is subject of much debate in modern times.

The first humans to reach the Americas were hunter-gathers who crossed the Bering Strait via a land bridge. Although pinpointing the date of arrival is difficult, the immigration of these groups took place in waves over many thousands of years, the last one occurring some 10,000 years ago.

Dance of the Aymaras Indians

Evidence from excavations at Monte Verde, just north of Puerto Montt in the Lake District, show that the earliest human settlement in Chile may date from more than 13,000 years ago. By 6000 BC, crops such as potatoes, squash, and beans had become the livelihood of the settled communities of Atacameño, Aymara, and Diaguita in the Atacama and foothills of the Andes. The Aymara also herded llamas and alpacas for meat and wool, bartering their goods with groups such as the Chango fisherfolk for products from the valleys and the coast. Farther south, the land was peopled by the Mapuche and the closely related Pewenche, Huilliche, and Puelche, all semi-sedentary agriculturalists who subsisted autonomously. In what is now Patagonia, the Chonos, Kawéskar, and Yámana – collectively known as Canoe Indians – lived off fish and shellfish from the fjords and channels along the Pacific coast and the Strait of Magellan. The Tehuelche hunted game on the Patagonian steppe, while the Selk'nam (Ona) were land-based hunters on the big island of the Tierra del Fuego archipelago.

Isolated from mainland Chile, Easter Island followed a separate trajectory of events, and its history is today a controversial subject. The first settlers arrived about 1,000 years ago from eastern Polynesia to what was then a densely forested island. Their descendents forged a complex society, best remembered by the iconic statues known as *moai* found at various locations around the island. However, the construction of the *moai*, coupled with a fast-growing population that reached unsustainable levels, deforested the island and led to clan warfare and the eventual collapse of this society.

TIMELINE

13,000 BC Establishment of Monte Verde, Chile's first-known settlement

Depiction of the settlement at Monte Verde

1000 Polynesian settlers arrive on Easter Island

14,000 BC | **AD1** | **400** | **800** | **AD 1200**

6000 BC Cultivation of crops such as potatoes, beans, and squash in the central Andes

Moai *on Ahu Akivi, Easter Island, c.1000–1600*

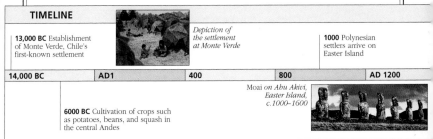

◁ **José de San Martín and Bernardo O'Higgins at the end of Chile's struggle for independence, April 5, 1818**

Valdivia at the foundation of Santiago, by Pedro Lira (1845–1912)

THE INCAN EMPIRE

During the 15th century, the Incas, the best known of the central Andean empires, extended their power southward up to the latitude of present-day Santiago, reaching a maximum extent around AD 1438. However, their control over peripheral areas, including modern-day Chile, was precarious, depending upon cooperation and tribute from the peoples. Intrigues within the empire, following the death of the emperor Huayna Capac (c.1527), led to a civil war that paved the way for the invading Spaniards.

EXPLORATION AND COLONIZATION

The voyages of Christopher Columbus (1451–1506) began an epoch of exploration and acquisition that brought most of what is now Latin America under Spanish control by the 1494 Treaty of Tordesillas. In 1520, Ferdinand Magellan (1480–1521) became the first European to reach Tierra del Fuego and navigate the passage now known as the Strait of Magellan. In the 1530s, the Spaniard Francisco Pizarro and his brothers divided and conquered the Inca empire. Pizarro's partner and rival Diego de Almagro was the first to explore and try to take what is now Chile, in an overland expedition in 1535, but poor planning and logistics stopped him from advancing beyond the Aconcagua valley in central Chile, and many of his men and animals died crossing the high Andes. Pedro de Valdivia's 1541 expedition was more successful, establishing the capital of Santiago, as well as the coastal cities of La Serena, Valparaíso, and Concepción, the interior town of Villarrica, and the riverside city of Valdivia. He also sent forces south to explore the Strait of Magellan from the western side, helping establish Chile's claim to the continent's southernmost areas.

Francisco Pizarro (c.1471–1541)

Initial good relations between the Mapuche and the Spanish soon deteriorated, leading to the Araucanian wars which lasted over three centuries. Valdivia himself died in the 1553 Battle of Tucapel against the Mapuche, but his exploits and organizational skills laid the foundation for the country that would become Chile.

The main goal of the conquistadores was to get rich and, when the gold they hoped for proved an illusion, they and their successors had to find alternatives. The Spanish Crown, with a vested interest in the new colonies, offered them wealth in the form of *encomiendas*, where power over large areas of land and its indigenous inhabitants were "entrusted" (*encomendado*) to Spanish settlers. At the same time,

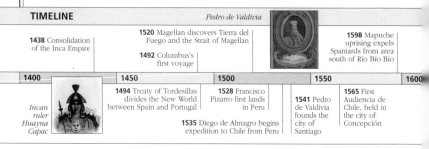

TIMELINE

Pedro de Valdivia

1438 Consolidation of the Inca Empire

1492 Columbus's first voyage

1520 Magellan discovers Tierra del Fuego and the Strait of Magellan

1598 Mapuche uprising expels Spaniards from area south of Río Bío Bío

1400 | 1450 | 1500 | 1550 | 1600

Incan ruler Huayna Capac

1494 Treaty of Tordesillas divides the New World between Spain and Portugal

1528 Francisco Pizarro first lands in Peru

1535 Diego de Almagro begins expedition to Chile from Peru

1541 Pedro de Valdivia founds the city of Santiago

1565 First Audiencia de Chile, held in the city of Concepción

the Catholic Church saw in this system an opportunity for evangelizing millions of possible converts. Both these factors became the basis of economic and social reorganization in the absence of Incan authority.

The *encomienda* lost its value as the indigenous population declined under the impact of smallpox (brought by the Spanish) and other diseases. In some cases, population numbers fell by more than 90 percent, and there were no more Indians to pay tribute. Mortality rates were highest in the coastal lowlands, where the climate favored the propagation of disease.

Chilean leader, Bernardo O'Higgins (1778–1842)

With no one to pay tribute, the Spaniards adapted by creating large rural estates, commonly known as haciendas, although their profitability was limited as there was no labor to work them. This changed as lower-class Spaniards cohabited with indigenous women, creating the mestizo population. However, this brought new social problems: the *latifundistas* (landowners) monopolized the best agricultural lands, while the mestizos became resident laborers, and neighboring *minifundistas* (peasants) struggled to put enough on the table.

COLLAPSE OF COLONIALISM

The issue of access to land divided Chileans well into the 20th century, but in the short term, it was less significant than their increasing alienation from Spain. Although there was a governor in Santiago, Chile was an administrative subdivision of the Lima-based Viceroyalty of Peru, which in turn depended on Spain for authority. Local criollos (South American-born Spaniards) grew restive with Madrid's rule, as their interests began to diverge from those of the Europeans. Events came to a head when Napoleon's invasion of Spain undercut the empire's control over its distant colonies. Figures on the empire's periphery, such as Chile's Bernardo O'Higgins, son of the Viceroy of Lima, and Argentina's José de San Martín, represented the aspirations of the criollo population, and led the campaign for independence.

A 19th-century lithograph depicting life on a Chilean hacienda

Captain James Cook

1722 Dutchman Jacob Roggeveen is the first European to land on Easter Island, at a time of peace between the island's inhabitants

1774 Captain James Cook visits Easter Island to find local society in disarray

1650 | 1700 | 1750 | 1800

1740 Corral bay, marking the river entrance to Valdivia, is secured with 17 forts

1778 Birth of Bernardo O'Higgins

1808 Napoleon invades Spain

The declaration of independence in 1818, painted by Chilean artist Pedro Subercaseaux in 1945

INDEPENDENCE AND REPUBLIC

As the tensions between Spain and the criollos exacerbated, and Spain's European relations grew problematic, Chilean patriots plotted to overthrow the Spaniards. Led by O'Higgins, they declared a governing junta in 1810. The declaration unleashed a Royalist reaction that culminated in the 1814 Battle of Rancagua, which resulted in the imprisonment of many high-profile rebels on the Juan Fernández archipelago. O'Higgins fled across the Andes to Mendoza, where he joined forces with Argentine liberator José de San Martín. Three years later, San Martín's Ejército de los Andes (Army of the Andes) defeated the Spaniards at Chacabuco and entered Santiago with an invitation for him to become Chile's Supreme Director. San Martín declined in favor of O'Higgins and proceeded north to liberate Peru. After overseeing Chile's declaration of independence in 1818, O'Higgins spent five tumultuous years as head of state, consolidating the country but angering conservatives who objected to his secularism and social activism. Over the following years, the influence of pro-business politicians and landowners grew until, after a brief civil war that ended in 1830, Santiago-born entrepreneur Diego Portales emerged as the power behind a new conservative regime. Portales was responsible for the Constitution of 1833, which created a centralized government and installed Roman Catholicism as the official religion. Portales's constitution lasted until 1925.

On the economic front, the country enjoyed a boom during this period, thanks to a silver strike at Chañarcillo, in the Atacama region, that enriched the national treasury. Additionally, the mid-19th century California Gold Rush made Valparaíso a major stopover for ships rounding Cape Horn, and San Francisco became a huge

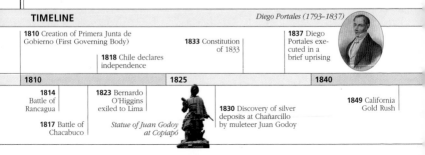

TIMELINE

1810 Creation of Primera Junta de Gobierno (First Governing Body)

1818 Chile declares independence

1833 Constitution of 1833

1837 Diego Portales executed in a brief uprising

Diego Portales (1793–1837)

1810 — **1825** — **1840**

1814 Battle of Rancagua

1817 Battle of Chacabuco

1823 Bernardo O'Higgins exiled to Lima

Statue of Juan Godoy at Copiapó

1830 Discovery of silver deposits at Chañarcillo by muleteer Juan Godoy

1849 California Gold Rush

market for Chilean wheat. The key beneficiaries of this boom were the landowners; resident laborers and the peasantry formed a permanent underclass of have-nots that would become one of Chile's great social dilemmas in the 20th century.

Nitrate extraction plant in the Atacama desert

TERRITORIAL EXPANSION

At the time of independence, Chile's territory stretched only from Copiapó in the Atacama to Concepción in the Central Valley, plus a few precarious outliers such as Valdivia and Chiloé. Beyond Copiapó, Bolivia and Peru held the Atacama's nitrate-rich lands. In Bolivia, these were controlled by Chilean investors, who balked at paying export taxes at the port-city of Antofagasta. In a move to negate this, Chilean military occupied the city in 1879. When Bolivia invoked Peruvian assistance, it unleashed a 4-year conflict, the War of the Pacific, that ended in an overwhelming Chilean victory. Not only did Chile gain Antofagasta, it also occupied Peru's southern provinces of Tacna, Arica, and Tarapacá, and even the capital, Lima. It eventually returned Lima and Tacna to Peru, but kept Arica and Tarapacá to form its present northern border. While consolidating its northern frontier, Chile also looked south, where just beyond Río Bío Bío, the Mapuche-controlled lands of Arauco were a dangerous frontier for settlers. Only the Patagonian territories, in and around Punta Arenas and in the vicinity of present-day Aisén, were under definitive Chilean control. In 1881, the government concluded a series of treaties with the Mapuche that finally ended the Araucanian wars. In the process, it opened the area south of the Bío Bío to European immigration, largely German, that left a visible impact on the landscape, with its shingled houses and dairy farms. At the same time, the country's growing navy solidified its presence from the desert north to Patagonia and beyond. A wool boom that started with the mid-1870s governorship of Diego Dublé Almeida made the Magallanes region especially prosperous. In 1888, Chile also annexed Easter Island.

Around this time President José Manuel Balmaceda faced a brief civil war for attempting to distribute the nation's newfound riches more evenly through the population. This ended with his suicide in 1891, and the consolidation of conservative power.

The 1879 Battle of Tarapacá, War of the Pacific

Naval combat between Chile and Peru, War of the Pacific

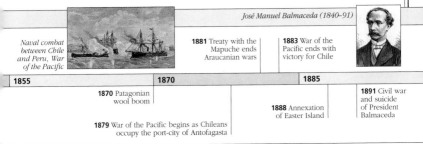

José Manuel Balmaceda (1840–91)

1881 Treaty with the Mapuche ends Araucanian wars

1883 War of the Pacific ends with victory for Chile

1855 | **1870** | **1885**

1870 Patagonian wool boom

1879 War of the Pacific begins as Chileans occupy the port-city of Antofagasta

1888 Annexation of Easter Island

1891 Civil war and suicide of President Balmaceda

Escuela Santa María de Iquique, site of the 1907 massacre

ECONOMIC DECLINE

With revenues booming from the profits of the mining and shipping industries, Chile had reason for optimism at the start of the 20th century. Yet there were clouds on the horizon. In 1907, one of the most notorious incidents in Chilean labor history occurred when the police and military slaughtered hundreds of striking workers and their family members, who had occupied a school in the mining town of Iquique to protest low salaries and poor working conditions. At the same time, synthetic nitrates began to replace the low-yield ores of the Atacama mines. As a result, many mining *oficinas* (offices) and ports withered from lack of traffic. Meanwhile, the opening of the Panama Canal in 1914 reduced commerce around Cape Horn, so that the then thriving port of Valparaíso went into sudden decline. Almost simultaneously, World War I nearly eliminated trade with traditional partners such as Great Britain and Germany. Chile was, in effect, on its own.

As the nitrate mines closed, many miners moved to Santiago and other cities, where they became part of an increasingly militant working class. The rural population found limited opportunities in the countryside, especially as large rural estates still monopolized the best land; smallholders, whose marginal properties often lacked basic amenities such as irrigation water, were unable to support growing families.

THE NEW CONSTITUTIONALISM

Despite the depressing social and economic conditions, the 1920s began auspiciously in Chile with the election of reformer Arturo Alessandri as president. Alessandri realized the

View of ships at Valparaíso harbor, depicted by Edward Willmann in 1840

TIMELINE

Arturo Alessandri (1868–1950)

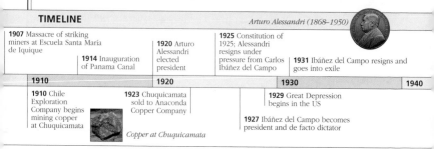

1907 Massacre of striking miners at Escuela Santa María de Iquique

1910 Chile Exploration Company begins mining copper at Chuquicamata

1914 Inauguration of Panama Canal

1920 Arturo Alessandri elected president

1923 Chuquicamata sold to Anaconda Copper Company

Copper at Chuquicamata

1925 Constitution of 1925; Alessandri resigns under pressure from Carlos Ibáñez del Campo

1927 Ibáñez del Campo becomes president and de facto dictator

1929 Great Depression begins in the US

1931 Ibáñez del Campo resigns and goes into exile

1910 | 1920 | 1930 | 1940

seriousness of the situation, but could not overcome a conservative congress. This soon provoked a military coup, which resulted in Alessandri's resignation and exile, as well as the new Constitution of 1925, which created a more powerful executive and separated church and state. However, the Great Depression of the 1930s combined with the authoritarian tendencies of the new president, army general Carlos Ibáñez del Campo, paved the way for Alessandri's return. The following decades brought political fragmentation with an electorate evenly divided among a radical left, a bourgeois center, and an authoritarian right.

Carlos Ibáñez del Campo (1877–1960)

During this period, copper became Chile's prime revenue earner, and the US-owned Anaconda Copper Company exerted an enormous influence in the country, even as urban and rural discontent festered. Elected in 1964, President Eduardo Frei Montalva tried to deal with these issues through land reform and by promoting the participation of Chilean investors in the mining sector. However, Frei's well-intentioned measures could not satisfy either side. The far left would accept nothing less than confiscation of the large estates and nationalization of the copper industry, while the landowners and mining magnates resisted any change to the status quo. In 1970, the election of the socialist Salvador Allende Gossens changed everything.

THE ALLENDE PRESIDENCY

Allende, who first ran for president in 1952, was a true radical who envisioned a total transformation of Chilean society. In 1970, in a close election, he finished first, though his leftist Unidad Popular coalition candidacy won 36.6 percent of the vote, while his opponents Jorge Alessandri Rodríguez and Radomiro Tomic took 34.9 percent 27.8 percent respectively. In the absence of a clear majority, the election passed to the Congress who, by custom, chose the leading candidate as president. Once in office, Allende nationalized the copper industry, but also confiscated some 7,700 sq miles (20,000 sq km) of agricultural land for redistribution, encouraging informal occupation of private landholdings that resulted in rural violence. At the same time, Allende tried to satisfy the urban working class with large wage increases and spending deficits that contributed to runaway inflation.

However, these measures failed to satisfy groups such as the rightist Patria y Libertad and leftist Movimiento de Izquierda Revolucionaria, who helped make the country ungovernable, with the result that political assassinations became commonplace. In the midst of this chaos, Allende appointed General Augusto Pinochet Ugarte as commander-in-chief of the army.

Salvador Allende elected president, October 24, 1970

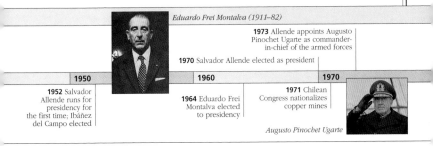

Eduardo Frei Montalva (1911–82)

1973 Allende appoints Augusto Pinochet Ugarte as commander-in-chief of the armed forces

1970 Salvador Allende elected as president

1950 | 1960 | 1970

1952 Salvador Allende runs for presidency for the first time; Ibáñez del Campo elected

1964 Eduardo Frei Montalva elected to presidency

1971 Chilean Congress nationalizes copper mines

Augusto Pinochet Ugarte

General Augusto Pinochet on a visit to Los Andes, July 1987

THE PINOCHET REGIME

A little-known careerist, Augusto Pinochet surprised almost everyone when, barely three weeks after his appointment as commander-in-chief, he led a sudden brutal coup that overthrew Salvador Allende, who committed suicide as the air force strafed Santiago's presidential palace on September 11, 1973. The following months were even more brutal, as the armed forces locked down the country with a curfew, banned political parties, imprisoned political dissidents, and executed many in campaigns such as General Sergio Arellano Stark's so-called Caravan of Death. At least 3,000 died or "disappeared," and many more were tortured. Pinochet also sent agents beyond Chile's borders to kill exiled Carlos Prats, his predecessor as commander-in-chief, and Allende's former foreign minister, Orlando Letelier.

Pinochet had no compunction about concentrating power in his person, or accumulating personal wealth despite cultivating an image of incorruptibility. However, he also tried to remake Chilean society. Implementing his beliefs in free-market capitalism, he oversaw a wholesale transformation of the economy, eliminating government regulations, privatizing health and pension plans, encouraging foreign investment, and selling off most state enterprises. An economic recovery gave him sufficient confidence to hold a plebiscite in 1980, to extend his "presidency" until 1989 and ratify a new constitution. Despite some dubious rules, he won the plebiscite by a wide margin and, even more confidently, permitted political parties to operate openly in 1987. Written by conservative lawyer Jaime Guzmán, the Constitution of 1980 stipulated another plebiscite, in 1988, that could extend his mandate until 1997. This time, however, a coalition of centrist and center-left parties rallied against him and, galvanized by a bold televised appearance from socialist politician Ricardo Lagos, the vote was emphatically against Pinochet.

RESTORING DEMOCRACY

In 1989, the center-left aligned Concertación coalition's candidate Patricio Aylwin won the presidency, but Guzmán's constitution limited political change to a snail's pace. Among other provisions, it created the lifetime position of Institutional Senator that allowed former presidents, such as Augusto Pinochet, to assume a congressional role that also stipulated legislative immunity. Four years later, the Concertación's Eduardo Frei Ruiz-Tagle won the presidency and, as the economy grew steadily, with only minor tinkering, there was neither demand nor

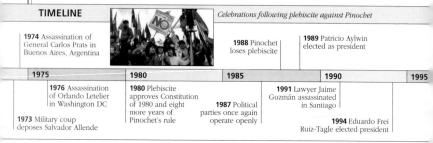

TIMELINE

Celebrations following plebiscite against Pinochet

1973 Military coup deposes Salvador Allende

1974 Assassination of General Carlos Prats in Buenos Aires, Argentina

1975

1976 Assassination of Orlando Letelier in Washington DC

1980

1980 Plebiscite approves Constitution of 1980 and eight more years of Pinochet's rule

1985

1987 Political parties once again operate openly

1988 Pinochet loses plebiscite

1989 Patricio Aylwin elected as president

1990

1991 Lawyer Jaime Guzmán assassinated in Santiago

1994 Eduardo Frei Ruiz-Tagle elected president

1995

Eduardo Frei Ruiz-Tagle, president 1994–2000

support for investigating the Pinochet dictatorship's human rights abuses. Convinced of his immunity, Pinochet traveled freely both at home and abroad, until, on a medical visit to London in October 1998, he found himself under house arrest on the order of Spanish judge Báltazar Garzón, who requested his extradition in an investigation into deaths and disappearances of Spanish citizens in the 1973 coup.

Garzón never managed Pinochet's extradition to Spain, but the London detention broke the spell. Soon thereafter, Chilean judge Juan Guzmán successfully challenged Pinochet's immunity and opened investigations into the Caravan of Death and other cases, as well as questionable overseas bank accounts that destroyed whatever credibility remained. While never convicted before his death in late 2006, Pinochet was effectively exorcised from public life.

POST-PINOCHET CHILE

The election of Ricardo Lagos marked the consolidation of Chilean democracy. Before his 6-year term ended, the third consecutive Concertación president managed to amend some of the constitution's most anti-democratic provisions, eliminating non-elected senators and restoring the president's authority to remove the commander-in-chief of the armed forces. It also reduced the presidential term to four years, but allowed ex-presidents to run for non-consecutive re-election. At the same time, the Concertación governments have largely continued the economic course set by their predecessor. While these policies have led to Latin America's most stable economy, the gap between the rich and poor has grown rather than diminished and unemployment remains higher than desirable.

In 2006, Chileans made history by choosing the Concertación's Michelle Bachelet, a former defense minister, as the country's first female president. After initial ups and downs, Bachelet has drawn praise for her handling of the Chilean economy during the global crisis of 2009, and her approval ratings have risen enormously. In March 2010, Bachelet's term expired and the opposition Alianza party's candidate Sebastián Piñera was elected to the post.

Ex-presidents Michelle Bachelet and Ricardo Lagos

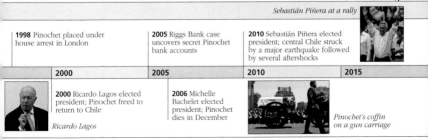

Sebastián Piñera at a rally

1998 Pinochet placed under house arrest in London

2005 Riggs Bank case uncovers secret Pinochet bank accounts

2010 Sebastián Piñera elected president; central Chile struck by a major earthquake followed by several aftershocks

2000 | 2005 | 2010 | 2015

Ricardo Lagos

2000 Ricardo Lagos elected president; Pinochet freed to return to Chile

2006 Michelle Bachelet elected president; Pinochet dies in December

Pinochet's coffin on a gun carriage

SANTIAGO AREA BY AREA

Santiago at a Glance

The capital, Santiago, is the largest city in Chile, home to more than one-third of the country's population. Urban Santiago covers an area of 248 sq miles (641 sq km) across a basin between the Andes to the immediate east and the coastal cordillera to the west. The Río Mapocho bisects the city, and Santiago's main points of interest lie along the river. These include the neighborhoods of Las Condes, Vitacura, Providencia, Bellavista, and El Centro (also known as downtown Santiago). Residential areas fan out into the foothills of the Andes, and toward the west, away from Parque Metropolitano de Santiago.

LOCATOR MAP

Catedral Metropolitana (see p58) *is an iconic landmark on the Plaza de Armas. It is the city's largest Catholic church and the seat of the Archdiocese of Santiago de Chile. The cathedral is built in a Neo-Classical style that can be seen in most of downtown's major buildings.*

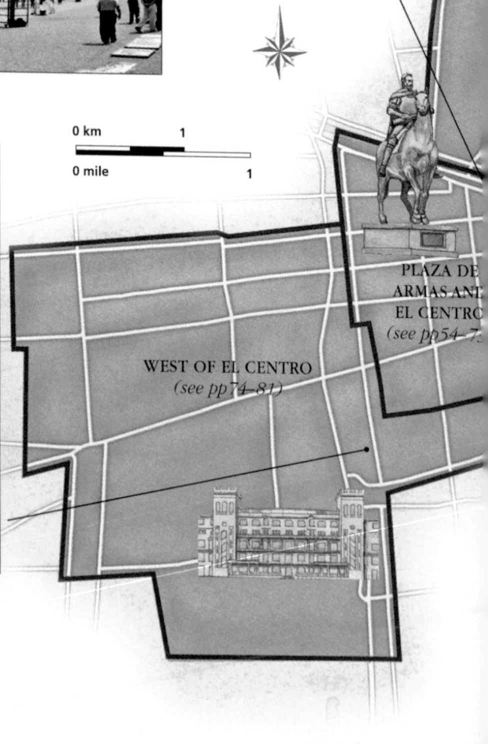

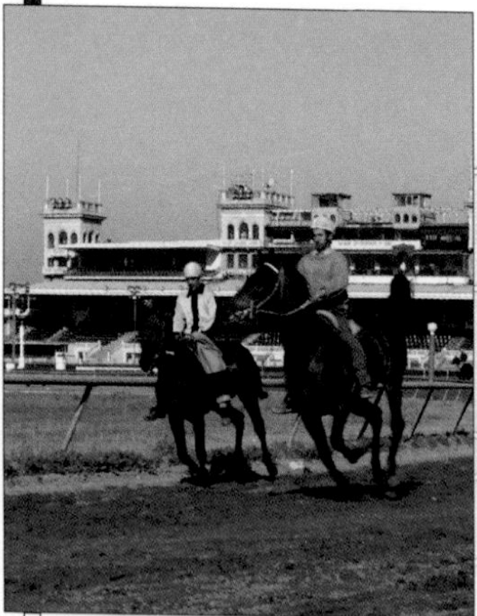

Club Hípico's *architectural grandeur* (see p81), *set amid the faded elegance of the Républica neighborhood, is a testament to Santiago's economic boom during the late 19th century.*

◁ **View of urban Santiago from Parque Metropolitano de Santiago**

Barrio El Golf (see p90) *is part of the larger neighborhood of Las Condes, which is nicknamed Sanhattan for its modern, glitzy skyscrapers. Dozens of excellent restaurants line Avenida Isidora Goyenechea and Avenida El Bosque in Barrio El Golf.*

Galería Isabel Aninat *is one of a dozen modern art galleries in the Barrio Vitacura* (see pp90–91) *that displays exhibits by both established artists and new Chilean talent.*

Parque Metropolitano de Santiago (see pp84–5) *is a forested recreational park and the lungs of Santiago. The park features walking trails, a botanical garden, swimming pools, the city zoo, and a cable car for aerial views.*

PLAZA DE ARMAS AND EL CENTRO

Established in 1541 by Pedro de Valdivia, the Plaza de Armas began as the civic and commercial nucleus of Santiago. The area around it became site of the court of law, the cathedral, the governor's palace, and the residential homes of Chile's principal conquistadores.

Mask at Museo Chileno de Arte Precolombino

Over the years, many of these buildings fell victim to earthquake or fire, and what remains today dates largely from the 18th century. The plaza and El Centro are now the major social hub of downtown Santiago, where people relax and are entertained by street performers.

SIGHTS AT A GLANCE

Historic Buildings, Streets, and Neighborhoods

Barrio Lastarría 24
Barrio París-Londres 17
Biblioteca Nacional 19
Bolsa de Comercio 15
Cancillería 11
Casa Colorada 5
Centro Cultural Estacíon Mapocho 31
Centro Cultural Palacio La Moneda 13
Club de la Unión 16
Correo Central 2
Ex Congreso Nacional 9
Mercado Central 30
Municipalidad de Santiago 4
Palacio Alhambra 10
Palacio de La Moneda 12
Palacio de la Real de la Audencia 3
Palacio de los Tribunales de Justicia 8
Paseos Ahumada and Huérfanos 7
Plaza Bulnes 14
Posada del Corregidor 28
Teatro Municipal 20

Churches and Cathedrals

Basilica y Museo de la Merced 22
Catedral Metropolitana 1
Iglesia de Santo Domingo 29
Iglesia San Agustín 21
Iglesia y Convento de San Francisco 18

Museums and Galleries

Museo de Arte Contemporaneo 27
Museo Chileno de Arte Precolombino pp60–61 6
Museo de Artes Visuales 25
Museo Nacional de Bellas Artes 26

Sites of Interest

Cerro Santa Lucía 23

SEE ALSO

- ***Where to Stay*** pp274–5
- ***Where to Eat*** pp294–5

KEY

- Street-by-street area *pp56–7*
- Metro de Santiago
- Visitor information
- Church

GETTING AROUND

The best way to see this area is on foot; there is ample public transport, but the distances are too short to warrant a taxi or metro ride.

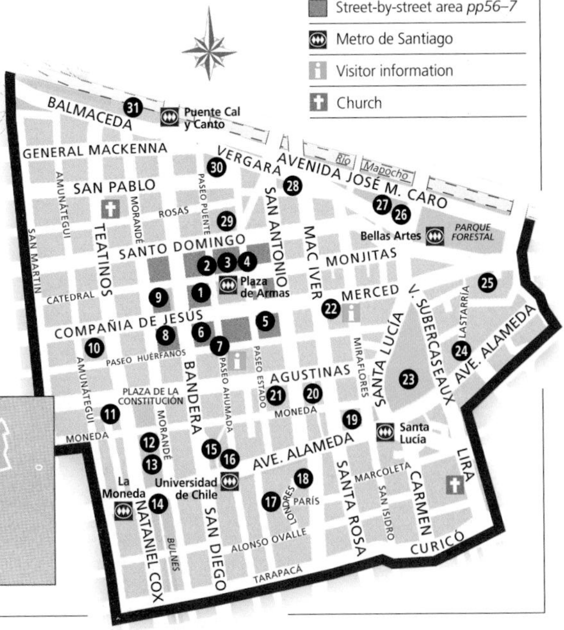

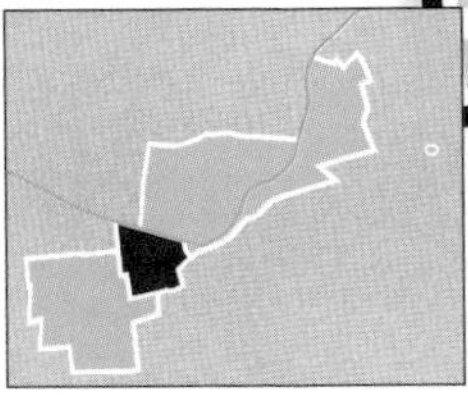

◁ **Equestrian statue of Spanish conquistador Pedro de Valdivia at the Plaza de Armas**

Street-by-Street: Plaza de Armas

Virgin statue, Ex Congreso Nacional

The symbolic heart of Santiago, the Plaza de Armas (Arms Plaza) was designed to suit the Spanish norm of leaving one block of a city grid empty for use as a parade ground. Government offices ringed the plaza during Colonial years, and in the 17th century, it became a thriving commercial area with shopping galleries stretching around the perimeter. In 2000, the square was cleared, leaving only a handful of tall trees and palms to create more open spaces in the city. Today, it is a vibrant social center drawing people who come here to rest on park benches, play chess, or enjoy the lively atmosphere and street performances.

The Ex Congreso Nacional, a venerable edifice, was constructed between 1858–76 in the Neo-Classical style with striking Corinthian columns ❾

Palacio de los Tribunales de Justicia
Chile's Supreme Court occupies a Neo-Classical building with French influences. An architectural masterpiece, its vaulted glass-and-metal ceiling runs the length of the edifice ❽

★ Museo Chileno de Arte Precolombino
Housed in the Palacio Real de la Casa Aduana, the Museo Chileno de Arte Precolombino highlights the arts and symbols of pre-Columbian cultures in the Americas ❻

KEY

– – – Suggested route

STAR SIGHTS

- ★ Museo Chileno de Arte Precolombino
- ★ Paseos Ahumada and Huérfanos
- ★ Palacio de la Real de la Audencia

★ Paseos Ahumada and Huérfanos
These two bustling pedestrian walkways are lined with shopping centers, cafés, and restaurants ❼

For hotels and restaurants in this area see pp274–5 and pp294–5

Catedral Metropolitana
Consecrated in 1775, Catedral Metropolitana is the fifth church to be built on this site. This cathedral was originally designed by Bavarian Jesuits, but received a Neo-Classical makeover between 1780–89 (1)

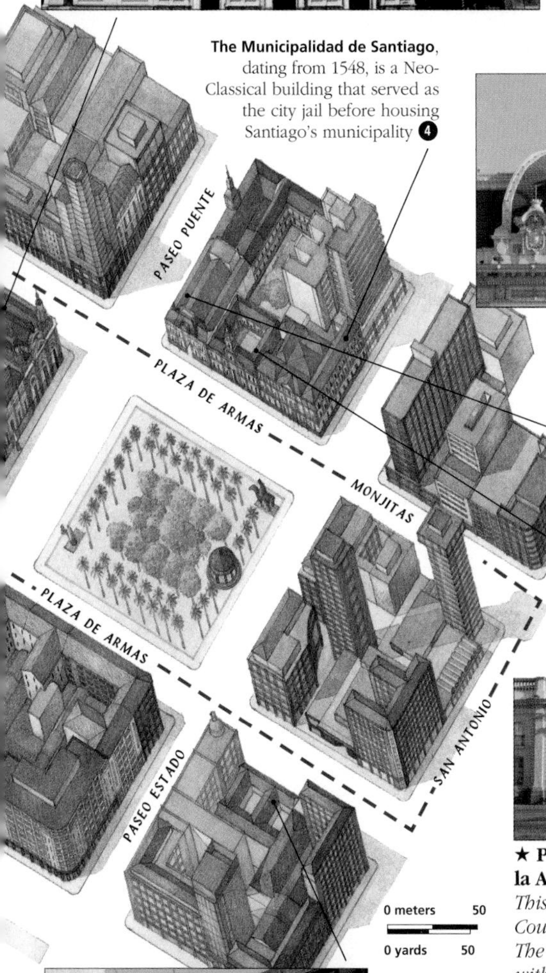

The Municipalidad de Santiago, dating from 1548, is a Neo-Classical building that served as the city jail before housing Santiago's municipality (4)

Correo Central
Chile's Correo Central (Post Office) occupies a French Neo-Classical edifice built in 1882 on the site of Pedro de Valdivia's residence (2)

★ Palacio de la Real de la Audencia
This served as Chile's Supreme Court until independence in 1810. The Museo Histórico Nacional within offers a walk through Santiago's Colonial past (3)

Casa Colorada
One of the last 18th-century structures left in Santiago, Casa Colorada features a second story, uncommon in its day. It now houses the Museo de Santiago (5)

Catedral Metropolitana ❶

Plaza de Armas. **City Map** 2 E2. *Plaza de Armas.* *9am–7pm Mon–Sat, 9am–noon Sun.*

Set on the western side of the Plaza de Armas, the Catedral Metropolitana was inaugurated in 1775 and is the fifth church to be built on this site, after previous structures were destroyed in earthquakes. The cathedral is considered the most important in Chile and is the seat of the Archdiocese of Santiago de Chile. The original design was conceived by Bavarian Jesuits, whose influence can be seen in the cathedral's imposing, hand-carved cedar doors and wooden pews, despite the church having undergone an endless series of renovations and architectural alterations.

The grand interior is 295 ft (90 m) long and divided into three naves. The right nave holds an urn that guards the hearts of war heroes who fought the Concepción battle during the War of the Pacific (1879–83). It also holds the vestige and altar of Santa Teresa de los Andes, Chile's first saint. Highlights in the central nave include the organ, imported from London in 1850; the cathedral's original 18th-century pulpit; and the central altar, constructed in Munich in 1912. Behind the altar is the crypt where Chile's past cardinals and archbishops are buried. The left nave is the Iglesia de Sagrario (Tabernacle Church), a national monument and site of the first parish that was founded in the country. The cathedral's Capilla del Centesimo Sacramento (the Hundredth Sacrament Chapel) is covered in beautiful silverwork crafted by Jesuits.

The cathedral houses Jesuit artwork and other religious imagery in the **Museo de Arte Sagrado**, a small yet atmospheric museum reached through the church.

Baroque grandeur of the nave at Catedral Metropolitana

Correo Central ❷

Plaza de Armas 983. **City Map** 2 E2. ***Tel*** *(02) 6971701.* *Plaza de Armas.* *9am–5pm Mon–Fri.* **www**.correos.cl

Historically known as the site of the first house built in early Santiago, Correo Central was initially the residence of the city's founding father, Pedro de Valdivia. Later it served as the Governing Council, and following independence, as the presidential residence until 1846. In 1881, a fire destroyed part of the edifice. Soon after, the government planned a grand post office at the Plaza de Armas, enlisting the help of architect and musician Ricardo Brown, who adapted his design using the actual base and partial walls of the existing building. He expanded the walls to a thickness of 4 ft (1 m) and topped the roof with metal. In 1908, in a bid to beautify the building, architect J. Eduardo Ferham renovated the façade in Renaissance style, adding a third floor and a glass cupola.

Today, the Correo Central has a small postal museum and stamp collection on the first floor to memorialize the history of Correos de Chile (Post Office of Chile).

Old post-office artifacts at the Correo Central

Palacio de la Real de la Audencia ❸

Plaza de Armas 951. **City Map** 2 E2. ***Tel*** *(02) 4117000.* *Plaza de Armas.* *10am–5:30pm Tue–Sun.* *cameras without flash allowed.* **www**.dibam.cl

Built between 1804 and 1808, the Neo-Classical Palacio de la Real de la Audencia has been witness to some of the most important events in Chile. In 1811, the palace was the site of Chile's first National Congress, and later it housed the governmental offices of Chile's first president and liberator, Bernardo O'Higgins. During the 20th century, the edifice housed the City Hall and the post office.

Located in this old palace, the **Museo Histórico Nacional** charts Chile's history through a chronolgical display of exhibits from the Colonial period to the military coup of 1973. Exhibit rooms are spread around a central courtyard and feature rare 18th-century paintings and furniture such as a sacristy wardrobe. Built in Baroque polychrome modeled in a Spanish-Renaissance style, the wardrobe guarded sacred ornaments for Catholic ceremonies. Reproductions of home interiors depict daily life in Colonial Chile, as do traditional clothing and agricultural instruments. There are also sections dedicated to transportation and education. The temporary exhibit hall, called Patrimonio Plaza de Armas (Heritage Square), features displays about Chilean culture and customs.

Sacristy wardrobe, c.1760, at the Museo Histórico Nacional

Municipalidad de Santiago ❹

Plaza de Armas s/n. **City Map** 2 E2. ***Tel*** *(02) 7136602.* Ⓜ *Plaza de Armas.* ● *to the public.* **www**.municipalidaddesantiago.cl

Although Santiago's municipal building is closed to the public, its exterior architecture is easily appreciated from the Plaza de Armas. Originally founded in 1548 as the *cabildo*, or Colonial town hall, this was also the site of the city's first jail. This first building suffered massive damage following a series of earthquakes. In 1785, Italian architect Joaquin Toesca, who had already put his signature Neo-Classical stamp on many of Santiago's buildings, rebuilt the town hall. In 1883, following the transfer of the jail to new premises, the town hall offices expanded, but within a decade the edifice succumbed to a major fire. Renovations began apace and by 1895, the Santiago Municipality was installed in the restored building. This still maintained the previous structure's Neo-Classical style, but now displayed touches of Italian Renaissance, in the form of arched doorways and three enormous frontal windows framed by columns. Today, the front façade bears a coat of arms given by Spain.

Casa Colorada ❺

Merced 860. **City Map** 2 E2. ***Tel*** *(02) 6330723.* Ⓜ *Plaza de Armas.* ◯ *10am–6pm Tue–Fri, 10am–5pm Sat, 11am–2pm Sun.* **www**.munistgo.cl

One of the few remaining Colonial structures in the capital, Casa Colorada (Red House) is highly regarded as a pristine example of Colonial architecture designed for the bourgeoisie of Chile. Built in 1770, it was the home of Don Mateo de Toro Zambrano (1727–1811), a wealthy entrepreneur and the first Count of the Conquest, a title he bought from the Spanish Crown. Toro Zambrano went on to serve as a senior military leader and Royal Governor during Spanish rule. On September 18, 1810, he was elected the first president of the newly formed government junta during Chile's fledgling struggle for independence. In 1817, after the battle of Chacabuco *(see p44)*, revolutionaries José San Martín and Bernardo O'Higgins stayed at the Casa Colorada, followed by Lord Cochrane *(see p203)*.

Modern-day façade of the Municipalidad de Santiago

Casa Colorada is unique in that it has two floors, which was unusual at the time. The family originally lived on the second floor and rooms on the first floor were used as Don Mateo's offices. The building was built with a brick façade painted red (hence the name) reinforced with decorative stone along the base, arched windows with forged iron balconies, and a central patio. Casa Colorada is now home to the prestigious **Museo de Santiago**, which charts the city's history from Colonial times to independence. There is also a library of books on Santiago's history and a salon for expositions.

Wax dolls in a *tertulia* (social gathering) at Museo de Santiago, Casa Colorada

Museo Chileno de Arte Precolombino ❻

Xipe Totec, Aztec god

Inaugurated in 1981, the highly regarded Museo Chileno de Arte Precolombino is dedicated exclusively to the study of the artistic and symbolic legend of cultures throughout Latin America. The museum is housed in the impressive Neo-Classical Palacio Real de la Casa Aduana, which was built between 1805 and 1807 as the Royal Customs House, and which later served as the National Library and Court of Law. The permanent exhibits are divided into six cultural regions. Of special interest is the valuable collection of pre-Columbian textiles and excellent ceramics. There are also interesting temporary exhibitions that in the past have included "Die to Govern: Sex and Politics in the Moche Culture".

Neo-Classical façade of the palatial building housing the museum

Ceramic Art
The Bahía, Tolita, and Jama-Coaque cultures of coastal Ecuador produced elaborate human and animal figurines, and representations of temples, in addition to ornate everyday items such as tripod vases and yucca graters.

★ Chinchorro Mummy
Now extinct, the Chinchorro (see p161) *lived in northern Chile and southern Peru, where they practiced mummification for over 3,500 years. They used sticks, vegetation, and mud to preserve bodies 2,000 years before the Egyptians began mummifying their dead.*

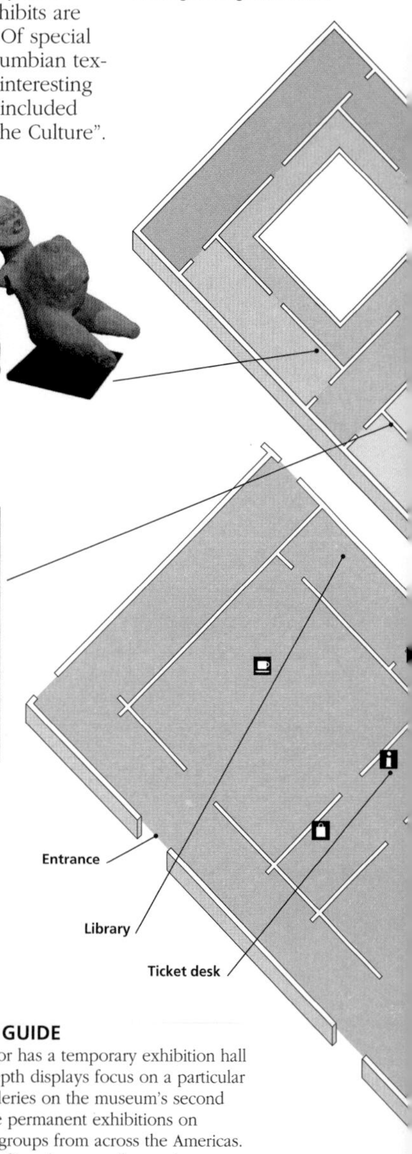

STAR EXHIBITS

- ★ Chinchorro Mummy
- ★ Incan Quipu
- ★ Andean Textiles

GALLERY GUIDE

The first floor has a temporary exhibition hall where in-depth displays focus on a particular culture. Galleries on the museum's second floor feature permanent exhibitions on indigenous groups from across the Americas. There is a café and a space for outdoor events at the museum's entrance patio.

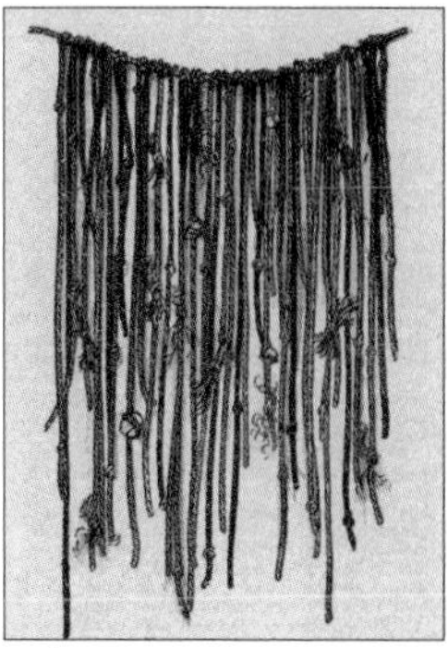

★ Incan Quipu
The expansive Incan empire kept complex judicial data and business transactions on record using the quipu, *a knotted counting instrument that could only be deciphered by the record keeper.*

VISITORS' CHECKLIST

Bandera 361. **City Map** 2 E2.
Tel *(02) 3527522.* *Plaza de Armas.* *10am–6pm Tue–Sun.*
Jan 1, May 1, Easter holidays.
free for students & children.
by prior arrangement only.
www.museoprecolombino.cl

SERGIO LARRAÍN GARCIA-MORENO

Hailed as a charismatic bon vivant and visionary advocate of Latin American and European art, Sergio Larraín Garcia-Moreno (1905–99) was the founder of the Museo Chileno de Arte Precolombino. An architect with a passionate interest in archaeology and ancient American cultures, Larraín began to trade and sell modern art to buy pre-Columbian relics. He convinced the Santiago municipality and the city mayor to let him convert the old, fire-damaged Royal Customs House into a museum, and employed experts to procure artifacts from private collections located across Europe and the Americas. The museum opened with 1,500 exhibits in 1981; today, the collection is double in size.

Chilean collector Sergio Larraín Garcia-Moreno

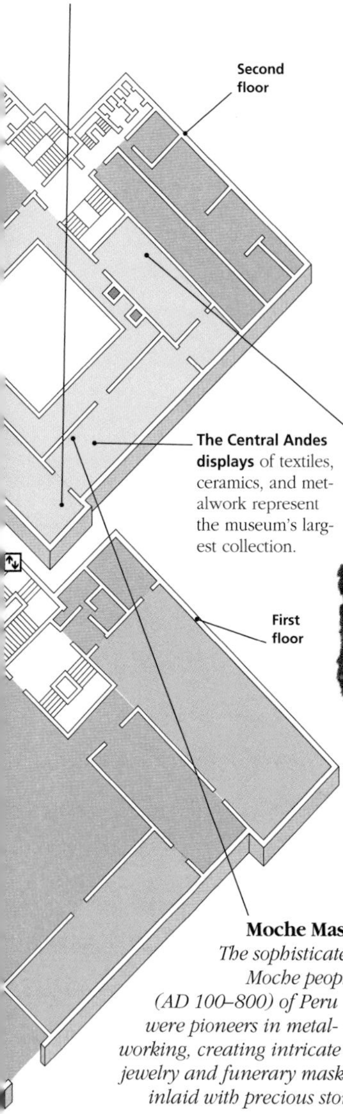

The Central Andes displays of textiles, ceramics, and metalwork represent the museum's largest collection.

★ Andean Textiles
The early domestication of alpacas and llamas allowed Central Andean cultures such as the Paracas and Nazca (100 BC–AD 300) to create aesthetic textiles. Culturally and politically symbolic designs conveyed a user's ethnic identity.

Moche Masks
The sophisticated Moche people (AD 100–800) of Peru were pioneers in metalworking, creating intricate jewelry and funerary masks inlaid with precious stones.

KEY

- Mesoamerican
- Caribbean
- Intermediate
- Amazonian
- Central Andes
- Southern Andes
- Temporary exhibition space
- Non-exhibition space

Paseos Ahumada and Huérfanos 7

City Map 2 E2. *Plaza de Armas.*

Pedestrianized in 1977 by closing 12 blocks to motor vehicles, Paseo Ahumada and Paseo Huérfanos are two walkways flanked by numerous shopping galleries, restaurants, electronic stores, and commercial businesses. Catering to a bustling downtown population, the *paseos* take on a lively ambience, with thousands of people walking to and fro all day. Street performers entertain passersbys and add to the excitement of a stroll here.

Paseo Ahumada stretches from Avenida del Libertador Bernardo O'Higgins, popularly called Avenida Alameda, to the Mercado Central *(see pp72–3)*. It is cut across by a number of roads, most notably by Agustinas, whose junction with Ahumada is the site of the former Hotel Crillón. The first story of this edifice is occupied by **Galería Crillón**, one of many downtown *galerías* – labyrinthine shopping centers brimming with stores selling everything from handicrafts to designer wear.

Paseo Huérfanos runs parallel to Agustinas and crosses Paseo Ahumada near the historic **Banco de Chile**. Built in 1921–25 by Viennese architect Alberto Siegel, the bank boasts ornate interiors and old-fashioned teller windows that are worth a look.

Pedestrians taking a break on the busy Paseo Ahumada

Palacio de los Tribunales de Justicia 8

Compañía de Jesús, esq. Morandé. **City Map** 2 E2. *Plaza de Armas.* *9am–2pm Mon–Fri.* **Note:** *IDs to be left at the front desk.*

Constructed between 1905 and 1930, the Palacio de los Tribunales de Justicia exhibits both Neo-Classical and Greco-Roman features. The colossal building stretches from *calles* Morandé to Bandera, covering an area of around 43,000 sq ft (4,000 sq m). Since its early days, it has been a site of public demonstrations against the government, most recently by school teachers seeking higher wages. In 1818, Chile's First National Government Assembly was convened here. Designed by the French architect Emilio Doyere, the building is entered through a marble stairway that is flanked by two fine caryatids. Although the edifice has a somber, institutional façade, its interior offers a stunning example of 20th-century architecture. An open three-story central hall is encircled with wraparound interior balconies and topped with a vaulted glass-and-metal ceiling. Located above the entrance is a bas-relief of a condor clutching a book inscribed with the letters LEX, the Latin term for Law.

Today, the palace houses Chile's Supreme Court, the Court of Appeals, the Military and Police Courts, as well as the Supreme Court Library.

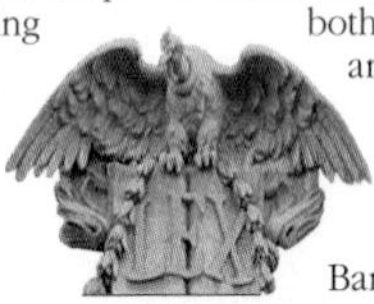

Sculpture of a condor, Tribunales de Justicia

Ex Congreso Nacional 9

Catedral 1158. **City Map** 2 E2. *Plaza de Armas.* *9am–2pm last Sun of May.*

An imposing Neo-Classical structure with massive columns similar to those of the Pantheon in Rome, the Ex Congreso Nacional was designated a National Monument in 1976. Beginning in 1858, the building's construction experienced a series of delays and was only completed in 1876, under the direction of architect Manuel Aldunate. In 1895, the building nearly burned to the ground and was rebuilt by architect Emilio Doyere in 1901.

Congressional sessions were held in this building until the dissolution of the Congress by former dictator Augusto Pinochet in 1973. Today, it houses the offices of the Senate as well as the Chamber of Deputies.

The edifice is surrounded by lush, exotic gardens that are open to the public. The statue of the Virgin that dominates the grounds was placed in memory of the 2,000 people who were killed in a fire at the Iglesia Compañía de Jesús in 1863, which was located nearby.

Formal gardens fronting the entrance to Ex Congreso Nacional

For hotels and restaurants in this area see pp274–5 and pp294–5

Palacio Alhambra ⑩

Compañia de Jesús 1340. **City Map** 2 D2. ***Tel*** *(02) 6980875.* *La Moneda.* *11am–1pm & 5–7:30pm Mon–Fri.* **www**.snba.cl

An extraordinary architectural gem, the Palacio Alhambra stands out in a neighborhood dominated chiefly by Neo-Classical structures and modern storefronts. Built between 1860 and 1862, Alhambra was modeled after the eponymous Moorish palace in Granada, Spain. The architect Manuel Aldunate designed the *palacio* for Francisco Ossa Mercado, a wealthy silver mine owner, politician, and military lieutenant. Aldunate traveled to Spain to study the original Alhambra Palace. Upon his return, he created a smaller version of it with elaborate plaster ceilings and carved pillars, and replicated the lion fountain from its Court of Lions. Following Mercado's death, the *palacio* was bought by Don Julio Garrido Falcón, a millionaire and renowned Chilean philanthropist, who donated the building to the National Society of Fine Arts in 1940.

Today, the palace houses the Society's offices and operates as a cultural center offering art classes and hosting exhibitions. The artworks displayed are dominated by traditional still lifes and Chilean landscapes.

Moorish motifs and arches at Santiago's Palacio Alhambra

Carving on Palacio Alhambra

Cancillería ⑪

Teatinos 180. **City Map** 2 E2. ***Tel*** *(02) 8274200.* *La Moneda.*

Chile's Ministry of Foreign Relations, or Cancillería, is located in an impressive 17-story building that was formerly the Hotel Carrera. Open from 1940 to 2003, this was the grandest hotel of its time. It was designed by architect Josué Smith Solar with help from his son José, who was already well known for his design of the Club Hípico *(see p81)*. The hotel's guests included luminaries such as Fidel Castro, Henry Kissinger, Charles de Gaulle, Nelson Rockefeller, Indira Gandhi, and Neil Armstrong among others.

Hotel Carrera was most famous for its proximity to the Palacio de la Moneda *(see p64)* during the infamous coup d'état in 1973 *(see 48)*, when it acted as a temporary home for nearly every international journalist reporting in the country. Most of the images of the presidential building being bombarded were taken from the hotel's windows and rooftop. The hotel itself was slightly damaged by the shelling.

In 2004, the hotel sold for US$24 million and was renovated to accommodate some 1,200 employees of the Ministry of Foreign Relations. Today, most of the building's interiors, other than the lobby, are unrecognizable from its hotel era. The lobby features beautiful marble columns that rise up to a towering 49 ft (15 m), and a striking mural made of opal glass. Painted by the Spanish artist Luis Egidio Meléndez, this mural is a depiction of the discovery of the Americas.

Opal-glass mural behind the gleaming marble columns in Cancillería's lobby

The palace guard outside the stately Neo-Classical Palacio de La Moneda

Palacio de La Moneda ⓬

Avenida Alameda, between Calles Morandé & Teatinos. **City Map** 2 E3. ***Tel*** *(02) 6904000.* *La Moneda.* *10:30am–6pm Mon–Fri.* **Note:** *passport needed to gain entry.*

The immaculately preserved Palacio de La Moneda is Chile's presidential headquarters. Built between 1784 and 1799 by the Spanish, this stately edifice was inaugurated in 1805 as the Casa de Moneda, the nation's mint. From 1846 onward, it housed the republican government offices, and also served as the presidential residence till 1958. Designed by Italian master architect Joaquin Toesca (1745–99), the palace was the largest building erected in any of Spain's colonies during the 18th century, and is considered one of the finest examples of Neo-Classical architecture in Chile.

At the northeastern side of the Palacio de La Moneda is the **Plaza de la Constitucíon**, an expansive grassy space crisscrossed by walkways and fronted by a triangular cement esplanade. Visitors can present their passports here and gain entrance to the palace. This easy access might seem odd to visiting foreigners used to more stringent security at other presidential headquarters. The plaza was designed in the 1930s to create Barrio Cívico, the country's poiltical and administrative center; other civic buildings around the plaza include the Ministry of Foreign Relations, Ministry of Labor, the Intendente, and the Central Bank of Chile. At the plaza's southern corner is a statue commemorating Chile's former president Salvador Allende, who perished here in the coup d'état of 1973 *(see p48)* that ushered in the Pinochet regime. It is possible to watch the ceremonial changing of the guard that takes place at the plaza at 10am every other day. From the plaza, visitors can enter the palace's interior courtyards that comprise the Patio de los Cañones – named for the two 1778 Peruvian-made cannons that are on display here – and the Patio de los Naranjos, named for the orange trees that adorn it.

Monument to Salvador Allende

Centro Cultural Palacio La Moneda ⓭

Plaza de La Ciudadania Nº 26. **City Map** 2 E3. ***Tel*** *(02) 3556500.* *La Moneda.* *9am–9pm daily.* **www**.ccplm.cl **Note:** *access is via elevators at ground level on the plaza or from sloping walkways at Calles Morandé and Teatinos.*

A pet project of former president Ricardo Lagos, the cutting-edge Centro Cultural Palacio La Moneda was inaugurated in 2006 as part of the 2010 Bicentennial Project that introduced new museums and improved road infrastructure in the capital. The cultural center is located just southwest of the Palacio de La Moneda, in what once served as the palace's basement.

Designed by noted Chilean architect Cristián Undurraga, the cultural center features three subterranean floors that surround a spacious central hall made of cement and glass. Three large salons host international traveling expositions as well as shows by well-known Chilean artists. This facility also houses the Arts Documentation Center library; the National Film Archive, with a digital library and a movie theater that can accommodate over 200 people; a number of restaurants and cafés; and a superb *artesanía* store that showcases arts and crafts from the length of Chile. The sprawling Plaza de la Ciudadanía, landscaped with gorgeous walkways and watery pools, acts as the roof for the underground cultural center.

Contemporary interior of the Centro Cultural Palacio de La Moneda

Fountain adorning the tree-lined walkway leading to Plaza Bulnes

Plaza Bulnes ⓮

Northern end of Paseo Bulnes. **City Map** 2 E3. *La Moneda*

Named for the six-block pedestrian esplanade at the end of which it stands, Plaza Bulnes has been the site of military and patriotic celebrations during the years of the Pinochet dictatorship as well as a center for dissident protests that continued long after the return to democracy *(see p49)*.

In 1975, General Pinochet established the controversial Eternal Flame of Liberty at the plaza. This flame was regarded by many as a visible monument to the dictatorship, and dissidents regularly attempted to extinguish it as a form of protest.

In 1979, the remains of revolutionary hero and Chile's first president Bernardo O'Higgins *(see p152)* were moved from the Cementerio General *(see p86)* to the plaza by the Pinochet regime. This was done in an attempt to create a patriotic altar that represented a supposed symbolic return to traditional historical values.

Plaza Bulnes was renovated in 2005 and now features an underground crypt holding the remains of Bernardo O'Higgins that can be viewed through a glass window. The Eternal Flame of Liberty was finally put out during the course of the renovations.

Bolsa de Comercio ⓯

La Bolsa 64. **City Map** 2 E3. ***Tel*** *(02) 3993000.* *Universidad de Chile.* *9am–5pm Mon–Fri.* **www**.bolsadesantiago.cl **Note:** *passport or ID needed to gain entrance.*

Launched in 1884 with only 160 incorporated companies, Chile's stock market expanded rapidly to include twice the number of companies within a decade. The early years of the 20th century continued to be a time of tremendous good fortune for the Chilean economy, mostly due to the boom in metal and nitrate mining in the northern desert.

Today, the financial nerve of the capital, **La City** is a micro-district comprising charming cobblestone streets and historic buildings. At the heart of this economic hub is the Bolsa de Comercio, Santiago's lively stock exchange. It is housed in a French Renaissance-style triangular structure, with Roman pillars and a slate roof with a cupola. This elegant old building was built in 1917 by Emilio Jecquier, who was already famous for his design of the Museo Nacional de Bellas Artes *(see p71)*. Visitors need to show their passports or IDs to enter the interiors of the building and witness the hustle and bustle of the stock market business. Although considerable modern technology has been installed during the past few decades, the interiors of the Bolsa de Comercio retain their original splendor.

Historic structures lining a cobblestone street in La City

Club de la Unión ⓰

Avenida Alameda 1091. **City Map** 2 E3. ***Tel*** *(02) 4284 600.* *Universidad de Chile.* **www**.clubdelaunion.cl **Note:** *entry via invitation only.*

The exclusive Club de la Unión is an architectural gem constructed between 1917 and 1925 by noted Chilean architect Alberto Cruz Montt (1879–1955) in French Neo-Classical style. The club boasts spacious dining rooms, halls, a private art gallery, and the longest carved oak bar in the country. The ornate interior of the club features gleaming marble walls, antique furnishings, crystal chandeliers, and other finery. The club operated as a men's-only association until 2006, when it invited its first female member.

Club de la Unión signage

Bolsa de Comercio's interior reflecting a mix of the old and new

Changing of the guard, in front of the Palacio de La Moneda ▷

Barrio París-Londres ⑰

Londres and París. **City Map** 2 F3. *Universidad de Chile.*

With small, artfully designed mansions, the tiny neighborhood known as Barrio París-Londres is an architectural oasis in an area cluttered with parking garages and utilitarian buildings that hark back to the 1960s and 70s. Laid out in 1922, the *barrio* was constructed over the gardens of the Convento de San Francisco. It was conceived by the architect Ernesto Holzmann, who believed that downtown Santiago lacked attractive neighborhoods that were within walking distance of services and shops. After purchasing the gardens of the Convento de San Francisco, he enlisted architects to create what he envisioned as a "model block residence," one he hoped to reproduce in other parts of the city.

The neighborhood is well preserved today, and is delightful for its elegant ambience, cafés, and courtyards. Within a four-block radius of winding, cobblestone streets are styles such as French Neo-Classical (Londres 70), Italian Renaissance (Londres 65), and Neo-Colonial (Londres 65). The building at Londres 38 was infamous during the dictatorship years (1973–90) as a torture center.

Old mansion on a quiet, cobbled street of Barrio París-Londres

Awe-inspiring magnificence of the Medina Library at Biblioteca Nacional

Iglesia y Convento de San Francisco ⑱

Londres 4. **City Map** 2 F3. ***Tel*** *(02) 6398737.* *Universidad de Chile.* *10am–1pm & 3pm–6pm Tue–Sat, 10am–2pm Sun.* **www**.museosanfrancisco.cl

The oldest surviving building in Santiago, the Iglesia y Convento de San Francisco is a national monument with distinct architectural details from various eras. Pedro de Valdivia first erected a chapel here in the 16th century in honor of the Virgen del Socorro, whose image he had brought with him and who, he believed, had protected the conquistadores against Indian attacks. In 1618, the Franciscan Order established a church of stone walls and coffered ceilings, expanding the complex to include cloisters, gardens, and an infirmary. With the exception of the church's bell towers, the structure survived two major earthquakes. The current tower was designed by Fermín Vivaceta in 1857 in Neo-Classical style.

The giant stones used to build the walls of the original church are still visible, as are the nave's intricately carved woodwork and the grand doors carved from cedar. The convent's lush and tranquil patio and tiled roofs are early examples of the traditional architecture of Chile *(see pp28–9)*. Set in the church is the **Museo San Francisco**, with an extremely valuable series of 17th-century paintings that narrate the life of St. Francis de Assisi. Also on display are antique locks, paintings representing the life of the Virgen del Socorro, a graph indicating the lineage of the Franciscans, and the Salon Gabriela Mistral, which houses the poet's Nobel Prize medal *(see p26)*.

Gabriela Mistral's Nobel medal

Biblioteca Nacional ⑲

Avenida Alameda 651. **City Map** 2 F3. ***Tel*** *(02) 3605232.* *Santa Lucía.* *Dec–Mar: 9am–5:45pm daily; Apr–Nov: 9am–7pm Mon–Fri, 10am–2pm Sat.* **www**.dibam.cl

An imposing building that occupies a whole city block, the Biblioteca Nacional was built over 1914–27 by architect Gustavo García Postigo in the style of the French Academy. Its interiors have marble staircases, bronze balustrades, painted murals, and carved wood detail in a highly ornamental style, unusual in a 20th-century building. The library boasts a most valuable collection of Colonial literary works in Latin America. It is estimated that 60 percent of everything printed during the Colonial-era in Latin America can be found in the handsome **Medina Library** on the second floor. Works include *Mística Teología* from Mexico (1547), *La Doctrina Cristina* from Peru (1584), and chronicles of explorers such as Sir Francis Drake.

Teatro Municipal ⓴

Agustinas 794. **City Map** 2 F2. ***Tel*** *(02) 4631000.* *Universidad de Chile.* **www**.municipal.cl

Built between 1853 and 1857, the Teatro Municipal is Chile's most important venue for classical music, opera, and theater. The theater was originally designed by architect Claude François Brunet des Baines in an elegant, French Neo-Classical style with a well-proportioned and symmetrical façade. Its first ever performance was an Italian production of Verdi's *Ernani*. Soon the theater became the cultural and social center of Santiago's elite, who contributed heavily to the production of important opera performances. In 1870, a raging fire nearly razed the theater. However, architect Lucien Henault successfully restored the building to its earlier splendor, and it was reopened in 1873.

The theater foyer, La Capilla, features two sculptures by Nicanor Plaza – *Prólogo* and *Epílogo*. The main concert hall has a capacity of 1,500, not including the private Sala Arrau salon on the second floor, with space for 250. The interior hall was designed after the Paris Opera house with lateral viewing boxes and a large ceiling cupola, whose grand crystal chandelier dates from 1930. The theater's massive curtain weighs 2,645 lb (1,200 kg) and was fabricated in Germany in 1995 using burgundy mohair velvet. Throughout the theater there are costume workshops, rehearsal studios, dressing rooms, and set design studios. The Philharmonic Orchestra, Santiago Ballet, and Municipal Theater Chorus are all permanent players at the theater. Many great artistes have graced this stage, including Plácido Domingo, Igor Stravinsky, Anna Pavlova, and Chilean pianist Claudio Arrau.

Simple, classical lines of the whitewashed Teatro Municipal

Iglesia San Agustín ㉑

Agustinas 828. **City Map** 2 E2. ***Tel*** *(02) 6380978.* *Universidad de Chile.*

The construction of the Iglesia San Agustín, formerly known as Templo de Nuestra Señora de Gracia, marked the founding of the Catholic Augustinian mission in Chile. Augustinians reached Chile from Peru in 1595 and erected their first church here in 1625. In 1647, an earthquake destroyed the church, along with most of the city. Rebuilt in 1707, the church was toppled again, by an earthquake in 1730. It was restored by architect Fermín Vivaceta, who added columns to the façade and bell towers. A curious aspect of San Agustín is the *Cristo de Mayo* statue. After the 1647 earthquake, priests salvaged the intact statue to find that the Christ's crown of thorn had fallen around his neck, which appeared miraculous given that the diameter of the crown was smaller than that of the head. Priests paraded through the rubbled streets of Santiago to celebrate this event, and in the ensuing decades the commemoration of May 13 grew into the city's most venerable religious festival. Today, followers still celebrate May 13, but on a much smaller scale.

Cristo de Mayo at Iglesia San Agustín

Colonnaded nave of the ornate Baroque Basilica de la Merced

Basilica y Museo de la Merced ㉒

Mac Iver 341. **City Map** 2 F2. ***Tel*** *(02) 6649181.* *Plaza de Armas.* *10am–6pm Tue–Sat, 10am–2pm Sun.* *Sun free.*

Established by the Order of the Blessed Mary of Mercy – who arrived with the first expedition to Chile – the Basilica de la Merced was built in 1566. During the city's early years, it was patronized by the elite, some of whom are buried within it walls. These include Governor Rodrigo de Quiroga and his wife Ines de Suarez, the first Spanish woman in Chile. The present-day basilica was built in 1760 and later adorned with Neo-Classical touches by architect Joaquín Toesca. The Baroque interiors feature a hand-carved pulpit and a Virgen la Mercedes from 1548. The church also boasts the largest organ in Chile. On the second floor of the basilica is the Museo de la Merced, an interesting collection of Easter Island artifacts, Colonial art, and 18th-century figurines.

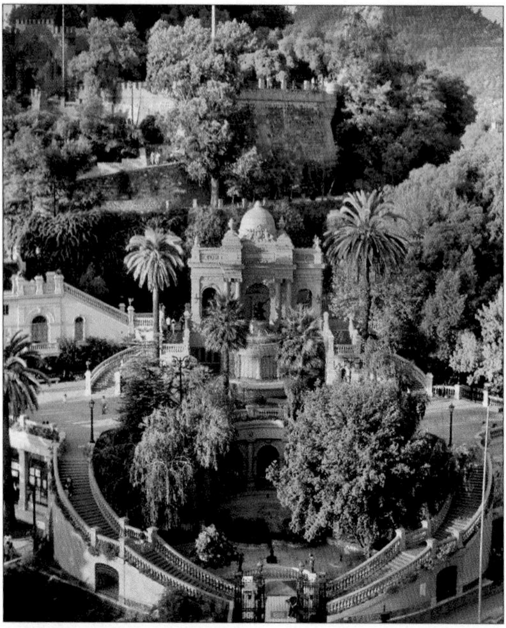

Aerial view of the lush and beautifully landscaped Cerro Santa Lucía

Cerro Santa Lucía ㉓

Avenida Alameda 499. **City Map** 2 F2. ***Tel*** *(02) 6331418.* *Santa Lucía.* *9am–7pm daily.*

Rising above the bustle of Santiago, the Santa Lucía hill is a lush park that was once the strategic defense point for conquistador Pedro de Valdivia, who founded Santiago at this very spot in 1541. Following the conquest, local Mapuches named the hill Huelén, meaning Sadness or Pain. In 1871, Mayor Benjamin Vicuña transformed the 226-ft (69-m) high denuded outcrop into a veritable Eden, with dense foliage, Gothic-style iron balustrades, stone walkways, statuary, fountains, and lookout points. Vicuña was buried here in the tiny chapel, **Capilla la Ermita**. Other historical curiosities include a 6-ft (2-m) high stone carved with a passage taken from a letter sent to Charles V, Holy Roman Emperor, by Pedro de Valdivia, chronicling the land features of Chile. There is also a statue representing the Dissidents Cemetery that was once part of Cerro Santa Lucía; dissidents referring to non-Catholics or to those who had committed suicide. At the summit sits **Castillo Hidalgo**, built by Royalists during the Chilean War of Independence (1814–17).

The principal access point to the hill, from Avenida Alameda, is at the **Plaza Neptune** monumental staircase, or up a cobblestone road across from Calle Agustinas. Visitors can also take the glass elevator from Calle Huérfanos, but that only operates occasionally. A tradition since the 18th century, there is a cannon boom at noon every day.

Weekly antiques fair at Plaza Mulato Gil de Castro, Barrio Lastarría

Barrio Lastarría ㉔

José Victorino Lastarría. **City Map** 3 B4. ***Tel*** *(02) 6383975.* *Universidad Católica.* **www**.barriolastarria.com **Plaza Mulatto Gil de Castro** Merced, esq. Lastarría. *11am–midnight Mon–Fri.*

Also known as Barrio Parque Forestal, the charming Barrio Lastarría is a fashionable neighborhood for artists, actors, and other young and creative members of society. On Calle Lastarría, and along the narrow streets that branch from it, there are cafés, restaurants, high-end *artesanía* shops, art galleries, bookstores, and a couple of boutique clothing stores, which together provide a wonderful atmosphere for shopping and strolling. Located in the middle of Calle Lastarría is the serene and sober **Iglesia de Veracruz** dating from 1857. The church was designed by architects Claudio Brunet des Baines and Fermín Vivaceta in Neo-Classical style using rich red and sunflower tones.

Barrio Lastarría's prime attraction is the tiny **Plaza Mulatto Gil de Castro**. Named for the famed 19th-century portrait painter José Gil de Castro who lived in the *barrio*, the plaza was once the patio of a former house. A small, outdoor book and antiques fair is held here from Thursdays to Saturdays.

Also worth viewing is the private gallery, **Observatorio Lastarría**, located at the corner of Calles Villavicencio and Lastarría. It is open to public and has a pleasant indoor café.

Art Nouveau ceiling and balconies at the Museo Nacional de Bellas Artes

Museo de Artes Visuales ㉕

José Victorino Lastarría 307. **City Map** 3 B4. ***Tel*** *(02) 6383502.* *Universidad Católica.* *10:30am–6:30pm Tue–Sun.* *Sun free.* **www**.mavi.cl

Opened in 1994, the Museo de Artes Visuales is the ideal place to view contemporary Chilean sculpture, painting, photography, and conceptual art. The museum's permanent collection comprises over 1,500 works by artists such as Samy Benmayor, a Neo-Expressionist painter; Gonzalo Cienfuegos, who uses a variety of media, including oil and acrylic; and Rodrigo Cabezas, best known for his three-dimensional assemblies. Located on the second floor, the **Museo Arqueológico de Santiago** is a compact salon with over 3,300 artifacts from pre-Columbian Chile, including a Chinchorro mummy, hallucinogenic tablets from Atacama, everyday utensils and tools, and decorative finery from the Aymara, Mapuche, Fuegino, and Rapa Nui cultures *(see pp22–3)*.

Museo Nacional de Bellas Artes ㉖

Palacio de Bellas Artes, Parque Forestal. **City Map** 2 F2. ***Tel*** *(02) 6334472.* *Bellas Artes.* *10am–6:50pm Tue–Sun.* *Sun free.* **www**.mnba.cl

First established in 1880 as the Museo de Pintura Nacional, and housed in the Parque Quinta Normal *(see pp76–7)*, the Museo Nacional de Bellas Artes is the oldest and one of the most important art museums in South America. The lovely palace in which it is housed today was built to celebrate Chile's centennial in 1910. It was designed by French-Chilean architect Emilio Jecquier, who created a French Neo-Classical edifice with Art Nouveau details, including a grand vaulted glass ceiling manufactured in Belgium and a façade modeled after the Petite Palais in Paris. In front of the museum is a large bronze sculpture by Chilean artist Rebeca Matte, the *Unidos en la Gloria y la Muerte* (United in Death and Glory), from 1922.

Unidos en la Gloria y la Muerte **by Rebecca Matte**

The museum's permanent collection numbers 2,700 works and is divided according to aesthetic, historic, and thematic criteria. Early works include Colonial art – which principally centered on religious themes and the fusion of Spanish and indigenous cultures – 19th-century paintings of landscapes, and portraits of major figures in Chilean history, the most famous of which are by José Gil de Castro. The most valuable paintings here are by Roberto Matta, the 20th-century Surrealist. Since 1990, the museum has drawn major traveling expositions from artists including Damien Hirst and David Hockney.

Museo de Arte Contemporaneo ㉗

Palacio de Bellas Artes, Parque Forestal. **City Map** 2 F1. ***Tel*** *(02) 9771755.* *Bellas Artes.* *11am–7pm Tue–Sat, 11am–6pm Sun.* **www**.mac.uchile.cl

Facing the tree-lined Parque Forestal, the Museo de Arte Contemporaneo (MAC) is housed in the Palacio de Bellas Artes, but is accessed by a separate western entrance. The museum, founded in 1947 by Marco A. Bontá, features over 2,000 works in its permanent collection. These include 600 paintings, 80 sculptures, and 250 photographs from the end of the 19th century to the present. There are also monthly expositions highlighting international and local artists, and shows such as the yearly Architecture Biennial. The museum has an auxiliary branch at Parque Quinta Normal. The collection features Latin American art, including works by members of the Grupo Signo and Generación del Trece groups *(see p28)*. The influence of Europe in the creation of Chilean artwork is vividly apparent, yet the art features indigenous viewpoints. This is seen in the work of Chilean Hugo Marín, who has melded European technique with pre-Colombian influences. Near the museum a tiny plaza draws street performers during weekends.

Classical colonnaded entrance to the Museo de Arte Contemporaneo

Vast colonnaded nave of the Iglesia de Santo Domingo

Posada del Corregidor ㉘

Esmeralda 749. **City Map** 2 F1. ***Tel*** *(02) 6335573.* *Bellas Artes.* *9:30am–1pm & 2–6pm Mon–Fri, 10am–2pm Sat.* **www**.municipalidaddesantiago.cl

A national landmark, Posada del Corregidor was built around 1750 and is one of the few Colonial buildings left in Santiago. Its thick adobe walls, stone base, and second-story balcony are outstanding examples of urban architecture in 18th-century Chile. In the 1920s, it became a social center for Santiago's bohemia. Although the building's name means the Magistrate's Inn, it was never actually the residence of a magistrate. The *posada* was christened as such – with a bogus plaque – in reference to the Colonial-era magistrate Luis Manuel Zañartu, whose descendent Darío Zañartu purchased the building in 1928. Today, it operates as an art gallery featuring temporary exhibits of emerging artists.

Iglesia de Santo Domingo ㉙

Santo Domingo 961. **City Map** 2 E2. ***Tel*** *(02) 6985933.* *Plaza de Armas.* **www**.dominicos.cl

The present-day Iglesia de Santo Domingo is the fourth church of the Dominican Order to be built on this site, on land that was initially granted by Spain to the church in 1557. The existing building was designed by architect Juan de los Santos Vasconcelos. Its construction began in 1747 – with the aid of Portuguese masons who were brought over to quarry stone – in a Doric Neo-Classical style that is distinct from other structures in downtown Santiago. In 1795–99, the Italian architect Joaquín Toesca intervened to complete the church's interiors and added brick towers in a Bavarian Baroque style. The church was finally inaugurated in 1808. Today, worshippers pray to the Virgin of Pompeii, whose statue occupies the central altar.

Virgin of Pompeii, Iglesia de Santo Domingo

Mercado Central ㉚

I.V. Vergara and Ave. 21 de Mayo. **City Map** 2 E1. ***Tel*** *(02) 6968327.* *Cal y Canto.* *6:30am–4pm Mon–Thu, 6:30am-8pm Fri & Sat, 6:30am–3pm Sun.* **www**.mercadocentral.cl

Built in 1872 for the National Exposition in Chile, Mercado Central (Central Market) stands on the site of the burned ruins of Plaza de Abastos. The old plaza had been set up in the early 1800s as a means of dispersing the flood of merchants who then occupied the Plaza de Armas. Designed by self-taught architect Fermín Vivaceta, the market is considered one of the most beautiful public structures of its era: the government briefly considered using the building for a fine arts museum. A firm in Glasgow, Scotland, was commissioned to build the grand cast-metal roof that now shelters the market space. The lattices and cutouts of the roof

Metalwork pilasters sheltering a busy and brightly lit restaurant at the Mercado Central

Intricate arches, cupolas, and metal-work fronting the Centro Cultural Estación Mapocho

were designed to suck air upward and ventilate the market. Part of the metal design features intertwined balustrades, and two reclining women who represent peace and agriculture. Upon the structure's completion, the firm first assembled the building in Glasgow, then took it apart and shipped the pieces in crates to Chile.

After the 1872 exposition, Mercado Central became a premier market. Although Santiago's major wholesale fish and vegetable market has since moved elsewhere, Mercado Central is still an important commercial center. It is frequented by locals and visitors alike who come to see, smell, and buy the bounty of fish and shellfish found along the Chilean coast, or dine on a local dish at one of the many restaurants in and around the market.

Centro Cultural Estación Mapocho ㉛

Plaza de la Cultura s/n, Balmaceda and Independencia. **City Map** 2 E1. ***Tel*** *(02) 7870000.* *Cal y Canto.* *10am–7pm Tue–Sun.* **www**.estacionmapocho.cl

Inaugurated in 1913, Estación Mapocho was built as a grand terminal for trains that connected Santiago to Valparaíso, northern Chile, and Mendoza in Argentina. The station was designed by renowned Chilean architect Emilio Jecquier, who had studied in France and returned greatly influenced by the Beaux-Arts movement and the teachings of Gustave Eiffel, architect of Paris's Eiffel Tower. The Beaux-Arts style can be readily appreciated in the details of the station's stunning façade, its cupolas, and the columns in the access hall. The station's vast steel roof and skeleton were produced in Belgium by the Haine Saint Pierre construction company, and its interior vaults and marquees were designed by the Paris-based company Casa Daydé. All were later shipped to Chile and assembled there.

Estación Mapocho was one of several public works projects to celebrate the country's centennial in 1910, and construction lasted from 1905 to 1912. It was declared a national monument in 1976. The station closed in 1987 when train service was entirely suspended. The building, abandoned, fell into a state of disrepair. Eventually, the government elected to convert it into a cultural center, reopening it in 1994 as the Centro Cultural Estación Mapocho.

During the restoration, architects rescued the station's façade and preserved most of the edifice's ornate details, including its domed ceilings, stained glass, and masonry. Indeed, much of the attraction of visiting the beautiful Estación Mapocho today is to marvel at the splendor of its architecture and decor.

The Centro Cultural now hosts all manner of events, including music concerts, theater performances, and cinema. Many of the original salons have been converted into galleries and spaces for temporary art, dance, and photography exhibits of Chilean artists.

Music workshop at the Centro Cultural Estación Mapocho

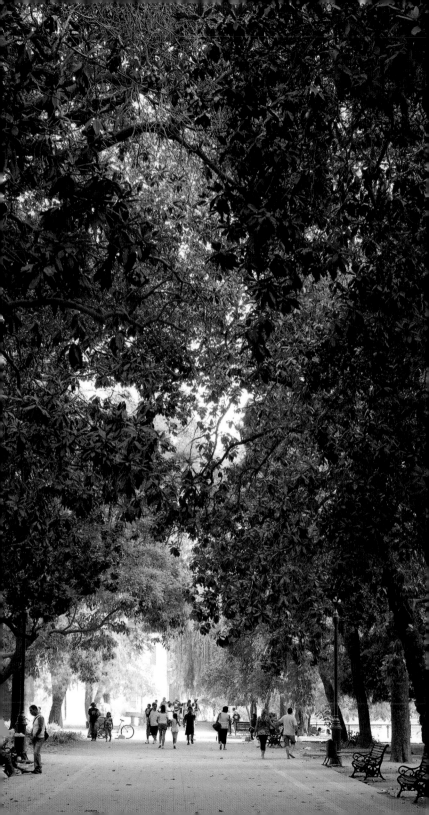

WEST OF EL CENTRO

The sprawling area west of El Centro incorporates Santiago's oldest neighborhoods, including Barrio Brasil, Barrio Concha y Toro, and Calle Dieciocho. These districts were home to the city's elite before they took flight northeast toward the Andean foothills. Few early Colonial buildings remain, but there are plenty of handsome and well-preserved examples of early 20th-century Neo-Classical and French architecture. Some of the capital's most interesting museums and galleries can also be found here, especially around the verdant Parque Quinta Normal, the cultural nucleus of this area.

Façade of Basilica de los Sacramentinos

SIGHTS AT A GLANCE

Historic Buildings, Streets, and Neighborhoods

Barrio Brasil 6
Barrio Concha y Toro 7
Biblioteca de Santiago 3
Calle Dieciocho 9
Confitería Torres 10
Palacio Cousiño 11

Churches and Cathedrals

Basilica de los Sacramentinos 12

Museums and Galleries

Matucana 100 4
Museo de la Solidaridad 8
Museo Pedagógico Gabriela Mistral 2

Parks and Sanctuaries

Parque Bernardo O'Higgins 13
Parque Quinta Normal pp76–7 1

Sites of Interest

Club Hípico 15
Fantasilandia 14
Planetario USACH 5

SEE ALSO

• ***Where to Stay*** p278

• ***Where to Eat*** p297

KEY

Train station
Metro de Santiago
Bus station
Church

0 meters 500
0 yards 500

GETTING AROUND

The area west of El Centro is best explored by metro, especially during office hours when the downtown streets are choked with traffic. Taxis are plentiful, but it can take more than 20–30 minutes to reach Barrio Brasil or Barrio Concha y Toro during rush hour.

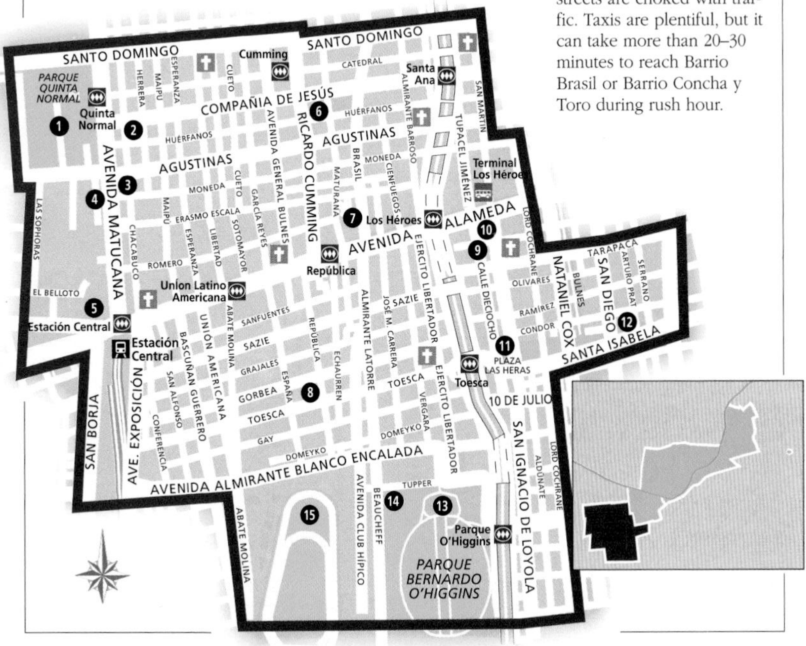

Tree-shaded avenue at the botanical garden, Parque Quinta Normal

Parque Quinta Normal ❶

Yak at the Museo Nacional de Historia Natural

Set up in 1842 to propagate foreign plants, Parque Quinta Normal is famous for its wide variety of tree species. Many of these were planted by French naturalist Claudio Gay whose extensive pioneering studies of Chilean flora and fauna gave birth to the city's Museo Nacional de Historia Natural and to the park itself. In its early years, Quinta Normal was also used for agricultural studies and in 1928, it was incorporated into the University of Chile as the School of Agronomy and Veterinary Sciences. Today, the park is only a fraction of its earlier size, but it remains popular owing to its large lawns and old, well-matured trees. The park is also home to a handful of scientific museums, picnic areas, and an artificial lake.

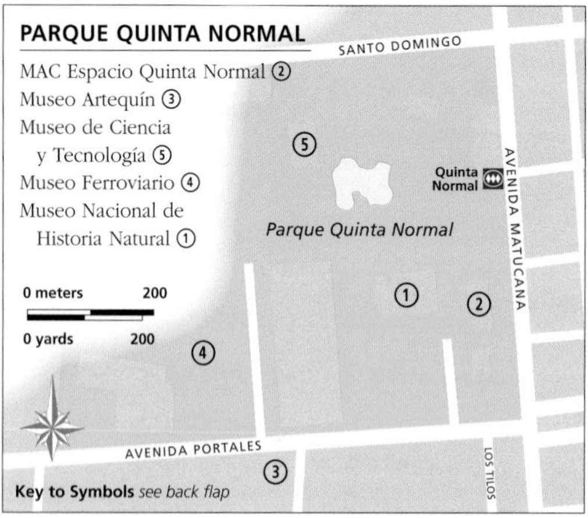

Museo Nacional de Historia Natural

Parque Quinta Normal. ***Tel*** *(02) 6804615.* *Quinta Normal.* *for restoration; phone for details.* **www**.dibam.cl

Santiago's museum of natural history is housed in a stately Neo-Classical edifice that was built in 1875 by French architect Paul Lathoud for the city's first International Exposition. In the following year, the building was handed over to the museum. Today, the institution focuses on research and technical work, but also has interesting displays for public viewing. The lofty main hall, near the entrance, is dominated by the skeleton of a juvenile fin whale. Displays are divided into 12 categories, including minerals, insects, biogeography, flora, and cultural anthropology. There is also a salon dedicated to the native forests of Chile, with massive wood slabs showing the age of such giants as alerce, the second-oldest tree in the world. In addition, the museum also has an interactive display for children. The building suffered structural damage in the 2010 earthquake *(see p19)* and is currently closed for repair.

MAC Espacio Quinta Normal

Avenue Matucana 464. ***Tel*** *(02) 6817813.* *Quinta Normal.* *for restoration; phone for details.* **www**.mac.uchile.cl

Housed in a Neo-Classical palace built in the early 1900s and called the Palacio Versailles, this museum is a branch of the Museo de Arte Contemporaneo *(see p71)*. In 2005, MAC was briefly relocated here while its salons in the Palacio de Bellas Artes were being renovated. Since then, this building has been retained by MAC for shows. With 12 spacious salons surrounding a central plaza, the museum now hosts large temporary expositions featuring up-and-coming national artists and large international expositions such as Germany's Fluxus and the Sao Paulo Biennial. Damage from the 2010 quake is now being repaired and the palace is awaiting designation as a national monument.

Museo Artequín

Avenue Portales 3530. ***Tel*** *(02) 6825367.* *Quinta Normal.* *9am–5pm Tue–Fri, 11am–6pm Sat & Sun.* *Feb.* **www**.artequin.cl

An offbeat museum featuring reproductions of the world's greatest painters, the Museo Artequín is located in the gorgeous Pabellón París that was designed to represent Chile at the 1889 Universal Exposition in Paris. Many erroneously

Mature trees in the popular Parque Quinta Normal

The eye-catching glass-and-metal exterior of Museo Artequín

believe that this building is the work of Gustave Eiffel, whose Eiffel Tower was inaugurated in the same year. The Pabellón's intricate Art Nouveau façade and interiors are in fact the creation of French architect Henri Picq. The structure was built using iron, steel, and zinc, in a clear reference to the Industrial Revolution – Chile highlighted its shipping, agriculture, and military industries during the exposition. Also featured were works by contemporary figures such as the influential writer and artist Pedro Lira. The Pabellón was built in Paris, taken apart, and later reassembled at Parque Quinta Normal where it housed a museum on minerals and metallurgy. In 1992, the Pabellón was renovated and reopened as the present-day Museo Artequín.

The purpose of the museum is to inspire and educate children and adults alike about art through a "real" version of the world's best paintings. On display are prints of some of the world's greatest artists, each represented by a piece for which he is best known. Among the most recognizable international names are Goya, Dalí, Kahlo, and Kadinsky.

Museo Ferroviario

Parque Quinta Normal. **Tel** *(02) 6814627.* *Quinta Normal.* *10am–6pm Tue–Fri, 11am–6pm Sat & Sun.* **www**.corpdicyt.cl

Housing one of the most important collections of steam locomotives in Latin America, the Museo Ferroviario is spread across 5 acres (2 ha) in the southwest corner of the Quinta Normal. Opened in 1984, the museum also contains a library and a sample train station where temporary expositions are held. On display at the museum are 16 locomotives and three wagons, the oldest of which is a Rogers locomotive type 22 built in 1893. Locomotive type 20, made by the now defunct Sociedad de Maestranza y Glavanizaciones from Caleta Abarca, is a pristine example of a locally built machine. Also on exhibit is a Kitson-Meyer locomotive built in 1909 in Leeds, UK. This served the Ferrocarril Transandino (Transandine Railway) that, until 1971, connected Los Andes *(see p134)* in Chile with Mendoza in Argentina – a distance of 154 miles (248 km) across the precarious peaks of the Andes. In all, there were nine locomotives used for the Andean passage, of which only two remain.

Visitors can also view the completely restored 1923 presidential carriage, which was utilized by ex-presidents such as Arturo Alessandri (1868–1950) and Carlos Ibáñez del Campo (1877–1960).

Museo de Ciencia y Tecnología

Parque Quinta Normal. **Tel** *(02) 6816022.* *Quinta Normal.* *10am–6pm Tue–Fri, 11am–6pm Sat & Sun.* **www**. museodeciencia.cl

Set up in 1985, the Museo de Ciencia y Tecnología is the first interactive museum in the country designed to actively engage children in learning about science and technology. The museum is housed in a building called the Parthenon, a Greco-Roman-style edifice built in 1884 by the Naples-born artist Alejandro Cicarelli and inaugurated by Chilean painter Pedro Lira, who sought to create a permanent exhibition hall for art. Museo de Ciencia y Tecnología offers interactive displays related to astronomy, geology, electromagnetics, mechanics, multimedia, and technology. Although interesting, it has since been overshadowed by the new Museo Interactivo Mirador *(see p101)*. In 1887, the Unión de Arte opened the city's first Fine Arts Museum here. It later became the Museo de Arte Contemporaneo (MAC) and in 1974, was transferred to its current location in Parque Forestal, in central Santiago.

VISITORS' CHECKLIST

Avenida Matucana 520. **City Map** 1 A2. **Tel** *(02) 6890119.* *Quinta Normal.* *9am–7pm daily.*

Interactive displays for children at the Museo de Ciencia y Tecnología

The 1909 Kitson-Meyer engine at Museo Ferroviario

Museo Pedagógico Gabriela Mistral ❷

Chacabuco 365. **City Map** 1 A2. ***Tel*** *(02) 6818169.* *Quinta Normal.* *10am–5pm Mon–Fri.* **www**.museodelaeducacion.cl

Housed in the Escuela Normal Brígada Walker, the Museo Pedagógico Gabriela Mistral tracks the history and development of education in Chile. The building, originally from 1886, underwent a two-decade renovation and reopened in 2006. The museum is named for Nobel laureate and literary artist Gabriela Mistral *(see p26)*, who was an educator throughout most of her life in spite of having left school at the age of 12. Self-taught and born with a natural verbal dexterity, Mistral became an advocate for education in response to the lack of opportunities for schooling in Chile.

This education museum was launched in 1941 as an exposition by the Museo Nacional de Bellas Artes *(see p71)* to celebrate Santiago's 400th anniversary. Its exhibitions explored the history of education from the Colonial period onward. Following the popular success of the exposition, director Carlos Stuardo combed through grade schools and even industrial and mining schools in search of material and furniture to establish a permanent collection. Today, the collection consists of more than 6,500 historical pieces, including antique maps, school desks, and skills-based teaching apparatus such as sewing machines, abacuses and more. There is also an extensive library of some 40,000 texts covering education, as well as a photo library of 6,000 digitalized images that track the history of education in the country.

Red-brick façade of the Museo Pedagógico Gabriela Mistral

Biblioteca de Santiago ❸

Avenida Matucana 151. **City Map** 1 A3. ***Tel*** *(02) 3282000.* *Quinta Normal.* *11am–8:30pm Tue–Fri, 11am–5pm Sat & Sun.* **www**.bibliotecadesantiago.cl

Opened in 2005, this was Chile's first major public library. It was built near Quinta Normal *(see pp76–7)* in an effort to create a center of cultural and educational development. Housed in a former government supply warehouse built in the 1930s, it has given the people of Santiago access to a vast range of literature, audiovisual and research materials, computer centers, auditoriums, conference rooms, ongoing lectures, and a children's section.

The children's reading room at Biblioteca de Santiago

Matucana 100 ❹

Avenida Matucana 100, Estación Central. **City Map** 1 A3. ***Tel*** *(02) 6824502.* *Quinta Normal.* *11am–1pm & 2pm–7pm Tue–Sun.* **www**.m100.cl

Another gallery founded near Parque Quinta Normal, Matucana 100 is set in a mammoth brick warehouse built in 1911 for the state railway company. The gallery was designed in 2001 to create a space in which a variety of art forms could participate simultaneously – whether cinema, theater, artwork, photography, or music. Over the past decade, the center has grown to include a large art gallery and a concert hall. It now focuses solely on contemporary works principally by national artists.

Planetario USACH ❺

Avenida Alameda 3349, Estación Central. **City Map** 1 C2. ***Tel*** *(02) 7182900.* *Estación Central.* *Sat & Sun; check website for scheduled events.* **www**.planetariochile.cl

The city's planaterium is one of the most prominent astronomy education centers in Latin America. Its projection dome, the Sala Albert Einstein, has an unusual conical design. Made of copper, it is 72 ft (22 m) in diameter, and has a Carl Zeiss model VI projector that uses 160 lenses, allowing visitors to observe the moon and the solar system, and over 5,000 stars in both hemispheres. Of particular interest are the special expositions that highlight discoveries by Chile's top astronomical observatories. The planetarium offers workshops, audiovisual salons, and expositions for both children and adults.

Barrio Brasil ❻

City Map 1 A2. *Los Héroes, Santa Ana.*

During the early 20th century, Barrio Brasil was a posh residential neighborhood. By the 1940s, wealthy residents began

International Freedom of the Press Fountain at Plazoleta de la Libertad de Prensa, Barrio Concha y Toro

migrating uptown, toward Barrio Alto. Later, the construction of the Norte-Sur Highway severed the neighborhood from the rest of the city, and Barrio Brasil was by and large forgotten. Thanks to this, the area escaped development and many of its grand early 20th-century Gothic and Neo-Classical mansions have been left intact. As a result, Barrio Brasil is now one of the most picturesque areas in Santiago. It has also experienced a cultural and architectural resurgence, due to the presence of many universities nearby. Artists and musicians have moved in, drawn by Barrio Brasil's eclectic ambience. Today, trendy lofts and funky restaurants sit alongside traditional *picadas* and bars. The streets near **Plaza Yungay** are especially well preserved, the most beautiful being **Pasaje Adriana Cousiño** between Huérfanos and Maipú, and **Pasaje Lucrecia Valdés** at the Compañía between Esperanza and Maipú. Both are cobblestone walkways that exude a strong European feel. Other vestiges of Barrio Brasil's past can be seen at the restaurant Boulevard Lavaud *(see p297)*.

A typical house from the early 1900s in Barrio Brasil

Barrio Concha y Toro 7

City Map 1 C3. *República.*
www.barrioconchaytoro.org

Dating from the 1920s, Barrio Concha y Toro is one of Santiago's best-preserved neighborhoods, comprising mansions built by the flourishing upper class in the early 20th century. The area was initially owned by engineer-entrepreneur Enrique Concha y Toro and his wife Teresa Cazotte, who reaped a fortune in mining in the late 1800s. They sought to replicate European towns with sinuous cobblestone streets, closely grouped buildings behind a continual façade, and a tiny plaza. The best Chilean architects of the time – Larraín Bravo, Siegel, González Cortés, Machiacao, and Bianchi – were entrusted with the design. They created a cohesive style incorporating influences such as Neo-Gothic, Neo-Classic, Baroque, and even Bauhaus. Highlights include the **Teatro Carrera**, built in 1926 by Gustavo Monckeberg and modeled after the Teatre des Presidents in Paris. The former home of poet Vicente Huidobro is now the popular Zully restaurant *(see p297)*. The picturesque **Plazoleta de la Libertad de Prensa**, often used as a set for television productions, was named in 1994 in honor of the World Press Freedom Day.

Museo de la Solidaridad 8

República 475. **City Map** 1 C4. ***Tel*** *(02) 6898761. República.* *10am–6pm Tue–Sun.* *Sun free.* **www**.museodelasolidaridad.cl

Set in the ex-headquarters of DINA, the secret police during the Pinochet military dictatorship *(see p48)*, Museo de la Solidaridad is the only museum in Latin America consisting entirely of works donated by artists. In an act of solidarity with the government of Salvador Allende *(see p47)*, artists in 1971 founded this museum with a collection of more than 400 pieces by such names as Joan Miró, Alexander Calder, Víctor Vasarely, and Roberto Matta. After Salvador Allende's overthrow, the works were hidden in the Museo de Arte Contemporaneo *(see p71)*. The museum's administration moved to Paris, where artists continued to donate until the collection reached some 1,500 pieces. The works date from 1950 to 1980, and many of them evoke the social struggle of Latin Americans.

19th-century façade of Confitería Torres, Santiago's oldest café

Calle Dieciocho 9

City Map 2 D4. *Los Héroes.*

During the turn of the 20th century Santiago's posh neighborhood was centered around Calle Dieciocho. Wealthy families erected opulent mansions here, as a means of flaunting their newfound fortune from shipping and mining. The constructions reflect the influence of European styles, principally French. Santiago's elite has since moved uptown, yet the architectural gems they built can still be seen, in spite of the fact that the neighborhood looks a little worse for the wear. Among its best are the Subercaseaux Mansion at No.190, Residencia Eguiguren at No.102, and the Palacio Astoreca at No.121. The grand buildings are now occupied by university groups, libraries, and other associations.

Confitería Torres 10

Avenida Alameda 1570. **City Map** 2 D3. ***Tel*** *(02) 6880751.* *Los Héroes.* *9:30am–11:30pm Mon–Thu, 10:30am–1:30pm Fri–Sat.* **www**.confiteriatorres.cl

Opened in 1879, the Confitería Torres is Santiago's oldest café. It served Santiago's politicians, intellectuals, and elite society when the Calle Dieciocho area was still considered fashionable. Renovations in 2004 salvaged the old red-leather booths, French doors, and long oak bar, and the café's antique ambience is still quite palpable. The Confitería is steeped in history and has produced several emblematic elements of Chile's culinary repertoire. The *barros luco*, a beef sandwich with melted cheese, is named for former president Barros Luco, who ordered one every time he came. The *cola de mono* aperitif of aguardiente, milk and coffee, was also invented here.

Palacio Cousiño 11

Calle Dieciocho 438. **City Map** 2 D4. ***Tel*** *(02) 6985063.* *Toesca.* *for restoration; phone for details.* **www**.palaciocousino.co.cl

Built between 1870 and 1878, the Palacio Cousiño was the most extravagant mansion of its day. It was designed by French architect Paul Lathoud for the Cousiño family, who had made a fortune in mining and shipping. From Europe, the Cousiños imported walnut and mahogany parquet floors, brocade tapestries, Italian marble, and French embroidered curtains, along with European artisans to install these fineries. The mansion also housed the country's first elevator. The palace was auctioned off to Santiago's mayor in 1940, who donated it to the city. Subsequently, it was used to house visiting dignitaries such as Golda Meir, Charles de Gaulle, and Belgian king Balduimo. In 1968, the mansion was converted into a museum that preserved the house as it was during the 19th century. Palacio Cousiño was majorly damaged during the 2010 earthquake and is currently closed for repairs.

Rich furnishings in the central hall of Palacio Cousiño

Distinctive cupola of Santiago's Basilica de los Sacramentinos

Basilica de los Sacramentinos 12

Arturo Prat 471. **City Map** 2 E4. *Toesca.* *for restoration; phone for details.*

Designed by architect Ricardo Larraín Bravo, the Basilica de los Sacramentinos was built as an imitation of the Sacré-Coeur of Paris, between 1919 and 1931. The church is notable for its Roman Byzantine architecture and the crypt, a 4,925-ft (1,500-m) long burial chamber that runs underneath. The parquet floors are the first of their kind to be made in Chile. The wooden pulpit, confessionals, and seats were all hand-carved by Salesians, a Roman Catholic order. Also of interest are the French stained glass and the organ

For hotels and restaurants in this area see p278 and p297

imported from Germany. The church, unfortunately, is often closed due to extensive damage from humidity, and more recently, the 2010 earthquake. However, the exterior is lovely, and made more pleasant by Parque Almagro, which lies stretched out before it.

Parque Bernardo O'Higgins ⓭

Between Avenida Beaucheff & Autopista Central. **City Map** 2 D5. *Parque O'Higgins.* *Fiestas Patrias (Sep 18 & 19).*

The capital's second-largest park is a popular recreation area for families and a major staging area for the Fiestas Patrias celebrations *(see pp32–3)*. Named for one of Chile's founding fathers, Bernardo O'Higgins, the park is home to tennis courts, soccer fields, an artificial lake, Santiago's largest indoor music stadium, and a public pool. A curious aspect of the park is the **Campos de Marte**, a gigantic strip of concrete that resembles a landing strip. Military parades take place here every September 19, drawing thousands of spectators.

Among the park's attractions is **El Pueblito**, a mock Colonial village with simple restaurants serving traditional cuisine. Located here are two museums. The first of these, **Museo de Huaso**, depicts the culture and history of cowboys of the Central Valley *(see pp114–55)*; while the second, **Museo de Insectos y Caracolas**, houses a collection of butterfly and insect displays. There are also artisan workshops and fairs at the **Plaza de las Artesanías**. During the Fiestas Patrias, the grounds are bloated to capacity with revelers who come for the *fondas*, or festival centers in tents – a hallmark of this popular park. For days, a veritable patriotic bacchanal takes over the park with nonstop *cueca* music, smoking barbecues, and excessive drinking – it is quite a sight to the ininitiated.

Entrance to Fantasilandia, Chile's largest amusement park

Fantasilandia ⓮

Beaucheff 938. **City Map** 2 D5. ***Tel*** *(02) 4768600.* *Parque O'Higgins.* *Dec–Feb: 11am–8:30pm daily; Mar–Nov: 11am–8:30pm Sat & Sun.* **www**.fantasilandia.cl

The second-largest amusement park in South America, Fantasilandia is often dubbed the Chilean Disneyland. It opened in 1978 as the brainchild of entrepreneur Gerardo Arteaga, who felt that Santiago had grown insufferably boring for families who were seeking amusement during their spare time. The park offers plenty of knee-trembling rollercoasters and stomach-churning rides such as Xtreme Fall, Raptor, and Boomerang. There are also more tranquil rides for younger children including a carousel, the Kids' Zone, and Villa Mágica, with music jamborees and magic acts.

Spectators following a horse race at Club Hípico

Club Hípico ⓯

Avenida Almirante Blanco Encalada 2540. **City Map** 1 C5. ***Tel*** *(02) 6939600.* *Unión Latino Americana.* *for races: Mon–Thu & Sun.* **www**.clubhipico.cl

First founded in 1870, Club Hípico is Chile's preeminent racetrack and home to South America's oldest stakes race, El Ensayo *(see p34)*, which takes place every November. It is part of the Triple Corona together with Hipódromo Chile and Valparaíso Derby.

The current racetrack was designed by architect Josue Smith and opened in 1923, the previous track house having succumbed to fire in 1892. The club building is a fine example of early 20th-century architectural grandeur, a result of Chile's economic boom during the late 1800s. Club Hípico features stylish terraces and viewing platforms, restaurants, formal gardens, and a picnic area, set amid the faded elegance of the old República neighborhood.

In total, there are about 1,500 races annually, including the famed Alberto Vial Infante and the Arturo Lyon Peña. The club also hosts major music concerts such as the 2009 Chilean Rock Summit, and international acts such as Elton John and Iron Maiden. Despite the racetrack's roots as an elite social club, it is now frequented by people from all backgrounds.

NORTHEAST OF EL CENTRO

The neighborhoods northeast of El Centro comprise residential areas built around a commercial center. Until the late 1950s, some of these were nothing more than *parcelas*, or country homes situated on large plots of land, interspersed with slums for Chile's poorer classes. Today, Barrio El Golf has glitzy skyscrapers and posh shops and restaurants; Barrio Bellavista, Santiago's bohemian quarter, sits at the foot of the recreational Parque Metropolitano; and in the north, Barrio Vitacura comprises leafy streets with 20th-century mansions mixed with towering condominiums.

Mask, Pueblo Los Dominicos

SIGHTS AT A GLANCE

Historic Buildings, Streets, and Neighborhoods
Barrio El Golf ⓮
Barrio Patronato ❺
Barrio Suecia ⓭
Barrio Vitacura ⓯
Plaza Camilo Mori ❼
Pueblo Los Dominicos ⓲

Museums and Galleries
Casa Museo La Chascona ❻
Museo de Arte Decorativo ❸
Museo de la Moda ⓱
Museo de Tajamares ⓫
Museo Ralli ⓰

Parks and Sanctuaries
Parque Balmaceda ❿
Parque de las Esculturas ⓬
Parque Metropolitano de Santiago pp84–5 ❶

Sites of Interest
Cementerio General ❷
Centro Cultural Montecarmelo ❾
La Vega ❹
Patio Bellavista ❽

SEE ALSO

• ***Where to Stay*** pp275–8
• ***Where to Eat*** pp295–7

KEY
Metro de Santiago
Funicular
Church

0 meters 800
0 yards 800

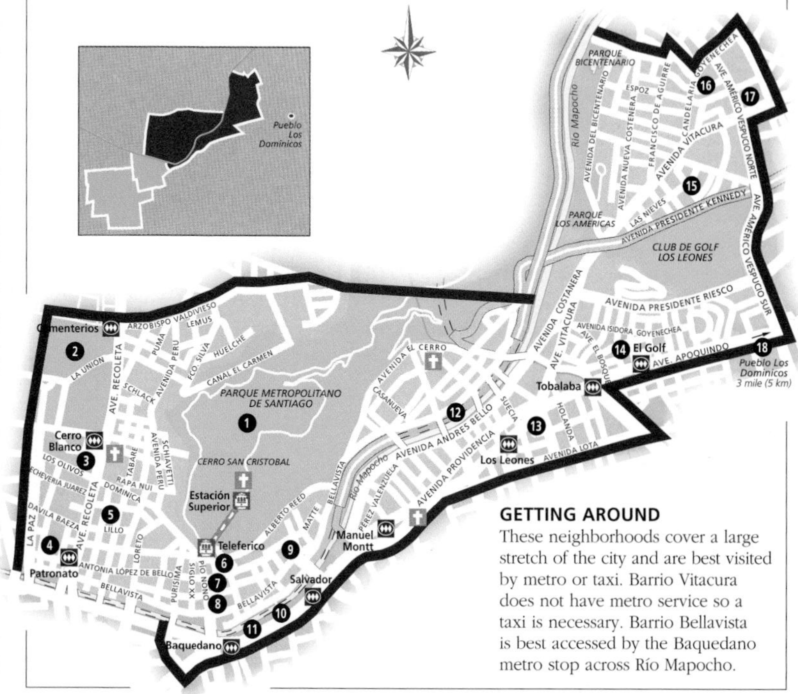

GETTING AROUND

These neighborhoods cover a large stretch of the city and are best visited by metro or taxi. Barrio Vitacura does not have metro service so a taxi is necessary. Barrio Bellavista is best accessed by the Baquedano metro stop across Río Mapocho.

◁ **Statue of the Virgin atop Cerro San Cristobal, in Parque Metropolitano de Santiago**

Parque Metropolitano de Santiago ❶

Garden artifact, Jardin Japones

Covering some 3 sq miles (7 sq km) of vegetation-clad slopes, Parque Metropolitano de Santiago was developed between 1903 and 1927 as the lungs of Santiago, encompassing the hills San Cristobal, Pirámide, Bosque, and Chacarillas. Previously bare and dry, the park was reforested with native plants and trees from across Chile and further developed with trails, picnic areas, swimming pools, a cultural center, and a cable car. It is now the city's recreational center and home to the Zoológico Nacional, and offers sweeping views of Santiago and the Andes.

★ Statue of the Virgin
This 45-ft (14-m) high statue was donated by France and erected in 1904. It can be seen from most of El Centro.

★ Funicular
This 1925 funicular takes visitors to the top of Cerro San Cristobal and past the park's zoo.

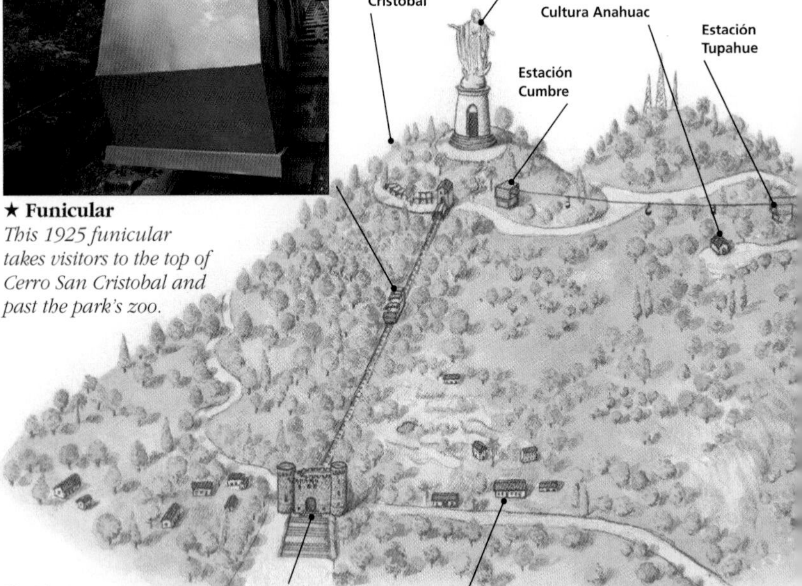

The Pío Nono entrance, leading directly to the Estación Funicular, forms part of the Plaza Caupolicán garden, with its medieval-style façade and souvenir stands.

★ Zoológico Nacional
Located on a slope with the metropolis as its stunning backdrop, the national zoo houses some 1,000 animals including native species such as condors, pumas, pudús, and llamas.

STAR SIGHTS

- ★ Statue of the Virgin
- ★ Funicular
- ★ Zoológico Nacional

For hotels and restaurants in this area see pp275–8 and pp295–7

Jardín Japonés
Inaugurated in 1997 by Prince Hitachi of Japan, the Japanese Garden features a lotus pond and water wheel. Filled with cherry trees and Japanese maples, this is a tranquil getaway from the bustle and noise of the city.

VISITORS' CHECKLIST

Entrance from Pío Nono & Ave. Pedro de Valdivia Norte. **City Map** 3 B2. ***Tel*** *(02) 7301300.* *Baquedano.* *8:30am–9pm daily.* *free on foot; vehicles pay 2,000 pesos.*
Piscina Antillen *Tue.*
Piscina Tapahue *Mon.*
Zoológico Nacional Entrance from Pío Nono funicular. *10am–6pm Tue–Sun.*
www.parquemet.cl

The alternative entrance to the park, from Pedro de Valdivia Norte, has two-way traffic open to ascending and descending vehicles. This is also the exit point for all vehicles.

Enoteca Wine Museum
Housed in the Camino Real restaurant (see p296)*, this museum is a good spot for sampling some of Chile's best vintages.*

Piscina Tupahue is one of the most popular pools in the capital.

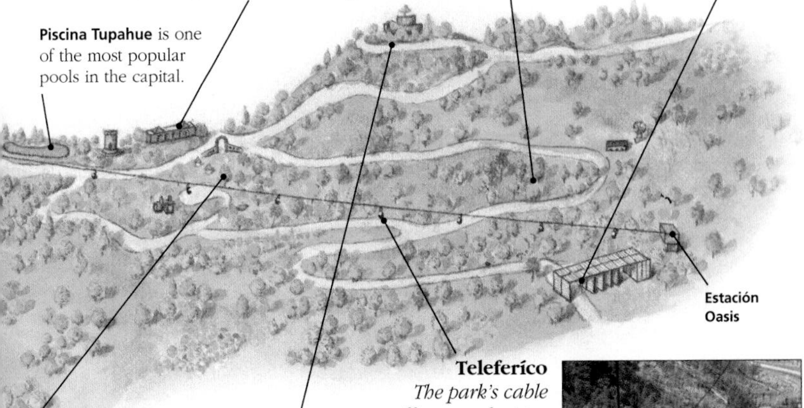

Estación Oasis

The Jardín Mapulemu covers over 8 acres (3 ha) of diverse Chilean flora, with interpretative information.

Teleferíco
The park's cable car offers superb vistas as it loops from Estación Cumbre to Estación Tupahue and Estación Oasis.

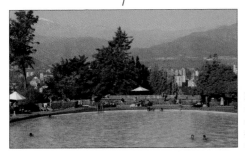

Piscina Antillen
Offering beautiful views of the city, this is the Santiago's highest swimming pool and a great respite from the summer heat.

Tombstones at Santiago's famous Cementerio General

Cementerio General ❷

Avenida Alberto Zañartu 951. **City Map** 3 A1. ***Tel*** *(02) 7379469.* *Cementerios.* *8:30am–6pm daily.* **www**.cementeriogeneral.cl

Santiago's principal cemetery is the final resting place for many of the country's historical figures. Most of the nation's past presidents are buried here, including Salvador Allende, who was moved to this site from Viña del Mar *(see pp128–9)* in 1990. The cemetery opened in 1821 and was inaugurated by Chile's first president, Bernardo O'Higgins, who now rests in a crypt fronting the Palacio de La Moneda *(see p64)*. The area was designed as a "city" for the dead, with tree-lined streets and elaborate mausoleums. These run the gamut of styles from Gothic to Egyptian to Greek, and the cemetery's aesthetic appeal is an integral part of its attraction. Among those buried here are legendary folk singer Violeta Parra; ex-Senator and leftist Orlando Letelier, who was murdered in Washington, D.C.; noted poet and singer Victor Jara; and more recently, former presidential candidate Gladys Marin. There is also a somber monument to the dictatorship era *(see p48)*, a mural by sculptor Francisco Gazitúa called *Rostros* (Faces) that lists thousands of Chileans who were executed. On the west side of the cemetery is the Dissenters' Patio, burial sector for the city's Protestants, who had been moved from their earlier burial site at Cerro Santa Lucía in the late 1800s.

Egyptian influence on a tomb at Cementerio General

Museo de Arte Decorativo ❸

Ave. Recoleta 683. **City Map** 3 A2. ***Tel*** *(02) 7375813.* *Cerro Blanco.* *10am–5:30pm Tue–Fri, 10:30am–2pm Sat & Sun.* **www**.museoartesdecorativas.cl

In 1982, the very valuable Coleccion Garcés was donated to the Chilean government and established as the Museo de Arte Decorativo. The museum was moved in 2005 to the old convent of the Centro Patrimonial Recoleta Dominica. The over 2,500 pieces here are divided into 20 thematic displays and include beautiful examples of 18th- and 19th-century porcelain, crystal glasses and vases, ornate silverwork, marble and ceramic objects, jewelry, and Greek, Roman, and Oriental art.

The center houses two other collections of interest. The **Museo Historíco Dominico** displays 18th- and 19th-century religious objects such as sacred goblets and priests' clothing. The **Biblioteca Patrimonial Recoleta Dominica** is one of the largest private libraries in Latin America with 115,000 historically important books, maps, and investigative papers covering science and religion.

La Vega ❹

Avenida Recoleta. **City Map** 2 E1. *Cal y Canto, Patronato.* **www**.lavega.cl

Located just across Mercado Central, La Vega is Santiago's principal fruit and vegetable market and a must-see for foodies. Amid its chaos of crates and stalls, and the buying, shouting, and negotiating, La Vega offers an earthy and colorful experience. The market is set in a huge warehouse that covers several city blocks and is surrounded by a 100 or more vendors selling everything from sandals to electronics and pet food. At the center of La Vega are the food stalls that sell typical and inexpensive meals such as chicken soup *cazuela*. This is an ideal place to look out for local fruits such as *chirimoya* (a custard apple), *pimienta dulce* (sweet pepper), which tastes like melon, *tuna* cactus fruit, and *lucuma*, a butterscotch-flavored fruit used in desserts such as ice cream.

Barrio Patronato ❺

Between Loreto, Bellavista, Dominica and Recoleta streets. **City Map** 3 A3. *Patronato.* *10am–7:30pm Mon–Fri, 9:30am–5:30pm Sat.* **www**.tiendaspatronato.cl

Occupying over a dozen blocks, Barrio Patronato is a bustling shopping area dominated by clothing stores and small eateries operated in large part by immigrants from Korea, China and the Middle

Stores and shoppers along a busy lane in Barrio Patronato

East. During the Colonial period, the *barrio* was a poor residential neighborhood. It was then called La Chimba, which means Other Side of the River. The area continues to be populated by the working class and many of the neighborhood's original adobe houses still stand.

During the late 19th century, Arab immigrants from Syria, Lebanon, and especially Palestine, settled in the Patronato neighborhood. They established the city's principal textile commercial center here, selling imported clothing and fabrics, as there was little national production of textiles at the time. Today, Patronato heaves with more than 10,000 shoppers per day, who pack the streets searching for T-shirts, shoes, ball gowns, suits, and trendy clothing at dirt-cheap prices.

Pablo Nerudo, Chile's iconic poet and diplomat

PABLO NERUDA

Chile's most beloved literary artist, Pablo Neruda has left an indelible mark the world over with his touching poetry about love, politics, history, and the beauty of life and the natural world. Born Neftalí Ricardo Reyes Basoalto on July 12, 1904, Neruda took his pen name from the Czech poet Jan Neruda, in part to hide his earliest works from his father, who did not consider writing a suitable career choice. Neruda was thrust into the limelight with the collection *Twenty Poems of Love and a Song of Despair*. Shortly thereafter, he was sent abroad in a series of diplomatic posts that included Argentina, Burma, Mexico, and Spain, where in the mid-1930s he became a vociferous opponent of the Spanish Civil War. In 1943, he was elected Senator and joined the Communist Party. During this time, Neruda wrote his opus *Canto General* (1950), an encyclopedic work encompassing the entire Latin American continent. In 1971, Neruda won the Nobel Prize for Literature. The poet died from cancer in 1973; his three homes, in Isla Negra, Santiago, and Valparaíso, are now treasured museums.

Casa Museo La Chascona ❻

Fernando Márquez de la Plata 192. **City Map** 3 A1. ***Tel*** *(02) 7778741.* *Baquedano.* *10am–6pm Tue–Sun.* *compulsory.* **www**.fundacionneruda.org

Built in 1953 on a steep slope of Cerro San Cristobal in the Bellavista neighborhood, the entrancing Museo La Chascona is one of 20th-century poet Pablo Neruda's three homes. The home was named La Chascona (Woman with Unruly Hair) for Matilde Urrutia, Neruda's secret mistress who lived here alone for a year; Neruda eventually married her in 1966. The house's original blueprints were drafted by Catalan architect, Germán Rodríguez. However, Neruda eschewed many of his designs and standard models of home-building. Instead, he used a deeply personal and notably whimsical design of intimate living areas connected by a labyrinth of winding staircases, passageways, and secret doors. His love of the sea is evident in La Chascona's maritime-influenced architectural details such as porthole windows, cozy spaces with creaking floors and arched ceilings, and a dining area that was once fronted by a stream to give the illusion of sailing while dining. The interiors exhibit Neruda's vast collection of art and artifacts, bought during his travels around the world.

Neruda was both a friend of ex-president Salvador Allende and a Communist. As a result, his home was vandalized and partially burned by Pinochet troops following the coup in 1973. The Fundación Pablo Neruda, which operates La Chascona and the poet's two other residences, later restored La Chascona to its original state. It now contains household items and decorative pieces rescued from the Santiago house, as well as furniture and personal objects from Neruda's office in France, where he was ambassador between 1970 and 1973. Neruda's library holds his Nobel prize medal along with photographs, letters, books, and other publications. The house can be seen only by guided tours. For visitors who arrive without a prior booking, the museum's café offers a pleasant area in which to relax, until another tour opens up.

Decorative cross at La Chascona

The quaint, almost lyrical grace of the garden at Casa Museo La Chascona

Castillo Lehuedé overlooking Plaza Camilo Mori

Plaza Camilo Mori ❼

Constitución, esq. Antonia López de Bello. **City Map** 3 B3. *Baquedano.*

Located in the heart of the bohemian neighborhood of Bellavista, Plaza Camilo Mori is named for the well-known Chilean painter whose house and studio stood here. The triangular plaza is dominated by the **Castillo Lehuedé**, a striking mansion, generally called the Casa Rosa (Red House) for the color of its façade. This beautiful stone edifice was built in 1923 by architect Federico Bieregel for entrepreneur Pedro Lehuedé. The plaza is also home to trendy boutiques and restaurants, as well as the **Centro Mori**, which hosts offbeat theater performances.

Patio Bellavista ❽

Constitución 30. **City Map** 3 B4. ***Tel*** *(02) 2498700. Baquedano.* *10am–10pm daily.* **www**.patiobellavista.cl

Inaugurated in 2006 as an urban renewal project, Patio Bellavista is a large collection of shops and restaurants that are spread around an interior square. This central plaza was originally a *cité*, a housing facility for the working class in the 19th century. Today, well restored, Patio Bellavista features over 80 stores selling high-end *artesanía*, or crafts, around two dozen restaurants and bars, book stores, art galleries, jewelry shops, as well as the boutique Hotel del Patio *(see p276)*. There are a number of outdoor cafés, which are popular with both locals and visitors. Patio Bellavista also hosts a variety of open-air cultural programs that include dance performances, live music shows, as well as exhibitions of paintings and photography.

Centro Cultural Montecarmelo ❾

Bellavista 0594. **City Map** 3 C3. ***Tel*** *(02) 7770882. Salvador.* *9am–6:30pm Mon–Sat.* *for events.* **www**.proviarte.cl

Barrio Bellavista's primary cultural center, the Centro Cultural Montecarmelo is located in the building of the former Montecarmelo Convent, which in the late 19th century belonged to the nuns of Carmelitas de Santa Teresa. The order was known for its humility, and its members were referred to as *descalzos* (barefoot). Today, operated by the Corporación Cultural de Providencia, the beautifully renovated center conducts workshops and classes in photography, art, music, and dance. It has a yearly calendar of concerts, cinematic events, and theater productions that take place on an outdoor stage, surrounded by the picturesque brick walls of the old convent.

Stark front façade of the Café Literario at Parque Balmaceda

Parque Balmaceda ❿

Avenida Providencia, between Baquedano and Del Arzobispo. **City Map** 3 C4. *Baquedano, Salvador.*

Built in 1927 following the canalization of Río Mapocho, Parque Balmaceda is named for José Manuel Balmaceda, Chile's erstwhile president and a central figure in the country's short-lived Civil War

Entrance to the popular shopping center, Patio Bellavista

Sculptures by Chilean artist Federico Assler Browne, Parque de las Esculturas

of 1891 *(see p45)*. A statue commemorating this national hero stands at the western end of the park.

Parque Balmaceda's central attraction is the relatively new **Fuente Bicentenario**, a fountain which lights up at night in a rainbow of colors. At the foot of the fountain is the **Monumento de Aviación**, an abstract scupture installed during the Pinochet dictatorship.

The **Café Literario**, located at the center of the park, is well stocked with newspapers and books. An enjoyable place for a stroll, Balmaceda attracts locals from the Providencia and Bellavista neighborhoods, and from downtown Santiago.

Museo de Tajamares ⓫

Avenida Providencia 222. **City Map** 3 C4. ***Tel*** *(02) 2232700.* *Baquedano.* *for restoration; phone for details.* **www**.proviarte.cl

Santiago's *tajamares* were a complex series of underground dikes and brick walls that held back Río Mapoche during the 18th century. Designed by master architect Joaquin Toesca, these prevented Santiago from flooding for many decades until the modern canal system was developed in the late 19th century. The mortar used for the construction of the *tajamares* was a mixture of egg white, limestone, and sand called *cal y canto.*

A part of the city's old *tajamares* was rediscovered during excavations in the Providencia neighborhod. The Museo de Tajamares, created in 1980, features well-preserved examples of these archaic thick walls and arched dikes. The museum suffered considerable damage during the 2010 earthquake and is currently closed for renovation.

Parque de las Esculturas ⓬

Avenida Santa María 2205, between Avenue Pedro de Valdivia and Padre Letelier. **City Map** 4 E2. ***Tel*** *(02) 3351832.* *Los Leones.* **www**.proviarte.cl

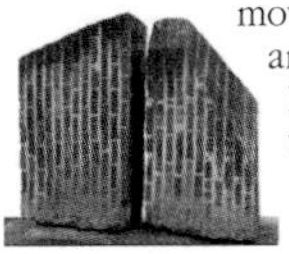

Part of old wall, Museo de Tajamares

Laid out after a massive flooding of Río Mapocho in 1982, Parque de las Esculturas was a creative response to the need to reinforce this area of the river shore. The park was landscaped between 1986 and 1988 by architect Germán Bannen with funds from the Corporación Cultural de Providencia. Serene walking paths meander through the area, which is dotted with some 30 valuable sculptures by contemporary Chilean artists, including *Pachamama* by Marta Olvín, *La Pareja* by Juan Egneau, and *Conjunto Escultorico* by Federico Assler. The park also offers views of the snow-capped Andes.

Barrio Suecia ⓭

Avenida Suecia, esq. Avenida Providencia. **City Map** 4 F2. *Los Leones.*

A micro-neighborhood, Barrio Suecia is packed with restaurants and bars that exude a North American flavor both in their design and cuisine. The area is dominated by bold and colorful façades.

During its heyday, Barrio Suecia was the city's most popular spot for nightlife, However, focus has now moved elsewhere to areas such as Bellavista. Despite this, young travelers, expatriates, and office workers flock to the neighborhood for happy-hour specials and for the clubs, which remain open until the wee hours of the morning. It can get rather brawly on the streets however, and pickpockets often take advantage of drunken revelers.

Busy outdoor café in the micro-neighborhood of Barrio Suecia

Barrio El Golf ⓮

Ave. El Bosque & Ave. Isidora Goyenechea. **City Map** 5 B4.
El Golf.

Often referred to as Sanhattan for its glitzy skyscrapers and North American feel, Barrio El Golf, a micro-neighborhood, is the city's most modern area and home to many major corporations and embassies. The avenues Isidora Goyenechea and El Bosque comprise the heart of the *barrio*, and are characterized by an abundance of restaurants and several five-star hotels. Little of the neighborhood's residential past can be seen, and most of the former mansions and large homes that remain are now upscale eateries. Two of the new office buildings include the stylish Titanium building and the megaproject Costanera Center, a 60-story complex designed to be South America's tallest skyscraper. The neighborhood's Civic Center and Municipal Theater is an ultra-modern cultural center that houses exposition halls and an underground theater for 800. The center, completed in 2010, is located on Avenida Apoquindo in front of the El Golf metro station.

Tiramisu restaurant and café on Avenida Isidora Goyenechea, Barrio El Golf

Barrio Vitacura ⓯

City Map 5 B2.
www.vitacura.cl

Named for the Mapuche chief Butacura (Big Rock) who lived here with his clan at the time of the conquistadores' arrival, Barrio Vitacura was expropriated in the mid-1500s as an *asentamiento* – Spanish settlements on indigenous land developed into haciendas.

Vitacura lies in the north of the city under the shadow of Cerro Manquehue (Place of the Condors), which is a popular day-hike. Today, Vitacura is the residential neighborhood of the affluent, the politicians, and the aristocracy. It is characterized by towering condominiums, Modernist homes, lush parks, and upscale stores and restaurants. The neighborhood is centered around Avenida Alonso de Cordova and Avenida Nueva Costanera. These two tree-lined streets are populated with luxury goods stores from Louis Vuitton to Longchamp, and exclusive Chilean and Argentine clothing and interior design stores. More recently, Avenida Nueva Costanera has become the focal point for Santiago's thriving gourmet restaurant scene, with posh eateries such as Tierra Noble, La Mar, and OX *(see p297)*.

The commune's sparkling new municipality building is part of a colossal urban renewal project that that also includes **Parque Bicentario**, a grassy expanse with lagoons and trails that has renovated the banks of Río Mapocho. This park is the staging center for outdoor festivals, especially wine galas and artisan fairs. An important institution here is the headquarters of **CEPAL**, the Spanish acronym for the United Nation's Economic Commission for Latin America, which is housed in an architectural landmark designed in the 1960s by Chilean architect Emilio Duhart (1917–2006).

Barrio Vitacura is Santiago's epicenter of high-brow art galleries, boasting more than two dozen venues whose expositions highlight Chile's finest artists. Housed in slick, Minimalist-style buildings with bookstores and fashionable cafés, the galleries are in constant motion, hosting exhibitions that provide a space for established and fresh talent. The best-known is **Galería Animal** *(see p95)*, the city's first cutting-edge gallery that launched the idea of presenting art in grand, airy spaces to give the works a more dramatic punch and draw a larger crowd. Galería Animal also offers an extensive range of Chilean art for sale, and frequently rotates its temporary exhibits. In 2008, several

Nativity scene on a hill in the Bicentennial Park, Barrio Vitacura

heavyweight galleries opened to the public, including the transnational Marlborough Chile, Isabel Aninat (known especially for new talent), Arte Espacio, and Patricia Ready. The Patricia Ready gallery hosts temporary art shows featuring top artists such as Carlos Capelan and Bruna Ruffa, and its inaugurations draw Santiago's elite society.

Modern glass exterior of the Patricia Ready art gallery, Barrio Vitacura

Museo Ralli ⓰

Alonso de Sotomayor 4110. **City Map** 5 B1. ***Tel*** *(02) 2064224.* *10:30am–7pm Tue–Sun* **www**.rallimuseums.org

One of the lesser-known museums in Santiago, the Museo Ralli boasts a small, yet impressive collection of Latin American and European art that includes a handful of works by Salvador Dalí, Marc Chagall, and Joan Miró. This transnational museum – there are other branches in Spain, Uruguay, and Israel – was founded in 1992 by Harry Recanati, an art collector and retired banker who shuns any profit from it. The museum is spread across 32,290 sq ft (3,000 sq m), and is located on a tranquil residential street, where it occasionally hosts temporary exhibits by contemporary European and Latin American artists.

Museo de la Moda ⓱

Avenida Vitacura 4562. **City Map** 5 C1. ***Tel*** *(02) 2193623.* *10am–7pm Tue–Sun.* **www**.museodelamoda.cl

Built to honor a family legacy and love of fashion, the Museo de Moda was established in 2007 by Juan Yarur, who converted his parents' Modernist home into one of the most important fashion museums in the world. Yarur, the grandson of a textile and banking mogul, scoured the globe for a decade to compile a nearly encyclopedic collection of more than 8,000 pieces of clothing. These range from the 18th century to modern day, from classic couture gowns by Chanel and Lanvin to modern frocks by Gaultier and Hollywood memorabilia such as Joan Collins' wardrobe from the 1980s TV series *Dynasty*. Madonna's cone bra and pieces owned by Marilyn Monroe also make an occasional appearance. The utterly stylish and low-lit museum rotates its collections in themes such as Rock and Roll and War and Love, with a special wing devoted to tennis, Yarur's sport of choice. The museum is also a tour through his family home preserved as it was in the 1960s and 70s, with a special interpretive area dedicated to his lineage and place in Chilean history. Many items on display are immaculately preserved clothing and accessories once owned by Yarur's mother, Raquel Bascuñán. There is also a restaurant, the Garage, occupying, of course, the family's former garage.

Dresses from the War and Love exposition, Museo de la Moda

Pueblo Los Dominicos ⓲

Apoquindo 9085. *Los Dominicos.* *10am–7:30pm daily.* **www**.pueblitolosdominicos.com

One of Santiago's best and most enticing shopping areas for local arts and crafts, the Pueblo los Dominicos is a rustic complex housed within the former grounds of the neighboring **Iglesia Los Dominicos**. In 1982, the *pueblo* was expanded and landscaped to resemble a Chilean Colonial village with whitewashed, low-slung adobe buildings that evoke a bygone era. The area was originally a Mapuche settlement headed by chief Apoquindo, whose name was given to the grand avenue that ends here.

Today, the *pueblo* offers 160 small shops to independent artisans for selling wares such as ceramics, leather goods, jewelry, folk art, stained glass, furniture, textiles, clothing, and even animals such as rabbits and birds. Part of the appeal here is that the shops double as workshops, giving visitors a glimpse of the artistic process and an opportunity to interact with the artisans.

The ambience is truly idyllic, enhanced by trickling creeks and the sound of flute music wafting through the village. Saturday and Sunday are the best days to come here, when the Iglesia Los Dominicos holds mass. The church is featured on the Chilean 2,000 peso bill and is a historical monument that provided shelter to revolutionaries during the nation's battle for independence in the 1810s.

GETTING AROUND SANTIAGO

Chile's dynamic capital city is well-connected by an efficient public transport system. Its outstanding metro service is the easiest and cheapest way to access the city's main attractions. Most of the capital's primary sights and services are located in or around central Santiago, which is served by metro lines 1 to 5. However, the metro tends to get crowded during rush hour, when it becomes preferable to use one of the numerous, reasonably inexpensive taxis, radio taxis, and *colectivos*. Santiago's bus service was overhauled in 2007, when its old buses were replaced with smart, environment-friendly vehicles. For the most part, short-term visitors will find the bus system less useful than the metro and, late at night, taxis are the better alternative.

Logo of Metro de Santiago

A metro shuttle through scenic Santiago

THE METRO AND RAIL NETWORK

The immaculate **Metro de Santiago** is mostly an underground system that covers nearly the entire city and many of its suburbs. Regarded the most contemporary and extensive metro network in South America, it offers an efficient, fast, and inexpensive way to get around the capital. The network has a total of four lines, but the central Línea 1 and, to a lesser degree, the intersecting Línea 5 are the most useful for visitors. Strangely, there is no Línea 3.

The metro operates from 5:40am to 11:30pm on all weekdays. On Saturdays, it starts operating at 6:30am and stops at 11pm; on Sundays and all holidays, it runs from 8am to 10:30pm. Fares vary according to the time of day, with morning and evening rush hours being slightly more expensive. Individual tickets are available, although rechargeable Multivía or Bip! tickets are cheaper and an easy way to avoid standing in long queues. Multi-trip tickets are bought for about US$2.50 and then charged to the required limit; an amount is deducted each time the card is used. These can also be used by multiple passengers, by passing them back and forth across the turnstile. The metro carriages are modern, but have a limited seating capacity. Passengers should stay vigilant about their possessions, as pickpocketing incidents in packed metro cars are not uncommon.

Starting at the Estación Central, a reasonably efficient southbound overland commuter rail system reaches Rancagua *(see p142)* and San Fernando *(see p146)*. This rail network is under the under the aegis of **Empresa de Ferrocarriles del Estado**.

BUSES

Transantiago is an ambitious attempt by Chile to eliminate the proliferation of poorly maintained, diesel-guzzling, private buses. The new bus system, introduced in early 2007, aimed to consolidate routes and replace the capital's worst polluters with larger, more comfortable buses. Passengers do not pay in cash, but use Bip! cards, which are also valid on the metro. When metro lines cease operations at night, Transantiago buses ply alongside the main metro routes.

DRIVING

Driving is mainly useful when leaving the city for excursions. Santiago's narrow streets mean congestion and slow travel times, and parking can be difficult. It is possible to

The eco-friendly green and white Transantiago buses

A commonly found black-and-yellow Santiago taxi

hire vehicles at international car rental companies including **Hertz** and **Budget**.

Chile follows strict driving laws – seat belts are compulsory, drunk driving is a serious offence, and drivers must not converse on cell phones.

TAXIS, RADIO TAXIS, AND COLECTIVOS

The capital has a number of metered yellow-and-black taxis. Fares are resonable, but passengers are charged more during the night. Taxi drivers are generally courteous and helpful, but some may take indirect routes to hike up the fare. A system of unmarked radio taxis, generally newer vehicles, also operates in Santiago. These do not have meters but charge customers per trip.

Colectivos are shared taxis that accommodate up to four passengers. These black taxis run on fixed prices and routes, and a placard on their roofs displays the destination.

WALKING

Central Santiago, with several mutli-block pedestrian malls, can be easily explored on foot. Parks such as Cerro Santa Lucía and the Parque Metropolitano, across the Río Mapocho, are also great for walkers. Neighborhoods such as Las Condes and Providencia are walkable, but in some parts of the city, the sidewalks need repair and have few wheelchair ramps at corners. Drivers in Santiago generally respect pedestrians, but walkers need to be careful crossing the multi-lane Alameda.

CYCLING

Many locals get around on bicycles, but it is better to avoid major avenues such as the Alameda and Avenida Vicuña Mackenna. The streets are often bumpy and there are many potholes, but new bicycle lanes and routes are being introduced.

DIRECTORY

THE METRO AND RAIL NETWORK

Empresa de Ferrocarriles del Estado (EFE)
Alameda Bernardo O'Higgins 3170, Estación Central.
Tel *600 585 5000.*
www.efe.cl

Metro de Santiago
Tel *800 730 073.*
www.metrosantiago.cl

BUSES

Transantiago
Tel *800 730 073.*
www.transantiago.cl

CARS

Budget
Avenida Francisco Bilbao 1439, Providencia. ***Tel*** *(02) 3623205.*
www.budget.com

Hertz
Andres Bello 1469, Providencia.
Tel *(02) 3608600.*
www.hertz.com

SHOPPING IN SANTIAGO

Chile's capital city offers a wide range of shopping options from high-end fashion to wine and local handicrafts. Traditional crafts include clay kitchenware, Mapuche-carved wooden utensils and bowls, and jewelry and art pieces made of *krill* (dyed horse hair). It is also possible to buy ponchos, alpaca and sheep's wool blankets, and thick woolen sweaters. Lapis lazuli, the unique blue stone found solely in Chile and Afghanistan, is used to create exclusive Chilean accessories. In recent years, young fashion designers have eschewed the shopping mall and set up independent, homespun boutique stores in areas such as Bellavista and Parque Forestal. In addition, the rising interest in Chilean gastronomy has spawned several gourmet delicatessens and wine stores in the city.

Lapis lazuli earrings

Textiles and ceramics on display at a shop in the capital

CRAFTS AND SOUVENIRS

Handicrafts from the Chilean provinces can be found in a range of stores across Santiago, although the choice may be restricted. The capital, however, is the best place to purchase the country's unique gemstone, lapis lazuli *(see p311)*, which is used in ornaments, decorative pieces, architectural fittings, and objects of daily use such as salt and pepper shakers. Lapis lazuli is sold in dozens of moderately priced stores lining Avenida Bellavista, between Calle Capellán Abarzúa and Calle Pío Nono. The **Lapis Lazuli House** offers finely crafted items made with this rare blue stone. For elegant lapis lazuli jewelry, it is ideal to visit any of the **Morita Gil** stores across the city or **Faba** in central Santiago.

Traditional ceramics, textiles, and decorative objects are available at the **Artesanías de Chile** shops in Bellavista and in the Centro Cultural Palacio La Moneda *(see p64)* in downtown Santiago. **Ona** offers some exciting artworks and fashionable clothing made from local products, and **La Verviene** in the Vitacura neighborhood boasts a wide selection of stylish *artesanía* that includes ornamental items for the home. Souvenirs such as T-shirts can be found at the stalls lining Patio Bellavista. The most distinctive souvenir shop, though, may be Santiago's **The Clinic El Bazar**, named for the English clinic in which Chile's former dictator, General Pinochet was arrested in 1998. The upscale **Pura Chile** store in the El Golf area carries a range of elegantly designed jewelry, throw rugs, leather work, and toys.

ANTIQUES

Shopping for antiques in Santiago is relatively easy as most antique shops are grouped into warehouses. Extensive bargains are on offer at **Antiguedades Balmaceda** where more than 200 independent antique dealers sell household items, furniture, chandeliers, decorative art, jewelry, and wares that date from the early 20th century. **Antiguedades Bucarest** is a shopping gallery that houses dozens of independent stores selling antique items such as gilded mirrors, paintings, wooden furniture, ornaments, and curios from a range of eras.

There are also a number of independent antique shops across Santiago. At the corner of Avenida Italia and Avenida Sucre, over a dozen antique furniture workshops sell mostly refurbished fittings and odd pieces. **Brainworks**, in the Parque Forestal area,

Antiques fair at Plaza Mulato Gil de Castro

The high-end Louis Vuitton store at Avenida Alonso de Córdova

specializes in household items, retro furniture, and reproductions dating from the 1960s and 70s.

Every Sunday at the Plaza Peru in El Golf, antique vendors display their wares for sale; another popular antique street fair takes place from Thursday to Saturday along the pocket-sized Plaza Mulatto Gil de Castro in the Parque Forestal area.

FASHION

Parque Forestal is the hub for fashion created by young Chilean designers. Among the popular designer stores here are **Parentesys** which displays menswear by Juan Jose Soto, **Atelier Carlos Pérez**, a contemporary fashion store, and **Tampu**, which sells modern clothing with indigenous patterns. **Galería Drugstore** in Providencia features more than 30 locally designed clothing and accessory outlets, including Kebo that sells frocks by designer Carla Godoy. The **Hall Central** offers clothing by local designers within the old parlor rooms of an ancient mansion.

Most middle-class Chileans buy the bulk of their clothing at shopping malls that stock national and international brands such as Zara, MNG, and Nine West. Vitacura's Avenida Alonso de Cordova and Avenida Costanera play host to luxury international brands such as Louis Vuitton, Armani, and Burberry, as well as national and Latin American brands such as **Casta & Devota** and **Zapatera**. Also located here, **Mor** is a premium women's clothier.

The epicenter of low-priced fashion is Barrio Patronato *(see p86)* in Recoleta, where shoppers descend each weekend in search of low-cost clothing at the hundreds of shops here. Shoppers head for **Óptica Bahía** for retro sunglasses, **Orange Blue** for funky clothing and footwear from the 60s and 70s, and **Nostalgic** on Calle Bandera for vintage wear and accessories.

ART GALLERIES

The uptown Barrio Vitacura in central Santiago is the heart of Chile's art gallery scene, with no fewer than 15 top galleries spread around Avenida Alonso de Córdova and Avenida Costanera. The most prominent of these is the **Galería Animal**, one of the city's first avant-garde galleries, offering an outstanding collection of contemporary Chilean art, including paintings, sculpture, conceptual pieces, and a handful of artworks by internationally acclaimed Surrealist painter Roberto Matta (1911–2002) and the Spanish artist Joan Miró. **Galería Patricia Ready** has vast spaces, a chic café, and a widespread selection of art books. Across the street is **Galería !sabel Aninat**, a long-time gallery that highlights the works of lesser-known Chilean artists. Another site for purchasing Chilean artworks is the **Galería La Sala**. Internationally renowned artists feature prominently at the **Galería A.M.S. Marlborough**. Located in downtown Santiago, **Galería Moro**, **Galería 13**, and **Galería Gabriela Mistral** feature mostly young artists who specialize in photography and painting.

Sculpture at the Galería Animal

BOOKS AND MUSIC

Street kiosks selling local magazines and newspapers are plentiful in Santiago. The stalls located on Paseo Ahumada, between Avenida Alameda and Paseo Húerfanos, sell publications from around the world at fairly reasonable prices.

English-language magazines are available mainly at the international airport, although some stalls and bookstores in crowded areas occasionally sell *Newsweek* or *Time*. However, a variety of English novels, magazines, guidebooks, and textbooks are available at the **Librería Inglesa** stores found throughout Santiago. **Librería Antartica** shops also have a range of English books.

Santiago's **Feria del Libro**, with many branches around the city, has a decent supply of books and magazines. Spanish books on geography, history, and, literature are available at **Librería Chile Ilustrado**. **Librería Eduardo Albers** is known for its travel-oriented selection.

Among the music stores in Santiago, **Feria del Disco** is the largest chain, with over a dozen shops in the city, each with a sizable selection of international and Latin music. There are also a number of pocket-sized music stores located throughout the capital.

Browsing through books at Patio Bellavista

WINE AND FOOD

The booming interest in Chile's wine and cuisine, as well as an increased production of gourmet food using local ingredients, has created a brand new culinary scene and shops that cater to it. Although many well-known Chilean wines can be found around the world, wine shops such as **La Vinoteca** and **El Mundo del Vino** offer boutique wines and little-known varieties that are not available elsewhere.

An upscale and modern store in Vitacura, **Wain** has four well-stocked floors of wine and food products, and organizes cooking demonstrations. In Bellavista, **Emporio Nacional** is designed to resemble a food shop from the early 1900s, and sells specialty food items from all over the country. On offer are cured meats, different kinds of cheese, and dried nuts and fruits. **World Delicatessen** is a popular deli-cum-gourmet restaurant in Vitacura that offers Chilean specialty food products and hosts occasional cooking demonstrations. The **Emporio La Rosa** serves many flavors of delicious homemade ice cream.

MARKETS

Many of Santiago's markets act as one-stop shopping centers for handicrafts, antiques, art, household items, pets, and plants. The Pueblo los Dominicos *(see p91)*, an outdoor market designed to resemble a Colonial adobe village, offers a variety of local arts and crafts, as well as a pleasing shopping ambience. At the centrally located, upscale Patio Bellavista *(see p88)*, it is possible to buy clothes, accessories, jewelry, and handicrafts. The **Feria Artesanal Santa Lucía** and the **Aldea de Vitacura** markets have moderately priced local handicrafts from all over Chile. Santiago's most accessible crafts market, **Centro de Exposición de Arte Indígena** sells Mapuche, Aymara, and Rapa Nui handicrafts. It is open daily, except on Sunday. The sprawling weekend flea market **Persa Bio Bio** sells a range of second-hand goods, but this chaotic market is recommended for the intrepid traveler who has at least a basic knowledge of Spanish.

SHOPPING MALLS

Santiago's shopping malls provide virtually the same stores and quality as most US shopping centers. The two most popular malls are **Parque Arauco** and **Alto los Condes**, housing many US, Latin American, and European chains, and departmental stores such as Ripley, Falabella, and Almacenes Paris *(see p310)*. Parque Arauco is a vast complex, with a dozen high-end gourmet restaurants, a bowling alley, and an indoor ice-skating rink for children. Both Parque Arauco and Alto los Condes have megaplex cinemas. The **Mall Apumanque** in Las Condes features mostly small boutiques with locally produced clothing and goods.

Handicrafts on display at one of the adobe shops in Pueblo los Dominicos

DIRECTORY

CRAFTS AND SOUVENIRS

Artesanías de Chile
Bellavista 0357.
City Map 2 F1.
Tel *(02) 7778643.*
www.artesaniasdechile.cl

The Clinic El Bazar
José Miguel de la Barra 459. **City Map** 3 A4.
Tel *(02) 6320736.*
www.theclinicelbazar.cl

Faba
Avenida Alonso de Córdova 4227.
City Map 5 C2.
Tel *(02) 2089526.*
www.lapislazulifaba.com

Lapis Lazuli House
Bellavista 04.
City Map 3 B4.
Tel *(02) 7321419.*
www.lapislazulihouse.cl

La Verviene
Avenida Las Tranqueras 1535. ***Tel*** *(02) 2010909.*
www.laverveine.cl

Morita Gil
Los Misioneros 1991.
City Map 4 E1.
Tel *(02) 2326853.*
www.moritagil.cl

Ona
Victoria Subercaseaux 295.
City Map 2 F2.
Tel *(02) 63201859.*
www.onachile.com

Pura Chile
Isidora Goyenechea 3226.
City Map 5 B4.
Tel *(02) 3310467.*

ANTIQUES

Antiguedades Balmaceda
Avenida Balmaceda & Brasil.
City Map 1 C1.

Antiguedades Bucarest
Avenida Providencia & Bucarest.
City Map 4 F2.

Brainworks
José Miguel de la Barra 454. **City Map** 2 F2.
Tel *(02) 6339218.*
www.brainworks.cl

FASHION

Atelier Carlos Pérez
Rosal 388. **City Map** 2 F2.
Tel *(02) 6641463.*

Casta & Devota
Avenida Nueva Costanera 3766. **City Map** 5 B1.
Tel *(02) 2073031.*

Galería Drugstore
Avenida Providencia 2124.
City Map 4 F2.
Tel *(02) 4901241.*
www.drugstore.cl

Hall Central
José Victorino Lastarria 316. **City Map** 3 A4.
Tel *(02) 6440763.*

Mor
Avenida Alonso de Córdova 4213. **City Map** 5 C2. ***Tel*** *(02) 571 5308.* **www**.mor.cl

Nostalgic
Bandera 721. **City Map** 2 E2. ***Tel*** *(02) 6988461.*
www.nostalgic.cl

Óptica Bahía
Merced 374. **City Map** 2 F2. ***Tel*** *(02) 6327031.*
www.opticabahia.cl

Orange Blue
Avenida Providencia 2455.
City Map 4 F2.
Tel *(02) 2325373.*
www.orangeblue.cl

Parentesys
Monjitas 359.
City Map 3 A4.
Tel *(02) 6644423.*

Tampu
Merced 327. **City Map** 3 B3. ***Tel*** *(02) 6387992.*

Zapatera
Avenida Alonso de Córdova 3834. **City Map** 5 B2. ***Tel*** *(02) 206 6585.* **www**.zapatera.cl

ART GALLERIES

Galería 13
Tegualda 1483.
Tel *(09) 92763700.*
www.galeria13.cl

Galería A.M.S. Marlborough
Avenida Nueva Costanera 3723. **City Map** 5 B2.
Tel *(02) 7993180.*

Galería Animal
Ave. Alonso de Córdova 3105. **City Map** 5 A1.
Tel *(02) 3719090.*
www.galeriaanimal.com

Galería Gabriela Mistral
Avenida Alameda 1381.
City Map 2 E3.
Tel *(02) 3904108.*

Galería Isabel Aninat
Espoz 3100. **City Map** 5 B1. ***Tel*** *(02) 4819870.*
www.galeriaisabel aninat.cl

Galería La Sala
Ave. Alonso de Córdova 2700. **City Map** 5 B2.
Tel *(02) 2467207.*
www.galerialasala.cl

Galería Moro
Merced 349, No. 12.
City Map 2 F2.
Tel *(02) 6338252.*

Galería Patricia Ready
Espoz 3125. **City Map** 5 B1. ***Tel*** *(02) 9536210.*
www.galeriapready.cl

BOOKS AND MUSIC

Feria del Disco
Avenida Providencia 2301.
City Map 4 F2.
Tel *(02) 5928702.*
www.feriadeldisco.cl

Feria del Libro
Huérfanos 623. **City Map** 2 F2. ***Tel*** *(02) 3458315.* **www**.feria chilenadellibro.cl

Librería Antartica
Avenida Kennedy 5413.
Tel *(02) 2420799.*
www.antartica.cl

Librería Chile Ilustrado
Avenida Providencia 1652.
City Map 4 E3.
Tel *(02) 2358145.*

Librería Eduardo Albers
Avenida Vitacura 5648.
Tel *(02) 2421839.*
www.albers.cl

Librería Inglesa
Avenida Pedro de Valdivia 47. ***Tel*** *(02) 2328853.*

WINE AND FOOD

El Mundo del Vino
Isidora Goyenechea 3000.
City Map 5 B4.
Tel *(02) 5841173.*
www.elmundodelvino.cl

Emporia La Rosa
Merced 291. **City Map** 3 B4. ***Tel*** *(02) 6389257.*

Emporio Nacional
Bellavista 0360. **City Map** 3 C4. ***Tel*** *(02) 7325612.*
www.emporionacional.cl

La Vinoteca
Isidora Goyenechea 2966.
City Map 5 A4.
Tel *(02) 3341987.*

Wain
Avenida Nueva Costanera 3955. **City Map** 5 B1.
Tel *(02) 9536290.*
www.wain.cl

World Delicatessen
Avenida Nueva Costanera 6664. ***Tel*** *(02) 7894047.*

MARKETS

Aldea de Vitacura
Avenida Vitacura 6838.
Tel *(02) 2193161.*

Centro de Exposición de Arte Indígena
Avenida Alameda 499.
City Map 2 E3.
Tel *(02) 6641352.*

Feria Artesanal Santa Lucía
Avenida Alameda & Carmen. **City Map** 2 F3.

Persa Bio Bio
San Francisco.

SHOPPING MALLS

Alto los Condes
Avenida Kennedy 9001.
Tel *(02) 2996965.* **www**.cencosudshopping.cl

Mall Apumanque
Manquehue Sur 31.
Tel *(02) 2462614.*
www.apumanque.cl

Parque Arauco
Avenida Kennedy 5413.
Tel *(02) 2990629.*
www.parquearauco.cl

ENTERTAINMENT IN SANTIAGO

Santiago is the culture capital of Chile, and nearly all of the country's major music, theater, and sports venues are concentrated within its limits. Jazz clubs, intimate bars, and mega stadiums play host to numerous national and international music acts, and the city's Teatro Municipal is home to national dance troupes and orchestras. Dramatic theater is hugely popular in Santiago. There are dozens of venues around the city and an international theater festival each February. Visitors looking for energy-packed entertainment will love the city's many soccer matches, played between national and visiting teams.

MALLSPORT

Logo of the sports shop, Mall Sport

Low-key ambience at the Bar 14

INFORMATION AND TICKETS

There are limited sources of entertainment information available in Santiago. The most reliable English-language source is the website of **Revolver Magazine**, which is run by a group of expatriates and offers a comprehensive guide to the thriving arts, cultural, and entertainment scene in the city. It features a calendar of events, restaurant guides, art show openings, previews and reviews of concerts and theater shows, and a smattering of fun pieces about travel in Chile as well as cultural-clash topics such as language blunders.

The most popular national newspapers, **La Tercera** and **El Mercurio**, publish entertainment listings in their Friday editions that are slightly more comprehensive and up-to-date than *Revolver Magazine's* website, but are available in Spanish only. Both newspapers also offer full listings, and reviews of music, arts and theater on their websites: *La Tercera* provides this on its Entretenimiento page, and *El Mercurio*, under Entretención. The website **Solo Teatro** focuses on theater reviews and performance schedules.

Tickets for major theater performances, music concerts, and sports events can be bought through **Ticketmaster** and **Feria del Disco** websites and sales points, and through Punto Ticket *(see p313)*, whose offices can be found in Ripley department stores and Cinemark movie halls. Tickets for performances and more intimate theater or music venues are generally purchased at the venue itself.

The Chilean Spanish-language dailies, *El Mercurio* and *La Tercera*

BARS AND CLUBS

There are relatively few true bars in Santiago as most double as full-scale restaurants given the city's licensing code that requires that food be served in all drinking establishments. The best "resto-bar," as they are known, is undoubtedly the Bar Liguria *(see p296)*, which has three addresses in the capital city. The bar pays homage to Chilean kitsch, serving potent drinks in a lively ambience that can get raucous after midnight. For expatriates, **Flannery's Geo Pub** serves pints and a convivial atmosphere. **Bar 14** serves up sushi and DJ music in a minimalist ambience with rooftop seating. Downtown, the sophisticated **Bar Catedral** draws fashionable businessmen and businesswomen for well-prepared cocktails. The establishment's second-story open-air bar is pleasant during the summer. In Bellavista, there are dozens of bars along Calle Pío Nono, although most cater to college students buying cheap beer in pitchers. Those seeking a low-key ambience will find plenty of bars to choose from at Patio Bellavista *(see p88)*. Bellavista's **Bar Constitución** is the city's newest hot spot with a sexy and sleek decor, electro pop DJ music and the occasional live band. After midnight, the dance floor kicks up and the place becomes packed. A number of Chilean DJs got their start at the stylish and low-lit **Club la Feria** lounge and dance club. Those seeking salsa dancing should head to

Havana Salsa for some racy stepping at this a tropical-style club. The 30- to 45-year-old singles crowd heads to **Las Urracas** to boogie the night away on one of the club's two dance floors, dine on Mexican food in the adjoining restaurant, and rub elbows with the city's TV stars and football players. Farther uptown is the **Sala Murano**, where the chic set goes to party and dance to reggaeton and 1980s hits, with a dash of electronica, in a packed ambience. Santiago's clubs do not get started until after midnight, and in most cases hit their peak at 2am.

CONTEMPORARY MUSIC

Santiago boasts a handful of large venues that pull in well-known international and national acts. The largest of such sites is **Estadio Nacional**, which is also a major sports stadium. Recent shows here have included performances by Madonna, U2, and Argentine rockers Soda Stereo. Equally large is the **Estadio San Carlos Apoquindo** in Las Condes, which has hosted the Black Eyed Peas and Pearl Jam. Santiago's newest large-scale music venue is located in the antique, 19th-century Club Hípico *(see p81)*, the city's oldest racetrack, which is occasionally adapted to showcase headlining acts such as Elton John, Depeche Mode, and the Jonas brothers. It is also the site of the yearly Cumbre de Rock Chileno (Chilean Rock Fest), held in January. Santiago's ultramodern venue **Espacio Riesco** is located on the outskirts of the capital. In addition to hosting bands such as Coldplay, the concert-cum-exposition hall is known for its yearly electronic and rock music festivals. The downtown district's Centro Cultural Estación Mapocho *(see p73)* features Chilean rock, pop, and folk bands, as well as DJ parties; however, the acoustics are not stellar.

U2's Bono performing at the Estadio Nacional

The Nuñoa district's **La Batuta** is ever popular for its more intimate music club experience. It highlights local bands or lesser-known international acts, hosting mostly rock and hip-hop acts, and some tribute bands. The **Teatro Caupolican** sponsors indie and alternative rock acts, and the edgy **Bar El Clan** hosts nightly acts that are mostly DJ parties and local rock and hip hop bands.

Santiago's famous **Club de Jazz** is considered one of the best jazz clubs in Latin America and has hosted a who's who of jazz greats during the more than 65 years that it has been open. Jazz enthusiasts will also do well at Bellavista's **El Perseguidor**, a supper club for just under 100 people that features young local and international talent. **La Casa en el Aire**, a tiny bar in the Bellavista area, books folk music acts with nightly live performances.

First-time visitors to the capital city will find that tickets for stadium concerts are not sold at the stadium itself and must be purchased through ticket vendors.

Live performance at the supper club El Perseguidor

Performers at the international theater festival of Santiago a Mil

CLASSICAL MUSIC, DANCE, AND THEATER

Performances of classical music, opera, and ballet are held at Santiago's Teatro Municipal *(see p69)* from April to December. These are led by the Santiago Philharmonic Orchestra and the Santiago Ballet, along with visiting orchestras and dance troupes. The **Teatro Oriente** often features performances by the Fundación Beethoven and Ballet Folklórico, while the **Teatro Universidad de Chile** puts on modern dance performances and boasts productions by the Chilean National Ballet and the Chilean Symphonic Orchestra.

Theater performances are widespread throughout the city, especially during the **Santiago a Mil** event each February. This grand celebration of theater brings street acts and local and international productions to the stage of more than 15 playhouses. During the rest of the year, cutting-edge productions can be seen at **Teatro Bellavista** and the **Centro Mori**, and comedic and contemporary acts at the **Teatro La Comedia**.

SPECTATOR SPORTS

Fútbol, or soccer, is Chile's most popular sport, attracting hordes of passionate fans to often thrilling matches. The three best-known teams are Universidad de Chile, Colo-Colo, and Universidad Católica, whose local stadiums are, respectively, Estadio Nacional, **Estadio Monumental**, and Estadio San Carlos de Apoquindo. Soccer matches are best attended with a local who is familiar with stadium procedures. Security guards will often close the gates to rowdy fans, even if they hold a paid ticket, so attendees are well advised to arrive no less than 3 hours early for the bigger or popular matches.

Major horse races take place at the Club Hípico *(see p81)* and the **Hipódromo Chile** year round, drawing large crowds of Chileans. El Ensayo, the major race of the year, and also the oldest stakes race in South America, is held at Club Hípico each November.

PARTICIPATION SPORTS

Most people in Santiago enjoy spending afternoons and weekends in city parks such as the Parque Metropolitano de Santiago *(see pp84–5)*, either jogging, walking, or cycling. Gymnasiums are very popular, and can be found throughout the city and in major hotels. On hot summer days, the outdoor public pools at Tupahue and Antilén atop the Parque Metropolitano, or the **Club Providencia**, which offers day passes, are ideal for swimmers. Indoor rock climbing, with classes for beginners, are available at **El Muro** in Las Condes, and **Mall Sport**, a shopping center dedicated exclusively to sports shops, features a climbing wall and skate park.

ENTERTAINMENT FOR CHILDREN

Santiago, like Chile in general, is very family-friendly, offering plenty of activities and attractions to keep children entertained and active. There are traveling circuses that often set up tents during the summer in the city limits. More permanent thrills include the amusement park Fantislandia *(see p81)* and the Parque Metropolitano de Santiago *(see pp84–5)*, where children ride a funicular and gondola, take a swim, or ride bikes. Also here, Santiago's

The outdoor swimming pool at Tupahue, Parque Metropolitano de Santiago

zoo, the Zoológico Nacional introduces children to native flora and fauna. Parque Quinta Normal *(see pp76–7)* has several child-friendly museums such as the Museo Nacional de Historia Natural, the Museo Ferroviaro, and the Museo Artequín. Farther afield, the **Museo Interactivo Mirador** and its adjoining **Aquarium Santiago** are designed to give children an introduction to science and technology via interactive exhibits, and learn about marine life through displays of over 200 species of sea animals. The shopping mall Parque Arauco *(see p97)* offers many attractions for children, including an indoor ice rink, a bowling alley, playground, and cinema.

Whale skeleton at the Museo Nacional de Historia Natural

DIRECTORY

INFORMATION AND TICKETS

El Mercurio
www.emol.cl

Feria del Disco
www.feriadeldisco.cl

La Tercera
www.latercera.cl

Revolver Magazine
www.santiago magazine.cl

Solo Teatro
www.soloteatro.cl

Ticketmaster
www.ticketmaster.cl

BARS AND CLUBS

Bar 14
Avenida Providencia 2563, Local14. **City Map** 4 F2. ***Tel*** *(02) 3332963.* **www**.bar14.cl

Bar Catedral
José Miguel de la Barra, esq. Merced. **City Map** 3 A4. ***Tel*** *(02) 6643048.* **www**.operacatedral.cl

Bar Constitución
Constitución 61. **City Map** 3 B4. ***Tel*** *(02) 2444569.* **www**.barconstitucion.cl

Club la Feria
Constitución 275. **City Map** 3 B3. ***Tel*** *(02) 7358433.* **www**.clublaferia.cl

Flannery's Geo Pub
Encomenderos 83. **City Map** 5 A4. ***Tel*** *(02) 2336675.* **www**.flannerys.cl

Havana Salsa
Calle Dominica 142. **City Map** 3 B3. ***Tel*** *(02) 7775829.* **www**.havanasalsa.cl

Las Urracas
Avenida Vitacura 9254. ***Tel*** *(02) 2293092.* **www**.lasurracas.com

Sala Murano
Avenida Las Condes 14950. ***Tel*** *(02) 2170959.* **www**.salamurano.com

CONTEMPORARY MUSIC

Bar El Clan
Bombero Nuñez 363. **City Map** 3 B3. ***Tel*** *(02) 7353655.* **www**.elclan.cl

Club de Jazz
José Pedro Alessandri 85. ***Tel*** *(02) 2741937.* **www**.clubdejazz.cl

El Perseguidor
Antonia López de Bello 0126. **City Map** 3 B3. ***Tel*** *(02) 7776763.* **www**.elperseguidor.cl

Espacio Riesco
El Salto 5000, Huerchuraba. ***Tel*** *(02) 4704400.* **www**. espacioriesco.cl

Estadio Nacional
Avenida Grecia 2001. ***Tel*** *(02) 2386477.*

Estadio San Carlos de Apoquindo
Camino Las Flores 13000. ***Tel*** *(02) 4124400.*

La Batuta
Jorge Washington 52. ***Tel*** *(02) 274 7096.* **www**.labatuta.cl

La Casa en el Aire
Antonio López de Bello 0125. **City Map** 3 B3. ***Tel*** *(02) 7621161.* **www**.lacasaenelaire.cl

Teatro Caupolican
San Diego 850. **City Map** 2 E5. ***Tel*** *(02) 6991556.* **www**.teatrocaupolican.cl

CLASSICAL MUSIC, DANCE, AND THEATER

Centro Mori
Constitución 183. **City Map** 3 B3. ***Tel*** *(02) 7776 246.* **www**.centromori.cl

Santiago a Mil
Juana de Arco 2012, oficiana 11. **City Map** 4 F3. ***Tel*** *(02) 9250300.* **www**.santiagoamil.cl

Teatro Bellavista
Dardignac 0110. **City Map** 3 B4. ***Tel*** *(02) 7352393.*

Teatro La Comedia
Merced 349. **City Map** 2 F2. ***Tel*** *(02) 6391523.*

Teatro Oriente
Avenida Pedro de Valdivia 099. **City Map** 4 E2. ***Tel*** *(02) 2312173.* **www**.teatroriente.cl

Teatro Universidad de Chile
Avenida Providencia 043, Plaza Italia. **City Map** 3 B4. ***Tel*** *(02) 9782480.* **www**.teatro.uchile.cl

SPECTATOR SPORTS

Estadio Monumental
Avenida Marathon 5300. ***Tel*** *(02) 6980806.*

Hipódromo Chile
Avenida Hipódromo Chile 1715. ***Tel*** *(02) 2709200.* **www**.hipodromo.cl

PARTICIPATION SPORTS

Club Providencia
Avenida Pocuro 2878. ***Tel*** *(02) 4266400.* **www**.clubprovidencia.cl

El Muro
Avenida Américo Vespucio 1647. ***Tel*** *(02) 4752851.* **www**.gimnasioelmuro.cl

Mall Sport
Ave. Las Condes 13451. ***Tel*** *(02) 4293030.* **www**.mallsport.cl

ENTERTAINMENT FOR CHILDREN

Aquarium Santiago
Sebastopol 90. ***Tel*** *(02) 7844210.* **www**. aquariumsantiago.cl

Museo Interactivo Mirador
Punta Arenas 6711. ***Tel*** *(02) 828 8000.* **www**.mim.cl

SANTIAGO STREET FINDER

The map given below shows the different areas of Santiago covered by the Street Finder maps – Plaza de Armas and El Centro; West of El Centro; and Northeast of El Centro. The map references given in the Santiago section for sites of interest, historic attractions, shopping areas, and entertainment venues refer to the maps on the following pages. Map references are also provided for Santiago hotels *(see pp274–8)* and restaurants *(see pp294–7)*. The first figure in the map reference indicates which Street Finder map to turn to, and the letter and number that follow refer to the map's grid. There is also an index of street names and attractions on page 109. The symbols used to represent sights and useful information on the Street Finder maps are listed in the key below.

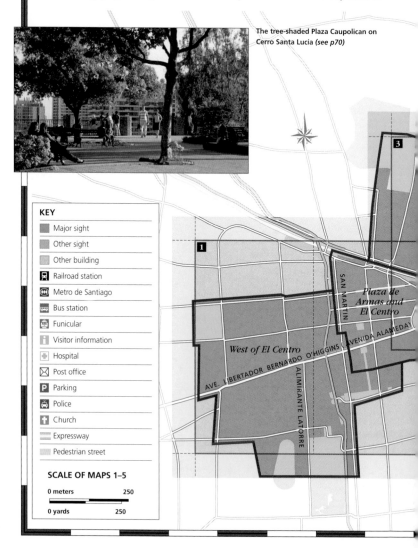

Information panel, Cerro San Cristobal

The tree-shaded Plaza Caupolican on Cerro Santa Lucía *(see p70)*

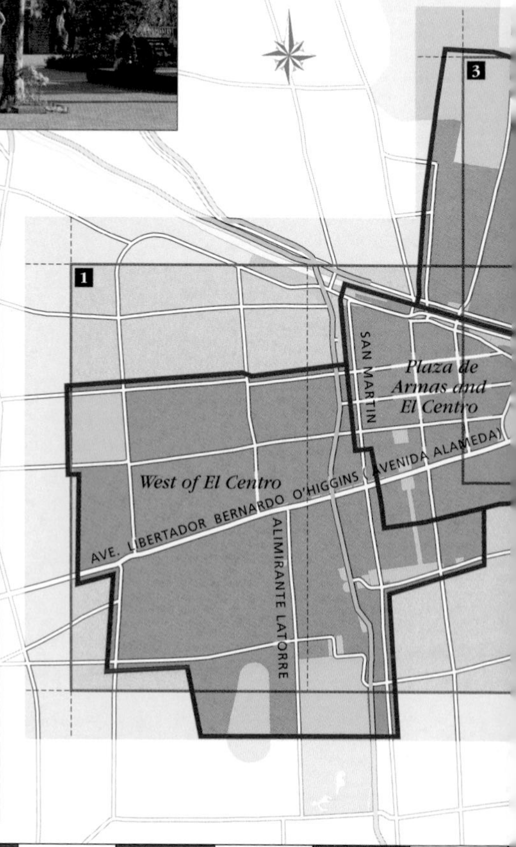

KEY

- Major sight
- Other sight
- Other building
- Railroad station
- Metro de Santiago
- Bus station
- Funicular
- Visitor information
- Hospital
- Post office
- Parking
- Police
- Church
- Expressway
- Pedestrian street

SCALE OF MAPS 1–5

0 meters 250

0 yards 250

Vehicles parked near an equestrian statue, adjacent to Avenida Libertador Bernado O'Higgins

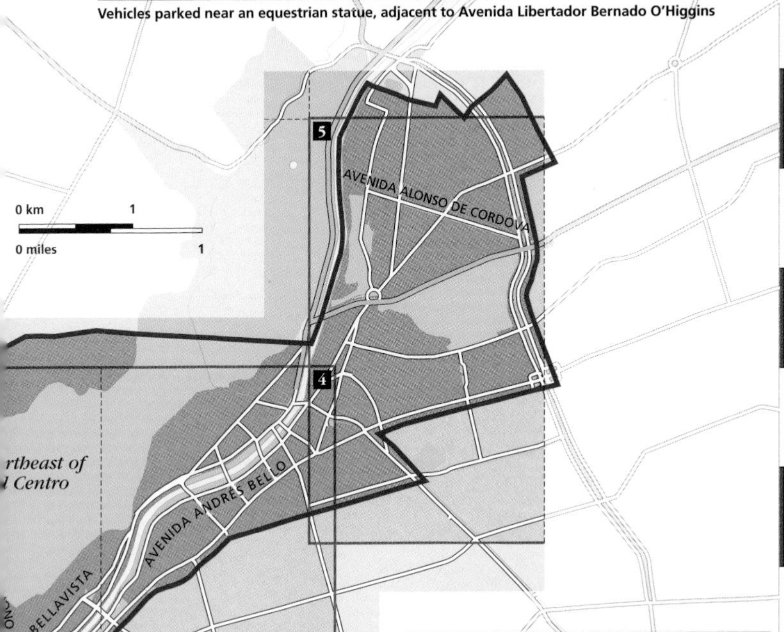

A green street sign outside a restaurant in Barrio Suecia *(see p89)*

1
A
B
C
1
2
3
4
5
AVENIDA MATUCANA
CHAÑARCILLO
HERRERA
CHACABUCO
ATACAMA
MAIPÚ
ESPERANZA
YUNGAY
PJE BALTRA
LIBERTAD
RAFAEL SOTOMAYOR
CUETO
CASTILLO
AVENIDA GENERAL BULNES
AVENIDA BALMACEDA
SAN NICOLAS
FRANCISCO BARDESSI
TRACCIÓN 21
CLENTARU
MATURANA
GENERAL BAQUEDANO
AVENIDA BRASIL
AVENIDA MAPOCHO
LOS ANDES
GENERAL MACKENNA
RIVAS VICUÑA
JUAN MIRANDA
PATRICIO LYNCH
MARTÍNEZ DE ROZAS
GARCÍA REYES
CAUTIN
PJE DELFINA
AVENIDA RICARDO CUMMING
SAN PABLO
ROSAS
PLAZA YUNGAY
SANTO DOMINGO
Museo de Ciencia y Tecnología
Quinta Normal
PARQUE QUINTA NORMAL
Museo Pedagógico Gabriela Mistral
CATEDRAL
Peluquería Francés
Cumming
COMPAÑIA DE JESÚS
BARRIO BRASIL
PLAZA BRASIL
PASEO HUÉRFANOS
Museo Nacional de Historia Natural
San Juan de Dios
Museo Ferroviario
MAC Espacio Quinta Normal
AVENIDA PORTALES
AGUSTINAS
AVENIDA GENERAL BULNES
Museo Artequín
LOS TILOS
Biblioteca de Santiago
MONEDA
SANTA MONICA
ERASMO ESCALA
Zully
Teatro Carrera
Matucana 100
LAS SOPHORAS
Universidad de Santiago de Chile
ROMERO
República
EL BELLOTO
ORIENTE
Planetario USACH
Union Latino Americana
AVENIDA LIBERTADOR BERNARDO O'HIGGINS (AVENIDA ALAMEDA)
AVENIDA ECUADOR
Estación Central
Universidad de Santiago
J.L. COO
Terminal de Buses San Borja
SAN ALFONSO
SALVADOR SANFUENTES
SAZIÉ
UNION AMERICANA
ABATE MOLINA
ESPAÑA
AVENIDA REPÚBLICA
ECHAURREN
ABDÓN CIFUENTES
PLAZA MANUEL RODRÍGUEZ
ALMIRANTE LATORRE
GRAJALES
GORBEA
Museo de la Solidaridad
CLUB HÍPICO
OBISPO JAVIER VASQUEZ VALENCIA
AVENIDA 5 DE ABRIL
SAN FRANCISCO DE BORJA
EXPOSICIÓN CENTRAL
SAN VICENTE
BACSUÑÁN GUERRERO
TOESCA
SAN JAVIER
DOLORES
GAY
DOMEYKO
TACNA
DEL NOGAL
LISPERGUER
OBISPO MANUEL UMAÑA SALINAS
CONFERENCIA
AVENIDA ALMIRANTE BLANCO ENCALADA
ARICA
LINCOLN
PUERTA DE VERA
MAQUINISTRA ESCOBAR

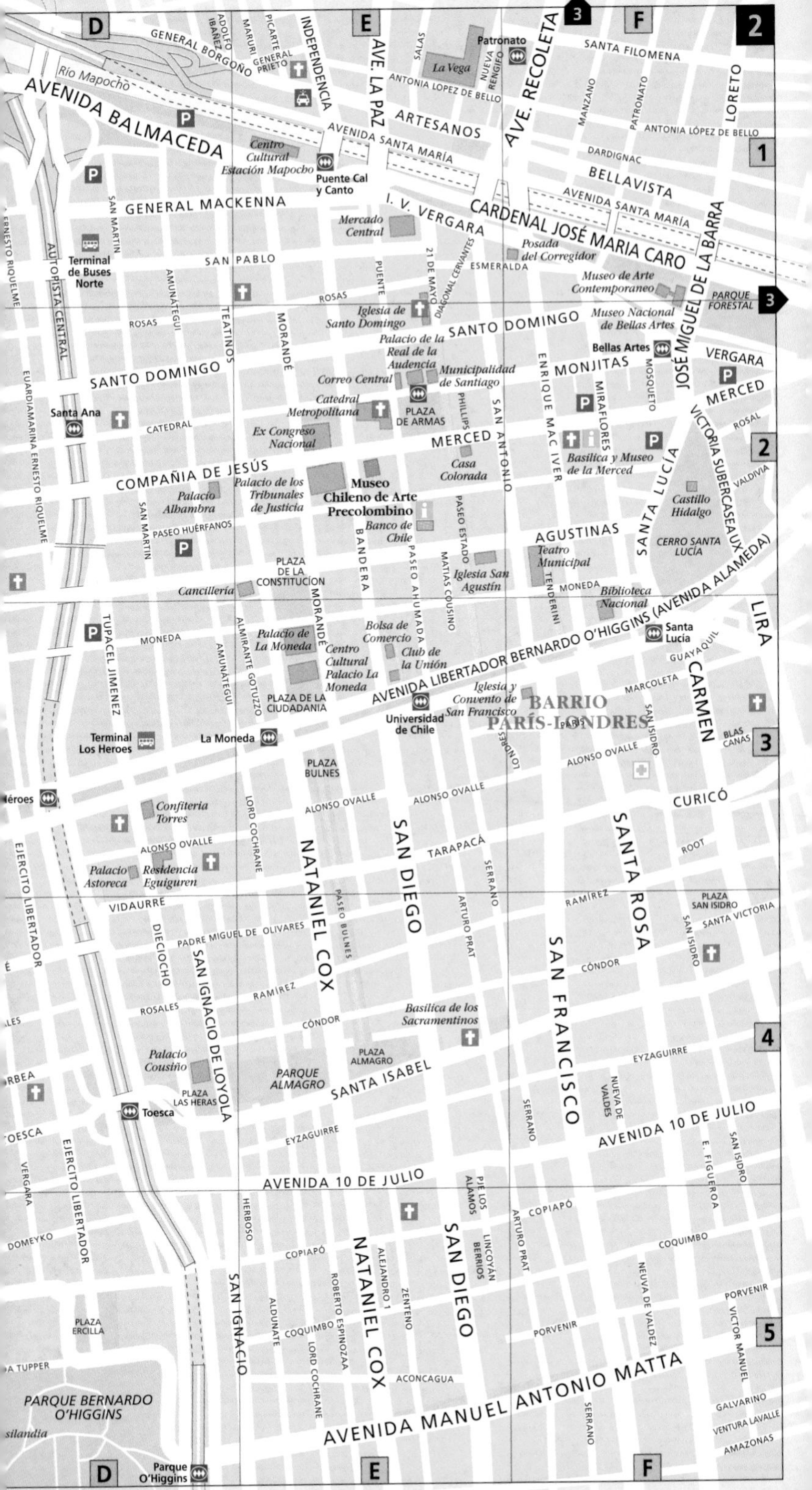
D
E
F
2
3
1
2
3
4
5
Río Mapocho
AVENIDA BALMACEDA
GENERAL BORGOÑO
ADOLFO IBAÑEZ
MARURI
PICARTE
GENERAL PRIETO
INDEPENDENCIA
AVE. LA PAZ
SALAS
La Vega
NUEVA RENGIFO
Patronato
AVE. RECOLETA
SANTA FILOMENA
LORETO
ANTONIA LOPEZ DE BELLO
ARTESANOS
MANZANO
PATRONATO
ANTONIA LÓPEZ DE BELLO
AVENIDA SANTA MARÍA
Centro Cultural Estación Mapocho
Puente Cal y Canto
DARDIGNAC
BELLAVISTA
AVENIDA SANTA MARÍA
CARDENAL JOSÉ MARIA CARO
GENERAL MACKENNA
I. V. VERGARA
Mercado Central
SAN MARTIN
Terminal de Buses Norte
SAN PABLO
21 DE MAYO
DIAGONAL CERVANTES
PUENTE
Posada del Corregidor
ESMERALDA
Museo de Arte Contemporaneo
JOSÉ MIGUEL DE LA BARRA
PARQUE FORESTAL
AUTOPISTA CENTRAL
ERNESTO RIQUELME
AMUNÁTEGUI
ROSAS
TEATINOS
MORANDÉ
ROSAS
Iglesia de Santo Domingo
Museo Nacional de Bellas Artes
SANTO DOMINGO
Palacio de la Real de la Audencia
Bellas Artes
VERGARA
SANTO DOMINGO
Correo Central
Municipalidad de Santiago
MONJITAS
EUARDIAMARINA ERNESTO RIQUELME
Catedral Metropolitana
PLAZA DE ARMAS
PHILLIPS
SAN ANTONIO
ENRIQUE MAC IVER
MIRAFLORES
MOSQUETO
MERCED
Santa Ana
CATEDRAL
Ex Congreso Nacional
MERCED
Casa Colorada
Basilica y Museo de la Merced
VICTORIA SUBERCASEAUX
ROSAL
COMPAÑIA DE JESÚS
Palacio de los Tribunales de Justicia
Museo Chileno de Arte Precolombino
SANTA LUCÍA
VALDIVIA
Palacio Alhambra
Castillo Hidalgo
SAN MARTIN
PASEO HUÉRFANOS
Banco de Chile
BANDERA
PASEO AHUMADA
PASEO ESTADO
MATIAS COUSIÑO
AGUSTINAS
Teatro Municipal
CERRO SANTA LUCÍA
PLAZA DE LA CONSTITUCÍON
Iglesia San Agustín
Cancillería
MORANDÉ
TENDERINI
MONEDA
Biblioteca Nacional
AVENIDA LIBERTADOR BERNARDO O'HIGGINS (AVENIDA ALAMEDA)
LIRA
TUPACEL JIMENEZ
MONEDA
AMUNÁTEGUI
ALMIRANTE GOTUZZO
Palacio de La Moneda
Bolsa de Comercio
Club de la Unión
Santa Lucía
GUAYAQUIL
Centro Cultural Palacio La Moneda
MARCOLETA
CARMEN
Iglesia y Convento de San Francisco
BARRIO PARÍS-LONDRES
PLAZA DE LA CIUDADANIA
Universidad de Chile
PARIS
SAN ISIDRO
LONDRES
Terminal Los Heroes
La Moneda
BLAS CANAS
ALONSO OVALLE
PLAZA BULNES
éroes
Confiteria Torres
LORD COCHRANE
ALONSO OVALLE
ALONSO OVALLE
CURICÓ
NATANIEL COX
SAN DIEGO
SANTA ROSA
EJERCITO LIBERTADOR
ALONSO OVALLE
TARAPACÁ
ROOT
Palacio Astoreca
Residencia Eguiguren
SERRANO
PASEO BULNES
ARTURO PRAT
RAMÍREZ
PLAZA SAN ISIDRO
VIDAURRE
SAN ISIDRO
SANTA VICTORIA
DIECIOCHO
PADRE MIGUEL DE OLIVARES
SAN IGNACIO DE LOYOLA
SAN FRANCISCO
CÓNDOR
RAMIREZ
ROSALES
Basilica de los Sacramentinos
CÓNDOR
Palacio Cousiño
PLAZA ALMAGRO
EYZAGUIRRE
PARQUE ALMAGRO
SANTA ISABEL
PLAZA LAS HERAS
NUEVA DE VALDES
Toesca
SERRANO
AVENIDA 10 DE JULIO
OESCA
EJERCITO LIBERTADOR
EYZAGUIRRE
E. FIGUEROA
SAN ISIDRO
VERGARA
AVENIDA 10 DE JULIO
PJE LOS ALAMOS
COPIAPÓ
DOMEYKO
HERBOSO
LINCOYÁN BERRIOS
ARTURO PRAT
COQUIMBO
COPIAPÓ
ALEJANDRO 1
ZENTENO
ROBERTO ESPINOZAA
SAN IGNACIO
NATANIEL COX
SAN DIEGO
PORVENIR
NUEVA DE VALDEZ
VICTOR MANUEL
PLAZA ERCILLA
ALDUNATE
COQUIMBO
LORD COCHRANE
PORVENIR
A TUPPER
ACONCAGUA
AVENIDA MANUEL ANTONIO MATTA
PARQUE BERNARDO O'HIGGINS
SERRANO
GALVARINO
VENTURA LAVALLE
AMAZONAS
silandia
Parque O'Higgins

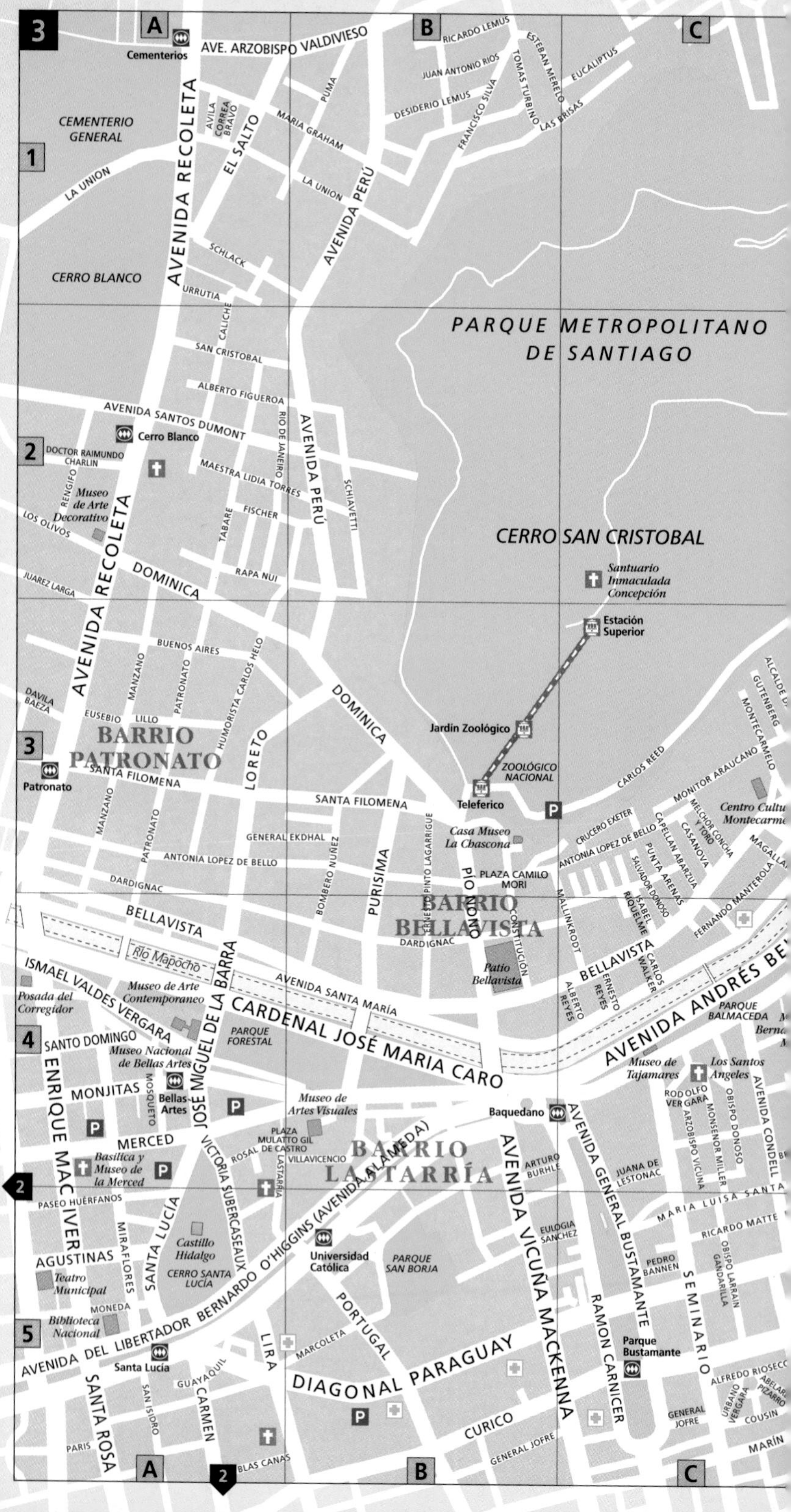
3
A
B
C
1
2
3
4
5
Cementerios
AVE. ARZOBISPO VALDIVIESO
RICARDO LEMUS
ESTEBAN MERELO
TOMAS TURBINO
EUCALIPTUS
JUAN ANTONIO RIOS
DESIDERIO LEMUS
FRANCISCO SILVA
LAS BRISAS
PUMA
MARIA GRAHAM
CEMENTERIO GENERAL
AVENIDA RECOLETA
AVILA
CORREA BRAVO
EL SALTO
LA UNION
AVENIDA PERÚ
SCHLACK
CERRO BLANCO
URRUTIA
CALICHE
SAN CRISTOBAL
PARQUE METROPOLITANO DE SANTIAGO
ALBERTO FIGUEROA
AVENIDA SANTOS DUMONT
Cerro Blanco
RIO DE JANEIRO
DOCTOR RAIMUNDO CHARLIN
MAESTRA LIDIA TORRES
SCHIAVETTI
RENGIFO
Museo de Arte Decorativo
LOS OLIVOS
FISCHER
TABARE
CERRO SAN CRISTOBAL
DOMINICA
RAPA NUI
JUAREZ LARGA
Santuario Inmaculada Concepción
Estación Superior
BUENOS AIRES
MANZANO
PATRONATO
HUMORISTA CARLOS HELO
DAVILA BAEZA
EUSEBIO
LILLO
BARRIO PATRONATO
LORETO
Jardín Zoológico
ALCALDE
GUTENBERG
MONTECARMELO
ZOOLÓGICO NACIONAL
CARLOS REED
MONITOR ARAUCANO
Patronato
SANTA FILOMENA
Teleferico
Centro Cultural Montecarmelo
MELCHOR CONCHA Y TORO
CRUCERO EXETER
CASANOVA
CAPELLAN ABARZUA
Casa Museo La Chascona
GENERAL EKDHAL
ANTONIA LOPEZ DE BELLO
PUNTA ARENAS
MAGALLANES
PLAZA CAMILO MORI
SALVADOR DONOSO
ISABEL RIQUELME
FERNANDO MANTEROLA
DARDIGNAC
BOMBERO NUÑEZ
PURISIMA
ERNESTO PINTO LAGARRIGUE
PÍO NONO
MALLINKRODT
BARRIO BELLAVISTA
CONSTITUCIÓN
BELLAVISTA
Río Mapocho
Patio Bellavista
CARLOS WALKER
ISMAEL VALDES VERGARA
Museo de Arte Contemporaneo
JOSE MIGUEL DE LA BARRA
AVENIDA SANTA MARÍA
ERNESTO REYES
ALBERTO REYES
AVENIDA ANDRÉS BELLO
Posada del Corregidor
CARDENAL JOSÉ MARIA CARO
PARQUE BALMACEDA
PARQUE FORESTAL
SANTO DOMINGO
Museo Nacional de Bellas Artes
Museo de Tajamares
Los Santos Angeles
ENRIQUE MAC IVER
MONJITAS
MOSQUETO
Bellas Artes
Museo de Artes Visuales
Baquedano
RODOLFO VERGARA
OBISPO DONOSO
AVENIDA CONDELL
PLAZA MULATTO GIL DE CASTRO
ROSAL
LASTARRIA
VILLAVICENCIO
MERCED
Basilica y Museo de la Merced
VICTORIA SUBERCASEAUX
BARRIO LASTARRÍA
ARTURO BURHLE
AVENIDA GENERAL BUSTAMANTE
ARZOBISPO VICUÑA
MONSEÑOR MILLER
JUANA DE LESTONAC
AVENIDA VICUÑA MACKENNA
2
PASEO HUÉRFANOS
MARIA LUISA SANTANDER
MIRAFLORES
SANTA LUCÍA
Castillo Hidalgo
AVENIDA DEL LIBERTADOR BERNARDO O'HIGGINS (AVENIDA ALAMEDA)
EULOGIA SANCHEZ
RICARDO MATTE
AGUSTINAS
Universidad Católica
PARQUE SAN BORJA
OBISPO LARRAIN GANDARILLA
PEDRO BANNEN
Teatro Municipal
CERRO SANTA LUCÍA
SEMINARIO
RAMON CARNICER
MONEDA
Biblioteca Nacional
PORTUGAL
LIRA
MARCOLETA
Parque Bustamante
DIAGONAL PARAGUAY
Santa Lucía
GUAYAQUIL
ALFREDO RIOSECO
ABELARDO PIZARRO
URBANO VERGARA
GENERAL JOFRE
COUSIN
SANTA ROSA
SAN ISIDRO
CARMEN
CURICO
PARIS
MARÍN
BLAS CAÑAS

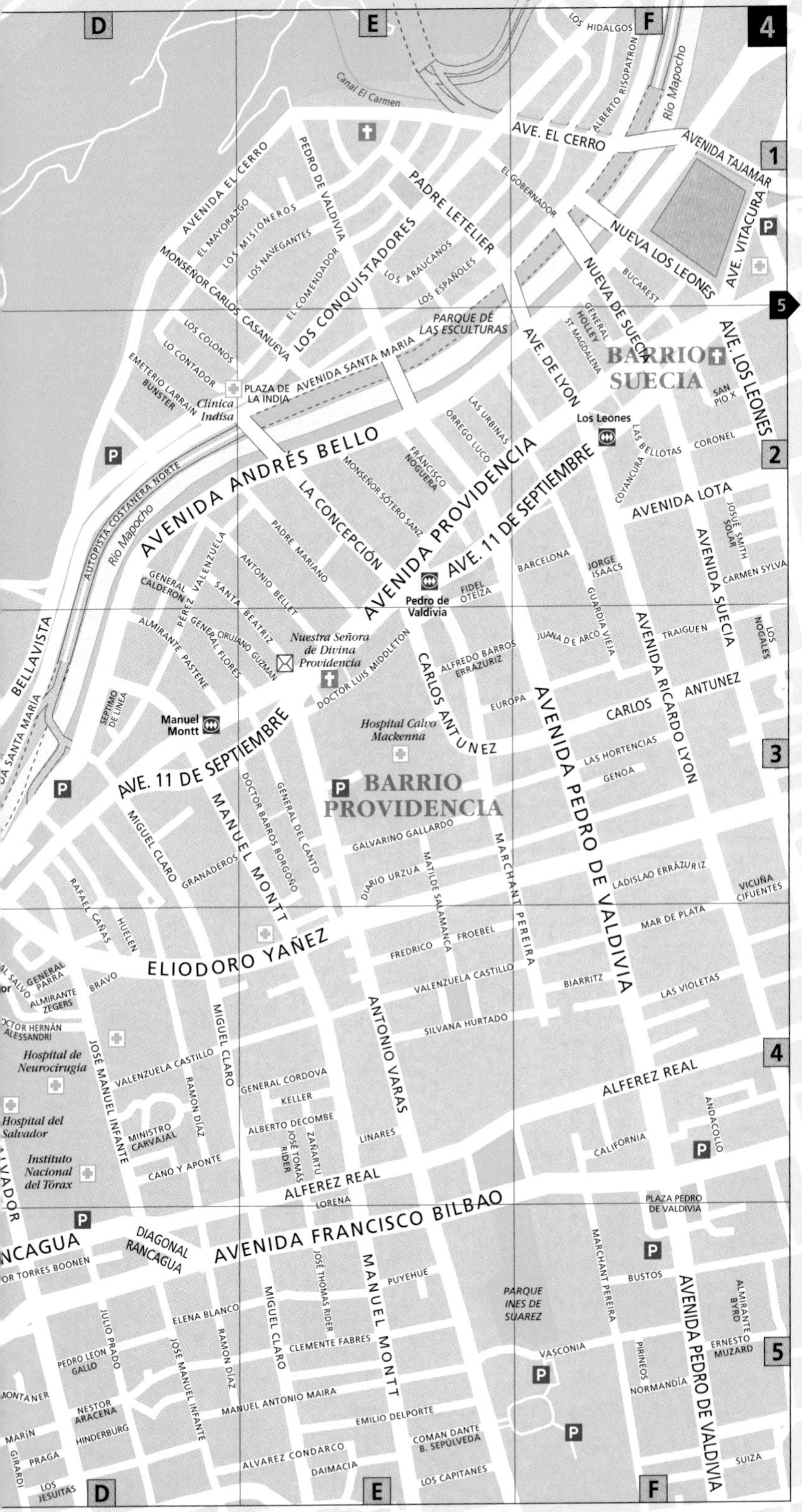
4
BARRIO SUECIA
BARRIO PROVIDENCIA
AVENIDA ANDRÉS BELLO
AVENIDA PROVIDENCIA
AVE. 11 DE SEPTIEMBRE
AVENIDA PEDRO DE VALDIVIA
AVENIDA RICARDO LYON
AVENIDA SUECIA
AVE. LOS LEONES
NUEVA LOS LEONES
AVENIDA TAJAMAR
AVE. VITACURA
AVE. EL CERRO
AVENIDA EL CERRO
AVENIDA SANTA MARIA
AVENIDA LOTA
CARLOS ANTUNEZ
ELIODORO YAÑEZ
ALFEREZ REAL
AVENIDA FRANCISCO BILBAO
DIAGONAL RANCAGUA
MANUEL MONTT
ANTONIO VARAS
MIGUEL CLARO
LOS CONQUISTADORES
PADRE LETELIER
PEDRO DE VALDIVIA
MONSEÑOR CARLOS CASANUEVA
LA CONCEPCIÓN
AVE. DE LYON
NUEVA DE SUECIA
PARQUE DE LAS ESCULTURAS
PLAZA DE LA INDIA
Clínica Indisa
Nuestra Señora de Divina Providencia
Hospital Calvo Mackenna
Hospital de Neurocirugía
Hospital del Salvador
Instituto Nacional del Tórax
PARQUE INES DE SUAREZ
PLAZA PEDRO DE VALDIVIA
Los Leones
Pedro de Valdivia
Manuel Montt
Río Mapocho
AUTOPISTA COSTANERA NORTE
BELLAVISTA
Canal El Carmen
MARCHANT PEREIRA
GENERAL DEL CANTO
DOCTOR BARROS BORGOÑO
JOSÉ MANUEL INFANTE
MIGUEL CLARO
RAMON DÍAZ
EMETERIO LARRAIN BUNSTER
LOS HIDALGOS
ALBERTO RISOPATRON
EL GOBERNADOR
BUCAREST
GENERAL HOLLEY
ST. MAGDALENA
SAN PIO X
CORONEL
LAS BELLOTAS
COYANCURA
JOSUÉ SMITH SOLAR
CARMEN SYLVA
LOS NOGALES
TRAIGUEN
BARCELONA
JORGE ISAACS
GUARDIA VIEJA
JUANA DE ARCO
FIDEL OTEIZA
ALFREDO BARROS ERRAZURIZ
EUROPA
LAS HORTENCIAS
GENOA
LADISLAO ERRÁZURIZ
VICUÑA CIFUENTES
MAR DE PLATA
LAS VIOLETAS
BIARRITZ
GALVARINO GALLARDO
DIARIO URZUA
MATILDE SALAMANCA
FREDRICO FROEBEL
VALENZUELA CASTILLO
SILVANA HURTADO
GENERAL CORDOVA
KELLER
ALBERTO DECOMBE
JOSÉ TOMAS RIDER
ZAÑARTU
LINARES
CALIFORNIA
ANDACOLLO
LORENA
CANO Y APONTE
MINISTRO CARVAJAL
BRAVO
GENERAL PARRA
ALMIRANTE ZEGERS
DOCTOR HERNÁN ALESSANDRI
RAFAEL CAÑAS
HUELEN
GRANADEROS
MIGUEL CLARO
SEPTIMO DE LINEA
ALMIRANTE PASTENE
GENERAL FLORES
CIRUJANO GUZMAN
SANTA BEATRIZ
ANTONIO BELLET
PADRE MARIANO
GENERAL CALDERON
PÉREZ VALENZUELA
DOCTOR LUIS MIDDLETON
MONSEÑOR SÓTERO SANZ
FRANCISCO NOGUERA
ORREGO LUCO
LAS URBINAS
LOS COLONOS
LO CONTADOR
EL MAYORAZGO
LOS MISIONEROS
LOS NAVEGANTES
EL COMENDADOR
LOS ARAUCANOS
LOS ESPAÑOLES
PUYEHUE
JOSÉ THOMAS RIDER
ELENA BLANCO
CLEMENTE FABRES
MANUEL ANTONIO MAIRA
EMILIO DELPORTE
COMAN DANTE B. SEPÚLVEDA
ALVAREZ CONDARCO
DAIMACIA
LOS CAPITANES
VASCONIA
BUSTOS
PIRINEOS
NORMANDÍA
ERNESTO MUZARD
ALMIRANTE BYRD
SUIZA
JULIO PRADO
PEDRO LEON GALLO
NESTOR ARACENA
HINDERBURG
PRAGA
LOS JESUITAS
GIRARDI
MARÍN
MONTANER
TORRES BOONEN
NCAGUA
ALVADOR
D
E
F
1
2
3
4
5

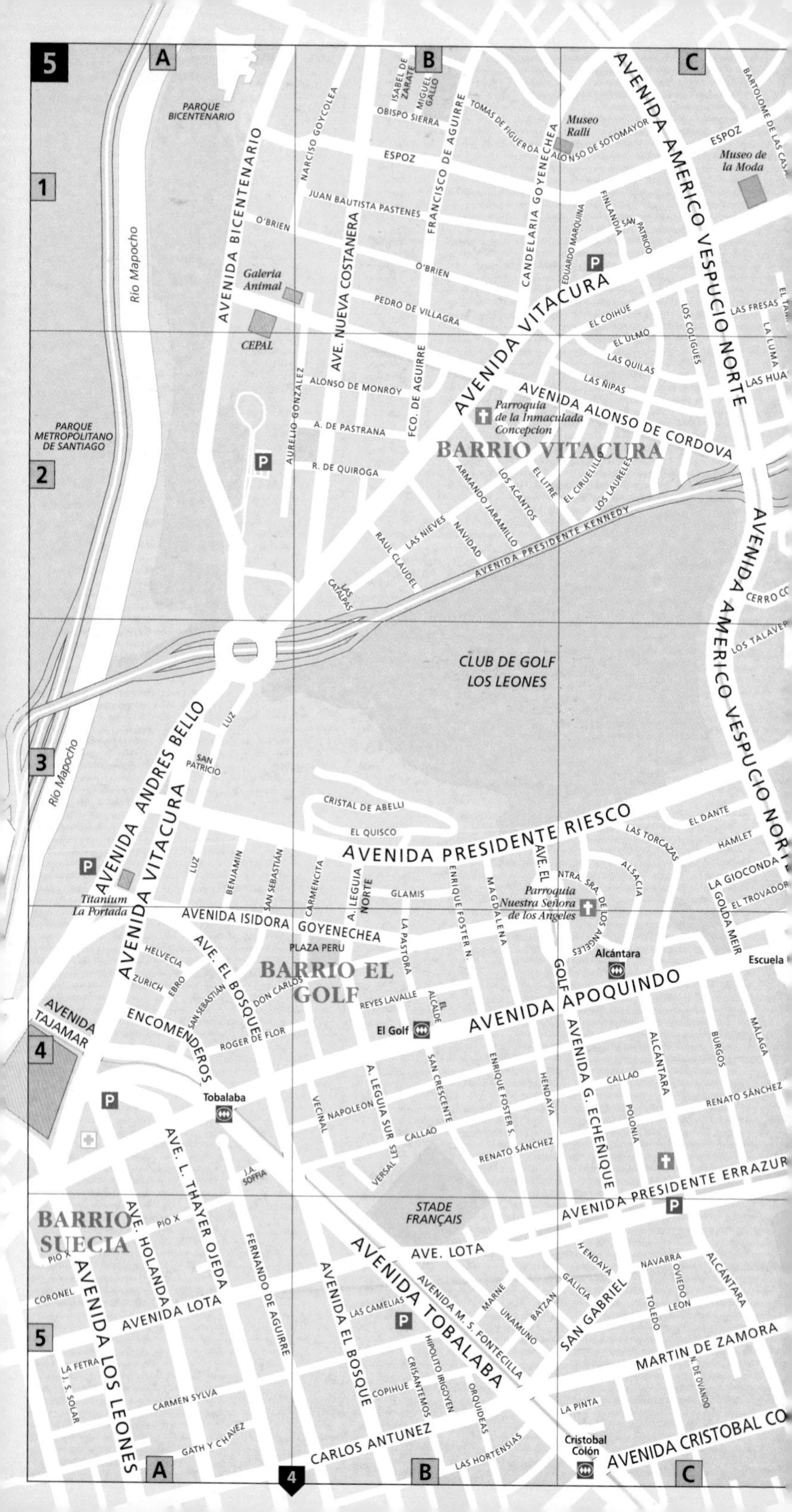
5
A
B
C
1
2
3
4
5
PARQUE BICENTENARIO
Río Mapocho
AVENIDA BICENTENARIO
NARCISO GOYCOLEA
ISABEL DE ZARATE
MIGUEL GALLO
OBISPO SIERRA
TOMAS DE FIGUEROA
Museo Ralli
ALONSO DE SOTOMAYOR
ESPOZ
JUAN BAUTISTA PASTENES
FRANCISCO DE AGUIRRE
CANDELARIA GOYENECHEA
AVENIDA AMERICO VESPUCIO NORTE
BARTOLOME DE LAS CASAS
Museo de la Moda
O'BRIEN
AVE. NUEVA COSTANERA
FINLANDIA
SAN PATRICIO
EDUARDO MARQUINA
Galeria Animal
CEPAL
PEDRO DE VILLAGRA
AVENIDA VITACURA
EL COIHUE
LOS COLIGUES
LAS FRESAS
EL ULMO
LA LUMA
LAS QUILAS
LAS ÑIPAS
PARQUE METROPOLITANO DE SANTIAGO
AURELIO GONZALEZ
ALONSO DE MONROY
FCO. DE AGUIRRE
AVENIDA ALONSO DE CORDOVA
Parroquia de la Inmaculada Concepcion
A. DE PASTRANA
BARRIO VITACURA
R. DE QUIROGA
ARMANDO JARAMILLO
LOS ACANTOS
EL LITRE
EL CIRUELILLO
LOS LAURELES
RAUL CLAUDEL
LAS NIEVES
NAVIDAD
AVENIDA PRESIDENTE KENNEDY
LAS CATALPAS
CERRO COLORADO
LOS TALAVERAS
CLUB DE GOLF LOS LEONES
AVENIDA ANDRES BELLO
LUZ
SAN PATRICIO
CRISTAL DE ABELLI
EL QUISCO
AVENIDA PRESIDENTE RIESCO
EL DANTE
LAS TORCAZAS
HAMLET
ALSACIA
LA GIOCONDA
EL TROVADOR
GOLDA MEIR
AVENIDA VITACURA
BENJAMIN
SAN SEBASTIÁN
CARMENCITA
A. LEGUIA NORTE
GLAMIS
ENRIQUE FOSTER N.
MAGDALENA
AVE. EL GOLF
NTRA. SRA. DE LOS ANGELES
Parroquia Nuestra Señora de los Angeles
Titanium La Portada
AVENIDA ISIDORA GOYENECHEA
LA PASTORA
Alcántara
Escuela
HELVECIA
AVE. EL BOSQUE
PLAZA PERU
BARRIO EL GOLF
ZURICH
EBRO
DON CARLOS
SAN SEBASTIÁN
REYES LAVALLE
EL ALCALDE
AVENIDA APOQUINDO
AVENIDA TAJAMAR
ENCOMENDEROS
ROGER DE FLOR
El Golf
AVENIDA G. ECHEÑIQUE
ALCÁNTARA
BURGOS
MALAGA
A. LEGUIA SUR
SAN CRESCENTE
ENRIQUE FOSTER S.
HENDAYA
CALLAO
POLONIA
RENATO SÁNCHEZ
Tobalaba
VECINAL
NAPOLEON
CALLAO
LAS VERSALLES
RENATO SÁNCHEZ
AVE. L. THAYER OJEDA
J.A. SOFFIA
AVENIDA PRESIDENTE ERRAZURIZ
STADE FRANÇAIS
BARRIO SUECIA
AVE. HOLANDA
PIO X
FERNANDO DE AGUIRRE
AVENIDA TOBALABA
AVE. LOTA
HENDAYA
NAVARRA
ALCÁNTARA
AVENIDA LOS LEONES
AVENIDA EL BOSQUE
AVENIDA M. S. FONTECILLA
GALICIA
OVIEDO
CORONEL
AVENIDA LOTA
LAS CAMELIAS
MARNE
UNAMUNO
BATZAN
SAN GABRIEL
LEON
TOLEDO
MARTIN DE ZAMORA
LA FETRA
J. S. SOLAR
HIPOLITO IRIGOYEN
CRISANTEMOS
COPIHUE
ORQUIDEAS
N. DE OVANDO
LA PINTA
CARMEN SYLVA
GATH Y CHAVEZ
CARLOS ANTUNEZ
LAS HORTENSIAS
Cristobal Colón
AVENIDA CRISTOBAL COLON
4

Street Finder Index

CHILE AND EASTER ISLAND REGION BY REGION

Chile and Easter Island at a Glance

With perhaps the greatest latitudinal extent that any country has, Chile is home to a huge geographical diversity. Its almost endless coastline is the source of some of the world's finest fish and shellfish, but the land rises rapidly eastward to form the towering Andes. In between, it has the world's driest desert, some of its most productive vineyards, a lushly forested Lake District studded with volcanoes, fjordlands, and ice fields. The land is inhabited by a polite, congenial people whose rich heritage can be experienced in traditional settlements, as well as in cities such as Valparaiso.

Street murals, *with their "surprise around every corner" quality, are major contributors to the bohemian air of Valparaíso* (see pp118–27). *This port-city's maze of hillside neighborhoods is also where Nobel Prize-winning poet Pablo Neruda once lived.*

Palafitos, *stilted fishermen's houses that once symbolized the Lake District and Chiloé archipelago, were mostly destroyed in the tsunami of 1960, but many remain in and around the city of Castro* (see pp216–7).

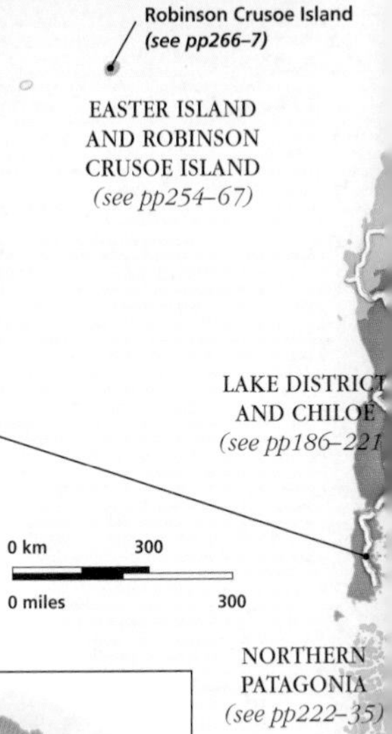

EASTER ISLAND

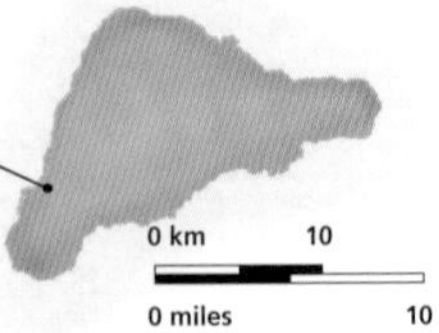

The *moai* of Easter Island (see pp254–65), *symbols of Polynesian culture, stand on ceremonial platforms such as Ahu Tahai. Many remain in their original quarry site at Rano Raraku.*

◁ **View from the port Mirador de la Cruz in Punta Arenas, Southern Patagonia**

Laguna Cejar, *in the Salar de Atacama* (see p176), *is proof that the world's driest desert can still boast wildlife-rich lagoons and grasslands. Visitors can float effortlessly in the saline waters of this lake.*

Parque Nacional Queulat (see p229) *is home to forests of southern beech and to the hanging glacier, Ventisquero Colgante. The latter is reached by a swinging pedestrian bridge over the rushing meltwaters of the Río Guillermo.*

The spectacular Torres del Paine National Park (see pp242–5) *in Southern Patagonia gets its name from the iconic granite peaks, shaped by glacial ice, that dominate the landscape. The park is rich in Patagonian flora and fauna, and is especially known for its robust populations of guanaco.*

CENTRAL VALLEY

The country's agricultural heartland, Central Valley is carpeted by lush vineyards and rich arable lands that are worked by the iconic Chilean cowboy, the huaso. *From the east, the arid Andes sweep down to the flat valley, which is dotted with wineries and old estates. The terrain yields in the west to coastal mountains and the Pacific littoral, where fishing villages alternate with luxury resorts.*

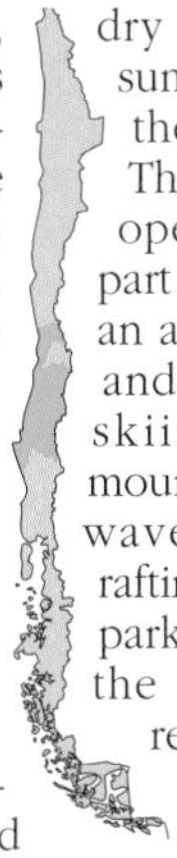

Inhabited since pre-Columbian times, Central Valley is considered Chile's oldest region and a bastion of its traditions. Its original settlers were the Mapuche, who resisted assimilation into the Incan Empire *(see p42)*. The Spanish arrived in 1541, founding Santiago at the foot of the Andes, Valparaíso on the coast, and later, towns across the valley floor. Central Valley became the center of Colonial Chile; the womb from which the country's north and south grew; its wealthiest area; and the political hub. The hacienda system, by which old families controlled vast tracts of land evolved here, spawning Chile's legendary *huaso*. Mining of silver, nitrates, and copper brought later wealth.

In modern times, agriculture, in particular viticulture, remains the greatest source of income here. The dry temperate climate and long summers make the region ideal for the production of noble wines. The valley's world-class wineries, open for tours and tastings, are part of a tourism sector that offers an array of other activities for locals and visitors alike. These include skiing and snowboarding at mountain resorts, surfing along big-wave beaches, and white-water rafting and horse riding in national parks. Forested spa retreats pepper the Andean foothills and beach resorts and idyllic fishing villages line the coast. The cities boast some of Chile's best fine-arts and decorative museums, complemeted by ornate parks, lush plazas, and fine seafood restaurants. Easily accessible from these cities are well-preserved haciendas and mines, and towns of Colonial charm.

Colorful street art, characteristic of the historic city of Valparaíso, a UNESCO World Heritage Site

◁ Costumed *huasos* participating in a rodeo in Rancagua's crescent-shaped corral

Exploring Central Valley

Most of the region's attractions are clustered around the northern part of the valley, and to a lesser extent in the south, with renowned vineyards in areas such as Casablanca and Colchagua valleys in the central lowlands. The region's main cities are the historic port of Valparaíso and Viña del Mar, which is characterized by French palaces and ornate museums. Easily accessed from both these urban centers are Pablo Neruda's house at Isla Negra and the surfers' haven Pichilemu. Away from the coast, in the eastern mountains, resorts such as Ski Portillo promise some of Chile's best skiing runs, while Termas de Jahuel and Termas de Cauquenes are renowned for their thermal pools. In the south, national parks including Reserva Nacional Altos de Lircay and Parque Nacional Laguna de Laja offer a gamut of activities.

People relaxing on a stretch of sandy beach in Tomé

SIGHTS AT A GLANCE

Villages, Towns, and Cities
Algarrobo 4
Cachagua 7
Cartagena 6
Chillán 35
Concepción 37
Los Andes 10
Lota 39
Papudo 9
Pichilemu 27
Quintay 3
Rancagua 19
Santa Cruz 25
Tomé 38
Valparaíso pp120–27 1
Viña del Mar pp128–9 2
Zapallar 8

Resorts and Spas
Ski Centers La Parva, El Colorado, Valle Nevado 16
Ski Portillo 11
Termas de Cauquenes 23
Termas de Chillán 36
Termas de Jahuel 13
Termas de Panimavida 34

National Parks, Reserves, and Natural Monuments
Parque Nacional La Campana 14
Parque Nacional Laguna de Laja 41
Parque Nacional Radal Siete Tazas 31
Reserva Nacional Altos de Lircay 33
Reserva Nacional Río de los Cipreses 24

Areas of Natural Beauty
Cajón del Maipo pp140–41 18
Lago Vichuquén 30
Saltos de Laja 40

Tours
A Tour of Wineries in the Casablanca Valley pp138–9 15
A Tour of Wineries in the Colchagua Valley pp148–9 28

Archaeological Sites and Ruins
Sewell pp144–5 21

Sites of Interest
Antique Wineries of Pirque 17
Casa Museo Isla Negra pp132–3 5
Cristo Redentor 12
El Teniente 22
Hacienda Los Lingues 26
Valle de Cachapoal 20
Valle de Curicó 29
Villa Cultural Huilquilemu 32

Artifacts and paintings at Casa Museo Isla Negra

SEE ALSO

• ***Where to Stay*** pp278–80
• ***Where to Eat*** pp298–300

GETTING AROUND

Comfortable buses connect Central Valley and Santiago. The Pan-American Highway, or Ruta 5, runs through the region, linking its main urban centers. The majority of wine routes and the more remote sights in the Andes mountains can only be visited by car or via organized tours. Mountain spa- and ski-resorts usually arrange transfers to and from Santiago.

KEY
Highway
Main road
Minor road
Untarred main road
Untarred minor road
Main railway
Minor railway
Regional border
International border
Peak
PACIFIC OCEAN
VALPARAÍSO
METROPOLITAN
LIBERTADOR
MAULE
BÍO BÍO
PAPUDO 9
ZAPALLAR 8
CACHAGUA 7
VIÑA DEL MAR 2
VALPARAÍSO 1
QUINTAY 3
ALGARROBO 4
CASA MUSEO ISLA NEGRA 5
CARTAGENA 6
TERMAS DE JAHUEL 13
PN LA CAMPANA 14
LOS ANDES 10
SKI PORTILLO 11
CRISTO REDENTOR 12
A TOUR OF WINERIES IN CASABLANCA VALLEY 15
SKI CENTERS LA PARVA, EL COLORADO, VALLE NEVADO 16
SANTIAGO
ANTIQUE WINERIES OF PIRQUE 17
CAJÓN DEL MAIPO 18
RANCAGUA 19
VALLE DE CACHAPOAL 20
SEWELL 21
EL TENIENTE 22
TERMAS DE CAUQUENES 23
RN RÍO DE LOS CIPRESES 24
A TOUR OF WINERIES IN COLCHAGUA VALLEY 28
SANTA CRUZ 25
HACIENDA LOS LINGUES 26
PICHILEMU 27
LAGO VICHUQUÉN 30
VALLE DE CURICÓ 29
VILLA CULTURAL HUILQUILEMU 32
PN RADAL SIETE TAZAS 31
RN ALTOS DE LIRCAY 33
TERMAS DE PANIMAVIDA 34
CHILLÁN 35
TERMAS DE CHILLÁN 36
TOMÉ 38
CONCEPCIÓN 37
LOTA 39
SALTOS DE LAJA 40
PN LAGUNA DE LAJA 41
Ingeniero Santa María
Río del Sobrante
Petorca
Maitencillo
Concón
San Felipe
San Antonio
San Juan
Pomaire
Talagante
San José de Maipo
Río Maipo
Longovilo
Río Rapel
La Compañia
Coipue
Rengo
Los Lobos
Cahuil
San Fernando
Chimbarongo
Morza
Volcán Tinguiririca 14,107 ft
La Capilla
Curicó
Los Quenes
Huaquén
Molina
Upeo
Lagunas de Teno
Carrizal
Camarico
El Bolsico
Constitución
Talca
San Javier
Lago Colbún
Chanco
Sauzal
Pelluhue
Linares
Los Rabones
Cauquenes
Laguna del Maule
Cerro Campanario 13,284 ft
Río Melado
Cobquecura
Santa Cruz
Pocillas
Parral
Colmuyao
Vegas de Itata
Río Itata
San Carlos
Río Cato
Talcahuano
Río Niblinto
San Miguel
Recinto
Santa Clara
Chiguayante
Pemuco
Isla Santa Maria
Coronel
Yumbel
Volcán Chillán 10,538 ft
Golfo de Arauco
Yungay
Laguna de la Laja
Llico
Río Laja
Polcura
Arauco
Diuquin
Volcán Antuco 11,761 ft
Los Ángeles
Lebu
Los Cambuchos
Mulchen
Cañete
Cayucupil
Río Renaico
Lago Lanalhue
Río Bío Bío
Volcán Copahue 9,776 ft
Lago Lleulleu
Quidico
Tirúa
0 km 50
0 miles 50

Valparaíso ❶

Founded in 1543, the hillside city of Valparaíso emerged as the South Pacific's greatest port in the 1800s. During this time, European immigrants flocked to the city, creating a cultural melting pot of raffish sailor bars and solemn Protestant churches. Valparaíso rises abruptly from a narrow strip of coast to cover over 45 steep hills, each a dense jumble of winding streets lined with colorful houses, post-Colonial edifices, and 19th-century museums. The city is a UNESCO World Heritage Site, and much of its rich architecture is beautifully preserved, even as it bursts with trendy restaurants, bars, and boutique hotels.

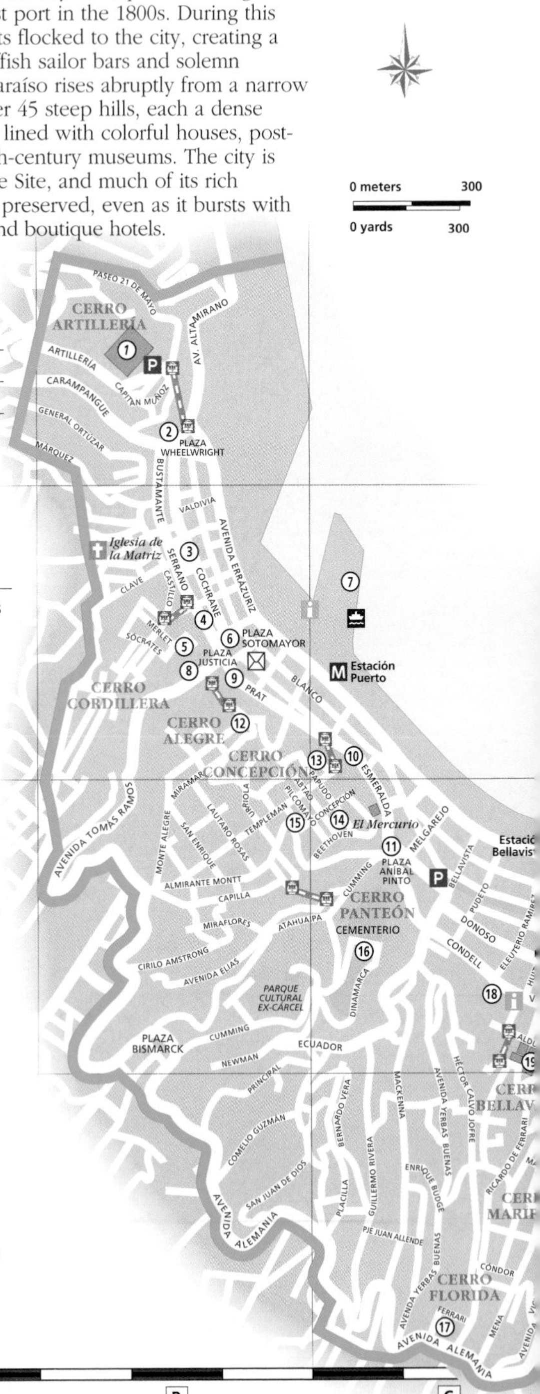

SEE ALSO

- ***Where to Stay*** pp279–80
- ***Where to Eat*** pp299–300

SIGHTS AT A GLANCE

Historic Buildings and Streets

Calle Esmeralda ⑩
Calle Prat ⑨
Congreso Nacional ㉑
Edificio de la Aduana ②
Palacio Baburizza ⑫
Palacio de la Justicia ⑧
Paseo Gervasoni ⑬
Plaza Aníbal Pinto ⑪
Plaza Echaurren ③
Plaza Sotomayor ⑥

Churches and Cathedrals

Iglesia Anglicana San Pablo ⑮
Iglesia de los Sagrados Corazones ⑳
Iglesia Luterana ⑭
Iglesia y Convento de San Francisco ㉒

Museums

Casa de Lord Cochrane ⑤
La Sebastiana ⑰
Museo a Cielo Abierto ⑲
Museo Naval y Marítimo ①
Palacio Lyon ⑱

Sites of Interest

Bar Inglés and Bar La Playa ④
Cementerios Católico and Disidentes ⑯
Muelle Prat ⑦

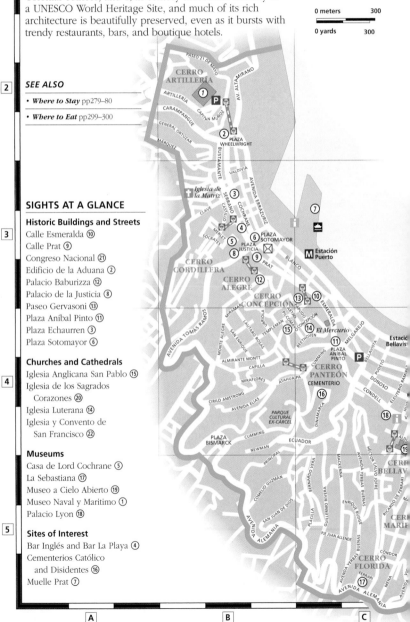

A view of Valparaíso's harbor and urbanized hillsides

VISITORS' CHECKLIST

Road Map B6. 75 miles (120 km) NW of Santiago. 276,000. *Municipalidad, Condell 1490; (032) 2939262. Glorias Navales (21 May); Carnaval Cultural de Valparaíso (end Dec).* **www.** ciudaddevalparaiso.cl

GETTING AROUND

Valparaíso consists of numerous hillside districts and a lower coastal section called El Plan. This coastal stretch can be explored on foot or by local buses and *trolebuses* *(see p125)*. However, most of Valparaíso's attractions are concentrated on the hillsides, which can be accessed from the lower section via funiculars *(see pp126–7)* and steep stairways. Cerro Concepción and Cerro Alegre are Valparaíso's main restaurant and hotel zones. An efficient metro system skirts Bahía de Valparaíso and links the city to neighboring Viña del Mar *(see pp128–9)*.

KEY

- Ferry port
- Metro station
- Coach station
- Funicular
- Visitor information
- Post office
- Parking
- Church

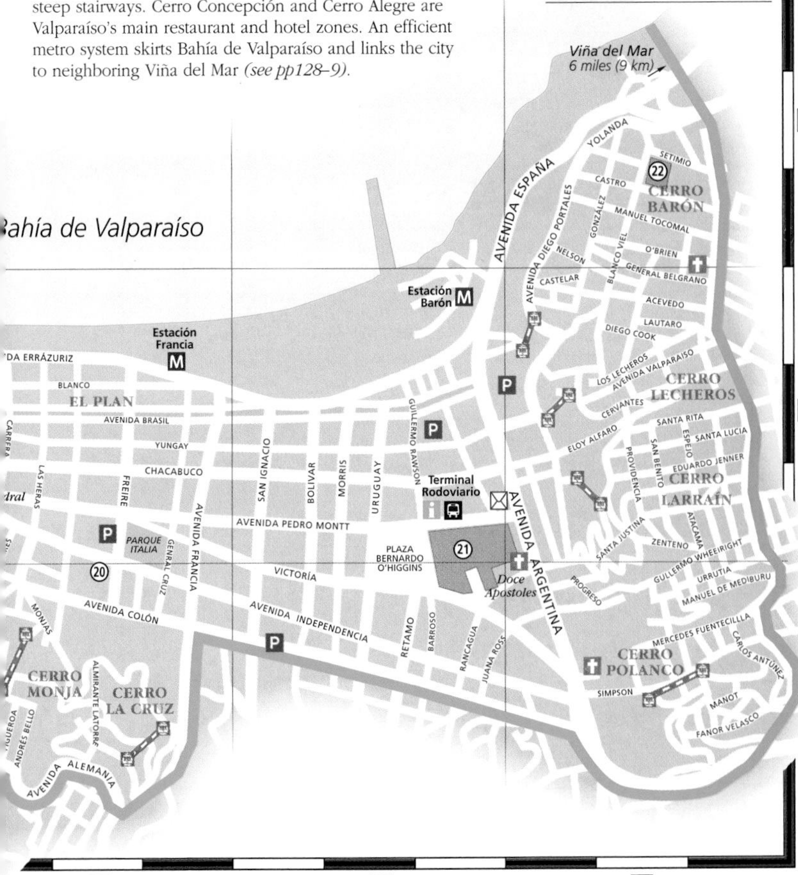

Bust of naval officer Arturo Prat at Museo Naval y Maritimo

Museo Naval y Maritimo ①

Paseo 21 de Mayo, Cerro Artillería. **City Map** B2. ***Tel*** *(032) 2437651.* *10am–6pm Tue–Sun.* **www**.museonaval.cl

Chile's excellent Museo Naval y Maritimo is housed in a building dating from 1893. It has 18 exhibition rooms, including salons dedicated to Chile's foremost naval heroes – Lord Thomas Cochrane, Arturo Prat, and Bernardo O'Higgins – and to Chile's key 19th-century naval battles. Exhibits include antique sabres and swords, pocket revolvers, bayonets, battle plans, and models of battleships. Items salvaged from Prat's schooner, *Esmeralda*, such as the clock which stopped at the precise time the ship sank during the Battle of Iquique (1879), are also displayed.

Edificio de la Aduana ②

Plaza Wheelwright. **City Map** B2. ***Tel*** *(032) 2200785.* *10:30am–4pm Thu.* **www**.aduana.cl

Built in 1855, the pink-painted Edificio de la Aduana (Customs Building) is a rare example of post-Colonial architecture. The institution's most famous employee was the Nicaraguan Modernist poet Rubén Darío, who worked here in the 1880s while writing his seminal work, *Azul* (1888). Guided tours visit a small museum, which displays objects from the building's history. Edificio de la Aduana overlooks **Plaza Wheelwright**, named for American industrialist William Wheelwright, who played a major role in building Chile's railroads and steamship fleet. His statue, raised in 1877, adorns the plaza.

Plaza Echaurren ③

Calle Cochrane, esq. Calle Serrano. **City Map** B3.

The birthplace and historic heart of Valparaíso, Plaza Echaurren marks the spot where Spanish explorer Juan de Saavedra first made landfall in 1543. Today, it is fronted by crumbling yet elegant mid-19th-century structures such as the beautiful old market building of Mercado Puerto.

Overlooking the plaza is the **Iglesia de la Matriz**, notable for its octagonal steeple. This adobe edifice was constructed in 1837 on the site of the city's first church.

Bar Inglés and Bar La Playa ④

City Map B3. **Bar Inglés** Cochrane 851. ***Tel*** *(032) 214625.* *10am–11pm Mon–Fri.* **Bar La Playa** Serrano 567. ***Tel*** *(032) 2594262.* *10–3am Mon–Wed, 10–5am Thu–Sun.* **www**.barlaplaya.cl

Two popular public bars, **Bar Inglés** and **Bar La Playa** evoke Valparaíso's halcyon days as the greatest port-city in the South Pacific. Bar Inglés was founded by English immigrants in 1926. Polished wood and brass embellish its appealing interior, which is hung with colossal wall mirrors, whirling ceiling fans, and forlorn portraits of Britain's royal family.

Located in the city's old port area, Bar La Playa was opened in 1934 as a raffish meeting spot for local working girls, sailors, and shipworkers, who would pass their time here between shifts. Today a bohemian drinking den, it hosts poetry readings on Wednesdays.

Well-stocked shelves of liquor behind the counter at Bar La Playa

Historic buildings overlooking the palm-lined Plaza Echaurren

Casa de Lord Cochrane ⑤

Calle Merlet 195, Cerro Cordillera. **City Map** B3. ***Tel*** *(032) 2939486.* *Ascensor Cordillera.* *Dec–Mar: 10am–7pm Tue–Sun; Apr–Nov: 10am–6pm Tue–Sun.* **www**.valparaisopatrimonio.cl

Located on a hilltop, Casa de Lord Cochrane was built in 1842 for Lord Thomas Cochrane, although the British naval officer never actually lived here. Open to visits, this house is a fine example of post-Colonial architecture with thick adobe walls and heavy oak doors that open inward on to a Spanish patio, adorned by a cast-iron drinking well. The sweeping front terrace, lined with cannon rows, offers glorious views of Valparaíso's bay. Occasional art exhibitions are hosted in the museum. At the back are sloping gardens with eucalyptus trees and shaded reading benches.

For hotels and restaurants in this region see pp279–80 and pp299–300

Plaza Sotomayor ⑥

Calle Cochrane, esq. Avenida Tomás Ramos. **City Map** B3.

Valparaíso's main square is the stately Plaza Sotomayor, a large area that holds parades on Glorias Navales or Navy Day *(see p37)*. The plaza is centered around the heroic **Monumento a los Heroes de Iquique**, raised in memory of the crew of the *Esmeralda* who were killed in the 1879 Battle of Iquique. The battle saw *Esmeralda*, the Chilean navy's oldest ship, fight the Peruvian fleet's most powerful vessel, *Huascar*, for 4 hours. Although the former was sunk, and her captain, Arturo Prat, killed, the battle was a turning point in the War of the Pacific *(see p45)*. Prat's bronze effigy crowns the monument and his body lies buried in a crypt here.

Towering over the southern end of Plaza Sotomayor is the elaborate façade of the Neo-Gothic **Comandancia Jefe de la Armada**. Built in 1910, its design was inspired by the Hôtel de Ville in Paris, and its interiors were multi-functional, serving both as a summer residence for Chile's presidents and as an office for the city's mayors and regional governors. Expropriated by the Chilean navy in the mid-1970s, the palace has since functioned as Chile's naval headquarters.

The Ministry of Culture, a Modernist building dating from 1936, is open daily to the public and hosts art exhibitions. Adjacent to this edifice, the Compañía de Bomberos, built in 1851, is the site of the oldest volunteer fire service in Latin America.

At the plaza's center, a staircase descends to the subterranean **Museo de Sitio Plaza Sotomayor**. This small archaeological museum displays remains of the pier that once stood where Plaza Sotomayor (built on land reclaimed from sea) now stands.

Monumento a los Heroes de Iquique dominating the Plaza Sotomayor

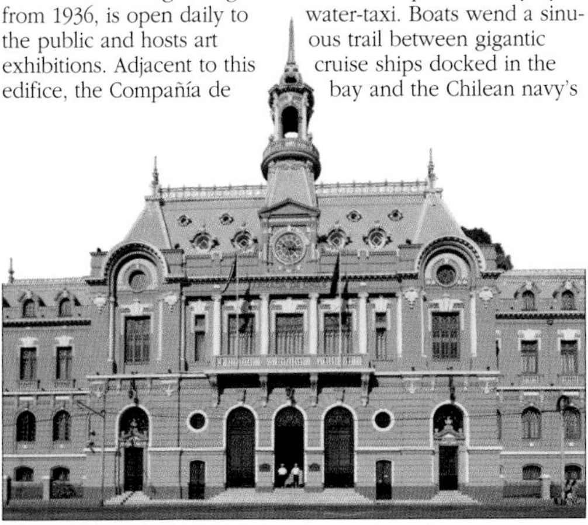

Imposing Neo-Gothic façade of the Comandancia Jefe de la Armada

Museo de Sitio Plaza Sotomayor
Plaza Sotomayor. *10am–2pm & 3:30–6pm daily.*

Muelle Prat ⑦

Avenida Errázuriz, in front of Plaza Sotomayer. **City Map** C3.

A busy pier, Muelle Prat is the departure point for half-hour tours of Valparaíso's bay by water-taxi. Boats wend a sinuous trail between gigantic cruise ships docked in the bay and the Chilean navy's battleships stationed offshore, before hitting open water. The tour offers tremendous views of the city's hillsides, densely built-up with rows of brightly colored houses.

Cruise ships and boats lining the waterfront at Muelle Prat

Palacio de la Justicia ⑧

Plaza Justicia. **City Map** B3. ***Tel*** *(032) 2258577.* *8am–2pm Mon–Fri.*

Built in 1939, the Palacio de la Justicia is Valparaíso's appeals court. The edifice has a sober, rectilinear façade, with a 10-ft (3-m) high statue of Justitia (Lady Justice) at its entrance. The figure is curiously anomalous in that she wears no blindfold, her customary symbol of objectivity, and her scales of truth dangle forlornly at her side, rather than at the end of her outstretched arm. According to legend, an angry merchant had the statue placed here to protest against a perceived injustice.

Plaza Aníbal Pinto dominated by the yellow and green Librería Ivens building

Calle Prat ⑨

City Map B3.

A narrow thoroughfare through the city's financial district, Calle Prat links Plaza Sotomayor and the monumental 1929 **Reloj Turri** (Turri Clock Tower), the city's Big Ben. Looming over both sides of the road are grand buildings of stone and black marble, constructed at the turn of the 20th century. Among these is the old Bank of London building, today the Banco de Chile (No. 698), which houses a monument built to commemorate British soldiers killed in World War I. Another evocative edifice here is Valparaíso's stock exchange, **La Bolsa de Valores**, the oldest stock exchange in South America. The old bidding wheel still stands inside the building's cavernous, domed interior.

Calle Esmeralda ⑩

City Map C3.

An extension of Calle Prat, Calle Esmeralda starts at the Turri Clock Tower, close to Ascensor Concepción *(see pp126–7)* and ends at Plaza Aníbal Pinto. The street's most beautiful construction is the **El Mercurio** building, home to the popular *El Mercurio de Valparaíso* newspaper. The ornate exterior of the edifice is crowned by a bronze statue of Mercury pointing skyward. Adjacent to El Mercurio, a stairway climbs up to the mystical **Cueva Chivito**, a natural rock cave, which according to local lore was once inhabited by the devil.

Plaza Aníbal Pinto ⑪

End of Calle Esmeralda. **City Map** C4.

Uniting Valparaíso's financial district and the commercial downtown area, Plaza Aníbal Pinto is a small, chaotic square fronted by beautiful buildings and the old **Cinzano** café *(see p299)*. A sepia-tinted bar, the café was founded in 1896 and features live tango shows.

On one side of the plaza is the striking **Librería Ivens** building. Founded in 1891, it is one of the city's oldest bookshops. At the entrance to this building is the plaza's attractive public artwork – a street fountain sculpted as Neptune in 1892.

Palacio Baburizza ⑫

Paseo Yugoslavo s/n, Cerro Alegre. **City Map** B3. ***Tel*** *(032) 2252332.* *Ascensor El Peral.* *call to check.*

An Art Nouveau mansion, Palacio Baburizza was constructed in 1916 for Italian saltpeter tycoon, Ottorino Zanelli. It was then bought by Pascual Baburizza, a Croatian immigrant and nitrates magnate, in 1925. Today, the structure houses Valparaíso's fine-arts museum, whose displays include the Baburizza family's collection of 19th- and-20th century European art.

The palace is situated on the summit of Cerro Alegre and overlooks the lovely Paseo Yugoslavo. A leafy promenade and viewing point, the street offers breathtaking vistas of neighboring hillsides, the city's port, financial districts, and the blue Bahía de Valparaíso.

View of the sprawling Art Nouveau Palacio Baburizza

Paseo Gervasoni ⑬

Cerro Concepción. Ascensor Concepción. **City Map** C3.

At the pinnacle of Cerro Concepción, the Concepción funicular spills out on to Paseo Gervasoni. A romantic cobbled promenade and vantage point edged with wild flowers, the *paseo* affords splendid views across the Bahía de Valparaíso to Viña del Mar in the north. Along the street are the elegant Café Turri *(see p299)*, the old Danish consulate building dating from 1848, and **Casa Mirador de Lukas**. The last is a 1900 house that holds a lovely museum dedicated to the life and works of Chile's best-loved cartoonist, Renzo Antonio Pecchenino Raggi (1934–88), popularly known as Lukas.

Casa Mirador de Lukas
Paseo Gervasoni 448, Cerro Concepción. ***Tel*** *(032) 2221344.*
11am–6pm Tue–Sun.
www.lukas.cl

Entrance to Casa Mirador de Lukas, Paseo Gervasoni

Iglesia Luterana ⑭

Abtao 689, Cerro Concepción. **City Map** C4. ***Tel*** *(032) 2975476.*
10am–1pm Mon–Fri.

Built by the city's German community in 1898, the Iglesia Luterana was South America's first Protestant church to be allowed a steeple and bell tower. Its beautifully austere façade tapers upward toward a slender, 115-ft (35-m) high steeple, which crowns Cerro Concepción and is visible from the city's lower sections. Inside, the nave fills with natural light and a sculpture of Christ on the cross, which is carved from a single pine trunk, hangs above the altar. A grand organ, brought from England in 1884, stands opposite the altar.

Soaring bell tower of the Protestant Iglesia Lutherana

Iglesia Anglicana San Pablo ⑮

Pilcomayo 566, Cerro Concepción. **City Map** B4. ***Tel*** *(032) 2975476.*
10:30am–1pm Tue–Fri.

The Neo-Gothic Iglesia Anglicana San Pablo was built in 1858 by British engineer William Lloyd. This church was established by Valparaíso's English community, but only after the city's Catholic archbishop imposed many conditions on what he considered a temple to a rival faith. Among the most curious was that this church's doors be smaller than those of the city's Catholic churches – and to this day visitors enter not via a grand portal, but by one of the two small side doors. The church's simple stone and wood interior houses a pipe organ donated in memory of Britain's Queen Victoria in 1903.

Cementerios Católico and Disidentes ⑯

Dinamarca s/n, Cerro Panteón. **City Map** C4. **Cementerio Católica** *8:30am–5pm daily.* **Cementerio Disidentes** *9am–1pm & 3–5pm Mon–Sat, 9am–1pm Sun.*

Spectacularly located high up on an overhanging hillside, the **Cementerio Católico** and **Cementerio Disidentes** are poignant evocations of this port-city's halcyon days in the 1800s as a melting pot of different cultures and creeds. The Cementerio Disidentes is the site of the simple, sometimes austere, graves of the city's Protestant communities, including American Mormons, English Anglicans, and German Lutherans. Many of the gravestones are engraved with tales of war and shipwreck. Opposite the Cementerio Disidentes, a grand portal enters the Cementerio Católico, otherwise known as Cementerio N°1. Valparaíso's most illustrious sons and daughters lie here in grand, marbled mausoleums. Among the luminaries buried are members of the Edwards-Ross family, owners of the *El Mercurio de Valparaíso* newspaper; José Francisco Vergara, founder of the town Viña del Mar; and Renzo Pecchenino, a popular Chilean cartoonist.

EL MERCURIO DE VALPARAÍSO

The oldest newspaper in continuous circulation in the entire Spanish-speaking world, *El Mercurio de Valparaíso* was founded in 1827 by Chilean journalist Pedro Felix Vicuña and the American typographer Thomas Well. Since the 1880s, it has been under the uninterrupted stewardship of Chile's eminent Edwards-Ross family, who continue to aspire to this newspaper's founding ideal: that it be "adequate enough to moderate the extreme passions that divide men".

Façade of the El Mercurio building

La Sebastiana, former residence of Chilean poet Pablo Neruda

La Sebastiana ⑰

Ferrari 692, Cerro Florida. **City Map** C5. ***Tel*** *(032) 2256606.* *Ascensor Espiritu Santo.* *Dec–Mar: 11:10am–6pm Tue–Sun; Apr–Nov: 10:30am–6:50pm Tue–Sun.* **www**.fundacionneruda.org

A must-see for devotees of Pablo Neruda *(see p87)*, La Sebastiana is the last of three houses bought by the poet in Chile. Neruda and two of his friends acquired the shell of the house in 1961 and named it for its architect and first owner, Sebastian Collado. They made extensive renovations to the structure, which resulted in an anarchic architecture that mirrored the city itself – the house became a jumble of narrow, twisting stairways and myriad nooks and crannies, painted in a range of colors.

In 1991, the structure was restored and converted into a museum that preserves the house as it was when Neruda lived there. It contains strange and wonderful objects bought by the poet, such as a Parisian carousel pony in the living room and an unfitted washbasin from England in the study. Pablo Neruda's rich imagination is also evident in the American oakwood stairway rescued from a demolition site, and a floor mosaic of uncut pebbles shaped into an antique map of Patagonia and Antarctica.

Palacio Lyon ⑱

City Map C4. **Museo de Historia Natural de Valparaíso** Condell 1546. ***Tel*** *(032) 2544840.* *10am–1pm & 2–6pm Tue–Sat, 10am–2pm Sun.* **www**.mhnv.cl **Galeria Municipal de Arte Valparaíso** Condell 1550. ***Tel*** *(032) 2939567.* *10am–5pm Mon–Fri.*

Built in 1887, Palacio Lyon houses the **Museo de Historia Natural de Valparaíso**, the city's natural history museum and Chile's second-oldest state museum. A construction of stone, cast iron, and glass, this edifice evokes the 19th century as a golden age of exploration, scientific discovery, and public education. Displays include exhibits from the early 1900s that feature Chile's marine flora and fauna, stuffed animals from around the world, and rows of curiosities including bovine conjoined twins conserved in tanks of formaldehyde. A separate side door leads to the palace's arched brick basement, where the **Galeria Municipal de Arte Valparaíso** showcases stimulating works by contemporary Chilean artists.

Museo a Cielo Abierto ⑲

Cerro Bellavista. **City Map** C4. ***Tel*** *(032) 593156.* *Ascensor Espiritu Santo.*

An outdoor museum on Cerro Bellavista, the Museo a Cielo Abierto comprises a maze of winding streets and passageways painted with giant, colorful street murals by some of Chile's best-known contemporary artists. There are about 20 murals, ranging from highly abstract works to humorous depictions of daily life in the city. The greatest concentration of murals is found on Calle Ferrari and on Pasaje Santa Lucía. The latter is a steeply stepped passageway and a whirl of kaleidoscopically vibrant motifs and figures.

Detailed murals painted on building walls along Calle Ferrari, part of Museo a Cielo Abierto

Iglesia de los Sagrados Corazones ⑳

Avenida Independencia 2050–2084. **City Map** D5. ***Tel*** *(032) 2746728.* *daily.*

Dating from 1874, the Iglesia de los Sagrados Corazones was the first church built in the Americas for the French Order of the Sacred Hearts. Most of its striking architectural elements, including the elegant clock tower, the wooden altar, pulpit, and confessional boxes, were brought from France. There is a stunning pipe organ made by Aristide de Cavalle-Coll, the most famous French organ maker of the time. Stained glass, a replica of the glass in the Church of Santa Gúdula in Belgium, adorns the church's upper reaches and thousands of tiny gold-painted stars decorate its vaulted ceiling.

Adjacent to the church, the **Colegio de los Sagrados Corazones** dates from 1837 and is Chile's oldest private high school. Several former presidents were educated here.

Manicured lawns fronting the entrance to the Congreso Nacional

Congreso Nacional ㉑

Victoría s/n. **City Map** E4. ***Tel*** *(032) 2505139.* *9:30am–12:30pm & 3–5pm Mon–Fri.* *reserve 24 hrs in advance.* **www**.camara.cl

In 1988, General Pinochet, Chile's military dictator, was obliged to return the country to democracy after 14 years of dictatorship *(see p48)*. In doing so, he chose Valparaíso, rather than Santiago, as the seat of the country's new National Congress. Two years later, the starkly modern and muscular Congreso Nacional building was inaugurated. The structure has met with divided opinion since its construction – some see it is a powerful symbol of democracy and of decentralized political power, while others question its aesthetic appeal. Tours of its halls and salons guide visitors through the rich allegory and symbolism of this building's architecture. Tours, both in Spanish and English, cover the National Senate, the Deputy chambers, and the Salón de Honor – the ceremonial hall where international statesmen including Mikhail Gorbachov and Bill Clinton, former Russian and US presidents respectively, have addressed dignitaries.

Iglesia y Convento de San Francisco ㉒

Blanco Viel s/n, Cerro Barón. **City Map** F3. ***Tel*** *(032) 2258735.* *9am–1pm & 4–8:30pm Tue, Wed, Fri & Sat; 7am–10pm Thu, 9am–2pm Sun.*

Established in 1846, the Iglesia San Francisco is one of Chile's most impressive examples of red-brick architecture. The church, designated a national monument in 1983, features an ornate façade topped with a distinct, rising bell tower, which used to be illuminated at night to guide ships to Valparaíso's port. The interior of the church is a study in beautiful simplicity, comprising modest whitewashed walls and a Spanish-tiled floor beneath an arched, dark-wood ceiling.

Towering steeple crowning the Iglesia y Convento de San Fransisco

Entered from the side of the church, the Convento de San Francisco was established as a boarding house for visiting priests. Constructed in Colonial style over two floors, the building surrounds a romantic Spanish courtyard lined with fruit trees and colorful flowers. This idyllic patio is accessible to the public and has several shaded benches.

THE TROLEBUSES

Valparaíso's fleet of electric *trolebuses* was imported from the US between 1946 and 1952, and includes the world's oldest trolleybuses still in service. Under the Pinochet regime, trolleybus systems deteriorated as funds for government-run transportation were cut. In 1982, some of the city's businessmen acquired the assets for the *trolebuses*, and then completely renovated them. Today, these vehicles ply between Avenida Argentina and Edificio de la Aduana *(see p120)*. Extremely low on noise and air pollution, they offer an easy and charming way to see the city.

Green *trolebuses* waiting for passengers on Avenida Argentina

Funiculars of Valparaíso

Logo on Ascensor Artillería

Valparaíso's funiculars are the cheapest, easiest, and most fun way of traveling between the city's residential hillsides and the port and financial districts of its El Plan (Lower Town). An antique form of transport, the funiculars were introduced between 1883 and 1912, and 15 of the original 20 still survive. They rattle up and down Valparaíso's steep hills past dense rows of houses and spill out on to dramatic promenades with beautiful city and ocean vistas. Many also access historic sights and tourist attractions, and together the funiculars themselves constitute a national historical monument.

Steep staircases accompanying the track of Ascensor Cordillera

Ascensor Concepción *was Valparaíso's first funicular. Very popular with visitors, its wooden cars connect the financial district with Cerro Concepción, a hillside of historical buildings, narrow alleyways, and hotels and restaurants. The funicular spills out on to the romantic Paseo Gervasoni promenade and its gorgeous vistas.*

Ascensor Polanco *is a wonderful curiosity. It is one of three urban elevators in the world whose ascent is totally vertical. It is accessed via a 500-ft (150-m) long tunnel, and rises 262 ft (80 m) through a yellow wooden tower to an upper station that is connected by a footbridge to Cerro Polanco.*

Ascensor Espiritu Santo *connects the city center with colorful Cerro Bellavista. Like all of Valparaíso's funiculars, it was once powered by steam and coal and now runs on electricity. Its upper station opens on to the Museo a Cielo Abierto and also provides easy access to the La Sebastiana museum.*

Ascensor Barón *climbs Cerro Barón on the eastern side of Valparaíso. It has the city's largest wooden cars and its first electric motors. Its upper station house is home to a small museum.*

Ascensor El Peral *is one of the busiest elevators, linking Plaza Sotomayor with the hotels and restaurants of Cerro Alegre. The funicular spills out on to the picturesque Paseo Yugoslavo promenade.*

ASCENSOR ARTILLERÍA

This funicular's wooden cars climb and descend parallel tracks between the port area near Edificio de la Aduana and Cerro Artillería. At the hilltop, a Victorian promenade offers fantastic port views, and the ex-machinist's house contains a museum and the Café Arte Mirador *(see p299)*. From a window table in the café, it is possible to watch the giant wheels of the funicular turning.

Ascensor Mariposas *is the city's longest funicular. It runs for 580 ft (177 m) and its dramatic climb squeezes between dense rows of colorful houses.*

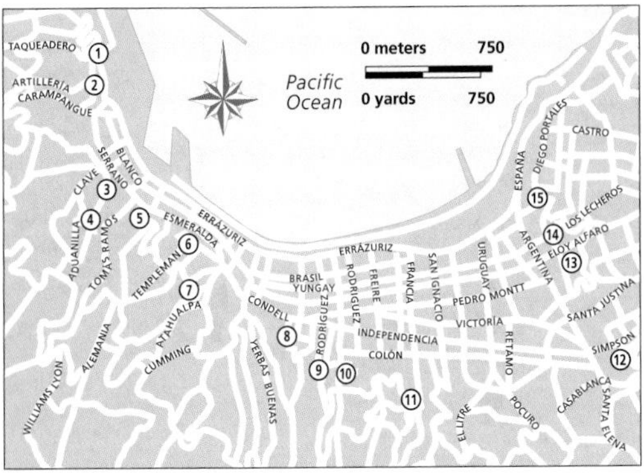

THE FUNICULARS

Ascensor Villaseca ①
Ascensor Artillería ②
Ascensor Cordillera ③
Ascensor San Agustín ④
Ascensor El Peral ⑤
Ascensor Concepción ⑥
Ascensor Reina Victoria ⑦
Ascensor Espiritu Santo ⑧
Ascensor Florida ⑨
Ascensor Mariposas ⑩
Ascensor Monjas ⑪
Ascensor Polanco ⑫
Ascensor Larraín ⑬
Ascensor Lecheros ⑭
Ascensor Barón ⑮

Viña del Mar 2

Coat of arms, Palacio Rioja

Founded in 1874, Viña del Mar (Vineyard of the Sea) has its origins in a Colonial hacienda whose vineyards faced the ocean. The area transformed into a city after the 1906 earthquake compelled Valparaíso's elite to relocate here. Its flat topography was ideal for building the French-style garden palaces that were then fashionable and the town became a resort for the rich. Today, it is Chile's Ciudad de Jardines (City of Gardens) – adorned with green spaces, great beaches, and fine palaces that house stunning museums.

Plaza José Francisco Vergara

Avenida Valparaíso, esq. Avenida Libertad.

Viña del Mar's elegant central square, Plaza José Francisco Vergara, is named for the city's founder, whose bronze statue stands on a marble plinth in a corner of the square. The plaza is decorated with pools, statues, and fountains, and lushly shaded by Chilean palms, Lebanese cedars, and Argentinian ombus.

Further grandeur is added by the Hotel Viña del Mar *(see p280)* and the Hotel O'Higgins. Built in 1930, the Neo-Classical **Teatro Municipal** is the most impressive structure in the square. Its façade of Corinthian columns hides a reception hall that is adorned with marble statues.

Palacio Vergara

Errázuriz 563–596. ***Tel*** *(032) 2269431.* *10am–1:30pm & 3–5:30pm Tue–Sun.*
Quinta Vergara *7am–6pm daily.*

Constructed in 1906–10 for José Francisco Vergara's family, Palacio Vergara now houses the Museo Municipal de Bellas Artes. The palace is built in a Venetian Neo-Gothic style with a stunning façade and an ornate interior that houses over 150 artworks. These include religious pieces from the 15th to 18th centuries; works by Chile's 19th-century masters; 20th-century Surrealist and Cubist paintings; and works of art donated by the Vergara family. The themed salons include a Salon Dorado ballroom, with Rococo mirrors, gold-and-silk wall tapestries, and Italian-marble statues.

Surrounding the palace are the parklands of **Quinta Vergara**, once the Vergara family's private gardens. These are planted with exotic trees and decorated with Classical statues. Dominating the grounds, the Anfiteatro Quinta Vergara is a strikingly contemporary amphitheater that hosts the annual Festival Internacional de la Canción de Viña del Mar *(see p36)*.

Reloj de Flores

Balmaceda, esq. Avenida Marina.

Planted in 1962 on a grassy hillock facing the ocean, the Reloj de Flores (Flower Clock) symbolizes Viña del Mar's status as the City of Gardens. The dial is a circular flower-bed planted with numerous bright Chilean flowers. The clock includes wooden hour, minute, and second hands that were brought from Switzerland.

Medieval tower and turrets of the stately Castillo Wulff

Castillo Wulff

Avenida Marina 37. ***Tel*** *(032) 2269741.* *10am–1:30pm & 3–5:30pm Tue–Sun.*

Located on the city's coastal avenue, Castillo Wulff was constructed for German industrialist Gustavo Adolfo Wulff in 1905. A national monument and architectural landmark, the edifice is built in the style of a typical medieval castle and features turrets, ramparts, a round tower, and a central courtyard. The courtyard stairs climb to a lookout point with marvelous ocean vistas. The castle also hosts art exhibitions.

Casino Municipal de Viña del Mar

Avenida San Martín 199. ***Tel*** *(032) 2500600.* *Dec–Mar: 24hrs daily; Apr–Nov: noon–4am daily.* **www**.enjoy.cl

Housed in an impressive Neo-Classical building, Casino Municipal de Viña del Mar opened in 1932 and sealed the city's reputation as Chile's playground for the rich. The casino has many game rooms that include roulette, blackjack, and over 1,200 slot machines. There are regular cabaret shows and for high rollers, a luxury hotel with a spa and restaurants. The casino also

Neo-Classical façade of the Teatro Municipal

offers family-oriented services such as a children's playroom and childminding staff.

Museo de Arqueológia e Historia Francisco Fonck
4 Norte N 784. ***Tel*** *(032) 2686753.* *Dec–Mar: 10am–6pm Mon–Sat, 10am–2pm Sun; Apr–Nov: 10am–6pm Mon–Fri, 10am–2pm Sat & Sun.* **www**.museofonck.cl
Housed in an old mansion, the Museo de Arqueológia e Historia Francisco Fonck features displays of pre-Hispanic objects collected from across Chile and Latin America. Rooms at this archaeological museum are dedicated to the major pre-Columbian civilizations of Chile as well as of Mexico, Peru, Ecuador, and other Latin American countries. Each salon boasts a rich selection of objects from the era it represents. Its standout collection was brought from Easter Island *(see p254–65)* in 1951. It includes rare artifacts, has informative panels in English and Spanish, and delves into the religious beliefs behind the erection of its famous *moai*. An original *moai*, one of the few on mainland Chile, stands at the entrance.

Easter Island *moai* outside the Museo Franciso Fonck

Palacios Rioja and Carrasco
Palacio Rioja Quillota 214. ***Tel*** *(032) 2483664.* *10am–1:30pm & 3–5:30pm Tue–Sun.* *on request.*
Palacio Carrasco Avenida Libertad 250. ***Tel*** *(032) 2269708.* *9:30am–1pm & 2–7pm Mon–Fri, 9am–2pm Sat.*
Constructed after the 1906 earthquake, both **Palacio Rioja** and **Palacio Carrasco** are national monuments. The Neo-Classical Palacio Rioja was inspired by Paris's Versailles Palace and built for tobacco baron Fernando Rioja in 1907. It is now a decorative arts museum that conserves the Rioja family home as it was a century ago. The visit includes a tour of its sumptuous rooms, including the ornate dining room, which has Corinthian columns and an orchestra balcony, and the magnificent central hall, which is embellished with classic Greek statues and pillars. A garden of exotic trees with paths and benches encircles the palace.

Built between 1912 and 1923 in the Beaux-Arts style, Palacio Carrasco houses the city's cultural center and hosts occasional art exhibitions. The entrance of the palace is adorned by *La Defensa*, a bronze statue by the famous French sculptor Auguste Rodin (1840–1917).

VISITORS' CHECKLIST

Road Map B6. 6 miles (9 km) N of Valparaíso. *290,000.* *Arlegui 755; (032) 2269092.* *Wed.* *Festival Internacional de la Canción de Viña del Mar (Feb).* **www**.vinadelmar.cl

Reñaca
3 miles (5 km) N of Viña del Mar. **www**.renaca.cl
A gorgeous stretch of golden sand, Reñaca is a popular holiday spot for the residents of Santiago during the summer months. This beach is overlooked by a number of hotels, and several bars and clubs operate at its southern end.

Environs
Some 6 miles (10 km) north of Reñaca, **Concón** is a small town with several good beaches, such as upscale Playa Amarilla and rustic Playa La Boca, a long, crescent-shaped beach popular with surfers. A surf school and numerous seafood restaurants front Playa La Boca. In summer, horseback rides cross its sands to dunes and coastal forest.

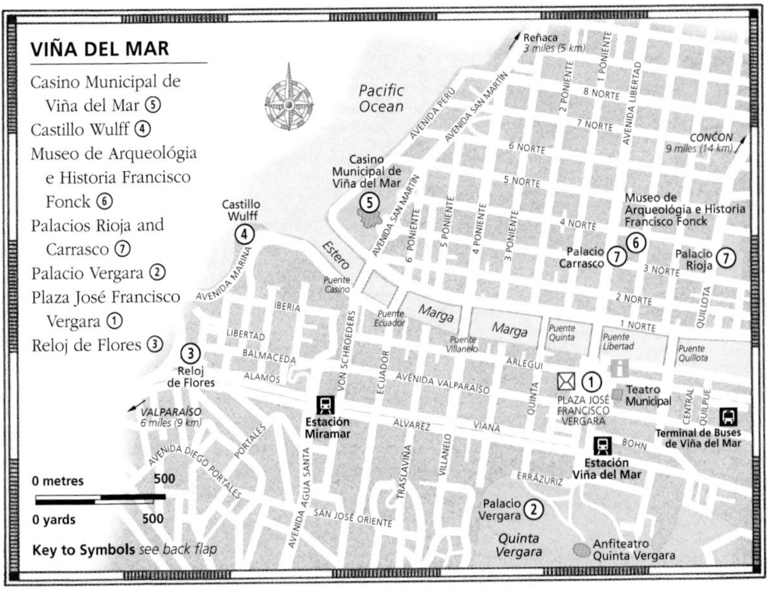

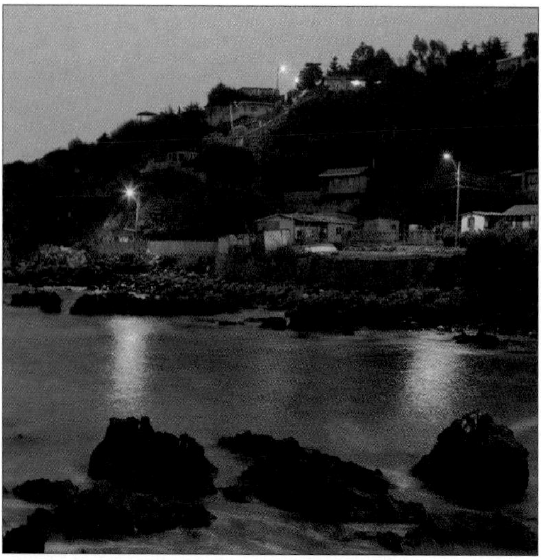

Calm waters along the rock-encrusted coastline of Quintay

Quintay ❸

Road Map B6. 29 miles (47 km) S of Valparaíso. *800.*

The fishing village of Quintay is an idyllic spot. Buses drop off visitors at its small plaza, from where sandy lanes wend down to the *caleta*. This is a horseshoe-shaped fishermen's harbor edged by a rocky beach and weatherboard seafood restaurants. Sea otters and birds congregate on the beach and fishermen unload their catch here from wooden boats.

Overlooking the *caleta* is the **Ballenera de Quintay**, Chile's biggest whaling station until its closure in 1967. Now a whaling museum, it includes the station's old and somewhat eerie whaling platform on to which the carcasses of 1,600 blue whale – the world's largest animal – were dragged year after year.

Quintay has two main beaches. From the plaza a 10-minute walk through cool pine and eucalyptus forest leads to the breathtakingly picturesque **Playa Chica**, a wave-pummelled beach ringed by high, rugged cliffs and wildflowers. North of the town centre, **Playa Grande** is a long stretch of golden sand, spoiled slightly by condominiums. For activities in Quintay, diving schools at the *caleta* run scuba-diving and kayaking excursions. These are ideal for beginners and enthusiasts alike.

Ballenera de Quintay
Caleta de Quintay. ***Tel*** *(032) 362511.* *Dec–Mar: 9am–9pm daily; Apr–Nov: 9am–6pm daily.* **www**.fundacionquintay.cl

Algarrobo ❹

Road Map B6. 43 miles (70 km) S of Valparaíso. *8,600.* **www**.vivealgarrobo.cl

The largest town along the section of Pacific coast south of Valparaíso, Algarrobo is a family-oriented resort that gets crowded in summer with families arriving from Santiago. This town boasts excellent tourist services and has some 14 separate beaches where activities include scuba-diving, windsurfing, and horseback riding. Its most popular beach, **Playa San Pedro**, is close to the town center and faces calm waters, ideal for swimming. **Playa Grande** is a more dramatic big-wave beach. South of the town center is **Playa El Canelo**, a stretch of fine sand washed by aquamarine waters, that backs on to thick pine forest. **Playa El Canelillo** is secluded and quieter. Reached by boat from Algarrobo, the **Isla de Pájaros Niño** is a rocky islet visited each September to April by nesting colonies of Humboldt penguins. Boats skirt the islet's shore, moving past birdlife such as pelicans, cormorants, and gulls.

Beach umbrellas lining a popular beach in Cartagena

Casa Museo Isla Negra ❺

See pp132–3.

Cartagena ❻

Road Map B6. 62 miles (100 km) S of Valparaíso. *17,000.* *Municipalidad, Plaza de Armas; (035) 200736.* **www**.cartagena-chile.cl

The delightful hillside town of Cartagena has narrow winding streets and colorful houses hanging from a hilltop overlooking a bay. The best time to visit is late spring or early autumn when the beaches are not as crowded as they are during summer.

From the lushly palm-shaded Plaza de Armas in Cartagena's upper town, twisting streets and stairways wend down to **Playa Chica**, south of the plaza, and to **Playa Grande**, north of the plaza. Set on a hillside east of Playa Chica is the home and tomb of Vicente Huidobro (1893–1948), a great Chilean poet who lived for several years in Cartagena. Sadly rundown, the spot is still a popular point of pilgrimage for Chilean poets and artists. The house is under private ownership and closed to public view.

Cachagua ❼

Road Map B6. 45 miles (73 km) N of Valparaíso. *1,500.*

A beautiful, rustic beach-town, Cachagua arrives as a welcome change along a stretch of coastline dominated by upscale resorts and condominiums. The town has a eucalyptus-shaded plaza from which sandy lanes flanked by thatched houses descend to the long, dramatic **Playa Grande**, Cachagua's main beach. Horse riding and surfing are popular activities here.

Visible from Playa Grande, the **Monumento Isla Cachagua** is a rocky islet that is refuge to a wide variety of birdlife, including nesting colonies of Humboldt penguins from September to April. Boat trips take visitors near the islet and offer a chance to observe this rare birdlife from a close range. Also of interest at Cachagua is **Playa Las Cujas**, a sheltered, rocky beach, popular with divers and anglers.

The long and scenic coastal walkway at Papudo

Humboldt penguins at Isla Cachagua

Zapallar ❽

Road Map B6. 50 miles (80 km) N of Valparaíso. *1,600.* *Municipalidad, Germán Riesgo 399; (033) 74200.* **www**.turismozapallar.cl

An exceptionally picturesque coastal town and an erstwhile high-end destination, Zapallar is small, secluded, and ringed by steeply forested coastal mountains. The town sits on a wooded hillside that sweeps dramatically down to rocky cliffs and a half-moon shaped sandy beach.

A number of weatherboard holiday villas dot the coastal mountains around Zapallar. Since the late 19th century, this town has been a favorite summer destination for the wealthy citizens of Santiago. From Zapallar's beach a 4-mile (6-km) long coastal path skirts clifftops and has wide ocean vistas. Boat launches make daily departures in summer, taking birdwatchers and holiday-makers southward to the Monumento Isla Cachagua.

A sandy path up the hillside from the beach leads to Zapallar's white-sand plaza, fronted by a clapboard theaterhouse. This dates from 1908 and was originally the town church. From the plaza, a number of lanes climb uphill to Zapallar's commercial center with shops, eateries, and tourist information.

The beach and town of Zapallar, sheltered by forested hills

Papudo ❾

Road Map B6. 56 miles (91 km) N of Valparaíso. *4,600.* *Chorrillos 9, 2nd Floor; (033) 790080.* *Wed & Sun.* *Feria Internacional de Integración Papudo (early Feb).* **www**.municipalidadpapudo.cl

Less exclusive than the neighboring beach-towns of Zapallar and Cachagua, Papudo is a small and unpretentious seaside town with great walks. A sweeping coastal boulevard runs parallel to the two main beaches: **Playa Grande**, a long open beach popular with surfers; and the smaller, sheltered **Playa Chica**, which is frequented by families. A number of attractive seaside walks strike out from both beaches, crossing sections of cliffs along the coast that are pitted with caves and caverns. On fine days, horses are available for those who wish to ride along the shoreline.

Among the buidings that line the main coastal boulevard, visitors will find the **Iglesia Nuestra Señora de las Mercedes**, a church and national monument built in 1918. Farther on, the honey-colored **Chalet Recart**, site of Papudo's town hall, is one of several alpine-chalet buildings that front the coast here.

Casa Museo Isla Negra ❺

African face mask

Attracted by its location facing the Isla Negra beach, Pablo Neruda bought the original building from a Spanish sailor in 1939. Neruda extended the house, creating a structure whose long, thin shape mirrored the geography of Chile, and filled it with over 3,500 weird and wonderful objects from across the globe. Today, the house is a museum and remains exactly as it was when the poet lived here with his third wife, Matilde Urrutia, prior to his death in 1973.

Isla Negra Beach
Named for its isolation and wild black rocks, Isla Negra beach is associated with the poet's love for the sea.

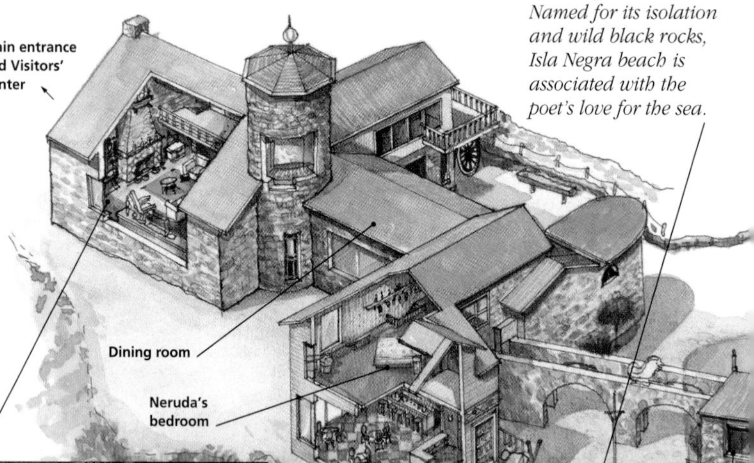

Living Room
Ship figureheads, stained glass, and wooden angels adorn this space. Neruda encrusted its floor with seashells to massage his feet.

Narrow wooden corridors like those on old ships run along the house. Neruda lined this one with African facemasks.

The Bar
The house bar conserves Neruda's collection of surreal and figuratively designed bottles. An array of colors, shapes, and sizes are displayed.

STAR SIGHTS

★ Neruda's Study

★ Neruda's Tomb

For hotels and restaurants in this region see pp278–80 and pp298–300

Seashell Collection

Neruda's collection of seashells occupies an entire room. The long, rapier-like tusk of a narwhal whale is also exhibited here.

VISITORS' CHECKLIST

Road Map B6. 56 miles (90 km) S of Valparaíso; Poeta Neruda s/n, Isla Negra. ***Tel*** *(035) 461284.* *Jan–Feb: 10am–8pm Tue–Sun; Mar–Dec: 10am–6pm Tue–Sun.* *mandatory; reserve 24 hrs in advance; tours, in English & Spanish, leave every 30 min from Visitors' Center.* **www**.fundacion neruda.org

Neruda entertained guests including other writers in this reception area. Eclectic collections fill its space.

The Stable

This was built for a papier-mâché horse. Neruda called it, "the world's happiest horse".

★ Neruda's Study

Crammed with miscellanea, Neruda's study displays model ships, butterfly collections, astrological charts, portraits, and an antique washbasin.

★ Neruda's Tomb

Two years after the museum's 1990 inauguration, Neruda was re-buried at Isla Negra. Matilde Urrutia is buried alongside him.

The convent building dedicated to Santa Teresa de Los Andes

Los Andes ⑩

Road Map B6. 87 miles (141 km) NE of Valparaíso. *60,000.* *Avenida Santa Teresa 333; (034) 902525.* *Wed, Sat, Sun.* *La Festival Nacional Folclórico "El Guatón Loyola" (mid-Sep).* **www**.losandes.cl

Ringed by the vineyards of Aconcagua valley, at the foot of the Andean cordillera, Los Andes was founded 1791 as a staging post on a Colonial trade route. Today, it is the first stop for many travelers making the road crossing of the Andes from Argentina to Chile's Central Valley. There are two museums of interest here. The **Museo Arqueológico de los Andes** is a Colonial house with pre-Columbian displays. The **Museo Histórico Religioso del Antiguo Monasterio del Espiritu Santu** is a convent building dedicated to Santa Teresa de Los Andes, Chile's first saint. Visitors can wander about the convent's old workrooms, sleeping quarters, cloistered courtyard, and orchard. Next door, the Capilla Espiritu Santo is a Neo-Gothic chapel and shrine to the saint. The Neo-Classical headquarters of the regional government, built over 1888–1891, overlooks Los Andes' pretty Colonial plaza. At the edge of town, the Cerro de la Vírgen is a hilltop lookout point with fine views.

Museo Arqueológico de los Andes
Avenida Santa Teresa 396–398.
Tel *(034) 420115.* *10am–6:30pm Tue–Sun.*

Museo Histórico Religioso del Antiguo Monasterio del Espiritu Santu
Avenida Santa Teresa 389.
Tel *(034) 421765.* *9:30am–1pm, 3–6:30pm Mon–Fri; 10am–6pm Sat & Sun.*

Ski Portillo ⑪

Road Map B6. 126 miles (203 km) E of Valparaíso; Renato Sánchez, Las Condes. ***Tel*** *(02) 2630606.* *from Santiago airport: Sat only.* *from Santiago.* *mid-June–Sep.* **www**.skiportillo.com

Spectacularly located at 10,000 ft (3,000 m) above sea level, Ski Portillo is South America's oldest ski resort. It has pistes for skiers and snowboarders of all levels. Expert and extreme skiers will find fantastic opportunities on slopes that descend from an altitude of 10,900 ft (3,270 m). Challenges include 50-degree descents, countless off-piste routes, heli-skiing and night-skiing. Views from the slopes are tremendous, embracing surrounding peaks and the Lago Inca, a frozen lake. The ski centre is a self-contained resort with packages that include hotel lodging, lift tickets, and facilities such as a cinema and a heated outdoor pool. Visitors can also choose to stay in cheaper mountain lodges or backpackers' lodges. There is a lively après-ski scene and excellent family-oriented services including babysitting and a ski camp for children aged 4–6 years.

Wooden benches lining the tree-shaded plaza at Los Andes

Cristo Redentor on the border between Chile and Argentina

Cristo Redentor ⑫

Road Map B6. 130 miles (210 km) E of Valparaíso; Camino Cristo Redentor. *from Santiago.* *Dec–Mar.*

The gigantic Cristo Redentor (Christ the Redeemer) marks one of the world's great frontier passes: the crossing of the central Andes between Chile and Argentina. Set against a backdrop of the snow-swathed Andes, the figure stands at a dizzying 12,539 ft (3,823 m) above sea level. The 23-ft (7-m) high statue of Christ is set on a 20-ft (6-m) high granite plinth weighing 8,800 lb (4,000 kg). Sculpted in 1904 in Buenos Aires, the Cristo Redentor was conveyed by train to the foot of the Andes, dismantled into various parts, and hauled up the mountains by mules. Its erection marked a historic signing of peace between Chile and Argentina following decades of border disputes that pushed both countries to the brink of war. Tour buses and private cars that pass the Chilean customs post reach the monument by

For hotels and restaurants in this region see pp278–80 and pp298–300

Chilean palms (*Jubaea chilensis*) at Parque Nacional La Campana

taking the Camino Cristo Redentor, a gravel turn-off en route to the **Túnel del Cristo Redentor**, a 2-mile (3-km) long tunnel crossing of the Andes.

Termas de Jahuel ⓭

Road Map B6. 87 miles (140 km) NE of Valparaíso; Jahuel s/n, San Felipe. ***Tel*** *(02) 4111720.* *from Los Andes.* **www**.jahuel.cl

Set on the slopes of the arid Andean foothills, overlooking the fertile Aconcagua valley, Termas de Jahuel is a modern, luxurious spa retreat that accepts both day and overnight guests. On offer are sophisticated natural therapies. The spa's signature massage treatment is an olive-oil therapy that uses organically grown plants. There is also an outdoor pool edged by palms, jasmine, and orange groves.

Jahuel's thermal properties were recognized in Colonial times when travelers crossing the Andes came to rest here. Today, guests reside in a Colonial-style pavilion or an exclusive boutique hotel with en suite thermal baths. The resort's activities include horse riding and mountain-biking. Trails climb to a plateau with fine valley views. Facilities include playrooms for children, tennis courts, and international and Chilean restaurants.

Mountain vizcacha at La Campana

Parque Nacional La Campana ⓮

Road Map B6. 37 miles (60 km) E of Valparaíso; Paradero 43, Avenida Granizo 9137. ***Tel*** *(033) 441342.* *from Santiago & Valparaíso.* *9am–6pm Sat–Thu, 9am–5pm Fri.* **www**.conaf.cl

A UNESCO-recognized area, La Campana harbors a wilderness habitat that is considered exceptional for its biodiversity. The park's signature flora is a relictual population of Chilean palms (*Jubaea chilensis*), the world's southernmost palm. The rich birdlife here includes numerous songbirds, and types of eagle, hawk, and falcon. Among mammals and reptiles, there is the vizcacha, a large burrowing rodent, as well as iguanas, snakes, and lizards. The park is named for its dominant natural feature, Cerro La Campana (The Bell Peak). From the entrance in the Granizo sector, **Sendero El Andinista** is a popular day-hike that reaches the summit of this peak. Charles Darwin once enjoyed 360-degree views from here – with the Andes to the east and the Pacific Ocean to the west. Less visited, the park's northern Odoa sector has its largest, densest concentrations of Chilean palms, including some 4,000-year-old specimens. Other areas feature rocky canyon scenery, pre-Hispanic archaeological sites and former coal mines that were abandoned in the 1930s.

DARWIN AND LA CAMPANA

Charles Darwin, English naturalist and pioneer

In August 1834, English naturalist Charles Darwin began a 2-night ascent of Cerro La Campana on foot and horseback. Accompanied by two cowboys, Darwin climbed the hill's northern flank and made camp at the Agua del Guanaco spring. Writing later in the *Voyage of the Beagle*, he noted, "the atmosphere was so clear the masts at anchor in the Bay of Valparaíso…could be distinguished as little black streaks." The group reached the summit on the second morning. Here, Darwin is gushing, "never has time seemed as short as at that moment. Chile lay at our feet as an immense landscape limited by the Andes and the Pacific Ocean." A plaque at the summit commemorates this ascent.

Bodegas and vineyards of Errazuriz, in the Aconcagua valley ▷

A Tour of Wineries in Casablanca Valley ⓯

Chardonnay and sauvignon blanc from Viña Mar

One of Chile's newest wine-growing regions, Casablanca Valley is fast winning an international reputation for its excellent white wines. Located between Santiago and the port-city of Valparaíso, this valley has a maritime-influenced climate of ocean breezes and cool temperatures that is ideal for the production of white varietals such as chardonnay and sauvignon blanc. Overlooked by the snowcapped Andes, the wineries feature grand estates and boutique bodegas that welcome group tours and private visits. Casablanca Valley is also home to Chile's first 100 percent organic winery.

Viña Casas del Bosque ②
Established in 1993, this highly rated boutique winery was the first in the valley to produce merlot. It has a gourmet restaurant and offers tractor-drawn trailer rides across its vineyards.

TIPS FOR VISITORS

Starting point: *Casablanca.*
Length: *15 miles (24) km. Allow 2 days for the full tour; it is best to hire a car.*
Getting there: *Tour agencies in Santiago and Valparaíso organize day-tours of the valley. Visitors arriving by car take the R68 highway that links these two cities and runs through the heart of the valley. Many buses depart daily from Valparaíso for Casablanca, from where taxis can be hired to reach nearby wineries*
Where to eat: *Restaurants at the Indomita, Matetic, Casas del Bosque, and Viña Mar wineries.*
Tours and tastings: *Tours, in English and Spanish, last 1–2 hours. Reserve 1–2 days in advance for private tours.*
www.casablancavalley.cl

Viña Kingston ③
Named for the American family that owns it, Viña Kingston is a rustic little bodega where wine-making is done by hand. They also grow a number of red varietals.

Viña Catrala ①
This tiny premium winery focuses on quality rather than quantity. Tastings take place in scenic surroundings amid vineyards.

Viña Matetic ⑪
Apart from tastings in a subterranean salon, the modern boutique Viña Matetic offers personalized tours and exciting horseback and bicycle rides through its vineyards.

Estancia El Cuadro ⑤
The wine museum at this winery displays antique wine-making machinery. Along with tastings, guests enjoy rodeo shows and horse-drawn carriage rides.

Viña William Cole ④
Founded in 1999, the family-run Viña William Cole specializes in premium wines. It runs small group tours, where resident wine experts lead the tastings.

Viña Veramonte ⑥
Tours at this large, modern winery take in the entire wine-making process. Its tastings pair wines with fruit, cheese, and chocolates amid the oak barrels of the winery's barrel room.

KEY FACTS ABOUT CASABLANCA VALLEY WINES

Location and Climate
Casablanca Valley is located in the Central Valley, close to the Pacific coast. The influence of the ocean and the Humboldt Current lends the valley a cool climate that is ideal for producing superior white wines.

Grape Varieties
The valley excels in cool-climate white varieties. The zesty sauvignon blanc has aromas of citrus fruits, grasses, and pines. Creamier chardonnays recall honey and tropical fruit flavors. Pinot noir, a red grape, also flourishes here.

Good Vintages
1998, 2000, 2002, 2004, 2007, 2008

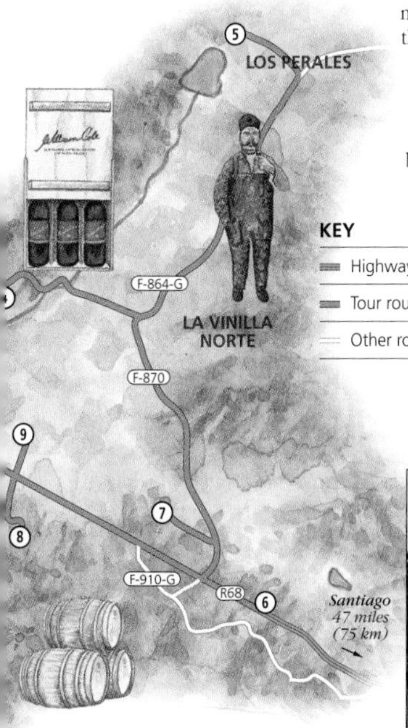

KEY

- Highway
- Tour route
- Other road

House of Morande ⑨
This contemporary restaurant serves regional dishes with wines from across the valley.

Viña Emiliana ⑦
This fully organic and biodynamic winery has been visited by the likes of Britain's Prince Charles. Visitors taste grapes from the vine before sampling the fine wines.

Viña Mar ⑩
Located atop a hillock, the award-winning Viña Mar is an eye-catching winery built to resemble a Venetian villa. A favorite with tour groups, it has a great gourmet restaurant and souvenir shop.

Viña Indomita ⑧
Among Casablanca Valley's most visited wineries, Viña Indomita is housed in a stunning Moorish-style building and features a state-of-the-art wine-making facility.

The El Colorado snowboard park encircled by the lofty Andes mountains

Ski Centers La Parva, El Colorado, Valle Nevado ⓰

Road Map B6. *from Santiago.* *Jun–Oct: 9am–5pm daily.* **El Colorado** 22 miles (36 km) E of Santiago. ***Tel*** *(02) 889 9260.* **www**.elcolorado.cl **La Parva** 25 miles (42 km) E of Santiago. ***Tel*** *(02) 2209530.* **www**. skilaparva.cl **Valle Nevado** 34 miles (55 km) E of Santiago. ***Tel*** *(02) 4777000.* **www**.vallenevado.com

Lying adjacent to one another in the central Andes are three ski resorts that are a big attraction with locals and visitors alike. Closest to Santiago, **El Colorado** is the most economical option of these three ski complexes. It has a ski school and a backpackers' lodge, and is particularly popular with beginners and snowboarders.

Located north of El Colorado, **La Parva** is ideal for a day visit and a number of the capital's wealthy residents own condominiums here. The resort caters to both beginners and experts and offers good off-piste skiing. Services include ski schools, restaurants, and hotels.

Chile's biggest, most modern ski center, **Valle Nevado** sits east of La Parva. It has drops for all levels of experience, breathtaking off-piste skiing across Andean slopes, and heli-boarding and heli-skiing at 14,760 ft (4,500 m) above sea level. It also boasts South America's biggest skiing surface, best snowboard park, as well as the continent's only super half-pipe. Each spring, the resort hosts a round of the annual Nokia Snowboarding World Cup. World-class facilities available at the complex include three hotels – one with ski-in, ski-out access – and a heated outdoor pool with mountain vistas. Family-oriented services here include a children's snow park.

Antique Wineries of Pirque ⓱

Road Map B6. *from Santiago.* *reservations required.* **Viña Cousiño-Macul** Ave. Quilín 7100, Peñalolén. ***Tel*** *(02) 351 4100.* *Línea 4, Estación Quilín.* *11am–4pm Mon–Fri, 11am–12pm Sat.* **www**.cousinomacul.cl **Viña Concha y Toro** Ave Virginia Subercaseaux 210, Pirque. ***Tel*** *(02) 4765269.* *Línea 4, Estación Plaza de Puente Alto.* *10am–5pm daily.* **www**.conchaytoro.com

Located in the Pirque area of the Maipo valley are two of Chile's oldest wine estates, both of which offer tours and tastings. Founded in 1856, the **Viña Cousiño-Macul** is the oldest family-run bodega in Chile. Antique wine-making machinery is displayed at the estate's museum. Tastings take place in a romantic candlelit 19th-century cellar.

The second of Pirque's wineries, **Viña Concha y Toro** is also the biggest in Chile. Established in 1883, it is the largest exporter of wine in all of Latin America. Guided tours take visitors through the estate's grounds, which include a stately 19th-century home and 80-year-old vineyards, as well as state-of-the-art production facilities.

Cajón del Maipo ⓲

Road Map B7. 20 miles (33 km) SE of Santiago. *from Santiago.* *Comercio 19788, San José del Maipo; (02) 8611275.* **www**.cajondelmaipo.com

Offering a gamut of outdoor activities, Cajón del Maipo is a popular weekend destination from Santiago. Trekking, camping, mountain-biking, and skiing are big draws for the adventurous. Rafting trips on the Río Maipo are popular between September and April.

Independent visitors usually make their base at **San José del Maipo**, the largest of several small towns in the area. Founded in 1791, San José del Maipo is an attraction in its own right, for its Colonial church and adobe houses.

Lagunillas

11 miles (17 km) NE of San José del Maipo. ***Tel*** *(09) 8253578.* *Jun–Oct.* **www**.skilagunillas.cl

The ski resort of Lagunillas has 13 slopes attracting skiers of all levels of experience during the winter months. It is also one of the few ski centers where night skiing is possible.

Santuario de la Naturaleza Cascada de las Animas

9 miles (14 km) SE of San José del Maipo; 31087 Camino al Volcán, San Alfonso. ***Tel*** *(02) 8611303.* **www**. cascadadelasanimas.cl

An adventure-tourism resort and sanctuary, the 14-sq-mile (36-sq-km) Santurio de la Naturaleza Cascada de las Animas protects an area of

Río Maipo slicing through the landscape of Cajón del Maipo

For hotels and restaurants in this region see pp278–80 and pp298–300

rugged mountains, rivers, and waterfalls. It lures visitors with adrenaline-charged activities that include white-water rafting on the Río Maipo, hiking and horse riding in the high Andes, and zip-lining over Cajón del Maipo. Hikes range from short nature trails to multi-day guided tours through mountain circuits. The most popular trek, **Cascada de las Animas**, finishes at three 160-ft (50-m) high waterfalls. Hikers can cool off with a dip in the pool at the foot of the cascades. The sanctuary organizes horse rides, ranging from 2-hour excursions to mountain plateaus to an 11-day circuit of the alpine lakes of central Andes or a 14-day ride across the Andes to Argentina.

The sanctuary also provides transport to and from Santiago for guests and offers many holiday package options. Accommodation options include well-equipped log-cabins set in the forest, a full-service guesthouse, and a scenically located campsite.

Visitors relaxing in the thermal pools at Termas Valle de Colina

Monumento Natural el Morado

26 miles (43 km) E of San José del Maipo. *Oct–Mar: 8:30am–6pm daily.* **www**.cajondelmaipo.com

A relatively compact reserve, Monumento Natural el Morado embraces the 16,597-ft (5,060-m) high **Cerro el Morado**. This snowcapped peak is best viewed on the 3-hour trek departing from the park entrance for the **Laguna el Morado**, an alpine lake from where a trail reaches the base of the electrifying **Glaciar San Francisco**. This glacier swathes the lower slopes of the park's second highest peak, the 14,255-ft (4,345-m) high Cerro San Francisco. South of this peak, the **Baños Morales** area has hot spring pools that attract weekend visitors from Santiago.

Termas Valle de Colina

37 miles (60 km) SE of San José del Maipo. ***Tel** (02) 2396797. Oct–May: daily.* **www**.termasvalledecolina.cl

A rustic hot springs resort, Termas Valle de Colina sits at the eastern end of Cajón del Maipo. It comprises a series of natural clay pools that bubble and steam on the slopes of a mountain overlooked by snowcapped peaks. Access to the pools is difficult, as the road that reaches the resort is closed to public transport. The Santiago-based Expediciones Manzur *(see p337)* runs round trips over weekends to the pools. Horses can be hired at the resort, and rides to the Argentine border, around 6 hours away, can be arranged with advance notice.

Environs

Located southwest of Cajón del Maipo, the **Reserva Nacional Río Clarillo** is an area of stunning natural beauty spread over some 40 sq miles (102 sq km). The reserve is ideal for bird-watching, hiking, horse riding, and rafting excursions throughout the year.

Reserva Nacional Río Clarillo

25 miles (40 km) SW of San José del Maipo. *Dec–Mar: 8am–7pm daily; Apr & Oct–Nov 8am–6pm daily; May–Sept 8am–6pm Tue–Sun.* **www**.conaf.cl

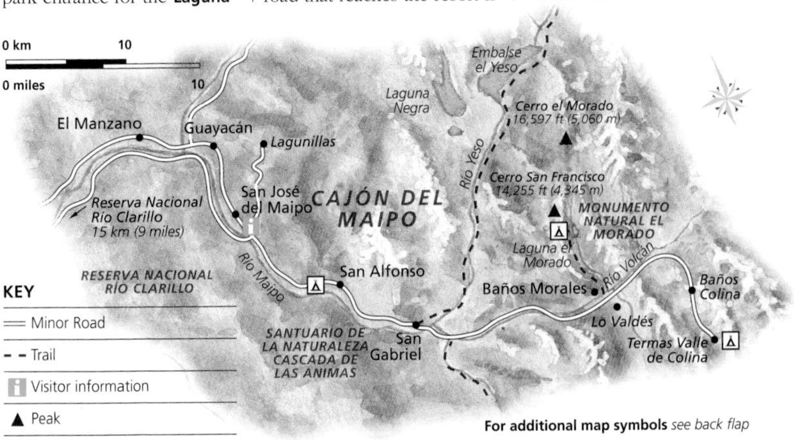

For additional map symbols *see back flap*

Costumed *huasos* gathering for the annual rodeo championship at Rancagua

Rancagua ⓳

Road Map B7. 54 miles (87 km) S of Santiago. *215,000.* *Germán Riesgo 350; (072) 584258.* *El Campeonato de Rodeo (early Apr).* **www**.rancagua.cl

Founded in 1743, Rancagua lies deep in *huaso* country and plays host to the Campeonato Nacional de Rodeo *(see p31)*, which is held here each year. Steeped in history, Rancagua is the site of one of Chile's bloodiest conflicts – the 1814 Battle of Rancagua, in which the patriot militia led by Bernardo O'Higgins *(see p153)* fought against vastly superior Spanish forces. The **Monumento a Bernardo O'Higgins** dominating the city's central plaza – focal point of the battle – is an equestrian memorial honoring Chilean soldiers who were killed at this spot.

Just north of the plaza, the **Iglesia de la Merced** is an adobe church built in 1778. O'Higgins directed his troops from its bell tower, which was rebuilt in 1857. The impeccably preserved interior of the church features whitewashed walls sheltered by dark, wooden rafters.

Located south of the plaza, the Paseo del Estado is an old Colonial street lined with fine historic structures. The highlight here is the **Museo Regional de Rancagua**, housed in two buildings that date from 1790 and 1800 respectively. The museum has engaging exhibits on religious art and on the Central Valley's weaving traditions and mining heritage. It also re-creates typical Colonial-era living quarters. At the southern end of Paseo del Estado, another large Colonial building houses Rancagua's **Casa de la Cultura**. Built in the early 1700s, it was the base for Spanish forces during the Battle of Rancagua. Today, it is a cultural center fronted by shaded gardens and hosting art exhibitions.

Museo Regional de Rancagua
Paseo del Estado 685. ***Tel*** *(072) 221524.* *10am–6pm Tue–Fri, 9am–1pm Sat & Sun.* **www**.museorancagua.cl

Casa de la Cultura
Corner of Avenida Cachapoal & Avenida Capitán Antonio Millán. ***Tel*** *(072) 584268.* *9am–6:30pm Mon–Sat.*

View of the ore-crushing and grinding plant at El Teniente

Valle de Cachapoal ⓴

Road Map B7. 60 miles (96 km) S of Santiago. *from Rancagua.* **www**.winesofchile.org

Located in Chile's agricultural heartland, Valle de Cachapoal is known for its production of two excellent red wine grapes, the cabernet sauvignon and the distinctive carménère *(see p293)*. Most of the valley's wineries are nestled in its cool eastern sector and are open for tours and tastings. The ultra-modern **Viña Altair**, inaugrated in 2001, features a contemporary, gravity-based design and offers moonlit tours of its vineyards. More traditional wineries include the **Viña Chateau Los Boldos**, built in the Spanish Colonial style.

Valle de Cachapoal lies in prime *huaso* territory and customized wine tours here include rodeo shows and horse rides through the mountains. Although the valley can be covered on a day trip from nearby Rancagua, overnight travelers will find accommodations at either the six-room guesthouse of sophisticated **Viña Porta**, or at Hacienda Los Lingues *(see p146)*, a family-run Colonial estate.

Sewell ㉑

See pp144–5.

El Teniente ㉒

Road Map B7. 49 miles (79 km) SE of Santiago; Carretera al Cobre. ***Tel*** *(072) 292000.* *from Santiago & Rancagua.* *9am–7:30pm Sat & Sun; call (072) 210290 for bookings.*

The biggest subterranean copper mine in the world, El Teniente comprises over 1,500 miles (2,400 km) of underground tunnels. In operation since the early 1800s, the mine produces around 485,000 tons (440,000 tonnes) of copper-ore each year. Guided excursions offered by tour operators take visitors through a maze of tunnels, past giant ore-crushing

The river valley at Reserva Nacional Río de los Cipreses surrounded by jagged Andean peaks

machinery. Also visible is an underground cave of glittering crystal that miners discovered while digging for copper.

Termas de Cauquenes ㉓

Road Map B7. 73 miles (117 km) S of Santiago. ***Tel*** *(072) 899010.* *from Rancagua.* *7:30am–6:30pm daily.* **www.**termasdecauquenes.cl

Nestled in the Andean foothills at 2,526 ft (770 m), Termas de Cauquenes has entertained such luminaries as English naturalist Charles Darwin (1809–82) and the revered Chilean hero Bernardo O'Higgins. This historic spa complex is set amid dense eucalyptus forests with numerous guided walks leading to a lookout point, an appealing place from where condors can be seen circling in the air. The 19th-century Neo-Gothic bathhouse of the spa is cathedral-like in size and ambition, with a soaring ceiling, stained-glass walls, and a mosaic floor between rows of private bathrooms. All rooms have exquisite Carrara-marble tubs, some of which are over 200 years old. Overnight guests to this accessible resort are housed in a Colonial-style hotel constructed around a Spanish courtyard with climbing vines and an elegant central fountain.

The resort also welcomes day visitors, who can luxuriate in the spa's thermal baths and enjoy a range of relaxing therapeutic treatments. Facilities include a heated outdoor pool, an outdoor playground for children, and a gourmet restaurant.

Interior of Termas de Cauquenes with decorative tiles and stained glass

Reserva Nacional Río de los Cipreses ㉔

Road Map B7. 81 miles (131 km) S of Santiago; Camino Chacayes s/n. *from Rancagua.* ***Tel*** *(072) 297505.* *8:30am–5:30pm daily.* **www.**conaf.cl

Created in 1985, Reserva Nacional Río de los Cipreses protects over 142 sq miles (367 sq km) of Andean wilderness, comprising river canyons and forests of mountain cypress. The reserve's popular northern sector has an administration center with displays on the area's wildlife. Starting at the center, paths cross the scenic Cajón Alto Cachapoal, from where the short **Sendero Tricahues** trail leads to a wildlife observation point. Here, colonies of the burrowing parrot, loro tricahue, can be seen nesting in the canyon wall.

Logo of the national reserve

The reserve's less-visited central and southern sectors can be reached by longer hikes and horse rides departing from the administration center. These trace the **Cajón Río Cipreses** that forms the spine of the reserve. Along the way, visitors traverse cypress forests and pass grazing guanaco herds. It is also possible to see pre-Hispanic petroglyphs and enjoy dramatic Andean vistas including views of the soaring 16,072-ft (4,900-m) high Volcán Palomo.

Sewell: The City of Stairs ㉑

Fire escape on a Sewell building

Clinging to Cerro Negro at 7,215 ft (2,200 m) above sea level, Sewell, or The City of Stairs, was established by the American Braden Copper Company in 1905 as a camp for workers of the nearby El Teniente mine. By 1960, it was a thriving metropolis, with around 15,000 inhabitants, a bank, a courthouse, a town hall, recreational clubs, and Chile's most advanced hospital. A UNESCO World Heritage Site, Sewell is now an eerily abandoned, but beautifully preserved city of multistoried wooden buildings.

Plaza Morgan, once Sewell's main commercial square

★ El Teniente Club

Once a recreational club for Sewell's US management, El Teniente Club is housed in a building featuring a neat Classical façade, a stuccoed ballroom, and a swimming pool.

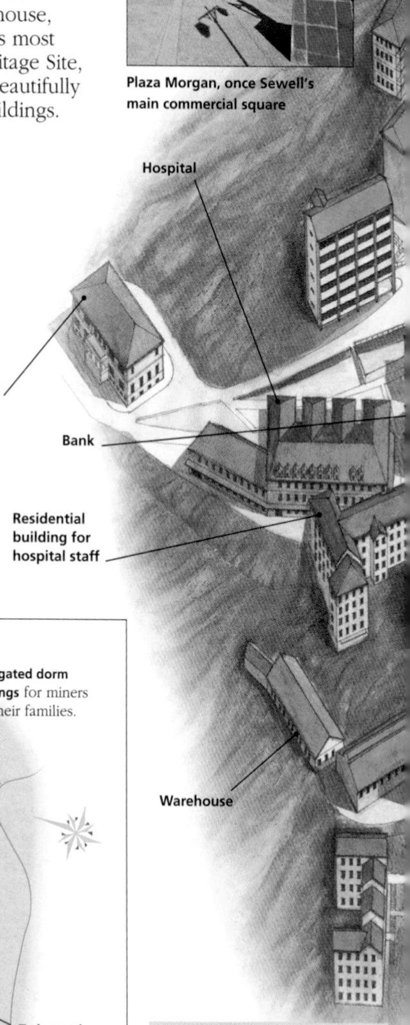

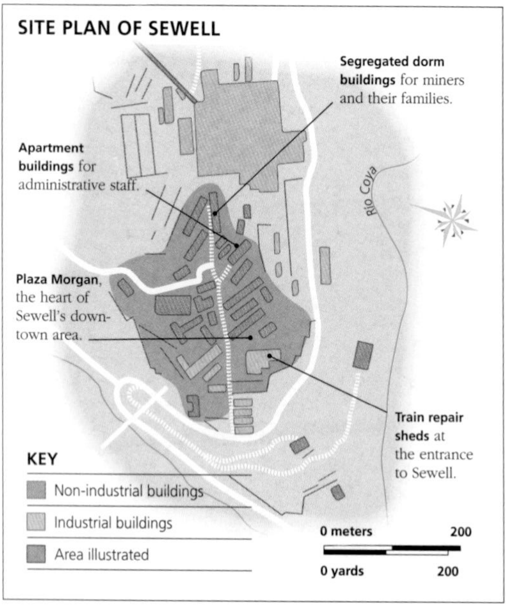

STAR SIGHTS

- ★ El Teniente Club
- ★ Iglesia de Sewell
- ★ Museo de la Gran Minería del Cobre

Escalara Central
A steep central staircase, the Escalara Central is the backbone of the abandoned city. Access paths and secondary stairs stem from it in a herring-bone pattern.

VISITORS' CHECKLIST

Road Map B7. 46 miles (75 km) SE of Santiago; Carretera al Cobre. ***Tel*** *(072) 292000.* **www**.sewell.cl **VTS Tour Operator** *Excursions from Santiago and Rancagua.* *9am–7:30pm Sat & Sun.* ***Tel*** *(072) 210290.* **www**.vts.cl

★ Iglesia de Sewell
Sewell's restored church dates from 1928. The Christ on the Cross above the altar is cast in copper excavated from the El Teniente mine (see pp142–3).

★ Museo de la Gran Minería del Cobre
Occupying the attractive Modernist building of the old Industrial School, Museo de la Gran Minería del Cobre displays historical and geological exhibits from Sewell's past.

Palitroque Bowling Alley
The preserved interior of this bowling alley features wooden bowling lanes and pins.

TIMELINE

1914 First school and social center founded

1967 State acquires majority share in company; toxic fumes from sulphuric plant cause workers and families to abandon Sewell for Rancagua

1915 Camp is named for Braden executive Bartin Sewell

1998 Sewell declared a national monument

1999 Temporary workers move to Rancagua; Sewell opens to tourists

1900 | 1920 | 1940 | 1960 | 1980 | 2000

1928 Iglesia de Sewell built

1905 Camp for miners set up by the US Braden Copper Company

Iglesia de Sewell

1971 El Teniente mine becomes fully nationalized

1982 Only temporary workers inhabit Sewell

2006 Sewell designated a UNESCO World Heritage Site

Santa Cruz ㉕

Road Map B7. 113 miles (182 km) SW of Santiago. *32,000.* *Plaza de Armas s/n.* *La Fiesta de la Vendimia (Mar).* **www**.santacruzchile.cl

One of the largest towns of the Colchagua Valley *(see pp148–9)*, Santa Cruz was founded in the 19th century and conserves some Colonial buildings, most notably the Municipalidad (Town Hall), a pink-painted arcaded house, and the Parroquía de Santa Cruz, a Spanish church built in 1817. Santa Cruz's outstanding highlight is the **Museo de Colchagua**, which houses over 5,000 objects relating to Chilean history. Displays range from rare objects that belonged to former president Bernardo O'Higgins to 18th-century Jesuit art, and antique 19th-century carriages.

Santa Cruz is the departure point for winery tours to Colchagua. A popular tour option is via the 1920s wine-themed steam train, **Tren del Vino**, which departs from San Fernando in the valley's north and ends at Santa Cruz in the south. On arrival at Santa Cruz visitors depart for two winery coach tours of Colchagua.

Museo de Colchagua
Avenida Errázuriz 145 **Tel** *(072) 821050.* *Dec–Mar: 10am–7pm Tue–Sun; Apr–Nov: 10am–6pm Tue–Sun.* *2 days' notice required.* **www**.museocolchagua.cl

Tren del Vino
San Antonio 65, Oficina 309A, Santiago. **Tel** *(02) 4707403.* *Sat.* **www**.trendelvino.cl

A wealth of historical exhibits at the Museo de Colchagua, Santa Cruz

Hacienda Los Lingues ㉖

Road Map B7. 78 miles (125 km) S of Santiago; Panamericana Sur 124 s/n, San Fernando. **Tel** *(02) 4310510.* *from Santa Cruz.* *daily.* **www**.loslingues.com

One of Chile's oldest, most prestigious estates, Hacienda Los Lingues dates from the end of the 16th century when it was gifted by King Philip III of Spain to Don Melchor Jufré del Águila. For over four centuries, it has remained in this Spanish nobleman's family, the current generation of which lives on the hacienda.

Overnight guests stay in sumptuous Colonial rooms that preserve the original architecture and furnishings. Antique family portraits hang from walls, and the sensation of staying at an old aristocratic home rather than simply at a luxury hotel is tangible. Visitors can also opt for the more economical day tour of the hacienda, which visits the courtyard, parks, wine cellar, stables, and the 1790-built chapel. Dating from 1760, the stables breed thoroughbred Aculeo horses, whose lineage can be traced to Moorish Spain. Day tours also feature a gourmet lunch, rodeo show, and horseback rides.

Pichilemu ㉗

Road Map B7. 161 miles (259 km) SW of Santiago. *13,000.* *Angel Gaete 365; (072) 841017.* *Wed & Sat.* *La Semana Pichilemina (Feb).* **www**.pichilemu.cl

Central Valley's surf capital, Pichilemu is a haven for surfers, bodyboarders, and hippies. Before the boarders arrived, Pichilemu was a luxury coastal resort, built in the 1900s by Chilean speculator Agustín Ross-Edwards. It was the site of Chile's first casino, but went into decline with the rise of Viña del Mar *(see pp128–9)* in the north. However, Pichilemu retains many charming vestiges of its aristocratic past. The old casino building is now occupied by a cultural center. Next to it, the lush coastal parkland, Parque Ross, has several viewing points and walking paths.

Today, Pichilemu is a small laid-back town that boasts several beaches, including the main **Las Terrazas** stretch, which has surf schools and is popular with novice boarders, owing to its small waves. About 2 miles (4 km) north of the town center, the **Los Lobos** beach's long, 8-ft (2-m) high leg breaks attract expert surfers. A stop on the international surfing circuit, Los Lobos has excellent infrastructure.

Crowds on one of Pichilemu's black-sand beaches

History of Wine in Chile

Grapes from a Chilean vineyard

Chilean wine-making began in the 16th century when Catholic missionaries brought vines from Spain to make wine for religious rites. By the 19th century, a secular demand for wine had blossomed in the nation's capital, Santiago, and it became fashionable for elite families to plant vineyards at their country estates. High-quality vines were introduced from France for the first time and Chile set up its first wineries. In the 1980s, economic liberalization sparked a new age of progress: foreign wine-makers and consultants, led by Spain's Miguel Torres in the Valle de Curicó and France's Michel Rolland in the Colchagua Valley, built ultra-modern wineries. Chile discovered its signature carménère grape and a new wine-tourism industry emerged.

Grapes were hand-plucked from vines and carried aloft in casks of native raulí wood.

Chile's first vineyards were planted in the Central Valley at the foot of the Andes.

Since the 1500s women have picked and de-stemmed grapes – female hands were deemed less likely to spoil grapes. This is still true today for premium wines

Antique wine-making machinery *in Chile was made of wood and operated by hand. It included wine presses, pumps, and corking machines.*

WINE-MAKING IN COLONIAL TIMES

Chile's first wines came from the Spanish país grape and were harvested on lands gifted to conquistadores by the Spanish Crown. Descendants of the first Spanish immigrants would clamor for more wine to whet their appetites.

Steel tanks *have replaced wooden vats in the fermentation process. Each has a capacity of 50,720 quarts (48,000 liters).*

Chile's world-class premium wines *are aged for up to two years in $1,000 barrels of French oak.*

MODERN WINE-MAKING IN CHILE

After independence, Chile turned to France for inspiration, introducing grapes such as merlot and pinot noir that are, today, emblematic of Chilean wine-making. Chile became the first New World country, ahead of California and Australia, to produce high-quality wines.

The avant-garde Clos Apalta *winery follows a vertical design and plunges underground to a depth of 115 ft (35 m). Its modern technology uses the flow of gravity, rather than pumps, to make the wine.*

New vineyards *are founded at high altitudes and at the edge of the Pacific, as the frontiers of Chilean wine-making continue to expand. Organic vineyards are also gaining ground.*

A Tour of Wineries in Colchagua Valley ㉘

Chile's premier wine-making region and its biggest wine-tourism destination, Colchagua Valley starts at the Andean foothills and sweeps westward toward the Pacific coast. The valley's fertile floor and rolling hills are sprinkled with many wineries; nearly all are open for tours and tastings. These wineries feature various architectural styles ranging from ultra-modern designs to Colonial-style estates. Among the valley's key attractions is the Tren de Vino, a steam train that takes visitors through the vineyard landscape.

The historic Tren de Vino chugging across the Colchagua Valley

Viña Los Vascos ⑧
Owned by the French Rothschild family, this winery runs small group tours. It is notable for its cabernet sauvignon that is aged in French oak barrels.

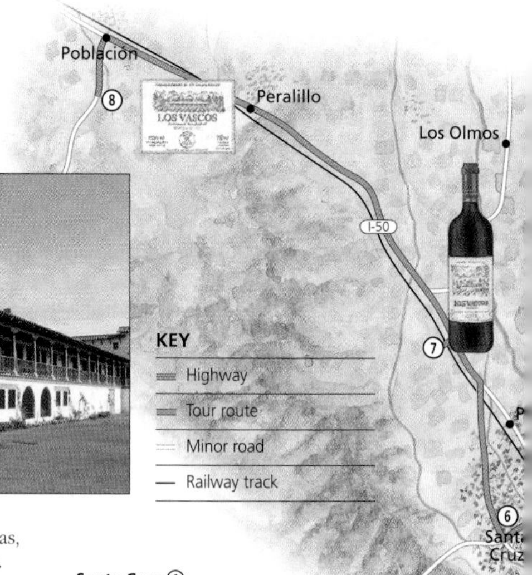

Viña MontGras ⑦
At the grand Colonial-style Viña MontGras, guests make and label their own wines. In early March visitors can take part in the valley's annual grape harvest festival, the Fiesta de la Vendimia.

Santa Cruz ⑥
Located at the center of Chile's leading wine-making region, Santa Cruz is the springboard for Colchagua's wineries. The town also serves as the terminal for the Tren de Vino.

TIPS FOR DRIVERS

Starting point: *San Fernando, 27 miles (43 km) E of Santa Cruz (see p146).*
Length: *47 miles (75 km). The tour needs at least 2 days.*
Getting There: *Ruta 5 runs from Santiago to San Fernando, which is linked to Santa Cruz by the Carretera del Vino, or I-50. Tours are arranged by Ruta del Vino.* **www**.rutadelvino.cl
Stopping-off points: *Viña Lapostolle (see p278) has a luxury hotel and gourmet restaurant. Viña Viu Manent is also a good place to stop for lunch.* **www**.colchaguavalley.cl

CHILE'S AWARD-WINNING WINE VALLEY

Owing to its superb terroir, ideal geographical and climatic conditions, and ultra-advanced technology, the Colchagua Valley produces more world-class wines than any other region in Chile and has been the recipient of innumerable awards since the year 2000.

- Viña Casa Silva – the Best South American Producer in London's 2000 Wine & Spirit Competition.
- Viña MontGras – the Best Chilean Wine Producer in UK's International Wine & Spirit Competition in 2002.
- In 2005, the international *Wine Enthusiast* magazine labeled the valley as the Best Wine Region In The World.
- *Wine Spectator* magazine voted Viña Lapostolle's Clos Apalta wine as the World's Best Wine in 2008.

Wine bottles from Colchagua Valley

KEY FACTS ABOUT WINES OF COLCHAGUA VALLEY

Location and Climate Set in Chile's fertile Central Valley, the sweeping Colchagua Valley features a climate similar to that of the Mediterranean regions, with dry, hot summers and cold, rainy winters.

Grape Varieties Common red grape varieties planted in the valley include Chile's signature grape, cabernet sauvignon, and others such as syrah, merlot, carménère, and malbec. The long summers allow grapes to develop rich aromas suggestive of red fruits, berries, and spices. Viognier, the only white wine grape to flourish here, has a sweet floral aroma.

Good Vintages (reds) 1995, 1997, 2002, 2005, 2007, and 2009.

Viña Casa Silva ①
Colchagua's oldest, most traditional winery, the family-run Viña Casa Silva is housed in a Colonial-style building. Tours include tastings within a century-old brick cellar, carriage rides through vineyards, and rodeo shows.

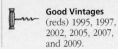

Viña Montes ④
Designed along feng shui principles, this winery grows only premium and icon wines. Tours include tractor-drawn trailer rides to a hilltop that offers spectacular panoramas.

Viña Viu Manent ②
Founded in 1935, this winery is housed in a romantic, Spanish-style hacienda. It offers vineyard carriage rides and has an excellent handicrafts shop and an equestrian club that gives riding lessons.

Viña Lapostolle ⑤
A state-of-the-art winery, Viña Lapostolle has a gravity-induced facility that descends six levels beneath the ground. Open to tours, its organic vineyards produce the award-winning Clos Apalta wine, manufactured exclusively at this winery.

Viña Las Niñas ③
Colchagua's smallest winery, Viña Las Ninas is run by three generations of women from a single French family. Activities include picnics, walks, and bike rides amid lushly planted vineyards.

Verdant banks and forested slopes surrounding Lago Vichuquén

Valle de Curicó ㉙

Road Map B7. 37 miles (60 km) S of Santa Cruz; Curicó. *from Santiago.* *from Santa Cruz.*

One of the less-visited wine valleys of central Chile, the Valle de Curicó carries one significant advantage for wine enthusiasts – personalized, unhurried tours and tastings hosted by wine experts. Valle de Curicó produces fine white wines, especially sauvignon blanc, as well as cabernet sauvignon reds – some from 80-year-old vines. Its wineries include the Spanish-owned Miguel Torres estate, which features a world-class restaurant. The wineries are visited on customized tours arranged by **Ruta del Vino Curicó**, which also organizes private tours.

Ruta del Vino Curicó
Prat 301-A, Curicó. ***Tel*** *(075) 328972.* *9am–2pm & 3:30–7:30pm Mon–Fri.*
www.rutadelvinocurico.cl

Lago Vichuquén ㉚

Road Map B7. 60 miles (96 km) SW of Santa Cruz. *from Curicó.* *Manuel Rodríguez 315, Vichuquén; (075) 400516.* **www**.lagovichuquen.com

Central Valley's most beautiful lake, Lago Vichuquén is an intensely blue tongue of water ringed by deep green, pine-swathed hills. The lake and its surrounds attract abundant birdlife, including species of swan, heron, and duck. In Colonial times, the rich suggestiveness of this area led to its notoriety as a supposed meeting place of sorcerers and witches. Today, it attracts bikers, windsurfers, water-skiers, anglers, horse-riding aficionados, and nature-watchers.

Some 4 miles (7 km) east of the lake is the historic settlement of Vichuquén, built by the Spanish in 1585 on the site of an old Incan colony. Today, it preserves warrens of winding Colonial streets lined with orange trees and fronted by adobe houses. Incan and Spanish-Colonial artifacts, which include a 3,000-year-old mummy, are displayed at its small **Museo Histórico de Vichuquén**. Both Vichuquén and its lake can be included on wine-tour itineraries of the Valle de Curicó.

Museo Histórico de Vichuquén
Rodriguéz s/n. *10am–1pm & 4–8pm Tue–Sun.*

Salto de la Novia in the Parque Nacional Radal Siete Tazas

Parque Nacional Radal Siete Tazas ㉛

Road Map B7. 78 miles (125 km) SE of Santa Cruz. *from Curicó, changing at Molina.* *Dec–Mar: 8:30am–1pm & 2–7:30pm daily; Apr–Nov: 8:30am–1pm & 2–6pm daily.* *from Curicó.* **www**.conaf.cl

This small national park is named for its most striking natural feature, the **Siete Tazas** (Seven Bowls). Located in the western section of the park, these are seven connected rock pools formed by the erosive waters of the Río Claro, which plunges down a narrow gorge here. Nearby are two breathtaking waterfalls: the 131-ft (40-m) high **Salto de la Novia** and the 82-ft (25-m) high **Salto de la Leona**. The trail linking Salto de la Leona with the Siete Tazas passes transition forest that features both Central Valley flora and temperate rain forest common to the Lake District farther south. A short distance from the pools, the Sector Parque Inglés has scenic walking, horse riding, and mountain-biking trails. The **Sendero El Bolsón** offers visitors a full day's hike. Nature-watching, swimming, and kayaking are popular activities here.

Villa Cultural Huilquilemu ㉜

Road Map B7. 47 miles (76 km) S of Santa Cruz; Km7, Camino San Clemente, Talca. ***Tel*** *(071) 242474.* *from Talca.* *9am–1pm & 3pm–6pm Tue–Fri, noon–6pm Sat & Sun.*

A true cultural highlight of the Central Valley, the Villa Cultural Huilquilemu is a large 19th-century hacienda whose Colonial-style house features a museum of religious items and crafts. The house, built in 1850 for a silver-mining baron, is a sprawling construction with thick adobe walls, red-clay floor tiles, and heavy wooden doors that open on to a Spanish patio centered around a cast-iron drinking well. The rooms ringing the patio display artifacts and old craftworks from across Chile. Exhibits include antique textiles, the font used to baptize Bernardo O'Higgins in 1778, and rare 18th-century statues of saints and the Virgin. In one salon, local women produce and sell textiles and handicrafts, including beautiful tapestries. Visits end in lush gardens that were planted in the 1800s with exotic trees such as Australian araucarias and French magnolias.

Environs

The villa, along with the town of Talca, is a springboard to the wineries of the surrounding Valle del Maule, Chile's largest wine-yielding region. The valley is dedicated to the mass production of table wines from Chile's traditional país grape. The **Ruta del Vino Valle del Maule** works with 15 wineries and organizes half-day valley tours, which include a guide and two winery tours.

Ruta del Vino Valle del Maule
Villa Cultural Huilquilemu. ***Tel*** *(071) 246460.* *9am–6:30pm Mon–Fri.*
www.valledelmaule.cl

Reserva Nacional Altos de Lircay ㉝

Road Map B7. 42 miles (67 km) E of Talca; Ruta Internacional Pehuenche, Cruce Vilches Alto. *from Talca.* *Dec–Mar: 8:30am–1pm & 2–7:30pm daily; Apr–Nov: 8:30am–1pm & 2–6pm daily.*
www.conaf.cl

Conserving a wilderness area of southern-beech forest and rugged river-canyon country, Reserva Nacional Altos de Lircay offers activities such as mountain-biking, hiking, and horse riding. From the administration center at the park entrance, there are several short nature-watching paths. Birdlife seen on these trails includes Andean condors and, in forests, loro tricahue (an endangered native parrot), and Magellanic woodpeckers.

The two most popular hiking trails also strike out from the park entrance. The **Sendero Laguna del Alto** is a 9-hour return trek of moderate difficulty, that climbs through southern-beech forests to the blue Laguna del Alto, which is ringed by craggy mountains. The **Sendero Enladrillado** is a 10-hour return trek, also of medium difficulty, that ascends through native woods to the Enladrillado, a soaring 7,544-ft (2,300-m) high platform of volcanic rock. A stunning vantage point, it overlooks a deep river canyon and has 360-degree vistas of an area that includes the peaks of three volcanoes – Cerro Azul, Volcán Quizapú, and Descabezado Grande (The Big Beheaded). Named for its truncated peak, the latter can be climbed on a 5-day long trekking circuit. Tour agencies such as Trekking Chile *(see p319)* organizes these treks.

Outdoor pool at the spa-resort Termas de Panamavida

Volcán Quizapu and Descabezado Grande, Reserva Nacional Altos de Lircay

Termas de Panimavida ㉞

Road Map B7. 55 miles (88 km) SE of Talca; Panimavida s/n, Linares. ***Tel*** *(073) 211743.* *from Linares.* *9am–9pm daily.*
www.termaspanimavida.cl

Set in pastoral farmlands in the Andean foothills, the spa-resort, Termas de Panimavida, occupies an old Colonial-style edifice surrounded by gardens with statues. On offer are large indoor and outdoor thermal pools, heated to temperatures of 97–104°F (36–40°C), as well as children's pools. Therapeutic treatments here include massages, hot rooms, and Jacuzzis, as well as wine therapies and herbal, Turkish, and mud baths.

Some 3 miles (5 km) to the south, **Termas de Quinamavida** is a spa with similar facilities and services. Its therapies also include steam treatments in cactus wood baths. The resort is set closer to the mountains and is a picturesque, modern complex of honey-colored buildings set in century-old eucalyptus and pine forests.

Termas de Quinamavida
Camino Linares-Colbún Km16. ***Tel*** *(073) 627100.* *from Termas de Panimavida.* *8am–1pm & 3–8pm daily.*
www.termasdequinamavida.cl

Crates of fruit and vegetables at stalls near Mercado Chillián

Chillán 35

Road Map D1. 252 miles (405 km) S of Santiago. 160,000. *18 de Septiembre 455; (042) 223272.* *Conmemoración Natalicio Bernardo O'Higgins (Aug).* **www**.municipalidadchillan.cl

The birthplace of Chile's founder Bernardo O'Higgins, Chillán is centered on a main square fronted by a Modernist cathedral that is supported by 11 giant parabolic arches made from reinforced concrete. Built after the 1939 earthquake, the cathedral has a tunnel-like interior. Above its altar, on a wooden cross pulled from the quake's rubble is a figure of Christ sculpted in Italy.

Also of interest is the **Escuela de México** primary school whose interior contains two giant murals painted in 1941–2 by Mexican artists David Alfara Siqueiros and Xavier Guerrero. Siqueiros's allegorical *Muerte al Invasor* (Death to the Invader) combines Cubist and Impressionist styles to symbolize the Mexican and Chilean peoples' independence struggle. Guerrero's Realist *De Mexico a Chile* (From Mexico to Chile) depicts, among many scenes, a Mexican woman pulling a Chilean baby from rubble.

Chillán's indoor food market, **Mercado Chillán**, is a delight for foodies. Eateries here serve regional specialties.

Escuela de México
Ave. O'Higgins 250. ***Tel*** *(042) 212012.* *10am–1pm & 3–6pm Mon–Fri, 10am–6pm Sat & Sun.*

Mercado Chillán
5 de Abril, Isabel Riquelme, esq. El Roble. *8am–7pm Mon–Fri, 8am–6pm Sat, 8am–2pm Sun.*

Termas de Chillán 36

Road Map D1. 51 miles (82 km) E of Chillán. ***Tel*** *(02) 2331313.* *from Chillán.* *daily.* **www**.termaschillan.cl

This year-round resort is best known for skiing but also has a state-of-the-art thermal spa complex. Its winter ski resort sits on the slope of Volcán Chillán and has 29 runs including the longest one in South America. Expert skiers can enjoy the excellent off-piste skiing here. The spa complex has thermal pools and outdoor hot springs that rise from natural geothermal fissures. Treatments include massages, mud baths, aromatherapy, and hydrotherapy. Two hotels sit at the foot of the resort – the posh Gran Hotel Termas de Chillán and the budget Hotel Pirigallo.

Concepción 37

Road Map D1. 322 miles (519 km) SW of Santiago. *216,000.* *Aníbal Pinto 460; (041) 274 1337.* *Aniversario de Concepción (mid-Nov).* **www**.concepcion.cl

A vibrant university city, Concepción was founded in 1550 as a frontier settlement on the banks of Río Bío-Bío, and in Colonial times acted as the springboard for Spanish attacks on the Mapuche-held Lake District south of this river.

Much of Concepción's architectural heritage was destroyed in the 19th century by earthquakes and tsunamis, leaving behind a rather bland metropolis. The outstanding historical highlight is the **Mural Historia de Concepción**, a 3,000-sq-ft (280-sq-m) mural in the regional government headquarters, the Edificio Gobierno Regiona. Painted in the Socio-Realist style in 1945 by Chilean artist Gregorio de la Fuente, this mural is a stunning visual description of this region's turbulent history from pre-Hispanic times onward.

Opposite this building, **Plaza España** is the city's lively bar and restaurant zone. To its north, **Plaza Independencia** is the historic square from where Bernardo O'Higgins proclaimed Chile's independence in 1818 *(see p44)*.

EARTHQUAKE OF 2010

In the early hours of February 27, 2010, an earthquake measuring 8.8 on the Richter scale struck central Chile, destroying homes and buildings, and flattening motorways across the region. The quake's epicentre was Concepción, one of Chile's most densely populated cities. Towns in its vicinity were the worst hit, but there was also widespread damage, reaching as far as the capital Santiago, 322 miles (520 km) away. In total, over 500,000 homes were destroyed or severely damaged and an estimated 500 people killed. Chile now faces overall recovery costs of US$ 15–30 billion.

Detail from the Mural Historia de Concepción at Edificio Gobierno Regional

Tomé 38

Road Map D1. 293 miles (472 km) SW of Santiago. *52,000.* *Municipalidad, Ignacio Serrano 1185; (041) 2406410.* *La Semana de Tomé (early Feb).* **www**.tome.cl

A tranquil, pleasant seaside town, Tomé was founded in 1875 as a port for shipping wine and maize from the Central Valley. Tomé later became Chile's main textile port. Today, its numerous sandy beaches attract visitors from the world over. Four blocks from the town center, **El Morro** is the most popular stretch of white sand. Within walking distance of the center, **Playa Bellavista** is a family-oriented beach fronted by good restaurants. Some 3 miles (5 km) north of the center, **Playa Cocholgüe** features high sand dunes and waves, which are a great draw for surfers.

Holiday-makers relaxing on a beach at the coastal town of Tomé

Lota 39

Road Map D1. 333 miles (537 km) SW of Santiago. *49,000.* *Municipalidad, P. Aguirre Cerda 200; (041) 2405002.* *mines.* **www**.lotasorprendente.cl

For 150 years, Lota lay at the heart of the Central Valley's coal-mining industry. Its mines were owned by the Cousiño-Macul family, who oversaw their investment from a grand villa in town. An earthquake in 1960 destroyed the villa, but its magnificent gardens, occupying a promontory overlooking the ocean, are open for visits. At their entrance, the **Museo Histórica de Lota** has historical displays on the Cousiño-Macul family. A long avenue, lined with wooden terraced houses built for miners' families, links the gardens to the mines. Closed in 1997, the mines can be seen on tours, booked at the museum. Former miners act as guides to its underground galleries.

The cascading white curtain of Salto de Laja

Museo Histórica de Lota
Avenida El Morro s/n, Lota Alto.
Tel *(041) 2871549.* *Dec–Mar: daily; Apr–Nov: Tue–Sun.*
www.lotasorprendente.cl

Saltos de Laja 40

Road Map D1. 298 miles (480 km) SW of Santiago. *from Concepción.* *daily.*

Natural marvels at the southern end of the Central Valley, the Saltos de Laja are four waterfalls plunging into a rocky canyon ringed by green forest. Vapor-drenched trails lie at the base and top of the falls. At 167 ft (51 m), **Salto de Laja** is the highest fall in the chain, forming a curtain of white water. Facilities around the falls include hotels and camps.

Parque Nacional Laguna de Laja 41

Road Map E1. 348 miles (561 km) S of Santiago. *from Los Angeles, 61 miles (98 km) W of park.* *Dec–Mar: 8am–9pm daily; Apr–Nov: 8am–6pm daily* **www**.conaf.cl

This compact park protects Chile's northernmost distribution of araucaria and mountain cypress. Its most grand natural feature is the 9,790-ft (2,985-m) high Volcán Antuco, whose summit is reached by an undemanding 8-hour return trek. The trail has great views of the glacier-hung Sierra Velluda range, just beyond the park's boundaries. A small ski center operates on the volcano's slopes between June and October. The park's namesake lake, the green **Laguna de Laja**, was formed by a 1752 eruption of the volcano. Easy trails skirt this lake and two gorgeous falls: **Saltos las Chicas** and **Saltos del Torbellino**. Along the trails, hikers can see plenty of birdlife – the park is refuge to over 50 bird species, including the Andean condor.

BERNARDO O'HIGGINS

Born in Chillán, Bernardo O'Higgins (1778–1842) was the illegitimate son of Ambrosio O'Higgins, a lieutenant-general in the Spanish army, and a local girl. His father rose to be Viceroy of Peru, the most powerful position in the Spanish Empire, and Bernardo was educated in Europe where he adopted liberal ideas and met revolutionaries intent on Spain's overthrow in Latin America. By 1814, O'Higgins was heading Chile's independence struggle, and eventually became the post-Independence leader *(see pp43–4)*.

Statue of O'Higgins

Regional Arts and Crafts de Artesania

The craft traditions of Central Valley date from pre-Columbian times and range from woodcarvings and weavings to ceramics and wickerwork. High-quality handicrafts can be browsed and bought at crafts markets across the region and at tiny villages, each famed for a century-long tradition in a particular craft. Pomaire, for instance, is known for its pottery, while Chimbarongo produces fine baskets. Visits to these hamlets reveal streets of crafts stalls and workshops where skilled artisans can be seen plying their trade. Most craftspeople in these villages and in other parts of Central Valley are represented by the non-profit Artesanías de Chile.

A range of handicrafts exhibited at a crafts' stall in Chillán

POTTERY

Villages located close to Santiago in the Central Valley have a long-standing tradition of making ceramics. Talagante is famous for its attractive porcelain creations. Pomaire, located 31 miles (50 km) southwest of Santiago, dedicates itself almost exclusively to red-clay pottery, the source of which are the clay-rich hills that surround this hamlet. Well-stocked pottery shops and busy workshops line both sides of Pomaire's main street.

Red-clay crockery displayed at a pottery shop in Pomaire

The metawe *(jug), shaped to resemble a duck, is part of the Mapuche tradition of using pottery for ritualistic ends. The duck is the Mapuche symbol for female fertility and the* metawe *is used in many rites-of-passage ceremonies for women.*

Cerámica Artensia de Los Andes *refers to the decorative ceramics crafted in Los Andes. These feature motifs from the Acanagua valley, for instance grapevines, or broader Chilean themes such as rodeos and haciendas. Potters shape their designs by hand at workshops such as CALA* (see p310).

Polychromatic figurine depicting a peasant woman

Talagante figurines *are porcelain miniatures that portray characters from daily Chilean life such as a washerwomen or an organ-grinder. Artists in Talagante, 27 miles (43 km) southwest of Santiago, make these multicolored figurines by hand. They continue a tradition begun by two sisters who lived here in the early 1900s.*

Some figurines feature Christmas motifs

CRIN FIGURINES

Skilled craftswomen from Chile's Central Valley weave multicolored miniatures using horse hair or *crin*. These are delicately woven figurines, each carefully dyed in a kaleidoscope of bright colors. Among the most popular items are ornamental figures of women, witches, butterflies, birds, the *huaso*, and the *huasa*. *Crin* products are found at markets and stalls throughout Central Valley, especially in the Maule area *(see p151)*.

Crin *statuettes of women in brightly-colored Colonial attire are popular.*

Butterflies, *among the most decorative items made of* crin, *reflect a fusion of fine craftsmanship with beautiful coloring.*

The poncho, *or* chamanto, *is a rectangular cloth with a horizontal opening for the head. It has been donned by Chileans since pre-Columbian times. Today, it is an essential garb for* huasos *and is functional for horse riding and rodeos.*

TEXTILES

Mapuche women use llama and sheep wool, or the more expensive alpaca wool, to weave ponchos, blankets, rugs, and scarves on rustic looms. These are then colored with natural vegetable dyes to create aesthetic and complex designs.

Multicolored blankets with abstract patterns

WEAVING

Artisans use wicker, straw, and reeds to weave baskets, furniture, decorative articles, and hats. Wicker from willow twigs is the most commonly used raw material. These are first soaked in water to separate the bark, and then dried before the fibers can be woven into intricate objects.

Basketry and wickerwork shops *in Chimbarongo, 95 miles (153 km) south of Santiago, showcase the skill of local craftsmen.*

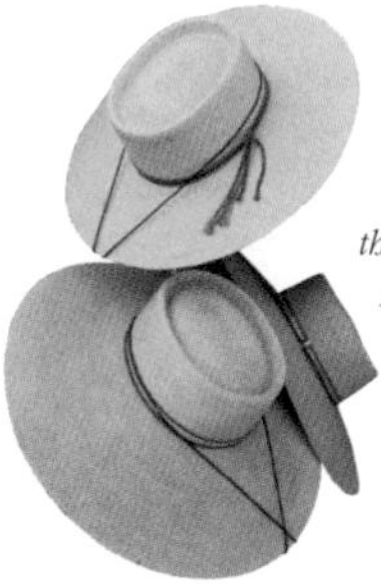

Hats *woven from straw are traditionally worn by* huasos. *The wide brim provides protection from the sun on Chile's open plains. These are also a crucial component of festive clothing and make excellent souvenirs.*

Simple Mapuche tray made with native wood

Handcrafted cutlery with intricate carvings

WOODWORK

Mapuche woodwork and carvings are central to the group's culture. Craftsmen use ancient techniques to carve both decorative and utilitarian objects. These are crafted from solid blocks of wood from the surrounding forests of raulí, pellín, and coigüe. The artisan's tools usually leave a characteristic tracing on the object's surface.

NORTE GRANDE AND NORTE CHICO

The north is Chile's vast desert region – an epic landscape of sand dunes, sun-baked ochre earth and white-sand cliffs. The land rises from the coast to the arid altiplano, where camelids roam, pink flamingos fly, and pointed volcanoes overlook brilliant blue lagoons. Port-cities line the coast, while indigenous hamlets and oasis villages with adobe churches bring the desert to life.

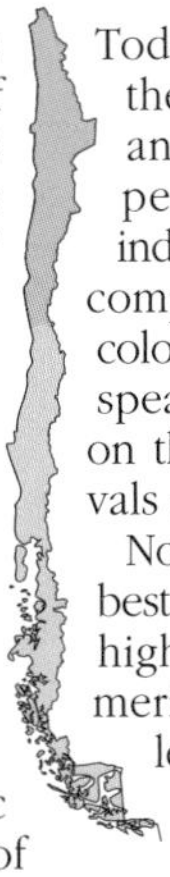

The hypnotically monotonous Atacama desert blankets much of the arid Norte Grande (Big North) and the semi-arid Norte Chico (Little North). The original inhabitants of this area belonged to the Diaguita, Aymara, and El Molle cultures, important pre-conquest societies ruled in the past by the Tiwanaku (AD 500–1000) and Incan (1450–1540) empires. The latter were supplanted by Spanish conquistadores and colonizers, who coveted the metal and mineral wealth of the desert, particularly gold, a symbol of power among the pre-Hispanic peoples. Swashbuckling pirates of this time sacked Colonial cities such as La Serena for silver. Even after independence, Chile waged war for the desert's nitrates *(see p45)*.

Today, mining in the Atacama is the bedrock of Chile's economy and many port-cities have prospered from the growth in this industry. However, the north mostly comprises oasis hamlets that hold colorful crafts markets and Quechua-speaking villages that herd llamas on the altiplano and celebrate festivals rooted in Incan culture.

Norte Grande and Norte Chico are best experienced on road trips to the high-altitutde wilderness of shimmering lagoons and to lunar valleys, hot springs, and salt lakes. Giant petroglyphs and stone fortresses can be seen on the hillsides by day, while stargazing is a huge nighttime attraction. On the coast, old cities have great beaches and splendid port architecture.

Flamingos by a shimmering salt lake in the Atacama desert

◁ **A 17th-century adobe church overlooked by snow-swathed peaks in Parque Nacional Volcán Isluga**

Exploring Norte Grande and Norte Chico

Chile's northernmost region of Norte Grande is a desert stretch, with the oasis village of San Pedro de Atacama serving as the gateway to the dazzling Salar de Atacama salt pan and the pre-Incan ruins of Aldea Tulor. The coast is lined with large cities including Arica, famed for its colorful crafts markets and mestizo culture, the old nitrate capital of Iquique, and the historic city of Antofagasta. Easily reached from these cities are the giant petroglyphs at Cerro Pintados and the massive telescope that draws stargazers to the Cerro Paranal Observatory. South of Río Copiapó, the scrubland of Norte Chico is punctuated by the pretty orchard town of Ovalle and the *pisco* distilleries and vineyards of Pisco Elqui. La Serena, a city of Colonial buildings, marks the desert's southern border.

Moorish designs and furnishings at the Casino Español, Iquique

SIGHTS AT A GLANCE

Villages, Towns, and Cities

Antofagasta 26
Arica pp160–61 1
Calama 13
Caldera 30
Caspana 17
Chiu-Chiu 15
Copiapó 29
Iquique pp166–7 6
La Serena pp180–81 34
La Tirana 10
Montegrande 37
Ovalle 39
Pica 11
Pisco Elqui 38
Putre 3
San Pedro de Atacama 19
Vicuña 35

Resorts and Spas

Termas de Socos 42
Baños de Puritama 20

National Parks, Reserves, and Natural Monuments

Monumento Nacional Valle del Encanto 41
Monumento Natural Pichasca 40
Parque Nacional Bosque Fray Jorge 43
Parque Nacional Lauca pp164–5 4
Parque Nacional Nevado de Tres Cruces 32
Parque Nacional Pan de Azúcar 31
Parque Nacional Volcán Isluga 8
Reserva Nacional Las Vicuñas 5

Areas of Natural Beauty

Laguna Verde 33
Salar de Atacama 23
Salar de Tara 22
Valle de la Luna 24
Valle de la Muerte 25

Archaeological Sites and Ruins

Aldea Tulor 21
Cerro Pintados 12
Humberstone and Santa Laura 7
Pukará de Lasana 16

Sites of Interest

Cerro Mamalluca Observatory 36
Cerro Paranal Observatory 28
Chuquicamata 14
Geisers de Tatio 18
Iglesia de San Gerónimo de Poconchile 2
La Portada 27
Mamiña Hot Springs 9

SEE ALSO

• ***Where to Stay*** pp280–81
• ***Where to Eat*** pp300–301

KEY

- Highway
- Main road
- Minor road
- Untarred minor road
- Minor railway
- Regional border
- International border
- Peak

The eroded arch of La Portada off the coast of Antofagasta

For additional map symbols *see back flap*

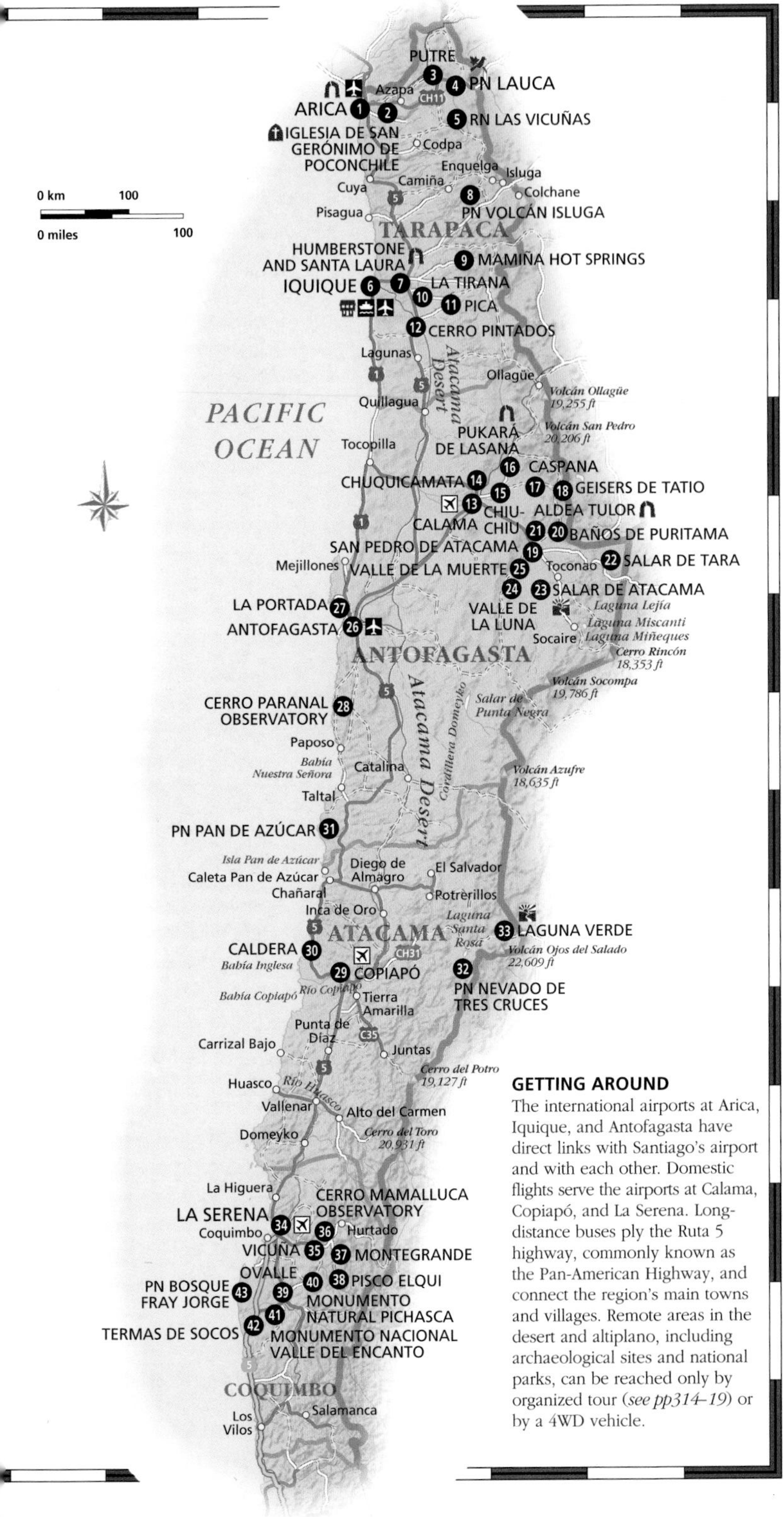

GETTING AROUND

The international airports at Arica, Iquique, and Antofagasta have direct links with Santiago's airport and with each other. Domestic flights serve the airports at Calama, Copiapó, and La Serena. Long-distance buses ply the Ruta 5 highway, commonly known as the Pan-American Highway, and connect the region's main towns and villages. Remote areas in the desert and altiplano, including archaeological sites and national parks, can be reached only by organized tour (*see pp314–19*) or by a 4WD vehicle.

Arica 1

Flag, Morro de Arica

The coastal city of Arica has palm-lined plazas and a vibrant indigenous flavor whose roots lie in the large mestizo and Quechua Peruvian populations. The city was part of Peru before its seccesion to Chile after the War of the Pacific (1879–83), and grand Peruvian-era buildings, including some by France's Gustave Eiffel, dot this compact grid of streets and plazas. Quechua crafts and markets add color, alongside sweeping beaches and outstanding archaeological highlights. Arica is also popular as a base for trips to Chile's altiplano, to the giant geoglyphs in the bordering Valle Azapa, and to Parque Nacional Lauca.

Latticed façade of Arica's Catedral de San marcos

Morro de Arica

Camino Al Morro, off Colón.
8am–2pm & 5:30–8pm daily.
Museo Histórico y de Armas
on request; in Spanish.

This 360-ft (110-m) high cliff towers above the city center and marks the end of Chile's coastal cordillera. It stands as a symbol of national glory, marking the site where, in 1880, Chilean forces stormed Peruvian fortifications to win possession of Arica in the War of the Pacific.

Located on the summit, the **Museo Histórico y de Armas** houses objects of war and other treasures. A monument to the unknown soldiers of Chile and Peru and a 33-ft (10-m) high bronze of Christ, raised as a symbol of peace between both countries, also adorn the cliff's summit.

Catedral de San Marcos

San Marcos 260. *8:30am–2pm & 6–10pm daily.*

Built by French engineer Gustav Eiffel, Arica's cast-iron, Neo-Gothic cathedral was prefabricated in France and assembled in Arica in 1876. Its latticed façade is a rich chocolate color, while the interior is notable for a delicate tracery that supports the cathedral's columns – a design flourish Eiffel used to replace the flying buttresses usually seen in Gothic churches. The bell near the entrance is from 1729 and belonged to the basilica that earlier stood on this site. Above the altar is a 17th-century sculpture of Christ.

Ex-Aduana

Manuel González. ***Tel** (058) 206366.*
8:30am–7pm Mon–Fri, 10am–2pm Sat & Sun.

Another building by Eiffel, the city's old customs house (officially called the Casa de la Cultura) was prefabricated in France and erected in Arica in 1874. This squat, brick building has an attractive pink and white striped exterior. Its interior, with cast-iron pillars and spiral staircase, houses art exhibitions. Photographs show pre-urban Arica, including shots of Morro de Arica with thousands of penguins.

Museo Ferrocarriles

21 de Mayo 51. *9am-6:30pm daily. on request.*

Arica's century-old train station houses the railroad museum. Built in 1906, the station was the western terminal for the now disused line between Arica and La Paz, Bolivia. This was the world's second highest railway, running over 283 miles (457 km), climbing to altitudes of 14,000 ft (4,275 m), and passing through some 70 mountain tunnels. The museum, in the former administrative offices, displays railway artifacts and its forecourt preserves antique trains from England and Germany. The interior of one of the old carriages has been restored and made into a restaurant.

Terminal Pesquero

Avenida Commandante San Martín.
5–8pm daily (boat tours).

In Arica's port area, Terminal Pesquero (Fishermen's Port), is a smelly but colorful experience. Boisterous water birds and sea lions vie over discarded scraps, while fishermen clean and gut the day's catch at stalls. Boat tours of the bay depart from here.

Beaches

Arica has four main beaches. Just south of the center, **Playa El Laucho** and **Playa La Lisera** have calm waters ideal for bathing; the former also has bars and restaurants. North of the center, **Playa Chinchorro** is popular for its big waves and amusement rides. Farther on, the rustic **Playa Las Machas** has more surfer waves.

Playa El Laucho, a view from the summit of Morro de Arica

For hotels and restaurants in this region see pp280–81 and pp300–301

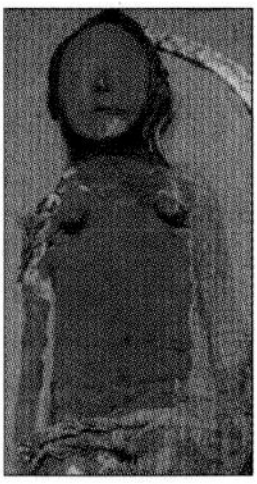
The mummy of a Chinchorro woman

CHINCHORRO MUMMIES

The Chinchorro populated Norte Grande during 6000–2000 BC and their mummies, buried in the Atacama desert, are the oldest in the world. The Chinchorro method of mummification was complex – it entailed the removal of the skin, extraction of the internal organs and extremities, and filling in of cavities with mud, ash, and resinous substances. The mummies were then buried in the extended position in collective tombs, which comprised adults, children, and fetuses.

Poblado Artesenal

Hualles 2825. ***Tel*** *(058) 228584.* *9:30am–1:30pm & 3:30–8pm daily.*

Arica's craftspeople's village is the place to buy multicolored Quechua crafts including weavings of alpaca and llama wools, ceramics, jewelry, and leather-ware. A walled space, the colony is built in the image of an altiplano village and includes workshops and lodging for local craftspeople.

Museo Arqueológico San Miguel de Azapa

Camino Azapa, Km12. ***Tel*** *(058) 205555.* *Dec–Mar: 10am–7pm daily; Apr–Nov: 10am–6pm daily.* **www**.uta.cl

Arica's outstanding museum of archaeology displays objects from up to 10,000 years ago and includes the world's oldest known mummies, the Chinchorro mummies. These comprise a man, woman, and two children buried in mass graves by the Chinchorro people between 4,000 and 8,000 years ago. The site also includes a display of severed heads, part of a "cult of the head" that existed between 500 BC and AD 500; utensils carved by the Tiwanaku people (AD 500–1000) to make hallucinogens; and ancient petroglyphs. There are also mummies of an Incan fisherman and a baby girl, with tiny hands and feet.

Painted ceramics arrayed on wooden shelves at the Poblado Artesanal

VISITORS' CHECKLIST

Road Map B1. 5,460 miles (1,664 km) N of Santiago.
190,000. *Aeropuerto Chacalluta.* *Serantur, San Marcos 101; (058) 252054.*
Sun. *Carnaval Andino con la Fuerza del Sol (end Jan).*
www.arica.cl

Geoglyph Cerro Sagrado

Alto Ramírez, Valle Azapa.

The great stone mosaic on the Cerro Sagrado hillside is the most eye-catching of several enormous geoglyphs in the Valle Azapa. A mosaic of anthropomorphic and zoomorphic motifs, it depicts giant human figures – adult and child – as well as mammoth lizards and llamas. The latter are composed in dynamic form, as if scaling up or bounding across this barren hillside. The geoglyphs date from this region's Incan period (AD 1450–1500), when farmers settled this green valley in the desert north.

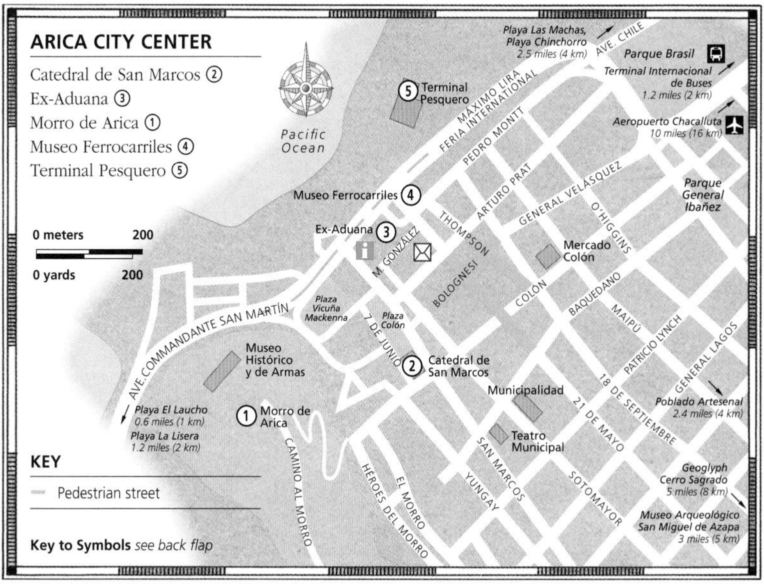

Putre's plaza, with views of the Chilean altiplano

Iglesia de San Gerónimo de Poconchile ❷

Road Map B1. 22 miles (35 km) E of Arica; Poconchile.

Located in the village of Poconchile, Iglesia de San Gerónimo is the oldest of northern Chile's early Colonial churches. It was built by Spanish priests in 1580, on a site along the old Camino del Inca (Inca Road), and served to evangelize the Aymara people of this area. The church's dazzlingly white exterior is faithful to the classic Spanish Colonial style – a thick adobe perimeter wall marks the boundary of this sacred site and twin bell towers flank its entrance. The restored interior is wooden and painted white. At the back of the church, a desert cemetery contains old graves marked by pebbles and simple wooden crosses.

Putre ❸

Road Map B1. 90 miles (149 km) NE of Arica. *1,200.*

The largest of the high-altitude settlements close to Arica, Putre is an oasis town ringed by the pointed peaks of several snow-swathed volcanoes. At 11,500 ft (3,500 m) above sea level, it is a stopover for travelers seeking acclimatization before continuing onward to higher altitude highlights such as the adjacent Parque Nacional Lauca and the more distant Reserva Nacional Las Vicuñas. Putre's roots lie in pre-Incan Chile, but the present town was founded by the Spanish around 1580 as a resting place for muleteers transporting silver from the mines of Potosí, in modern-day Bolivia, to the Pacific coast. The town's most attractive structure is the heavily restored Colonial church fronting the plaza. This edifice dates from 1670 and stands on the site of the original temple that was destroyed by earthquake, and which, according to Spanish chronicles, was completely clad in silver and gold. The rest of Putre is a compact grid of dirt streets lined with relatively new concrete-and-zinc buildings and old Spanish adobe houses. A selection of hotels and restaurants dot this pleasant altiplano town; tour agencies are found on Calle Baquedano.

Parque Nacional Lauca ❹

See pp164–5.

Reserva Nacional Las Vicuñas ❺

Road Map B1. 143 miles (230 km) E of Arica. *4WD from Putre; tours from Putre and Arica.* *CONAF, Guallatire.* **www**.conaf.cl

Spectacular and remote, the Reserva Nacional Las Vicuñas protects a vast wilderness of giant volcanoes, high-altitude tablelands, abandoned Aymara settlements, and diverse indigenous fauna. This reserve has a stepped landscape that rises from 13,120 ft (4,000 m) above sea level at its lowest elevation to 18,370 ft (5,600 m) at its highest. It is overlooked by three 20,000-ft (6,000-m) volcanoes – Volcán Acotango, Volcán Capurata, and Volcán Guallatire. Vicuñas, for whose protection this park was founded in 1983, can be seen bounding across the puna; ñandus, an ostrich-like bird, sprint over open plains; pink flamingos congregate on the banks of high lagoons; and vizcachas (a large chinchilla-like rodent) scurry across rocks. In the central sector of the reserve, the llama-herding hamlet of **Guallatire** has lodgings, the CONAF administrative center, and a 17th-century church. South of this hamlet, the **Monumento Natural Salar de Surire** is a dazzlingly white salt plain. Three different species of flamingo nest on its shores in the summer months, and on its western bank a CONAF *refugio* offers rustic accommodations.

Ñandu, Reserva Nacional Las Vicuñas

The snow-bound peak of Volcán Guallatire at Reserva Nacional Las Vicuñas

Pukarás and the Camino del Inca

Northern Chile's pre-Incan fortresses, built between AD 1000 and 1450, are known as *pukarás*. In the 11th century, the reigning Tiwanaku Empire, whose seat was in present-day Bolivia, collapsed, returning autonomy to Norte Grande's Aymara and Atacameño peoples. However, the peace of empire was replaced by intermittent warfare as local warlords rose to compete for resources. To protect ancestral trading routes, the warlords built *pukarás* on strategic hillsides. The *pukará's* role as a power-base continued until the 1450s, when Incan forces sacked them and incorporated their routes into the Camino del Inca (Inca Road), a 3,720-mile (6,000-km) highway that ran the length of the Incan Empire.

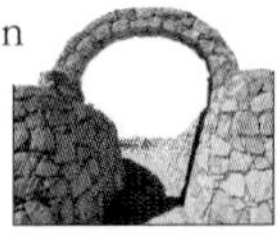

Stone archway at Pukará de Quitor

A long perimeter wall marked the *pukará's* boundary and was its first line of defense.

Pukarás occupied strategic positions on hillsides in rocky canyons and oasis valleys.

PUKARÁ ARCHITECTURE

In peacetime, *pukarás* were used by warlords to wield authority over surrounding *aldeas* (villages). In wartime, they became defensive fortresses, where villagers relocated for their own safety. Accordingly, *pukarás* at Lasana *(see p171)* and Quitor *(see p174)* include not only defensive fortifications but domestic neighborhoods as well.

Family quarters *in the fortress could be circular or square, with dry-stone or stone-and-mud walls. Smaller storehouses adjoined them for stocking timber, maize, and other provisions.*

Narrow stone passages *connected the* pukará's *maze of fortifications and its residential neighborhoods. The latter comprised numerous houses, storehouses, patios, communal squares, and animal pens for llamas.*

Pukarás climbed hillsides *in terraces. The hill's crest was an ideal vantage point for spotting enemy approach; its steep slopes a further defense against attack.*

Parque Nacional Lauca ❹

Flamingo at the national park

Northern Chile's most scenic sanctuary, Parque Nacional Lauca protects around 532 sq miles (1,378 sq km) of altiplano wilderness. The park climbs a stepped ecology that starts at 10,500 ft (3,200 m) in its western zone and rises to over 20,700 ft (6,300 m) in the east. The accessible, high-altitude attractions include brilliantly colored lakes, snowy volcanoes, lava islands, stretches of high tableland, and tiny Aymara villages. There is also an abundance of wildlife. Over 140 bird species find refuge in this area, key among them, the ostrich-like ñandu and three species of flamingo, which feed and nest on lakeshores. Wild populations of vicuña are also easily spotted.

Llareta, a cushion plant found at high altitudes

Jurasi Thermal Baths

These hot springs are scenically situated within a rocky gorge. They include many small baths of bubbling hot water, a large pool, changing rooms, and toilets.

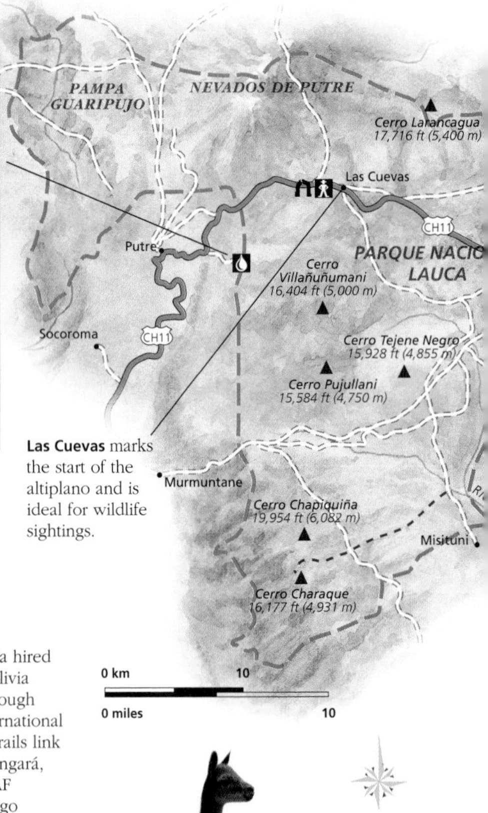

Las Cuevas marks the start of the altiplano and is ideal for wildlife sightings.

EXPLORING THE PARK

Parque Nacional Lauca can be reached via hired vehicles, organized tours, or the Arica-Bolivia international bus, whose route passes through this area. Within the park, the CH-11 international highway runs east to west, and walking trails link the popular sites of Parinacota, Lago Chungará, and Lagunas Cotacotani. There are CONAF stations at Las Cuevas, Parinacota, and Lago Chungará. The last of these has *refugio* accommodation and Parinacota has a visitors' center.

STAR SIGHTS

- ★ Volcán Parinacota
- ★ Parinacota
- ★ Lago Chungará

Vicuña

Parque Nacional Lauca protects wild herds of vicuña, which bound across the puna and graze at lakeshores. Vicuña numbers in the park have increased from barely 1,000 in the 1970s to over 20,000 today.

For hotels and restaurants in this region see pp280–81 and pp300–301

★ Volcán Parinacota
The twin peaks of Volcán Parinacota and Volcán Pomerape form a glorious backdrop to Lago Chungará. At a height of 20,762 ft (6,330 m), dormant Volcán Parinacota is a target for climbers, who scale its summit on 2-day expeditions.

VISITORS' CHECKLIST

Road Map B1. 102 miles (165 km) E of Arica. ***Tel*** *(058) 585704.* *from Arica.* *CONAF, Parinacota.* *daily.* *from Arica & Putre.* **www**.conaf.cl

Laguna Cotacotani
Visible from the CH-11, this area is a network of jade-green lagoons patterned with black lava flows and cinder cones. The banks can be explored on scenic trails.

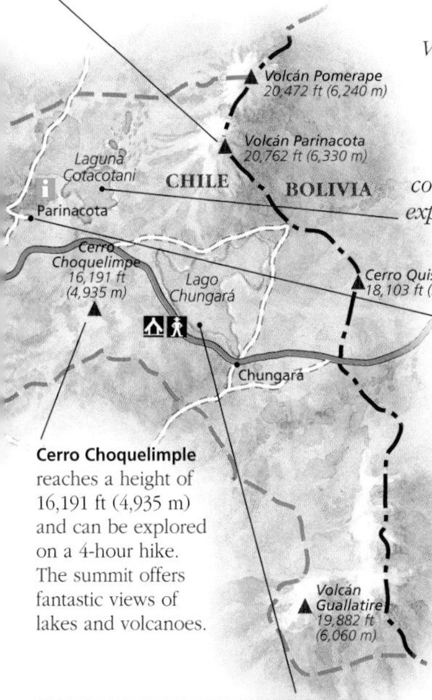

Cerro Choquelimple
reaches a height of 16,191 ft (4,935 m) and can be explored on a 4-hour hike. The summit offers fantastic views of lakes and volcanoes.

★ Parinacota
A small Aymara hamlet, Parinacota is visited for its handicrafts market and a 17th-century church, where frescoes depict the tortures of hell.

★ Lago Chungará
At 14,990 ft (4,570 m), Lago Chungará is one of the world's highest lakes. It is stunningly beautiful: metallic-blue and ringed by snowy volcanoes. Colorful birdlife feeds on its shores.

KEY

- Main road
- Untarred minor road
- Trail
- Park boundary
- International border
- Visitor information
- Ranger station
- Hostería/Refugio
- Spa
- Cave
- ▲ Peak

Iquique ❻

Moorish tile at Casino Español

Originally a part of Peru, Iquique was annexed by Chile during the War of the Pacific (1879–83). This coastal city, already well-developed due to its rich mineral deposits, subsequently emerged as Chile's nitrate capital. Opulent buildings and streets from the nitrate-era stand testament to the city's decadent golden past, a period when Iquique is said to have consumed greater quantities of champagne per capita than any other city in the world. Today, this important port-city is the springboard for excursions to nearby national parks, nitrate ghost towns, and oasis villages.

The Iquique skyline seen from Playa Cavancha

Palacio Astoreca

*O'Higgins 350. **Tel** (057) 425600. 10am–1pm & 4–7pm Mon–Fri, 11am–2pm Sat. for group visits only.*

One of Iquique's extravagant mansions, Palacio Astoreca is a beautiful 27-room house that was built in Bristish Georgian style for a nitrate magnate in 1903. It was constructed with Oregon pine that was shipped from the US. The house retains vestiges of a glorious past that include silk wallpaper, a grand staircase, and a stained-glass skylight in its reception hall. Today, this grand building serves as Iquique's cultural center, and hosts occasional art exhibitions and workshops. Permanent exhibitions include re-creations of nitrate-era living quarters with original Art Nouveau furnishings. On display is a collection of seashells of varying sizes from around the world.

Teatro Municipal

*Calle Thompson 269. **Tel** (057) 544734. 9am–6pm daily.*

Built in 1890 at the height of the nitrate boom, Iquique's Teatro Municipal is housed in a magnificent wooden structure, whose Neo-Classical façade is ornamented with female stone figures symbolizing theatrical elements such as costume and dance. The foyer, topped by a cupola, has a ceiling painted with cherubic allegories of music, dance, painting, and theater, as well as depictions of famed literary and musical masters including Shakespeare, Chopin, and Mozart. A domed ceiling crowns the auditorium and is painted with more theatrical motifs, including musical instruments and theater masks symbolizing comedy and tragedy. Adjacent to the stage,

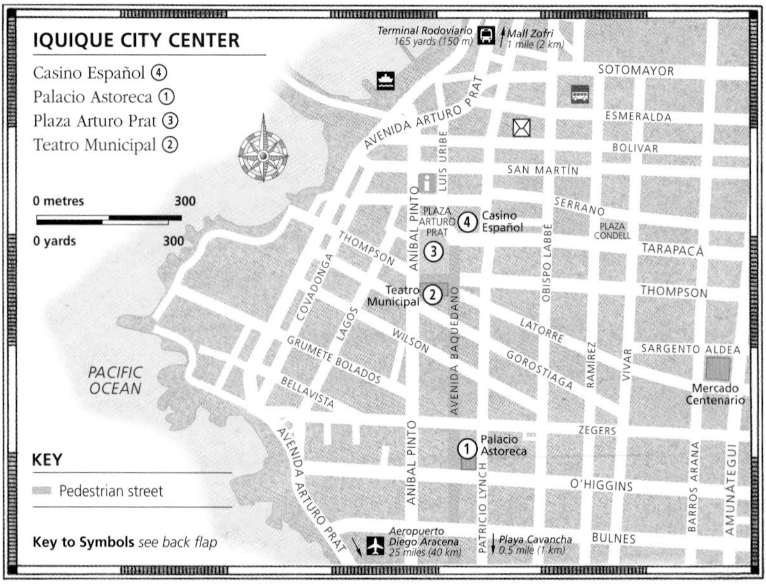

Interior of the Teatro Municipal displaying luxurious furnishings

stairs descend to the bowels of this edifice, where century-old wooden pulleys and wheels still serve as stage machinery.

Plaza Arturo Prat

Between Calle Aníbal Pinto & Avenida Baquedano.

Iquique's main square, Plaza Arturo Prat is located in the heart of the city's historic center. Dominating the plaza is the city's emblematic landmark, the flamboyant **Torre Reloj**. Built from Oregon pine by the English community in 1877, this clock tower is made up of three tapering tiers that are painted white and rise to 82 ft (25 m). The tower's arched base features a bust of Arturo Prat, considered Chile's greatest naval hero. He captained the *Esmeralda* schooner that was sunk by the Peruvian battleship *Huascar* at the Battle of Iquique during the War of the Pacific. This battle ended with the death of Prat and much of his crew, but proved to be the turning point in a war that secured possession of Iquique for Chile and dominion over this area's lucrative nitrate deposits.

Running south from the plaza, **Avenida Baquedano** preserves some of Iquique's finest nitrate-era buildings, including several wooden mansions built by wealthy English and German nitrate magnates in the late 1800s.

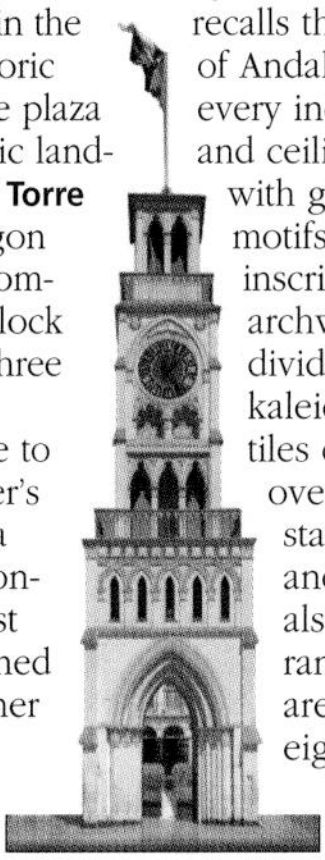

The historic Torre Reloj at Plaza Arturo Prat

Casino Español

Plaza Prat 584. ***Tel*** *(057) 333911.* *noon–4pm & 8–9:30pm daily.*

Constructed by the city's Spanish community in 1904, the Casino Español occupies a Moorish-style wooden edifice with an arched, Arabesque façade. Its domed interior recalls the Moorish palaces of Andalusian Spain with every inch of floor, wall, and ceiling space decorated with glittering Moorish motifs, patterns, and inscriptions. Arabesque archways and columns divide the salons, and kaleidoscopically glazed tiles decorate floors overlooked by Spanish stained glass, mirrors, and statues. There is also a public restaurant, the walls of which are embellished with eight giant oil paintings by well-known Spanish artist Antonio Torrecilla. Completed in 1907, these depict scenes from Miguel de Cervantes' famous novel *Don Quijote de la Mancha* (1605).

Mall Zofri

Edificio de Convenciones, Zona Franca Zofri. ***Tel*** *(57) 515100.* *11:30am–9pm Mon–Sat.* **www**.zofri.cl

Starting at Iquique's center, *colectivos* take people on the short trip north to the Zona Franca Zofri, the city's gigantic tax-free zone. The most attractive shopping center here is Mall Zofri, a glossy shopping mecca located amid scores of giant wholesale warehouses. It comprises over 400 stores selling electrical goods, perfumes, toys, clothing, and sportswear. Goods purchased here are free of Chile's 20 percent direct tax.

VISITORS' CHECKLIST

Road Map B2. 196 miles (316 km) S of Arica. *220,000.* *Aeropuerto Diego Aracena.* *Sernatur, Aníbal Pinto 436; (057) 419241.* *Festival de la Canción de Iquique (end Jan).* **www**.iquique.cl

Playa Cavancha

1 mile (2 km) S of city center. **Casino de Iquique** Avenida Arturo Prat 2755. ***Tel*** *(057) 577500.* *daily.* **www**.casinoiquique.cl

Located within walking distance from the city center, Playa Cavancha is Iquique's main beach. A long stretch of golden sand edged by a beachside boulevard, Playa Cavancha is popular with swimmers and surfers. At its southern end, the **Casino de Iquique** is housed in a mock nitrate-era building, while the family-oriented **Parque Temático** has a small animal farm with llamas and alpacas, and hosts marine-life shows. Also located here is the **Peninsula Cavancha**, a modern hotel and restaurant zone. It is also possible to take a taxi farther south to the quieter, windswept Playa Brava, a favorite with sunbathers.

Shops selling a variety of goods at Iquique's duty-free Mall Zofri

Humberstone and Santa Laura ❼

Road Map B2. 30 miles (48 km) E of Iquique; Ruta A16, Km3. ***Tel*** *(057) 760626.* *from Iquique.* *9am–6pm daily.* *Tue–Sat; on request.*

In the 1930s, British investors built the towns of Santa Laura and Humberstone to provide housing and leisure for the workers and management of the area's nitrate mines. By 1960, the advent of artificial nitrates had closed the mines, leaving these two towns eerily abandoned. Today, these UNESCO-protected nitrate ghost towns have become popular visitor attractions. The more-visited Humberstone is a silent grid of named roads, empty plazas, creaking street signs, and shells of deserted buildings and facilities. These include quarters that once housed 3,700 employees, a hospital and school, an outdoor pool, sports fields, a marketplace, a church, clock tower, and a theater that could seat up to 800 people. Each of these desolate structures is signposted with panels bearing historical information that help visitors explore the town independently. Adjacent to these buildings stands the rusting machinery of the town's nitrate mine.

About one mile (1.5 km) east of Humberstone, the smaller ghost town of Santa Laura, feels all the more abandoned for receiving fewer visitors. Its hulking processing facilities – which include giant chimneys and mills – are perfectly preserved.

Empty quarters for workers at the nitrate ghost town of Humberstone

Parque Nacional Volcán Isluga ❽

Road Map B1. 155 miles (250 km) NE of Iquique. *CONAF; (057) 421 352.* *from Iquique to Colchane: 10 miles (16 km) from park.* *from Colchane.* *8am–8pm daily.* **www**.conaf.cl

Isolated from northern Chile's beaten track, Parque Nacional Volcán Isluga protects around 674 sq miles (1,741 sq km) of altiplano wilderness that embraces brilliantly hued lagoons, forgotten Aymara villages, and soaring volcanoes, including the 17,115-ft (5,218-m) high Volcán Isluga. The park's highlights are in its eastern sector, accessible via the paved A-55 international highway that connects Iquique with neighboring Bolivia. Close to the park entrance, **Isluga** is an Aymara village with a beautiful 17th-century church as well as the Pukará de Isluga, a ruined fortress dating from pre-Columbian times. Also located in the eastern sector, the Aymara village of Enquelga is the gateway to the park's hot springs. This sector has two pristine lakes: Laguna Arabillo has a walking trail along its shore, while Laguna Parinacota is popular for sightings of wildlife such as pink flamingos, camelids, and the taruca, a small endangered deer.

The arid slopes of Volcán Isluga in Parque Nacional Volcán Isluga

One of the thermal swimming pools at Mamiña Hot Springs

Mamiña Hot Springs ❾

Road Map B2. 78 miles (125 km) E of Iquique; Mamiña. *from Iquique.* **www**.termasdemamina.cl

Located 8,860 ft (2,700m) above sea level, these hot springs have been used to cure afflictions ranging from eczema to anxiety and respiratory illnesses since the age of the Incas. They comprise a number of hot springs such as **Baños de Ipla** that has sodium-rich waters and **Baños Chinos Manantial**, famous for its mud baths. Adjacent to the springs is the village of Mamiña, with stone houses, terraced fields, and Incan ruins. The village's restored **Iglesia de San Marcos**, dating from 1632, is unique among Andean churches for its twin bell towers.

La Tirana ⑩

Road Map B2. 45 miles (72 km) SE of Iquique. *1,300.* *Festival de La Tirana (mid-July).*

A somnolent oasis village with adobe houses, La Tirana springs to life each July for the lively Festival de La Tirana, a religious celebration, drawing some 200,000 devotees to the village from across Chile.

The origins of the village can be traced to the 1500s when an Incan princess, notorious for killing Christians, ruled the area. The princess, who was known as La Tirana (The Tyrant), eventually fell in love with a Portuguese prisoner and converted to Christianity, only to have her irate subjects kill them both on their wedding day. In 1540, a Jesuit missionary found the cross marking the princess's grave and ordered the construction of a church on the site. Named the Iglesia de la Virgen del Carmen de la Tirana in honor of Chile's patron saint and the Incan princess, the church became the progenitor of the cult of La Tirana. The **Santuario de la Tirana** comprises the present-day wooden church, a sweeping plaza adorned with effigies of the Virgin and the princess, and the Museo de la Virgen de la Tirana, which displays costumes and masks from the Festival La Tirana. Inside the church is a polychrome shrine to the Virgin.

Santuario de la Tirana
Tel *(057) 532836. 9:30am–1pm & 3:30–8pm Mon–Fri, 9am–8pm Sat & Sun.*

FESTIVAL DE LA TIRANA

Chile's biggest religious event, Festival de La Tirana has its roots in pre-Columbian rituals and offers a peek at Andean culture. It venerates the Virgen del Carmen via costume and dance. On its first day, dancers enter La Tirana's church to percussion and brass bands and ask the Virgin's permission to dance. They then embark on a week of frenetic dancing which culminates on the Day of the Virgin, when a hoisted image of the saint leads a mass procession through the village. On the final day, they visit the church to bid farewell to the Virgin, before exiting on their knees.

Costumed performer at the Festival La Tirana

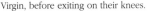

Fruit-laden tree in one of Pica's orange and lemon groves

Pica ⑪

Road Map B2. 71 miles (114 km) E of Iquique. *6,100.* *Balmaceda 299; (057) 741841.* *La Fiesta de San Andrés (end Nov).* **www**.pica.cl

Called the Flower in the Sand, Pica is an oasis village famed for its orchards. Regional and local varieties thrive in Pica's micro-climate, and fruit trees and adobe houses line its sleepy streets. Facing the main plaza, the beautiful Iglesia de San Andrés was built in 1886. Its polychrome interior holds a life-size representation of the Last Supper carved from wood. Just east of the plaza, **Museo de Pica** displays millennia-old preserved Chinchorro mummies *(see p161)*. At the edge of town, the warm waters of **Cocha Resbaladero** thermal pools have attracted visitors since the 16th-century.

Museo de Pica
Balmaceda 178. ***Tel*** *(057) 741665. 9am–2pm & 3:30–6:30pm Mon–Fri.*

Cocha Resbaladero
Balneario Cocha Resbaladero.
Tel *(057) 741173. 8am–9:30pm daily.*

Cerro Pintados ⑫

Road Map B2. 59 miles (96 km) SE of Iquique; El Cruce de Geoglifos de Pintados, La Panamericana.
Tel *(057) 751055. from Iquique. 9am–4pm daily.*

The barren hillsides of Cerro Pintados are etched with more than 350 gigantic geoglyphs. Dating from AD 500–1450, when this region was part of a caravan route to the Pacific coast, the geoglyphs comprise huge geometric shapes as well as anthropomorphic and zoomorphic figures including depictions of fish, llamas, and the ñandu, a native ostrich-like bird. These are accessible via a 3-mile (4-km) long path that skirts the base of the hillsides.

Façade of La Tirana's Iglesia de la Virgen del Carmen de la Tirana

Calama ⓭

Road Map B2. 242 miles (390 km) SE of Iquique. *140,000.* *El Aeródromo El Loa de Calama.* *J. J. Latorre 1689; (055) 531707.* *Aniversario de la Ciudad de Calama (end Mar).* **www**.calamacultural.cl

The city of Calama is the base for visits to the great copper mines of Chuquicamata. An oasis city in the driest zone on the planet's driest desert, Calama has its roots in pre-Columbian Chile, and derives its name from the Atacameño word *kara ama*, meaning water haven. In the 1920s, Calama boomed as a service town and provider of debauched diversion to pit workers. Today, the city is fairly unremarkable, its single daytime attraction being the **Parque El Loa**, a riverside tourist park featuring a replica of the Colonial church at Chiu-Chiu. The grounds are also the site of the city's Museo Arqueológico y Etnografico Parque el Loa, which houses artifacts belonging to this area's pre-Incan oasis villages.

Parque El Loa
Avenida Bernardo O'Higgins s/n.
Tel *(055) 531771.* *daily.*

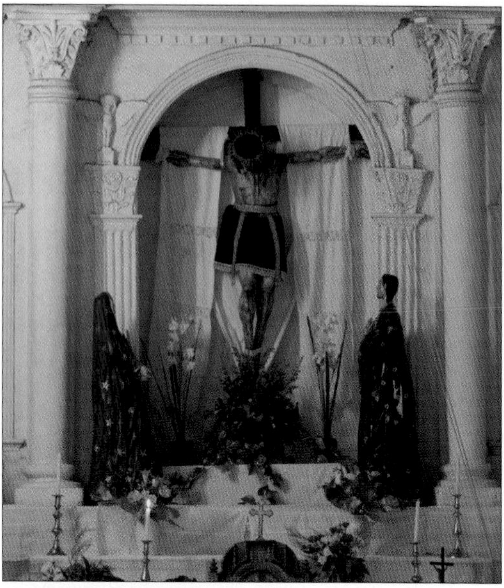

Altar at the Iglesia San Francisco de Chiu-Chiu

Chuquicamata ⓮

Road Map B2. 10 miles (16 km) N of Calama; Entrada al Campamento, J.M. Carrera. ***Tel*** *(055) 322122.* *from Calama.* *2pm Mon–Fri.* **www**.codelco.cl

Visited only by guided tour, Chuquicamata is the world's biggest open-pit mine. This huge copper quarry is almost about 2 miles (3 km) wide, 3 miles (5 km) long, and an impressive 2,300 ft (1,000 m) deep. The mine is to copper what Saudi Arabia is to oil – any blip in the production process here strikes panic in world copper markets. Chile's biggest state company, Codelco, oversees the mine. It employs 20,000 workers, operates 24 hours per day, and is the single biggest contributor to Chile's state coffers, bankrolling the country's public health and education systems. Each year this massive hole in the Andes mountains is gouged ever deeper, a phenomenon brought into stunning perspective on one-hour coach tours of the site. Tours pass refineries, and crushing and smelting plants to a viewpoint that overlooks the open pit. Here, visitors can peer into the depths of Chuquicamata, and see from a distance the giant 400-tonne (394-ton) dump trucks that ascend and descend its terraced walls like worker ants, carrying the almost pure copper deposits excavated from the mine's rocky bed to its top.

Stepped quarry and gravel roads at the copper mine of Chuquicamata

Chiu-Chiu ⓯

Road Map B2. 22 miles (36 km) NE of Calama. *Festival de Nuestra Señora de Lourdes (mid Feb).* **www**.sanfranciscochiuchiu.com

Founded by the Spanish around 1610, Chiu-Chiu is an oasis village of whitewashed adobe houses and cactus-wood doors. Visited on tours from Calama, or more usually from San Pedro de Atacama *(see p174)*, the village conserves one of Chile's oldest, most beautiful churches, the **Iglesia San Francisco de Chiu-Chiu**. This whitewashed adobe church was built in 1674 in the Spanish Colonial style, with two bell towers, walls over 3 ft (1 m) thick, and a well-preserved interior of mini altars and polychrome statues of saints and virgins. The church's small grounds, protected by a thick perimeter wall, contain a tiny cemetery.

One block from the main plaza of Chiu-Chiu is the **Museo Geológico de Chiu-Chiu**, housing some interesting rock and fossil exhibits.

Museo Geológico de Chiu-Chiu
10am–1pm & 3–6pm Thu–Mon.
www.sanfranciscochiuchiu.com

Pukará de Lasana ⑯

Road Map B2. 28 miles (45 km) N of Calama; Pueblo Lasana, Valle Lasana. *9:30am–5pm daily.*

The stone ruins of the pre-Inca Pukará de Lasana occupy a natural promontory that overlooks the green Valle Lasana from within a rocky canyon. The people of the Atacameño civilization (400 BC–AD 1400) erected this fortress from a pre-existing village during a period of war in the 11th century. Today, the well-preserved ruins are a hilly maze of perimeter walls, roofless houses, storehouses, patios, narrow passageways, and fortifications. Incan forces sacked this site in 1447, and converted it into a strategic administrative center for control of the valley. They abandoned it in the 16th century on the arrival of the Spanish to this region.

Jets of steam rising from the Geisers de Tatio

Caspana ⑰

Road Map C2. 52 miles (84 km) E of Calama. 480. *La Virgen Candelaria (early Feb).*

One of the oasis villages that dot the high mountain pass between Calama and San Pedro de Atacama, Caspana is spectacularly situated 11,870 ft (3,260 m) above sea level in a steep gorge irrigated by a tributary of the Río Salado. The village is an adobe jewel, with monochrome stone-and-mud houses that were inhabited by the Atacameño people before the arrival of the Incas and Spanish. Today, it subsists on farming, and sinuous rows of green terraces can be seen along the contours of the lower slopes of the gorge. These are planted with root vegetables, grown to be sold at the market in Calama.

At the edge of the village, the adobe and cactus-wood **Iglesia San Lucas** dates from 1641 and backs on to a small cemetery. The **Museo Etnográfico** has archaeological and ethnographic exhibits. The tiny village plaza offers shaded benches and lovely vistas of the rocky gorge, pale houses, and verdant terraces.

Museo Etnográfico
Los Tres Alamos s/n. ***Tel*** *(055) 692147.* *10am–1pm & 2:30–6pm Tue–Sun.*

Terraced cultivation around the village of Caspana

Geisers de Tatio ⑱

Road Map C2. 74 miles (119 km) E of Calama; Camino a Tatio. *4WD.* *daily.*

A natural spectacle, the Geisers de Tatio shoot skyward in columns of white vapor at an altitude of 14,200 ft (4,320 m) above sea level. There are some 40 geysers and 70 fumaroles here, each a scar on the surface of a flat geothermic basin that is ringed by rust-colored mountains and pointed volcanoes. Their origin lies in the contact of a cold river with hot, magmatic rock deep underground. This contact causes jets of vapor to stream upward through fissures in the earth's crust and to exit here, in white-vapor streams that rise to a height of 33 ft (10 m) and reach a temperature of 185°F (85°C). It is best to visit the geysers on 4WD excursions that depart from San Pedro de Atacama at 4am, reaching the geysers at around 5am when they are at their most impressive. Visitors who make this early trip will be able to view the geyser field at its most elemental; hear it groan, grumble, spit, and ultimately, both audibly and visibly, exhale. Half-day trips to the Geisers de Tatio end with a dip in sulfur-rich hot springs. Full-day excursions continue to Calama, visiting Caspana, Chiu-Chiu and the Pukará de Lasana, before returning to San Pedro de Atacama.

Geisers de Tatio in the Atacama desert ▷

Entrance to the Museo Arqueológico Gustavo Le Paige, San Pedro de Atacama

San Pedro de Atacama ⓳

Road Map C3. 304 miles (490 km) SE of Iquique. *5,000.* *Toconao esq Gustavo Le Paige.* *La Celebración de San Pedro (end Jul).* **www**.sanpedroatacama.com

Lovely San Pedro de Atacama is northern Chile's most popular tourist destination. A small oasis village of clay-colored adobe houses and dirt streets, this is the picturesque springboard for trips into a region of stunning natural highlights and rich archaeological interest, and as such is a magnet to adventure-hungry visitors. Its location is a geological basin at 7,990 ft (2,436 m) above sea level, overlooked from its west by the Domeyko mountains and from its east by the younger Andes range. Both basin and mountains are part of a stepped ecology that rises to over 19,700 ft (6,000 m) at its highest altitude and features jaw-dropping highlights such as dazzlingly white salt lakes, lunar valleys, Chile's biggest volcanoes, smoking geyser fields, high-altitude lagoons and hot springs, and the ruins of pre-Incan forts and villages. These can be visited on 4WD tours, mountain-bike rides, and horseback excursions.

An important settlement in pre-Incan Chile, San Pedro de Atacama retains a beguiling, authentic charm despite the year-round presence of tourists and the large number of accommodations, from backpacker hostels to luxury hotels, which line its narrow streets. The **Iglesia San Pedro de Atacama** overlooks its pretty, tree-lined plaza. A brilliant white adobe edifice with cactus-wood doors, the church dates from the early 1600s. Standing opposite it, the **Casa Incaica** was built for Chile's founder Pedro de Valdivia in 1540 and is the town's oldest house.

The adobe church, Iglesia San Pedro de Atacama

The superb **Museo Arqueológico Gustavo Le Paige** houses archaeological objects such as stone paraphernalia sculpted with images of animalistic deities, which the decadent Tiwanaku (AD 500–1000) used to make hallucinogens. There are also millennia-old basketry, ceramics, and woodcarvings. Tour agencies line the town's main street, Caracoles.

Environs

Reached on horseback or by mountain bike from San Pedro de Atacama, the **Pukará de Quitor** comprises ruins of a red-stone pre-Incan fortress, built in the 12th century during a period of war. The ruins sprawl across a steep hillside which overlooks the stunning San Pedro river canyon and consist of an outer wall, narrow passageways, living quarters, grain storehouses, herding pens, and communal squares. A walking trail climbs to the top of the fortress for wonderful views of the canyon, volcanoes, and the Valle de la Muerte.

From Pukará de Quitor, determined visitors can continue 3 miles (4 km) north to **Catarpe**, site of the ruins of a *tambo* (Incan administrative center). These are less intact than the *pukará*, but the journey to them traverses breathtakingly wild canyon country.

Museo Arqueológico Gustavo Le Paige
Gustavo Le Paige 380. ***Tel*** *(055) 851002.* *9am–6pm daily.*

Pukará de Quitor
2 miles (3 km) N of San Pedro de Atacama; Avenida Pukará. *8:30am-6:30pm daily*

Hedges and pepper trees lining the main plaza at San Pedro de Atacama

Baños de Puritama ⓴

Road Map C3. 19 miles (30 km) NE of San Pedro de Atacama; Camino al Tatio, Km32. *from San Pedro de Atacama.* *9:15am–6pm daily.* **www**.explora.com

A half-day excursion from San Pedro de Atacama, the Baños de Puritama are terraced hot springs that tumble down a narrow canyon. At 77–86°F (25–30°C), these natural volcanic pools are perfect for bathing. There are changing rooms nearby, and wooden footbridges link the stepped, interconnected pools.

People in the secluded thermal pools at Baños de Puritama

The world's most powerful telescope at Cerro Paranal Observatory

STARGAZING IN THE NORTHERN DESERT

Chile's northern desert boasts some of the world's clearest night skies and its most hi-tech astronomical observatories. Open to visits, these include the facilities at Cerro Mamalluca *(see p182)* and Cerro Paranal *(see p177)*. The latter is the location of the gigantic VLT, the world's most powerful telescope. Yet by 2011, this awe-inspiring instrument will be eclipsed when ALMA, a multi-billion-dollar facility, opens on a 16,400-ft (5,000-m) high plateau near San Pedro de Atacama. Financed by North American, European, and Asian governments in cooperation with Chile, ALMA will become the single biggest astronomical project on the planet. It will comprise a mind-boggling 50 antennae, each 39 ft (12 m) in diameter, that will act as a single telescope and offer vision 10 times sharper than the Hubble Space Telescope. ALMA astrophysicists will, for the first time, see planets and super-massive black holes formed 10 billion years ago.

Aldea Tulor ㉑

Road Map C3. 6 miles (9 km) NE of San Pedro de Atacama; Ayllo de Tulor, RN Los Flamencos. *from San Pedro de Atacama.* *Dec–Mar: 8:30am–8pm daily; Apr–Nov: 9am–5:30pm daily.*

Excavated as recently as 1982, after desertification had left it buried beneath sand for 1,600 years, Aldea Tulor comprises the 2,800-year-old red-clay ruins of one of Chile's first sedentary settlements. The Atacameño abandoned this site in AD 500 owing to the encroaching desert. Today the walls of their settlement and its doorways, passageways, and large honeycomb-like patterns of rooms lie partially or fully exposed to view. Most visitors choose to reach Tulor from San Pedro de Atacama independently on horseback or by mountain bike, crossing the Atacama desert in the shadows of impressive volcanoes.

Neolithic settlement of adobe mud brick preserved at Aldea Tulor

Salar de Tara ㉒

Road Map C3. 62 miles (100 km) E of San Pedro de Atacama; Reserva Nacional Los Flamencos. *4WD from San Pedro de Atacama.* *Control de CONAF.* **www**.conaf.cl

Adventurous travelers make the arduous yet memorable excursion from San Pedro de Atacama to the Salar de Tara; a salt lake located 14,100 ft (4,300 m) above sea level. Tough roads lead to this breathtaking white spectacle decorated by jewel-like lakes and green vegetation with abundant fauna. Its birdlife includes Chile's three species of flamingo, which rest on the shores of the lagoons, horned coots (*Fulica cornuta*) and Andean geese (*Chloephaga melanoptera*). Herds of vicuña can be seen grazing at the edge of the salt pan.

Salar de Atacama ㉓

Road Map C3. 6 miles (10 km) S of San Pedro de Atacama; RN Los Flamencos. *from San Pedro de Atacama.* *Control de CONAF, Sector Soncor.* **www**.conaf.cl

Occupying 1,160 sq miles (3,000 sq km) of surface area, Salar de Atacama is Chile's largest, and the world's third largest, salt flat. It lies 7,700 ft (2,350 m) above sea level in a great geological depression between the Domeyko and Andes mountain ranges. The *salar* formed when lakes that orignially filled this basin evaporated, leaving a thick coat of silver-gray salt crystals on the flat earth. Not blindingly white like other salt pans in this region, the Salar de Atacama is neverthless a vision of color and beauty, with salt-water lagoons of intense hues decorating its surface. **Laguna Cejar** is a brilliantly blue lake whose high salt and lithium content allows bathers to float weightlessly on its surface. **Laguna Chaxa** has shallow waters, a volcanic backdrop, sure flamingo sightings, and brilliant sunsets.

Environs

Lying 13,100 ft (4,000 m) above sea level, just east of the Salar de Atacama, are the arrestingly beautiful **Laguna Miscanti**, **Laguna Miñeques**, and **Laguna Lejía**, famous for their birdlife. Also east of the *salar* are **Toconao**, **Peine**, and **Socaire**, oasis villages with early Colonial churches, pre-Incan ruins, and petroglyphs.

A view of dunes and volcanoes at the Valle de la Luna

Valle de la Luna ㉔

Road Map B3. 12 miles (19 km) SW of San Pedro de Atacama; Sector 6, Reserva Nacional Los Flamencos. *from San Pedro de Atacama.* *9am–7pm daily.*

This lunar valley is a stark landscape of otherworldly rock formations, salt caves, natural amphitheaters, and sweeping sand dunes. Set 7,870 ft (2,400 m) above sea level in the Cordillera de Sal (Salt Mountain Range), it is explored via a well-marked circuit. This path includes **Las Tres Marias**, eroded rock sculptures that resemble three praying women, and the **Duna Mayor**, the greatest of this valley's massive sand dunes. Most tours climb the Duna Mayor at dusk for stupendous views of the Andean peaks and volcanoes washed in indigo, orange, and red tones. The vistas include Volcán Licancabur and Volcán Láscar; the latter being one of Chile's most explosive peaks.

A flock of Andean flamingos on the Laguna Chaxa

Valle de la Muerte ㉕

Road Map C3. 6 miles (10 km) SW of San Pedro de Atacama; Camino a Calama. *from San Pedro de Atacama.* *9am–7pm daily.*

A barren bed of huge sand dunes and red-rock pinnacles, Valle de la Muerte (Valley of Death) was thrust upward from the earth's crust 23 million years ago during the violent upheaval that created the Andes. This valley's death tag is no misnomer – though rich in mineral deposits, it is one of the driest, most inhospitable places on the planet and no known life exists here. Guided tours to Valle de la Luna stop briefly en route at Valle de la Muerte. Travelers with more time can join horseback excursions, including full-moon rides, as well as trekking expeditions from San Pedro de Atacama. Treks feature sandboarding runs down the valley's great dunes.

Antofagasta ㉖

Road Map B3. 194 miles (313 km) SW of San Pedro de Atacama. *297,000.* *Aeropuerto Cerro Moreno.* *Ave. Prat 384; (055) 451819.* *El Día del Aniversario de Antofagasta (mid-Feb).* **www**.municipalidaddeantofagasta.cl

A historic port-city, Antofagasta is the sea outlet for the metals and minerals mined in the Atacama desert. Founded in 1869 as part of Bolivia, it was absorbed by Chile in the War of the Pacific (1879–83) and used to ship silver, nitrates and, from 1915, copper from the great Chuquicamata mine (*see p170*). Chile's most progressive city by the 1930s, it appears today as a somewhat grimy place, but there is still plenty of historic charm.

Set in the city center, the Neo-Gothic cathedral dates from 1917 and faces the Plaza Colón. The clock tower adorning the plaza was donated in 1910 by the city's English community and is a tangible reminder of British influence in Antofagasta. Just

Ruinas de Huanchaca, with Antofagasta's tower blocks in the backdrop

north of the plaza, the former Customs House, dating from 1869, is home to the **Museo Regional de Antofagasta**. The museum's collection of over 9,000 objects includes fossils from the region, objects salvaged from the old nitrate mines, and period furniture.

At the end of the same road is **Ex-Estación El Ferrocarril de Antofagasta a Bolivia**, the city's disused train station. Built in 1873 using British capital, this was the terminus for the Antofagasta-Bolivia railway. It conserves Scottish steam trains, English clocks, and red telephone boxes. Trains carrying copper from the Chuquicamata mine still pass through this station on their way to the port. Also near the port is the **Muelle Histórico Salitrero** (Nitrates Wharf), which dates from 1872, and the Terminal Pesquero, Antofagasta's rustic fish market. The roof of the market forms the perch for dozens of pelicans.

Facing the Pacific Ocean, some 5 miles (8 km) south of the city center, are the massive stone remnants of a silver refinery dating from 1888–92. Known as the **Ruinas de Huanchaca**, this fascinating and intact site occupies a desert hillside in stepped terraces, and features a steep central staircase, a round tower, narrow passageways, and rows of stone storehouses. The Casino Enjoy Antofagasta, opposite the ruins, runs tours (including night tours) for visitors. The casino's glitzy architecture mirrors the ruins with a round tower and terraced façade that lends a quasi-Aztecan symmetry to this site.

A small on-site museum displays geological, archaeological, and anthropological objects, including antique silver-refining machinery.

Museo Regional de Antofagasta
Balmaceda 2786. ***Tel** (055) 227016.*
9am–5pm Tue–Fri, 11am–2pm Sat & Sun. **www** dibam.cl

Ex-Estación El Ferrocarril de Antofagasta a Bolivia
Bolívar 255. ***Tel** (055) 206101.*
9am–6:30pm daily.

Ruinas de Huanchaca
Ruta 5, Lado Sur. ***Tel** (055) 653000.*
from Antofagasta. from Antofagasta. daily.
www.hoteldellago.cl

La Portada 27

Road Map B3. 10 miles (16 km) N of Antofagasta; Ruta 5, Lado Norte. *from Antofagasta. from Plaza Colón in Antofagasta. Mar–Dec: daily.*

A natural spectacle, La Portada (The Gateway) is a rock arch that faces dramatic coastline. The arch, eroded over seven million years, is visible from two distinct coastal trails – the first runs along the top of facing cliffs and offers panoramic views of arch and coast; the second descends these high cliffs to cross dramatic beaches to the foot of the archway.

Cerro Paranal Observatory 28

Road Map B3. 75 miles (120 km) S of Antofagasta; Cerro Paranal, B-70 Old Pan-American Highway. ***Tel** (055) 435335. from Antofagasta.*
Jan–Nov: 2pm Sat, 10am & 2pm Sun; last two weekends of the month only. mandatory. **www**.eso.cl

The world's most advanced astronomical facility, the Cerro Paranal Observatory is housed in a futuristic complex of brilliant-white buildings, sharp lines, and curved domes. This state-of-the-art observatory stands at 8,500 ft (2,600 m) above sea level atop Cerro Paranal and is overseen by the European Southern Observatory (ESO). Its star attraction is the **Very Large Telescope** (VLT). The world's most powerful optical instrument, the VLT comprises four separate telescopes that combine to form one gigantic lens measuring 650 ft (200 m) in diameter. This lens can define objects four billion times fainter than any that are visible to the naked eye – that is the equivalent of distinguishing car headlights from the surface of the moon. Fascinating 2-hour guided tours follow a presentation on astronomy with visits to the VLT and its control room.

Stargazing facilities at the Cerro Paranal Observatory

Shoreline of La Piscina, a stretch along the Bahía Inglesa, south of Caldera

Copiapó 29

Road Map B4. 351 miles (566 km) S of Antofagata. *120,000.* *Sernatur, Los Carrera 691; (052) 212838.* *Festival de la Virgen de la Candelaria (Feb).* **www**.copiapo.cl

Capital of Chile's Atacama (III) region, Copiapó is a low-key city whose attractions are linked to its silver-mining heritage. Silver was first found here in 1832 by the muleteer Juan Godoy. His statue stands in a plaza fronting the Iglesia de San Francisco, an 1872 church with ornate paintings. Chile's first (and now defunct) railway was built in 1851 to take silver from Copiapó to the port at Caldera, and silver built the lovely wooden buildings from the 1800s that survive on Avenida Manuel Matta.

Copiapó is centered around a plaza, which is fronted by a wooden cathedral from 1851. The Neo-Classical design of this edifice features an unusual three-tiered bell tower. Set at the city's western end is its grandest mansion, the **Palacio Viña de Cristo**, built in 1860 in the Georgian style for a silver baron. The city's two museums, **Museo Mineralógico** and **Museo Regional de Atacama**, recount the Atacama region's history and mineral wealth.

Museo Mineralógico
Colipi 333. ***Tel*** *(052) 206606.*
10am–1pm & 3:30–7pm Mon–Fri; 10am–1pm Sat.

Museo Regional de Atacama
Atacama 98. ***Tel*** *(052) 212313.*
daily; see website for details.
Sun free. *with reservation only.* **www**.dibam.cl

Caldera 30

Road Map B4. 50 miles (80 km) W of Copiapó. *14,000.* *Plaza Carlos Condell; (052) 316076.* *Sat.* *La Fiesta de Recreación (mid-Jul).* **www**.caldera.cl

The colorful harbor-town of Caldera grew in the late 1800s as a port for shipping silver brought in by the railway from Copiapó. Today, it has a picturesque waterfront of sparkling ocean and sandy beaches where pelicans congregate. On the waterfront, the **Terminal Pesquero** is the fishermen's harbor and market, where small ma-and-pa eateries serve fresh seafood specialties. Located next to it, the **Museo Palaeontológico** is housed in Caldera's recycled railway station, built in 1850, and displays mammoth marine fossils. Its standout exhibit is a fossilized skull of a bearded whale that lived 10 million years ago. A short walk south of the museum is an Easter Island *moai* facing the sea on Caldera's waterfront. At the heart of the town, the Neo-Gothic 1862 **Iglesia de San Vicente de Paul** overlooks the plaza. Its interior contains an image of the Virgin of Dolores, patron saint of the Peruvian army, plundered by Chilean forces during the War of the Pacific (1879–83).

Environs

Just south of Caldera is northern Chile's most beautiful beach, named **Bahía Inglesa** (English Bay) for the swashbuckling English pirates and corsairs who dropped anchor here during the 17th century. This magical long sweep of bleach-white sand is fronted by a turquoise ocean, rolling white waves, and blissfully little construction save a smattering of upscale hotels and restaurants.

Museo Palaeontológico
Centro Cultural Estación Caldera, Wheelwright s/n. ***Tel*** *(052) 535604.*
Jan–Feb: 10am–2pm & 4–10pm Tue–Sun; Mar–Dec: 10am–2pm & 4–8pm Tue–Sun. *on request.*

Bahía Inglesa
4 miles (6 km) S of Caldera. *next to Hotel Rocas de Bahía.* **www**.bahiainglesa.com

Parque Nacional Pan de Azúcar 31

Road Map B4. 120 miles (194 km) NW of Copiapó; Ruta C-120, Km27 de Chañaral. *from Copiapó.* **www**.conaf.cl

Created in 1985 to protect 169 sq miles (438 sq km) of coastal desert, this park has

Desert scenery in Parque Nacional Pan de Azúcar

For hotels and restaurants in this region see pp280–81 and pp300–301

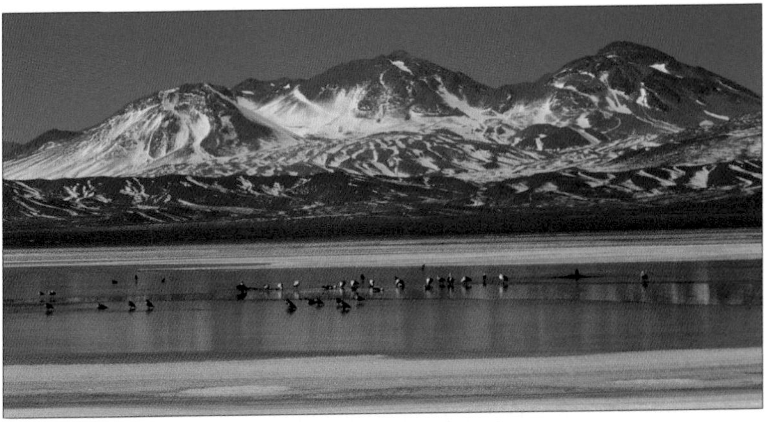

A flock of birds on Laguna Santa Rosa, in Parque Nacional Nevado de Tres Cruces

long white beaches, sheltered coves, and vertiginous sand cliffs. The dramatic coastline plays refuge to magnificent, easily sighted marine fauna. Dolphins, southern sea lions, Humboldt penguins, gulls, cormorants, and pelicans populate the shoreline. Coastal attractions include the offshore **Isla Pan de Azúcar**, a refuge to penguins and other seabirds, that is reached by boat excursion; and **Caleta Pan de Azúcar**, a picturesque fishermen's hamlet with campsites and cabins. Farther inland the flora and fauna includes guanacos, foxes, eagles, condors, and over 20 species of cactus. Scenic highlights include the Quebrada del Castillo and Quebrada Pan de Azúcar canyons; as well as the Mirador and Las Lomitas viewpoints, which offer vistas of desert, coast, and the blue ocean.

Parque Nacional Nevado de Tres Cruces ㉜

Road Map B4. 94 miles (151 km) E of Copiapó. ***Tel*** *(052) 213404.* *4WD from Copiapó.* *CONAF, Laguna del Negro Francisco.* *8:30am–6pm daily.* *from Copiapó.* **www**.conaf.cl

This remote but stunning national park conserves some 228 sq miles (591 sq km) of altiplano wilderness typified by brilliantly colored lakes, snowy volcanoes, and abundant native fauna. Most visits focus on the northern sector, where **Laguna Santa Rosa**, an intensely blue saltwater lake, fills a depression ringed by the snowy peaks of the Nevados de Tres Cruces massif. Next to the lake, the dazzlingly white Salar de Maricunga is Chile's southernmost salt flat.

Accessed via a 4WD route from Laguna Santa Rosa, the park's southern sector is less visited. Its greatest natural feature is **Laguna del Negro Francisco**, a lake with mirror-like waters which reflect the pointed cone of Volcán Copiapó and the giant wings of flapping flamingos. Chile's three flamingo species are present on the lakeshore here, part of a wildlife bonanza that features some 30 bird species and easily sighted mammals, including vicuñas, guanacos, vizcachas, and Andean foxes.

Sea lion resting at the Isla Pan de Azúcar

Vicuñas on the altiplano at Parque Nacional Nevado de Tres Cruces

Walking trails circle around Laguna Santa Rosa and Laguna del Negro Francisco, where a 12-bed CONAF *refugio* offers lodging and hot showers.

Laguna Verde ㉝

Road Map C4. 164 miles (265 km) NE of Copiapó. *along the CH31 toward the San Francisco border pass to Argentina.* *Cernatur, Los Carrera 691, Copiapó; (052) 212838.* *from Copiapó.* **Volcán Ojos del Salado** *Oct–Mar.*

Located high in the Andes, at 13,780 ft (4,200 m) above sea level, Laguna Verde is a breathtaking lake of green and turquoise tones that change hue according to the light and time of day. On the lake's western shore, rustic hot springs provide blissful relaxation. Mighty volcanoes, including El Muerto, Peña Blanca, Incahuasi, Barrancas Blancas, and Vicuñas, encircle the area. Their snowy peaks and the brown, red, and ochre tones of their flanks complete an artist's palette of sharply contrasting colors. However, most of these peaks are challenging and hard to climb.

At 22,609 ft (6,893m), **Volcán Ojos del Salado** towers over the southern basin of Laguna Verde. This is the world's highest active volcano as well as Chile's highest peak. The climb to its summit is physically challenging but technically undemanding.

La Serena 34

Statue, Plaza de Armas

Founded in 1544, La Serena is Chile's second oldest city and one of its biggest coastal resorts. Soon after it was established, the city was destroyed in an Indian attack, resettled in 1549, and later sacked by pirates, most famously by England's Bartholomew Sharp. Today, at La Serena's historical heart, the bell towers of Colonial stone churches ring out amid beautiful Spanish architecture. On the coast are golden beaches and rolling white waves, with modern buildings lining the avenues. Situated at the mouth of Río Elqui, La Serena is also the gateway to the lush Valle del Elqui.

Granite fountain at the center of Plaza de Armas

Plaza de Armas

Casa Gabriel González Videla Matta 499. ***Tel*** *(051) 215082.* *10am–6pm Mon–Fri, 10am–1pm Sat.* *on request, in Spanish only.*

La Serena's central plaza marks the site of the city's second founding by conquistador Francisco de Aguirre (1507–81). Located here is the limestone Catedral de La Serena as well as the Neo-Colonial Tribunales de la Justicia (Law Courts) and Municipalidad (City Hall). Both date from the 1930s and have extravagant red-and-white exteriors. A Modernist granite fountain by Chilean sculptor Román Rojas adorns the center of this square. On a corner of the plaza is the 19th-century mansion-house **Casa Gabriel González Videla**, family home of the former Chilean president whose name it bears. The mansion's first floor displays personal objects of the late president, and a regional historical museum occupies the floor upstairs.

Catedral de La Serena

Plaza de Armas. **Museo Sala de Arte Religioso** Los Carrera 450. ***Tel*** *(051) 225388.* *Dec–Mar: 10am–2pm & 5–8pm Mon–Fri, 10am–1pm Sat; Apr–Nov: 10am–2pm & 4–7pm Mon–Fri, 10am–1pm Sat.*

Catedral de La Serena

The Neo-Classical façade and proud, prow-like tower of La Serena's cathedral stand majestically over the Plaza de Armas. Built from limestone under the direction of French architect Juan Herbage in 1844, this cathedral preserves the tomb of conquistador Francisco de Aguirre. The building itself stands on the site of a previous cathedral destroyed in 1680 by English pirate Bartholomew Sharp, who sacked the city over three days before razing it to the ground. Beautiful stained-glass windows from France ornament the cathedral's walls. Located on the building's grounds, the **Museo Sala de Arte Religioso** displays religious art and objects from the 17th to 19th centuries.

Iglesia de San Francisco

Balmaceda 640. ***Tel*** *(051) 224477.* *8am–1pm & 4–9pm Tue–Fri.*
Museo de Arte Religioso *10am–1pm & 4–7pm Tue & Thu.*

Built between 1590 and 1627, the Iglesia de San Francisco is the oldest of La Serena's stone churches, and the only one of the city's temples to escape destruction at the hands of the pirate Sharp. The church is crowned by a bell tower and cupola, and its exterior walls are flamboyantly carved with Baroque motifs: a design that is considered mestizo for its South American influences. Adjacent to the church, the **Museo de Arte Religioso** holds a collection of religious art and imagery dating from the arrival of the Franciscan Order to Chile in the 16th century, including a bible penned in 1538.

Museo Arqueológico

Cordovez, esq. Cienfuegos. ***Tel*** *(051) 224492.* *9:30am–6pm Tue–Fri, 10am–1pm & 4–7pm Sat, 10am–1pm Sun.* *on request, in Spanish only.* **www**.dibam.cl

Entered via an 18th-century Baroque portal, La Serena's archaeological museum displays pre-Columbian objects from Norte Chico, Norte Grande, and Easter Island. Artifacts include petroglyphs carved by the Molle civilization (AD 1–700) and ceramics painted by the Diaguita between AD 1000 and 1536. The most eye-catching exhibits include the 1,500-year-old mummy of a contorted body dug up in the Atacama desert close to Chiu-Chiu *(see p170)*, and a 10-ft (3-m) tall *moai* from Easter Island.

Baroque entrance to the city's Museo Arqueológico

DESIERTO FLORIDO

Glory-of-the-sun in the Desierto Florido

Every 4–5 years, the sparse rainfall on a section of the Atacama causes dormant seeds beneath the sands to explode into a profusion of life and color in a phenomenon called the Desierto Florido (Flowering Desert). When this happens, the monochrome desert floor turns overnight into a carpet of flamboyant flowers of vibrant blues, purples, yellows, and reds that attracts a rich bird and insect life, as well as thousands of visitors from across Chile. It is impossible to predict the year of the Desierto Florido, only that it occurs between September and November. It last happened in 2008.

Museo Mineralógico

Benavente 980. ***Tel*** *(051) 204096.*
Mar–Jan: 9:30am–12:30pm Mon–Fri; Feb: 9:30am–2pm Mon–Fri.
non-Chileans only. *on request, in Spanish only.*

Set in the Universidad de La Serena, the museum of mining and metallurgy features over 2,000 mineral and rock samples collected by Polish mineralogist Ignacio Domeyko, who arrived to Chile at the height of its 19th-century mining boom. Displays include samples from each of Chile's major mining zones and exhibits of all their minerals, from gold to magnesium, which glitter and shine in glass display boxes. The most compelling exhibits are great boulder-sized, multicolored crystallized rock samples, and a meteorite that crashed into the Atacama desert in 1861. Displays also include mineral samples collected from Europe, Asia, and Africa.

View of the modern city blocks and sandy beach at La Serena

VISITORS' CHECKLIST

Road Map B5. 435 miles (700 km) S of Antofagasta. *160,000.* *Aeropuerto La Florida.* *Sernatur, Matta 461; (051) 225138.* *Aniversario de La Serena (end Aug).* **www**.turismolaserena.cl

Avenida del Mar

La Serena's 4-mile (6-km) long coastal boulevard is the city's thriving restaurant and bar zone. The avenue, lined by sandy beaches and big white waves on one side and by modern hotels, apartment blocks, bars, and restaurants on the other, is a frenzy of day- and night-time activity in summer. In the off-peak season, it offers dramatic sea walks, especially at sunset. A 20-minute walk from the center, west along the city's main Avenida Francisco de Aguirre, leads to **El Faro Monumental**, a lighthouse marking the northern end of Avenida del Mar. Beaches around this area are rustic, with big waves that attract surfers. Just south of the lighthouse are the main bathing beaches, **Playa 4 Esquinas** and **Playa Canto del Agua**, with plenty of bars and restaurants.

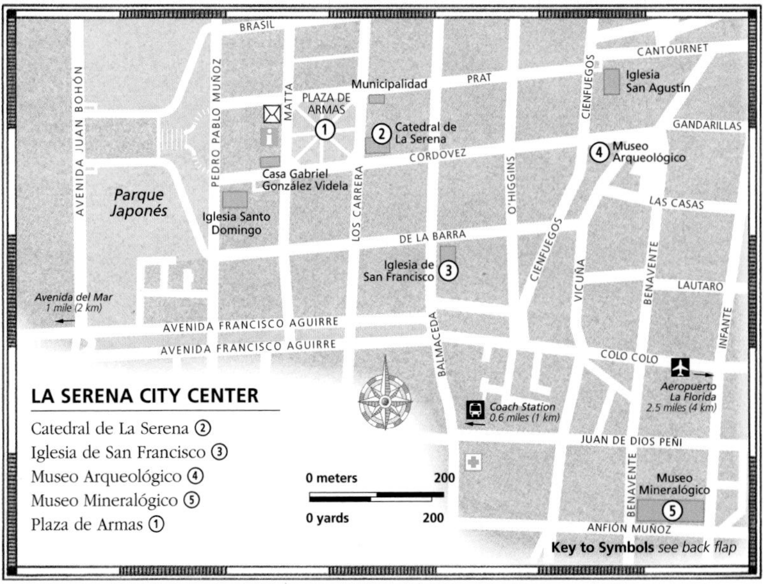

Vicuña 35

Road Map B5. 39 miles (63 km) E of La Serena. *24,000.* *Gabriela Mistral, esq. San Martín; (051) 419105.* *Fiesta de la Vendimia (Feb).* **www**.munivicuña.cl

Set in the valley of Río Elqui, Vicuña is a small town of adobe houses ringed by rippled mountains. Birthplace of Chile's Nobel-prize-winning poet, Gabriela Mistral *(see p26)*, it is a popular pilgrimage site for writers and artists. The **Museo Gabriela Mistral** displays personal items of the celebrated poet, including books, paintings, and awards. At the center of town, sculptures inspired by Mistral's works adorn Vicuña's plaza. Overlooking the plaza is the landmark **Torre Bauer**, an incongruous yet charming, red Bavarian tower. It was constructed in 1905 at the behest of Vicuña's former mayor of German descent, Alfonso Bauer. Adjacent to the tower, the *cabildo* (town hall) dates from 1826 and houses a small, historically themed museum as well as an information office for visitors. Also bordering the plaza, the **Iglesia de la Concepción** was built in 1909 and has a luminous interior with beautiful frescoes on the ceiling. The font here was used to baptize Mistral in 1889.

Located two blocks east of the plaza, the **Museo Casa El Solar de los Madariaga** is a restored adobe house from 1875 with period furnishings, photographs, and artifacts. At the edge of town is **Planta Capel**, Chile's biggest *pisco* distillery. Guided tours take visitors to its vineyards, plant facilities, and a *pisco* museum, and end with tastings.

Painted façade and tapering steeple of Iglesia de la Concepción, Vicuña

Museo Gabriela Mistral
Gabriela Mistral 759. ***Tel*** *(051) 411223.* *Jan–Feb: 10am–7pm Mon–Sat, 10am–6pm Sun; Mar–Dec: 10am–5:45pm Mon–Fri, 10:30am–6pm Sat, 10am–1pm Sun.* **www**.dibam.cl

Museo Casa El Solar de los Madariaga
Gabriela Mistral 683. ***Tel*** *(051) 411220.* *Dec–Mar: 10am–7:30pm daily; Apr–Nov: 10am–6:30pm daily.* *on request; in Spanish, English, & French.*

Planta Capel
Camino a Peralillo s/n. ***Tel*** *(051) 554396.* *Jan–Feb: 10am–6pm daily; Mar–Dec: 10am–12:30pm, 2:30–6pm Tue–Sun.* **www**.piscocapel.cl

Cerro Mamalluca Observatory 36

Road Map B5. 6 miles (9 km) NE of Vicuña. *Gabriela Mistral 260, Vicuña; (051) 411352.* *mandatory; reservations & departures at observatory's information center in Vicuña.* **www**.mamalluca.org

One of the greatest attractions of visiting Valle del Elqui is stargazing at the fascinating Cerro Mamalluca Observatory. A futuristic complex of enormous telescopes and white domed buildings that sit like giant golf balls on the mountainside, this observatory overlooks the nearby town of Vicuña from Cerro Mamalluca. The facility is seen on guided tours that are conducted in English and Spanish and last up to 2 hours. During the tour, visitors can observe the Milky Way, star constellations thousands of light years away, planets, nebulae and clusters, as well as blue and red stars, through the lens of powerful telescopes. Other highlights of the visit include watching the rings on Jupiter and Saturn, and craters on the surface of the moon, all of which appear with a crisp, photographic clarity in a night sky that is regarded as one of the clearest in the world.

A hi-tech and fun visual presentation precedes the telescopic gazing. Visitors can choose from a presentation on the planets, stars, and the universe, or on the ancient cosmology of this region's indigenous peoples.

Part of the Cerro Mamalluca Observatory complex near Vicuña, Valle del Elqui

Statue honoring poet Gabriela Mistral in Montegrande

Montegrande 37

Road Map B5. 63 miles (101 km) E of La Serena. *600.* *from La Serena & Vicuña.*

The tiny Andean village of Montegrande lies at the eastern, exceptionally scenic, end of Valle del Elqui at 3,600 ft (1,100 m) above sea level. Here, the valley narrows to a width of just 1,312 ft (400 m) and is surrounded by the steep, arid slopes of the Andean pre-cordillera, behind which the snowcapped peaks of the mighty Andean mountain range form a backdrop.

Montegrande was also the hamlet where poet Gabriela Mistral spent her childhood, having moved here from Vicuña with her mother and stepsister when she was three years old. The small adobe house in which Mistral grew up is preserved as the **Museo de Sitio Casa-Escuela Gabriela Mistral**. The house doubled as the village school when Mistral lived here and includes furniture and personal belongings of the poet.

Prior to her death from cancer in 1957, Mistral had requested that she be laid to rest in her "beloved Montegrande"; her tomb lies on the crest of a low hill near the village plaza. Facing this small tree-lined plaza is an adobe church. Built in 1879, it is crowned by a tall bell tower. Mistral took her first communion in its highly decorative interior.

Museo de Sitio Casa-Escuela Gabriela Mistral
Dec–Mar: 10am–1pm & 3–6pm Tue–Sun; Apr–Nov: 10am–1pm & 3–7pm Tue–Sun.

Pisco Elqui 38

Road Map B5. 65 miles (105 km) SE of La Serena. *500.* *from La Serena & Montegrande.*

Set 4,100 ft (1,250 m) above sea level, Pisco Elqui is one of the prettiest villages of Valle del Elqui. It was originally christened La Unión by the Spanish, but renamed in 1936 as part of a government initiative to boost the area's most famous commodity, *pisco*. Among the best-known distilleries here is the **Destileria Pisco Mistral**, formerly the Solar de Pisco Tres Erres. Set facing the plaza, this facility has been making *pisco* for over a century. Guided tours take visitors to its *pisco* museum and to the production, barrelling, and bottling salons, and end with tastings.

An architectural hightlight of the village is the **Iglesia Nuestra Señora de Rosario**, whose elegant wooden tower rises above the lush plaza. A web of streets with lodgings is spread around this square.

Destileria Pisco Mistral
O'Higgins 746. ***Tel*** *(051) 451358.*
Jan–Feb: 11:30am–7:30pm daily; Mar–Dec: 10:30am–6pm Tue–Sun.
hourly.
www.piscomistral.cl

Sprawling *pisco* vineyards on the slopes of Pisco Elqui

PISCO

First developed by Spanish settlers in the 16th century, *pisco* is an aromatic, fruity brandy made from distilled Muscat grape wine. Chile's unrivalled national drink, it is commonly consumed as pisco sour, a refreshing aperitif made by mixing *pisco*, lemon juice, and sugar. It is also drunk neat and as piscola, a fashionable highball cocktail that mixes *pisco* with cola and is a favorite among nightclubbing Chileans. Travelers can taste *pisco* in its many guises during visits to distilleries in the Valle del Elqui.

Bottled *pisco* produced at Planta Capel in the Valle del Elqui

Ovalle ㊴

Road Map B5. 53 miles (86 km) S of La Serena. 98,100. *Victoria, esq. Independencia; (053) 622108.* *La Fiesta de Vendimia (Mar).* **www**.ovalleencantonativo.cl

Little visited, Valle del Limarí is a fertile area of orchards and farms that feeds much of the arid Norte Chico. The valley's largest settlement is Ovalle, a small city ringed by monochrome peaks. Farmers from the valley sell their produce at **Feria Modelo de Ovalle**, the city's great food market. On any day, the floor space is stacked with rows of spices, mounds of goat's cheese, fruit pyramids, and hanging fish. In the city center, the **Iglesia de San Vicente Ferrer** faces Ovalle's tree-lined plaza. Built in 1888, it has a strikingly tall bell tower and an ornate interior. The city's big draw is the outstanding **Museo del Limarí** which exhibits pre-Hispanic items from the local area and features Chile's most impressive displays of Diaguita ceramics (AD 1000–1536).

Environs

Ovalle is a springboard for visits to Valle del Limarí's wineries and villages. West of the city is the picturesque oasis village of **Barraza**, with narrow adobe streets and a church that dates from 1681. The upright tombs of former priests are encased in its adobe walls. Also in the western sector are the wineries **Viña Tabalí** and **Viña Casa Tamaya**, which open for tours and tastings. North of Ovalle, the **Hacienda Los Andes** is a horse-riding ranch with Colonial-style rooms, a large nature reserve, and trails to an abandoned gold mine. Some 2 miles (3 km) north of this ranch, **Hurtado** is a beautiful village of fruit orchards which specializes in semitropical fruits and jams.

One of the historic lava caves at Monumento Natural Pichasca

Museo del Limarí
Covarrubias, esq. Antofagasta, Ovalle. ***Tel*** *(053) 433680.* *9am–6pm Tue–Fri, 10am–1pm Sat & Sun.* *Sun free.* *on request.* **www**.museolimari.cl

Viña Tabalí
Hacienda Santa Rosa de Tabalí, Ruta Valle del Encanto. ***Tel*** *(02) 4775535.* *10am–6pm Mon–Fri; on request Sat & Sun.* **www**.tabali.com

Viña Casa Tamaya
Camino Quebrada Seca Km 9, Ovalle. ***Tel*** *(053) 686014.* **www**.tamaya.cl

Hacienda Los Andes
Río Hurtado, Hurtado. ***Tel*** *(053) 691822.* **www**.haciendalosandes.com

Monumento Natural Pichasca ㊵

Road Map B5. 34 miles (55 km) NE of Ovalle, Valle del Limarí. ***Tel*** *(09) 89230010.* *from Ovalle up to 3 miles (5 km) before entrance.* *9am–6pm daily.* *from Ovalle.* **www**.conaf.cl

Rich in palaeontological and archaeological finds, the Monumento Natural Pichasca is a site with petrified forests of fossilized tree trunks, gigantic dinosaur fossils, and 11,000-year-old rock paintings in ancient lava caves. The area was also a refuge for hunter-gatherers around 8000 BC. Tours begin at a visitors' center that has displays on the area's fauna, flora, palaeontology, and archaeology. From here, a 2-mile (3-km) long walking trail explores the site, which also includes life-size replicas of the gigantic dinosaurs that once roamed this region.

The tree-shaded Plaza de Armas at Ovalle

For hotels and restaurants in this region see pp280–81 and pp300–301

Monumento Nacional Valle del Encanto 41

Road Map B5. 16 miles (25 km) SW of Ovalle; D45, Valle del Encanto. ***Tel*** *(09) 4685400.* *from Ovalle to 3 miles (5 km) from entrance.* *Jan–Feb: 8:30am–8pm daily; Mar–Dec: 8:30am–6pm daily.* *from Ovalle.*

An ancient ceremonial and hunting ground, this site has Chile's finest collection of El Molle petroglyphs, dating from around AD 700. Viewed from a marked circuit, there are more than 30 petroglyphs, etched on to rockfaces using sharp stones. Most are line drawings depicting human, zoomorphic, abstract, and geometric shapes. The human portraits are most interesting: entire families are shown in various poses with fingers pointing upward at the sun or downward, at Mother Earth. The shamans and deities in these carvings are crowned with tiaras and headdresses. The petroglyphs are best seen at noon, when the sharp mid-day light shows them at their most impressive.

Piedras tacitas **in Valle del Encanto**

Another enigmatic highlight of the site is the *piedras tacitas* – slabs of flat rock gouged with large patterns of identical, circular, and deep holes that align with nighttime star constellations. Experts have several theories on their existence – that they were used for preparing hallucinogens, or offerings to gods; or that they were filled with water to create terrestrial reflections of the constellations. Travelers can camp under the stars.

Termas de Socos 42

Road Map B6. 24 miles (38 km) SW of Ovalle; Panamericana Norte, Km370. ***Tel*** *(053) 1982505.* *8:30am–7pm daily (spa).* **www**.termasocos.cl

Encircled by rugged canyons in the Valle del Limarí, Termas de Socos is a family-owned spa retreat open to day and overnight visitors. Its amenities include massage treatments, saunas, thermal baths, and an exterior pool that is ringed by cacti as well as pepper and eucalyptus trees. There is a rustic but refined feel to this place – poolside vistas rise to rocky canyons, wild honey grows in the spa's ample gardens, hummingbirds abound, and guests are accommodated in comfortable, woody rooms. For budget travelers, there is a separate campsite with its own thermal baths. Staff run trips to Monumento Nacional Valle del Encanto and Parque Nacional Bosque Fray Jorge. At night, guests can gaze at the stars from this spa's canyon-top observatory.

Parque Nacional Bosque Fray Jorge 43

Road Map B5. 56 miles (90 km) W of Ovalle; Km26 de la Ruta Patrimonial. ***Tel*** *(09) 3462706.* *from Ovalle & La Serena.* *9am–4pm daily.* *CONAF, park entrance.* **www**.conaf.cl

The highlight of this UNESCO biosphere reserve is a relictual Valdivian rain forest – a remnant of the temperate rain forest that cloaked all Norte Chico prior to the southward advancement of the Atacama desert, some 30,000 years ago. The forest is located in the park's western sector, on the 1,600-ft (500-m) high cloud summit of Cerro Concovado. Indeed, it owes its freak and continued existence to the high rainfall that hits the mountain peak each year – around 47 inches (120 cm) per year compared with just 4 inches (10 cm) on the semi-arid lowlands directly to the mountain's east. The park is at its most impressive between October and December, when, after heavy rainfall, the forest floor is carpeted with brightly colored flowers.

Boardwalk through the forest at Parque Nacional Bosque Fray Jorge

A vehicle route and a 6-mile (10-km) long walking trail strike out for the summit from the park entrance, where a CONAF center has displays on the area's flora. At the peak, a short boardwalk traverses the lush forest. Visitors who time their walk up the slope for mid-morning will see the park at its best, with mist shrouding the rain forest.

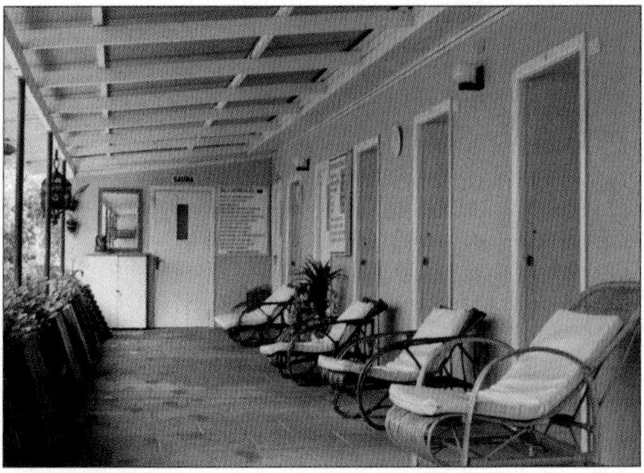

A veranda with cane furnishings at the Termas de Socos

LAKE DISTRICT AND CHILOÉ

Named for the string of blue lakes that spreads across its entirety, Chile's Lake District features emerald forests, smoldering volcanoes, bubbling thermal springs, and tumbling rivers and waterfalls. Immediately south of the district, and separated from it by a narrow channel, lies enchanting Chiloé, an island archipelago of misty bays, quaint palafitos, *and historic Jesuit churches.*

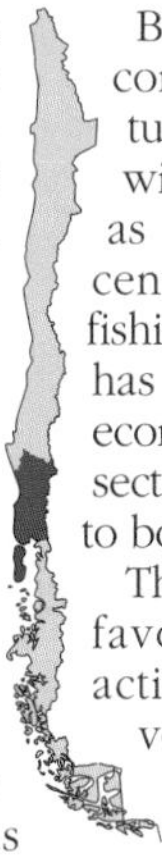

The Lake District is bounded to its north by the Río Bío-Bío and to its south by the Canal Chacao, the sea-channel that links it to the Chiloé archipelago. In pre-Columbian times, the Lake District was populated by Mapuche communities, and Chiloé, by the seafaring Chono. The Spanish arrived in 1552 and established what are today the region's largest cities, including Valdivia, Villarrica, and Osorno. However, much of the area remained a Mapuche stronghold until independence, when Chile launched the Araucanian wars *(see p45)* to supress all indigenous resistance. Subsequently, the area opened up to European immigrants, notably German settlers, who greatly influenced the architecture, art, and cuisine of the urban centers they established in the Lake District.

By the late 19th century, railroad construction had sparked agriculture, forestry, and port industries, with the city of Temuco emerging as Lake District's main commercial center. In the Chiloé archipelago, fishing, in particular salmon farming, has always been the bedrock of the economy. Today, a booming tourism sector has brought added prosperity to both the Lake District and Chiloé.

The region's national parks are a favored destination for outdoor activities, including skiing down volcano slopes and horse riding through ancient araucaria (monkey-puzzle) forests. These parks are accessible from lakeshore towns that also offer splendid examples of Teutonic-style architecture, while the Chiloé archipelago fascinates with its rich mythology, distinct cuisine, and vibrant festivals.

The wooden 17th-century Jesuit church of Degan in Ancud, Chiloé

◁ **Serene Lago Verde encircled by forests of native araucaria, Parque Nacional Huerquehue**

Exploring Lake District and Chiloé

The Andean foothills in the Lake District's eastern section embrace lake, volcano, and forest scenery in reserves such as Parque Nacional Conguillío, Parque Nacional Vicente Pérez Rosales, and Parque Nacional Villarrica. Lakeshore towns and cities provide ideal stopovers: Pucón is the area's adventure-tourism capital, Frutillar and Puerto Varas its German heartland, and Temuco and Villarrica its historic Mapuche towns. West of the mountains, the land dips, crossing a central valley to the Pacific coast, to Valdivia, a beautiful port-city encircled by historic fortresses. Farther south, a short ferry ride from the city of Puerto Montt leads to the Chiloé archipelago, where Jesuit churches alternate with wooden *palafitos*.

Rafting on Río Petrohué, Parque Nacional Vicente Pérez Rosales

SIGHTS AT A GLANCE

SEE ALSO

- ***Where to Stay*** pp281–3
- ***Where to Eat*** pp302–303

Castro's colorful houses on stilts lining the water's edge, Chiloé

GETTING AROUND

The well-paved Pan-American Highway (Ruta 5) runs through the Lake District, making traveling by bus the best way to explore the area. Long-distance buses link major cities, while smaller *micros* connect lakeshore towns with major national parks, although a sturdy car, preferably a 4WD, is needed to reach more distant destinations in the Andean foothills. Daily flights connect Santiago to the airports at Temuco and Puerto Montt. From Puerto Montt, ferries take buses across Canal Chacao to Chiloé. Frequent bus and ferry services link sites in the archipelago.

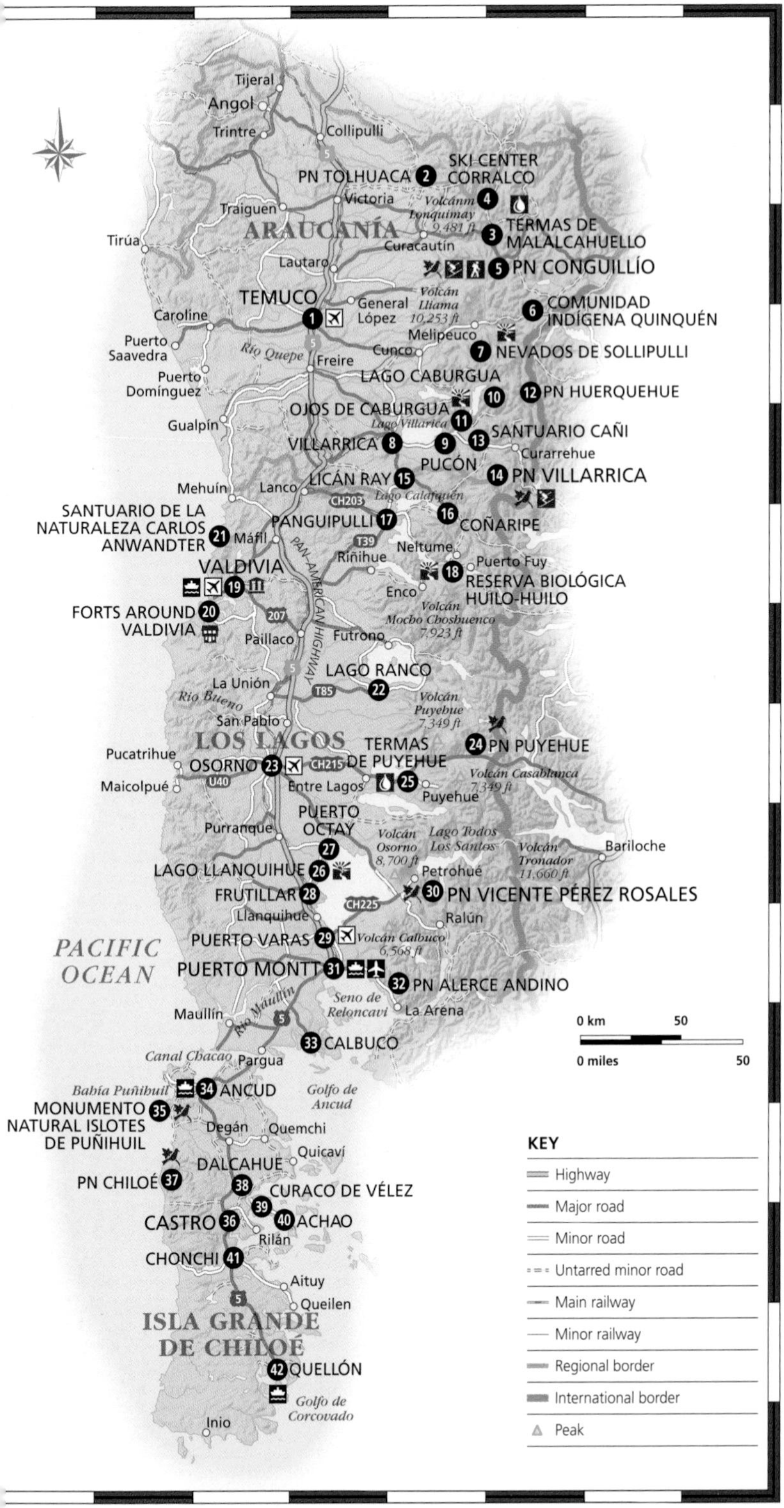
Tijeral
Angol
Trintre
Collipulli
PN TOLHUACA 2
SKI CENTER CORRALCO
Victoria
Traiguen
Volcánm Lonquimay 9,481 ft
4
3 TERMAS DE MALALCAHUELLO
Tirúa
ARAUCANÍA
Curacautín
Lautaro
5 PN CONGUILLÍO
TEMUCO
1
General López
Volcán Llaima 10,253 ft
6 COMUNIDAD INDÍGENA QUINQUÉN
Caroline
Puerto Saavedra
Río Quepe
Freire
Cunco
Melipeuco
7 NEVADOS DE SOLLIPULLI
Puerto Domínguez
LAGO CABURGUA
10
12 PN HUERQUEHUE
OJOS DE CABURGUA
11
Lago Villarica
Gualpín
13 SANTUARIO CAÑI
VILLARRICA 8
9
Curarrehue
PUCÓN
14 PN VILLARRICA
LICÁN RAY 15
Mehuín
Lanco
CH203
Lago Calafquén
16
SANTUARIO DE LA NATURALEZA CARLOS ANWANDTER 21
Máfil
PANGUIPULLI 17
COÑARIPE
T39
Neltume
Riñihue
PAN-AMERICAN HIGHWAY
VALDIVIA
Puerto Fuy
18
19
RESERVA BIOLÓGICA HUILO-HUILO
Enco
FORTS AROUND VALDIVIA 20
207
Volcán Mocho Choshuenco 7,923 ft
Paillaco
Futrono
LAGO RANCO
La Unión
Río Bueno
T85
22
Volcán Puyehue 7,349 ft
San Pablo
LOS LAGOS
TERMAS DE PUYEHUE
24 PN PUYEHUE
Pucatrihue
OSORNO 23
CH215
Maicolpué
U40
Entre Lagos
25
Volcán Casablanca 7,349 ft
Puyehue
PUERTO OCTAY
Purranque
Volcán Osorno 8,700 ft
Lago Todos Los Santos
Volcán Tronador 11,660 ft
Bariloche
27
LAGO LLANQUIHUE 26
Petrohué
FRUTILLAR 28
30 PN VICENTE PÉREZ ROSALES
CH225
Llanquihue
Ralún
PUERTO VARAS 29
Volcán Calbuco 6,568 ft
PACIFIC OCEAN
PUERTO MONTT 31
32 PN ALERCE ANDINO
Seno de Reloncaví
La Arena
Maullín
Río Maullín
5
0 km 50
0 miles 50
33 CALBUCO
Canal Chacao
Pargua
Bahía Puñihuil
34 ANCUD
Golfo de Ancud
MONUMENTO NATURAL ISLOTES DE PUÑIHUIL 35
Degán
Quemchi
Quicaví
DALCAHUE
PN CHILOÉ 37
38
CURACO DE VÉLEZ
39
CASTRO 36
40 ACHAO
Rilán
CHONCHI 41
Aituy
Queilen
ISLA GRANDE DE CHILOÉ
42 QUELLÓN
Golfo de Corcovado
Inio
KEY
Highway
Major road
Minor road
Untarred minor road
Main railway
Minor railway
Regional border
International border
Peak

Temuco ❶

Statue at Cerro Nielol

Set in the former Mapuche heartland, Temuco traces its origins to a fort settlement established during the 19th century – the city itself was officially founded in 1881. The construction of the railroad and European immigration in the 20th century brought about rapid growth. Today, Temuco is a commercial hub with busy plazas and museums. Famous for colorful markets attended by Mapuche traders and artisans, the city is also an ideal base for exploring the natural beauty of the surrounding countryside.

View of urban Temuco from the crest of Cerro Nielol

Museo Regional de la Araucanía

Avenida Alemania 084. ***Tel*** *(045) 739952.* *Tue–Sun.*
www.museoregionalaraucania.cl

Housed in a 1924 mansion, this museum records the often bloody history of Chile's Araucanía region *(see p189)* through a collection of some 3,000 archaeological, ethnographic, and historical objects. Among them is the country's most impressive collection of Mapuche objects, including stunning 19th-century weavings and jewelry. Also on display are conquistador firearms, 17th-century religious objects, pioneer-era photographs of Temuco, and a life-size reconstruction of a *ruca* (grass hut).

Monumento Natural Cerro Ñielol

Avenida Arturo Prat s/n. ***Tel*** *(045) 298222.* *Dec–Mar: 8am–10:30pm daily; Apr–Nov: 8am–6pm daily.* *on request.*

A protected hillside, Cerro Ñielol harbors a species-rich temperate rain forest that once covered the Araucanía region. Walking trails explore native evergreen woods of coigüe and arrayan, and lagoons that provide refuge for an abundant birdlife. One of the trails leads to **La Patagua del Armisticio**, a site commemorating the signing of an armistice in 1881 between the Mapuche and the Chilean government, by which the Mapuche ceded territory for the founding of Temuco. The hill's crest offers panoramic city vistas.

Plaza Teodoro Schmidt

Avenida Arturo Prat, esq. Lautaro.

Shaded by lime, oak, and palm trees, Plaza Teodoro Schmidt is named for the 19th-century city architect whose bust adorns one side of the square. In another corner stands the pretty **Iglesia Anglicana Santa Trinidad**, one of Temuco's oldest surviving structures. A steepled church with a weatherbeaten, white-clapboard façade, the church was built in 1920 by Anglican missionaries from England in an effort to evangelize the Mapuche. The plaza is best known as the site of the city's **Feria Arte**. This important crafts fair, held each year in February, features woodcarvings, ceramics, and weavings made by artisans from across the country.

Mercado Municipal

Between Calles Diego Portales, M. Rodríguez, Aldunate, & Ave. M. Bulnes. ***Tel*** *(045) 973445.* *Dec–Mar: 8am–8pm Mon–Sat, 8am–4pm Sun; Apr–Nov: 8am–7pm Mon–Sat, 8:30am–4pm Sun.*

A sprawling indoor market, Mercado Municipal combines the grandeur of early 20th-century European architecture with the vibrancy of modern Chile. The market building dates from 1930 and features a central fountain under an English-style cast-iron roof. Along the perimeter, traders stack stalls with pyramids of exotic fruit, racks of freshly cut meats, and rows of aromatic spices. At the heart of the market, local craftsmen sell high-quality woollens, weavings, and woodcarvings. The market is also the best place in Temuco to feast on shellfish and seafood specialties.

Plaza Aníbal Pinto

Avenida Arturo Prat, esq. Claro Solar.

The city's main plaza is planted with native trees and exotic palms, and centered on the **Monumento a la Araucanía**, a bronze-and-stone sculpture that pays homage to this area's principal colonizers. The figure of a robed *machi* (female Mapuche shaman) crowns the monument and is flanked by four other figures – a Mapuche hunter with a spear;

The arched entrance to Temuco's bustling Mercado Municipal

For hotels and restaurants in this region see pp281–3 and pp302–303

Fruit and vegetable stalls at the Feria Libre Aníbal Pinto

a Spanish conquistador with a Christian cross; a 19th-century soldier; and a settler farmer. A stylized rock-face symbolizing the Andes forms the base of the monument. Behind this structure stands the **Galería Municipal de Arte Plaza Aníbal Pinto**, a small art gallery with a roof terrace with seating. The city cathedral overlooks one corner of the square.

Feria Libre Aníbal Pinto

Ave. Aníbal Pinto, esq. Balmaceda. *Dec–Mar: 8am–5pm daily; Apr–May: 8am–6pm daily.*

Temuco's rustic open-air market is a high-energy nexus of feverish trading and stimulating smells. Traders here sell pungent cheese, herbs, spices, vegetables, and fruit, including *pehuen* (araucaria fruit), a staple part of the Mapuche diet. Mapuche women travel in from outlying districts to sit in groups selling flour, eggs and *mote* (husked wheat). Small restaurants in the center of the market serve regional specialties such as *pastel de choclo* *(see p291)* and seafood dishes. More stalls stocking traditional *huaso* hats, stirrups, and spurs ring this market's outer limits.

Museo Nacional Ferroviaria Pablo Neruda

Avenida Barros Arana 0565. ***Tel*** *(045) 973940.* *9am–6pm Tue–Sun.* **www**.museoferroviariotemuco.cl

Chile's national railway museum occupies the old headquarters of the country's

The Presidential Train at Museo Nacional Ferroviaria Pablo Neruda

VISITORS' CHECKLIST

Road Map D1. 385 miles (620 km) S of Santiago. *245,000.* *Ave. Bulnes 586;* ***Tel*** *(045) 211969.* *El Show Aniversario de Temuco (mid-Feb).* **www**.temucochile.com

national railroad, a UNESCO World Heritage Site. Its great attraction is the old **Casa de Máquinas** (Locomotive Hall), a cavernous oval construction built in 1929–43 for the maintenance of locomotives. Today, the hall preserves rows of old trains, such as the Presidential Train, built in Germany in 1920 and used by all Chilean presidents between 1924 and 2004, barring General Pinochet. Tours of the train's sumptuous interior include the presidential quarters, linked to the First Lady's bedroom via a hidden door. The old Administrative Hall is worth visiting for its photographic displays.

The museum is named for Temuco's most celebrated son, Pablo Neruda *(see p87)*, whose father José del Carmen Reyes Morales was a lifelong employee of the railways. Neruda's many odes to Chile's railroad adorn plaques throughout this large and beautifully curated museum.

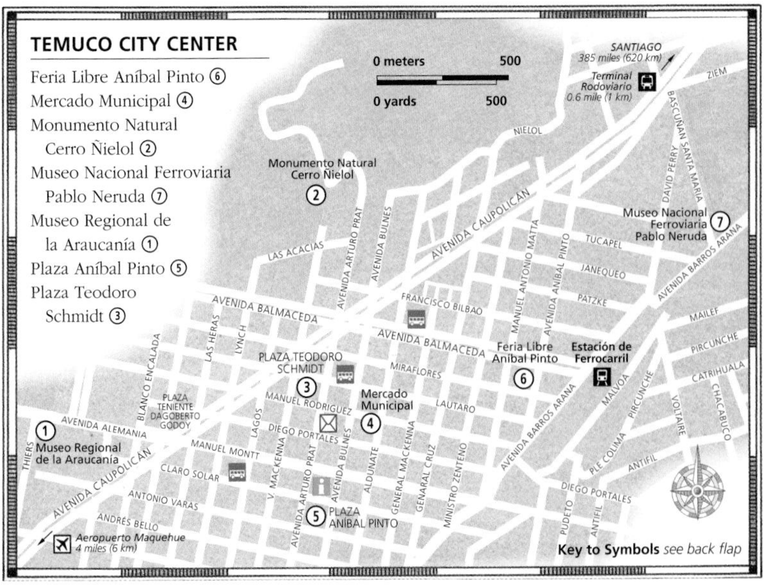

Parque Nacional Tolhuaca ❷

Road Map D1. 81 miles (130 km) NE of Temuco; Acceso 1, road via village of Inspector Fernández. ***Tel*** *(02) 1960480.* *from Temuco.* *CONAF office near southeastern entrance to park.* *8:30am–7pm daily.* **www**.conaf.cl

Set in the far north of the Lake District and distant from the region's more traveled routes, Parque National Tolhuaca conserves a highly scenic area of the Andean foothills, where altitudes vary from 2,200 ft (700 m) to 5,800 ft (1,800 m) above sea level. The park encompasses wild temperate rain forest famous for the prehistoric araucaria (*Araucaria araucana*), also called the monkey-puzzle tree. Attractive trails through the pristine forests offer great bird-watching; among the more easily observed species are the Chilean parakeet (*Microsittace ferruginea*), several types of duck, and the Andean condor. Swimming, fishing, and hiking are also popular activities in this park. Tolhuaca's most hiked trail, the **Sendero Salto Malleco**, skirts the northern shore of Lago Malleco, the park's dominant feature, before crossing native forest to the stunning 164-ft (50-m) high Salto Malleco waterfalls.

Another picturesque hike edges along the **Laguna Verde**, which lies 4,264 ft (1,300 m) above sea level and is ringed by small waterfalls and spindly araucaria woods. Other treks in the area include the **Sendero Lagunillas** and the **Sendero Mesacura**. The first is an undemanding climb to a set of mountain lagoons, where 360-degree views encompass the 2,800-ft (850-m) high Volcán Tolhuaca. The second passes through dense forest. Both are full-day hikes and require advance planning.

Just south of the park lie the thermal pools of **Termas de Tolhuaca**. Located in a canyon, the natural sauna created by the rocks and sulfurous steam provide the ideal spot to relax after a long hike.

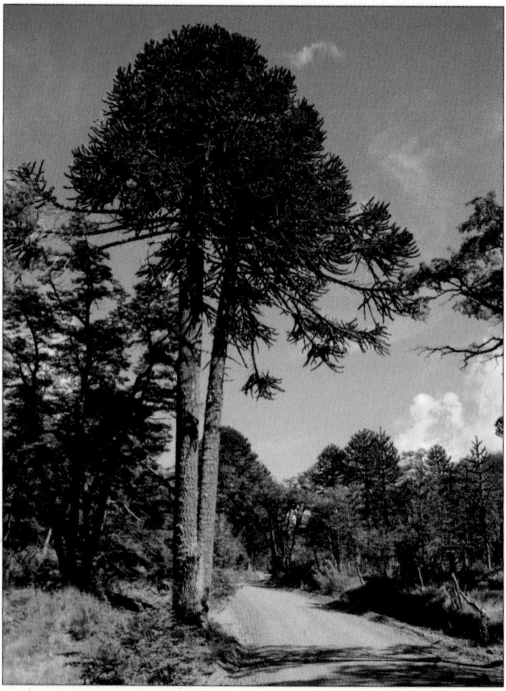

The distinctive monkey-puzzle tree, *Araucaria araucana*

The spa Termas de Malacahuello, at the foot of Volcán Lonquimay

Termas de Malalcahuello ❸

Road Map E1. Ruta Bioceánica 181-CH, Km86, Región de la Araucanía, Malalcahuello. ***Tel*** *(045) 1973550.* *from Temuco.* *9am–9pm daily.* **www**.malalcahuello.cl

The serene location for the modern spa complex of Termas de Malalcahuello is a lushly forested valley at the foot of the 9,395-ft (2,865-m) high Volcán Lonquimay. Both day and overnight visitors are welcome here. On offer are three indoor thermal pools, each filled with mineral-rich water that bubbles up from deep beneath the earth's crust – the temperature of the water ranges from 37°C (99°F) to 43°C (109°F). Floor-to-ceiling windows surround the pools and offer bathers dreamy views of the fertile Lonquimay valley and the snow-covered peak of its volcano. There is also a broad sun-terrace overlooking the valley.

Therapeutic treatments at the resort include wine, honey, and hot-stone massages, as well as herbal and mud baths, and steam rooms. Accommodation options at the complex include a mountain lodge-style hotel, log cabins, and family-sized bungalows. Local bus services and private transfers connect the Termas de Malalcahuello to the nearby Ski Center Corralco.

Ski Center Corralco 4

Road Map D1. Volcán Lonquimay, Camino a RN Malalcalhuello. ***Tel*** *(02) 2029326.* *from Termas de Malalcahuello.* *mid-Jun–Sep: 9am–5pm Fri–Sun; Oct–mid-Jun: 9am–5pm daily.* **www**.corralco.com

The scenic Ski Center Corralco is one of Chile's newest resorts. Skiers can descend Volcán Lonquimay on seven pistes that have a maximum drop of 1,053 ft (321 m). The off-piste opportunities are best suited for experts. There are snowboarding runs as well, some with steep drops, and Nordic skiing circuits. Summer activities include trekking, horse riding, and mountain-biking. The resort also offers a ski school, mountain lodge, and equipment rental.

Parque Nacional Conguillío 5

See pp194–5.

Comunidad Indígena Quinquén 6

Road Map E2. I. Carrera Pinto 110. ***Tel*** *(045) 891110.* *from Lonquimay.* **www**.pewenche.cl

High in the Andean foothills, the Comunidad Indígena Quinquén comprises five communities of a Mapuche group known as Pewenche. Visitors are received on the banks of the Galletué and Icalma lakes, and are invited to dine on traditional Mapuche fare and browse handicrafts. Prehistoric araucaria forests surround the area and can be explored via five treks during which guides explain the sacredness of this tree for the Mapuche, who use its fruit as a source of food and medicine. Guests with camping gear can set up tent nearby.

Ice-hiking on the steep slopes of Nevados de Sollipulli

Nevados de Sollipulli 7

Road Map E2. Nevados de Sollipulli Dome Camp, Camino hacía Carén Alto. ***Tel*** *(045) 276000.* *transfer service from Temuco.* **www**.sollipulli.cl

There are few places in Chile where travelers can witness nature's powerful geological forces more clearly than at **Volcán Sollipulli**, part of the Nevados de Sollipulli range, close to Chile's border with Argentina. This volcano's ancient crater, and the 5-sq-mile (12-sq-km) glacier that fills it, are two of the primal elements responsible for the formation of the great Andes mountain range.

Visitors can climb to the crater on a day-long hike that passes through dense forests of araucaria, with sweeping vistas of the Andean peaks, crystalline rivers, and countless parasitic craters. There is also a 2-day trekking circuit, which includes ice-hikes on the glacier. All hikes start at the **Nevados de Sollipulli Dome Camp**. Situated next to a forested lake on the volcano's northeastern face, this camp comprises five superbly equipped, centrally-heated domes. Among the many luxuries found here are hot tubs in the open air.

Boats docked at the banks of Galletué lake, at Comunidad Indígena Quinquén

Parque Nacional Conguillío 5

Young araucaria tree in the park

One of Lake District's great natural attractions, Parque Nacional Conguillío stretches over 235 sq miles (609 sq km) of volcanic wilderness crowned by the smoking cone of the 10,253-ft (3,125-m) high Volcán Llaima. A diverse, spectacular landscape surrounds this colossal peak and features ancient araucaria forests, rolling sierras, crystalline lakes, and deep valleys scarred by jagged lava flows. The park abounds with rich wildlife, including pumas, smaller wildcats, red and gray foxes, woodpeckers, hawks, and condors. Splendid hiking trails, skiing down volcanic slopes, and boat trips across serene lakes draw a large number of visitors to the park throughout the year.

Magellanic woodpecker in Parque Nacional Conguillío

Laguna Captrén
This shallow lake was formed when lava flows from Volcán Llaima obstructed the Río Captrén. Upright trunks of a submerged forest pierce its surface.

Centro de Esquí las Araucarias
Functioning on Volcán Llaima's western slope, this popular ski center is surrounded by thick araucaria forest. Services include a snow-boarding park, accommodations, a ski-school, and an equipment rental shop.

STAR SIGHTS

- ★ Volcán Llaima
- ★ Lago Conguillío
- ★ Sendero Sierra Nevada

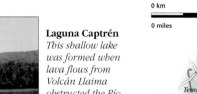

★Volcán Llaima
The glacier-swathed cone of this active volcano dominates the park's landscape. Seasoned climbers can make the guided ascent to its summit.

★ Lago Conguillío
The beautiful Lago Conguillío, the park's biggest lake, was created when lava flow blocked Río Captrén. Bordered by forests, its shores offer fantastic vistas. Lakeside services include shops, cabins, campsites, and boat trips.

VISITORS' CHECKLIST

Road Map E1. 74 miles (120 km) E of Temuco. *from Temuco.* *from Melipeuco & Curacautín.* *Oct–Apr: CONAF, Sector del Lago Conguillío, (045) 298210; May–Sep: Visitors' center, Melipeuco.* *Oct–Apr: 8:30am–8pm daily; May–Sep: 8:30am–5pm daily.* *from Temuco.*
www.conaf.cl

EXPLORING THE PARK

Parque Nacional Conguillío comprises two sectors separated from each other by Volcán Llaima. The western sector, Sector Los Paraguas, offers winter skiing, while the bigger eastern sector, Sector del Lago Conguillío has great hiking trails including the popular Sendero Sierra Nevada. This sector is served by the gateway towns of Melipeuco in the south and Curacautín in the north. Heavy snowfall usually makes this sector impassable between May and September.

★ Sendero Sierra Nevada
The park's most popular trail, the Sendero Sierra Nevada climbs to pure araucaria forests and offers splendid views of Volcán Llaima, Lago Conguillío, and the snowy Sierra Nevada.

Laguna Verde, named for its intense green color, is a small lake with a walking path linking its shore to the park's main road.

The Salto del Truful Truful waterfall cascades amid solidified lava flows and rocks.

KEY

- Minor road
- Trail
- Park boundary
- Visitors information
- Ranger station
- Viewpoint
- Campsite
- *Hosteria/ Refugio*
- Peak

THE WRATH OF VOLCÁN LLAIMA

Smoldering Volcán Llaima is one of Chile's two most explosive volcanoes; the other being Volcán Villarrica *(see p198)*. Over 40 eruptions have been recorded since 1640, and Volcán Llaima's boiling lava has shaped most of Parque Nacional Conguillío's landscape. The eruptions in 2008–09 created 9,800-ft (3,000-m) high smoke columns, forced the evacuation of villages, and dumped ash on Argentina. Over the years, lava flows blocked rivers, turning forests into lakes. Today, lava fields scar the earth where lush forests once stood, and dense woods are still visible in the water.

Volcán Llaima spewing lava, smoke, and ash

Villarrica ❽

Road Map D2. 54 miles (87 km) SE of Temuco. 🏙 *45,000.* 🚌 🛈 *Pedro de Valdivia 1070; (045) 206619.* 🎪 *La Semana de la Chilenidad (mid-Feb).* **www**.villarrica.org

Originally founded in 1552 by the Spanish, Villarrica (Rich Town) was named for the abundant gold and silver deposits discovered here. In 1598, the town was razed in a Mapuche uprising and only resettled in 1883. Today, it is a laid-back, family-oriented destination on the western shore of a sapphire lake of the same name and at the foot of the majestic 9,338-ft (2,847-m) high Volcán Villarrica. Lago Villarrica, a big attraction in its own right, has shores lined by beaches of black volcanic sand. Boat trips from the lake's El Pescadito beach are extremely popular.

Villarrica's Mapuche heritage finds expression at the **Museo Arqueológico Municipal Mapuche** where pre-Columbian exhibits include ceramics and weaponry. Next to it, the **Centro Cultural Mapuche** features a Mapuche crafts market in the summer months. At the edge of town, the **Mirador Canela** is a lookout point with great views of the lake and volcano.

Exhibit, Centro Cultural Mapuche

🏛 **Museo Arqueológico Municipal Mapuche**
Pedro de Valdivia 1050. **Tel** (045) 415706. ⏲ Dec–Mar: Mon–Sat; Apr–Nov: Mon–Fri. 🎫 ✦

Pucón ❾

Road Map D2. 69 miles (112 km) SE of Temuco. 🏙 *21,000.* 🚌 🛈 *O'Higgins 483; (045) 293003.* 🎪 *Ironman (mid-Jan).* **www**. pucononline.cl

Set on the eastern shore of Lago Villarrica, Pucón is the Lake District's adventure-tourism capital. It was founded in 1883 as a fort settlement at the foot of Volcán Villarrica; and today its compact grid of dusty streets still possesses the makeshift air of a Western

The snowcapped Volcán Villarrica rising above the landscape

film set, lined as it is by low wooden buildings that serve the booming tourism industry. Nestled in an area of natural beauty, Pucón is a base for trips to nearby hot spring and national parks, and visitors heading out to these areas will find the city's CONAF office helpful. Pucón is also the starting point for many adrenalin-charged activities such as white-water rafting on Río Trancura and Río Bío Bío; horse riding in Huerquehue and Villarrica national parks; hikes up Volcán Villarrica; kayaking and sport fishing on nearby lakes; light-aircraft trips over Volcán Villarrica; and parachuting, paragliding, and zip-lining excursions. Pucón has two black-sand beaches where swimming and watersports are possible. The main beach, **Playa Grande**, is overlooked by forested peaks. To its west, the smaller **La Poza** beach faces a protected inlet. In summer, boat rides from La Poza are a popular way of touring Lago Villarrica. Amid the fun-filled adventure and the beaches, visitors will find a small concession to culture – **Museo Mapuche**, a private collection of 19th-century Mapuche silverware and pre-Colonial stone artifacts. At the edge of town, the **Monasterio Santa Clara** is a functioning monastery that is open to the public and offers breathtaking lake vistas.

Environs
To the east of Pucón are a number of *termas*, ranging from luxurious spa complexes to rustic hot springs. These are usually visited as day trips, either with a tour operator or in a hired car or taxi.

Among the best is **Termas de Huife**, concealed within native forest. This offers smart log cabins on the banks of Río Liucura, thermal pools, therapeutic treatments, and activities such as horse riding. Located in the same valley, **Termas Los Pozones** is a great economical choice. Nestled in the shadow of craggy peaks, it has seven stone-walled pools on the forested banks of Río Liucura.

🏛 **Museo Mapuche**
Caupolicán 243. **Tel** (045) 441963. ⏲ Jan–Feb: 11am–1pm & 6–8pm Tue–Sun; Mar–Dec: 11am–1pm & 3–7pm Tue–Sun. 🎫 ✦ ✦ **www**.museomapuche.cl

♨ **Termas de Huife**
20 miles (33 km) E of Pucón; Camino Pucón-Huife Km33, Valle del Liucura. **Tel** (045) 1975666. 🎫 ♿ 🍴 🅿 🛍 ✦ **www**.termashuife.cl

♨ **Termas Los Pozones**
22 miles (35 km) E of Pucón; Valle del Liucura. **Tel** (045) 412379. 🎫 ♿ 🍴 🅿 🛍 △

Boats for rent on the black-sand Playa Grande at Pucón

For hotels and restaurants in this region see pp281–3 and pp302–303

Lago Caburgua ⑩

Road Map D2. 76 miles (122 km) SE of Temuco via Pucón. *from Pucón.*

Ringed by forested mountains, Lago Caburgua is a crystalline lake with this region's only white-sand beaches. Thermal activity in the depths of the lake make its waters warmer than those of the district's other lakes. Popular beaches here are **Playa Negra**, a black-sand beach, and **Playa Blanca**, a stretch of white, crystallized sand. Boat tours of the lake depart from Playa Negra, from where paddle-boats can also be rented. A scenic lakeside walk links these two beaches.

Forested slopes surrounding Lago Tinquilco, Parque Nacional Huerquehue

Ojos del Caburgua ⑪

Road Map D2. 73 miles (117 km) SE of Temuco via Pucón. Camino Internacional 7, Km17 or Km20. ***Tel*** *(09) 0677420. from Pucón.* *9am–9pm daily.*

The waters of Lago Caburgua flow southward and underground for 3 miles (5 km) before gushing out to form the Ojos del Caburgua (Eyes of Caburgua). This necklace of aquamarine rock pools lies at the base of cascading waterfalls and is shrouded in pristine forest. Travelers to the site access the pools at a sign-posted entrance on the main road from Pucón. A second entrance lies 2 miles (3 km) north on the same road and offers a more intimate view of the pools, falls, and forest. This approach is marked solely by a wooden roadside statue of Christ on the cross.

Parque Nacional Huerquehue ⑫

Road Map E2. 94 miles (152 km) SE of Temuco via Pucón;Camino a Caburgua. *from Pucón.* *CONAF Pucón, Lincoyán 336; (045) 443781.* *8:30am–8pm daily.* **www**.conaf.cl

Created in 1967, the compact Parque Nacional Huerquehue protects around 48 sq miles (124 sq km) of native forest that includes 2,000-year-old araucaria woods. The park has some of the Lake District's best short treks and offers spectacular views of Volcán Villarrica and its surroundings. A must-do trail is the **Sendero Los Lagos**, which traverses forests of Chilean yew and beech, skirts five different lakes, and two waterfalls. Along the way there are breathtaking vistas of the volcano and of Lago Tinquilco, the park's largest body of water. The trail ends at Lago Chico, a small alpine lake surrounded by steep cliffs crowned by araucaria.

Between hikes, visitors can enjoy swimming in the lakes and nature-watching. Birdlife abounds in this area, the highlight being the different species of eagle. Among the mammals here are the puma; the pudú (*Pudu pudu*), the world's smallest deer; and the brown-gray mouse opossum (*Dromiciops gliroides*), one of the southern Andes' few surviving marsupials.

One of the falls plummeting into the rock pools of Ojos del Caburgua

Santuario Cañi ⑬

Road Map D2. 83 miles (133 km) SE of Temuco via Pucón; Camino Termas de Huife, Km21, Pichares. ***Tel*** *(09) 8373928. from Pucón.* *9am–6pm daily.* **www**.santuariocani.cl

Protecting a lush swathe of temperate Valdivian rain forest, Santuario Cañi is home to some of Chile's oldest stands of araucaria. Day hikes climb through forests of southern beech (*Nothofagus*) to reveal hidden mountain tarns and, at higher elevations, pure forests of araucaria. Together, these habitats harbor a rich variety of birdlife and many shy mammals that are usually difficult to spot, including the puma and pudú. Hiking trails end at a lookout point about 5,084 ft (1,550 m) above sea level. This has 360-degree views of the area's four volcanoes – Lanín, Villarrica, Quetrupillán, and Llaima – as well as its three biggest lakes – Caburgua, Villarrica, and Calafquén. Travelers on overnight treks can stay at rustic *refugios* and camping grounds.

Parque Nacional Villarrica ⓮

South American gray fox

Conserving 243 sq miles (629 sq km) of stunning wilderness, Parque Nacional Villarrica extends from south of Pucón to Chile's frontier with Argentina. The smoking, snow-swathed cone of the grand 9,341-ft (2,847-m) high Volcán Villarrica forms the park's centerpiece, crowning a landscape that embraces two other volcanoes, several small lakes, steep gorges, and dense forests of southern beech and araucaria. The park provides shelter to a rich wildlife, including the rare Chilean shrew opossum. Activities include skiing, horseback riding, wildlife-watching, trekking across lava fields and native forests, and helicopter rides over Volcán Villarrica's crater.

Spindly araucaria flourishing on the slopes of Volcán Villarrica

Centro de Ski Pucón
Volcán Villarrica's northern face is the stunning location for this popular ski resort. It has slopes for all levels of skiers, and offers off-piste skiing, an impressive snowboard park, and excellent amenities.

Volcanic caves in the par[k] are well-lit lava tubes th[at] can be explored by hik[ers]

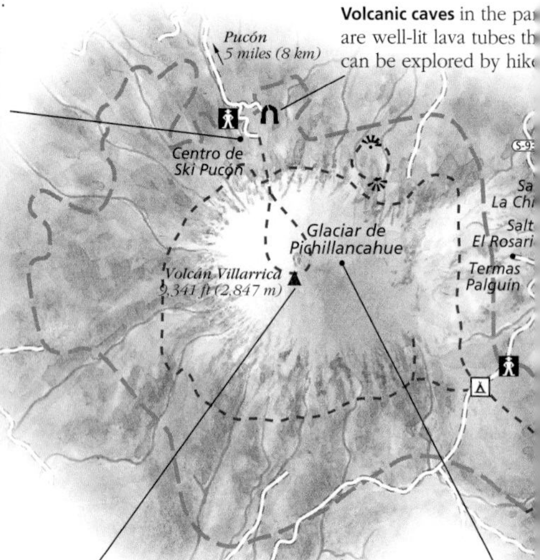

Glaciar de Pichillancahue, the park's largest glacier, is a sweeping body of blue ice with waterfalls cascading down its front wall. It is reached by the main walking trail in the park's western sector.

★ Volcán Villarrica
The trek to Volcán Villarrica's crater features a physically challenging, but technically undemanding hike through icy glaciers and a slide down the slopes via snow tunnels. Climbers enjoy stupendous vistas, including views of the volcano's bubbling lava lake.

STAR SIGHTS

★ Volcán Villarrica

★ Laguna Azul

HOUSE OF THE DEVIL

The Mapuche of the area refer to Volcán Villarrica as Rucapillán, or House of the Devil – an apt description for one of Chile's most explosive peaks. The volcano erupted 16 times in the 20th century alone. A major explosion in 1971 almost destroyed the nearby village of Coñaripe *(see p200)*. It last erupted in 1999, but remains constantly active. Its crater smokes, hisses, and belches, and is one of the only four craters on the globe that has an active lava lake.

Bubbling and flaming lava in Volcán Villarrica's crater lake

VISITORS' CHECKLIST

Road Map D2. 5 miles (8 km) SE of Pucón. 🚌 from Pucón. 🛈 *CONAF, Lincoyán 336, Pucón; (045) 443781.* ⏰ *Oct–Apr: 8am–8pm daily; May–Sep: 8am–6pm daily.* 🅿️ 🍴 📷 🅰️ www.conaf.cl

KEY

━━ Major road

＝＝ Untarred road

－ － Trail

━ ━ Park boundary

━ ▪ International border

🏃 Ranger station

🔆 Viewpoint

🅰️ Campsite

⋂ Cave

▲ Peak

Volcán Quetrupillán is a dormant, snowcapped volcano. Its name means mute devil in the Mapuche tongue.

Lago Quilleihue is a tranquil lake reached by a hiking trail through thick araucaria forest.

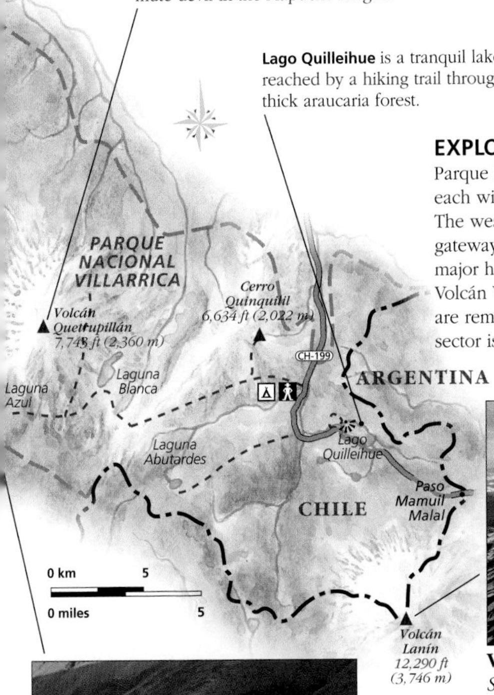

EXPLORING THE PARK

Parque Nacional Villarrica has three sectors, each with hiking trails and a ranger station. The westernmost sector, accessible from the gateway town of Pucón, features the park's major highlights, including the magnificent Volcán Villarrica. The two sectors to the east are remote, yet beautiful; the park's wildest sector is in the area bordering Argentina.

PARQUE NACIONAL VILLARRICA

Volcán Quetrupillán 7,743 ft (2,360 m)

Cerro Quinquilil 6,634 ft (2,022 m)

Laguna Azul

Laguna Blanca

CH-199

ARGENTINA

Laguna Abutardes

Lago Quilleihue

Paso Mamuil Malal

CHILE

0 km 5

0 miles 5

Volcán Lanín 12,290 ft (3,746 m)

Volcán Lanín
Shared by Chile and Argentina, the snow-topped Volcán Lanín is southern Chile's biggest volcano. The hike from Laguna Abutardes to Lago Quilleihue offers fabulous vistas of this volcano.

★ **Laguna Azul**
A mirror-like sheet of water edged by a forested flank of the majestic Volcán Quetrupillán, Laguna Azul can be reached by the 9-mile (15-km) long Los Venados trail that starts at the ranger station in the Quetrupillán sector.

Boardwalk past a waterfall at the Termas Geómetricas, near Coñaripe

Licán Ray ⓯

Road Map D2. 70 miles (113 km) SE of Temuco. *2,100.* *General Urrutia, esq. Cacique Marichanquin; (045) 431516 (Dec–Mar only).* *La Semana de Licán Ray (Feb).* **www**.lican-ray.cl

Small and tranquil, Licán Ray is the main resort on the hauntingly beautiful **Lago Calafquén**. The village is a quiet oasis, except in February when the people of Santiago arrive in large numbers to holiday by Lago Calafquén's mist-shrouded warm waters.

There are two beaches at this miniature retreat – **Playa Grande** and the more picturesque **Playa Chica**, which is ringed by rolling forested peaks that sweep down to a shore of black volcanic sand. A wooded peninsula divides these two beaches and is crossed by walking paths that ascend to lookout points with great vistas. Catamaran tours of the lake depart from Playa Chica. At the village center, the main plaza is edged by sandy sidewalks and artisans' fairs.

Coñaripe ⓰

Road Map D2. 83 miles (134 km) SE of Temuco. *1,500.* **www**.coñaripe.com

Set on the eastern shore of Lago Calafquén, and away from the region's more traveled routes, Coñaripe is a tiny village with a soporific air and a couple of black-sand beaches. The area around the village offers ample opportunities for adventure sports, including white-water rafting on the Río San Pedro, and horseback, mountain-bike, and trekking trips. Coñaripe has many accommodation options for overnight guests; budget-travelers in particular will enjoy the well-equipped campsites by the beaches.

Environs

The hills around Coñaripe are dotted with more than a dozen thermal springs which are scenic, relaxing, and well worth visiting. They range from very basic, rustic pools to modern hotel-and-spa complexes. One of the best among these is the **Termas Geómetricas**. Nestled within a forested ravine, this stylish spa comprises 60 thermal fountains that gush into bubbling bathing pools through a network of wooden water channels. Visitors simply walk across the ravine on a 1,476-ft (450-m) long catwalk, and descend via wooden stairs to the pool of their choice.

The **Termas Coñaripe** is a good choice for an overnight stay. This modern hotel and spa made of glass and wood offers indoor pools, semi-covered pools, and outdoor thermal pools. Guests can also slather around in mud baths and enjoy walks and horseback rides to nearby waterfalls and lagoons.

A road route links Coñaripe to Parque Nacional Villarrica *(see pp198–9)*, some 11 miles (18 km) to the north.

Termas Geómetricas
10 miles (16 km) NE of Coñaripe.
Tel *(02) 2141214.* *day visits only; Dec–Mar: 10am–9pm daily; Apr–Nov: 11am–7pm daily.*
www.termasgeometricas.cl

Termas Coñaripe
9 miles (15 km) SE of Coñaripe; Camino Coñaripe-Liquine, Km15
Tel *(045) 411111.*
www.termasconaripe.cl

Tour boats on Lago Calafquén, moored by the forest-lined Playa Chica at Licán Ray

For hotels and restaurants in this region see pp281–3 and pp302–303

Panguipulli ⑰

Road Map D2. 90 miles (145 km) SE of Temuco. 33,000. *Bernardo O'Higgins s/n, in front of Plaza A. Prat; (063) 310435. La Semana de las Rosas (mid-Feb).* **www**.panguipulli.cl

Overlooking the tranquil waters of its eponymous lake, Panguipulli is a popular stop-over for visitors heading on to the Reserva Biológica Huilo-Huilo. A pleasant lakeshore destination of brightly painted clapboard houses on undulating hillside streets, the town's biggest attraction is the landmark **Iglesia Capuchina**. A twin-towered wooden construction, the church was built by German Capuchin missionaries in 1947 and stands on the site of a German mission from the 1890s. The building is fronted by an extravagantly latticed façade that is painted red, yellow, and black – the colors of the German national flag. Religious statues brought from Germany adorn the church's interior. Overlooking the altar is a large high-relief, beautifully sculpted from native raulí and mañío woods, depicting Christ's ascension to heaven.

Environs

Panguipulli and its namesake lake lie at the heart of Chile's **Seven Lakes** region. These lakes – Calafquén, Pallaifa, Pullinque, Ruñihue, Neltume, Panguipulli, and Pirhueico – are linked to each other by rivers, which together comprise a single hydrological system. A chain of beautiful and generally uncrowded villages face the shores of these lakes. Although this area receives only a fraction of the visitors that head for nearby Pucón *(see p196)*, it offers good infrastructure and tourist services. Panguipulli is the ideal springboard for exploring the Seven Lakes – local tour agencies run day trips to the lakeshores and more active travelers can make their own way around the region on mountain bikes rented in town.

Iglesia Capuchina with its twin towers rising above Pangiupulli

Reserva Biológica Huilo-Huilo ⑱

Road Map D2. 130 miles (210 km) SE of Temuco; El Portal, Camino Internacional Panguipulli-Puerto Fuy, Km56. ***Tel*** *(02) 3344565.* *from Temuco & Valdivia.* **www**.huilohuilo.cl

Run by a private foundation dedicated to sustainable tourism, Reserva Biológica Huilo-Huilo preserves 232 sq miles (600 sq km) of temperate rain forest that was once the target of large-scale logging. Within the reserve boundaries, there is some truly compelling scenery. By far the most impressive is the **Volcán Mocho-Choshuenco**, which is in fact two volcanoes bridged by a large glacier. The surrounding landscape comprises glacial lakes, rivers, and Andean prairies.

Chilean firebush at the private reserve

Visitors to the reserve first need to choose a base from which to explore this area. There is a range of lodging options, from an upscale mountain lodge in the woods, to more inexpensive accommodations in the small towns of Neltume and Puerto Fuy. These were built in the 1930s to house employees of the logging companies. Puerto Fuy is situated near the beautiful Lago Pirehueico and is the starting point for fly-fishing, kayaking, and boating trips.

The reserve's mountain lodge, **La Montaña Mágica** (The Magic Mountain), is worth a visit even for non-guests. Built by ex-forestry workers, it rises above the forest like a fantasy castle from a Grimm Brothers' fairy-tale, and has a cascading waterfall that plunges down its side. The interior is constructed almost entirely from native woods. Activities at the reserve are mostly guided and arranged at La Montaña Mágica or at the administration center close to the reserve's main entrance. These include horse rides across forest, prairie, and mountain terrain, and wildlife observation of re-introduced fauna – such as the camelid species, guanaco – that once roamed freely here. Travelers looking for more rugged activites will also find zip-lining, mountain-biking, and trekking excursions. Hiking trails range from a gentle walk through indigenous forest that ends at the gushing, 115-ft (35-m) high **Salto del Huilo-Huilo** waterfall, to the thrilling full-day trek to the crater of Volcán Mocho.

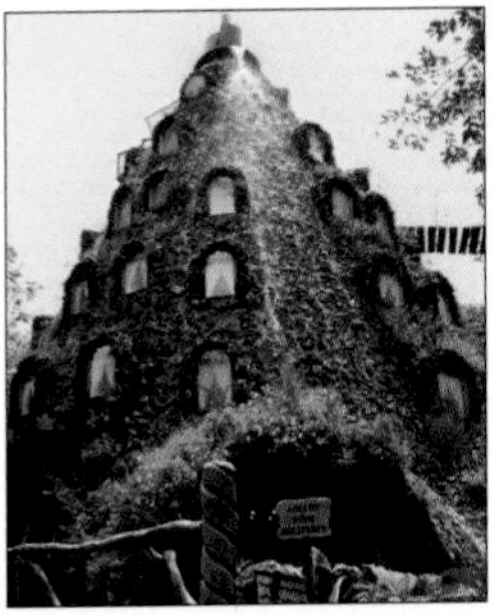

The whimsical La Montaña Mágica at Reserva Biológica Huilo-Huilo

Valdivia ⓳

A waterfront city, Valdivia is named for its founder, the Spanish explorer Pedro de Valdivia. Established in 1552, the colony spread along the banks of three rivers – Río Cau Cau, Río Calle Calle, and Río Valdivia, the last of which links this port-city to the Pacific Ocean. Valdivia was a prized possession of the Spanish, who guarded it with military forts for over 200 years until its defenses were breached in the War of Independence (1810–26). In 1960, a massive earthquake devastated Valdivia, but today, it is a vibrant city whose lush riverside is fronted by fine museums and 19th-century Teutonic architecture.

Boats docked along the Río Valdivia, near the lively Mercado Fluvial

Mercado Fluvial

Avenida Arturo Prat s/n.
10am–8pm daily.

Located on the banks of Río Valdivia, Mercado Fluvial, the city's bustling fish market, is a colorful snapshot of coastal Chilean life as well as the prime industry that sustains it. Traders clean the day's catch for customers, while live crabs scuttle about in huge crates and bobbing sea lions bellow for scraps by the water's edge. In this scuffle over discarded odds and ends are hundreds of screaming seabirds. Picturesque seafood restaurants serving local specialties edge the market.

Centro Cultural El Austral

Yungay 733. ***Tel** (063) 213658.*
10am–1pm & 4–7pm Tue–Sun.

Set in a large, beautifully restored house, Valdivia's Centro Cultural El Austral dates from the period of German settlement in the Lake District. Built in the 1870s for a pioneer family, it was made entirely from local wood in the German chalet style and features a striking Bavarian steeple. The interiors reflect typical living quarters of early German settlers. Dazzlingly furnished, the rooms feature Art Nouveau chandeliers, extravagant wall mirrors, and stately 19th-century European furniture. Other salons in the building showcase works by contemporary artists.

Museo de Arte Contemporaneo

Los Laureles s/n, Isla Teja. ***Tel** (063) 221968. Jan–Feb: 10am–2pm & 4–8pm Tue–Sun; Mar–May & Sep–Dec: 10am–1pm & 3–7pm Tue–Sun.*
www.macvaldivia.uach.cl

A recycled brewery building with a strikingly modern glass façade is the post-Industrial

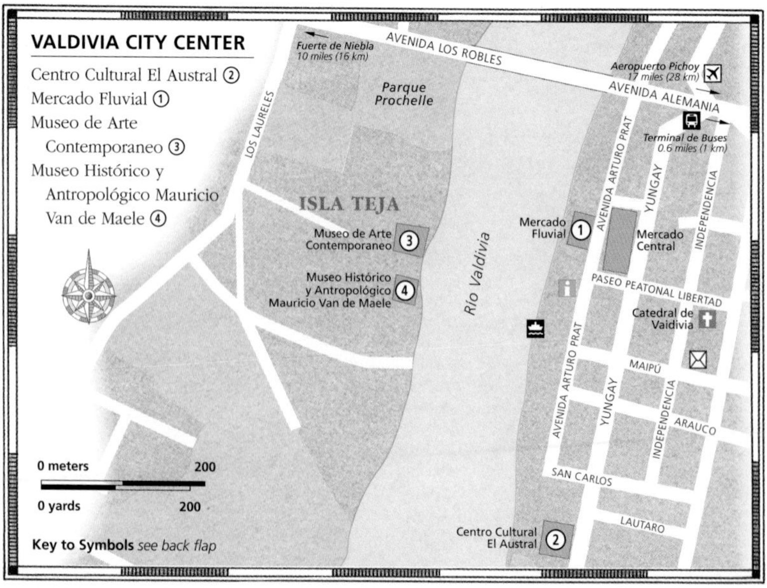

The busy outdoor thermal pool at Aguas Calientes, Parque Nacional Puyehue

the **Termas Aguas Calientes** is a rustic hot-springs resort featuring sulfur-rich outdoor rock pools that are edged by forest and tumbling rivers. In the park's Antillanca sector, **Volcán Casablanca**, rising to a height of 6,337 ft (1,932 m), has one of the Lake District's least demanding ascents. The base is the starting point for several trails, both easy and challenging, that wind through native forests of lenga, ulmo, and coigüe trees. The park is home to a rich and varied birdlife, including hummingbirds, condors, and kingfishers. Hikers can also hear the loud, distinctive call of the endemic, onomatopoeically named chucao (*Scelorchilus rubecula*). Among the park's mammals are pumas, foxes, the native and endangered huemul, as well as the tiny, tree-dwelling mouse possum.

Volcán Casablanca is also the location for the highly rated **Centro de Ski Antillanca** which operates on the volcano's western wall. This popular ski resort attracts a large number of skiing enthusiasts. Offering excellent off-piste skiing, it features 14 slopes for all levels, snowboard runs, and a maximum drop of 1,640 ft (500 m). The slopes afford panoramic views of the blue skyline pierced by the snow-capped cones of surrounding volcanoes. Services available include an equipment rental shop, a ski-school, and a snow park for children. Summertime activities at Antillanca feature mountain-biking, horse riding, caving, and trekking on the volcano, as well as kayaking and fishing excursions. Snowmobile rides through virgin forest are an added draw during the winter months.

In the less trodden northern sector of the national park, the 7,334-ft (2,236-m) high **Volcán Puyehue** offers a difficult 2-day ascent, and is for experienced hikers only. The stunning trails here pass geysers, steaming fumaroles, and gurgling hot springs.

Kingfisher, Parque Nacional Puyehue

Termas Aguas Calientes
Km4 Camino Antillanca.
Tel *(064) 331700.*
www.termasaguascalientes.cl

Centro de Ski Antillanca
Volcán Casablanca. ***Tel*** *(064) 235114. Jun–Oct: 8am–5:30pm daily.*
www.skiantillanca.cl

Termas de Puyehue ㉕

Road Map D2. 114 miles (183 km) SE of Valdivia; Ruta 215, Km76, Puyehue. ***Tel*** *(064) 331400. from Puyehue. 8am–8pm Mon–Fri, 8am–9pm Sat & Sun.*
www.puyehue.cl

A five-star spa-resort, the Termas de Puyehue is the ideal place to soothe aching limbs after long treks in the nearby Parque Nacional Puyehue. Hidden within forests at the edge of the park, this luxurious, yet accessible, mountain lodge and spa receives both day and overnight guests. It is possible to relax in the therapeutic waters of three large thermal pools – covered, semi-covered, and outdoor – whose temperatures range from a comfortable 22°C (72°F) to a warm 41°C (106°F). There are hot rooms and hydrotherapy pools, and a tempting variety of indulgent treatments that include honey, algae, and herbal massages, as well as sulfur-rich mud baths. The spa has a daily program of children's activities and a well-equipped playroom. Other facilities include two gourmet restaurants, a small art gallery, and outdoor tennis courts. Visitors can enjoy exhilarating horse rides to the forested shore of the nearby Lago Puyehue, where the spa arranges several watersports for its guests.

Entrance to the popular hot-springs resort, Termas de Puyehue

Lago Llanquihue ㉖

Road Map D2. 99 miles (160 km) SE of Valdivia.

Resembling a small sea in its size, the breathtakingly beautiful Lago Llanquihue is South America's third largest natural lake. It covers a surface area of 338 sq miles (875 sq km), plunges to a depth of 1,148 ft (350 m), and its crystal blue waters are bound by Volcán Osorno and Volcán Calbuco. The Mapuche believed this lake and its dominions to be a realm of monsters and evil spirits. The Spanish discovered it in 1552, but it was not until the arrival of German immigrants in the 19th century that Europeans finally colonized the lake's shores. Since then, Llanquihue has been the German heartland of the Lake District and is today fronted by steepled Bavarian towns. Of these, Puerto Octay has the most authentically Teutonic feel, while Frutillar is famous for its beaches and volcanic vistas, and Puerto Varas offers great restaurants and nightlife.

Volcán Osorno overlooking the azure waters of Lago Llanquihue

Puerto Octay ㉗

Road Map D2. 99 miles (160 km) SE of Valdivia. *10,000.* *Pedro Montt 378; (064) 391860.* *Festival de la Leche (Jan).* **www**.puertooctay.cl

Set on the northern shore of Lago Llanquihue, Puerto Octay was founded in 1852 by German immigrants who were attracted by its location on a sheltered bay. The town grew into an important lake port and staging post on the trade route between Osorno and Puerto Montt. Today, it is a charming holiday destination with a stunning natural setting and streets of well-conserved German architecture. Wooden houses and civic buildings from the settler era front streets such as Avenida Pedro Montt, Calle G. Wulf, and Calle Amunategui. Occupying an old settler's house, the excellent **Museo de Puerto Octay** exhibits period objects. Another noteworthy building is the landmark 1907-built **Iglesia Parroquial**, constructed in a simple Gothic style.

Puerto Octay faces the peaks of three volcanoes – Calbuco, Puntiagudo, and Osorno. Each is visible from the town's main beach, **Playa La Baja**, a stretch of volcanic black sand fringed by eucalyptus and pine forests. Puerto Octay's hilltop cemetery, which holds the graves of the original German settlers, offers even more magnificent views of the lake and its surrounding volcanoes.

Museo de Puerto Octay
Avenida Independencia 591.
***Tel** (064) 643327. Dec–Mar: 10am–1pm & 3–7pm daily; Apr–Nov: 10am–1pm & 3–5pm daily. on request.*
www.museopuertooctay.cl

Frutillar ㉘

Road Map D2. 105 miles (170 km) SE of Valdivia. *16,000.* *Avenida Philippi s/n.* *Wed, Fri.* *Semana Musical de Frutillar (late Jan–early Feb).* **www**.frutillarchile.cl

Said to be the Lake District's loveliest town, Frutillar was founded in 1856 by German colonists on the western shore of Lago Llanquihue. The town's charming district Frutillar Bajo (Lower Frutillar) has stunning views of Volcán Osorno, whose perfect snow-capped cone seems to float ethereally above the far shore of the sapphire lake.

A mix of hotels, crafts markets, restaurants, and old Germanic architecture line the long sandy shores of Frutillar Bajo. The **Museo Colonial Alemán** is set in landscaped gardens and re-creates the pioneer era with life-size buildings that include a mill, farmhouse, and blacksmith's

The tower of Iglesia Parroquial rising above Puerto Octay, on the banks of Lago Llanquihue

For hotels and restaurants in this region see pp281–3 and pp302–303

forge. Period objects furnish these buildings and multilingual information panels provide historical detail.

On the waterfront, the **Teatro del Lago** is a contemporary theater venue and site of the Semana Musical de Frutillar, a week-long festival featuring opera, jazz, and classical music. At the town's northern edge, the **Reserva Forestal Edmundo Winkler** preserves Valdivian rain forest. A short walking path here climbs to a lookout point with lake and volcano vistas.

Museo Colonial Alemán
Avenida Vicente Pérez Rosales, esq. Arturo Prat, Frutillar Bajo. ***Tel*** *(065) 421142.* *Dec–Mar: 10am–7:30pm daily; Apr-Nov: 10am–2pm & 3–5:30pm daily.* **www**.museosaustral.cl

Reserva Forestal Edmundo Winkler
Calle Concepción s/n, Frutillar Bajo. ***Tel*** *(065) 422307.* *8:30am–6pm daily.*

Traditional German buildings at Museo Colonial Alemán, Frutillar

Puerto Varas 29

Road Map D2. 118 miles (190 km) S of Valdivia. *33,000.* *El Muelle, Avenida Vicente Pérez Rosales; (065) 237956.* **www**.puertovaras.org

Fronting the southern shores of Lago Llanquihue, Puerto Varas is the biggest town on the lake. It was founded in 1854 by German immigrants, and pioneer-era homes can still be seen on streets such as Prat, Miraflores, and Decker. The tourist information office offers a walking tour, the Paseo Patrimonial, which encompasses 28 different houses. The town's most remarkable Teutonic building, the **Iglesia Sagrado Corazón de Jesús**, was built in 1915–18 as a to-scale replica of a church in Germany's Black Forest. Made entirely from wood, its Baroque interior boasts two cupolas, built to the maximum height possible without metal supports.

Puerto Varas's only museum, the small **Museo Pablo Fierro**, houses an eclectic display of objects, from pinball machines to antique pianos.

Most visitors are attracted to Puerto Varas for its black-sand beaches. The most popular of these is **Playa de Puerto Chico** with views of Volcán Osorno. At the town's edge, a vehicle path climbs Cerro Phillipi, which offers lacustrine views.

Iglesia Sagrado Corazón de Jesús
Verbo Divino, esq. San Francisco. *9:30am–1.30pm & 4:30–9pm Mon–Sat, 10am–1pm & 7–9pm Sun.*

Museo Pablo Fierro
Costanera Vicente Pérez Rosales s/n. *9:30am–1pm & 3–8pm Mon–Sat.* **www**.pablofierro.cl

GERMAN IMMIGRANTS OF THE LAKE DISTRICT

An original settler house in Frutillar

In 1845, the Chilean government passed the Badlands Law, a regulation that aimed to loosen Mapuche control over the Lake District via colonization. Some 150 German Catholic families accepted Chile's invitation to populate the area; a trickle that became a torrent as more Germans sought to escape poverty and authoritarian rule at home. Between 1846 and 1875, 66 ships made the 5-month journey from Hamburg in Germany to Valdivia *(see pp202–203)*. Families of artisans and farmers settled first in Valdivia and, as thousands more arrived, in Osorno *(see p204)*, and finally in the area around Lago Llanquihue. Here, German settlers founded three lakeshore towns – Puerto Octay, Frutillar, and Puerto Varas – that became the German heartland of the region. German immigration fizzled out in the 1880s, but the towns around Lago Llanquihue continued to thrive as main stops on the route from Osorno to Puerto Montt *(see pp212–13)*.

The Teutonic-style Iglesia Sagrado Corazón de Jesús at Puerto Varas

Colorful boats sailing on Lago Villarrica, overlooked by the snowy Volcán Villarrica ▷

Parque Nacional Vicente Pérez Rosales ㉚

Green-backed firecrown

Created in 1926, Parque Nacional Vicente Pérez Rosales is one of Chile's most breathtaking parks. Its landscape of lost-world beauty encompasses volcanoes, crystalline lakes and lagoons, gushing waterfalls, and evergreen forest. Its crowning glory is the perfect cone of the active Volcán Osorno. Two more great volcanoes – Tronador and Puntiagudo – pierce the skyline here. They, along with Lago Todos Los Santos and Saltos de Petrohué, protect an abundant bird and mammal life, and offer activities such as boat rides, horse riding through forests, lava treks, and volcano skiing.

KEY

☐ PN Vicente Pérez Rosales

★ Volcán Osorno

The park's most striking feature, Volcán Osorno is the focus of many hikes and horseback rides. A vehicle road climbs its flank to Estación Base, site of a spectacular viewpoint, as well as a modern ski and snowboard center. Summer activities here include mountain-biking and zip-lining.

Laguna Verde is an intensely green lagoon surrounded by black lava rock and emerald forest. Trails cross lava fields to Lago Llanquihue, the great lake whose waters seep into Laguna Verde.

★ Saltos de Petrohué

White-water torrents, emerging from where a lava field splits Río Petrohué, form the gushing Saltos de Petrohué. Walkways gouged from lava rock skirt the rapids and powerboats depart for their swirling base. A number of trails snake through the surrounding forest to jade lagoons.

STAR SIGHTS

- ★ Volcán Osorno
- ★ Saltos de Petrohué
- ★ Lago Todos los Santos

Río Petrohué

Originating at the Lagos Todos Los Santos, Río Petrohué is one of Chile's most popular rivers for activites such as sport fishing, kayaking, and rafting.

For hotels and restaurants in this region see pp281–3 and pp302–303

★ Lago Todos Los Santos
This beautiful glacial lake ringed by forested mountains and black beaches is explored on catamarans and small wooden boats. Three volcanoes are visible from the lake.

VISITORS' CHECKLIST

Road Map D2. 28 miles (45 km) NE of Puerto Varas. *from Puerto Montt & Puerto Varas, via Ensenada & Petrohué.* *CONAF, Ochagavía 458, Puerto Montt; (065) 486115.* *8:30am–6:30pm daily.* www.conaf.cl

KEY

- Minor road
- Trail
- Park boundary
- International boundary
- Visitor information
- Campsite
- Peak

Peulla is a single-hotel hamlet reached by catamaran. It offers lake-fishing, plus hikes and horseback riding on the slopes of Volcán Tronador.

EXPLORING THE PARK

The park's star sights are concentrated in its western section, which is served by road and local bus, and is linked to the gateway city Puerto Varas *(see p207)*. Located in this sector, the villages of Ensenada and Petrohué have hotel and campsite accommodations. From Petrohué, catamarans make the daily 2-hour crossing to the park's eastern sector, called Peulla, where the eponymous hamlet has a hotel.

CRUCE DE LOS LAGOS

This spectacular crossing over the Andes, between the lake districts of Chile and Argentina, traverses two national parks and four lakes. The 2-day journey, beginning at Petrohuè, over both land and lakes ends at Bariloche, Argentina. En route, there are four volcanoes, many waterfalls, and abundant wildlife.

A catamaran crossing the waters of Lago Todos Los Santos

Volcán Tronadór
The awesome 11,351-ft (3,460-m) high peak of this extinct volcano straddles the border between Chile and neighboring Argentina.

Puerto Montt 31

The port-city of Puerto Montt is where the Lake District meets the Pacific Ocean. Founded in 1853 on a hillside overlooking the Seno de Reloncaví, the city grew rapidly around its port, which was used to ship grains and alerce wood. Puerto Montt was badly hit by the 1960 earthquake and much of it was rebuilt thereafter. Today, it has a booming salmon-farming industry and is the departure point for south-bound ferries and cruise ships sailing through Chile's fjords. At the city's center are busy markets, fine museums, and conserved Jesuit architecture.

Shoppers in downtown Puerto Montt

Plaza Buenaventura Martínez

Built on the site of the city's foundation, Puerto Montt's main plaza is also Chile's first public square with a garden. Remodeled many times since its inauguration in 1853, the plaza is a broad space with an open southern side that offers panoramic views of Seno de Reloncaví. The northern end of the plaza is overlooked by the Neo-Classical **Iglesia Catedral**. Built in 1856–96, the cathedral is modelled on Greece's Parthenon, with Doric pillars of alerce adorning the façade and a simple interior. One of these columns conceals the city's founding stone. The San Francisco de Sales, a Neo-Gothic side chapel, is entered from inside the cathedral.

Campanario de los Jesuitas

Colegio San Javier, Guillermo Gallardo 269. ***Tel*** *(065) 366000.*
4:30–6pm Mon–Fri, 11–11:30am Sat.

The centerpiece of a complex of 19th-century Jesuit buildings, the Campanario de los Jesuitas is a bell tower built by Jesuit missionaries in 1894. A national monument, the Neo-Gothic tower features a steeple and smaller minarets crowned with crosses. The *campanario* was built entirely from native woods, including alerce, coigüe, and mañio, and wooden pegs join its component parts. This flexible construction enabled the bell tower to survive the 1960 earthquake. Wooden ladders climb its interior to a belfry that houses two 8,800-lb (4,000-kg) bells brought from Austria in 1890. Visits to the tower start at the **Colegio San Javier**, a Jesuit college, and include the **Iglesia Jesuita**, a wooden church from 1872.

Museo Municipal Juan Pablo II

Avenida Diego Portales 997. ***Tel*** *(065) 261822.* *Dec–Mar: 10am–7pm Mon–Fri, 10am–6pm Sat & Sun; Apr–Nov: 10am–7pm Mon–Fri.*

Named for Pope John Paul II, who celebrated mass with thousands of Chileans at this

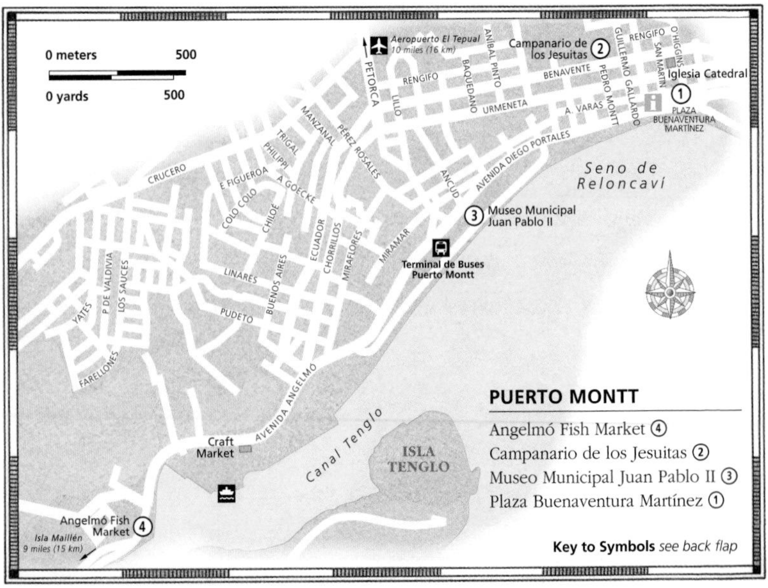

VISITORS' CHECKLIST

Road Map D2. 130 miles (210 km) S of Valdivia. *176,000.* *Aeropuerto El Tepual.* *San Martín s/n; (065) 223016.* *La Semana Puertomontina (mid-Feb).* **www**.puertomonttchile.cl

site in 1987, this museum traces the history of Puerto Montt, Chiloé, and the Lago Llanquihue areas. Exhibits date from pre-Columbian times to the present day and include Jesuit artifacts as well as a rich selection of objects brought by 19th-century German immigrants. Among these are antique toys and German-language newspapers and bibles. Also on display are moving photographic accounts of the 1960 earthquake and tsunami, showing Puerto Montt before and after the disaster.

Old wooden cart exhibited at the Museo Municipal Juan Pablo II

Angelmó Fish Market

Avenida Angelmó s/n. ***Tel*** *(065) 261825.* *8am–11pm daily.*

Located on the waterfront, the raucous Angelmó Fish Market is the city's biggest attraction. A whirl of vibrant colors and aromas, the market is a maze of narrow, guttered passageways along which traders sell fish, spices, algae strings, and local delicacies. Wooden stairs climb to numerous small restaurants that serve the best seafood platters in the city. On streets bordering the market, craftspeople sell woolens and woodcarvings. From a jetty behind the market, boats leave for Tenglo and Maillén, islands in the Seno de Reloncaví.

Parque Nacional Alerce Andino 32

Road Map D2. 25 miles (40 km) SE of Puerto Montt; CONAF, Sector Correntoso, E of Correntoso village. *Dec–Mar: 9am–7pm daily; Apr–Nov: 9am–6pm daily.* **www**.conaf.cl

Covering an area of around 150 sq miles (390 sq km), Parque Nacional Alerce Andino protects the magnificent alerce tree, *Fitzroya cupressoides*. Native and exclusive to southern Chile and Argentina, the alerce is a majestic species that grows up to 170 ft (50 m) in height and can live for up to 4,000 years. The national park also embraces a dramatic landscape of rolling mountains, deep valleys, southern beech forests, and some 50 mountain lagoons. Nature-watching, river kayaking, and trekking are popular activities here. The most hiked trails are two undemanding paths to the Sagaso and Fría lagoons, ringed respectively by 800- and 300-year-old alerce woods. Birdlife abounds along both trails.

Calbuco 33

Road Map D3. 32 miles (52 km) S of Puerto Montt. *31,000.*

The scenic seaside town of Calbuco, named with the Mapuche word for Blue Water, is where Chile's long, thin mainland begins to break up into a medley of archipelagos.

Trail through stands of alerce trees at Parque Nacional Alerce Andino

Spanish forces founded the town as a fort settlement in 1603 when retreating southward from a Mapuche uprising. The colony later became an important port used to ship alerce trunks felled in nearby forests. Today, it is a small, picturesque stopover whose main attraction is a plaza facing the open sea with dramatic views of islands and three volcanoes. The plaza is fronted by a mustard-colored church that contains a statue of Archangel Michael, brought from Spain by Calbuco's founders.

The town faces the 14 islands of the Calbuco archipelago, where colonies of Magellanic penguins and other sea birds congregate between September and April. Boat trips from Caleta La Vega, Calbuco's fishermen's harbor, visit these colonies.

Excursion boats moored at the waterfront of Calbuco

Chiloé

Green, rainy, and dotted with wooden churches, the enchanting archipelago of Chiloé lies south of the Lake District and comprises one large island, Isla Grande, and several smaller ones. In pre-Colonial times, it was occupied by the seafaring Chono, and later by the Huilliche, a sedentary Mapuche sub-group. The Spanish arrived in 1567 and, over the next 200 years, steered Chiloé along a historical course distinct from that of mainland Chile. During this period, Chiloé saw ethnic mixing between the Spanish and indigenous peoples, evolved a unique culture, and was the last Spanish stronghold to fall in the War of Independence. Today, Chiloé's Jesuit churches and numerous coastal towns and villages, distinct in character from their mainland counterparts, are visited on day-trips from the historical regional capital of Castro.

The city of Ancud with its surrounding greenery and waterways

Ancud ㉞

Road Map D3. 54 miles (87 km) S of Puerto Montt; Isla Grande. *40,000.* *from Puerto Montt.* *Libertad 665; (065) 622 800.* *Festival Costumbrista Chilote (last week of Feb).* **www**.ancud.cl

A picturesque fishing town, Ancud is the first stop for most visitors crossing the Canal de Chacao, from the Lake District to Chiloé. The town was set up by the Spanish in 1768 as a fort settlement on the Bahía de Ancud, a tongue of water dotted with wooden fishing boats, edged by algae-strewn beaches and colorful houses, and ringed by emerald hills. This compact town is easily explored on foot. Its coastal Avenida Ignacio Carrera Pinto runs parallel to the bay, which is overlooked by the ruins of **Fuerte San Antonio**. This Spanish fort marks the site where Royalist forces made their last stand in Chile's War of Independence in 1826. An obelisk at the fort commemorates the Spanish Crown's final defeat. Beneath rocky cliffs nearby is **Playa Arena Gruesa**, a horseshoe-shaped beach and bathing spot.

In the town itself, **Museo Regional de Ancud** in the central plaza displays archaeological and ethnographic exhibits. It includes an ornate collection of 17th- and 18th-century Jesuit artifacts; carved demons from Chilote mythology; and a life-size replica of *Goleta Ancud*, the Ancud-built schooner that carried the first Chilean settlers to the Strait of Magellan in 1843. Adjacent to the museum is the town's cathedral, whose shingled exterior resembles the façade of a typical Chilote home.

Fuerte San Antonio
Cochrane esq San Antonio.
8.30am–9pm Mon-Fri, 9am–8pm Sat & Sun

Museo Regional de Ancud
Libertad 370. ***Tel*** *(065) 622002.*
10am–5.30pm Tue-Fri; 10am–2pm Sat & Sun.
10am–noon & 3.30–5pm.
www.museoancud.cl

Monumento Natural Islotes de Puñihuil ㉟

Road Map D3. 17 miles (27 km) W of Ancud; off Playa de Lechagua, Bahia Puñihuil, Isla Grande. *from Bahia Puñihuil: Sep–Apr: 10am–7pm daily.* *Sep–Apr: 10am–7pm daily.* **www**.conaf.cl

Three rocky islets of volcanic origin, the Monumento Natural Islotes de Puñihuil are refuge to colonies of Humboldt and Magellanic penguins that nest here each year. These islets are among the world's few places where the vulnerable Humboldt shares the same habitat as its close Magellanic relative. Small-boat excursions depart from Bahía Puñihuil on Isla Grande's northwestern coast to observe the penguins and other fauna. This includes marine otters, which scramble across the black rock at the water's edge; red-legged cormorants, agile flyers that can be seen dive-bombing the water for crustaceans; flightless steamer ducks; and American oystercatchers.

Nesting colony of penguins at Monumento Natural Islotes de Puñihuil

For hotels and restaurants in this region see pp281–3 and pp302–303

Myths and Folklore of Chiloé

Folktales and myths have long enriched Chilote life, with stories handed across centuries, from one generation to the next, through oral storytelling. Goddesses who protect the land, an evil forest dweller who tricks adolescent girls into surrendering their virginity, a serpent that sucks the lifeblood from a household, and witches disguised as owls that are seen as harbingers of death: these are just a few of the benevolent and evil spirits, sorcerers, witches, and monsters believed by the islanders to roam Chiloé. The origin of these tales lies in thousands of years of Mapuche legend and its later blurring with Spanish superstition and Roman Catholic beliefs. In addition, the archipelago's landscape forms an ideal background; the mist-shrouded bays, silent forests, craggy peaks, and low, lead-gray skies are evocative of fantastical worlds.

Metal silhouette of El Trauco

The evil El Trauco *is a little forest-dwelling man, without toes and heels, who walks with a stick and carries an axe that can fell a tree in just three blows. He roams his domain searching for youthful virgins walking the forest alone. On seeing one, his axe becomes a flute, the woman is mesmerized into submission and left with child. These children are later called to the forest to replace their father when he is absent.*

La Pincoya, *a woman of incomparable beauty, appears at midnight to dance frenetically on Chiloé's beaches. A dance facing the sea signals abundance of fish; facing the beach means scarcity.*

El Basilisco *hatches from a hen's egg, but is a snake with a rooster's red crest. Concealing itself beneath floorboards it feeds on the saliva of its host family as they sleep. The family members develop dry coughs and die before El Basilisco abandons their house.*

El Coo *is a witch disguised as an owl-like creature, whose nighttime appearance on the windowsill of a Chilote house announces the death of a loved one.*

El Camahueto, *a single-horned calf born in marshland, emigrates seaward on reaching adulthood. It destroys farmland as it goes, and causes disastrous tidal waves on its submergence into the sea.*

Castro ㊱

An island gem, Castro is the capital of Chiloé and an inevitable stop on any visit to the archipelago. The third oldest settlement in Chile, Castro was founded by the Spanish in 1567 on a hill overlooking the mist-swathed Fiordo Castro. It became the southernmost city in the world and the point for Spanish endeavors to conquer the Chiloé archipelago, as well as for Jesuit attempts to evangelize it. Today, it is a picturesque destination of hilly lanes, gorgeous sea views, and historic *palafitos*.

Statue, Iglesia San Francisco

Brightly painted wooden *palafitos* along the shores of Fiordo Castro

🏛 Museo Regional de Castro

San Martín 261. **Tel** (065) 635967.
◯ Dec–Mar: 9:30am–7pm Mon–Sat, 10:30am–1pm Sun; Apr–Nov: 9:30am–1pm & 3–6:30pm Mon–Sat, 10:30am–1pm Sun. 🎟 📷 ♿
📷 cameras without flash allowed.
The small Museo Regional de Castro traces Chiloé's history right from the arrival of hunter-gatherer groups to the archipelago – around 6,000 years ago – to modern times. Historical objects and information panels record the islands' colonization by the Chono and Huillichie communities; the subsequent Spanish conquest during the 16th century; and the primary role played by Chiloé as a Royalist stronghold during Chile's War of Independence (1810–18). The exhibits on modern history feature photographs of the destruction caused by the 1960 earthquake and tsunami, which battered coastal villages throughout the archipelago. Thematic sections in the museum explore Chiloé's rich mythology *(see p215)*, its religious architecture, and the origins of Chilote culture.

🔒 Iglesia San Francisco

Plaza de Armas. ◯ 9:30am–9:30pm daily. 🔔
Chiloé's most iconic landmark, the beautiful Iglesia San Francisco is an extraordinary work of local craftsmanship. A UNESCO-protected building, it was designed by Italian architect Eduardo Provasoli in 1910, constructed entirely from native woods such as cypress, alerce, and coigüe, and finished in flamboyant polychrome fashion. The edifice's striking Neo-Gothic façade is clad with sheets of beaten tin, painted lilac and vanilla, and features two 130-ft (40-m) high bell towers. For decades, these towers were used to guide ships arriving at the port and today, their status as Castro's tallest structures is protected by law. The church's vaulted

CASTRO CITY CENTER

Iglesia San Francisco ②
Museo Regional
 de Castro ①
Palafitos ③

0 metres 500
0 yards 500

Key to Symbols *see back flap*

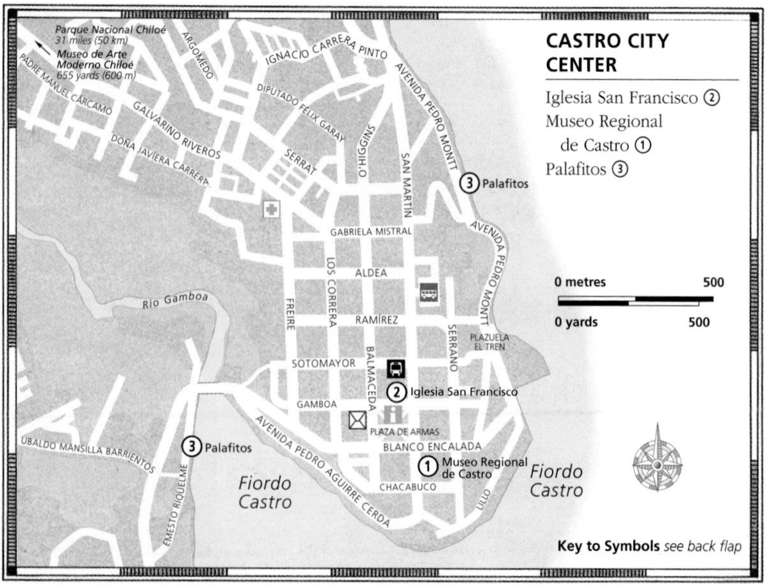

interior is ornamented with opulent religious imagery and the altar, pulpit, and confessional boxes are exquisitely hand-carved from native woods by local artisans.

Impressive Neo-Classical façade of Iglesia San Francisco

Palafitos

Shore of Fiordo Castro.

Castro's *palafitos*, the city's favorite postcard image, are traditional wooden houses built on stilts along the edge of the Fiordo Castro. These picturesque homes are constructed from local woods and painted in vibrant colors. Each *palafito* has two façades: one facing the street and the other overlooking the water. Exquisite examples of vernacular architecture, the *palafitos* were originally built in the 19th century for local fishermen, who would moor their boats in the water before climbing a wooden ladder to their family home.

VISITORS' CHECKLIST

Road Map D3. 48 miles (77 km) S of Ancud. 39,000. *Plaza de Armas.* *Festival Costumbrista Chilote (Feb).* **www**.municastro.cl

Prior to the 1960 earthquake, the *palafitos* lined most of Isla Grande's eastern shore. However, their numbers have greatly reduced and they are now concentrated on Castro's coastal Avenida Pedro Montt. Boat tours departing from the jetty offer spectacular views of these unique structures.

Museo de Arte Moderno Chiloé

Galvarino Riveros s/n, Parque Municipal. ***Tel*** *(065) 635454.* *Jan–Feb: 10am–6pm daily; Nov–Mar: 11am–4pm daily.* *on request.* **www**.mamchiloe.cl

Housed in a former grain warehouse, the Museo de Arte Moderno Chiloé sits atop a windswept hillside that offers spectacular views of the city. This excellent contemporary art museum showcases a wide range of styles such as installation, graffiti, and digital art. The permanent collection includes works by well-known Chilean artists, Arturo Duclos and Ricardo Yrarrázaval.

Many of the displays at the museum make use of indigenous materials such as sheep's wool and native woods. The exhibits also explore local themes that emphasize Chiloé's identity as distinct from that of continental Chile.

Parque Nacional Chiloé 37

Road Map D3. 32 miles (52 km) SW of Castro; Sector Chanquín, Cucao. *CONAF, Gamboa 424, Castro; (065) 532501.* *from Castro.* *8:30am–6pm daily.* **www**.conaf.cl

The scenic Parque Nacional Chiloé is fringed by the Pacific Ocean on its west and by Chile's coastal mountain range on its east. In between, it protects over 164 sq miles (426 sq km) of indigenous forest, including Chile's southernmost forests of alerce. The park has abundant wildlife and its coastal sections harbor colonies of southern sea lions, Magellanic and Humboldt penguins, and several seabirds.

Most visits to the park focus on the southern sector, where the Cucao village offers rustic accommodations at the park entrance. The village is the trailhead for the **Chanquín-Cole Cole Trail**, which skirts past a stretch of the Pacific coastline, marked by white beaches, big surf, and sand dunes edged by native forest. At the end of the trail, members of a Huilliche community organize horseback rides through the verdant woods.

The park's northern sector, although less visited, has forests of greater size and density. Here, the outstanding 11-mile (18-km) long **Castro-Abtao Trek** crosses through thick alerce forest and ends at the Pacific Ocean.

Windswept landscape of cliffs and dunes fringing the Pacific Ocean at Parque Nacional Chiloé

Local crafts on sale at the market near the harbor, Dalcahue

Dalcahue 38

Road Map D3. 17 miles (28 km) NE of Castro. *11,000.* *Ramón Freire s/n; (065) 642376.* *Sun.* *La Fiesta del Ajo y de las Tradiciones (mid-Feb).* **www**.dalcahue.cl

Located on the eastern coast of Isla Grande, the town of Dalcahue faces the smaller islands of the Chiloé archipelago. Dalcahue was not founded on any particular date; rather it evolved from the 1700s onward as a stop on the Jesuits' Circular Mission – annual trips made by the Jesuits across Chiloé.

The town's chief draw is the UNESCO-protected **Iglesia Dalcahue**. This Neo-Gothic structure was built in 1903 on the site of the Jesuits original mission. Close to it, the **Museo Cultural de Dalcahue** has local historical exhibits.

Dalcahue is also a sales hub for craftsmen from the nearby islands, who arrive daily by boat to offer their wares at the artisans' market.

Museo Cultural de Dalcahue
Avenida Pedro Montt 105. ***Tel*** *(065) 642375.* *Dec–Mar: 8am–5pm Mon–Fri, 10am–5pm Sat & Sun; Apr–Nov: 8am–5pm Mon–Fri.*

Curaco de Vélez 39

Road Map D3. 23 miles (37 km) E of Castro. *3,400.* *from Castro.* *from Dalcahue.* *Entrada a Curaco de Vélez, Plazoleta la Amistad.* *Festival Costumbrista Chilote (Feb).* **www**.curacodevelez.cl

From Dalcahue, boats cross Canal Dalcahue – part of the Mar Interior (Inner Sea) that separates Chiloé from mainland Chile – to reach Isla de Quinchao, an island dotted with tiny coastal villages.

Facing the canal on this island is the exceptionally pretty village of Curaco de Vélez, the smallest settlement in the Chiloé archipelago. Its origins can be traced to the 1600s, when Jesuit priests first dropped anchor here on their missionary route. Although the town's original Jesuit church was destroyed in a fire in 1971, a wealth of century-old vernacular architecture can still be seen. **Calle Errázuriz** is lined with gray wooden houses clad with alerce tiles in the typical Chilote style. These stand as a testament to Curaco de Vélez's prosperous past, when forestry brought wealth and fine craftsmanship. Today, life in this sleepy village revolves around a small plaza where the **Museo Municipal de Curaco de Vélez** has displays on the town's local history. The plaza backs on to a dramatic sweep of shell-strewn beach facing the narrow stretch of sea. Colonies of black-necked swans dot the water's surface in summer. Isla de Quinchao is also visited for its old Jesuit churches, historic wooden houses, seafood restaurants, and crafts markets.

Museo Municipal de Curaco de Vélez
Calle 21 de Mayo s/n. ***Tel*** *(065) 667223.* *10am–6pm daily.*

Achao 40

Road Map D3. 28 miles (45 km) E of Castro. *9,000.* *from Castro & Curaco de Vélez.* *Amunátegui s/n, Plaza de Armas.* *Encuentro Folclórico de las Islas del Archipiélago (Feb).*

Nestled on Isla de Quinchao's eastern coast, the small town of Achao makes for a good half-day visit. **Iglesia Santa María de Loreto**, the archipelago's oldest church, is the single surviving structure from the Jesuits' original mission. Built in 1754, the church fronts the town's main plaza and is a completely wooden structure: even the pegs and nails used in its construction are made of wood. The vaulted interior features Baroque columns and a beautifully carved altar and pulpit. The church's Neo-Classical façade is clad in alerce tiles in the traditional Chilote style. Also facing the plaza, the **Museo de Achao** has engaging exhibits on the Chono, the nomadic people who colonized Chiloé in the pre-Columbian era, and colorful displays of Chilote weavings.

Façade of Achao's wooden church

Museo de Achao
Amunátegui 014. *Dec–Mar: 10am–6pm daily.*

Bust of local naval hero adorning the tree-lined plaza of Curaco de Vélez

For hotels and restaurants in this region see pp281–3 and pp302–303

Fishing and excursion boats docked at Chonchi's sheltered harbor

Chonchi ㊶

Road Map D3. 14 miles (23 km) S of Castro. *13,000.* *Centenario, esq. Sgto. Candelaria.* *Festival Costumbrista Chilote (Feb).*

Referred to as the City of Three Floors for its abrupt topography, Chonchi is actually a hillside village overlooking a scenic bay on Isla Grande. The town, seen by Jesuit priests as a beachhead from where they could evangelize the archipelago's southern zones, evolved around the Jesuits' Circular Mission in the 17th century.

In the late 19th century, Chonchi reached its commercial peak as a major timber port and wooden buildings still line its gravel streets, particularly on Calle Centenario. Dating from 1883, the **Iglesia de Chonchi** is one of 16 UNESCO-protected churches on the archipelago. Its wooden façade, painted vanilla and powder-blue, hides a vaulted interior decorated with thousands of tiny white stars.

Also of interest, the **Museo de las Tradiciones Chonchinas** is housed in a family mansion that was built for a logging baron in 1910. Inside, it recreates the rooms of a typical pioneer-era Chilote home.

Museo de las Tradiciones Chonchinas
Centenario 116. ***Tel*** *(065) 672802.* *Jan–Feb: 8:30am–1pm & 2–7:30pm Mon–Fri, 9am–1pm Sat; Mar–Dec: 9am–1pm & 2–6pm Mon–Fri, 9am–2pm Sat.* *cameras without flash allowed.*

Quellón ㊷

Road Map D3. 62 miles (99 km) S of Castro. *22,000.* *22 de Mayo 251; (065) 683500.* *Festival Costumbrista Chilote (Feb).*

A commercial fishing port, Quellón grew at the turn of the 20th century around an alcohol and acetone distillery. Although the town was battered by the 1960 earthquake and tsunami, as well as by the subsequent economic decline, its nascent whale-watching industry attracts several vacationers each year. The most popular site for this activity is the Golfo de Corcovado, just southeast of Quellón, which lies on the annual migratory path of the blue whale. In the town itself, a sight well worth visiting is the **Museo Inchin Cuivi Ant**, which has exhibits on Chilote technology and history, and sculptural representations of Chiloé's mythological figures *(see p215)*. The town also serves as a starting point for ferries departing for Northern Patagonia *(see pp222–35)*, and as the end point for the great Pan-American Highway. This road network travels 12,400 miles (20,000 km) across both the North and South American continent before terminating at Quellón's town center, where the site is marked by the Monumento Hito Cero.

Museo Inchin Cuivi Ant
Avenida Juan Ladrilleros 225. ***Tel*** *(065) 681213.* *Dec–Mar: 9:30am–1pm & 2:30–6pm daily.*

FESTIVAL COSTUMBRISTA CHILOTE

A vibrant celebration of Chilote culture, the Festival Costumbrista Chilote is Chiloé's biggest annual event, and is held across towns and villages in the archipelago in January and February. Festivities feature folk music and dance, crafts fairs, and demonstrations of traditional island activities. Visitors can try their hand at shearing sheep, driving oxen, making jams, as well as learn traditional Chilote weaving methods. Food stalls serve Chilote food and drinks, including shellfish empanadas, *curanto* (*see p291*), *licor de oro* (a fermented cow-milk liqueur), and sweet ulmo honey, made from the native ulmo tree. The festivities involve a number of events held at different times and places, so it is advisable to ask a tourist information office for details.

Costumed children dancing, Festival Costumbrista Chilote

Jesuit Churches in Chiloé

Christ on the cross, Iglesia de Castro

In 1608, Jesuit priests arrived at Chiloé to evangelize the indigenous Huilliche. In the process, they established the Circular Mission and built wooden churches across the archipelago. Their construction represented a new form of religious architecture – the Chilote School – whose roots lay in the Jesuit-church architecture of 17th-century Central Europe. Today, over 60 Jesuit churches survive on the archipelago, some of which were rebuilt in the 18th and 19th centuries following fire or earthquake. Each church shares essential architectural features, though they differ in size and detail. Sixteen constitute a UNESCO World Heritage Site.

A vaulted ceiling *covers the central nave, such as in Iglesia de Castro. This elegant feature might be brightly painted or left bare and unadorned.*

The altar table *stands at the church's northern end. Crafted from native alerce, cypress, and mañio trunks by local artisans, it is often richly carved with Catholic imagery. Brightly painted, wooden saints adorn the space above the altar.*

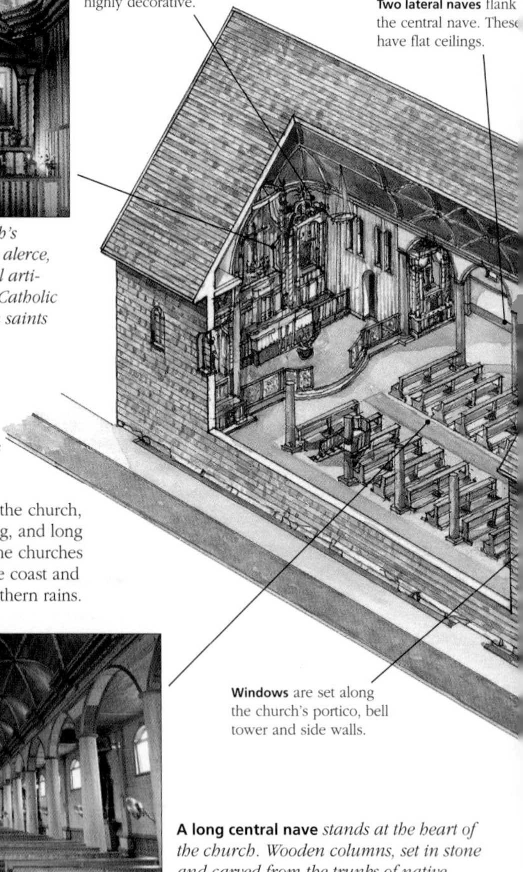

The interior of the church can be simple and austere or highly decorative.

Two lateral naves flank the central nave. These have flat ceilings.

Windows are set along the church's portico, bell tower and side walls.

CHURCH ARCHITECTURE

Chilote churches have similar key characteristics, all of which can be seen in Iglesia de Achao. Most distinctive are the bell tower and symmetrical façade. The shape of the church, with its angled roof, vaulted ceiling, and long nave suggests an inverted boat. The churches overlook a natural harbor from the coast and face south for protection from northern rains.

A long central nave *stands at the heart of the church. Wooden columns, set in stone and carved from the trunks of native island trees, separate this part from two lateral naves. Only the central nave reaches the back of the church and the altar.*

Façade of Iglesia de Tenaun

THE JESUITS' CIRCULAR MISSION

Jesuit priests faced two major obstacles to the evangelization of Chiloé: the exceptional isolation of its islands and of its Huilliche populations. In an effort to overcome these, the Jesuits made round, annual trips of the archipelago by sea. On this Circular Mission, priests disembarked at each indigenous settlement, converted its people, deposited a layman for continued spiritual assistance, and returned the following year. A church was built at each new mission – 200 were built in total – around which villages grew. After the Jesuits' expulsion from the Spanish New World in 1767, Franciscans continued the Circular Mission.

A cross crowns the tower. It acts as a guiding beacon for fishermen and sailors at sea.
A bell tower rises above the choir at the center of the façade, lending the church a symmetrical design. The tower consists of a rectangular base and a tapering, windowed octagonal tower.
The façade is beautiful for its simplicity and symmetry. It features a gabled roof and is sometimes shingled with alerce tiles.
The choir lies above the entrance, forming a triangular shape when viewed from outside.

The entrance *may have a columned and arched arcade in the Neo-Gothic or Neo-Classical style, as seen in Iglesia de Dalcahue. The Jesuits laid out squares in front of entrances for religious processions.*

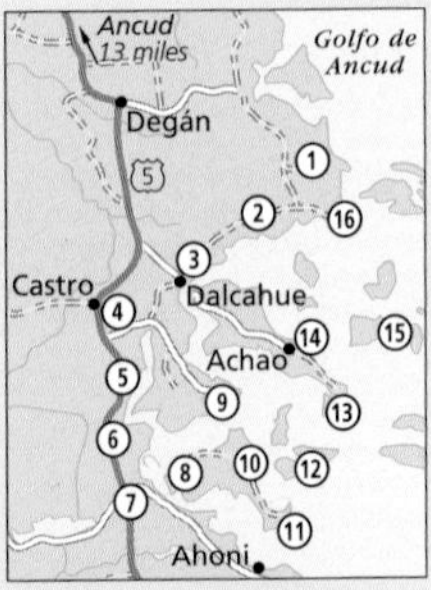
Ancud
13 miles
Golfo de Ancud
Degán
5
Castro
Dalcahue
Achao
Ahoni
1
2
3
4
5
6
7
8
9
10
11
12
13
14
15
16

UNESCO-PROTECTED CHURCHES IN CHILOÉ

Iglesia de Colo ①
Iglesia de San Juan ②
Iglesia de Dalcahue ③
Iglesia de Castro ④
Iglesia de Nercón ⑤
Iglesia de Vilupulli ⑥
Iglesia de Chonchi ⑦
Iglesia de Ichuac ⑧
Iglesia de Rilán ⑨
Iglesia de Aldachildo ⑩
Iglesia de Detif ⑪
Iglesia de Chelín ⑫
Iglesia de Quinchao ⑬
Iglesia de Achao ⑭
Iglesia de Caguach ⑮
Iglesia de Tenaun ⑯

VISITS AND TOURS

Many churches grace the center of Chiloé's towns. These are open all day and easily accessible. For visitors arriving in Chiloé by car, the Ruta de las Iglesias is a half-day driving tour of Chiloé's UNESCO-protected churches. Organized tours of selected churches run from Castro and Ancud. Details are available at **www**.rutadelasiglesias.cl

NORTHERN PATAGONIA

Thinly populated Northern Patagonia is home to some of the continent's wildest country, including Chile's single most scenic highway, the Carretera Austral. The region embraces icy-blue glaciers and icebergs, rugged Andean pinnacles, and large forest reserves. Scattered hamlets and small towns such as Coyhaique serve as ideal bases for exploring the region's myriad attractions.

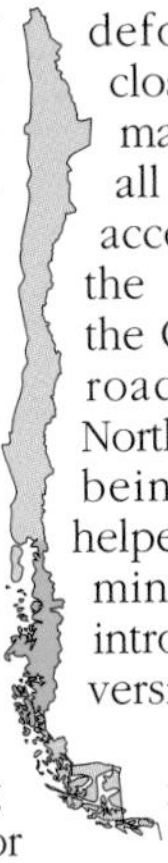

The fjords, forests, and steppes of Northern Patagonia were originally inhabited by a handful of Tehuelche hunter-gatherers and Kawéskar fisherfolk. During the age of exploration, few Europeans penetrated the area, apart from Jesuit missionaries based in Chiloé. British seafarers and scientists such as John Byron (1723–86) and Charles Darwin (1809–82) left some of the best early records. Even after independence, Chile was slow to colonize Northern Patagonia. It was not until the early 20th century that a huge land grant for sheep ranching and forestry provided the impetus for economic growth in the region.

The Chilean government's 1903 grant was made to private agricultural companies in and around the budding regional capital of Coyhaique. This initially led to large-scale fires, deforestation, and erosion that closed up Puerto Aisén, the area's main port, at a time when virtually all transport was seaborne. Road access began to be established in the 1970s with the construction of the Carretera Austral – a longitudinal road that extends the length of Northern Patagonia and is gradually being paved. The new highway helped promote tourism, encouraged mining and salmon farming, and introduced massive, though controversial, hydroelectric projects.

Northern Patagonia's many national parks conserve large swathes of old native forests, wild rivers, rugged peaks, and plunging waterfalls. Explored via scenic ferry routes and road trips off the Carretera Austral, these are ideal for a gamut of activities, from white-water rafting to fly-fishing and trekking.

One of the tree-lined streets in downtown Coyhaique

◁ Stream flowing through verdant forest in Parque Nacional Queulat, near Puerto Puyuhuapi

Exploring Northern Patagonia

The region is characterized by the absence of large towns, other than the provincial capital of Coyhaique, which is the gateway to the glacier-swathed Parque Nacional Laguna San Rafael and the trekkers' paradise, Reserva Nacional Cerro Castillo. Most travelers explore Northern Patagonia on the Carretera Austral, which stretches across the length of the region. Among the attractions accessible via this highway are the top white-water destinations of Río Futaleufú and Río Baker, the forest reserves of Parque Pumalín and Reserva Nacional Lago Jeinemeni, and the orchard-town of Chile Chico. The highway ends near Villa O'Higgins, where an adventurous overland trekking route leads into Argentina. Ferries and catamarans navigate island channels to reach the fishing hamlet of Melinka and the secluded Puerto Edén.

Kayaking on the waters of Lago Bertrand, off the Carretera Austral

SIGHTS AT A GLANCE

Villages, Towns, and Cities

Caleta Tortel 21
Chaitén 3
Chile Chico 17
Cochrane 19
Coyhaique 11
Futaleufú 4
Hornopirén 1
Melinka 6
Palena 5
Puerto Chacabuco 12
Puerto Cisnes 10
Puerto Edén 23
Puerto Puyuhuapi 7
Villa O'Higgins 22

Resorts and Spas

Puyuhuapi Lodge & Spa 8

National Parks, Reserves, and Natural Monuments

Parque Nacional Laguna San Rafael 16
Parque Nacional Queulat 9
Reserva Nacional Cerro Castillo 15
Reserva Nacional Lago Jeinemeni 18
Reserva Nacional Río Simpson 14

Areas of Natural Beauty

Parque Aiken del Sur 13
Parque Pumalín 2
Río Baker 20

KEY

- Main road
- Minor road
- Untarred minor road
- Regional border
- International border
- Peak

SEE ALSO

- ***Where to Stay*** pp283–5
- ***Where to Eat*** p304

Rugged landscape rising behind the lakeshore town of Chile Chico

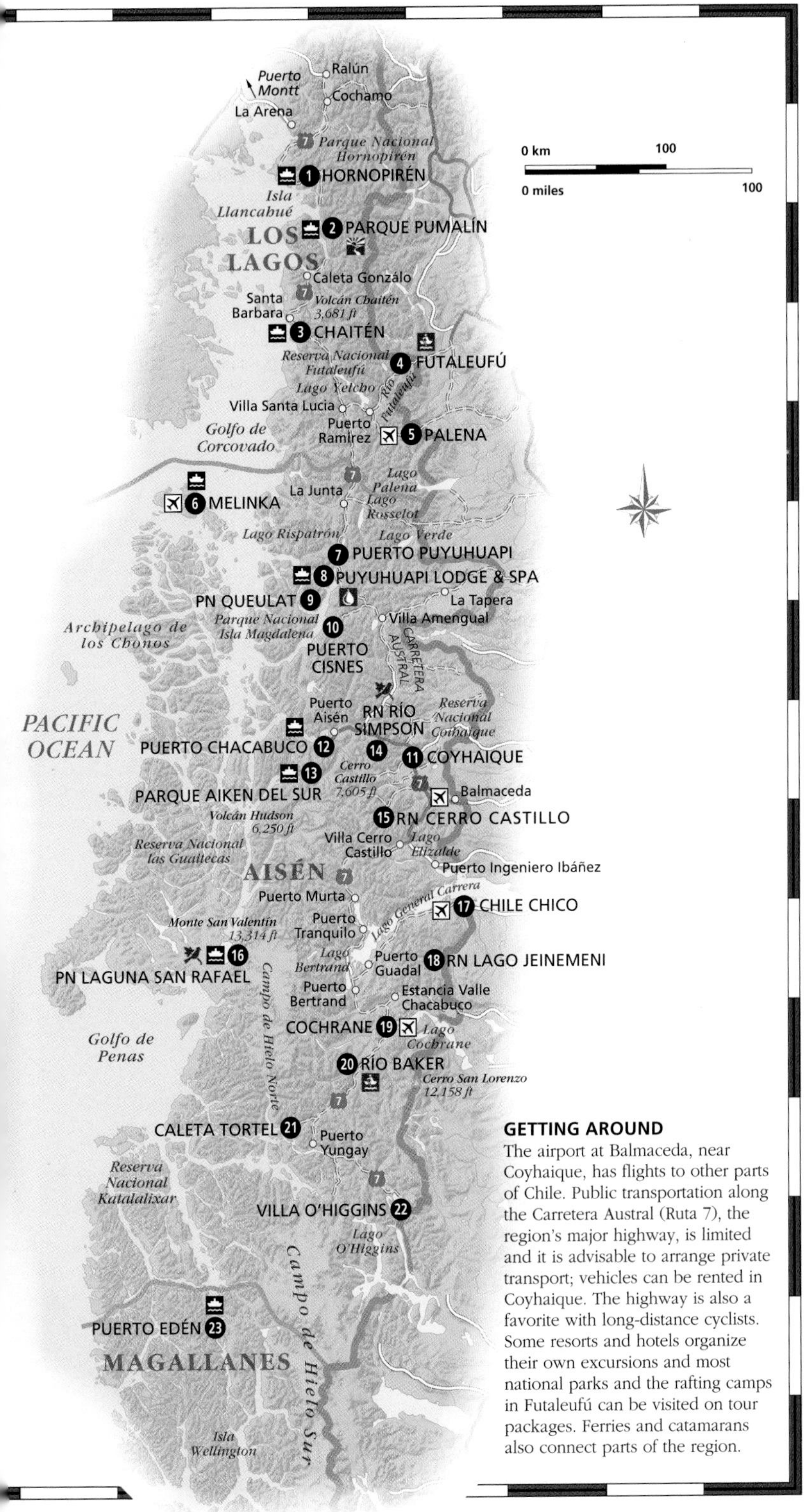

GETTING AROUND

The airport at Balmaceda, near Coyhaique, has flights to other parts of Chile. Public transportation along the Carretera Austral (Ruta 7), the region's major highway, is limited and it is advisable to arrange private transport; vehicles can be rented in Coyhaique. The highway is also a favorite with long-distance cyclists. Some resorts and hotels organize their own excursions and most national parks and the rafting camps in Futaleufú can be visited on tour packages. Ferries and catamarans also connect parts of the region.

Boats at Hornopirén's quay, surrounded by dramatic fjord scenery

Hornopirén ❶

Road Map D3. 581 miles (936 km) S of Santiago. *2,400.* *from Puerto Montt.*

Scenically set on the edge of a serene fjord, Hornopirén is named for the towering, 5,150-ft (1,570-m) high Volcán Hornopirén that looms over the town. Hornopirén has been prosperous since the 19th century, despite being hard hit by the Volcán Chaitén eruption in 2008. Today, it is the gateway to Parque Nacional Hornopirén, 7 miles (12 km) to the northwest, which offers good wildlife-watching and hiking. Local launches docked at the ferry port take visitors to hot-spring pools nearby. Harborside vendors sell fresh fish.

Parque Pumalín ❷

Road Map D3. 82 miles (132 km) S of Puerto Montt; Caleta Gonzalo. ***Tel*** *(09) 2566624.* *from Hornopirén: Jan & Feb only.* *Klenner 299, Puerto Varas; (065) 250079.* **www**.parquepumalin.cl

The world's largest privately owned nature reserve, Parque Pumalín protects over 1,224 sq miles (3,170 sq km) of temperate rain forest in an area of rugged mountains rising out of deep fjords. Established in 1991, the park was the result of the conservation initiatives of its founder, US environmental millionaire and entrepreneur, Doug Tompkins. The project initially faced stiff resistance from some of Chile's nationalists, who were against the idea of a foreigner aquiring such a massive piece of land in the country. However, the park's gradual opening to the public, complete with campgrounds, *cabañas*, and hiking trails, has delighted many Chileans. Since 2003, the park has been under the aegis of the Chilean Fundación Pumalín, and in August 2005, it was declared a nature sanctuary.

Parque Pumalín is a favored destination with hikers, owing to the many trails that snake through its stunning landscapes of verdant alerce forests, cascading waterfalls, and pristine fjords. Most of these trails are short but some are truly challenging, and require hikers to climb steep ladders while attached to ropes. There are also many hot springs within the park; some are freely available to the public, while others can be accessed for a fee. The eruption of Volcán Chaitén in May 2008 disrupted the park's services, but these are now being restored.

Cabañas **amid the lush vegetation in Parque Pumalín**

Chaitén ❸

Road Map D3. 100 miles (160 km) S of Puerto Montt.

Located along Chile's Ruta 7, better known as the Carretera Austral, the town of Chaitén was popular for its scenic blend of seaside and sierra until the Volcán Chaitén, barely 6 miles (10 km) away, erupted on May 2, 2008. This catastrophe was followed by massive flooding, which swept many houses off their foundations and buried several others in soggy ash.

The Chilean government has begun to relocate the residents of Chaitén to a more sheltered location 6 miles (10 km) northwest of town. In spite of the volcano's presence, the area continues to attract many visitors. Ferries from Puerto Montt and the Chiloé archipelago still arrive at Chaitén's port, and many accommodations and other services remain open.

Kayaking on the calm waters of Río Azul, near Futaleufú

Futaleufú 4

Road Map E3. 96 miles (154 km) SE of Chaitén. 1,200. from Chaitén. O'Higgins 536; (065) 721241. **www**.futaleufu.cl

Nestled in a secluded and picturesque valley close to the Argentine border, the village of Futaleufú is famous for its eponymous river. Popularly called the Fu, Río Futaleufú is one of the internationally popular destinations for white-water rafters and kayakers. Operators maintain riverside camps for the adventurous who travel to this river to test its Class 5 rapids, which include the Gates of Hell, Terminator, and The Perfect Storm. Novices can try their hand at calmer sections of the river, or head to the less demanding Río Azul and Río Espolón nearby. Sea kayaking is possible on Lago Yelcho, which merges with the Pacific Ocean via Río Yelcho. Other activities around Futaleufú include hiking, horse riding, and mountain-biking.

The village, as well as a large part of the area east of Río Futaleufú, is part of the 19-sq-mile (49-sq-km) **Reserva Nacional Futaleufú**. This reserve is home to lush forests of lenga, coigüe, and the Chilean cedar, and offers sanctuary to a number of animal species, including the endangered huemul deer.

The May 2008 eruption of Volcán Chaitén covered the village in ash, but, in spite of a couple of secondary ashfalls, Futaleufú has managed to recover quickly.

SAILING THE FJORDS OF NORTHERN PATAGONIA

The 3-day voyage from Puerto Montt *(see p212)* south to Puerto Natales *(see p240)* aboard the M/V *Magallanes*, operated by Navimag Ferries *(see p337)*, is one of Northern Patagonia's top attractions and an experience in itself. The exhilarating journey passes through innumerable fjords, channels, and thousands of uninhabited islands along the length of Patagonia. From the deck, passengers can admire an electrifying landscape – dense temperate rain forests, serene lakes, massive glaciers, and snowcapped mountains. It is also possible to spot some wildlife including the odd colony of sea lions. Pods of dolphins occasionally follow the boats, and seagulls and albatrosses soar above in the skies. Entertainment on board includes talks on natural history and screenings of Chilean documentaries. As the ferry passes south of Chiloé, the lights of Melinka can be seen in the distance.

Navimag's ship M/V *Magallanes*

Palena 5

Road Map E3. 160 miles (257 km) SE of Puerto Montt. *1,700.* *from Chaitén.* *O'Higgins 740; (065) 741217.* *Rodeo de Palena (Jan).*

Close to the Argentine border, the village of Palena is named for the river that flows past it, but is untouched by the white-water frenzy that has transformed neighboring Futaleufú. Instead, the village is notable for the **Rodeo de Palena**, which showcases Chile's *huaso* heritage. The main event at this rodeo involves costumed *huasos* on horseback, trying to pin a calf to a padded ring.

The Sendero de Chile *(see p314)*, a web of trails across Chile, passes through Palena en route to the little-known Reserva Nacional Lago Palena, from where the road continues to the Argentine border.

Fly-fishing from a wooden bridge across the meandering Río Palena

Melinka 6

Road Map D3. 171 miles (276 km) SW of Puerto Montt. *1400.* *from Puerto Montt.* *from Puerto Montt & Quellón.*

Off the mainland west of Palena, the Guaitecas archipelago is made up of several tiny islands. Of these, Isla Ascensión is home to the fishing village of Melinka, the archipelago's main settlement. The village overlooks Golfo de Corcovado, known for its sizable blue whale population; these are often visible from shore. Melinka has some simple, but comfortable lodgings and a few small eateries.

Puerto Puyuhuapi 7

Road Map D3. 269 miles (434 km) SE of Puerto Montt. *830.* *Otto Übel s/n; (067) 325244.* **www**.puertopuyuhuapi.cl

Most settlements along the Carretera Austral are, like the highway itself, relatively new and nondescript. However, the small fishing village of Puerto Puyuhuapi is an exception. Sitting on the edge of a scenic fjord, the village was founded by German immigrants from the Sudetenland (later, part of Czechoslovakia) in the 1930s. As a result, a large number of the houses in this area are distinctly Teutonic in style.

The village is best known for the **Alfombras de Puyuhuapi**, a family-owned factory that produces custom-made carpets for export. Set up in 1945 by German textile engineer Walter Hopperdietzel, the factory employs women from the archipelago of Chiloé to weave a range of exquisite hand-knotted woolen carpets. Unique vertical looms are used to create these beautiful rugs that are available in different designs and sizes. The plant, which is open for tours, sells readymade pieces and also takes special orders.

Puerto Puyuhuapi also serves as an ideal base for those who want to explore nearby destinations such as the Parque Nacional Queulat and the adjacent Reserva Nacional Lago Rosselot. Also in the vicinity are the hot springs of the luxurious Puyupuapi Lodge & Spa.

Guests relaxing in the indoor thermal pool at Puyuhuapi Lodge & Spa

Environs

Located 4 miles (6 km) south of Puyuhuapi, the **Termas Ventisquero de Puyuhuapi** is open for day visits. This excellent mid-range spa also has outdoor pools and a café.

Alfombras de Puyuhuapi
Aisén s/n. ***Tel*** *(09) 3599515.*
8:30am–noon & 1:30–7pm Mon–Fri. **www**.puyuhuapi.com

Termas Ventisquero de Puyuhuapi
Carretera Austral Sur Km6.
Tel *(07) 9666862.* *8am–11pm daily.* **www**.termasventisqueropuyuhuapi.cl

Puyuhuapi Lodge & Spa 8

Road Map D4. 277 miles (447 km) SE of Puerto Montt; Bahía Dorita s/n. ***Tel*** *(067) 325103.* *from reception at Carretera Austral, 9 miles (14 km) S of Puyuhuapi.* **www**.patagonia-connection.com

In a country known for its hot-springs resorts, Puyuhuapi Lodge & Spa is one of the top choices. Located in a secluded spot on the western side of the gorgeous Seno Ventisquero inlet, the lodge blends smoothly into the fern- and flower-filled rain forest: site of exquisite flora such as the rhubarb-like nalcas, which attract the eye with their enormous umbrella-sized leaves.

Puyuhuapi Lodge & Spa welcomes both day and overnight guests. The complex is made up of charming units, whose façades recall the shingled houses often seen on the islands of Chiloé. Rooms at the lodge boast polished wooden interiors and face the Bahía Dorita. Day visitors have access to three outdoor thermal pools and a café, while hotel guests can also use the heated indoor pool and enjoy a wide range of therapies, body treatments, and massages.

An interesting variety of package options are available for overnight guests. These include outdoor activities such as hiking through the pristine landscape of Parque Nacional Queulat, fly-fishing on the nearby rivers, and a visit to the village of Puerto Puyuhuapi and its famous carpet factory. Most stays conclude with a day trip south to Parque Nacional Laguna San Rafael *(see p233)*, sailing on the high-speed catamaran *Patagonia Express*, which passes through serene fjords and canals. The boat then returns north to Puerto Chacabuco, from where the lodge's guests are transfered to Coyhaique *(see p232)* and its airport at Balmaceda.

Casa Ludwig, a Teutonic-style house characteristic of Puerto Puyuhuapi

Parque Nacional Queulat ❾

Road Map D4. 269 miles (434 km) SE of Puerto Montt. *CONAF, Sector Ventisquero Colgante, Carretera Austral.* *from Puerto Puyuhuapi.* **www**.conaf.cl

Covering some of Northern Patagonia's most rugged terrain, Parque Nacional Queulat stretches from La Junta in the north to Puerto Cisnes in the south, and almost to the Argentine border in the east. Its dense rain forests, limpid lakes, clear trout streams, and steep-sided mountains cover an area of more than 5,800 sq miles (15,000 sq km). Altitudes in the park vary significantly – from sea level to a height of 6,500 ft (2,000 m), where much of the abundant precipitation falls as snow.

Although the national park fronts the Carretera Austral, its trackless backcountry is generally unexplored. However, Queulat's Sector Ventisquero Colgante offers good hiking trails. An eastbound lateral off the Carretera Austral leads to CONAF's office for visitors. From here, a couple of nature trails offer breathtaking views of the **Ventisquero Colgante**, a hanging glacier that in the early 19th century nearly reached the sea. From this mass of solid ice, waterfalls

Narrow bridge across Río Guillermo at the Parque Nacional Queulat

plunge into the jade-colored **Laguna Témpanos** (Iceberg Lake), which, in spite of its name, has no icebergs. The lake can be reached via the **Sendero Río Guillermo**, a 1,969-ft (600-m) long route that crosses a suspension bridge over the river from which it takes its name.

From the lake, a 2-mile (4-km) long trail, called the **Sendero Ventisquero Colgante**, climbs through dark and dense temperate rain forest to an overlook. When the sun warms the glacier's face, it is possible to see blocks of ice fall and shatter on to the rock debris below.

Near the park's southern entrance, the **Sendero Río de las Cascadas** is a short path leading to a fascinating natural granite amphitheater. Another road in the southern sector zigzags over the 1,650-ft (500-m) high Portezuelo Queulat pass. An offshoot from this point leads to the **Salto Padre García**, an attractive, tumbling waterfall.

Located in the northern part of the park, **Lago Risopatrón** is a popular point for fly-fishing. While the park itself has only campgrounds, there are several fishing lodges along the highway, and other accommodations at La Junta and Puerto Puyuhuapi.

Puerto Cisnes ❿

Road Map D4. 320 miles (520 km) SE of Puerto Montt. *2500.* *Sotomayor s/n; (067) 346423.*

Sitting at the mouth of the eponymous river, Puerto Cisnes was founded in 1929 as a humble lumber factory. Today it is a pretty fishing village, with colorful boats lining its waterfront. The wooden Neo-Classical **Biblioteca Pública Genaro Godoy**, the village library, is a notable landmark. Its façade is adorned with figurines from Greek mythology. Puerto Cisnes is also the access point to the **Parque Nacional Isla Magdalena**, and local fishermen shuttle visitors to this lushly forested park.

Waterfalls from the Ventisquero Colgante glacier plunging into Laguna Témpanos, Parque Nacional Queulat

Visitors on inflatable boats approach a glacier, Parque Nacional Laguna San Rafael ▷

Cerro Macay rising above one of Coyhaique's tree-lined streets

Coyhaique ⓫

Road Map E4. 286 miles (461 km) SE of Puerto Montt. *50,000.* *Bulnes 35; (067) 240290.* **www**.coyhaique.cl

Capital of Chile's Aisén region, and Northern Patagonia's only sizable city, Coyhaique is a labyrinth of concentric roads that encircle the pentagonal Plaza de Armas and change names on every other block. Despite this bewildering orientation, the city's setting beneath the basalt massif of Cerro Macay gives it visual appeal. Coyhaique also offers the region's best tourist infrastructure and easy access to destinations such as Lago Elizalde and the Reserva Nacional Río Simpson.

Coyhaique's most notable attraction, the **Museo Regional de la Patagonia** has competently arranged collections on history, mineralogy, plant paleontology, archaeology, and regional zoology.

Just beyond city limits, **Reserva Nacional Coyhaique** is a 10-sq-mile (27-sq-km) large park with hiking trails through forests of coigüe and lenga. It has a campground and offers great panoramas of the city and its environs.

Museo Regional de la Patagonia
Eusebio Lillo 23. ***Tel*** *(067) 213174.*
8:30am–6pm Mon–Fri.

Reserva Nacional Coyhaique
Ruta 7 Norte. ***Tel*** *(067) 212225.*
Dec–Mar: 8:30am–9pm daily; Apr–Nov: 8:30am–5:30pm daily.
www.conaf.cl

Puerto Chacabuco ⓬

Road Map D4. 37 miles (60 km) W of Coyhaique. *1,200.* *from Coyhaique.* *from Puerto Montt & Quellón.*

Located on the shores of an attractive natural harbor, Puerto Chacabuco is a small but lively port-town, and the center of a thriving fishing industry. It superseded nearby Puerto Aisén as the Aisén region's main port in the 1940s; by this time, deforestation of Patagonia's forests had filled Río Aisén's outlet with sediments that made it impossible to anchor at Puerto Aisén.

Today, Puerto Chacabuco serves as the gateway to nearby sights such as Parque Aiken del Sur and Parque Nacional Laguna San Rafael.

Parque Aiken del Sur ⓭

Road Map D4. 54 miles (87 km) SW of Coyhaique. *from Puerto Chacabuco.* *from Puerto Chacabuco.* *J.M. Carrera 50, Puerto Chacabuco; (067) 351115.* *reservations required.* **www**.aikendelsur.cl

The privately owned nature reserve and botanical garden of Parque Aiken del Sur covers a densely forested area of 1 sq mile (3 sq km). It has four good hiking trails featuring informational panels and viewpoints, as well as an arboretum with a number of helpfully labeled plant species. Parque Aiken is under the same ownership as Puerto Chacabuco's Hotel Loberías del Sur, which organizes guided trips to the park. Tours end with a *parrillada* (barbecue) lunch and folkloric entertainment that includes performances of Chile's national dance, the *cueca* *(see p24).*

The plunging Cascada La Vírgen at Reserva Nacional Río Simpson

Reserva Nacional Río Simpson ⓮

Road Map D4. 15 miles (25 km) W of Coyhaique. *from Coyhaique & Puerto Chacabuco.* *CONAF, Ruta 240, Km37.* *8:30am–5:30pm daily.* **www**.conaf.cl

Straddling both the Carretera Austral and the Río Simpson are the humid wooded mountains of Reserva Nacional Río Simpson. This reserve protects

Entrance through forested hills to the Parque Aiken del Sur

For hotels and restaurants in this region see pp283–5 and p304

an area of over 256 sq miles (426 sq km) and is characterized by deep canyons, gushing waterfalls and forests of tepa, coigüe, and lenga. The park is also an important sanctuary for the pudú and the endangered huemul deer.

CONAF's visitor center features a small natural history museum that offers interesting information on native flora and fauna. A short trail leads from the center to the attractive **Cascada La Vírgen** waterfall, which is encircled by wild ferns and shrubs.

Lago Elizalde in the Reserva Nacional Cerro Castillo

Reserva Nacional Cerro Castillo ⓯

Road Map D4. 28 miles (45 km) S of Coyhaique. *from Coyhaique.*

Covering over 517 sq miles (1,340 sq km) of rugged Andean landscape, Reserva Nacional Cerro Castillo is named for the impressive 7,605-ft (2,318-m) high Cerro Castillo, which crowns this reserve. A popular destination for hikers, the reserve offers several nature trails that snake through forests of lenga and around cascading waterfalls and icy glaciers. Wildlife spotted on these hikes includes the huemul, puma, and fox.

The reserve's big attraction is a 3-day trek through dense vegetation that ends at the tiny hamlet of Villa Cerro Castillo. A short distance south from this village is **Alero de las Manos**, a natural rock shelter that is home to spectacular pre-Columbian paintings. Exquisite examples of rock art, these paintings date from 3,000 years ago.

Situated along the northern border of Reserva Nacional Cerro Castillo, **Lago Elizalde** is a narrow lake that stretches for 15 miles (25 km), but is less than a mile (2 km) wide at any point. Verdant woodlands of coigüe and lenga fringe this lake, which is a popular spot for fishing, sailing, and kayaking. Boats can be rented at the small yacht harbor on the lake's eastern banks. In the summer, tour operators based here organize outdoor activities such as horse riding, trekking, and biking in the scenic surroundings of the lake.

Southeast of the reserve, the port-town of **Puerto Ingeniero Ibáñez** sits at the edge of Chile's largest lake, Lago General Carrera. While notable for its orchards, the town is also a springboard for neighboring fruit-growing areas.

Alero de las Manos
3 miles (5 km) S of Villa Cerro Castillo. *10am–6pm daily.*

Parque Nacional Laguna San Rafael ⓰

Road Map D4. 118 miles (190 km) SW of Coyhaique. *from Coyhaique.* *from Puerto Chacabuco.*
www.conaf.cl

A UNESCO World Biosphere Reserve, Parque Nacional Laguna San Rafael is one of Chile's largest national parks. Almost half of this sprawling 6,726-sq-miles (17,420-sq-km) reserve is covered by the **Campo de Hielo Norte**, the second-largest ice sheet in the southern hemisphere. This sheet embraces the towering Monte San Valentín, which at 13,314 ft (4,000 m) is the highest summit in Patagonia. Campo de Hielo Norte feeds over 18 glaciers including the park's highlight, the 200-ft (60-m) high **Ventisquero San Rafael**, which overlooks Laguna San Raphel. From the face of this receding glacier, massive chunks of blue ice spill into the lagoon below.

Several tour operators *(see p319)* arrange sailing excursions to the glacier through a maze of fjords and channels. While boats usually keep a safe distance from the glacier, passengers can enjoy a closer look from inflatable dinghies. A plane ride over the park also offers breathtaking panoramas of the ice field.

Famous names associated with this place include that of renowned British naturalist Charles Darwin (1809–82), who visited the glacier during his voyage on board the HMS *Beagle*. John Byron, grandfather of famous British poet Lord Byron, was shipwrecked here in 1742 and gave extensive descriptions of the place.

Mist-swathed glacier in Parque Nacional Laguna San Rafael

Chile Chico 17

Road Map E4. 68 miles (110 km) SE of Coyhaique. *4,500.* *from Puerto Ingeniero Ibañez.* *O'Higgins s/n; (067) 411638.* **www**.chilechico.cl

Located close to the Argentine border, Chile Chico is part of a fruit-growing belt near Lago General Carrera. The town is best approached by a scenic and precipitous road from the Carreta Austral, a trip that is an experience in itself.

Chile Chico dates from 1909, when Argentines crossed over to settle in this area. It was briefly famous in 1917, when the colonizers faced the ranchers in a conflict, known as the War of Chile Chico. In 1991, the eruption of Volcán Hudson nearly smothered the area's apple and pear orchards. This past and the area's natural history are documented in the **Museo de la Casa de Cultura**, part of which occupies the grounded *Los Andes* steamer, which once toured the lake.

Museo de la Casa de Cultura
Calle O'Higgins and Lautaro. ***Tel*** *(067) 411123.* *10am–7pm daily.* *Dec–Mar: Sun.*

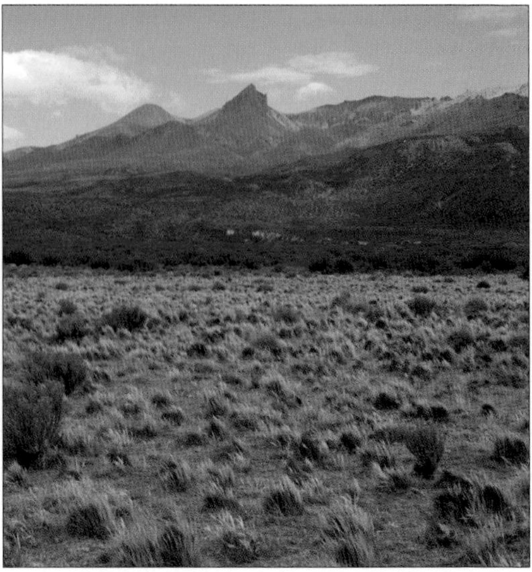

Broad, mountainous landscape in Reserva Nacional Lago Jeinemeni

Reserva Nacional Lago Jeinemeni 18

Road Map E4. 89 miles (143 km) S of Coyhaique; Blest Gana 121, Chile Chico. ***Tel*** *(067) 411325.* *from Chile Chico.* **www**.conaf.cl

Hugging the Argentine border, and accessible only by high-clearance vehicles, Reserva Nacional Lago Jeinemeni is an enormous 622-sq-mile (1,600-sq-km) sanctuary named for its lake, which is popular with fly-fishers. In the north-eastern sector, a footpath leads to pre-Columbian rock art at the **Cueva de las Manos**.

Cochrane 19

Road Map D4. 119 miles (192 km) S of Coyhaique. *2,200.* *Dr. Steffen and Esmeralda; (067) 522326.* **www**.cochranepatagonia.cl

Situated at the western edge of the eponymous lake, the tidy town of Cochrane is the last major service center on Carretera Austral. Visitors, notably motorists, will find the highway's last gasoline station here, but the fuel is more expensive than anywhere else in the country. Cochrane is also the gateway to **Reserva Nacional Lago Cochrane**, a major sanctuary for the endangered huemul deer. Guided huemul-watching tours by boat can be arranged with the help of CONAF, the national forestry authority.

Reserva Nacional Lago Cochrane
4 miles (6 km) E of Cochrane; CONAF, Río Nef 417. ***Tel*** *(067) 522164.* **www**.conaf.cl

The *Los Andes* steamer outside Museo de la Casa de Cultura at Chile Chico

Río Baker 20

Road Map D5. 146 miles (235 km) S of Coyhaique. *from Cochrane.*

Flowing between Caleta Tortel and Lago Bertrand, the 116-mile (170-km) long Río Baker is Chile's largest river in terms of volume. Owing to its flow, and the mountainous terrain through which it runs, this wild and scenic river is also under threat from a massive hydroelectric project that could devastate the natural landscape and destroy the region's nascent ecotourism industry. For the moment however, the lands just south of **Puerto Bertrand**, especially at the stunning confluence

For hotels and restaurants in this region see pp283–5 and p304

of the Baker and the Río Nef, are a paradise for campers, hikers, rafters, fly-fishers, and other recreationists. In a tributary valley to the east, toward the Argentine border, environmental philanthropist Doug Tompkins *(see p226)* and his wife have acquired the former Estancia Chacabuco, and plan to make it part of a new national park connecting it with Reserva Nacional Lago Jeinemeni in the north, and Reserva Nacional Lago Chacabuco in the south.

Río Baker, forming a ribbon of blue through the verdant hills of Patagonia

Caleta Tortel ㉑

Road Map D5. 172 km (277 miles) SW of Coyhaique. 430. *from Coyhaique.*

Located on an inlet off the Río Baker's Fiordo Mitchell, Caleta Tortel is arguably Patagonia's most picturesque village. The settlement was unreachable by road until 2003. It still has no streets as such, but boardwalks and staircases that link its bay side *palafitos (see p112)*. These homesteads show the influence of the folk architecture of the Chiloé archipelago *(see pp214–21)*. Most of the buildings are made of guaiteca cypress, the world's southernmost conifer species.

In recent years, the tourism industry has grown, with hiking to nearby sites such as **Cerro La Bandera** – accessible by land – and **Cascada Pisagua**, a waterfall that requires a boat shuttle to reach the trailhead.

The village is also an ideal base for visiting the nearby Parque Nacional Laguna San Rafael, Parque Nacional Bernardo O'Higgins, and Reserva Nacional Katalalixar, all of which can be reached by basic motor launches.

Villa O'Higgins ㉒

Road Map E5. 204 miles (328 km) S of Coyhaique. 465. *from Coyhaique.* *from Cochrane.* *from Puerto Yungay.* *Carretera Austral 267, (067) 431821.* **www.** villaohiggins.com

Beyond Cochrane, services are nearly non-existent on the last 120 miles (200 km) of the Carretera Austral. There is, however, a free ferry shuttle from Puerto Yungay, near the Río Bravo, which takes visitors to the end of the highway: at Villa O'Higgins. This village dates from 1966 and is named for the Chilean hero Bernardo O'Higgins *(see p153)*. Since the arrival of the Carretera Austral in 1999, the village has grown due to tourism. Surrounded by wild mountain scenery, and within sight of the **Campo del Hielo Sur** (Southern Icefield), Villa O'Higgins offers ample hiking trails including a part of the Sendero de Chile, an ongoing project to connect major trails across the country. The area has also become a destination for an adventurous route, by vehicle or on foot, to the Argentine trekking mecca of El Chaltén.

***Palafitos* and boardwalks at the secluded riverside village of Caleta Tortel**

Puerto Edén ㉓

Road Map D5. 272 miles (438 km) SW of Coyhaique. 275. *Ferry and cruise ship days.*

Located on Isla Wellington, in one of the rainiest sectors of the Pacific fjords, the town of Puerto Edén owes its origin to an air force initiative that contemplated a stop for seaplanes between Puerto Montt *(see pp212–13)* and Punta Arenas *(see pp246–7)*. However, the site soon became the last outpost of Kawéskar hunter-gatherers, who settled here after the air force abandoned it. Today, Puerto Edén is home to the few surviving members of the Kawéskar community, who have re-created some of their traditional shelters. It is possible to purchase a sample of their crafts here. Weather and schedule permitting, the town is a stop for Skorpios cruise ships and Navimag ferries that sail out of Puerto Natales *(see p240)*.

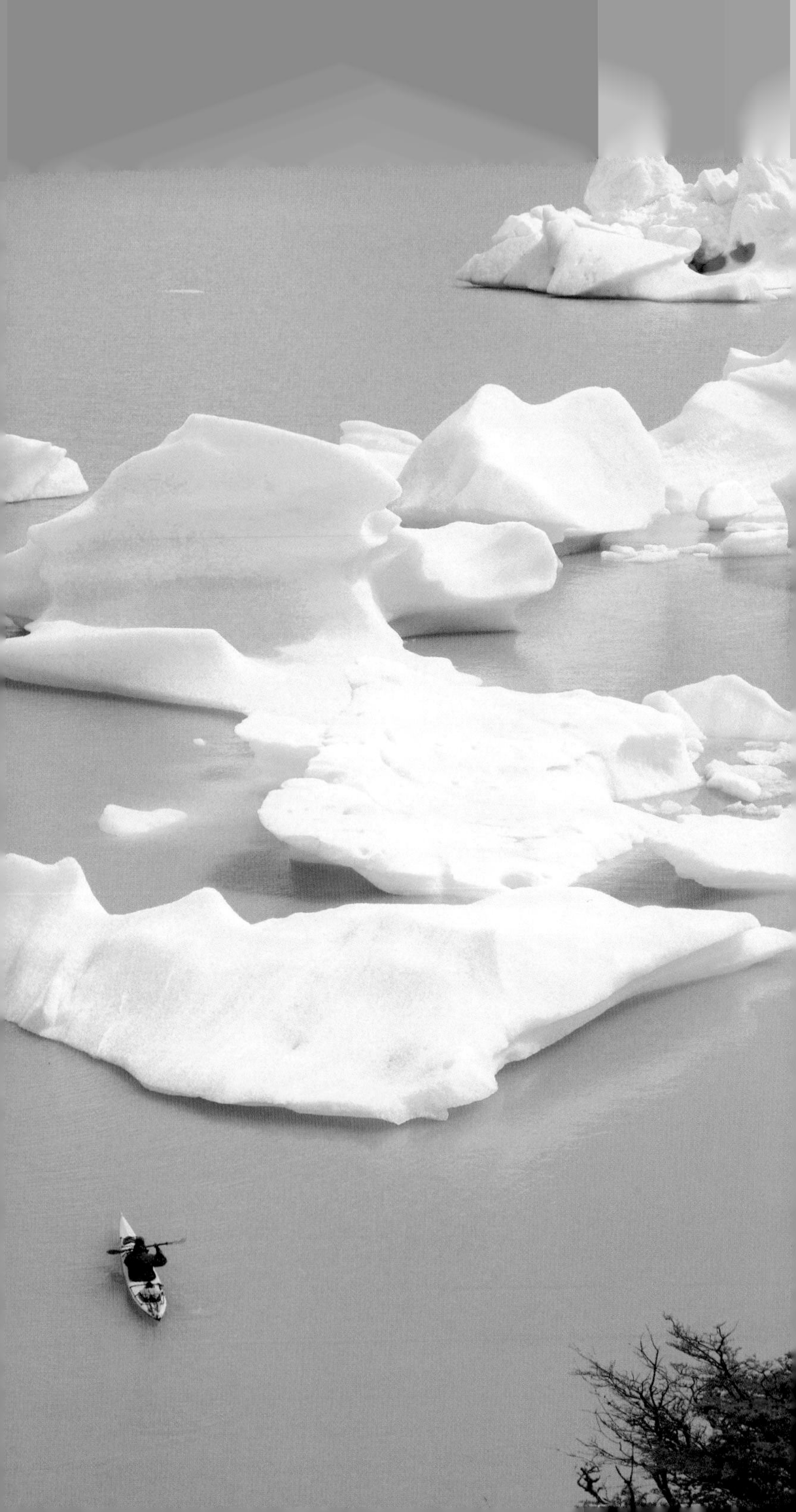

SOUTHERN PATAGONIA AND TIERRA DEL FUEGO

An archipelagic labyrinth and a thin strip of continental land, Southern Patagonia is a dramatic wilderness of emerald fjords, vast ice fields, rugged peaks, and windswept prairies. Separated from the mainland by the Strait of Magellan, Tierra del Fuego stretches across untamed and largely unpopulated territory to Cape Horn, the awe-inspiring tip of South America.

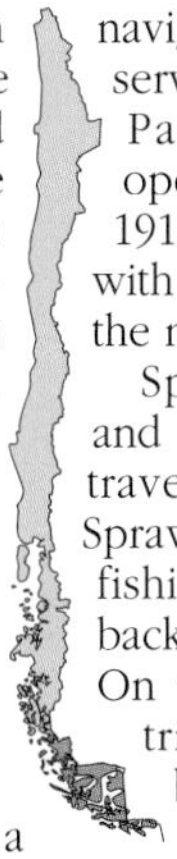

The original inhabitants of Southern Patagonia and Tierra del Fuego were the Ona, Yamana, Tehuelche, and Alacalufe communities, who are now extinct or greatly reduced in number. In 1520, Portuguese navigator Ferdinand Magellan became the first European to discover the area. However, permanent settlements were not established until the 19th century, when missionaries, adventurers, and merchants arrived from Spain, Britain, Croatia, and northern Chile. Immigrants also came to work on sheep estancias that emerged across the region.

The late 19th century witnessed a rise in prosperity as a result of large-scale sheep ranching. At the same time, a thriving shipping industry developed, benefitting from the navigable Strait of Magellan, which served as a passage between the Pacific and Atlantic until the opening of the Panama Canal in 1914. Today, sheep farming, along with oil extraction and tourism, are the mainstays of the economy.

Spectacular natural attractions and a wide range of activities draw travelers to the region each year. Sprawling parks offer excellent fly-fishing, trekking, kayaking, horseback riding, and mountain climbing. On the coast, whale-watching and trips to penguin rookeries are becoming increasingly popular. Cruise ships take passengers through magnificent channels and past the craggy scenery of Tierra del Fuego, where they can spot sea lions, albatrosses, and flamingos.

Sea lions off a fjord near Puerto Williams in Tierra del Fuego

◁ **Kayaking between floating icebergs on Lago Grey, Parque Nacional Torres del Paine**

Exploring Southern Patagonia and Tierra del Fuego

The region's Magallanes district is known for its fjords and dense forests. The Campo de Hielo Sur (Southern Ice Field) blankets much of Southern Patagonia and sends forth glaciers that can be visited from Puerto Natales. The town is also a good base to explore the top trekking destination of Torres del Paine National Park, the archaeological site of Cueva del Milodón, and the private zoo near Villa Tehuelche. Punta Arenas is the gateway to the national monument of Puerto Hambre and the large colonies of Magellanic penguins at Isla Magdalena. Across the Strait of Magellan, Chilean Tierra del Fuego is the least-visited destination, home to a handful of lodges and the southernmost city in the world, Puerto Williams.

SIGHTS AT A GLANCE

Villages, Towns, and Cities

Porvenir ⓫
Puerto Hambre ❾
Puerto Natales ❶
Puerto Williams ⓬
Punta Arenas pp246–7 ❻
Villa Tehuelche ❺

National Parks, Reserves, and Natural Monuments

Parque Nacional Bernado O'Higgins ❹
Torres del Paine National Park pp242–5 ❸

Areas of Natural Beauty

Isla Magdalena ❽
Seno Otway ❼
Strait of Magellan ❿

Archaeological Sites and Ruins

Cueva del Milodón ❷

Sights of Interest

Cape Horn ⓭

KEY

- Main road
- Minor road
- Untarred minor road
- International border
- △ Peak

SEE ALSO

• ***Where to Stay*** pp285–7
• ***Where to Eat*** pp305–307

Boardwalk to the Monumento al Navegante Solitario on Cape Horn

For additional map symbols *see back flap*

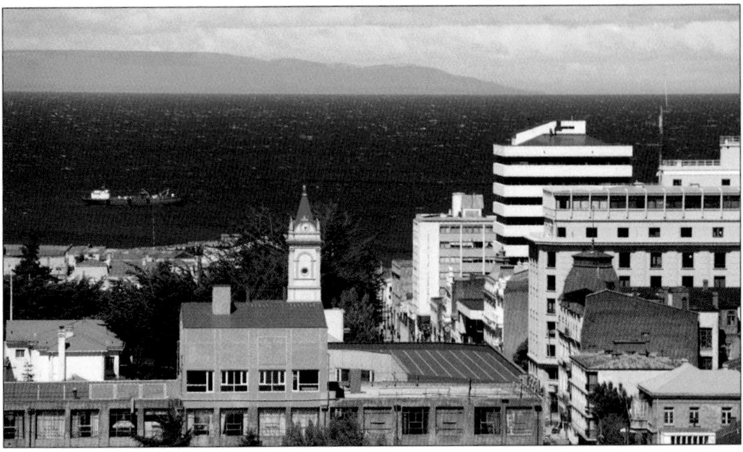

View across Punta Arenas to the Strait of Magellan, with Tierra del Fuego in the distance

GETTING AROUND

It is possible to get around Southern Patagonia by air, ship, or long-distance bus. A large number of visitors arrive at the airport in Punta Arenas. Puerto Natales and Puerto Williams also have local aerodromes served by charter flights. Bus services are plentiful and reliable. Most roads are unpaved and gas stations are scarce, so motorists and drivers should consider carrying a canister of gas. Ferries and cruise ships go to destinations in Tierra del Fuego.

Puerto Natales ❶

Road Map E6. 1,268 miles (2,040 km) S of Santiago. *Ave. Puerto Montt 19, (061) 412125.* *17,000.* **www.**torresdelpaine.com

Historic locomotive in the Plaza de Armas, Puerto Natales

Black-necked swan at Puerto Natales

Capital of the Última Esperanza Province of Chile, Puerto Natales is a windswept town backed by the Sierra Dorothea range. The town overlooks the Seno Última Esperanza (Last Hope Sound) – so called because this was the site that Spanish explorer Juan Ladrilleros considered his last hope while attempting to locate the Strait of Magellan in 1557. The region was originally inhabited by the indigenous Tehuelche and Kawéskar tribes; the present town was only founded in 1911 when a sheep-ranching boom and the subsequent establishment of two mutton processing factories nearby led to the influx of Croatian, British, and German immigrants, as well as of people from the Chiloé archipelago. Today, the economy of Puerto Natales is primarily based on its flourishing tourism industry.

At the town's center, **Plaza de Armas** is adorned by an old locomotive that stands testament to the region's flourishing sheep-ranching days. This rail engine was used to transport workers back and forth from the abattoir in nearby Puerto Bories. Located a few blocks west of the plaza, **Museo Histórico Municipal** features displays of antique tools and household items, as well as photographs of the Kawéskar and Aonikenk indigenous communities, who no longer exist in the region. The town's main road, Avenida Pedro Montt, popularly called the Avenida Costanera, affords splendid views of glacier-topped peaks and the turquoise sound, which is dotted with cormorants, native black-necked swans, and other seabirds.

Puerto Natales serves as the main gateway to Southern Patagonia's famous Torres del Paine National Park. As a result, the town caters to hundreds of travelers who stop here en route to the park.

Environs

Located 3 miles (5 km) north of Puerto Natales is **Puerto Bories**, a small housing community and site of the Frígorifico Bories, an old sheep processing plant founded in 1915. This factory was part of the Sociedad Explotadora de Tierra del Fuego, once the largest sheep-ranching operation in Patagonia which extended for some 11,584 sq miles (30,000 sq km) across Chile and Argentina. Today, the Frígorifico Bories is a national monument and a portion of the building has been converted into a hotel. However, its locomotive garage, blacksmiths' workshop, offices, and boiling and tannery facilities can still be viewed from the outside. Most notable is the architectural style of this brick factory, which is reminiscent of post-Victorian England.

Around 12 miles (20 km) northwest of Puerto Natales, **Puerto Prat** is the remains of the first immigrant settlement of the area. Established in 1897 as the main port of the Seno Última Esperanza, it is now a scattering of quaint buildings and an old cemetery.

A short distance northwest of Puerto Pratt, **Estancia Puerto Consuelo** was founded by German immigrant Hermann Eberhard. Among the earliest

The sprawling town of Puerto Natales fronting the waters of the Seno Última Esperanza

For hotels and restaurants in this region see pp285–7 and pp305–307

Replica of the Pleistocene-era ground sloth outside Cueva del Milodón

ranches in Chilean Patagonia, the estancia offers spectacular views of Torres del Paine National Park. Visitors can ride horses, hike in the surrounding countryside, kayak in the series of waterways close by, observe ranch hands at work, and finish with a delicious barbecue.

Museo Histórico Municipal
Manuel Bulnes 285. ***Tel*** *(061) 209534. 8:30am–12:30pm & 2:30–6pm Tue–Sun.*

Cueva del Milodón ❷

Road Map E6. 15 miles (24 km) NW of Puerto Natales. *from Puerto Natales. Oct–Apr: 8am–8pm daily; May–Sep: 8:30am–6pm daily.*

Arguably the most important paleontological and archaeological site in Southern Patagonia, the Cueva del Milodón is named for the now-extinct ground sloth, or milodón *(Mylodon listai)*, whose partial remains were discovered here by immigrant Hermann Eberhard in 1895. The slow-moving milodón, measuring up to 10 ft (3 m) in height when on its hind legs and weighing around 400 pounds (181 kg), roamed Patagonia till the Pleistocene period, about 10,000 years ago. Today, a replica of this sloth dominates the cave entrance. A small visitors' center displays fossil remains of the sloth and other extinct animals such as the dwarf horse and saber-toothed tiger.

Torres del Paine National Park ❸

See pp242–3.

Parque Nacional Bernardo O'Higgins ❹

Road Map D6. 90 miles (145 km) NW of Puerto Natales. *CONAF, Manuel Baquedano 847, Puerto Natales; (061) 411438. by Turismo 21 de Mayo from Puerto Natales; call (061) 411978 for details. included in catamaran price.* **www**.turismo21demayo.cl

Created in 1969, Parque Nacional Bernardo O' Higgins is bordered on the east by the mammoth ice field Campo de Hielo Sur and comprises a maze of small islands, fjords, and channels. Covering an area of 13,614 sq miles (35,260 sq km), it is Chile's largest national park, but the lack of land access also makes it one of the least visited. Navimag's ship *(see p337)* which links Puerto Montt and Puerto Natales, stops near the park at Puerto Eden *(see p235)*. The park is also reached on a full-day catamaran cruise from Puerto Natales. Retracing the 16th-century voyage of Juan Ladrilleros through the Seno Última Esperanza, the trip offers views of sea lions, cascades, and rugged scenery. The trip includes a visit to the hanging Glaciar Balmaceda and a short trek to the iceberg-laden lagoon of Glaciar Serrano. From the lagoon, kayaks and dinghies navigate up the Río Serrano through a little-known route marked by untrammeled scenery of glaciers, peaks, and dense forest, and ends at Torres del Paine National Park's administration center. This trip can also be made in the opposite direction from Torres del Paine.

Villa Tehuelche ❺

Road Map E6. 96 miles (154 km) SE of Puerto Natales. *700. from Puerto Natales. Festival de la Esquila (third weekend of Jan).*

The pocket-sized outpost of Villa Tehuelche was founded in 1967 as a service center for the regional population with shops, a post office, church, school, and police station. This village is famous for the annual Festival de la Esquila, or Shearing Festival, that draws hundreds of people from across Patagonia and features rodeos, sheep-shearing competitions, and lamb barbecues.

Some 36 miles (58 km) south of Villa Tehuelche, the old **Estancia Lolita** has fashioned itself as an attraction, most notably as a private zoo, with exhibits of local fauna including pumas, guanacos, a rare Geoffrey's cat, and foxes.

A view of the sleepy village of Villa Tehuelche

Torres del Paine National Park ❸

Chile's most dazzling national park, Torres del Paine (Towers of Blue) is a UNESCO World Biosphere Reserve. The park is named for the Paine massif, a cluster of granite peaks and needles backed by the Southern Ice Field and situated between the Andes and the Patagonian steppe. The name itself is a mix of Spanish and indigenous Patagonian words: *paine* being the Tehuelche term for blue, a color frequently seen throughout the area in the form of turquoise glaciers, icebergs, rivers, and lakes. The park is Chile's trekking mecca, with numerous day hikes as well as 2- to 10-day backpacking routes.

Laguna Amarga entrance to Torres del Paine National Park, Patagonia

★ Glaciar Grey
The 2-mile (4-km) wide Glaciar Grey descends from the Southern Ice Field. Boats cruise up to the glacier face; visitors can also trek across the glacier in crampons, or kayak past the icebergs on Lago Grey.

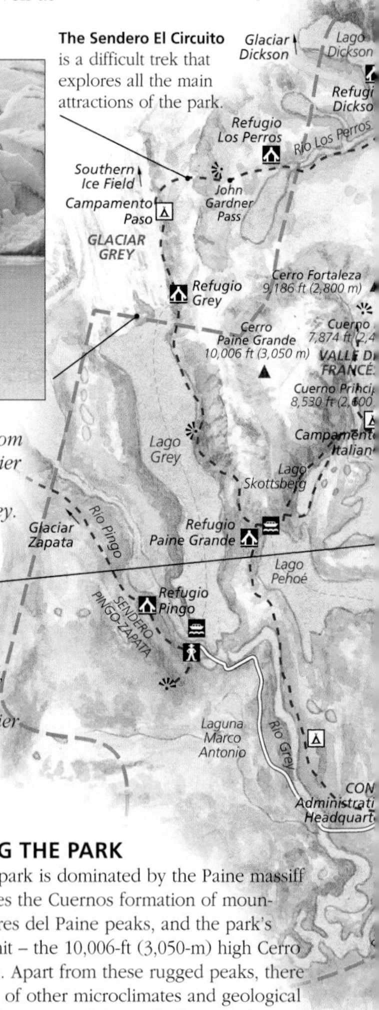

The Sendero El Circuito is a difficult trek that explores all the main attractions of the park.

Salto Grande
This waterfall connects Lago Nordenskjold with Lago Pehoé, which drains water from glacier meltoff in the northern sector.

STAR SIGHTS

★ Glaciar Grey

★ Torres del Paine

★ Los Cuernos

EXPLORING THE PARK

The national park is dominated by the Paine massiff which includes the Cuernos formation of mountains, the Torres del Paine peaks, and the park's highest summit – the 10,006-ft (3,050-m) high Cerro Paine Grande. Apart from these rugged peaks, there are a number of other microclimates and geological features that form part of the park. These include glaciers, granite spires, beech forests, lakes, and steppe, and can be explored by foot, by vehicle, aboard a catamaran, or on horseback. The park also offers a series of campgrounds and *refugios*, in addition to several hotels *(see pp286–7)*.

Valle de Ascencio
The valley leads up to a granite moraine and the last leg of the Torres hike, continuing on to Valle de Silencio.

VISITORS' CHECKLIST

Road Map D6. 43 miles (70 km) NW of Puerto Natales. ✈ from Punta Arenas. 🚌 from Punta Arenas or Puerto Natales. 🚢 Navimag. ℹ CONAF; all ranger stations. ◯ daily. 🏳 ⊞ ◻ ◻
www.torresdelpaine.com

Lago Paine
Río Paine
SENDERO EL CIRCUITO
Campamento Serón ◻

ORRES DEL PAINE
NATIONAL PARK

Río Paine

Laguna Azul

LE DE NCIO

VALLE DE ASCENCIO

Torre Norte Monzino
▲ 8,530 ft (2,600 m)

▲ Torre Central
9,186 ft (2,800 m)

rre Sur i Agostini
350 ft (2,850 m)

Refugio Chileno

▲ Cerro Almirante Nieto
8,753 ft (2,668 m)

Hostería Las Torres

uerno Este
217 ft (2,200 m)

Refugio Los Cuernos

SENDERO

Lago Nordenskjold

Laguna Amarga

Lago Sarmiento

Punta Arenas
— 207 miles (334 km)

Laguna Verde

SIERRA DEL TORO

ro

erto Natales
miles (70 km)

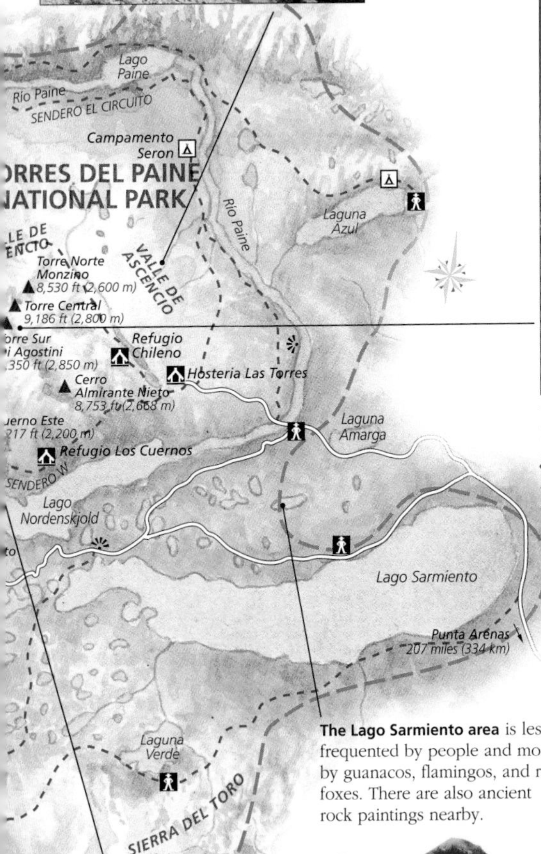

★ Torres del Paine
Three gigantic, salmon-pink granite towers, the Torres del Paine can only be seen in their entirety from the Laguna Azul sector, or by climbing to their base on the last leg of a full-day hike through Valle de Ascencio.

The Lago Sarmiento area is less frequented by people and more by guanacos, flamingos, and red foxes. There are also ancient rock paintings nearby.

0 km		5
0 miles		5

KEY

═══	Minor road
– – –	Trail
▬ ▬	Park boundary
- - -	Ferry route
🚢	Riverboat pier
ℹ	Visitor information
🚶	Ranger station
❉	Viewpoint
◻	Campsite
◣	Hostería/Refugio
▲	Peak

★ Los Cuernos
The park's centerpiece, Los Cuernos is made up of three granite peaks: Cuerno Norte, Principal, and Este. These are part of the 120-million-year-old Paine massif and have been formed as a result of erosion by glaciers, wind, and rain.

Exploring Torres del Paine National Park

Patagonia's gray fox

Access to the park is from Punta Arenas via road, or from Puerto Natales by one of two roads or by inflatable boat along the Río Serrano. There are five separate entrances to the park, all manned by CONAF ranger stations. Within its boundaries, some 155 miles (250 km) of the sanctuary is covered by clearly marked trails. The most popular of these is Sendero El Circuito, a hike that needs roughly 8 days and takes visitors to the Paine massif, passing by the brilliant lakes of Paine, Dickson and Grey. There are also trails to Lago Paine, the Torres peaks, and the Valle del Francés, which can be combined into a single hike, named after its shape as Sendero W.

A heard of guanacos at Torres del Paine National Park

CONAF Administracion Headquarters

Lago del Toro sector, southern entrance of park. ***Tel*** *(061) 691931.*

8:30am–8:30pm daily.

The southern road from Puerto Natales is the most beautiful of all routes into the park, and leads to the CONAF Administration Headquarters. This center provides general information about the park and also has educational displays on the flora, fauna, and geological features of the sanctuary. The outdoor platform here is an excellent place from which to spot aquatic birds. A small kiosk sells maps, books, and sundry items.

Sendero W

This medium-difficult trail follows the shape of a W, hence its name. The Sendero W is the most popular multi-day trek because it takes visitors to the three major highlights of the park: the Torres del Paine, the Valle del Francés (French Valley), and Glaciar Grey. Most trekkers begin at the Las Torres *(see p287)*, a ranch-style complex that has campgrounds and a hostel, the **Hosteria Las Torres**. The 7- to 8-hour roundtrip hike to the iconic Torres del Paine is difficult, first traversing the beautiful beech forests of the **Valle de Ascencio** and ending with a steep, 45-minute hike up a moraine of boulders to the torres, three stunning granite towers that rise majestically in front of a glacial lake.

The Sendero W continues southwest from Hosteria Las Torres along the shores of the turquoise **Lago Nordenskjold** and skirting the flank of the park's famous two-toned granite Los Cuernos.

About 7 miles (11 km) along this route are the hostel and campgrounds of Refugio Los Cuernos. Trekkers may either spend the night here or, if camping, continue onward another 4 miles (6 km) to the **Valle del Francés** and its Campamento Italiano. However, there are no services here. The trail up and into the Valle del Francés is about 5 miles (8 km) long, climbing high into the valley ringed with granite peaks and offering sweeping views of the Patagonian steppe.

From the base of the Valle del Francés, it is some 5 miles (8 km) to the Refugio Paine Grande and campground, and to the docking area for a catamaran that crosses **Lago Pehoé** to the Pudeto sector. From this point, the trail heads north for the final leg of the Sendero W, 7 miles (11 km) to Refugio Grey. Visitors to the *refugio* can arrange trekking excursions to Glaciar Grey. Most trekkers return to Lago Pehoé and take the catamaran to Pudeto,

Forests of southern beech carpeting Valle de Ascencio

Hikers on the Sendero El Circuito, near Laguna Azul

from where transportation is available to Puerto Natales. However, it is also possible to walk 11 miles (18 km) of flat terrain to the park's administration center.

Sendero El Circuito

For a thorough exploration of the park, hikers should consider the Sendero El Circuito (The Circuit Trail), which circumnavigates the Paine massif. This hike takes about 6 to 8 days depending on individual ability and weather conditions. The trail is undertaken in a counter-clockwise direction, starting at the Hosteria Las Torres or from the Laguna Amarga ranger station. Alternatively, backpackers may begin the hike from the Laguna Azul sector, though this requires a river crossing at the Refugio Dickson via boat.

The trail from Hosteria Las Torres begins with a 4-hour hike through the Valle de Ascencio with grazing cattle and forest to Campamento Seron. It then continues for 12 miles (19 km) to Refugio Dickson, which offers direct views of **Glaciar Dickson**.

The trail grows increasingly difficult from this point. However, the views are far more dramatic, with glaciers, peaks, and beech forest. About 6 miles (9 km) through forest and swampy terrain from Refugio Dickson lies the campground Los Perros. The 7-mile (12-km) climb from here, up to **John Gardner Pass** can be difficult during bad weather. The electrifying views of Glaciar Grey and the **Southern Ice Field** from the pass are the highlights of the Sendero El Circuito; the vast stretch of ice is breathtaking. Recreational hikers can spend the night at the Campamento Paso, as the next 6 miles (10 km) to Refugio Grey are difficult, with steep, rocky gorges and fallen tree trunks. Hikers then trek from Refugio Grey to Lago Pehoé, for the journey back to Puerto Natales.

Blossoming porcelain orchid in the park

Sendero Pingo-Zapata

This infrequently visited trail is good for bird-watching, and has an easy-medium difficulty level. The trail begins at the Lago Grey CONAF station and follows the Río Pingo past prairie, scrub, and views of the western granite walls of the Paine massif. After about 5 hours, visitors arrive at the Campamento Zapata, with a decrepit *refugio*, and a half-hour later to a lookout point with views of the stunning **Glaciar Zapata** and its numerous rows of glacial moraine.

Glaciar Grey

Although it has receded greatly during the past decade, Glaciar Grey is one of the largest and most easily accessed glaciers in Patagonia. The icebergs that break off from the glacier float to the end of Lago Grey. These can be seen along a short walk on flat beach from the Grey sector's ranger station, near Refugio Grey. At the end of the beach, reached by about a half-hour walk, a peninsula with a viewing platform offers vistas of Glaciar Grey in the distance. A popular journey here is aboard the catamaran *Grey II*, which leaves Refugio Grey twice daily and sails to the face of the glacier in summer.

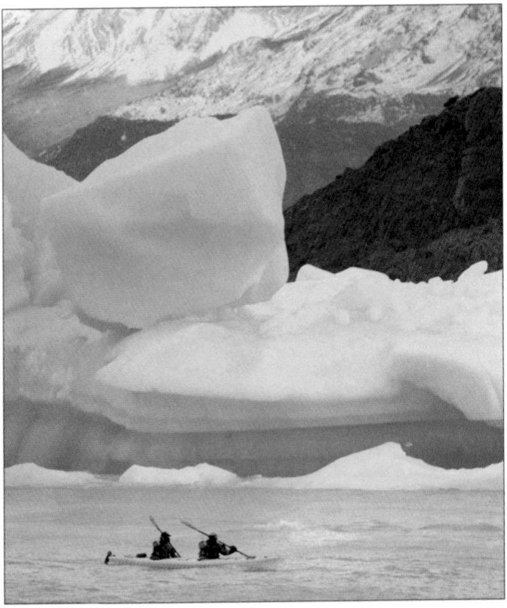

Kayaking near the floating icebergs on Lago Grey

Punta Arenas ❻

Braun Menéndez museum display

The capital of the Magallanes region, Punta Arenas is the jumping off point for cruises to Tierra del Fuego and Antarctica. Set up in 1848, the city was initially a penal colony and a disciplinary center for military personnel. During the early 20th century, it drew thousands of Europeans escaping World War I and seeking fortunes in sheep ranching, gold and coal mining, and the shipping industry. Today, the best place to begin exploring the town is at the Plaza Muñoz Gamero.

Drawing room at the Museo Regional Braun Menéndez

Museo Regional Braun Menéndez

H. de Magallanes 949. ***Tel*** *(061) 244 216.* *May–Sep: 10:30am–2pm daily; Oct–Apr: 10:30am–5pm Mon–Sat, 10am–2pm Sun and hols.* *reservation required.* **www**.dibam.cl

Travelers to Punta Arenas can appreciate the staggering wealth of the Braun-Menéndez family – owners of a mammoth ranching operation in the early 20th century – at the Museo Regional Braun Menéndez. Dating from 1903, the edifice is preserved with its original furniture and finery, which was imported from Europe and includes marble fireplaces, French tapestries, crystal chandeliers, and examples of some of the best European craftsmanship from that time. The museum also features a salon dedicated to the ethnographic history of the region.

Just south of the museum is the main square, Plaza Muñoz Gamero, with the Magellan Monument at its center. The ritual here is to kiss the toe of the Indian statue on the monument, for good luck or, as legend goes, so that visitors return to Punta Arenas. Also on the square is **Palacio Sara Braun**, another mansion of the Braun-Menéndez family that is now home to a hotel and the Club de la Unión.

Museo Regional Salesiano Maggiorino Borgatello

Ave. M. Bulnes & Maipú. ***Tel*** *(061) 221001.* *10am–12:30pm & 3–5:30pm Tue–Sun.*

Founded in 1893, the Museo Regional Salesiano Maggiorino Borgatello charts the history, ecology, and anthropology of the Magallanes region. Visits begin at the lobby, which displays stuffed local fauna, pickled marine life, and geological samples collected by Salesian missionaries of the early 20th century. There are also ethnographic exhibits of Kawéskar and Selk'nam Indians that include tools,

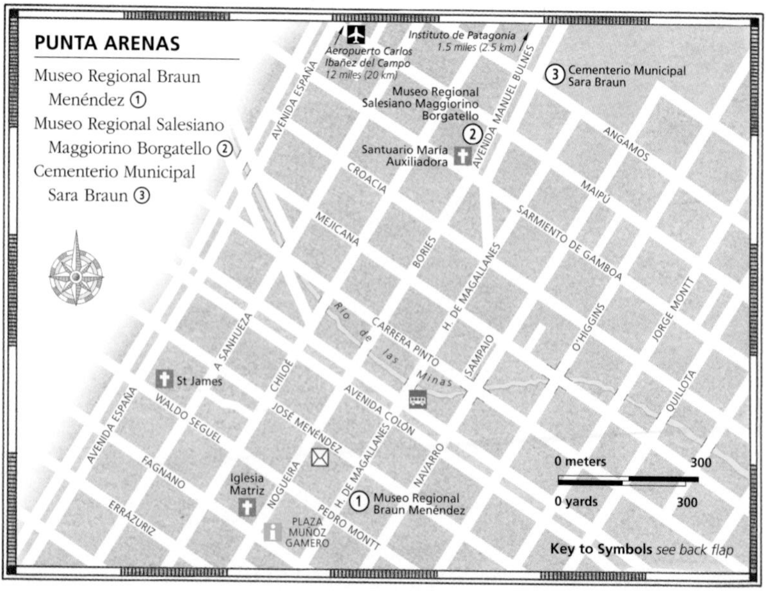

VISITORS' CHECKLIST

Road Map E6. 153 miles (247 km) S of Puerto Natales. *146,000.* *Plaza Muñoz Gamero.* *Winter carnival (Jul).* **www**.puntaarenas.cl

Cypress trees and tombs at the Cementerio Municipal Sara Braun

clothing, and black-and-white photographs; a history of missionary work in the area and Catholic religious artifacts; and a floor devoted to the industrial history of Punta Arenas.

Cementerio Municipal Sara Braun

Ave. M. Bulnes & Rómulo Correa. *Oct–Mar: 7:30am–8pm daily; Apr–Sep: 8am–6:30pm daily.*

This antique mausoleum is the site of a number of family tombs and simple graves with extravagantly pruned cypress trees along the pathways. Of special interest is the Indiecito (Little Indian) statue, located on the northwest side, that represents deceased indigenous groups and is a totem for good luck.

Instituto de Patagonia

Ave. M. Bulnes 1890. ***Tel** (061) 217173.* *8:30am–11:30am & 2:30pm–6:30pm Mon–Fri, 8:30–12:30pm Sat.*

Set at the edge of the city, the Instituto de Patagonia is run by the University of Magallanes and features artifacts and antiques from the early days of Punta Arenas. The complex consists of mock houses and businesses built in the style of early 20th-century architecture. Each building has exhibits ranging from carpentry workshops to a dry goods store, the interior of a residence with household appliances, and the residence of a ranch hand. Scattered around the property are examples of old carriages and ranching machinery.

Seno Otway 7

Road Map E6. 40 miles (65 km) N of Punta Arenas. *mid-Oct–Mar: 8am–7pm daily.*

A delightful half-day tour from Punta Arenas is a visit to the penguin rookery at Seno Otway, which is accessible by a mostly unpaved road. Every year, between November and March, some 2,500 pairs of Magellanic penguins come to burrow nests here before heading north to Argentina or the south-central Chilean coast.

The 110-acre (45-ha) reserve at Seno Otway features roped walkways and lookout platforms, and a store with penguin souvenirs. On the way to the reserve, it is possible to spot birds such as the flightless Darwin's rhea.

Isla Magdalena 8

Road Map E6. 22 miles (35 km) NE of Punta Arenas. *from Punta Arenas; Dec–Feb: 4pm Tue, Thu & Sat.*

The 2-hour boat trip to Isla Magdalena is worth the effort given that the island hosts up to 60,000 breeding pairs of Magellanic penguins. In addition, each pair produces two chicks over November–March, bringing the population on the island to some 240,000 penguins. A roped walkway runs across the area, and an old lighthouse acts as a ranger and research station. Adult penguins take turns guarding the nest and fishing, and every morning and afternoon visitors can watch the birds waddling along narrow paths to and from the sea, passing just inches from them.

Chilean flag fluttering above Fuerte Bulnes, near Puerto Hambre

Puerto Hambre 9

Road Map E7. 36 miles (58 km) S of Punta Arenas. *8.30am–6pm daily.*

The first attempt to establish a settlement on the Strait of Magellan took place in 1584 when the Spanish captain Pedro Sarmiento de Gamboa left several hundred colonists about 20 miles (50 km) south of Punta Arenas. He called the settlement Rey Felipe, but it was changed to Puerto Hambre (Port Hunger) in 1587 by British captain Thomas Cavendish, who landed here to find just one survivor – the rest had starved or succumbed to the elements. The traces of these ruins are now considered a national monument.

About 2 miles (4 km) to the south is the national monument **Fuerte Bulnes**, set up in 1843 by colonists from Chiloé who were later transplanted to present-day Punta Arenas in 1848. It was the second, and first successful, colonization of the strait, and the well-reconstructed site offers an interesting look into the colonists' lives.

Walking among Magellanic penguins on Isla Magdalena

Boats anchored alongside a yacht club in Puerto Williams, near the mountains of Isla Navarino ▷

Tormenta-II

Fishing boat trawling across the Strait of Magellan

Strait of Magellan ⓾

Road Map E7. 62 miles (100 km) S of Punta Arenas. *from Punta Delgada to Puerto Espora and from Punta Arenas to Porvenir.*

A navigable sea route linking the Atlantic with the Pacific Ocean, the Strait of Magellan is named for Ferdinand Magellan, the first European to discover this passage in 1520. Measuring 354 miles (570 km) in length, this strait separates Tierra del Fuego from the Chilean mainland, and, in spite of currents and strong winds, offers a safer route for ships rounding the South American continent than the Drake Passage farther south. Until the opening of the Panama Canal in 1914, the Strait of Magellan served as the principal route for steam ships traveling between the Atlantic and Pacific oceans.

The strait is a breeding ground for humpback whales, sea lions, penguins, and other marine fauna during the summer months. Breeding colonies are easily spotted at Isla Carlos III, near the strait's western entrance. The waters surrounding the island comprise the 259-sq-mile (670-sq-km) large **Parque Marino Francisco Coloane**, Chile's first marine reserve. Boat trips to Isla Carlos III include a stop at Cabo Froward, the southernmost tip of the Chilean mainland, and the Cabo San Isidro. Located on the southeastern coast of the Brunswick Peninsula, this cape has a lighthouse dating from the 8th century. Once used to guide ships through the Strait of Magellan, the lighthouse has now been converted into a museum that charts the culture and history of the region's indigenous groups such as the Selk'nam and Yamana Indians.

Porvenir ⓫

Road Map E6. 25 miles (40 km) SE of Punta Arenas. *7,000.* **www**.muniporvenir.cl.

Dating back to 1834, but officially established as a town only in 1894, windswept Porvenir first grew as an outpost for miners working in the Baquedano mountain range during a local gold rush in the mid-19th century. Later, during the 20th-century boom in wool production, the town acted as a service center for the region's sheep estancias that had been established principally by Croatian immigrants. Today, Porvenir is the capital of the Tierra del Fuego province. The town's tin-walled homes are interspersed with buildings erected in the 1930s and its main highlight is the **Museo Provincial Fernando Cordero Rusque**. The museum has displays on local fauna and archaeological and anthropological exhibits on the indigenous cultures that once inhabited the region. Four blocks north of the museum, the **Cementerio Municipal** features antique mausoleums in the shade of cypress trees pruned into cylindrical shapes. Located on the town's main coastal road, Avenida Manuel Senoret, **Parque del Recuerdo** displays antique machinery and vehicles from the 19th century. On the same road, the Plaza de las Américas features a monument constructed to commemorate the Selk'nam Indians, the original inhabitants of the region.

View of the brightly painted houses in Porvenir

Environs

Located some 4 miles (6 km) north of Porvenir, **Monumento Natural Lagunas de los Cisnes** is known for large flocks of pink flamingos and black-necked swans. Farther south, Lago Blanco is a scenic lake renowned for rainbow trout and brown trout fishing. The lake sits on the northeastern edge of Parque Natural Karukinka, a privately run nature reserve founded by the Wildlife Conservation Society with funding from Goldman Sachs in 2004 to protect the region's endangered beech forests from exploitation by international timber agencies.

Museo Provincial Fernando Cordero Rusque

Padre Mario Zavattaro 402.
Tel *(061) 581100. 9am–5pm Mon–Thu, 9am–4pm Fri, 10:30am–1:30pm & 3pm–5pm Sat, Sun & holidays.* **www**.museoporvenir.cl

For hotels and restaurants in this region see pp285–7 and pp305–307

THE WORLD'S SOUTHERNMOST PRISON

Following the military coup of 1973 *(see p48)*, the Pinochet regime sent deposed government leaders to the tiny Isla Dawson in the Strait of Magellan. Characterized by cold, wretched weather and a remoteness that made escape nearly impossible, the island held up to 400 prisoners who were subjected to torture, harsh living conditions, and brutal forced labor. These prisoners were either executed or transferred to other jails in 1974. Many who survived played a major role in the restoration of democracy in Chile. The prisoners' experience was documented in the 2009 film *Dawson: Isla 10*, directed by former exile Miguel Littín. The film was inspired by the autobiographical work of former Minister of Mining, Sergio Bitar, one of Allende's cabinet ministers who was imprisoned on the island from 1973 to 1974.

Poster of documentary, *Dawson: Isla 10*

Puerto Williams ⓬

Road Map F7. 182 miles (293 km) SE of Punta Arenas. *2,500.* *from Punta Arenas.*

The solitary town on Isla Navarino, south of mainland Chile, Puerto Williams is the capital of the Magallanes and Chilean Antarctic region, and also the southernmost town in the world. Founded in 1953 as a Chilean naval base, it was later named Puerto Williams in honor of Irish-born officer Juan Williams, who captured the Strait of Magellan for Chile in 1843. The town boasts a stunning backdrop of the granite peaks of Dientes de Navarino, a rugged area that offers some of the best trekking in the region. The town's main attraction, **Museo Martín Gusinde**, established in 1974, is dedicated to the eponymous Austrian anthropologist and clergyman (1886–1969) who did significant research on the region's indigenous Yamana and Selk'nam Indian communities. The museum features ethnographic exhibits on these groups and has displays on local geology, fauna, and flora. The island is a favored destination for sailors and yachtsmen, who meet at the Club de Yates Milcalvi, an antique boat retrofitted as a bar.

Located around 20 miles (32 km) east of Puerto Williams, a village known as Villa Ukika is home to the handful of surviving members of the Yamana community.

Cape Horn ⓭

Road Map F7. 437 miles (703 km) S of Punta Arenas. *from Punta Arenas & Puerto Williams.* *from Punta Arenas & Puerto Williams.*

The southernmost "point" of the South American continent, Cape Horn, or the Horn as it is often called, actually comprises a group of islands that form the Parque Nacional Cabo de Hornos. Cape Horn was discovered by Europeans during a Dutch sailing expedition in 1616 and named for the town of Hoorn in the Netherlands. From the 18th century until the opening of the Panama Canal in 1914, it served as an important trade route for cargo ships.

The waters around the Cape Horn islands are treacherous due to choppy swells, rogue waves, strong currents, notorious gales, and in particular, the williwaws, blasts of wind that appear out of nowhere. Inhospitable sailing conditions make it difficult to reach the very tip, and **Isla Hornos**, to its northwest, is usually as far as people can go.

Monument on Isla Hornos

The moss-covered Isla Hornos is home to a naval station, a lighthouse, and a chapel. Shaped to resemble an albatross, the Monumento al Navegante Solitario honors sailors who died while sailing around the Horn. The island has a rich birdlife, including Magellanic penguins, condors, and albatrosses. Dolphins and whales can be seen offshore.

The coastal town of Puerto Williams, overlooked by the jagged peaks of Dientes de Navarino

Visiting Argentina

Visitors to Chile's Patagonia have the option of traveling to the Argentinian Patagonia given that both the countries' star attractions are so close to each other. In just a few hours, travelers to Torres del Paine National Park can visit the Argentine town El Calafate, a tourism-oriented town that forms the base for visits to Argentiana's Glaciar Perito Moreno and Los Glaciares National Park. Cruise ship passengers often have the option of stopping over for a day or night in the Argentine port-city Ushuaia, a phenomenally beautiful town backed by jagged peaks.

KEY

- International airport
- Domestic airport
- Highway
- Other road
- International border

SIGHTS AT A GLANCE

Cerro Castor ④
PN Los Glaciares ①
PN Tierra del Fuego ③
Ushuaia ②

Parque Nacional Los Glaciares ①

227 miles (336 km) NW of Puerto Natales; 50 miles (80 km) W of El Calafate. *El Calafate.* *El Calafate.* *Avenida del Libertador 1302, El Calafate; (02902) 493004.* www.losglaciares.com

Created in 1937, Parque Nacional Los Glaciares is an add-on destination favored by most travelers to Torres del Paine National Park, as there are two border crossings near it. Named for the glaciers that cascade down from the Southern Ice Field, this reserve is Argentina's second-largest national park and a trekking and climbing mecca. The park, most of it inaccessible, covers 1.5 million acres of rugged mountains, turquoise lakes, glaciers, and thundering rivers. Dominating the whole is the dramatic Fitz Roy massif, a towering cluster of granite needles. Trekkers to this area can take part in camping-based trips over many days, or on shorter day hikes that last between 2 and 6 hours. Trips begin at the tiny mountain village of **El Chaltén**, a scattering of hotels and restaurants that sprang up in the 1990s along the Río Las Vueltas.

The major crowd-puller at Parque Nacional Los Glaciares is the **Glaciar Perito Moreno**, which flows for some 18 miles (29 km) before making contact with a peninsula that provides visitors with ideal lookout points from which to view the glacial marvel. The glacier is, in fact, one of the few in Patagonia that is not receding, although it cannot grow very far either as its terminus is obstructed by land. Every several years, pressure that has built up from the ice's contact with land causes the glacier to calve in a crashing fury, a sight many travelers aspire to see when visiting this park. Several agencies offer trekking on the glacier with crampons and ropes, along with a selection of nature walks, and boat rides to the neighboring glaciers of Upsala and Spegazzini, and around floating icebergs.

Los Glaciares is accessed from **El Calafate**, a tourism-based town on the shore of Lago Argentino, a 5-hour drive from Puerto Natales, Chile. Antique *estancias* (sheep ranches) here have been converted into hotels and restaurants and give visitors a taste of Patagonian gaucho life and culture.

Visitors at the Glacier Perito Moreno, Parque Nacional Los Glaciares

An early morning view of Ushuaia, Argentina's southernmost city

Ushuaia ②

351 miles (564 km) SE of El Calafate. *64,000.* *Avenida San Martin 674; (02901) 424 550.* *Festival Música Clásica de Ushuaia (Apr).* **www**.e-ushuaia.com

Hugging the shore of the Beagle Channel with the broken peaks of Parque Nacional Tierra del Fuego rising majestically behind it, Ushuaia is Argentina's southernmost city. Visited for its natural beauty, Ushuaia is a popular port of call for major cruise lines and the jumping off point for trips to Antarctica.

The city is named in the language of the region's first indigenous inhabitants, the Yamana; Ushuaia translates as the City Facing West. It was formally established as the capital of Tierra del Fuego in 1904. British missionaries first settled the area in the mid 1800s, and in 1896, President Julio Argentino Roca founded a penal colony here for serious and repeat offenders from the north and Buenos Aires. The colony not only served as a means of hiding away society's most dangerous criminals, it was also a way of establishing a strong Argentine presence in Tierra del Fuego. The sprawling prison was shut down in 1947 and now houses the **Museo Marítimo y Presidio**, a vast collection of historical, nautical, scientific, and cultural exhibits of the area. There are also exhibits of prison-era artifacts and interpretative displays depicting the life of prisoners and their guards.

Parque Nacional Tierra del Fuego ③

18 miles (11 km) N of Ushuaia. *from Ushuaia.* *Ruta Nacional 3, Km.3047; (02901) 421315.* *24hrs daily.* **www**.tierradelfuego.org

Founded in 1960 to protect some 235 sq miles (610 sq km) of southern beech forest and rugged terrain, Parque Nacional Tierra del Fuego is the only park in Argentina featuring a maritime coast and two large sea bays – Lapataia and Ensenada. Though most of the park is inaccessible, it is still popular with Ushuaia locals as a recreational area offering picnic grounds, trails, boating, bird-watching, and trout fishing. Short pedestrian paths and longer hikes pass through thick forest and past dark-water *turbales* (swamps). Visitors may see guanacos and red foxes, or the island's scourge, the Canadian beaver, which was introduced in the 1940s to harvest pelts. They have now vastly multiplied and represent a huge environmental threat.

The area is especially lovely in autumn, when the beech trees turn colors. Children and adults enjoy riding the park's **Tren del Fin de Mundo**, a steam locomotive that once took prisoners to the forest to chop wood, during Ushuaia's stint as a penal colony. The train leaves from Estación de Tren, outside the park, for an hour-long journey, passing forest, waterfalls, and rivers.

VISITORS' CHECKLIST

El Calafate *charter flights from Punta Arenas.* *from Puerto Natales via Control Fronterizo Dorotea at Río Turbio or Control Frontrizo Río Don Guillermo at Cerro Castillo.* **Ushuaia** *from Santiago; charter flights from Punta Arenas.* *from Punta Arenas & Porvenir via border control at Paso San Sebastian.*

Cerro Castor ④

16 miles (26 km) NE of Ushuaia; Ruta Nacional 3, Km.3047. ***Tel** (02901) 422244.* *from Ushuaia.* *mid-Jun–mid-Oct.* **www**.cerrocastor.com

Argentina's southernmost ski resort attracts not only locals from Ushuaia, but skiers and snowboarders from Buenos Aires, and Chile too. The base is just 640 ft (195 m) above sea level, with the highest elevation at 3,468 ft (1,057 m), yet Cerro Castor receives prodigious snowfall.

The exclusive and modern retreat comprises the Castor Ski Lodge, with 15 rustic-chic and cozy cabins, four restaurants, and four *refugios* or mountain cafés. The resort offers nearly 1,500 acres (607 ha) of skiable terrain and 2,630 ft (800 m) of vertical drop, a snowpark, and seven lifts. Numerous activities are on offer, including a series of ski and culinary events that extend throughout the season.

Boardwalk to Lapataia bay, Parque Nacional Tierra del Fuego

EASTER ISLAND AND ROBINSON CRUSOE ISLAND

Chile's borders extend over two of the planet's most isolated, remote, and exotic islands. Easter Island, known as Rapa Nui to its inhabitants, is most visited for its moai *statues, world-renowned icons of archaeology and enigmatic remnants of a vanished society. Closer to the mainland, Robinson Crusoe Island is site of one of the world's great true adventure sagas.*

Four hours from the mainland by jet, Easter Island is a tiny volcanic triangle whose culture, despite its political link to Chile, is more Polynesian than Latin American. The original settlers island-hopped their way across the Western Pacific and arrived at Easter Island around AD 1000. What they lacked in numbers they made up for with ingenuity and creativity, carving giant monuments that have since made the island famous. Restored to their original platforms, if not their former glory, the *moai* attract tens of thousands of visitors each year. Activities such as hiking, diving, riding, and surfing, not to mention the Polynesian ambience, complement its unique cultural resources.

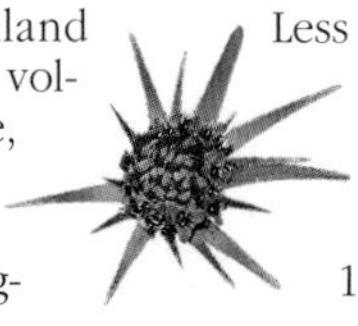

Endemic *Ochagavia elegans* in bloom

Less visited by tourists, Robinson Crusoe Island is part of the Juan Fernández archipelago, named for the Spanish navigator who landed here in 1574. The island itself takes its name from the novel *Robinson Crusoe*, which was inspired by the real-life story of 18th-century Scotsman, Alexander Selkirk *(see p267)*. The first permanent settlements were set up in the mid-18th century and Chilean authority was established in the early 19th century. The present inhabitants, concentrated in the tiny town of San Juan Bautista, live off lobster fishing and tourism. The town is also the base for exploring endemic forests on the island's north and the trails that were familiar to Selkirk.

Thick forest, home to numerous endemic species, Robinson Crusoe Island

◁ View from the rim of Rano Kau's crater on Easter Island

Exploring Easter Island and Robinson Crusoe Island

The ideal base for exploring Easter Island is Hanga Roa, a rather spread out village with some of the island's main sights located close by, notably the crater and cultural village at Rano Kau. More remote sights, such as the *moais* at Rano Raraku, Playa Anakena, and Península Poike, can be seen on a full-day loop along the island's eastern shores before returning to Hanga Roa. Robinson Crusoe Island is primarily a summer destination, as flights to the island are most frequent in January and February. Here, the village of San Juan Bautista is a good base. The rugged terrain is ideal for hiking, especially along Sendero Salsipuedes and Mirador Selkirk. Limited transportation makes sightseeing time-consuming – though always rewarding.

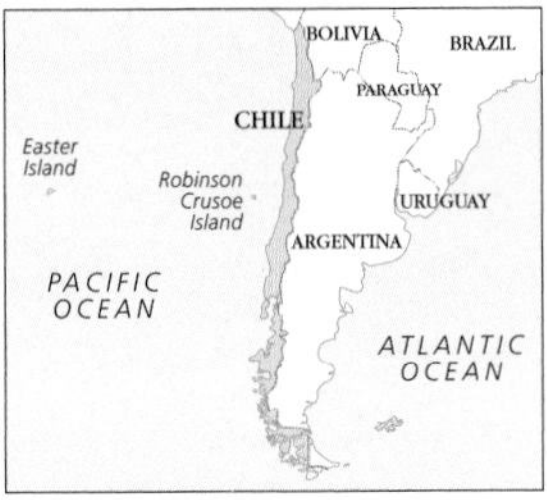

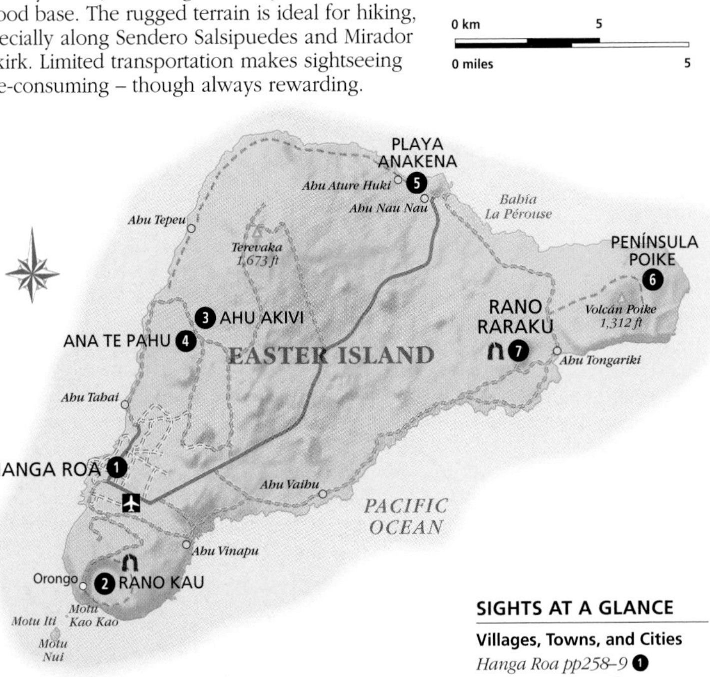

SIGHTS AT A GLANCE

Villages, Towns, and Cities

Hanga Roa pp258–9 ❶
San Juan Bautista ❽

Areas of Natural Beauty

Mirador Selkirk ⓫
Península Poike ❻
Playa Anakena ❺
Sendero Salsipuedes ❾

Archaeological Sites

Ahu Akivi ❸
Ana Te Pahu ❹
Rano Kau ❷
Rano Raraku pp262–3 ❼

Sites of Interest

Cueva Robinson ❿
Plazoleta El Yunque ⓬

Moais **at Ahu Nau Nau on Playa Anakena, Easter Island**

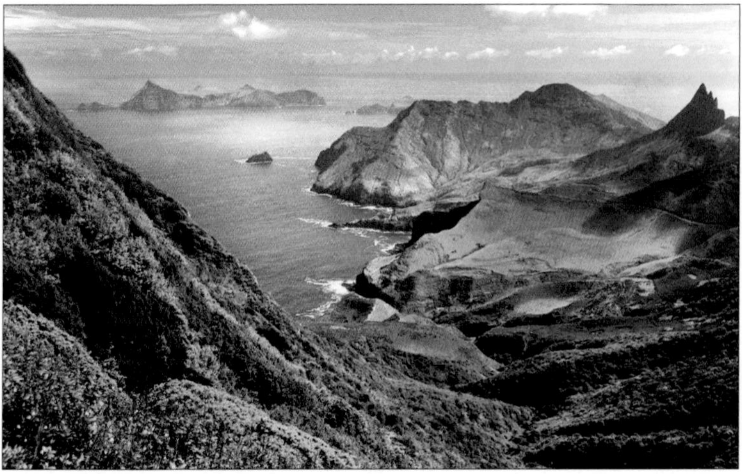

View from Mirador Selkirk, on Robinson Crusoe Island

GETTING AROUND

Both Easter Island and Robinson Crusoe Island are small in area, but getting around each of them is different. Easter Island has a good road system, suitable for cars, motorbikes, and bicycles. However, not all roads are paved and some are potholed. Hanga Roa has a taxi fleet, as well as tour companies that shuttle clients to and from the main sights. Horses can also be rented for excursions. There are many routes suitable for hiking, though camping is not permitted outside Hanga Roa. On Robinson Crusoe Island, there are no roads to speak of. The terrain is usually tackled on hikes, some of which can be challenging. It is possible to hire boats to sights that are not easily accessible by foot.

KEY

- Major road
- Untarred major road
- Untarred minor road
- Track
- Boat route
- Peak

SEE ALSO

- ***Where to Stay*** p287
- ***Where to Eat*** p307

Hanga Roa ❶

Moai exhibit at Hanga Roa

Easter Island's only permament settlement, Hanga Roa is a sprawling subtropical village housing nearly all of the island's inhabitants. Most of its wide streets are lined with compact homes fronted by gardens. The population is mainly Polynesian but there are also expatriates, many from mainland Chile, who participate in the island's growing tourism industry. The village is a hub for visitors who come to enjoy the area's unique attractions, including its sophisticated cuisine that blends fresh ingredients with South Pacific touches.

Iglesia Sagrado Corazón

Tuukoihu, esq. Avenida Te Pito Ote Henua.

Originally a simple structure, the village church of Iglesia Sagrado Corazón underwent a major renovation in 1982, and now stands out from Hanga Roa's other mainly utilitarian buildings. It boasts an attractive façade with bas-reliefs of Rapa Nui imagery, including the Birdman *(see p260)*, and figures of fish, frigate birds, and turtles. On one side, the church is flanked by the crypt of the Capuchin priest and scholar Sebastián Englert (1888–1969), who took active interest in the island's history and culture. His tomb lies next to that of the island's first missionary, Eugene Eyraud, who died here in 1864.

Within the luminous interior of the church, woodcarvings blend traditional Christian imagery with Rapa Nui symbols – the Birdman here is depicted as an angel. The church is also the center of vibrant Easter Sunday celebrations, with the local priest's arrival on horseback being the high point of the ceremonies. Church services include chants in the Rapa Nui language, with decidedly Polynesian rhythms.

Mercado Artesanal

Tuukoihu, esq. Ara Roa Rakei.
9am–7pm Mon–Sat, 10am–2pm Sun.

Located opposite the Iglesia Sagrado Corazón, Mercado Artesanal is Hanga Roa's lively artisans' market. It is the perfect place to purchase local handicrafts, textiles, ornaments, as well as custom-made souvenir *moai*, which are either carved of wood or made of volcanic tuff. Shoppers are also offered wooden replicas of the ancient inscribed stone tablets known as *rongorongo* and of wooden *moai kavakava*, which are skeletal *moai* with prominent ribs. The market is best visited during the early hours of the morning, before the area gets hot and crowded.

Souvenir at the Mercado Artesanal

Rapa Nui imagery on the entrance of Iglesia Sagrado Corazón

Well-tended graves with colorful flowers at Cementerio Hanga Roa

Cementerio Hanga Roa

Near Petero Atamu.

Situated at the northern end of the village, Cementerio Hanga Roa officially dates from 1951, although the site has been used for burials since the early 20th century. Lovingly maintained, the cemetery overlooks the Bahía Cook inlet and is surrounded by a wall of volcanic stones. Simple, home-crafted headstones marked with crosses and decorated with artificial flowers dot the cemetery's grounds. This is a good place to appreciate the island's contemporary local history, in addition to its enigmatic pre-European epic.

Ahu Tahai

Tahai.

Located north of Hanga Roa's cemetery, Ahu Tahai is the most notable archaeological site within walking distance of the village. It is actually a complex of three *ahus* (stone platforms) that were restored by US anthropologist William Mulloy in the 1960s and 70s. The central platform, Ahu Tahai proper, has a single standing *moai*. To its north, the *moai* at Ahu Ko Te Riku has a restored topknot and ceramic eyes. To the south, Ahu Vai Ure is crowned with five standing *moai*.

The Ahu Tahai complex also marks the foundations of several *hare paenga* (boat-shaped houses) and a boat ramp. Mulloy, who died in 1978, is buried in the complex next to his wife Emily.

For hotels and restaurants in this region see p287 and p307

Museo Antropológico P. Sebastián Englert
Tahai s/n. ***Tel*** *(032) 2551020.* *9:30am–12:30pm & 2–5:30pm Tue–Fri, 9:30am–12:30pm Sat, Sun & holidays.* **www.**museorapanui.cl

Founded in 1973, Museo Antropológico P. Sebastián Englert is named for the benevolent Capuchin priest who spent many years on the island. The museum displays focus on trans-Pacific navigation and migration and on iconic Rapa Nui artifacts such as the *moai* and *rongorongo* tablets created by this people upon settling on the island. The museum also explores the crisis, probably demographic, that led to the toppling of several *moai* in the 18th century.

The museum's anthropology section offers information on most of Oceania, the geographical region comprising the Pacific islands from New Guinea and Australia to the tiny atolls of Polynesia.

In 2003, Viña del Mar's **Biblioteca William Mulloy**, named for the pioneer archaeologist, was shifted to this museum. This scientific research library is well stocked with photographs, videos, and literature that document the island's rich history and culture.

Red and white painted birds on the ceiling of Ana Kai Tangata

Ana Kai Tangata
Near Avenida Policarpo Toro.

An impressive rock-art site, Ana Kai Tangata is a coastal cavern that features painted terns on its ceiling. Legend has it that cannibalism may have been practiced here, and the cave's ambiguous name, according to American archaeologist Georgia Lee, could mean cave where men eat, cave where men are eaten, or cave that eats men. However, the evidence to support this theory is tenuous. A carved ceremonial skull has been found on this site, but without cut marks on bones that could indicate cannibalistic practices. Ana Kai Tangata is also the starting point of Sendero Te Ara O Te Ao, a network of trails that climbs to Rano Kau *(see p260)* and Orongo.

VISITORS' CHECKLIST

2,340 miles (3,765 km) NW of Santiago. *3,800.*
Aeropuerto Mataveri.
Avenida Policarpo Toro, at Tuu Maheke; (032) 2100255.
Tapati Rapa Nui (early Feb).

TAPATI RAPA NUI

Easter Island's biggest annual event for the past 30 years, Tapati Rapa Nui, has filled the streets of Hanga Roa with folkloric music, dance, and competitive events. Celebrated each February, the festival is a chance for islanders to showcase their skills and crafts, which include stone and woodcarvings, body-painting, and cooking in the Polynesian style. Tapati Rapa Nui focuses on tradition and identity despite the use of imported elements such as drums and guitars.

Performers with traditional costumes

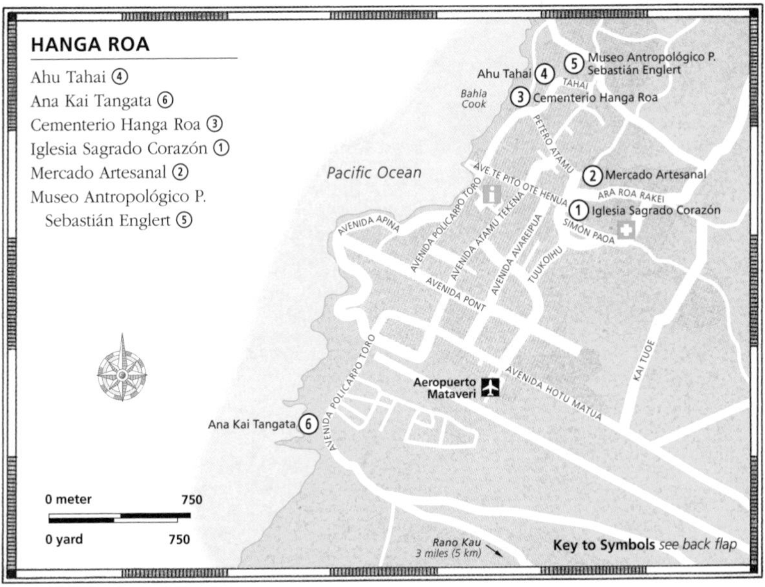

The water-filled crater of Rano Kau, with the Pacific beyond

Rano Kau ❷

3 miles (5 km) S of Hanga Roa; Sector Orongo. 🚗 ◯ *9am–6:30pm daily.* 🎫

Part of a national park on Easter Island, the water-filled crater of Rano Kau is the island's most striking natural sight – the panorama from its rim, with the seemingly endless Pacific Ocean on the horizon, is one of the most unforgettable sights of the island. Descending into the crater is no longer permitted, but walking around its undulating rim is a true top-of-the-world experience. On the crater's southwest side, the ceremonial village at **Orongo** is a complex of 53 houses that were linked to this island's Birdman sect in the 18th and 19th centuries. The sect gets its name from the Birdman, an influential post whose incumbent was chosen each year in a ritual that culminated in the collection of a sooty tern egg. Visitors to this historic and fragile site are requested not to leave the marked path or enter the houses, which consist of earth and overlapping slabs, with doors so low that entering them would require crawling.

Rano Kau and Orongo are reached by a road that passes by the west end of Mataveri airport and loops around its south side. However, it is also possible to hike there, and back, on the Te Ara O Te Ao footpath that starts at Ana Kai Tangata *(see p259)*. The admission fee for Rano Kau, collected by CONAF, is also valid for entry to Rano Raraku *(see p262–3)*.

Environs

Some 2 miles (4 km) northeast of Rano Kau, **Ahu Vinapu** is one of the sites that was once held to be proof of South American influence on Easter Island, because its closely fitted stones superficially resemble Incan sites in Peru. Ahu Vinapu actually consists of three separate platforms, whose *moai* tumbled over in conflicts during the 18th and 19th centuries. The site is also known for the discovery of fossilized palm, believed to be evidence of early island settlement, around AD 1300. Theory holds that the tree became extinct as islanders cleared woods to make space for erecting *moai*.

Large, compact boulders forming the platform at Ahu Vinapu

LEGEND OF THE BIRDMAN

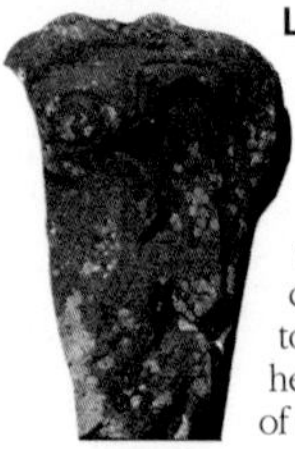

Petroglyph of a Birdman, Orongo

Around the 16th century, Rapa Nui's culture, rooted in ancestor worship, was replaced by a system of beliefs known as *makemake*, after the creator god of that belief. One of this new sect's key customs was an annual competition held to elect the Tangata Manu (Birdman), who held a position of power on the island. Each of the contestants would sponsor an islander, a *hopu*, whose task was to scramble down the 1,300-ft (400-m) slope of Rano Kau, swim through shark-infested waters to the islet of Motu Nui, and retrieve the egg of a sooty tern. The first *hopu* to do so, would climb back to Orongo and be greeted by his sponsor, who became that year's Birdman. The Birdman people disappeared with the slave raids of the 1860s and the arrival of Christian missionaries.

Ahu Akivi ❸

4 miles (6 km) NE of Hanga Roa; Sector Akivi. 🚗 ♿

With seven standing *moai*, restored in 1960 by American anthropologist William Mulloy and his Chilean colleague Gonzalo Figueroa García-Huidobro, Ahu Akivi is one of few inland *ahu* (stone platforms) and, unlike most other *ahus*, its *moai* look toward the sea. They also look toward the platform's ceremonial center and, during both equinoxes, directly into the setting sun.

Ana Te Pahu ❹

4 miles (6 km) NE of Hanga Roa; Sector Ahu Akivia.

Today, much of Easter Island's food is imported from the mainland, but before this became an option, the islanders used lava tube caves called *manavai*, or sunken gardens, to grow their produce. Ana Te Pahu is one such cave. Owing to the total absence of surface streams on Easter Island's porous volcanic terrain, large-scale agriculture has always been a challenge. The humid microclimate and relatively deep soils in the caves permitted the cultivation of crops such as bananas; these are still grown in Ana Te Pahu and in similar sites around the island. Visitors can easily descend into the cave, but a flashlight is necessary.

Playa Anakena ❺

10 miles (16 km) NE of Hanga Roa; Sector Anakena.

Located on the northeastern shores of Rapa Nui, Playa Anakena is the island's only broad sandy beach and, with its tall palms and turquoise waters, is almost a caricature of a South Pacific idyll. The beach is a perfect spot for swimming and sunbathing. It also has barbecue pits, picnic tables, changing rooms, and several snack bars that make it the most popular choice with locals for a day's outing.

According to Easter Island's oral tradition, Playa Anakena is the place where the first Polynesian settlers, under chief Hotu Motu'a, landed. Anakena has one thing that no part of Polynesia can match – the seven standing *moai* of **Ahu Nau Nau**, four of them with *pukao* (topknots) that were restored in 1979 under the direction of island archaeologist Sergio Rapu. Two of these *moai* are badly damaged, but the remainder are in excellent condition. Also located on the same beach is the smaller **Ahu Ature Huki** with a single *moai*. From Anakena, it is possible to hike around the little-visited north coast, returning to Hanga Roa via two other sites – Ahu Tepeu and Ahu Tahai. However, this is a full day's trip and demands an early start.

The impressive row of standing *moai* at Ahu Tongariki

Península Poike ❻

13 miles (21 km) NE of Hanga Roa; Sector Poike.

The peninsula at the island's eastern end takes its name from Volcán Poike, which marks this area's highest point. In pre-European times there was a village here, and petroglyphs from the period include a turtle, a Birdman, and a tunafish. The area also has fascinating landmarks associated with legends of the island. Key among these is a 2-mile (4-km) long westerly "ditch" believed to mark a line of defensive fortifications during a war between rival clans. On the peninsula's southwestern edge is Poike's most stunning asset – **Ahu Tongariki**, with its 15 *moai*, is the island's largest platform.

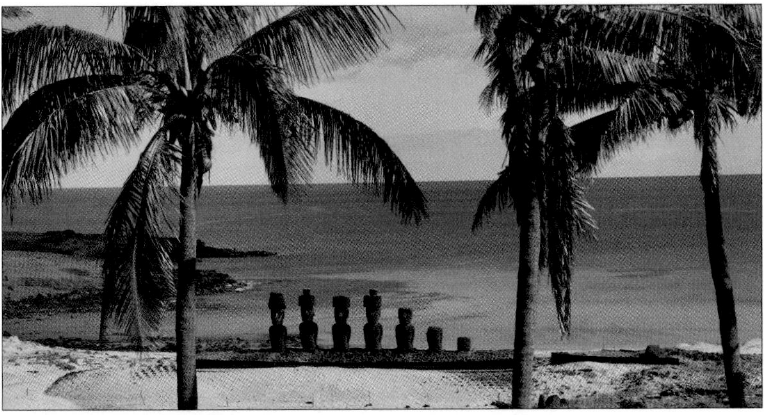

***Moai* of Ahu Nau Nau on the palm-lined Playa Anakena, backed by the Pacific Ocean**

Rano Raraku ❼

Among Easter Island's most breathtaking features are the crater lake and *moai*-studded slopes of Rano Raraku. In fact, the southeastern rim and banks of this volcano are the cradle of the island's iconic *moai*. It was here, long before the arrival of Europeans, that Rapa Nui carvers crafted their massive statues from volcanic tuff and, with substantial effort, freed them from the quarry to be transported across the island. Today, nearly 400 of these can still be seen standing or toppled beside their *ahu* (stone platform). While they differ in detail, the *moai* have much in common. The CONAF-built trails around the crater's outer slopes is an ideal, and indeed the only, way to explore the area.

A tilting *moai* head on the crater slopes of Rano Raraku

★ Crater Lake

The vast center of Rano Raraku is occupied by a serene lake whose edges are lined with totora reeds. The crater can only be reached through a gap in the western end of this site. Hordes of feral horses often visit this area, and can be seen trampling over the green beds of totora.

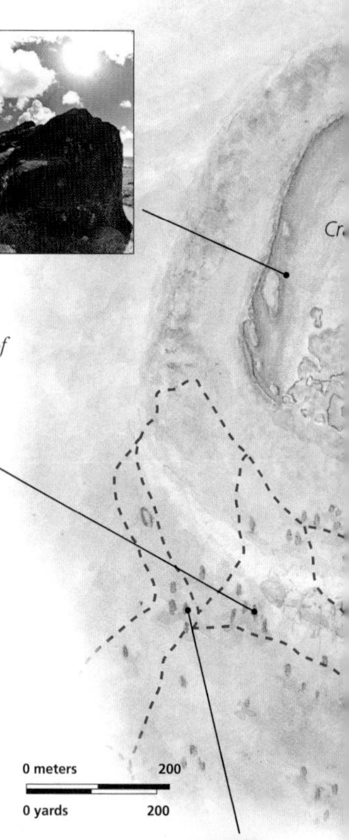

★ Hinariru

Located on one of the lower points of the trail, the much-photographed, 13-ft (4-m) high Hinariru is also called the moai *with the twisted neck, in reference to its bulging base. According to various folktales, Hinariru was the brother-in-law of Hotu Motu'a, legendary leader of the first island settlers, and perhaps also the master who brought the* moai *to the island.*

STAR SIGHTS

- ★ Crater Lake
- ★ Hinariru
- ★ El Gigante

Piropiro

Just west of Hinariru is another 13-ft (4-m) high moai *known as Piropiro. About 22 ft (7 m) of this* moai's *body is buried beneath volcanic soil.*

For hotels and restaurants in this region see p287 and p307

VISITORS' CHECKLIST

11 miles (18 km) E of Hanga Roa. *from Hanga Roa.* *ranger station and rangers on-site.* *9am–6:30pm daily.* **www**.conaf.cl

★ El Gigante
Climbing to the upper slopes of Rano Raraku, the trail reaches El Gigante, which, at 65 ft (20 m), is the largest moai *ever carved. Still attached to bedrock, its estimated weight is about 270 tons (240 tonnes).*

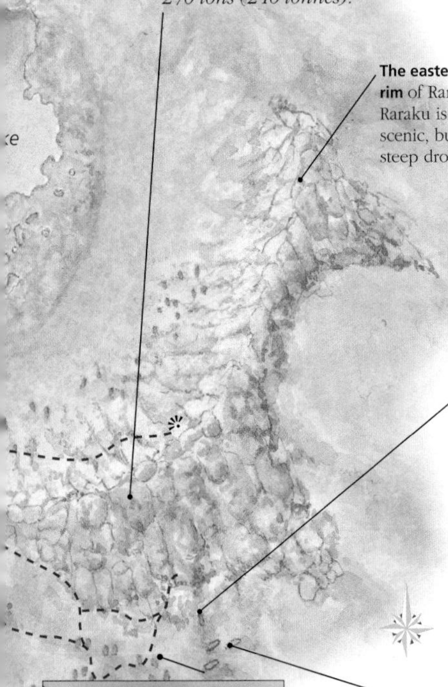

The eastern rim of Rano Raraku is scenic, but has steep dropoffs.

Tukuturi
The fenced-off Tukuturi is the singular kneeling, bearded moai *that apparently mimics the posture of Polynesian ceremonial singers. According to American archaeologist Joanne van Tilburg, it may be the last* moai *ever made, with links to the Birdman cult* (see p260).

KEY

- - Trail

Viewpoint

Ko Kona He Roa
The moai *known as Ko Kona He Roa bears evidence of European contact in the carved image of a three-masted sailing ship roughly etched on its trunk.*

Hare Paenga
Immediately east of Tukuturi are the basalt foundations of many hare paenga, *thatched boat-shaped houses that were reserved for chiefs and priests. Several others are scattered around the crater.*

***Moai* statues on the slopes of Rano Raraku ▷**

Robinson Crusoe Island

The Juan Fernández firecrown

Covering a land mass of only 36 sq miles (93 sq km), Robinson Crusoe Island is a rugged volcanic speck with a rich natural heritage – about 70 percent of its plant species are endemic. Originally known as Isla Masatierra, the island was renamed for Daniel Defoe's 1719 novel *Robinson Crusoe*, which was partially inspired by the tenure of the Scottish castaway Alexander Selkirk on the island. Today, Robinson Crusoe Island is home to a small fishing community that subsists mainly on lobster exports to Santiago. Much of the island is part of the Parque Nacional Archipélago de Juan Fernández, a UNESCO World Heritage Site, and its many hiking trails are the prime draw for adventurous visitors.

San Juan Bautista ❽

472 miles (759 km) W of Santiago. *650. from Santiago. from Valparaíso.* *Larraín Alcalde s/n.* *Día de la Isla (Nov 22).* **www**.comunajuanfernandez.cl

Robinson Crusoe Island's only permanent settlement, San Juan Bautista is nestled on the curving shoreline of the scenic Bahía Cumberland. Located just south of the village plaza, the small **Fuerte Santa Barbara** stands atop a hill. Dating from 1770, this stone fort was constructed by the Spanish in response to the presence of the British in the South Pacific. It was later rebuilt in 1974, but the fort's several cannons, pointing at the harbor, still stand here.

Next to the fort, the **Cuevas de los Patriotas** (Caves of the Patriots) was where, in the early 19th century, the Spanish held Chilean leaders fighting for independence. At the village's western end, the **Cementerio San Juan Bautista** has tombs of early settlers, and of German sailors who stayed on the island after the scuttling of the *Dresden* in 1915. This battleship had been cornered by the British navy in the Bahía Cumberland. Local historic relics are on display in the **Casa de Cultura Alfredo de Rodt**, named for an early Swiss settler.

Casa de Cultura Alfredo de Rodt
Larraín Alcalde s/n. *10am–noon & 4–8pm Mon–Fri.*

Sendero Salsipuedes ❾

1 mile (2 km) W of San Juan Bautista. ***Tel** (032) 2751004.* **www**.conaf.cl

Starting at Calle La Pólvora, just west of San Juan Bautista, the Sendero Salsipuedes is a nature trail with multiple switchbacks. The path snakes through dense vegetation and verdant forests of acacia, eucalyptus, Montrey cypress, Montrey pine, and the native murtilla before culminating at the jagged Salsipuedes ridge. The views from here are exceptional and include sweeping panoramas of San Juan Bautista and of the blue waters of Bahía Cumberland that surround the village.

Cueva Robinson ❿

2 miles (3 km) NW of San Juan Bautista by boat; Puerto Inglés. **www**.conaf.cl

From the Salsipuedes ridge, a steep pathway descends to the beach at Puerto Inglés and to the Cueva Robinson, the ostensible site of Alexander Selkirk's shelter. This precipitous approach can be dangerous, and it is advisable to hire the services of a local guide. While there is no clear evidence that Selkirk

THE TSUNAMI OF 2010

The massive earthquake of February 27, 2010, unleashed a tsunami that struck the village of San Juan Bautista, demolishing shoreline constructions and claiming several lives. Most of the island's trails and sights, such as Mirador Selkirk and Plazoleta El Yunque, remain unaffected because they are inland. However, many hotels have been destroyed and visitors will need to check with Chile's toursim board, Sernatur *(see p325)*, for details on lodging options.

The settlement of San Juan Bautista on the shores of Bahía Cumberland

For hotels and restaurants in this region see p287 and p307

inhabited this cave, a replica of his supposed refuge dominates the site. From 1995 onward, American treasure hunter Bernard Keiser spent several years in the area around Cueva Robinson searching for a massive, 18th-century Spanish treasure, allegedly found by the British and then re-hidden here.

Cueva Robinson, Alexander Selkirk's alleged cave house

Mirador Selkirk ⓫

2 miles (3 km) S of San Juan Bautista. www.conaf.cl

A popular hiking destination, Mirador Selkirk is the saddle from where, in despondency and hope, castaway Alexander Selkirk watched for the ship that would rescue him from his lonely exile. The trek to this lookout starts at the southern end of San Juan Bautista's central plaza and climbs steeply through an eroded zone dotted with blackberry bushes. As the trail gains altitude, it passes through thick endemic rain forest, studded with towering tree ferns, before culminating at the saddle.

Two metal plaques on the saddle, one placed by the Royal Navy in 1868 and the other by a distant relative in 1983, commemorate Selkirk's exile. This site offers great views of Bahía Cumberland and San Juan Bautista to the east. To the south, the landscape changes dramatically from dense rain forest to desert at Tierras Blancas, where the rugged shoreline provides habitat to the endemic Juan Fernández fur seal, *Arctocephalus philippii.*

A colony of native Juan Fernández fur seal basking in the sun

Plazoleta El Yunque ⓬

2 miles (3 km) S of San Juan Bautista. www.conaf.cl

Starting at San Juan Bautista's power plant, a short southbound road turns into a gentle nature trail that leads to the Plazoleta El Yunque, a serene forest clearing with a campsite. The site is also the spot where Hugo Weber, a German survivor of the *Dresden* sinking, built a house whose foundations are still visible.

A steep and challenging hike beginning at the Plazoleta El Yunque traverses dense forest to reach the saddle of El Camote, which offers sweeping views of the island. Farther ahead, a more strenuous hike culminates at **Cerro El Yunque** (The Anvil Hill), which, at 3,002 ft (915 m), is the highest point on Robinson Crusoe Island. CONAF organizes guides for those who wish to undertake this hike.

Cerro El Yunque rising above the island's forested shoreline

ALEXANDER SELKIRK

The story of Alexander Selkirk, who was marooned on Isla Masatierra in the 18th century, served as the template for Daniel Defoe's novel *Robinson Crusoe* (1719). Selkirk, a Scotsman who had served under the British privateer William Dampier, was abandoned on the island in 1704 by Dampier's former associate Thomas Stradling after Selkirk complained about the seaworthiness of Stradling's vessel, *Cinque Ports*. During his years as a castaway, Selkirk subsisted on feral goats, fish, and wild plants, clothed himself with animal skins, and stayed hidden from Spanish vessels until his rescue in 1709 by the British privateering ship *Duke*, under Woodes Rogers. Interestingly, as Selkirk had predicted, the *Cinque Ports* sank within a month and most of its crew drowned.

Castaway Alexander Selkirk rescued by the *Duke* in 1709

TRAVELERS' NEEDS

WHERE TO STAY

Chile offers lodging options for every preference and budget, ranging from five-star international chains and cutting-edge boutique hotels to campgrounds and hostels. Most of the large chains are located in the capital city and beach resorts. Boutique hotels are generally found in large cities, in and around the temperate wine-growing areas, and in Patagonia. Many boutique hotels in the Lake District have their own hot springs. Chile also has some good estancias – cattle and sheep ranches that have been turned into accommodations. Mid- and upper-range hotels usually offer guests the option of paying for their stay in US dollars. Budget lodgings, especially hostels, are worth consideration as their private rooms are sometimes less expensive yet better than comparable quarters in one- or two-star hotels. Prices for all accommodations rise steeply in the main resorts and urban centers during tourist season.

Signage at La Tetera Hostal in Pucon

Spa, gym, and pool on the top floor of the Ritz-Carlton, Santiago

GRADINGS

Hotels in Chile are ranked on a scale of one to five stars by the national tourist board. However, this system can be misleading as the grading is dependent on the facilities offered by a hotel, not on the quality of its hospitality. As a result, some two- and three-star options may be better than their four-star competitors, and boutique hotels may be downgraded for lacking amenities such as abundant parking. Nor do *cabaña* (cabin) accommodations, which can be a bargain for families, fit within the traditional categories. Generally, however, international five-star chains live up to their billing.

PRICING AND BOOKING

Pricing is mainly dependent on three factors – season, location, and the prevailing economic situation, the last of which includes both macroeconomics and the exchange rate between the US dollar and the Chilean peso.

The most costly locations are in the capital city of Santiago, the desert oasis of San Pedro de Atacama, beach resorts such as Viña del Mar and La Serena, lakeside locales such as Pucón and Puerto Varas, and Patagonian national parks such as Torres del Paine. That said, all these areas also have budget options.

Luxury five-star hotels can cost upward of US$ 300 per night, while exclusive fishing lodges in the southern Lake District and Patagonia range beyond US$ 500 per night. Luxury chains such as Explora, and even some boutique hotels, sell only multi-day packages. Though prices in the capital are usually not seasonal, rates are highest in the months of January and February – when most Chileans take their vacations – and lower over November–December and March–April. Prices can also rise in July, the winter school holidays, especially at the Andean ski resorts, which hit their peak rates at this time.

TAXES

Hotel prices may or may not include the 19 percent *impuesto de valor agregado* (Value Added Tax), also known as the IVA. Bona fide travelers to the country are exempt from this tax if they pay in US dollars or with a foreign credit card. Hotels may not volunteer this information and guests need to ask for the exemption and present their passport and tourist card *(see p322)*. In addition, this is an optional program and not all hotels in Chile participate; budget accommodations are mostly ineligible. Before making a

Hotel Explora at Torres del Paine National Park

◁ Colorfully patterned fabrics typical of altiplano Chile

payment, it is best to verify whether the advertised rates are inclusive of taxes.

CHAIN HOTELS

Marriott, **Ritz-Carlton**, **Hyatt**, and **Sheraton** are among the big-name international chains with representation in Santiago and, occasionally, in other areas of Chile. National chains include the business-oriented **Hoteles Diego de Almagro**, which offers a scattering of utilitarian but comfortable and reliable hotels throughout the country. There is also **A y R Hoteles**, a loosely affiliated group of hotels that range from fairly modest business-oriented accommodations to intimate boutique and luxury five-star hotels.

Living room at the modern Clos Apalta winery, Colchagua valley

LUXURY AND BOUTIQUE HOTELS

Santiago is the site of most of Chile's luxury hotels which, in this seismically active country, tend to be new constructions with state-of-the-art amenities. The finest are in the eastern boroughs of Vitacura and Las Condes, and are invariably high-rises with pools, fitness centers, business facilities, and top restaurants. In the rest of the country, luxury hotels are smaller, but often include more extensive gardens and access to ocean or lake beaches.

Boutique hotels are becoming abundant throughout the country, and offer some of the best lodging options, especially in the Central Valley, Lake District and Patagonia regions. Some

Entrance to Hostería Las Torres at the Torres del Paine National Park

of these, Puerto Natales's Hotel Indigo *(see p285)* for instance, are also Chile's most eco-friendly accommodations.

BODEGAS

The boom in wine tourism has led a number of wineries to install their own luxurious, even super-luxurious, accommodations. The best are found on Colchagua's wine tour, Ruta del Vino *(see p148)*. These serve as an excellent base to explore the area by road, or by rail on the Tren de Vino. The Ruta del Vino Valle del Maule *(see p151)* also offers vineyard lodgings.

BUDGET ACCOMMODATIONS

The range of Chile's budget accommodation includes basic one- and two-star hotels, or cheaper family-run *hospedajes* and *residencias*, which are likely to have a choice of shared or private bath. Some of these are dismal, others surprisingly good, but they are always inexpensive. Such accommodations usually include a basic breakfast.

HOSTALES AND HOSTERÍAS

Relatively small dwellings, *hostales* and *hosterías* are Chile's closest counterpart to bed-and-breakfast options. With rarely more than a dozen rooms, these accommodations vary widely in quality, but the best of them are very good indeed. Those in national parks are usually fine new constructions. They are often, but not always, oriented toward the tastes of Chilean rather than foreign clientele. Some occupy historic homes that have been remodeled, while others are utilitarian and even bland. However, they frequently offer better value for money than comparably priced hotels.

ESTANCIAS AND HACIENDAS

Estancias and haciendas are ranches and farms that have chosen to open their often historic facilities to paid guests. These accommodations are mainly found in Patagonia, and a handful are located in temperate central Chile. In some cases, the estates are remodeled to appeal to affluent tastes, and may include the services of gourmet chefs. Most ranches offer activities such as horse riding, and their isolation implies a certain exclusiveness, although not all of them are elite options.

Room with veranda at Hacienda Tres Lagos in Patagonia

Yurt-style accommodation on campgrounds in Southern Patagonia

HOSTELS

The best-value hostels are represented by **Backpacker's Best**, **Hostelling International Chile**, and **Backpackers Chile**, most of which have excellent private rooms in addition to dorms, at a fraction of the cost of a hotel. The latter two are loose alliances that also include some classy B&Bs.

SELF-CATERING AND CABAÑAS

Apart-hotels in Chile usually offer fine accommodations at lower prices than full-service hotels. Apart-hotels have a reception desk, kitchenettes, living rooms, and cleaning staff, but lack concierges, restaurants, and other facilities.

Cabañas are suitable for couples or families and range from one to three bedrooms, plus a kitchen. They can be found throughout Chile but are most common in the Lake District and Patagonia.

APARTMENT RENTALS

Short-term apartment rentals for vacationers are not usual, but German-run **Contact Chile** has a selection of more than 300 in Santiago, Viña del Mar, and Valparaíso. In general, rentals are for two or three months at the minimum.

CAMPGROUNDS AND REFUGIOS

To most Chileans, camping does not mean roughing it in the backcountry, but rather parking the van or pitching the tent in an organized campground with electricity, firepits, and bathrooms with hot showers. Such sites, often run by **CONAF**, are common in the Lake District, Patagonia, and some national parks. Many campgrounds charge for a minimum of four or five people, and solo travelers or couples may find them an expensive option.

Refugios in national parks such as Torres del Paine range from basic to surprisingly elaborate dormitory accommodations along backcountry trails. These are ideal for hikers who do not care to sleep in tents. The *refugios* also offer meals and hot showers, which usually cost extra for tent campers.

DISABLED TRAVELERS

In recent years, Chilean hotels, primarily at the upper end of the price spectrum, have become wheelchair-friendly. Many now have at least one room designed with accessibility for disabled travelers in mind. In cases where there are no dedicated facilities, Chilean hoteliers will do everything possible to accommodate the wheelchair-bound with first-floor rooms and assistance with overcoming steps when necessary.

TIPPING

The practice of tipping in Chile resembles that in much of the rest of the world. Hotel bellmen and porters are given a small gratuity: a 500-peso coin should be enough except for special efforts. In restaurants, a 10 percent tip is customarily left on the table, even if this has been included in the bill.

DIRECTORY

CHAIN HOTELS

A y R Hoteles
Tel (032) 2681424.
www.ayrhoteles.cl

Hoteles Diego de Almagro
www.dahoteles.com

Hyatt
Tel (02) 9501234.
www.hyatt.cl

Marriott
Tel (02) 4262000.
www.marriott.com

Ritz-Carlton
Tel (02) 4708500.
www.ritzcarlton.com

Sheraton
Tel (02) 2335000.
www.starwoodhotels.com

HOSTELS

Backpacker's Best
Tel (02) 4112050.
www.backpackersbest.cl

Backpackers Chile
www.backpackerschile.com

Hostelling International Chile
Hernando de Aguirre 201, Oficina 602, Providencia, Santiago
Tel (02) 4112050.
www.hostelling.cl

APARTMENT RENTALS

Contact Chile
Huelén 219, second floor, Providencia, Santiago.
Tel (02) 2641719.
www.contactchile.cl

CAMPGROUNDS AND REFUGIOS

CONAF (Corporación Nacional Forestal)
Avenida Bulnes 285, Santiago.
Tel (02) 6630000.
www.conaf.cl

Chile's Best: Boutique Hotels

Small-scale boutique hotels with individualized attention are a recent phenomenon in the country, and there is no real consensus about what they are. Some are recycled buildings in historic locales, such as the hills of Valparaíso and the central wine country, while others are purpose-built design hotels in Lake District and Patagonia. Others are a combination of the two: custom-built accommodations in a style that respects tradition but incorporates contemporary comforts, as in San Pedro de Atacama and Easter Island.

Hotel Awasi, *despite its luxury rooms and chic common areas, has adobe walls and thatched roofs. These help it fit inconspicuously into the heart of the traditional village of San Pedro de Atacama (see p174).*

Zero Hotel *(see p280), in a Victorian-style mansion, offers fine views of Valparaíso's scenic harbor, in a pedestrian-friendly neighborhood with touches of Mediterranean Europe.*

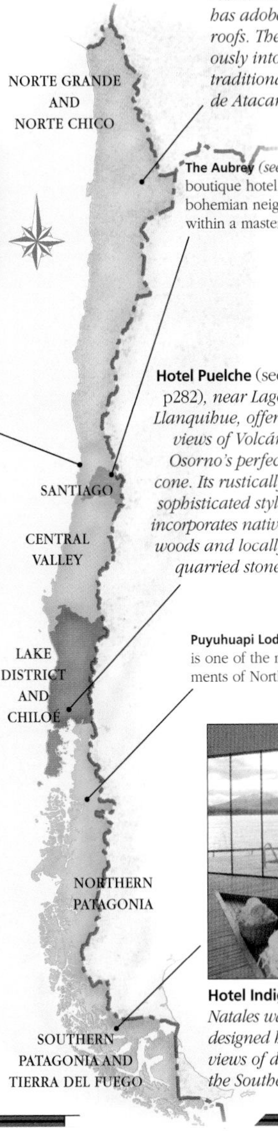

The Aubrey *(see p277)*, Santiago's first true boutique hotel, is located in the charming, bohemian neighborhood of Bellavista, within a masterfully restored 1927 mansion.

Hotel Puelche (see p282), *near Lago Llanquihue, offers views of Volcán Osorno's perfect cone. Its rustically sophisticated style incorporates native woods and locally quarried stone.*

EASTER ISLAND

Posada de Mike Rapu *is a luxurious hotel that mimics the traditional architecture of the island.*

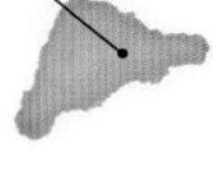

Puyuhuapi Lodge & Spa *(see p228)* is one of the most stylish establishments of Northern Patagonia.

Hotel Indigo (see p285), *on the Puerto Natales waterfront, is an audaciously designed hotel whose rooftop spa offers views of distant Torres del Paine and the Southern Ice Field.*

Choosing a Hotel

Most of the hotels and resorts in this guide have been selected across a wide price range for their good value, facilities, and location. Hotels are listed by area and arranged alphabetically within the same price category. For map references see pages 102–109 for Santiago, pages 118–19 for Valparaíso, and the inside back cover for others.

PRICE CATEGORIES
The following price ranges, in US dollars, are for a standard double room per night, including taxes, service charges, and breakfast.

$ Under $75
$$ $75–$100
$$$ $100–$150
$$$$ $150–$200
$$$$$ Over $200

SANTIAGO

EL CENTRO Andes Hostel — $

Monjitas 506 **Tel** *(02) 6329990* **Rooms** *16* — **City Map** *2 F2*

In the heart of the artsy Bellas Artes neighborhood, this trendy, youthful, and highly recommended hostel offers maid service, plentiful private and shared restrooms, a kitchen, laundry, bike rentals, a rooftop terrace, and a bar with a pool table. Sunny rooms look out on to bustling streets. Shared rooms. **www.andeshostel.com**

EL CENTRO Hostal Plaza de Armas — $

Portal Fernandez Concha, Compañía 960, No.607 **Tel** *(02) 6714436* **Rooms** *11* — **City Map** *2 E2*

Overlooks the grand Plaza de Armas from the sixth story of a late 19th-century apartment building, with spectacular city views. Stylish decor and backpacker amenities such as a kitchen, BBQ area, lockers, and laundry. Four private double rooms and one single; shared dorms are also available. **www.plazadearmashostel.com**

EL CENTRO Hotel Foresta — $

Victoria Subercaseaux 353 **Tel** *(02) 6396261* **Fax** *(02) 6322996* **Rooms** *35* — **City Map** *2 F2*

Superb location overlooking leafy Cerro Santa Lucía in a charming neighborhood. Art museums and cafés are a short walk away. Good low-cost option that feels like a European economy hotel; however, decor is kitschy and service minimal. Spanish speakers fare better here as they do not have bilingual staff.

EL CENTRO Hotel Las Vegas — $

Londres 49 **Tel** *(02) 6322514* **Rooms** *20* — **City Map** *2 E3*

A funky, 1970s-era hotel with an English-tavern decor, Hotel Las Vegas is housed in a converted mansion on a charming cobblestone street. Nearly all the rooms are wood-paneled, some are thinly carpeted, and the beds are of average quality. The hotel is a good bet for budget travelers who are not too picky. **www.hotelvegas.net**

EL CENTRO Hotel Montecarlo — $

Victoria Subercaseaux 209 **Tel** *(02) 6339905* **Fax** *(02) 6335577* **Rooms** *65* — **City Map** *2 F2*

One of the capital's funkiest hotels, with 1970s furniture, shag carpeting, and smoked glass tables. Excellent location, close to the Bellas Artes neighborhood; rooms with views of Cerro Santa Lucia park are the best. Budget travelers who are not too fussy will be comfortable here. **www.hotelmontecarlo.cl**

EL CENTRO Residencial Londres — $

Londres 54 **Tel** *(02) 6339192* **Fax** *(02) 6382215* **Rooms** *25* — **City Map** *2 E3*

The mainstay of cheap lodging in Santiago, located on a cobblestone street in the charming Barrio París-Londres. Antique charm with floor-to-ceiling windows, vintage furniture, parquet floors. Private rooms, some with shared bathrooms. Interior courtyard and TV salon. No kitchen and no heating in winter. **www.londres.cl**

EL CENTRO Hotel Blue Tree Fundador — $$$

Paseo Serrano 34 **Tel** *(02) 3871200* **Fax** *(02) 3871300* **Rooms** *147* — **City Map** *2 E3*

Renovated in a vibrant, airy style with hardwood floors and tonal shades of vibrant lime and white, Hotel Blue Tree Fundador is situated on the edge of Barrio París-Londres. Hallways and common areas are a tacky combination of graffiti-like paint and ponchos, but overall a good retreat from downtown bustle. **www.hotelfundador.cl**

EL CENTRO Hotel Galerias — $$$

San Antonio 65 **Tel** *(02) 4707400* **Rooms** *172* — **City Map** *2 F3*

Good-value downtown hotel popular with Latin American travelers. Located on a bustling street, but the attractive and well-appointed rooms have double-paned windows and are quiet. Thematic decor, with imitation *moai* statues and hotel staff dressed as *huasos*. Rooftop pool a plus during the summer. **www.hotelgalerias.cl**

EL CENTRO Hotel Majestic — $$$

Santo Domingo 1526 **Tel** *(02) 6909400* **Fax** *(02) 6974051* **Rooms** *49* — **City Map** *2 D2*

A Best Western affiliate, Hotel Majestic is located on a bustling street about six blocks from Plaza de Armas. With cookie-cutter decor, standard comfortable rooms, and full guest services, including concierge, business center, cable TV, and room service. The hotel is locally renowned for its Indian restaurant. **www.hotelmajestic.cl**

Key to Symbols *see back cover flap*

EL CENTRO Hotel San Francisco Plaza $$$

Avenida Alameda 816 **Tel** *(02) 6393832* **Fax** *(02) 6397826* **Rooms** *155* **City Map** *2 E3*

An upscale hotel equally popular with tourists and businessmen, and arguably the nicest hotel in El Centro. Full-service amenities and attentive service, and decor that is slightly buttoned-up, with Victorian influences. Rooms are soundproofed and hotel is set near tranquil Barrio París-Londres. **www.plazasanfrancisco.cl**

EL CENTRO Hotel NH Ciudad de Santiago $$$$

Avenida Condell 40 **Tel** *(02) 341-7575* **Fax** *(02) 269-1079* **Rooms** *122* **City Map** *3 C4*

A solid four-star chain hotel featuring snazzy decor, spacious and clean guest rooms, and delicious buffet breakfast, but little local flavor. Service is bilingual and friendly. Located on the edge of Providencia within walking distance of Bellavista, in a safe residential neighborhood close to the Salvador metro station. **www.nh-hotels.com**

EL CENTRO Hotel Cesar Business $$$$$

Avenida Alameda 632 **Tel** *(02) 5956622* **Fax** *(02) 5956600* **Rooms** *142* **City Map** *2 F3*

A Latin American chain hotel geared toward traveling executives. Very convenient for downtown attractions, but the neighborhood dies at night and the facing avenue is loud. Attractive, modern decor in communal areas; plain, spacious rooms. Full services include a business center and full breakfast buffet. **www.caesarbusiness.com**

NORTHEAST OF EL CENTRO Hostel Bellavista $

Dardignac 184 **Tel** *(02) 7328737* **Rooms** *17* **City Map** *3 B4*

One of Santiago's best hostels for its location alone – in Bellavista and close to night clubs, restaurants, and the Parque Metropolitano. The trendy, laid-back, and colorful style mirrors the neighborhood, and features friendly service and decently sized rooms; although some are noisy. **www.bellavistahostel.com**

NORTHEAST OF EL CENTRO L'Ambassade $$

Suiza 2084, Providencia **Tel** *(02) 7619711* **Rooms** *5* **City Map** *4 F5*

Run by a French-Chilean couple, this pretty bed-and-breakfast occupies a converted home in a residential area close to the metro but a good walk from businesses. Each light and airy room is decorated differently with contemporary decor and antiques. Facilities include a sauna. Warm, personalized service. **www.ambassade.cl**

NORTHEAST OF EL CENTRO Director Suites Hotel $$

Carmencita 45 **Tel** *(02) 4983000* **Fax** *(02) 4983010* **Rooms** *49* **City Map** *5 B4*

In spite of its bland exterior and frumpy furnishings, the Director Suites Hotel boasts an upscale address and offers good value for its suites that come with a kitchenette. Families will find the Executive Suite set-up ideal given the generous living room space and cooking facilities. **www.director.cl**

NORTHEAST OF EL CENTRO Apart-Hotel Bosque Tobalaba $$

Luis Thayer Ojeda 027, Los Condes **Tel** *(02) 2322337* **Rooms** *20*

RQ Hotels offers five properties in Santiago, of which, this apart-hotel is one of the most reasonably priced and within walking distance of restaurants, the metro, and shops. Slightly frumpy country decor, but all units come with kitchenettes and a living space, and the happening Bar Liguria is on the first floor. **www.rq.cl**

NORTHEAST OF EL CENTRO Hotel Kennedy $$

Avenida Kennedy 4570 **Tel** *(02) 2908100* **Rooms** *133*

Compared to its competition, the five-star status this hotel claims seems dubious. That said, the premises are upscale enough to make the price tag seem like a steal. Located on a major thoroughfare near a shopping mall and visitors need only a short taxi ride to reach nearby restaurants. **www.hotelkennedy.cl**

NORTHEAST OF EL CENTRO Hotel Orly $$

Avenida Pedro de Valdivia 027 **Tel** *(02) 2318947* **Fax** *(02) 3344403* **Rooms** *28* **City Map** *4 E2*

Housed in a sizable French-style mansion with a compact lounge and glass-enclosed patio, Hotel Orly is one of the few boutique hotels in the city. Guest rooms range in size and rooms at the back are quieter. Attentive service. One of the coziest spots to lodge in Santiago, just steps away from good restaurants. **www.orlyhotel.com**

NORTHEAST OF EL CENTRO Hotel Torremayor $$

Ricardo Lyon 332 **Tel** *(02) 2342000* **Fax** *(02) 2343779* **Rooms** *80* **City Map** *4 F2*

A three-star hotel that is comfortable and clean. The hotel sees a lot of group travelers and is perfectly adequate for a night or two in Santiago, but too generic for a week-long stay. Guest rooms are decorated in country floral, and are quiet given the hotel's location on a residential street. **www.hoteltorremayor.cl**

NORTHEAST OF EL CENTRO La Sebastiana Apart Hotel $$

San Sebastian 2727 **Tel** *(02) 6587220* **Rooms** *54*

This apart-hotel has rooms that come with kitchenettes; standard rooms also have a living room with sofa bed. The decoration is exceptionally hip; however, guests here tend to be more independent and service is minimal. Lower rates available for stays of 2 weeks or more. **www.lasebastiana.cl**

NORTHEAST OF EL CENTRO Vilafranca Petit Hotel $$

Pérez Valenzuela 1650 **Tel** *(02) 2351413* **Rooms** *8* **City Map** *3 E2*

Charming B&B on a quiet street, a few blocks away from restaurants. Decorated in French country style with earth tones and local art, and cozy guest rooms that are on the small side. No elevator. Good value for the price, and features a living room and patio terrace. Highly recommended. **www.vilafranca.cl**

NORTHEAST OF EL CENTRO Atton Las Condes $$$

Roger de Flor 2770 **Tel** *(02) 9473600* **Fax** *(02) 9473601* **Rooms** *211*

Decorated in fetching modern geometric prints and bold colors, this business-oriented hotel is one of two Atton Hotels in Santiago; the new El Bosque location is far more convenient for dining and shopping. Lots of public spaces for lounging or meetings. Excellent value. **www.atton.cl**

NORTHEAST OF EL CENTRO Holiday Inn Express $$$

Avenida Vitacura 2929 **Tel** *(02) 4996000* **Fax** *(02) 4996200* **Rooms** *168*

Surrounded by skyscrapers, this amenity-heavy hotel is a safe bet for US travelers seeking an upscale neighborhood and no surprises, but as part of the chain, Holiday Inn, it lacks any Chilean character. Gleaming marble lobby, stylish rooms, and a sauna. Children under 18 can share room with parents. **www.holidayinnexpress.cl**

NORTHEAST OF EL CENTRO Hotel Bonaparte $$$

Mar de Plata 2171 **Tel** *(02) 7966900* **Fax** *(02) 2048907* **Rooms** *65* **City Map** *4 F4*

Mid-range, comfortable hotel that feels more like an inn, with individually sized rooms and pleasant service. The hotel sports somewhat generic country decor, and is located in a lush residential section of Providencia, about five blocks from the commercial area. The pool is more for a dip than laps. **www.hotelbonaparte.com**

NORTHEAST OF EL CENTRO Hotel del Patio $$$

Pío Nono 61 **Tel** *(02) 7327571* **Rooms** *10* **City Map** *3 B4*

A charming, U-shaped hotel on the second story of an antique building in the Patio Bellavista market. Ideal for younger travelers seeking smart accommodation. Lovely wooden floors, a window gallery overlooking the patio, small outdoor deck, cozy dining area, and spacious rooms with contemporary decor. **www.hoteldelpatio.cl**

NORTHEAST OF EL CENTRO Hotel Director $$$

Avenida Vitacura 3600 **Tel** *(02) 3891900* **Fax** *(02) 2460088* **Rooms** *95*

The well-maintained 70s-era Hotel Director is part of a chain of hotels. It is within walking distance of Barrio Vitacura's plethora of gourmet restaurants and art galleries, but away from public transportation. The hotel is good-value accommodation, with economical rates for a suite or junior suite. **www.hoteldirector.cl**

NORTHEAST OF EL CENTRO Hotel Neruda $$$

Avenida Pedro de Valdivia 164 **Tel** *(02) 6790700* **Rooms** *112* **City Map** *4 F2*

Notable for its handy location, Hotel Neruda has spacious but sparsely furnished rooms, a bright, glossy lobby, well-lit café, a large indoor pool, and friendly staff. This is the best bet for travelers seeking clean, average accommodation rather than a hotel with zest. Cheaper rates are available on their website. **www.hotelneruda.cl**

NORTHEAST OF EL CENTRO Hotel Rugendas $$$

Callao 3123 **Tel** *(02) 8569800* **Fax** *(02) 8569861* **Rooms** *51*

Tucked away on a tree-lined residential street, Hotel Rugendas is just two blocks away from shops and restaurants in El Bosque. The hotel commonly offers discounts, and includes use of their sauna and other perks in the price. Standard rooms are small, and it is better to opt for a junior suite. **www.hotelrugendas.cl**

NORTHEAST OF EL CENTRO Le Reve $$$

Orrego Luco 023 **Tel** *(02) 7576000* **Rooms** *28* **City Map** *4 E2*

Occupying a refurbished mansion, this boutique hotel combines French decor and a convenient location near shops and transportation. Notable are the many lounges and sitting areas, including an outdoor patio. Le Reve has a hint of sophistication but is cozy and ideal for both business travelers and tourists. **www.lerevehotel.cl**

NORTHEAST OF EL CENTRO Los Españoles $$$

Los Españoles 2539 **Tel** *(02) 2321824* **Fax** *(02) 2331048* **Rooms** *48* **City Map** *4 F1*

A Best Western franchise with friendly service and extensive amenities, Los Españoles includes a minibar, gym, sauna, and room service. The hotel is in a residential area and faces the wonderful Sculpture Park, which has walking paths, but is a 10-minute walk to a commercial center. **www.losespanoles.cl**

NORTHEAST OF EL CENTRO Meridiano Sur Petit Hotel $$$

Santa Beatriz 256 **Tel** *(02) 2353659* **Rooms** *8* **City Map** *4 D2*

A B&B-style hotel featuring fresh, contemporary decor and personalized service. The *meridiano* (deluxe) rooms are brighter and larger, and there is a third-story loft for five with a kitchenette. Small reading lounge, breakfast and dining area, and terrace. The hotel is a few blocks away from Providencia's restaurants. **www.meridianosur.cl**

NORTHEAST OF EL CENTRO Novotel Santiago $$$

Avenida Américo Vespucio Norte 1630 **Tel** *(02) 4992200* **Fax** *(02) 4992230* **Rooms** *144*

European-style hotel aimed at business travelers. Close to Barrio Vitacura's gourmet restaurants, luxury shopping district, and art galleries, in an upscale neighborhood far from tourist attractions. Rooms are on the small side, but with fresh, contemporary, and simple furniture. **www.novotel.com**

NORTHEAST OF EL CENTRO Radisson Santiago $$$

Avenida Vitacura 2610 **Tel** *(02) 4339000* **Fax** *(02) 4339001* **Rooms** *159*

The chic, modern decor of this Radisson group hotel pairs well with the avant-garde architecture of the building that houses it: the World Trade Center. West-facing rooms can be avoided as they overlook a construction project that will be completed in 2011; east facing rooms above the eighth floor offer great Andean views. **www.radisson.cl**

Key to Price Guide *see p274* **Key to Symbols** *see back cover flap*

NORTHEAST OF EL CENTRO Río Bidasoa $$$

Avenida Vitacura 4873 **Tel** *(02) 2421525* **Rooms** *33*

Family-run hotel, ensconced in a residential area far from tourist attractions, and ideal for travelers seeking a home away from home. The hotel, with its patio, lawn, and pool, is engulfed by greenery. Interiors have a handsome, earthy decor, with leather chairs, crisp ecru-colored linens, and halogen lights. **www.hotelbidasoa.cl**

NORTHEAST OF EL CENTRO Sheraton Four Points $$$

Santa Magdalena 111 **Tel** *(02) 7500300* **Fax** *(02) 7500350* **Rooms** *128* **City Map** *4 F2*

Another international chain hotel with clean and pleasant yet corporate-style decor. Surrounded mostly by office buildings. Some rooms are affected by noise emanating from the street bars of Barrio Suecia on weekends. Friendly staff, good breakfast, and many other amenities. **www.starwoodhotels.com**

NORTHEAST OF EL CENTRO The Park Plaza $$$

Ricardo Lyon 207 **Tel** *(02) 3724000* **Fax** *(02) 3724010* **Rooms** *104* **City Map** *4 F2*

The conservatively designed Park Plaza boasts dark-wood interiors with low lights, and plaid and brocade fabrics. Service here is hit-or-miss, so do not expect to be overly pampered. The quiet residential location just two blocks away from the attractions of Avenida Providencia is a plus, and rooms are quite spacious. **www.parkplaza.cl**

NORTHEAST OF EL CENTRO Hotel Panamericano $$$$

Francisco Noguera 146 **Tel** *(02) 2332230* **Fax** *(02) 2332494* **Rooms** *66* **City Map** *4 E2*

A good bet for generic comfort and at a reasonable price, often with discounts and deals, this hotel is best in the summer for its outdoor pool. Perfect for families, and just minutes from a park and commercial center. The hotel features clean but unremarkable rooms, and polite but minimal service. **www.panamericanahoteles.cl**

NORTHEAST OF EL CENTRO Intercontinental Hotel $$$$

Avenida Vitacura 2885 **Tel** *(02) 3942000* **Fax** *(02) 3942075* **Rooms** *296* **City Map** *5 A3*

There are two faces to this hotel: the old tower, with cramped decor, and the new tower, with spacious rooms. Outstanding location, close to restaurants and transportation, though some rooms sit face to face with buildings. Glossy marble lobby, polite service, a rooftop pool, and many other amenities. **www.ichotelsgroup.com**

NORTHEAST OF EL CENTRO Marriott Santiago $$$$

Avenida Kennedy 5741 **Tel** *(02) 4262000* **Fax** *(02) 4262100* **Rooms** *280*

One of Santiago's top hotels, with great views of the Andes, but far from major attractions. Ideal for skiers heading up to ski resorts such as the one at Valle Nevado *(see p140)*. Housed in a skyscraper with chic Mediterranean-influenced decor, this largely business-oriented hotel offers access to a local golf club. **www.marriott.com**

NORTHEAST OF EL CENTRO Sheraton Santiago H&C Center $$$$

Avenida Santa María 1742 **Tel** *(02) 2335000* **Fax** *(02) 2341729* **Rooms** *379* **City Map** *4 E2*

Updated rooms and a sprawling outdoor pool complex are the highlights of the Sheraton Santiago Hotel and Convention Center, which shares a lobby with the Sheraton Tower but is a separate property. A vast lobby, several restaurants, shops, and spectacular Andean views. **www.starwoodhotels.com**

NORTHEAST OF EL CENTRO The Aubrey $$$$$

Constitución 299 **Tel** *(02) 9402800* **Rooms** *15* **City Map** *3 B3*

This gorgeously renovated 1927-era mansion is Santiago's first boutique hotel. Immensely cozy, with intricate, hand-carved molding, polished parquet floors, and upgraded with dark wood, copper lamps, fine linen, balconies, and contemporary furniture. Fabulous on-site restaurant, Pasta e Vino. **www.theaubrey.com**

NORTHEAST OF EL CENTRO Boulevard Suites $$$$$

Avenida Kennedy 5749 **Tel** *(02) 4215000* **Fax** *(02) 4265073* **Rooms** *50*

Boutique-style hotel on the upper floors of the Marriott building, offering glitzy, sophisticated apartment suites that vary in size from one to three bedrooms and include a kitchen. Granite counters, black-leather couches, chic decor, and glass-wrapped walls with Andean views. **www.boulevardsuites.cl**

NORTHEAST OF EL CENTRO Grand Hyatt Regency Santiago $$$$$

Avenida Kennedy 4601 **Tel** *(02) 9501234* **Fax** *(02) 9503155* **Rooms** *336*

Santiago's first five-star hotel and still the grand dame, with over-the-top amenities, peerless service, and sweeping views. Even standard rooms are huge. The sprawling, tropical-style pool area and spa are idyllic, restaurants world class, and the decor sophisticated. Glamorous yet comfortable. **www.hyatt.cl**

NORTHEAST OF EL CENTRO Hotel Plaza del Bosque $$$$$

Ebro 2828 **Tel** *(02) 4981800* **Fax** *(02) 4981801* **Rooms** *179*

Little-known business-oriented hotel. The 17th-story restaurant, with its spectacular views, is open to all guests, not just to business travelers. All rooms are suites, with a separate living area. Service is attentive, and the style leans toward crystal and marble traditional decor. **www.plazaelbosque.cl**

NORTHEAST OF EL CENTRO Sheraton San Cristobal Tower $$$$$

Josefina Edwards de Ferrari 0100 **Tel** *(02) 7071000* **Fax** *(02) 7071010* **Rooms** *127* **City Map** *4 D2*

Part of the Sheraton chain's luxury hotels. It shares a lobby with the regular Sheraton, but there is a separate check-in area. Executive lounge, access to the hotel's spa and indoor pool, and sumptuous guest rooms with marble baths, and butler service. Good access to Bellavista, and amenities galore. **www.starwoodhotels.com**

NORTHEAST OF EL CENTRO The Ritz-Carlton Santiago $$$$$

El Alcalde 15 **Tel** *(02) 4708500* **Fax** *(02) 4708501* **Rooms** *205* **City Map** *5 B4*

One of the lowest-priced Ritz-Carlton hotels with understated luxury, floral brocades, Oriental carpets, and a hushed ambience. Spectacular rooftop pool offers Andean views. The concierge is the best in town, offering unique day trips and stellar advice. Convenient location close to restaurants and the subway. **www.ritzcarlton.com**

NORTHEAST OF EL CENTRO W Hotel $$$$$

Isidora Goyenechea 3000 **Tel** *(02) 7700000* **Rooms** *196*

The most exciting hotel to open in Chile in a decade, W Hotel offers fabulous, cutting-edge decor designed to impress even the most jaded traveler. Best rooftop pool and bar in the city, excellent cuisine, modish guest suites with an unexpected range of amenities and personal service. **www.starwoodhotels.com**

WEST OF EL CENTRO Happy House Hostel $

Catedral 2207 **Tel** *(02) 6884849* **Rooms** *10* **City Map** *1 B2*

Old-world charm and trendy decoration are the hallmark of this hostel, housed in a mansion with high ceilings and polished parquet floors. Spacious communal areas include a rooftop terrace, library, and kitchen. Rooms feature balconies and huge windows. Friendly, if sometimes inconsistent, service. **www.happyhousehostel.cl**

WEST OF EL CENTRO Hostal Río Amazonas $

Rosas 2234 **Tel** *(02) 6719013* **Fax** *(02) 6719013* **Rooms** *8* **City Map** *1 C2*

A folksy hostel painted a rainbow of colors, in a converted 19th-century home. Family-run and very personable service. Private rooms and shared dorms, recommended during the summer. However, rooms can be cold during the winter due to drafty hallways and high ceilings. **www.hostalrioamazonas.cl**

WEST OF EL CENTRO La Casa Roja $

Agustinas 2113 **Tel** *(02) 6964241* **Rooms** *12* **City Map** *1 C3*

Australian-run and housed in a renovated 19th-century mansion with high ceilings and parquet floors, this hostel has every amenity a backpacker needs, and more: clean bathrooms, spacious communal areas, a modern kitchen, Internet, even an outdoor swimming pool, Jacuzzi, and bar. **www.lacasaroja.cl**

CENTRAL VALLEY

CAJÓN DEL MAIPO Residencia Iniesta $

Comercio 19321, San José de Maipo **Tel** *(02) 8611012* **Rooms** *9* **Road Map** *B7*

This modest *residencia* is the only hotel accommodation in the biggest town of Cajón del Maipo. Located a short walk from the plaza, it has pleasant, if dated, rooms and includes three doubles with private bathrooms. Tasty homemade breakfasts, prepared by the friendly owner who fusses over guests like a mother hen.

CASABLANCA VALLEY La Casona $$$$$

Fundo Rosario, Lagunillas Casablanca **Tel** *(02) 2323134* **Fax** *(02) 2311254* **Rooms** *7* **Road Map** *B6*

The Viña Matetic *(see p138)* guesthouse is a recycled Colonial building set amid lush vineyards. Sophisticated suites with white walls, polished wood furnishings, and private terrace. There is a stately dining area, an outdoor pool, and an honesty bar. Rates include dinner for two with wine, plus wine tour and tastings. **www.matetic.com**

CHILLÁN Hotel Paso Nevado $$

Avenida Libertad 219 **Tel** *(042) 237666* **Fax** *(042) 221827* **Rooms** *20* **Road Map** *D1*

Excellent mid-range choice five blocks from the city center. A small, purpose-built building featuring spotless, spacious rooms painted in creamy tones and simply appointed with wooden furnishings. There is a comfortable café-bar area. Garden with sun terrace at the back of the building. **www.hotelpasonevado.cl**

CHILLÁN Gran Hotel Isabel Riquelme $$$

Constitución 576 **Tel** *(042) 434400* **Fax** *(042) 211541* **Rooms** *70* **Road Map** *D1*

The city's largest, best-rated hotel is a pleasing mix of modern design and pleasant informality. Rooms come as single, double, triple, and quadruple. International restaurant, business center, late-night bar, and big buffet breakfasts. Reception has city road maps and can advise on the area's attractions. **www.hotelisabelriquelme.cl**

COLCHAGUA VALLEY The Lapostolle Residence $$$$$

Viña Lapostolle, Apalta Km4 **Tel** *(072) 953360* **Fax** *(072) 953369* **Rooms** *4* **Road Map** *B7*

This boutique residence has four luxury suites, each effortlessly stylish and massive in size. There is an infinity pool, gourmet restaurant, and sumptuous sun terrace with vineyard vistas. Visitors can choose from one- and two-night programs with tours, tastings, vineyard walks, and picnics all included. **www.lapostolle.com**

CONCEPCIÓN Hotel Alborada $$

Barros Arana 457 **Tel** *(041) 2911121* **Rooms** *70* **Road Map** *D1*

Popular with business travelers, this glossy, glass and steel hotel has five floors of modern rooms with king-size beds, dark-wood workstations, and marbled bathrooms. The pleasing color scheme varies from salmon-pink to apple-green and strawberry-red according to floor. Good downtown location. **www.hotelalborada.cl**

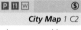

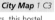

LOS ANDES Hotel Plaza Los Andes $

Manuel Rodriguez 368 ***Tel*** *(034) 421929* ***Fax*** *(034) 426029* ***Rooms*** *40* ***Road Map*** *B6*

Los Andes's single three-star hotel is situated one block away from its main plaza and has two floors of rooms, which ring a central space that serves as the hotel car park. Rooms are functional and comfortable, though service is haphazard. This hotel's best feature is an outside pool with breakfast terrace. **www.hotelplazalosandes.cl**

PAPUDO Hotel Carande $

Chorillos 89 ***Tel*** *(033) 791105* ***Fax*** *(033) 791118* ***Rooms*** *30* ***Road Map*** *B6*

The three-star Hotel Carande is a traditional wooden building and the best option in this seaside town. A warm lobby with open fireplace sets an inviting tone. Clean, comfortable, well-equipped rooms, in particular, the eight doubles, which have lovely ocean views. Well-stocked bar adjoining the restaurant. **www.hotelcarande.cl**

PICHILEMU Hotel Asthur $

Avenida Ortuzar 540 ***Tel*** *(072) 841072* ***Rooms*** *23* ***Road Map*** *B7*

Excellent budget choice in the heart of town. This old Colonial-style building has two floors of rooms built around an interior patio. Rooms are big, comfortable, and very clean. The lounge area offers great beach and ocean views. There is also an outdoor pool and sun terrace. The staff here is very friendly. **www.hotelasthur.cl**

PICHILEMU Pichilemu Surf Hostal $

E. Diaz Lira 164 ***Tel*** *(072) 842350* ***Rooms*** *8* ***Road Map*** *B7*

This cool beachside B&B has brightly decorated double rooms with private bathrooms and ocean views. Guests can arrange for surf lessons, hire bikes, sign-up for horse riding, and lounge in hot tubs on the terrace. Reception is inside the El Puente Holandes restaurant, directly across the road. **www.pichilemusurfhostal.com**

RANCAGUA Hotel Rancagua $

San Martín 85 ***Tel*** *(072) 232663* ***Fax*** *(072) 241155* ***Rooms*** *19* ***Road Map*** *B7*

A converted family house that is both smart and homely. Painted a fun tangerine-orange, inside and out, it has simple but clean and comfortable rooms spread over two floors. Communal areas include a patio, a flowered garden, and a lounge with well-stuffed sofas. A great budget choice in the heart of the city.

RANCAGUA Hotel Mar Andino $$

Bulnes 370 ***Tel*** *(072) 645400* ***Fax*** *(072) 645401* ***Rooms*** *54* ***Road Map*** *B7*

Located four blocks away from the city plaza, this is a charming combination of contemporary style and traditional Chilean hospitality. Rooms are large and well equipped. The front-of-house restaurant and spacious lobby display colorful surrealist artworks. Outside pool and sun terrace. **www.hotelmarandino.cl**

SANTA CRUZ Hotel Vendimia $$$$

Ismael Valdez 92 ***Tel*** *(072) 822464* ***Rooms*** *8* ***Road Map*** *B7*

A family-run boutique hotel. Vintage pianos, mirrors, paintings, and furnishings adorn the lounge and dining areas. Rooms have four-poster, brass-framed beds, bathroom suites with stand-alone tubs, and discreetly placed modern conveniences. The garden has a pool and terrace. Big, homemade breakfasts. **www.hotelvendimia.com**

SANTA CRUZ Hotel Santa Cruz Plaza $$$$$

Plaza de Armas 286 ***Tel*** *(072) 209600* ***Rooms*** *113* ***Road Map*** *B7*

This busy, upscale hotel is a popular base for wine enthusiasts planning visits to Colchagua Valley. A Colonial-style construction with traditionally styled rooms, Hotel Santa Cruz Plaza offers numerous facilities including indoor and outdoor pools, spa, casino, childcare services, and in-house tour agency. **www.hotelsantacruzplaza.cl**

VALPARAÍSO Hostal Luna Sonrisa $

Templeman 833, Cerro Alegre ***Tel*** *(032) 2734117* ***Rooms*** *6* ***City Map*** *B4*

This funky little hostel has a limited number of doubles with en suite bathrooms. It is an old period building on a hillside street with a hippy-chic, artsy interior. Serves the best breakfast in town, with fresh fruit, homemade breads, jams, fruit pies, and unlimited freshly brewed coffee. Helpful staff. **www.lunasonrisa.cl**

VALPARAÍSO Harrington B&B $$

Templeman 535, Cerro Concepción ***Tel*** *(032) 2121338* ***Rooms*** *5* ***City Map*** *B4*

This eco-friendly B&B is a converted 1920s house run by a French couple. It has a mustard-yellow façade and spacious, minimalist suites, one with a street-facing balcony. Rooms are woody, chic, and with Art Nouveau decor. Recycled wood is used for the furnishings and solar panels heat the water. **www.harrington.cl**

VALPARAÍSO Hotel Casa Thomas Somerscales $$$

San Enrique 446, Cerro Alegre ***Tel*** *(032) 2331379* ***Fax*** *(032) 2331006* ***Rooms*** *8* ***City Map*** *B4*

Boutique hotel in an 1874 hilltop house built for English painter Thomas Somerscales. Rooms ooze vintage style: white walls, lacy iron bedsteads, stand-alone wardrobes, velvet drapes, and stripped floorboards. Each has bright color schemes and modern appliances. Rooftop balcony has views of the Pacific. **www.hotelsomerscales.cl**

VALPARAÍSO Robinson Crusoe Inn $$$$

Héctor Calvo 389, Cerro Bellavista ***Tel*** *(032) 2495499* ***Rooms*** *12* ***City Map*** *C5*

A colorful design hotel whose façade is a jigsaw of corrugated zinc sheets, wooden window frames, and polished brass doors. Interiors are cool countryside chic. Rooms with rustic motifs, including patterned rugs and wood-fired stoves. Balconies on fourth-story rooms. Huge, healthy breakfasts. **www.robinsoncrusoeinn.com**

VALPARAÍSO Zero Hotel $$$$$

Lautaro Rosas 343, Cerro Alegre ***Tel*** *(032) 2113113* ***Fax*** *(032) 2113114* ***Rooms*** *9* ***City Map*** *B3*

A luxury boutique hotel in a wooden townhouse built in 1890. Large, light rooms and modern, elegant decor. Suites have high ceilings, chic color schemes, wooden floors, and king-size beds with Egyptian linen. There is an honesty bar and a secluded garden terrace with pool, wisteria, and beautiful bay vistas. **www.zerohotel.com**

VIÑA DEL MAR Hotel Reloj de Flores $

Los Baños 70 ***Tel*** *(032) 2967243* ***Fax*** *(032) 2485242* ***Rooms*** *10* ***Road Map*** *B6*

A friendly bed-and-breakfast tucked away on a hilly side street close to the coastal avenue, Hotel Reloj de Flores is a pink-painted house with rooms built around a small central patio. Most rooms are spacious and have private bathrooms with showers. Comfortable lounge and a fully-equipped kitchen. **www.relojdefloresbb.com**

VIÑA DEL MAR Hotel Viña del Mar $

Francisco Vergara 191 ***Tel*** *(032) 2698906* ***Rooms*** *23* ***Road Map*** *B6*

A gorgeous retreat in a 1913 house fronting the main plaza. The Baroque façade leads into a lobby with a sweeping staircase, extravagant chandeliers, and stuccoed ceiling. The spacious double rooms are irregularly shaped and come with gilded mirrors and stand-alone antique furnishings. **www.hotelvinadelmar.cl**

VIÑA DEL MAR Hotel Cap Ducal $$$

Avenida Marina 51 ***Tel*** *(032) 2626655* ***Fax*** *(032) 2665478* ***Rooms*** *22* ***Road Map*** *B6*

Built in 1936 in the style of an ocean liner, this hotel actually stands on the ocean floor on a reinforced concrete base. Spiral wooden staircases and a wooden lift with stained glass and concertina door ascend to passageways of spacious doubles with wonderful ocean vistas. There is also a "floating" restaurant. **www.capducal.cl**

ZAPALLAR Hotel Isla Seca $$$$

Camino Costero Ruta F-30-E N°31 ***Tel*** *(033) 741224* ***Fax*** *(033) 741228* ***Rooms*** *42* ***Road Map*** *B6*

A boutique hotel built in the style of a mountain lodge, overlooking the coast. Rooms have period furnishings, checkerboard floor tiles, and bright color schemes, including red and yellow walls. Suites offer a private terrace and ocean vista. Palm-fringed pool. The hotel's Cala restaurant serves delicious seafood. **www.hotelislaseca.cl**

NORTE GRANDE AND NORTE CHICO

ANTOFAGASTA Panamericana Hotel Antofagasta $$$

Balmaceda 2575 ***Tel*** *(055) 228811* ***Fax*** *(055) 268415* ***Rooms*** *159* ***Road Map*** *B3*

A modern hotel located close to the historic port area. The standard doubles, in soft green and brown tones, are comfortably equipped with plasma TV, easy chair, and full-length mirror. Amenities include an international restaurant, business center, and a curved pool that edges a private beach. **www.panamericanahoteles.cl**

ARICA Panamericana Hotel Arica $$$

Avenida Comandante San Martín 599 ***Tel*** *(058) 254540* ***Fax*** *(058) 231133* ***Rooms*** *114* ***Road Map*** *B1*

This highly rated resort hotel faces Playa El Laucho. Its impressive services include two pools, a spacious sundeck with ocean and mountain vistas, a private beach, tennis courts, and on-site masseurs. Service is pleasingly informal, rooms are modern and spacious, and there are excellent childcare facilities. **www.panamericanahoteles.cl**

COPIAPÓ Hotel La Casona $

O'Higgins 150 ***Tel*** *(052) 217278* ***Fax*** *(052) 217277* ***Rooms*** *12* ***Road Map*** *B4*

Picturesquely contained in an adobe house, La Casona (Little House) is warm and welcoming. Rooms are snug, traditionally furnished, and set around a tree-shaded garden.The breakfast salon doubles as an evening restaurant specializing in regional dishes. Advance booking is recommended. **www.lacasonahotel.cl**

IQUIQUE Hotel Arturo Prat $$

Aníbal Pinto 695 ***Tel*** *(057) 520000* ***Fax*** *(057) 520050* ***Rooms*** *92* ***Road Map*** *B2*

Fronting Iquique's main plaza, this hotel is a decent mid-range choice with good services and amenities. The front wing overlooks the plaza and has comfortable, if slightly dated, singles and doubles. A second, more modern wing stands at the back and has brighter, more inviting, but pricier rooms. **www.hotelprat.cl**

IQUIQUE Gavina Hotel $$$$

Avenida Arturo Prat 1497 ***Tel*** *(057) 393030* ***Fax*** *(057) 391111* ***Rooms*** *82* ***Road Map*** *B2*

A glossy five-star tower, excellently located, Gavina Hotel offers luxury services. Amenities include two pools (one a natural seawater pool ringed by rock), a spa, a mini-cinema, a private beach, and sports facilities. Rooms are equipped with modern conveniences and most open on to balconies with dazzling ocean views. **www.gavina.cl**

LA SERENA Hotel Del Cid $$

O'Higgins 138 ***Tel*** *(051) 212692* ***Fax*** *(051) 222289* ***Rooms*** *35* ***Road Map*** *B5*

Owned by a Scottish ex-pat, this delightful hotel is an early 1900s house on a quiet street close to the city center. Rooms have wooden floors, elegant furnishings, and tasteful, period-style wallpapering. Each opens on to a patio of big flower pots, checkerboard floor tiles, and wicker furniture. **www.hoteldelcid.cl**

LA SERENA Hotel Campanario del Mar $$$

Avenida del Mar 4600 **Tel** *(051) 245516* **Fax** *(051) 245531* **Rooms** *14* **Road Map** *B5*

An excellent four-star choice fronting the Pacific coast. The floorplan of this small, modern hotel mimics the old Colonial blueprint: rooms are set around a central patio with fountain. The super spacious rooms are well equipped; most have balconies and ocean views. Huge breakfasts with brewed coffee. **www.hotelcampanario.cl**

OVALLE Hotel Plaza Turismo $$

Victoria 295 **Tel** *(053) 662500* **Fax** *(053) 662548* **Rooms** *29* **Road Map** *B5*

A raspberry colored edifice facing Ovalle's main plaza. The lobby has crystal chandeliers, marbled floor, and leather sofas. Carpeted corridors access large, smartly appointed rooms with period-style furnishings. A stylish restaurant serves traditional fare in an interior patio decorated with colorful wall murals. **www.plazaturismo.cl**

SAN PEDRO DE ATACAMA Hostal Sonchek $

Gustavo Le Paige 170 **Tel** *(055) 851112* **Rooms** *13* **Road Map** *C3*

This popular backpackers' escape has an unassuming exterior and an interior that is big on character. Rooms are clean, carpeted, hippy-chic, and open on to an oasis garden slung with hammocks and dotted with shaded areas. There are doubles, triples, and dorms, a laundry service, and a small restaurant serving homemade dishes.

SAN PEDRO DE ATACAMA Hotel Tulor $$$

Domingo Atienza 523 **Tel** *(055) 851027* **Fax** *(055) 851063* **Rooms** *8* **Road Map** *C3*

Owned by a Chilean archaeologist and inspired by the ancient settlement of Tulor. Rooms are thatched, built from adobe, wood, and stone, yet have bright colors and modern furnishings. The outside spaces include a pool, a garden with native trees, and a spacious sun terrace looking out to Volcán Licancabur. **www.hoteltulor.cl**

SAN PEDRO DE ATACAMA Hotel Altiplánico $$$$

Domingo Atienza 282 **Tel** *(055) 851212* **Fax** *(055) 851238* **Rooms** *29* **Road Map** *C3*

The sumptuous suites of this hotel are adobe houses built in the traditional Atacameño style. Interiors are warm and luxurious, with thick llama-wool rugs, alpaca-wool bedspreads, and leather flourishes. Amenities include a garden, an exterior pool with terrace, and a first-rate modern Chilean restaurant. **www.altiplanico.com**

LAKE DISTRICT AND CHILOÉ

ANCUD Hotel Galeón Azul $$

Libertad 751 **Tel** *(065) 622567* **Fax** *(065) 622543* **Rooms** *15* **Road Map** *D3*

Perched on a bluff overlooking the ocean, this bright yellow-and-blue hotel is a refurbished old weatherboard building. The interior mixes modern styling with wooden staircases and floors. Rooms are big, especially on the first floor, light, and contemporary. Ten rooms have floor-to-ceiling ocean views. **www.hotelgaleonazul.cl**

CASTRO Hostal Casa Blanca $

Los Carrera 308 **Tel** *(065) 632726* **Rooms** *10* **Road Map** *D3*

A top choice, occupying a large pink-painted wooden house dating from 1910. Fancy windows face the still waters and beached fishing boats of the Fiordo Castro. The interior is beautifully appointed with pale wood and salmon-pink colors characterizing the decor. Rooms are bright, spacious, and modern. Eight have sea views.

CASTRO Hotel Unicornio Azul $$

Avenida Pedro Montt 228 **Tel** *(065) 632359* **Fax** *(065) 632808* **Rooms** *17* **Road Map** *D3*

This white, wooden guesthouse has cozy doubles and singles equipped with cable TV and private bathrooms. Tasty breakfasts prepared by the gregarious septuagenarian owner. Comfortable lounge, a picture-book pretty garden in front of the house, and five family-sized wood cabins at the back. **www.hotelgaleonazul.cl**

CHONCHI Hotel Huildín $

Centenario 102 **Tel** *(065) 671388* **Rooms** *12* **Road Map** *D3*

A century-old house with a swinging street sign and fancy wooden veranda recalling the houses of America's Wild West. Atmospheric interior: each room is woody and dressed in cheerful paint schemes and brightly colored bed linen. The inviting lounge has a wood-stove fire and antique wall clocks. **www.hotelhuildin.cl**

FRUTILLAR Hotel Ayacara $$

Avenida Philippi, esq. Pedro Aguirre Cerda, Frutillar Bajo **Tel** *(065) 421550* **Rooms** *8* **Road Map** *D2*

Aptly named Ayacara (Jewel on the Lake), this boutique hotel on the shores of Lago Llanquihue is a period construction whose weatherboard façade is painted yellow and black. Stylish, spacious rooms, four with views of the lake and Volcán Osorno. Smart restaurant with terrace. Lounge with great vistas. **www.hotelayacara.cl**

LICAN RAY Hostal Hofmann $

Camino Coñaripe 100 **Tel** *(045) 431109* **Rooms** *5* **Road Map** *D2*

Owned by a family of German descent, this is a welcoming B&B with a teahouse in one wing. Comfortable, woody rooms, sprawling front and back gardens, and three lolloping dogs. Children's swings and play frames in the garden. An apiary here provides honey for homemade breakfasts.

OSORNO Hotel Lagos del Sur $$$

O'Higgins 564 **Tel** *(064) 243244* **Fax** *(064) 242396* **Rooms** *20* **Road Map** *D2*

A three-star hotel located one block from Osorno's main square. It has a modern, brick exterior and a traditionally furnished interior. Wallpapered corridors access three floors of large, well-equipped rooms with big bathroom suites. Pleasant, professional staff; secretarial service for business travelers. **www.hotelagosdelsur.cl**

PANGUIPULLI Hostal Chabunco $

Diego Portales 72 **Tel** *(063) 311847* **Rooms** *15* **Road Map** *D2*

This well-located great-value *hostal* offers clean, comfortable rooms with carpeted floors, cable TV, warm blankets, and showers. There is a small lounge area and a sun terrace with tables and chairs. The owner is a friendly woman, happy to direct guests on what to do and see in Panguipulli. **www.chabunco.cl**

PN VICENTE PÉREZ ROSALES Petrohué Hotel & Cabañas $$$$

Ruta 225, Km64 **Tel** *(065) 212025* **Rooms** *20 + 4 cabins* **Road Map** *D2*

An upscale hotel overlooking Lago Todos Los Santos. Guests choose from rooms with lake, volcano, or river view, or stay in one of the well-equipped, family-sized log cabins. Amenities include a restaurant and indoor and outdoor pools. Helpful staff arrange activities within the national park. **www.petrohue.com**

PUCÓN Hostería ¡école! $

General Urrutia 592 **Tel** *(045) 441675* **Rooms** *22* **Road Map** *D2*

A funky, hugely popular guesthouse. There are brightly painted, shared and private rooms to suit a variety of budgets. Amenities include a vegetarian restaurant, a bar-café, a book-stuffed lounge, and a garden slung with hammocks. The hotel organizes daily trips to nearby natural highlights. Book well in advance. **www.ecole.cl**

PUCÓN Hotel La Casona de Pucón $$

Lincoyan 48 **Tel** *(045) 443179* **Rooms** *8* **Road Map** *D2*

This boutique hotel is a refurbished house built in the 1930s. Traditional weatherboard exterior, and the interior has been expertly restored by local craftsmen. Rooms are elegant, light, and airy; three with spacious wooden terrace and mountain views. The garden has shaded areas and furnishings. **www.lacasonadepucon.cl**

PUCÓN Hotel Malalhue $$

Camino Internacional 1615 **Tel** *(045) 443130* **Fax** *(045) 443132* **Rooms** *24* **Road Map** *D2*

An Alpine-chalet building, Hotel Malalhue fuses the smart services of a hotel with the friendliness of a Chilean guesthouse. Rooms are cozy, with thick floor rugs, Mapuche ornamentation, flat-screen LCD TVs, and woody furnishings. Communal spaces include a homely lounge, restaurant, and exterior pool. **www.malalhue.cl**

PUCÓN Villarrica Park Lake Hotel $$$$$

Camino Villarrica Pucón, Km13 **Tel** *(045) 450000* **Fax** *(045) 450202* **Rooms** *70* **Road Map** *D2*

Lavish luxury on the Villarrica lakeshore with sleek, contemporary design. The hotel has standard category suites featuring king-size beds, bathroom suites with hydro-massage baths and walk-in showers, and furnished balconies with lake views. Sumptuous spa with heated pool and massage therapies. Huge sun terrace. **www.vplh.cl**

PUERTO MONTT Hotel Millahue $

Copiapó 64 **Tel** *(065) 256317* **Rooms** *25* **Road Map** *D2*

An excellent budget choice. Fishing-themed paintings hang in the snug lobby, from where arched staircases climb to carpeted, cocoon-like rooms with cable TV and private bathroom. Covered parking and Internet access. The hotel's excellent Los Arcos restaurant serves delicious seafood specials. **www.hotelmillahue.cl**

PUERTO MONTT Don Luis Hotel $$$

Quillota 146 **Tel** *(65) 259001* **Fax** **Rooms** *60* **Road Map** *D2*

This hotel oozes old-fashioned charm. A lobby with open fireplace and well-stuffed sofas greets guests. Heavy timber doors open on to warmly decorated suites that feature workstations and wall-mounted LCD TVs. Floors seven and eight have ocean views. On the top floor is a fitness center and sauna. **www.hoteldonluis.cl**

PUERTO OCTAY Hotel Viento Sur $

Camino Osorno-Puerto Octay, Km49, Cruce Purranque-Corte Alto **Tel** *(064) 264650* **Rooms** *3* **Road Map** *D2*

This gorgeous guesthouse is a pioneer-era house built for a German immigrant family. There is a comfortable lounge and dining area downstairs. A rickety wooden staircase climbs to brightly painted, contemporarily styled rooms. Guests can ride the owner's horses through the surrounding forest and fields. **www.vientosurhotel.cl**

PUERTO VARAS The Guest House $$

O'Higgins 608 **Tel** *(065) 231521* **Rooms** *9* **Road Map** *D2*

An American-owned guesthouse with a powder-blue clapboard exterior. The smell of homemade bread pervades the restful living and dining areas. On the second floor are beautifully appointed rooms with sloping ceilings, and antique ragdolls and teddy bears on pillows ring a second lounge. Sunny patio. **www.vicki-johnson.com**

PUERTO VARAS Hotel Puelche $$$$

Imperial 695 **Tel** *(065) 233600* **Fax** *(065) 233350* **Rooms** *21* **Road Map** *D2*

This Alpine-style building has a central location and excellent services. Polished wood and cool stone are recurring motifs. The standard doubles are light and spacious, with large beds and bathrooms. Amenities include a modern Mediterranean restaurant and a spa with sauna, Jacuzzi, and masseurs. **www.hotelpuelche.com**

Key to Price Guide *see p274* **Key to Symbols** *see back cover flap*

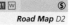

TEMUCO Hotel RP $$$

Portales 779 ***Tel*** *(045) 977777* ***Rooms*** *23* ***Road Map*** *D2*

Aimed at the hip traveler, Hotel RP is a sleek design hotel whose lobby has red sofas and road Mapuche weavings on the walls. Modish, air-conditioned rooms mix luxury leather touches with smart steel-and-chrome appliances. Suites also have living-room space and a Jacuzzi. Services include covered parking space. **www.hotelrp.cl**

TEMUCO Hotel Terraverde $$$$

Avenida Prat 0220 ***Tel*** *(045) 239999* ***Fax*** *(045) 239455* ***Rooms*** *74* ***Road Map*** *D2*

An excellently located modern five-star hotel with spacious grounds. Amenities include a fitness room, sauna, and an exterior pool shrouded by weeping willows. Rooms are large and well equipped; those on upper floors have pleasant views across Temuco's rooftops to the Andean foothills. **www.panamericanahoteles.cl**

VALDIVIA Hostal Río de Luna $

Avenida Prat 695 ***Tel*** *(063) 253333* ***Rooms*** *14* ***Road Map*** *D2*

Set on the banks of Río Calle Calle, close to the city center, this weatherboard house has an attractive blue-and-white exterior and a contemporary interior. Standard rooms receive plenty of natural light, and have modern decor. Suites with boutique-style furnishing and spacious terrace with views. **www.hostalriodeluna.cl**

VALDIVIA Hotel Melillanca $$$

Avenida Alemania 675 ***Tel*** *(063) 212509* ***Rooms*** *73* ***Road Map*** *D2*

Situated close to shops and services. Inviting atmosphere includes complimentary pisco sour on arrival and a tourist information desk in the lobby. Balconied rooms with modern conveniences and appliances. Supervised children's playroom, a restaurant with children's menu, and a gym with sauna. **www.hotelmelillanca.cl**

VILLARRICA Hotel El Ciervo $$$

General Körner 241 ***Tel*** *(045) 411215* ***Fax*** *(045) 413884* ***Rooms*** *13* ***Road Map*** *D2*

This excellent value-for-money hotel is a sprawling period house whose charming, traditional design embraces embossed wallpaper, hardwood beds, and open fireplaces. Spacious grounds include a sweeping lawn, an outdoor pool, and a sun terrace with garden furniture. Homemade German breakfasts. **www.hotelelciervo.cl**

NORTHERN PATAGONIA

CALETA TORTEL Hostal Costanera $

Antonio Ronchi 141 ***Tel*** *(067) 234815* ***Rooms*** *7* ***Road Map*** *D5*

Opened to tourism in 2003 by the road link to Carretera Austral, the town of Caleta Tortel offers only B&B accommodation. Hostal Costanera is the best of these for its setting and room quality in a Chiloé-style shingle house. Children pay half. Patrons must tote their luggage from the town parking lot.

CHILE CHICO Hostería de la Patagonia $

Camino Internacional s/n ***Tel*** *(067) 411337* ***Fax*** *(067) 222147* ***Rooms*** *7* ***Road Map*** *E4*

Founded by a Franco-Belgian pioneer family on Chile Chico's outskirts, this *hostería* is set in verdant gardens surrounded by tall poplars and spreading willows. Sparsely but attractively decorated rooms with natural light. Rooms upstairs have private bath; cheaper rooms downstairs have shared bath. **www.hosteriadelapatagonia.cl**

CHILE CHICO Hacienda Tres Lagos $$$$$

Cruce El Maitén, Carretera Austral Km274 Sur ***Tel*** *(067) 411323* ***Fax*** *(02) 3345294* ***Rooms*** *20* ***Road Map*** *E4*

An expanding resort with its own beach on Lago Negro. Rooms are spacious free-standing units with wood-burning stoves or fireplaces, and even iPods. Facilities include a spa with hot tubs and Jacuzzis. There are two restaurants, one international and the other a grill for lamb barbecues. **www.haciendatreslagos.com**

COCHRANE Hotel Último Paraíso $$

Lago Brown 455 ***Tel*** *(067) 522361* ***Fax*** *(067) 522361* ***Rooms*** *6* ***Road Map*** *D4*

Set in a shockingly barren landscape in an otherwise lush natural region, this stylishly designed building in a quiet residential area has well-kept, well-heated rooms that often house groups of fly fishermen, but is open to everyone. In a town where fine food is hard to find, its guests-only restaurant sets a standard.

COYHAIQUE Hostal Español $

Sargento Aldea 343 ***Tel*** *(067) 242580* ***Fax*** *(067) 242580* ***Rooms*** *11* ***Road Map*** *E4*

This is a spotless new alternative, with luminous rooms, though those on the upper story are more so. However, some of those rooms are barely wider than the length of their beds, even if all of them have cable TV. Close enough to walk to restaurants, but comfortably distant from traffic congestion. **www.hostalcoyhaique.cl**

COYHAIQUE Hostal Gladys $

General Parra 65 ***Tel*** *(067) 245288* ***Rooms*** *6* ***Road Map*** *E4*

Simple but friendly family accommodation in central Coyhaique, within easy walking distance from everything. All rooms well heated, with cable TV, but some have shared rather than private baths. Abundant, diverse breakfast available at additional charge. Limited parking at no extra charge.

COYHAIQUE Hotel El Reloj $$

Baquedano 828 **Tel** *(067) 231108* **Fax** *(067) 231108* **Rooms** *9* **Road Map** *E4*

Overlooking the river, set back from a busy avenue, Hotel El Reloj is Coyhaique's closest thing to a boutique hotel. Attractive common areas with natural wood and large fireplace, cozy rooms with views of greenery and the nearby canyon, but close enough to walk to the Plaza de Armas. Fine restaurant. **www.elrelojhotel.cl**

COYHAIQUE Hostal Belisario Jara $$$

Bilbao 662 **Tel** *(067) 234150* **Fax** *(067) 425694* **Rooms** *8* **Road Map** *E4*

Vaguely Francophile, with intriguing nooks and crannies, this centrally located three-story hotel is set back from the street and that gives it some privacy and quiet. Rooms on the small side, though they vary, but luminous and well-heated in cool climate. Breakfast and WiFi included; separate bar. **www.belisariojara.cl**

COYHAIQUE Hostal Espacio y Tiempo $$$

La Junta, Carretera Austral s/n **Tel** *(067) 314141* **Fax** *(067) 314142* **Rooms** *9* **Road Map** *E4*

Camouflaged by conifers, this cozy roadside *hostal* has a bar-restaurant open to non-guests as well. The friendly management and rustic style draws fishing enthusiasts in particular, but it is also possible to arrange horseback rides and road trips by motor vehicle. Game dishes such as venison on the menu. **www.espacioytiempo.cl**

FUTALEUFÚ Hotel El Barranco $$$

O'Higgins 172 **Tel** *(065) 721314* **Fax** *(065) 721314* **Rooms** *10* **Road Map** *E3*

At the quiet west end of town, Hotel El Barranco overlooks a lushly forested canyon and is built of native woods, with common areas that include a bar-restaurant. Organizes activities such as fishing, rafting, and kayaking on Río Futaleufú and smaller rivers nearby. Abundant small-pane windows keep it bright. **www.elbarrancochile.cl**

PARQUE PUMALÍN Cabañas Caleta Gonzalo $$$

Carretera Austral s/n **Tel** *(065) 250079* **Fax** *(065) 255145* **Rooms** *9* **Road Map** *D3*

The impeccable taste of Parque Pumalín founder Doug Tompkins is on display at his Caleta Gonzalo cabins, which lodge up to six people at a time in style. Easy access to the visitors' center, trails, and other services. However, there are no kitchens; the nearby excellent café is the only food option. **www.parquepumalin.cl**

PUERTO CHACABUCO Hotel Loberías del Sur $$$$$

Jose Miguel Carrera 50 **Tel** *(067) 351115* **Fax** *(02) 2311993* **Rooms** *60* **Road Map** *D4*

Sprawling resort hotel that is the gateway for catamaran trips to Laguna San Rafael and Parque Aiken del Sur. Easily the best hotel in the region, with an excellent restaurant and large rooms with bay windows. Ample common areas including heated pool and bar. Gym also has a sauna. **www.catamaranesdelsur.cl**

PUERTO INGENIERO IBÁÑEZ Hostería Shehen Aike $

Risopatrón 055 **Tel** *(067) 423284* **Fax** *(067) 423284* **Rooms** *5* **Road Map** *E4*

A friendly Swiss-Chilean family operates these free-standing *cabaña*-style B&B accommodations on a large poplar-lined lot in the center of Puerto Ibáñez. Common areas are in the main house, where breakfast and other meals are served. English and German spoken here. Rental bikes and excursions available. **www.aike.cl**

PUERTO PUYUHUAPI Casa Ludwig $

Avenida Übel 202 **Tel** *(067) 325220* **Rooms** *10* **Road Map** *D3*

A chalet-style B&B owned by the Ludwig family, one of the pioneers in this region. The house can lodge a variety of budgets as accommodation ranges from spacious private rooms on lower floors to attic bunks for backpackers. The house loans out its rowboat for excursions on the fjord nearby. **www.casaludwig.cl**

PUERTO PUYUHUAPI Cabañas El Pangue $$$

Carretera Austral Km240 **Tel** *(067) 325128* **Rooms** *12* **Road Map** *D3*

Set in a densely wooded site on the shores of Lago Risopatrón, El Pangue has scattered *cabañas* and a central clubhouse with a fine restaurant, heated indoor-outdoor pool, and diversions such as a billiard table. Accommodations are spacious. Excursions include fishing and horseback riding. **www.elpangue.cl**

PUERTO PUYUHUAPI Puyuhuapi Lodge & Spa $$$

Bahía Dorita s/n **Tel** *(067) 325103* **Fax** *(067) 325103* **Rooms** *39* **Road Map** *D3*

Reached only by motor launch *(see p228)*, this is Northern Patagonia's top spa hotel. Large rooms with sea views, indoor and outdoor pools, and a spa with massage therapy services. Offers multiple excursions, including hiking at Parque Nacional Queulat and catamaran to Laguna San Rafael. **www.patagonia-connection.com**

RESERVA NACIONAL LAGO JEINEMENI Terra Luna Lodge $$$

Puerto Guadal, Camino a Chile Chico Km1.5 **Tel** *(067) 431263* **Fax** *(067) 431264* **Rooms** *16* **Road Map** *E4*

This hillside hotel sits on 15 acres (6 ha) of private land with panoramas of Lago General Carrera. There are several buildings with different types of accommodations – for couples, families, and even backpackers. The main lakeside building includes a restaurant. Offers packages that include activities. **www.terra-luna.cl**

RÍO BAKER Lodge Río Baker $$

Carretera Austral Sur Km247, Puerto Bertrand **Tel** *(067) 411499* **Rooms** *6* **Road Map** *D5*

Situated in the cozy hamlet of Puerto Bertrand, Lodge Río Baker is named for the river on whose edge it stands. The lodge is built from native woods and surrounded by forest on all sides. Gracious Argentine ownership and personal attention. Welcomes all guests, not just fishing enthusiasts.

RÍO BAKER Patagonia Baker Lodge $$$

Carretera Austral, 2 mile (3 km) S of Puerto Bertrand ***Tel*** *(067) 411903* ***Rooms*** *6* ***Road Map*** *D5*

This is a fly-fishing lodge located directly on the Río Baker. The six double rooms are comfortable, well furnished and heated electrically but also have woodstoves. Amenities include a central clubhouse with restaurant, bar, fireplace, and other common areas such as riverside decks. **www.pbl.cl**

VILLA O'HIGGINS Hostal Runín $

Pasaje Vialidad s/n ***Tel*** *(067) 431870* ***Fax*** *(067) 431822* ***Rooms*** *8* ***Road Map*** *E5*

A two-story house surrounded by tall southern beeches on a large plot of land, with outdoor *quincho* (barbecue). The *hostal* is operated by the town's ex-mayor and offers useful information on the area. Six of its rooms have private bath, the other two shared bath. Rates include American-style breakfast; other meals on request.

SOUTHERN PATAGONIA AND TIERRA DEL FUEGO

PORVENIR Hostería Yendegaia $

Croacia 702 ***Tel*** *(061) 581919* ***Rooms*** *7* ***Road Map*** *E6*

Housed in a 1926 traditional home perched on the corner of a residential street, this small hotel has a warm, homey feel with tin walls painted sunflower yellow. The simplicity of the exterior belies the charming and modern decor within. Tasty breakfasts. Travel planning help available. **www.hosteriayendegaia.com**

PORVENIR Hotel Rosas $

Phillipi 296 ***Tel*** *(061) 580088* ***Rooms*** *11* ***Road Map*** *E6*

Despite a plain exterior, Hotel Rosas offers clean, spacious, and pleasant rooms with cable TV, and one of Porvenir's most popular restaurants. The owner, a local, can provide in-depth information about the region and assist in planning excursions around Tierra del Fuego.

PUERTO NATALES Hostal Lili Patagonicos $

Arturo Prat 479 ***Tel*** *(061) 414063* ***Rooms*** *8* ***Road Map*** *E6*

Youthful energy pervades this *hostal*, mostly due to the wall climbing and zip lining on offer. Comfortable, no-frills rooms; some are en suite and there is a shared dorm as well. Active outdoor enthusiasts on staff, who can help with planning trips; they also rent equipment such as tents and backpacks. **www.lilipatagonicos.com**

PUERTO NATALES Keoken $$$

Señoret 267 ***Tel*** *(061) 413670* ***Rooms*** *7* ***Road Map*** *E6*

A cozy, family-run B&B ideal for people who like to feel at home when traveling. The owners can help guests book lodging and reserve campgrounds in the Torres del Paine National Park. Guests can also rent bikes for exploring the town. The decor is understated, and some rooms have bay views. **www.keokenpatagonia.com**

PUERTO NATALES Hotel Altiplánico $$$$$

Huerto Familiar 282 ***Tel*** *(061) 412525* ***Rooms*** *22* ***Road Map*** *E6*

A low-slung hotel on a grassy slope that overlooks the Seno Última Esperanza, a 15-minute walk from town. The hotel uses lots of stone and cement, colorful textiles, and sheepskin throw rugs. Rooms have tiled floors and heat, and there are outdoor Jacuzzis. Staff can book excursions to Torres del Paine NP. **www.altiplanico.cl**

PUERTO NATALES Hotel Cost Australis $$$$$

Pedro Montt 262 ***Tel*** *(061) 412000* ***Rooms*** *110* ***Road Map*** *E6*

A contemporary hotel, in cream and gray tones, with peaked roofs and a grand, yellow façade adorned with angular wooden beams; reminiscent of a mountain lodge. Half the rooms face the Seno Última Esperanza and are more expensive. The hotel is popular with tour groups and business travelers. **www.hoteles-australis.com**

PUERTO NATALES Hotel Indigo $$$$$

Ladrilleros 105 ***Tel*** *(061) 413609* ***Rooms*** *29* ***Road Map*** *E6*

One of Chile's most chic properties. Most rooms, though small, feature views of the Seno Última Esperanza. Stripped-down decor with bare walls, elevated metal walkways, and plush lounge couches. The rooftop spa has sweeping views. Beds have down comforters and are warmed every evening. **www.indigopatagonia.com**

PUERTO NATALES Remota $$$$$

Ruta 9, Km1.5, Huerta 279 ***Tel*** *(061) 414040* ***Rooms*** *77* ***Road Map*** *E6*

Perched high above the sound, with views from several fire-warmed lounges, the stunning Remota was inspired by estancia architecture. Light and spacious interiors, decorated with an impressive collection of indigenous artifacts. All-inclusive packages with gourmet meals, excursions, and use of the sumptuous spa. **www.remota.cl**

PUERTO WILLIAMS Hotel Lakutaia $$$$$

Seno Lauta s/n ***Tel*** *(061) 621721* ***Rooms*** *24* ***Road Map*** *F7*

Puerto Williams' best hotel has its own horse stables and a pier. Handsome, elegant interiors provide a sumptuous respite, and there is plenty of information and an on-staff anthropologist guide. Trekking, sailing trips to Cape Horn, and horseback riding can be planned as well. **www.lakutaia.cl**

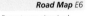

PUNTA ARENAS Hostal Calafate $

Magallanes 671 **Tel** *(061) 710100* **Rooms** *20* **Road Map** *E6*

A long-standing *hostal*, popular for its convenient location and clean, standard rooms, which come with cable TV. Amenities include an Internet café, laundry, and trip-planning services. The hotel faces the Museo Regional Braun Menéndez *(see p246)* on a busy city street. **www.calafate.cl**

PUNTA ARENAS Hotel Chalet Chapital $

Armando Sanhueza 974 **Tel** *(061) 730100* **Fax** *(061) 730101* **Rooms** *11* **Road Map** *E6*

Well located one block from the main plaza, this budget hotel has spartan yet clean and comfortable rooms that are all en suite. Housed in an attractive, early 20th-century building, the small hotel has a lounge with television, and extremely helpful staff. **www.hotelchaletchapital.cl**

PUNTA ARENAS Ilaia Hotel $$

Ignacio Carrera Pinto 351 **Tel** *(061) 223592* **Rooms** *9* **Road Map** *E6*

Built in an eye-catching, contemporary design, this new hotel is a favorite among travelers for its friendly, attentive service and focus on recharging travelers' batteries with yoga, meditation, and reiki sessions. There are also organic breakfasts, city tours, and good views from the hotel lounge. **www.ilaia.cl**

PUNTA ARENAS Patagonia Pionera Hotel $$

Arauco 786 **Tel** *(061) 222045* **Rooms** *8* **Road Map** *E6*

This lovely B&B is located on a quiet residential street seven blocks from the main plaza. Housed in a renovated, early 20th-century home fronting a pretty garden, the hotel has parquet floors, antique furniture, and comfortable beds, and is impeccably clean. **www.ilaiapatagonia.cl**

PUNTA ARENAS Hotel Rey Don Felipe $$$

Armando Sanhueza 965 **Tel** *(061) 295000* **Fax** *(061) 295002* **Rooms** *45* **Road Map** *E6*

A good-value hotel, the Rey Don Felipe is centrally located and offers pleasant, spacious rooms and tasteful, earthy decor in beige and coffee tones. The hotel is adorned with framed photos of the city's early days. For the price, the hotel offers more amenities than its competitors. **www.hotelreydonfelipe.com**

PUNTA ARENAS Dreams Hotel $$$$$

O'HIggins 1235 **Tel** *(02) 2033091* **Rooms** *72* **Road Map** *E6*

Located on the waterfront, the stunning glass-and-steel Dreams Hotel has a trendy yet sophisticated decor and features luxurious guest rooms with views of the Strait of Magellan. Amenities include children's activities, a casino, spa, three restaurants, and shops. Every kind of traveler is catered to. **www.mundodreams.com**

PUNTA ARENAS Hosteria El Faro $$$$$

Near Cabo Froward **Tel** *(099) 3493862* **Rooms** *6* **Road Map** *E6*

A gem of a *hostería*, El Faro sits on the strait and is reached by a one-hour drive from town and a short boat ride. Interiors with driftwood furniture, natural art, cozy leather couches, and panoramic views from the windows. All-inclusive packages with meals, kayaking, trekking, and whale-watching. **www.hosteriafarosanisidro.cl**

PUNTA ARENAS Hotel Cabo de Hornos $$$$$

Plaza Muñoz Gamero 1039 **Tel** *(061) 715000* **Rooms** *111* **Road Map** *E6*

Renovated in 2008, Hotel Cabo de Hornos now has the feel of a mountain lodge, with slate flooring, cowhide furniture, and earthy decor. This grand hotel is one of the most luxurious in town, yet can be a bargain during the low season. Full amenities. Rooms on the upper levels feature sweeping views. **www.hoteles-australis.com**

PUNTA ARENAS Whale Sound $$$$$

Near Cabo Froward **Tel** *(061) 710511* **Rooms** *5* **Road Map** *E6*

A scientific base that arranges whale-watching journeys from its remote camp, 2 hrs from Punta Arenas. Comfortable domed tents connected by elevated boardwalks, and a main lounge and dining area. Programs include boat trips to view humpback whales and other fauna, kayaking, and trekking. **www.whalesound.com**

TORRES DEL PAINE NATIONAL PARK Cerro Lodge Guido $$$$$

25 miles (40 km) from Laguna Amarga Ranger Station **Tel** *(02) 1964807* **Rooms** *15* **Road Map** *D6*

A working estancia that places as much importance on horseback riding as on touring and meeting ranch hands at work. Rooms in the old manor home are exquisite, with rich linen and antique furniture. Meals are prepared using organic produce grown on the premises, and are served with premium wine. **www.cerroguido.cl**

TORRES DEL PAINE NATIONAL PARK Explora Hotel Saltochico $$$$$

Lago Pehoé sector **Tel** *(02) 2066060* **Rooms** *50* **Road Map** *D6*

The Explora hotel chain virtually launched the all-inclusive adventure lodge concept in Chile with this exclusive accommodation. Outstanding location, with mesmerizing views. Guided excursions, a private *quincho* (barbecue), horse stables, and a full spa. Warmly decorated interiors with plenty of lounge areas. **www.explora.com**

TORRES DEL PAINE NATIONAL PARK Hostería Grey $$$$$

Lago Grey sector **Tel** *(061) 712100* **Rooms** *30* **Road Map** *D6*

Nestled in a grove of beech trees, this tidy white *hostería* has backdoor access to spectacular views of peaks and icebergs. Like all park lodging, this three-star hotel is overpriced given the so-so decor and sometimes drafty rooms. Excellent outdoor terraces. Packages include catamaran tours to Glaciar Grey. **www.turismolagogrey.com**

TORRES DEL PAINE NATIONAL PARK Hotel Rio Serrano $$$$$

Serrano sector ***Tel*** *(02) 4345352* ***Rooms*** *99* ***Road Map*** *D6*

This hotel offers magnificent views and handsome decor. Located at the edge of the park, it is the largest hotel in the area, with conference rooms, an interpretive center, library, and guided excursions. Rooms feature beautiful views, are well appointed, spacious, and have full amenities. **www.hotelrioserrano.cl**

TORRES DEL PAINE NATIONAL PARK Las Torres $$$$$

Torres sector ***Tel*** *(061) 360362* ***Rooms*** *84* ***Road Map*** *D6*

This sprawling, ranch-style hotel is a former estancia that sits at the trailhead of the Torres hike. Standard rooms, airy lounges, an interpretive center, stables, and excursions booked separately or as part of a package. The hotel also has a campground and cheaper hostel with shared dorms. **www.lastorres.com**

TORRES DEL PAINE NATIONAL PARK Patagonia Camp $$$$$

Km74, road to Puerto Natales ***Tel*** *(02) 3349255* ***Rooms*** *17* ***Road Map*** *D6*

The only yurt-based lodging in Chile. The luxurious "tents" come with decks, tiled bathrooms, comfortable beds, and a desk. The yurts occupy a beech forest overlooking a lake, and are connected by boardwalks. Stylish main lounge and dining area. Information center helps plan daily excursions. **www.patagoniacamp.com**

EASTER ISLAND AND ROBINSON CRUSOE ISLAND

HANGA ROA Aloha Nui Guest House $

Avenida Atamu Tekena s/n ***Tel*** *(032) 2100274* ***Fax*** *(032) 2100274* ***Rooms*** *6*

A short walk from the airport, this congenial B&B is operated by tour guide Ramón Edmunds and his wife Josefina Mulloy, granddaughter of the pioneering archaeologist, William Mulloy (1917–78). While less than luxurious, it is definitely a local experience, but with more sophistication than that normally implies.

HANGA ROA Residencial Kona Tau $

Avareipua s/n ***Tel*** *(032) 2100321* ***Fax*** *(032) 2100321* ***Rooms*** *6*

Two blocks north of the airport, Easter Island's Hostelling International representative has a main house with comfortable private rooms, dorms for backpackers, plus common areas for everybody. The lush garden is most notable for its abundant mangoes, which are free for the taking. **www.hostelling.cl**

HANGA ROA Hostal Martín y Anita $$

Simón Paoa s/n ***Tel*** *(032) 2100593* ***Fax*** *(032) 2100593* ***Rooms*** *5*

A garden-style B&B with an out-of-the-way location, across from the hospital and set back from the street, which means less traffic and noise. The rooms are less than luxurious, but the owner-hosts are solicitous of their guests, and help arrange excursions, car rentals, and other services. **www.hostal.co.cl**

HANGA ROA Hotel Otai $$$

Te Pito o Te Henua s/n ***Tel*** *(032) 2100560* ***Fax*** *(032) 2100482* ***Rooms*** *40*

Located in the center of Hanga Roa, Hotel Otai is a garden hotel set back from the street, which gives it an air of privacy. Rooms are relatively plain and moderately sized, but have either a small deck or porch. Some have desks. All rooms have wheelchair access, but the baths are not equally well outfitted. **www.hotelotai.com**

HANGA ROA Hotel Tahatai $$$$

Apina Nui s/n ***Tel*** *(032) 2551192* ***Fax*** *(032) 2551192* ***Rooms*** *40*

Offering access to both the shoreline and the village of Hanga Roa, Hotel Tahatai has a luminous central building with hotel rooms and separate bungalows, with up to three beds, on sprawling grassy grounds. All rooms have patios. Modest swimming pool, and a bar-restaurant in a separate building. **www.hoteltahatai.cl**

HANGA ROA Hotel Taura'a $$$$

Atamu Tekena s/n ***Tel*** *(032) 2100463* ***Fax*** *(032) 2551310* ***Rooms*** *11*

Though not up to the service level of Hanga Roa's more elaborate hotels, the Taura compensates with soothing, colorfully decorated rooms and personal attention from its owners, an Australian-Rapa Nui couple. Surrounded by subtropical gardens, and within walking distance to restaurants and shops. **www.tauraahotel.cl**

HANGA ROA Hotel Iorana $$$$$

Ana Magaro s/n ***Tel*** *(032) 2100312* ***Fax*** *(032) 2100608* ***Rooms*** *52*

Located on the coast near the cave of Ana Tai Kangata, Hotel Iorana has motel-style rooms that enjoy access to large gardens and ocean views through sliding glass doors. More expensive suites offer Jacuzzis, but actor Kevin Costner was contented with a smaller "superior" room when he stayed here. **www.ioranahotel.com**

HANGA ROA Posada de Mike Rapu $$$$$

Sectoo Te Miro Oone ***Tel*** *(02) 2066060* ***Fax*** *(02) 2284655* ***Rooms*** *30*

Explora group's hotel occupies an isolated site in the middle of the island, but with views of the coast. Despite its luxuries, this all-inclusive resort is subdued both in setting and architecture. Open for multi-day packages only, it includes full board and a diversity of excursions visiting every major island sight. **www.explora.com**

WHERE TO EAT

Chile offers an increasingly sophisticated cuisine that uses an assortment of ingredients from the fertile farmlands of its Central Valley and the seas off its endless coastline. Though underrated as a gastronomic destination, the country has a huge diversity of restaurants that range from the roadside *parrilla*, or steakhouse, to eateries serving the freshest possible seafood. Major cities also offer a number of international choices that would draw attention anywhere in Europe or North America. Santiago and other major cities offer outstanding dishes based on beef, lamb, and seafood, but dining can be fairly simple in many smaller towns and in the countryside. Fast food often takes the form of burgers and pizza, but there are also a number of street food stands selling sandwiches and *completos* (inexpensive hot dogs slathered with mayonnaise).

Lamb chops served with sautéed potatoes

Parrilla at the Pehoe campsite, Torres del Paine National Park

RESTAURANTS

The simplest eateries found in markets across Chile are the *comedores* or *cocinerías*, which usually serve fresh seafood that is remarkably good given the price. A *picada* is an informal family restaurant, often starting as a room in the house, that expands as its gains a reputation beyond the neighborhood. A *fuente de soda*, literally, a soda fountain, refers to a simple place that does not serve liquor, while a *salon de té* or a teahouse is more of a café. A *restaurante* proper is a formal eatery, usually with an elaborate menu. *Parrillas* specialize in grilled beef, but in larger cities, they may also serve other meats, seafood, and pastas. Primarily a seafood restaurant, the *marisquería* also serves traditional meat dishes. Reservations are genarally required only in upscale restaurants, or on busy weekend evenings and holidays. Guests who are looking for specifics such as smoke-free seating should call in advance.

CHAIN RESTAURANTS

In Chile's liberal economic environment, international fast food chains, such as KFC, McDonald's, Pizza Hut, and Burger King, have spread from the northern deserts to the southern tundra regions. However, Chile has its own counterparts, such as Dino's and Bavaria, that are as good as the US fast food chains.

EATING HOURS

At most restaurants, and even at some B&Bs, it is hard to get breakfast before 9am. Lunch is served relatively late, around 2pm, and even later on weekends. Chileans often take a third meal of sandwiches and sweets, known as *onces*, between 5 and 7pm; this is accompanied with tea or coffee, and sometimes runs into the dinner hour. Dinner is generally served between 8pm and midnight. However, smaller restaurants in the countryside usually do not stay open beyond 9 or 10pm.

PAYMENT AND TIPPING

In addition to the à la carte menu, many restaurants have fixed-price lunches that are often bargains, but this practice is less common at dinnertime. Prices are inclusive of the 19 percent *Impuesto al Valor Agregado* (IVA) or VAT, but not the service tax. Most restaurants accept MasterCard, Visa, and American Express,

Dining room at Ancud's upscale Hostal Mundo Nuevo

Diners at the atmospheric and popular Ricer Restaurant, Coyhaique

although the latter is less common. Payment with traveler's checks is rare. In small, informal eateries, especially outside larger cities, payment in cash is the rule.

There is no fixed standard regarding tipping; where the service tax is not incorporated in the bill, it is customary for guests to leave a tip up to 10 percent, depending on the quality of service.

FOOD HYGIENE

Chilean health standards are generally high, but it is always worth taking precautions. It is best to avoid eating uncooked shellfish, as algae flourishing along the coast can make them toxic. Raw vegetables and salads are usually safe. Fresh meat and fruit are invariably reliable, and there is little concern beyond the normal precautions visitors would take elsewhere. Tap water is generally dependable, but people with sensitive stomachs may prefer bottled water. Avoid purchasing food and beverages in shabby open-air markets and street stalls.

DISABLED TRAVELERS

In Santiago and a few other cities, upscale restaurants have ramps or other means of access, but few traditional buildings have been suitably retrofitted for guests with limited mobility. In general, Chileans will try to make the wheelchair-bound feel comfortable and welcome, but toilet access can be a problem. It is advisable to enquire ahead of time about the facilities available.

CHILDREN

Chile is a child-friendly nation and children are welcome almost everywhere. However, restaurants that permit smoking may not admit anybody under 18. Separate menus for children are not usual at most eateries, but restaurants do not mind if parents share the often generous portions of food with their children.

VEGETARIANS

Although Chile's fertile valleys produce abundant ingredients for vegetarian dining, Chilean diet is based on meat and seafood. Despite this, there are exceptional vegetarian restaurants in Santiago and in tourist destinations such as Pucón; elsewhere visitors may need to insist on salads and pasta with meatless sauces.

SMOKING

Chile's tobacco laws allow restaurants to decide whether or not they will permit smoking, but even if they do, no one under the age of 18 is permitted to smoke. Some eateries prohibit smoking entirely, while others have set up smoking and non-smoking sections. There is no ban on smoking in bars and clubs, since 18 is the minimum age for obtaining entrance to these establishments. Smoking is prohibited on public transport, including both local and long-distance buses *(see p324)*.

Café Caribe on Paseo Huerfanos, Santiago

The Flavors of Chile

The heritage of the high Andes is present in Chilean food with the potato; quinoa, the native Andean grain; and the meat of the llama. Chileans are committed carnivores, and eat beef whenever they can, but lamb, primarily from Patagonia, is also popular, as are chicken and pork. Game, such as boar and the ostrich-like rhea, is also gaining popularity. It is the extraordinary marine life of Chile's coastline, however, which is the star of Chilean cuisine – the cool Humboldt current yields an array of fish and shellfish hard to match anywhere else in the world.

Andean quinoa

Baked meat empanadas on display in a traditional Chilean bakery

CREOLE CUISINE

Comida criolla or Creole cooking is Chilean country cuisine, using staples such as potatoes, sweet corn, onions, garlic, and olives. Stewing is the most common method of cooking them. *Humitas*, similar to Mexican tamales, are steamed corn wraps and can be made with or without meat. Stemming from the Spanish tradition, and common throughout Latin America, the empanada is a pastry turnover, usually filled with ground beef or cheese. The Chilean version is larger and a bit heavier than in most other countries.

Chilean food in general is quite lightly spiced, if at all. In recent years, however, Mapuche *merkén* (a ground spice mix of dried, smoked red chilies, toasted coriander, and cumin) has grown in popularity, adding some bite to otherwise bland dishes.

FISH AND SEAFOOD

Chile's long coastline is the source of some of its greatest seafood. Chilean fish includes superb *congrio* (conger eel), *corvina* (sea bass), *lenguado* (sole), and *merluza* (hake), among

Selection from the vast range of superb Chilean seafood

CHILEAN DISHES AND SPECIALTIES

Aji chilies

The best Chilean dishes are seasonal, linked to the harvests of both land and sea. Chileans tend to eat their largest meal at lunchtime – Santiaguinos throng into the city's restaurants for business lunches, while country dwellers may take two or three hours over a home-cooked meal. Popular dishes include *pastel de papas* (potato casserole), *caldillo de congrio* (conger eel soup), *chupe de locos* (abalone stew) and *palta reina* (an appetizer of avocado stuffed with tuna, chicken, or ham, heavy on the mayonnaise). A favorite condiment, served with bread or spooned over barbecued meat, is *pebre*, a tangy dipping sauce of chopped onion and tomato, fresh coriander, olive oil, garlic, and mildly spicy Aji chili peppers.

Cazuela de Ave *is a thin stew of chicken (usually leg or thigh) with corn on the cob, potato, and rice.*

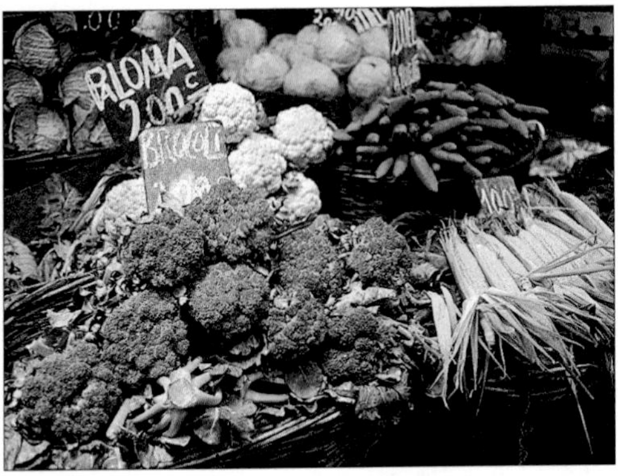

Fresh vegetables at the central fruit and vegetable market in Santiago

other kinds. However, it is shellfish that sets Chilean seafood cuisine apart from the ordinary. Everyone will recognize such standards as clams, crab, oysters, scallops, shrimp, and squid. The novelties, for first-time visitors in particular, are the many variety of mussels, including the *choro zapato* (shoe mussel, so named for its size), *erizos* (sea urchins), *locos* (giant abalone), and *picoroco* (giant barnacle). Some of these, of course, are acquired tastes.

Salmon is widely, and controversially, farmed in the lake regions, and trout from there is extremely delicious.

When ordering fish, avoid the *frito* (deep fried) options, often prepared using heavy oils – *a la plancha* (grilled) and *al vapor* (steamed) are healthier options.

MIXED GRILL

Chileans enjoy a *parrillada* or barbecue. In addition to cuts of beef, the meal usually includes a variety of sausages such as *morcilla* (blood sausage) and *chunchules* (chitterlings), and sometimes pork or chicken. Salads and red wine are both essential accompaniments.

***Chanco* cheese and *longaniza* sausage in a market stall**

SNACKS

Chile's favourite snack, the *completo* is a hot dog smothered in mayonnaise, ketchup, mustard, and sauerkraut. Sandwiches are very popular, usually eaten at *onces* or late afternoon tea. German settlers have given Chile *kuchen*, thick-crusted pastries topped with fruit. *Sopaipilla* (fried sweet or savory flatbread) is a favorite street food.

THE PERUVIAN CONNECTION

Chile and Peru undoubtedly have a contentious political relationship – much of the northern third of Chile was once Peruvian territory, and the two countries even dispute the historical roots of the grape brandy known as *pisco*. But, just as North Americans have embraced Mexican food, so Chileans flock to Peruvian restaurants. In the capital, Santiago, some of the best kitchens have Peruvian chefs. To discover what Chileans see in their neighbor's cuisine, look out for dishes such as *aji de gallina* (strips of chicken in a creamy walnut sauce with potatoes and olives) and *lomo saltado* (stir-fried steak and vegetables) For those who enjoy spicier food, the Peruvians use a variety of peppers in their dishes; *papa a la huancaína* is a typically spicy potato appetizer.

Pastel de chocio, *served in a traditional earthenware bowl, is ground meat topped with corn purée and baked.*

Porotos Granados, *a thick stew of whole beans and squash, draws its origins from the high Andes.*

Curanto, *a typical southern dish of seafood, pork, and vegetables, is simmered for hours in an earth oven.*

What to Drink

While Chile's superb wines are renowned globally and are the traditional favorite among people from across the country, beer consumption has also increased dramatically in recent times. *Pisco*, the grape brandy of Norte Chico's deserts, is the basis of pisco sour, the national cocktail. Non-alcoholic drinks include a number of standard sugary soft-drinks. Tap water is almost always potable, but for those who have any doubts, bottled water is readily available. Chileans drink both black and herbal teas but, except in the capital and major tourist destinations, soluble coffee powder is the default option for caffeine addicts.

Pisco sour, a popular cocktail

Diners at the popular Cinzano restaurant in Valparaíso

PISCO

Distilled from the Muscatel grapes grown in Norte Chico, *pisco* is a clear brandy-like liquor. The final product varies according to its alcoholic content, stated in terms of degrees. Lower quality *pisco* ranges from *selección* (30° or 60 proof) to *especial* (35° or 70 proof), while better versions vary from *reservado* (40° or 80 proof) to *gran pisco* (up to 50° or 100 proof). In general, *reservado* is considered ideal for the emblematic pisco sour, Chile's favorite cocktail. This is a potent blend of grape brandy flavored with lime juice, egg white, and Angostura bitters and, at best, a dash of sugar. Chileans also mix *pisco* with cola drinks to create the piscola, Chile's counterpart to the Cuban libre. Both lower and higher quality *piscos* may be consumed straight, or mixed as cocktails.

BEER

Chile has marketed its wines brilliantly and they are widely available overseas. Chileans themselves, however, tend to consume more beer than wine. The most commonly drunk beers are run-of-the-mill lagers produced by companies such as Cristal and Escudo, but increasingly, Chilean breweries are offering microbrews of greater diversity and flavor. For instance, Valdivia's Compañía Cervecera Kunstmann makes excellent ale, honey beers, and bock, while Santiago's Szot has found a niche with its pale ale, amber ale, and stout. However, many of these products can be difficult to find except in specialized markets and restaurants.

A worker labelling bottles of beer at the Szot brewery in Santiago

NON-ALCOHOLIC DRINKS

Chilean tap water is drinkable almost everywhere, but short-term visitors with sensitive stomachs may want to stick with bottled water, which comes as either *con gas* (carbonated) or *sin gas* (non-carbonated). Good coffee is not easily available throughout the country. However, coffee-enthusiasts will find espresso and brewed coffee in most major cities and tourist destinations, especially in the better hotels and B&Bs.

Chile boasts a variety of unique herbal teas such as *boldo* and *cachamai*. These are gleaned from the southern forests and, with their unique aroma and woody flavors, are a good substitute to the country's commonly found packaged black tea. In Patagonia, many Chileans drink *mate*, a slightly bitter Argentine brew concocted from a relative of the wild holly and sipped from a bulbous gourd through a metal *bombilla* or straw.

Chilean Wines

Luscious grapes and red wine

Much of Chile enjoys wet winters and dry summers, that are ideal for cultivating grapes and, by extension, for producing quality wines. In general, whites predominate in the north and give way to reds toward the south, but there are many exceptions to this rule – the Casablanca Valley, northeast of Santiago, produces some of the finest sauvignon blanc and chardonny, but also offers pinot noir and other reds. The country's main wine-growing areas welcome visitors for tours and tastings, but lesser-known vineyards in regions such as the Valle del Elqui are also worth a visit. Chile's wineries range from large, industrial operations such as Viña Concha y Toro to tiny boutique businesses that produce a few thousand bottles of premium wine per annum.

Sought-after varietals *include whites such as Castillo de Molina's sauvignon blanc and Cono Sur's chardonny. Viña Casa Silva* (see p149) *produces its reds from old vines.*

POPULAR VARIETALS

Cabernet sauvignon is probably the country's most widely planted grape, but carménère is the most distinctive – the root disease phylloxera nearly killed it in Bordeaux in the 19th century, but French enologists rediscovered it among merlot plantings in Chile in the 1990s. This unintended blending has given Chilean merlot a unique flavor. Other reds cultivated here include syrah and, increasingly, pinot noir. The most common whites, of course, are chardonnay and sauvignon blanc, which are highly regarded.

Casa Silva's Dona Dominga label

Label of Falerina's syrah

BUYING AND DRINKING WINE IN CHILE

Good drinkable wines are available at most supermarkets for around US$5, but finer vintages can be purchased at a slightly higher price from specialist wine stores. Top vintages, from wineries such as Viña Montes and Viña Lapostolle in the Colchagua Valley *(see pp148–9)*, can be hard to find except at the wineries themselves. In Santiago and other major cities, restaurants usually have extensive wine lists. Wine is generally served by the bottle; the traditional *botellín* or *vino individual* is a single serving bottle. Wine by the glass, however, is not usually served.

Clos Apalta, *the only wine manufactured by the Franco-Chilean Viña Lapostolle* (see p149), *is a unique blend of petit verdot, merlot, cabernet sauvignon, and carménère.*

Merlot, sauvignon blanc, and syrah served at Tanino in Viña Casas del Bosque

Choosing a Restaurant

The restaurants in this guide have been selected across a range of price categories for their location, atmosphere, good food, facilities, and value. Entries are arranged alphabetically within price categories by area. For map references, see pages 102–109 for Santiago, pages 118–19 for Valparaíso, and the inside back cover for others.

PRICE CATEGORIES
Price ranges, in US$, are for a meal for one, inclusive of tax and service charges, and a half bottle of house wine.

- $ Under $10
- $$ $10–$15
- $$$ $15–$25
- $$$$ $25–$35
- $$$$$ Over $35

SANTIAGO

EL CENTRO El Rápido — $
Bandera 347 **Tel** *(02) 6722375* — **City Map** *2 E2*

Aptly named, El Rápido whips up empanadas and sandwiches in a matter of minutes. Greasy but good, the empanadas are served hot with a variety of fillings including meat, seafood, and cheese. Diners normally stand at a large bar, gobble down their lunch, and continue on their way. Open Monday to Saturday for lunch.

EL CENTRO El Hoyo — $$
San Vicente 375 **Tel** *(02) 6894528* — **City Map** *1 B5*

Tucked away at the edge of downtown Santiago, El Hoyo has served some of the city's best Chilean fare for decades. El Hoyo is a *picada*, akin to a dive, whose simple, country-style cooking includes *arrollado* (a pork roll) and *terremoto* (a drink made of white wine, pineapple juice, and ice cream). Open daily for lunch and dinner.

EL CENTRO El Naturista — $$
Moneda 846 **Tel** *(02) 3905942* — **City Map** *2 E3*

Opened in 1927, El Naturista is South America's oldest and downtown Santiago's most popular vegetarian restaurant. The fare is ovo-, lacto-, and vegan-friendly, and includes empanadas, crepes, sandwiches, and quinoa risotto. Spread over two floors, El Naturista serves lunch and dinner on weekdays, and lunch on Saturdays.

EL CENTRO Fuente Alemana — $$
Avenida Alameda 58 **Tel** *(02) 6894528* — **City Map** *3 B4*

One of Santiago's most traditional restaurants, the Fuente Alemana has branches across Santiago, but this is the original. The casual eatery serves lunch and dinner from Monday to Saturday, and is famous for its enormous sandwiches and *completos*, the famous Chilean hot dog topped with sauerkraut and globs of condiments.

EL CENTRO Ambrosia — $$$
Merced 838 A **Tel** *(02) 6972023* — **City Map** *2 E2*

The family-run Ambrosia specializes in eclectic, fusion cuisine that is innovatively prepared and served in a cozy, artsy ambience. The shrimp and mushroom crepe lasagna is a favorite, but the menu also leans heavily on seafood. Quieter than other downtown venues, Ambrosia is open from Monday to Saturday for lunch and dinner.

EL CENTRO Bar Nacional — $$$
Paseo Huérfanos 1151 **Tel** *(02) 6965986* — **City Map** *2 E2*

Among the most traditional restaurants in Chile, Bar Nacional has been serving classic Chilean dishes for more than 50 years. The interior has a diner-like decor with formica tables and metal chairs. Menu features chicken stew, broiled razor clams, and *pastel de choclo* – a corn and beef pie. Open Monday to Saturday for lunch and dinner.

EL CENTRO Blue Jar — $$$
Almirante Gotuzzo 102 **Tel** *(02) 6998399* — **City Map** *2 D3*

This restaurant has a chic, upscale ambience and offers cuisine that is creatively prepared using only seasonal products. Dishes run the gamut from tasty burgers to tamarind garbanzo beans, gravlax (cured salmon), and peanut and chicken curry. The Blue Jar is open for lunch and dinner on weekends.

EL CENTRO Confitería Torres — $$$
Avenida Alameda 1570 **Tel** *(02) 6880751* — **City Map** *2 D3*

Dating from 1879, Confitería Torres *(see p80)* is Santiago's oldest restaurant and was the haunt of the elite during the early 20th century. It has been renovated since with red leather booths and a cellar for wine-tasting, but much of the recipes hearken from early days. Lunch and dinner served from Monday to Saturday.

EL CENTRO Donde Agusto — $$$
Mercado Central **Tel** *(02) 6714558* — **City Map** *2 E1*

Set in the jovial ambience of a bustling fish market, Donde Agusto offers the freshest seafood available anywhere in Santiago. Guests can splurge on an entire king crab or savor one of the dozen types of fish fillets. Specialties include the *Caldillo de Congrio* fish stew, but the mushy seviche is best avoided. Lunch and dinner served daily.

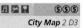

EL CENTRO Fulano Zutano Mengano $$$

Agustinas 1352 **Tel** *(02) 6971000* **City Map** *2 D2*

An attractive downtown restaurant, favored by businessmen, with an airy dining room featuring linen tablecloths and colorful art on the walls. Fulano Zutano Mengano offers both Chilean and international cuisine, including a barbecue *parrillada* (mixed grill). Open on weekdays for breakfast, lunch, and dinner.

EL CENTRO Japon $$$

Barón Pierre de Coubertine 39 **Tel** *(02) 2224517* **City Map** *3 B5*

Popular with the local Japanese community, Japon serves some of the best sushi in Santiago. On offer are hard-to-find seafood items, delicious udon soups, and a good selection of micro beers. Separate sushi bar and private dining spaces. Open from Monday to Saturday for lunch and dinner; closed on Sundays for dinner.

NORTHEAST OF EL CENTRO Café Melba $$

Don Carlos 2898 **Tel** *(02) 2324546* **City Map** *5 A4*

The most popular restaurant with expatriates, principally because it is one of the few eateries that serves a full and delicious breakfast. Lunch specials change seasonally and are creatively prepared, for which reason, there is often a 15-minute wait for a table. Open daily until 6pm, the restaurant doubles as a café with Internet service.

NORTHEAST OF EL CENTRO Dominó $$

Pedro de Valdivia 28 **Tel** *(02) 4110600* **City Map** *4 E2*

A sandwich joint with 19 branches across the city, Dominó is known for its condiment-laden *completo* hot dogs and *lomitos* (pulled-pork sandwiches). The diner is open from Monday to Saturday for lunch and dinner. Staff behind the U-shaped counter offer fast service and huge sandwiches that need to be eaten with a fork and knife.

NORTHEAST OF EL CENTRO El Huerto $$

Orrego Luco 54 **Tel** *(02) 2332690* **City Map** *4 E2*

This vegetarian eatery has a wide range of healthy dishes, including salads, soups, Mexican enchiladas, and Indian curries served in a relaxed yet upscale ambience. The fresh fruit juices are especially good, and the desserts are mouthwatering. El Huerto is open from Monday to Saturday for lunch and dinner, and on Sundays for lunch only.

NORTHEAST OF EL CENTRO Galindo $$

Dardignac 098 **Tel** *(02) 7770116* **City Map** *3 B4*

A Bellavista classic, Galindo is a casual eatery serving simple Chilean cuisine at reasonable prices. On weekends, the restaurant tends to fill up with university students and young artists and journalists. The fixed-price menu at lunch offers good value for money, and there is pleasant outdoor seating as well. Open daily for lunch and dinner.

NORTHEAST OF EL CENTRO Akarana $$$

Reyes Lavalle 3310, esq. La Pastora **Tel** *(02) 2319667* **City Map** *5 B4*

This restaurant boasts a delightful wraparound patio that is popular with the happy hour crowd. The owner, a New Zealander, has crafted a menu focusing on Pacific Rim cuisine, from Asian fare to fish and chips. The contemporary decor and delicious cocktails are a highlight. Akarana serves lunch and dinner daily, with occasional live music.

NORTHEAST OF EL CENTRO Barandarian $$$

Constitución 38 **Tel** *(02) 7370725* **City Map** *3 B4*

Set in the buzzing Patio Bellavista *(see p88)*, Barandarian serves lunch and dinner daily, and is a favorite for savory Peruvian cuisine such as seviche, lamb stewed in beer, and *parihuela* (a seafood stew). The pisco sours are both delicious and potent. Chef Marco Barandiaran is a TV personality and former chef of the Peruvian embassy.

NORTHEAST OF EL CENTRO Danubio Azul $$$

Reyes Lavalle 3240 **Tel** *(02) 2344688* **City Map** *5 B4*

Chinese restaurants are common in Santiago, but few are as good as Danubio Azul. Menus here feature photos of the dishes and make ordering easy. Standard fare includes chop suey, dim sum, and duck cooked in orange sauce. The decor is refined and service excellent. The restaurant serves lunch and dinner daily.

NORTHEAST OF EL CENTRO Divertimiento $$$

Avenida El Cerro, esq. Pedro de Valdivia **Tel** *(02) 2331920* **City Map** *4 E1*

Sitting at the foot of Cerro San Cristobal, Divertimiento offers standard Chilean cuisine. To sample some of the country's most classic dishes, share the Chilean platter that comes with miniature versions of crab casserole, corn and meat pie, and smoked salmon. The restaurant serves lunch and dinner, but is closed on Sundays for dinner.

NORTHEAST OF EL CENTRO El Parrón $$$

Avenida Providencia 1184 **Tel** *(02) 2518911* **City Map** *4 D3*

One of Chile's oldest *parrilla*, or steakhouse, El Parrón is a casual restaurant serving heaped platters of beef, pork, and chicken. It has an antique, wooden bar and a modest dining area under a faux grapevine. Try the razor clams with parmesan, a Chilean specialty. Open for lunch and dinner from Monday on Saturday; closed on Sundays for dinner.

NORTHEAST OF EL CENTRO Opera and Catedral $$$

José Miguel de la Barra, esq. Merced **Tel** *(02) 6643048* **City Map** *3 A4*

Located in a single building are the two restaurants Opera and Catedral. On the first floor, Opera tempts with outstanding, French-influenced gourmet cuisine and an on-site sommelier. Upstairs, the hip Catedral attracts a trendy crowd and serves good Chilean food and cocktails. Both serve lunch and dinner from Monday to Saturday.

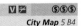

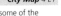

NORTHEAST OF EL CENTRO Patagonia $$$

Lastarria 96 **Tel** *(02) 6643830* **City Map** *3 A4*

A charming street scene gives this eatery a pleasant and relaxed ambience. Patagonia serves creative Chilean fare using local products such as boar, salmon, and lamb. It is open daily for lunch and dinner and is especially known for its excellent weekend brunch buffet. Good selection of local beers. Service, however, is slow and inattentive.

NORTHEAST OF EL CENTRO Tiramisú $$$

Isidora Goyenechea 3141-A **Tel** *(02) 5194900* **City Map** *5 B4*

This swanky pizzeria serves several kinds of thin-crust pizzas baked in a wood-burning oven. Also on offer are well-made calzones and delicious salads, and the house specialty – tiramisu. Open for lunch and dinner daily, the restaurant is perennially busy for its delicious fare and cozy, candlelit ambience.

NORTHEAST OF EL CENTRO Amorio $$$$

Constitución 181 **Tel** *(02) 7771454* **City Map** *3 B4*

Ensconced in Barrio Bellavista and owned by two young actors, Amorio is one of Santiago's trendiest restaurants. The lunch and dinner menu includes artfully presented cuisine made from local products such as lamb and sea bass, as well as tuna from Easter Island. There is an upstairs bar with a short menu. Closed on Sundays.

NORTHEAST OF EL CENTRO A Pinch of Pancho $$$$

General del Canto 45 **Tel** *(02) 2351700* **City Map** *4 E3*

Serves expertly prepared American cuisine, from clam chowder and braised short ribs to Philly cheese steak. The relaxed yet refined decor features modern art mixed with American memorabilia. Gracious and attentive service. The lip-smacking apple pie à la mode is worth a try. Open from Monday to Saturday for lunch and dinner.

NORTHEAST OF EL CENTRO Baco $$$$

Nueva de Lyon 113 **Tel** *(02) 2314444* **City Map** *4 F2*

Tucked away in a courtyard on a bustling street, Baco serves lunch and dinner daily. The menu features classic French fare such as cassoulet and duck confit, as well as steak and fries. Excellent list of wines served by the glass. Inviting and warm decor, with wooden walls and floors, paper table coverings, and chalkboard wine menus.

NORTHEAST OF EL CENTRO Bar Liguria $$$$

Avenida Providencia 1373 **Tel** *(02) 2357914* **City Map** *4 D3*

One of Santiago's best restaurants for its lively atmosphere, attentive service, and delicious cuisine. Bar Liguria offers lunch and dinner daily. The menu features hearty Chilean dishes, filling sandwiches, and salads, served in an early 19th-century ambience. There are five dining areas within the restaurant.

NORTHEAST OF EL CENTRO Camino Real $$$$

Cerro San Cristobal **Tel** *(02) 2323381* **City Map** *4 D1*

Sweeping views of the capital are the hallmark of this hilltop restaurant. The food served is good and simply prepared, yet follows an international style that focuses on Chilean specialty products such as salmon and lamb. Camino Real is open for lunch and dinner throughout the week.

NORTHEAST OF EL CENTRO Cienfuegos $$$$

Constitución 67 **Tel** *(02) 2489080* **City Map** *3 B4*

The stylish Cienfuegos is part restaurant, part lounge. Only dinner is served here (Tuesdays–Satudarys), accompanied by a DJ act or live music on Fridays and Saturdays. The menu offers little explanation of the cuisine, just the main ingredients, but the waiters can elaborate on the dishes. Desserts by the two Spanish-trained chefs are superb.

NORTHEAST OF EL CENTRO Etniko $$$$

Constitución 172 **Tel** *(02) 7320119* **City Map** *3 B3*

A Pan-Asian restaurant serving lunch and dinner from Monday to Satuday, Etniko attracts the capital's trendy crowd and many American expatriates, who love the bar and interior atrium seating. An in-house DJ spins music late into the night. The menu has Vietnamese and Thai specialties, and there is also a sushi bar.

NORTHEAST OF EL CENTRO Fabula $$$$

Marin 0285 **Tel** *(02) 2223016* **City Map** *3 C5*

Occupying a two-story, converted home, Fabula features a softly lit and intimate dining area. The menu, whipped up by a friendly Bolivian chef, changes almost weekly but is always delicious, with interesting combinations that incorporate Chilean and Bolivian flavors. Fabula serves lunch and dinner from Monday to Saturday.

NORTHEAST OF EL CENTRO Le Flaubert $$$$

Orrego Luco 125 **Tel** *(02) 2319424* **City Map** *4 E2*

Arguably the coziest restaurant in Santiago, Le Flaubert is a French-style bistro on the first floor of an antique apartment building. Every day, the restaurant lists a dozen dishes on a chalkboard menu, including different preparations of meats and fish. The service is excellent and attentive. Open daily for lunch and dinner.

NORTHEAST OF EL CENTRO Pinpilinpausha $$$$

Isidora Goyenechea 2900 **Tel** *(02) 2336507* **City Map** *5 A3*

With over 40 years in the business, Pinpilinpausha serves Basque cuisine that focuses on seafood. Two can order a hearty plate of Valencia rice, a paella, which takes 30 minutes to arrive as it is freshly prepared each time. The pork with apricot sauce and ginger is another highlight. The restaurant serves lunch and dinner from Monday to Saturday.

Key to Price Guide *see p294* **Key to Symbols** *see back cover flap*

NORTHEAST OF EL CENTRO Sukalde $$$$

Avenida Francisco Bilbao 460 ***Tel*** *(02) 6651017*

Young chef Matias Palomo brought his knowledge of molecular cuisine to Chile after learning the technique in Spain. A hole-in-the-wall gourmet gem, this restaurant serves lunch and dinner from Monday to Saturday. Specialties include tuna tartare with soy caviar and konzo fish wrapped in banana served with a grapefruit salad.

NORTHEAST OF EL CENTRO Astrid y Gaston $$$$$

Antonio Bellet 201 ***Tel*** *(02) 6509125* — ***City Map*** *4 E2*

The outstanding Astrid y Gaston, which first opened in Peru, serves classic Peruvian dishes such as seviche with a gourmet upgrade. Its unique preparations of seafood, including sea urchin ravioli and tuna with sweet potato, are also great. Desserts are made to order. On-site sommelier. Open for lunch and dinner from Monday to Saturday.

NORTHEAST OF EL CENTRO Boragó $$$$$

Avenida Nueva Costanera 3467 ***Tel*** *(02) 9538893* — ***City Map*** *5 B2*

At the award-winning Boragó, food is as much about taste as it is about presentation. The outlandishly artful concoctions beg to be photographed before eaten. Among the interesting items on the menu are salads presented to resemble minature forests. Boragó serves lunch and dinner from Monday to Saturday.

NORTHEAST OF EL CENTRO Europeo $$$$$

Alonso de Córdova 2417 ***Tel*** *(02) 2083603* — ***Map*** *5 B2*

Among the finest restaurants in Santiago, the Swiss-owned Europeo serves German and Swiss influenced cuisine. Open for lunch and dinner from Monday to Saturday, it has a refined and elegant ambience. Dishes change seasonally, but typically include ultra-fresh fish, beef from *wagyu* cattle, truffles, and foie gras. On-site sommelier.

NORTHEAST OF EL CENTRO La Mar $$$$$

Avenida Nueva Costanera 3922 ***Tel*** *(02) 2067839* — ***City Map*** *5 B1*

A branch of Astrid y Gaston, La Mar also began in Peru and serves the best seviche in Santiago. Also on offer is fresh seafood such as grouper, tuna, and sole. Guests can order and share an entire fish, which is either steamed, fried, or stewed. Delicious cocktails and great service. Open for lunch and dinner; closed on Sundays for dinner.

NORTHEAST OF EL CENTRO Mestizo $$$$$

Avenida Bicentenario 4050 ***Tel*** *(02) 4776093* — ***City Map*** *5 A1*

The airy Mestizo has glass walls that slide open, making it one of the city's best summertime venues. The large open kitchen presents gourmet takes on classic Chilean dishes, and there is also a *parrillada* (barbecue). Start with a gingery pisco sour and try the abalone casserole. Mestizo serves lunch and dinner; closed on Sundays for dinner.

NORTHEAST OF EL CENTRO OX $$$$$

Avenida Nueva Costanera 3960 ***Tel*** *(02) 2083458* — ***City Map*** *5 B1*

The city's best bet for gourmet meats, OX is open for lunch and dinner from Monday to Saturday. Virtually every cut and kind of meat can be ordered here, including an outstanding foie gras, tender *wagyu* steak, roast beef, and arguably the best short ribs in Santiago. However, service is not always reliable.

NORTHEAST OF EL CENTRO Puerto Fuy $$$$$

Avenida Nueva Costanera 3969 ***Tel*** *(02) 2088908* — ***City Map*** *5 B1*

Chef Giancarlo Mazarelli brought the concept of molecular cooking to Santiago, offering dishes such as abalone ravioli with champagne foam and liquid nitrogen sorbet. Dishes are artfully presented, and there is tasting menu for a fixed price. Sophisticated yet cozy ambience. Serves lunch and dinner from Monday to Saturday.

NORTHEAST OF EL CENTRO Tierra Noble $$$$$

Avenida Nueva Costanera 3872 ***Tel*** *(02) 7614861* — ***City Map*** *5 B1*

This eatery places heavy emphasis on the natural flavors of Chilean favorites such as salmon, shellfish, and lamb. The chef chooses the freshest, best-quality ingredients and uses simple, earthy cooking techniques such as grilling. The delectable desserts are also a feast for the eye. Tierra noble is open daily for lunch and dinner.

WEST OF EL CENTRO Boulevard Lavaud $$$

Compañia de Jesús 2789 ***Tel*** *(02) 6825243* — ***City Map*** *1 B2*

This endearing eatery is known as the *peluquería francésa* (french barbershop) for its past life as an elegant hair salon. It is filled with early 20th-century artifacts that add to a memorable dining experience. Open for lunch and dinner from Monday to Saturday, the restaurant focuses on French and Chilean cuisine, and strong cocktails.

WEST OF EL CENTRO Ocean Pacific's $$$$

Avenida Ricardo Cumming 221 ***Tel*** *(02) 6972413* — ***City Map*** *1 C3*

This restaurant is crammed with all sorts of fascinating marine and military memorabilia, including watertight bathroom doors, hanging torpedos, and whale bones. In fact, one wing is designed to resemble the interior of a submarine. Fairly good seafood on the menu. Serves lunch and dinner; closed on Sundays for dinner.

WEST OF EL CENTRO Zully $$$$

Concha y Toro 34 ***Tel*** *(02) 6961378* — ***City Map*** *1 C3*

Set in a charming neighborhood, the American-owned Zully is housed in an antique, four-story mansion renovated with trendy interiors. The cuisine features high-concept Chilean and international fare. There is also a bar, and the wine cellar offers tastings. The Zully serves lunch and dinner from Monday to Saturday.

CENTRAL VALLEY

CACHAGUA Los Coirones $$$$

Playa Grande ***Tel*** *(096) 668597* ***Road Map*** *B6*

Occupying a thatched, wooden house, Los Coirones has a pleasing rustic ambience. The daily lunch and dinner menus feature great seafood, fresh salads, and both white and red meats. Tables on the outside face a long, wave-battered sweep of sandy beach. The beachside bar serves delicious pisco sours and offers great views.

CASABLANCA VALLEY Tanino $$$$

Viña Casas del Bosque, Hijuela 2, Ex Fundo Santa Rosa ***Tel*** *(02) 3779431* ***Road Map*** *B6*

Set in an idyllic location amid lush vineyards, the Tanino features contemporary decor and an award-winning cuisine paired with fine wines. It also offers a tasting menu, terrace seating, and cocktail bar, as well as a children's menu and play area. Open for lunch only; closed on Mondays between April and December.

CHILLÁN Sureño $$$

5 de Abril 263 ***Tel*** *(042) 221784* ***Road Map*** *D1*

Traditional Chilean ingredients are used at the Sureño to create refreshingly modern dishes. The salmon and shellfish pancakes are a highlight, as are the pastas and crepes. Lunch and dinner are served on weekdays and only dinner on Saturdays. The relaxed, smart interior has bright white walls hung with colorful art. Closed on Sundays.

CHILLÁN Fuego Divino $$$$$

Avenida Gamero 980 ***Tel*** *(042) 430900* ***Road Map*** *D1*

An upscale steakhouse serving quality red meats in a stylish and modern setting. The restaurant has a fine black and white interior with low lighting. At the center, prime beef cuts sizzle and smoke on an open flame grill. Salads and Chilean wines accompany the steaks. Fuego Divino serves lunch and dinner from Tuesday to Saturday.

COLCHAGUA VALLEY Restaurant Casa Silva $$$$$

Viña Casa Silva, Hijuela Norte, San Fernando ***Tel*** *(072) 710180* ***Road Map*** *B7*

Set in the 1896 hacienda house of the oldest winery in Colchagua Valley. The outdoor tables ring a Spanish patio, while inside, tables overlook the winery's barrel room. The international and Chilean fare served here includes wild mushroom soup, lamb ribs, and duck smoked in wine barrels. Open for lunch and dinner from Tuesday to Sunday.

COLCHAGUA VALLEY Restaurante Viña Viu Manent $$$$$

Viña Viu Manent, Carretera del Vino Km 37 ***Tel*** *(072) 858751* ***Road Map*** *B7*

Occupying a 120-year old Colonial-style house, this romantic winery restaurant has tables in a salon and outside in a cobbled courtyard amid antique wine-making gear. Its French-Catalan cuisine is inspired by a recipe book brought from Europe by the Viu Manent family a century ago. The restaurant is open daily for lunch and dinner.

CONCEPCIÓN Choripan $$

Plaza España, Arturo Prat 524 ***Tel*** *(041) 253004* ***Road Map*** *D1*

Situated in Concepción's main bar-restaurant zone, Choripan offers burgers, chorizos, and *lomo a la pobre* – steak topped with ham and fried eggs – served in huge portions that can be shared by two. The place gets crowded by midnight. Smoky, grungy atmosphere. Blues and rock bands play live at night. Serves dinner daily.

CONCEPCIÓN Centro Español $$$$

Barros Arana 675 ***Tel*** *(041) 2224249* ***Road Map*** *D1*

A sweeping staircase, overlooked by old portraits of conquistadores, leads to a salon where the decor evokes bygone days with delicate chandeliers, heavy drapes, polished wood, and gilded mirrors. Traditional Chilean fare is on offer, including steaks and seafood paella served for lunch and dinner from Monday to Saturday.

LOS ANDES Casa Vieja $$$

Maipú 151 ***Tel*** *(034) 460367* ***Road Map*** *B6*

Among the best eating options in Los Andes, Casa Vieja is open daily for lunch and dinner. Rustic interior features a timber roof, wooden beams, stacked hay bales, and a clay floor. Sizzling grilled steaks are whisked to tables by gregarious waiters; portions are huge and can be shared between two. Live folkloric music on weekends.

PAPUDO Restaurant Gran Azul $$$$

Avenida Irarrázabal 86 ***Tel*** *(033) 791584* ***Road Map*** *B6*

Sitting on Papudo's coastal avenue, this restaurant faces the gorgeous Playa Chica and serves organic and locally sourced seafood. Tables on the terrace offer great views of fishing boats on the water. Impressive wine selection. Open for lunch and dinner daily, but closed from Monday to Thursday between April and November.

PICHILEMU Casa Roja $$$

Avenida Ortúzar 215 ***Tel*** *(072) 841555* ***Road Map*** *B7*

A blend of classic Italian cuisine and stylish, modern ambience. Seafood carpaccio and soup starters precede pasta and pizza. Tables look out to the sea. Inside, artworks decorate the walls and acid-jazz music accompanies the dining experience. Casa Roja is open daily for lunch and dinner, but is closed on Mondays between April and November.

Key to Price Guide *see p294* **Key to Symbols** *see back cover flap*

PICHILEMU Puente Holandes $$$

Eugenio Diaz Lira 167 ***Tel*** *(072) 842350* ***Road Map*** *B7*

Owned by a Dutch surfer and his Chilean wife, the popular Puente Holandes serves classic Chilean staples at moderate prices. The grilled salmon, sweetcorn pie, and shellfish empanadas are especially good. A bamboo-thatched terrace faces the beach and has seawater hot tubs for relaxing. Open daily for lunch and dinner.

QUINTAY Restaurant Miramar $$$$

Costanera, Caleta Quintay ***Tel*** *(032) 2362046* ***Road Map*** *B6*

Set on the beach, Restaurant Miramar serves seafood caught fresh each morning. The creamy crab stew, in particular, is excellent. Terrace tables overlook fishing boats wedged in the sand and fishermen unloading the day's catch. Chilean dining at its picturesque best. Open daily for lunch and also for dinner on weekends.

RANCAGUA El Viejo Rancagua $

Paseo del Estado 607 ***Tel*** *(072) 227715* ***Road Map*** *B7*

Occupies a Colonial-style house dating from 1830. Decor features low wooden ceilings and thick adobe walls decorated with antique clocks, farming tools, and pictures, and chandeliers hanging above wooden tables. Serves traditional Chilean fare for lunch from Monday to Saturday, and for dinner from Thursday to Saturday.

RANCAGUA Sapore Italiano $$$

Avenida Miguel Ramires 96 ***Tel*** *(072) 768417* ***Road Map*** *B7*

Lunch and dinner at this pizzeria feature pastas and pizzas with regional and Italian toppings and sauces, such as black truffles, smoked salmon, crab, shellfish, and squid. Decor features opera posters, prints of Italian artworks, and photos of Rome on the walls. Closed on Sundays for dinner, and all day on Mondays.

SANTA CRUZ Club Social de Santa Cruz $$$

Plaza de Armas 178 ***Tel*** *(072) 822529* ***Road Map*** *B7*

Loved by locals since its opening in 1933, Club Social de Santa Cruz occupies a Colonial-era house. Lunch and dinner, served daily, features classic Chilean cuisine with regional delicacies such as quail, ox tongue, and figs-in-syrup desserts. A great spot for a long, lazy Sunday lunch. Wines from the Colchagua Valley wineries available.

VALPARAÍSO Café Arte Mirador $$

Paseo 21 de Mayo 214, Cerro Artillería ***Tel*** *(032) 2280944* ***City Map*** *B2*

This arty café and restaurant sits in the old machine house of Ascensor Artillería. The psychedelic interior is painted with graffiti art and murals depicting Valparaíso's port life. Tables either face the port area or look inward toward the giant wheels that turn the funicular. Classic Chilean food served daily for lunch and dinner.

VALPARAÍSO Le Filou de Montpellier $$

Almirante Montt 382, Cerro Alegre ***Tel*** *(032) 2224663* ***City Map*** *B4*

A corner house on a cobbled hillside street, this French-owned eatery oozes Gallic charm. The bijou interior of wooden floors, low ceilings, and whirling ceiling fans hosts an intimate, convivial atmosphere. Lunch and dinner feature excellent French and international dishes; daily specials at reasonable prices. Closed on Mondays.

VALPARAÍSO Allegretto $$$

Lautaro Rosas 540, Cerro Alegre ***Tel*** *(032) 2968517* ***City Map*** *B4*

English-owned Allegretto is a fun pizzeria with a retro-kitsch interior, a functioning 1950s jukebox, tiger-print lampshades, and wall-mounted TVs with mirrors as screens. Pizzas have both usual and unusual toppings, including curry sauce and river salmon. Good pastas and risottos. Lunch and dinner served daily.

VALPARAÍSO Cinzano $$$

Plaza Aníbal Pinto 1182 ***Tel*** *(032) 2213043* ***City Map*** *C4*

Sepia-tinted Cinzano has changed little since its inception in 1896. Old shipping pictures plaster the walls, ceiling fans whirl above the long bar, and bow-tied septuagenarian waiters attend tables. Chilean seafood dishes and grilled meats are served here for lunch and dinner. Live tango music on Thursdays and weekends. Closed on Sundays.

VALPARAÍSO Restaurant Gato Tuerto $$$$

Museo a Cielo Abierto, Héctor Calvo 205, Cerro Bellavista ***Tel*** *(032) 2220867* ***City Map*** *C4*

The exotic lunch and dinner menus at Gato Tuerto includes Indian, Thai, and Moroccan dishes. There is also fusion cuisine, featuring regional specialties such as barbecued lamb and Chilean sea bass spiced with tangy red and green curry sauces. The balcony tables offer lovely views of the port and neighboring hillsides. Closed on Mondays.

VALPARAÍSO Hamburg $$$$

O'Higgins 1274 ***Tel*** *(032) 2597037*

Opened in the 1980s by a retired German sailor, Hamburg is filled with shipping memorabilia. Ship figureheads, nautical bells, and replica ships adorn every corner of the restaurant. The menu features Chilean and German cuisines. Items include pork chops and pickled herring. Open for lunch and dinner from Monday to Saturday.

VALPARAÍSO Café Turri $$$$$

Templeman 147, Cerro Concepción ***Tel*** *(032) 2365307* ***City Map*** *C4*

Set in a 1897 hillside residence, Café Turri serves Chilean and French dishes for lunch and dinner with foie gras starters and entrées such as wild boar and grilled eel. The hanging terrace affords nighttime views across Bahía de Valparaíso to Viña del Mar. Closed for dinner on Sundays and Mondays between April and November.

VALPARAÍSO Pasta e Vino $$$$$

Templeman 352, Cerro Concepción ***Tel*** *(032) 2496187* ***City Map*** *B4*

Offers imaginative pasta dishes such as gnocchi stuffed with fresh strawberries and served with a champagne and clams sauce. Desserts include homemade ice creams. There are just 13 tables, so reservations are recommended. Open for dinner from Wednesday to Saturday, and for lunch on Saturdays. Closed Sunday to Tuesday.

VIÑA DEL MAR Hampton Deli $

Etchevers 174–176 ***Tel*** *(032) 2714910* ***Road Map*** *B6*

A small, family-run deli in downtown Viña del Mar serving excellent-value set-menu lunches. The food is wholesome, simple, and delicious. Chalkboard menus feature daily specials including lasagne, shepherd's pie, fish stews, and tasty vegetarian fare such as spinach tortilla. Efficient and attentive service. Closed on Sundays.

VIÑA DEL MAR Restaurant Cap Ducal $$$

Hotel Cap Ducal, Avenida Marina 51 ***Tel*** *(032) 2626655* ***Road Map*** *B6*

First opened in 1936, Restaurant Cap Ducal has a timeless dining space with a circular floor, large windows, and near 360-degrees ocean views. The sound of crashing waves accompanies cuisine that is mostly seafood, but also features a variety of well-prepared pastas and meat-based dishes. Cap Ducal serves lunch and dinner daily.

VIÑA DEL MAR Delicias del Mar $$$$$

Avenida San Martín 459 ***Tel*** *(032) 2901837* ***Road Map*** *B6*

An upscale restaurant, Delicias del Mar uses local ingredients to whip up mouthwatering dishes. Basque seafood paella is the house specialty, and the salmon and eel entrées and king crab starters are excellent. Guests are requested to switch off their mobile phones while dining. The restaurant is open daily for lunch and dinner.

VIÑA DEL MAR Fellini $$$$$

3 Norte 88, Frente al Casino ***Tel*** *(032) 2975742* ***Road Map*** *B6*

Open daily for lunch and dinner, Fellini covers all culinary bases with great aplomb, though the menu leans toward Italian cuisine. Pastas come with rich sauces. Also on offer are beefsteaks, fish, shellfish, and game. Bow-tied waiters serve tables covered with red-and-white cloths and bearing heavy cutlery.

ZAPALLAR Restaurant El Chiringuito $$$$$

Caleta Zapallar s/n ***Tel*** *(033) 741024* ***Road Map*** *B6*

A choice combination of simple shellfish and fish is on the menu at this picturesque restaurant. The shrimp omelette, grilled salmon, and swordfish are good. Seating in a spacious interior and on a bayside terrace. Views of bobbing fishing boats, and a backdrop of forested coastal mountains. Serves lunch and dinner daily.

NORTE GRANDE AND NORTE CHICO

ANTOFAGASTA El Horno de Barro $$$

Washington 2356 ***Tel*** *(055) 229031* ***Road Map*** *B3*

Close to the old port, El Horno de Barro (The Clay Oven) serves Chilean cuisine for lunch and dinner. Popular dishes include beefsteaks, shepherd's pie, and sweetcorn pie. Charming interior with wooden beams and cowhide decorations. Folkloric bands play live on weekends. Closed on Sundays and Mondays for dinner.

ARICA Restaurant Maracuyá $$$

Avenida Comandante San Martín 0321 ***Tel*** *(058) 227600* ***Road Map*** *B1*

This smart restaurant serves lunch and dinner everyday. A short stroll from the city center, it fronts the Playa El Laucho and has terrace tables within earshot of breaking waves. A picturesque interior, with a relaxed, warm, and welcoming atmosphere. The menu is traditional Chilean, with a focus on fish and seafood dishes.

ARICA Terra Amata $$$$$

Yungay 201 ***Tel*** *(058) 259057* ***Road Map*** *B1*

A contemporary restaurant, Terra Amata occupies a whitewashed Mediterranean-style building. Lunch and dinner feature Chilean dishes such as *parihuela* and Peruvian specialties. The wine cellar specializes in emerging wineries. The restaurant is closed on Sundays. A jazz club, in a separate wing, has live music on weekends.

CALAMA Delight $$$

Avenida Granaderos 1798 ***Tel*** *(055) 312045* ***Road Map*** *B2*

Centrally located, Delight has an interior of pinewood floor, red-and-black furnishings, and abstract art on the walls. Lunch and dinner include pastas, salads, fish and meat dishes, and Thai specialties. The young owners prepare the dishes and attend tables. Closed on Saturdays for dinner, and all day on Sundays.

CALDERA El Miramar $$$

Gana 090 ***Tel*** *(052) 315381* ***Road Map*** *B4*

Situated near the harbor, El Miramar features Norte Chico specialties such as sweetcorn pie, hearty *cazuela* broth, and numerous seafood staples. There are great omelets too. Old-fashioned ambience and decor and postcard views of the ocean and colorful fishing boats. Open all day, El Miramar is a great place for a quick coffee.

COPIAPÓ Legado $$$$$

O'Higgins 12 ***Tel*** *(052) 523895* ***Road Map*** *B4*

Set in a Colonial-style house, Legado is the best place in Copiapó for classic Chilean dinners. The scrumptious grilled steaks are the specialty, but the menu also features good wild boar, lamb, venison, quail, and many fish entrées. An old-fashioned, colorful vibe, quick and attentive service, and a fine wine list. Closed on Sundays.

IQUIQUE Puerto Camaron $$$

Paseo Baquedano 801 ***Tel*** *(057) 763391* ***Road Map*** *B2*

As its names suggests, Puerto Camaron (Shrimp Port) serves delicious shrimps, one of several great seafood items on the menu. There are filling pizzas and empanadas too, genuinely friendly service, and a pretty dining area of apple-green walls, wooden furniture, and tabletops decorated with seashells. Closed for dinner on Sundays.

IQUIQUE El Tercer Ojito $$$$

Patricio Lynch 1420-A ***Tel*** *(057) 426517* ***Road Map*** *B2*

A cute restaurant where tables are spread around a central patio and its surrounding bamboo-thatched cloisters. Colorful flowers, cacti big and small, and hippy oriental art on the walls create a fun ambience. The Chilean-Latin American cuisine includes salads, pastas, and even sushi. Closed for dinner on Sundays, and all day on Mondays.

LA SERENA Café Mistral $

Avenida Francisco de Aguirre 0306 ***Tel*** *(051) 216586* ***Road Map*** *B5*

This bohemian restaurant and café has a large terrace and serves lunch and dinner. Excellent vegetarian fare, including soya burgers and stir-fries, as well as great salmon and shellfish pancakes. A good selection of *pisco*. Blues and rock music adds to the casual mood. Popular with local students. Closed for dinner on Sundays.

LA SERENA La Casona del Guatón $$$

Brasil 750 ***Tel*** *(051) 211519* ***Road Map*** *B5*

A classic Chilean restaurant, La Casona del Guatón occupies an old adobe family home. The house is impeccably preserved with its original mosaic flooring. Chilean staples, dominated by grilled meats which crackle on an open flame grill. Service is a little slow, but the ambience is cozy. Open daily for lunch and dinner.

LA SERENA Porota's $$$$

Avenida del Mar 900-B ***Tel*** *(051) 210937* ***Road Map*** *B5*

Beachside Porota's apple-green house has a rustic-chic interior. Food arrives on frosted-glass plates, the table linen has fruity motifs, and napkins are bound in bamboo. The lunch and dinner menus are creative, featuring items such as albacore with aniseed and papaya jam. Closed on Mondays from April to November.

OVALLE Restaurante Los Braseros $$$

Vicuña Mackenna 595 ***Tel*** *(053) 624917* ***Road Map*** *B5*

The arched interior of this restaurant has firewood stoves, checkerboard floor, log-beamed ceiling, and bare brick walls. Lunch and dinner feature classic Chilean and regional cuisine such as grilled meats with rice and salads, and river prawns in a tangy garlic sauce. Attentive service. Closed for dinner on Sundays.

PUTRE Cantaverdi $$

Arturo Pérez Canto 339 ***Tel*** *(09) 85127200* ***Road Map*** *B1*

Set in an adobe house with mustard colored walls, a clay floor, and wooden tables, Cantaverdi offers pizzas, meats, salads, tapas, seafood, and sandwiches for lunch and dinner daily. Pizzas come with Peruvian toppings such as spiced meats and chorizo. Contemporary art on the walls contrasts with the traditional Andean setting.

SAN PEDRO DE ATACAMA La Cave $$

Toconao 447 ***Tel*** *(055) 851073* ***Road Map*** *C3*

A good dining choice, La Cave is a cozy pizzeria owned by a French expatriate. The five-tabled interior is decorated with posters of French pop-culture idols. Outside, a spacious, thatched terrace has seating around an open fire. On offer are daily lunch and dinner promotions as well as fixed menu items such as pizzas and crepes.

SAN PEDRO DE ATACAMA Etnico $$$

Tocopilla 423 ***Tel*** *(055) 851377* ***Road Map*** *C3*

An eatery with a relaxed vibe and funky interior, Etnico occupies an adobe house with a low, thatched roof, rustic-cool tables, and jazz music. Open daily, it has a fixed, inexpensive menu at midday and a varied one in the evening, with pastas, fish, meats, and salads. The friendly owners attend to customers.

SAN PEDRO DE ATACAMA Todo Natural $$$

Caracoles 271 ***Tel*** *(055) 851585* ***Road Map*** *C3*

The cuisine at this vegetarian restaurant is completely free of preservatives and additives. Pastas, risottos, pancakes, and tortillas are on the menu. Drinks include fresh juices, smoothies, *piscos*, and wines. The ambience is relaxed and rustic, with a low ceiling, stone floor, and wooden tables around a clay-fired oven. Open daily for dinner.

SAN PEDRO DE ATACAMA Café Adobe $$$$$

Caracoles 211 ***Tel*** *(055) 851132* ***Road Map*** *C3*

The upscale Café Adobe features imaginative lunch and dinner menus. Traditional ingredients such as quinoa, a highland herb, are used to create original, modern dishes paired with premium wines. A uniquely designed ethnic-modern interior, where tables and artworks ring a roaring fire that is dug into the sandy floor. Open daily.

LAKE DISTRICT AND CHILOÉ

ANCUD Restaurant Kurantón $$$

Avenida Prat 94 ***Tel*** *(065) 623090* **Road Map** *D3*

A comfortable, colorful place with tangerine walls, Restaurant Kurantón is decorated with a plethora of collectables such as woodcarvings, basketry, fishing nets, and old photographs. The menu leans toward seafood – the grilled cod is superb – but there are also meats, salads, pastas, and rice dishes. Serves lunch and dinner daily.

CASTRO Años Luz $$$

San Martín 309 ***Tel*** *(065) 532700* **Road Map** *D3*

Facing Castro's main square, Años Luz is a popular eatery serving fish, shellfish, tapas, and meat dishes. A chalkboard menu lists the day's lunch and dinner specials. Lively bar in the front of the restaurant. Regular live music performed by rock, Latino, and Mapuche folkloric bands. Closed on Sundays.

CASTRO Restaurant Octavio $$$

Avenida Pedro Montt 261 ***Tel*** *(065) 632855* **Road Map** *D3*

Housed in a *palafito*, Restaurant Octavio overlooks the Fjordo Castro. The daily lunch and dinner menus are dominated by seafood, although there are meat-based options, salads, and rice dishes as well. The *curanto*, a preparation of shellfish, meat, and potatoes, is a specialty. Fruity desserts include papaya with cream.

CURACO DE VÉLEZ Restaurant Los Troncos $

Avenida del Mar 5 ***Tel*** *(09) 5210324* **Road Map** *D3*

The menu at Restaurant Los Troncos features oysters, salmon, and seafood empanadas, with oysters being the star attraction. Caught the same day, these are huge, salty and served raw – staff slice them open in front of guests – with a lemon. Wash down with wine or beer. Pleasant garden setting. Open for lunch and dinner daily.

DALCAHUE Restaurant Chiloé $$

Avenida Pedro Montt 120 ***Tel*** *(065) 641284* **Road Map** *D3*

Opposite Dalcahue's handicrafts market, the small, family-run Restaurant Chiloé is set in a shingled house. Serves seafood, beef, and pork mains as well as entrées with fiery sauces, pastas, and salads. A good range of *pisco* drinks on the menu too. Window tables offer spectacular views of the sea. Serves lunch and dinner daily.

FRUTILLAR Club Alemán Frutillar $$$

Avenida Philipi 747 ***Tel*** *(065) 421249* **Road Map** *D2*

The town's German Club has a large dining floor and an international menu with many traditional German dishes. The kuchen desserts are a must-try. The drinks menu features Chilean wines, pisco sours, and German-origin bock beers. Window tables offer views of Lago Llanquihue and Volcán Osorno. Lunch and dinner served daily.

OSORNO La Parrilla de Pepe $$$$

Mackenna 1095 ***Tel*** *(064) 249653* **Road Map** *D2*

A *parrilla* set in a German settler's 19th-century house. Features a low timber ceiling and an interior of many archways. The lunch and dinner menus feature Chilean and regional dishes, meats cooked to order, and German desserts. Closed all day on Sundays from December to March, and for Sunday dinner from April to November.

PANGUIPULLI Restaurant Gardylafquen $$

Martínez de Rosas 722 ***Tel*** *(09) 4587612* **Road Map** *D2*

The family-owned Restaurant Gardylafquen serves classic Chilean cuisine such as excellent *lomo* or tenderloin, and grilled fish with homemade breads and spicy sauces. Tasty tapas and German desserts as well. The tables are set amid wine racks and walls are hung with photographs from the region. Open for lunch and dinner daily.

PUCÓN Coppa Kabana $

General Basilio Urrutia 407 ***Tel*** *(045) 444371* **Road Map** *D2*

An inexpensive corner restaurant, Coppa Kabana serves lunch and dinner daily. It has just six tables and a bar, plus a street terrace with more tables. The juicy *churrascos* (grilled steaks) and *lomos* are the pick of the menu; but there are also good sandwiches, empanadas, and salads. Wine comes by the bottle or the *copa* (glass). Good pisco sours.

PUCÓN Restaurant ¡école! $$$

Hostería ¡école, General Urrutia 592 ***Tel*** *(045) 441675* **Road Map** *D2*

Welcoming service accompany lunch and dinner at this bustling restaurant. The menu boasts creative salads, freshly baked breads, flavorsome quiches and crepes, curried trout, and vegetable lasagna. Desserts include homemade tarts stuffed with local fruits. Enjoy it all in the snug dining room or on the tree-shaded patio.

PUCÓN Madre Tierra $$$$

Lincoyan 199 ***Tel*** *(045) 449099* **Road Map** *D2*

A delightful *parrilla*, Madre Tierra has a modern-rustic interior of woody furnishings. The lunch and dinner menus list Lake District specialties such as wild boar, trout, salmon, and venison. Guests choose their own wine from the in-house wine cellar. Closed on Tuesdays from July to November, and for Sunday dinner from April to June.

Key to Price Guide *see p294* **Key to Symbols** *see back cover flap*

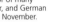

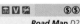

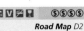

PUERTO MONTT La Estrella de Angelmó $$$
Angelmó fish market, Local 2 ***Tel*** *(08) 843028* **Road Map** *D2*

Wooden stairs at the Angelmó fish market lead to the small seafood restaurant, La Estrella de Angelmó (The Star of Angelmó), which serves clams, stewed crabs, and sea urchins. Everything is very fresh, netted each morning by fishermen. Menus in English and Spanish. The service is friendly. Open daily for lunch and dinner.

PUERTO MONTT Club de Yates $$$$$
Avenida Juan Soler Manfredini 200 ***Tel*** *(065) 284000* **Road Map** *D2*

The upscale Club de Yates juts into the ocean on its own pier. It has a modern interior, with floor-to-ceiling windows offering wide ocean vistas. The long menu is devoted almost entirely to seafood. Try the house specialty shellfish, the tangy seviche, or the delicious king crab and swordfish mains. Lunch and dinner served daily.

PUERTO OCTAY Puerto Muñoz Gamero $$
Muñoz Gamero 107 ***Tel*** *(064) 391435* **Road Map** *D2*

Family-run Puerto Muñoz Gamero is set in a wooden house built for a German pioneer family in 1908. It is charming and old-fashioned, with wooden furnishings and pictures decorating the walls. Lunch and dinner, served daily, feature traditional Lake District fare such as river trout and salmon, as well as red and white meats.

PUERTO VARAS La Rada $$$
Santa Rosa 040 ***Tel*** *(065) 718316* **Road Map** *D2*

A cozy seafood restaurant housed in a small weatherboard building on the city's coastal avenue, La Rada has a romantic interior and an outside deck with fabulous views of Lago Llanquihue and Volcán Osorno. The seviche here is excellent. The shellfish dishes and homemade pastas are also good. Serves lunch and dinner daily.

PUERTO VARAS Mediterraneo $$$$$
Santa Rosa 068 ***Tel*** *(065) 237268* **Road Map** *D2*

The lunch and dinner menu at the lakefront Mediterraneo features southern European dishes made with local ingredients. Items include seafood risottos, paellas, lasagnes, grilled meats, and fish. Spanish as well as Chilean varietals feature on the wine list. Stylish, modern-rustic ambience. Closed on Sundays from April to November.

QUELLÓN Restaurant Madero $$$
Ramón Freire 430 ***Tel*** *(065) 681330* **Road Map** *D3*

Centrally located, Restaurant Madero has a varied lunch and dinner menu with meats and fish dishes. The pizzas and pastas come with enticing seafood toppings and sauces – the creamy oyster sauce for pastas is scrumptious. Reserve wines and limited edition bottles on the wine list. A stone-and-wood interior. Closed on Sundays.

TEMUCO El Criollito $$
Interior, Mercado Municipal, Local 113 ***Tel*** *(045) 911254* **Road Map** *D2*

One of the oldest and most atmospheric restaurants in Temuco's Mercado Municipal, El Criollito features a woody decor, and fantastic lunch and dinner menus that includes fish stews, shellfish, salmon dishes, juicy red meats, and salads. Open during market hours only *(see p190)*; closed for dinner on Sundays.

TEMUCO Madonna Pizza & Pasta $$$
Avenida Alemania 0660 ***Tel*** *(045) 329393* **Road Map** *D2*

A popular hangout, this pizzeria and pasta house serves great Italian cuisine for lunch and dinner daily. Classic Italian toppings and sauces, but regional influence too – seafood pastas and salmon-topped pizzas. Quick service, a good wine list, and a bustling atmosphere. Sidewalk seating available. Reservations recommended.

VALDIVIA La Terraza $$$
Between Niebla and Los Molinos, Playa Los Enamorados ***Tel*** *(063) 282195* **Road Map** *D2*

Set within an old family home on Valdivia's riverside, La Terraza serves classic coastal cuisine, including fresh oysters. Pretty and welcoming decor with mustard yellow- and red-painted walls, a timber roof, and stained-glass lampshades above tables. Outdoor tables dot a grassy patio. Serves lunch and dinner daily.

VALDIVIA La Perla del Sur $$$$
Arturo Prat 500 ***Tel*** *(063) 245531* **Road Map** *D2*

Set in an atmospheric location on Valdivia's waterfront, La Perla del Sur occupies a brightly painted corner building from 1910 with a charmingly dated interior. Emphasis on simple yet exquisite seafood, such as oysters dipped in olive oil or grilled cod with lemon. Decent wine selection. Open for lunch and dinner daily.

VILLARRICA The Travellers International Restaurant $$
Valentín Letelier 753 ***Tel*** *(045) 413617* **Road Map** *D2*

This restaurant is a favorite with young backpackers. Pop-culture images and memorabilia such as Marilyn Monroe posters and old vinyl records decorate the scarlet walls. Lunch and dinner served daily include Mexican burritos, Thai curries, and tasty burgers. Happy hour at the horseshoe-shaped bar from 6:30–9:30pm everyday.

VILLARRICA El Rey del Marisco $$$$
Valentín Letelier 1030 ***Tel*** *(045) 412093* **Road Map** *D2*

The town's lakeshore is the location for this little seafood restaurant whose big windows offer beautiful lake views. The owner-chef's signature dish is a fantastic eel in a garlic, asparagus, and white-wine sauce. The salmon and trout entrées and king crab and oyster starters are also fabulous. Open for lunch and dinner daily.

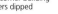

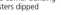

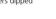

NORTHERN PATAGONIA

CALETA TORTEL El Mirador $$

Sector Centro s/n ***Tel*** *(067) 445482* **Road Map** *D5*

In a town with no real haute cuisine, El Mirador manages to make simple preparations of salmon, beef, and grilled chicken, plus fries, rice, or salad, into something memorable. Premium meats and fish are a little more expensive. Open for lunch and dinner daily, El Mirador offers sweeping mountain and harbor vistas.

COCHRANE Ñirrantal $$$

O'Higgins 652 ***Tel*** *(067) 522604* **Road Map** *D4*

The last good dining experience on the southbound Carretera Austral, Ñirrantal is a family-run and moderately priced eatery. The kitchen pays close attention to a range of delicious homemade dishes, from hearty sandwiches to beef and fish, mostly salmon. Well-intentioned but inconsistent service. Lunch and dinner served daily.

COYHAIQUE Cafetería Alemana $

Condell 119 ***Tel*** *(065) 231723* **Road Map** *E4*

An attractive eatery, Cafetería Alemana whips up delicious sandwiches, *lomos, bistec a lo pobre* (steak and potatoes topped with a fried egg), and pastries for lunch and dinner. This family-oriented cafeteria also offers German specialties such as kuchen. The midday lunch is excellent value for money.

COYHAIQUE Café Ricer V $$

Paseo Horn 48 ***Tel*** *(067) 232920* **Road Map** *E4*

Coyhaique's classic restaurant is in a pedestrian mall opposite the town's pentagonal Plaza de Armas. Does almost everything well, from sandwiches and pastas to meats and ice cream, but the specialty is the Patagonian lamb. The upstairs salon, with attractive historic decor, permits smoking. Open for lunch and dinner daily.

COYHAIQUE La Fiorentina V $$

Francisco Bilbao 547 ***Tel*** *(067) 238899* **Road Map** *E4*

Serves pizza with a diverse range of toppings, but guests can also savor delicious versions of standard Chilean dishes such as *pastel de choclo,* a preparation of ground corn and basil, and *cazuela de ave,* a meat and vegetable stew. The decor is utilitarian; a TV broadcasts popular channels. Serves lunch and dinner daily.

COYHAIQUE La Olla V $$

Prat 176 ***Tel*** *(067) 234700* **Road Map** *E4*

The lunch and dinner menu at La Olla features the best pastas in town as well as good Spanish fare, including well-prepared paellas. The fixed-price lunches offer good value for money, but the service can be inconsistent. The pisco sours are delicious, but tend to be on the sweeter side; guests can ask the staff to hold the sugar.

COYHAIQUE La Casona V $$$

Obispo Vielmo 77 ***Tel*** *(067) 238894* **Road Map** *E4*

A family-style restaurant, La Casona serves Chilean and regional specialties such as lamb, crab casseroles, and seafood dishes for lunch and dinner. On offer are delicious pisco sours and an impressive selection of wines. The service never falters even when the restaurant is packed. Utilitarian decor.

COYHAIQUE Lito's $$$

Lautaro 147 ***Tel*** *(067) 234361* **Road Map** *E4*

Behind a nondescript exterior, Lito's serves well-made beef, fish, and seafood dishes. The restaurant's fixed-price menu is an excellent deal. There is a bar with an impressive selection of wines. Service is quick and diners are accommodated in a spacious dining room. Open for lunch and dinner daily.

COYHAIQUE El Ovejero V $$$$

Hotel El Reloj, Baquedano 828 ***Tel*** *(067) 231108* **Road Map** *E4*

Specializes in regional dishes, particularly lamb, but also salmon and game such as the Patagonian hare. The intimate ambience, individual attention paid to each dish, and cozy dining room overlooking the Río Coyhaique valley make El Ovejero the best place in town for a romantic dinner. Serves lunch and dinner daily.

FUTALEUFÚ Martín Pescador $$

Balmaceda 603 ***Tel*** *(067) 721279* **Road Map** *E3*

Most of Futaleufú's best food is served at the rafting and kayaking camps outside town, but Martín Pescador offers excellent dining for those not camping on the river. Spacious dining area and stylish ambience. Guests can sprawl on sofas and enjoy their drinks before relishing a salmon dinner. Open daily for lunch and dinner.

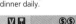

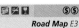

PUERTO PUYUHUAPI Café Rossbach $$

Ernesto Ludwig s/n ***Tel*** *(067) 325203* **Road Map** *D3*

Occupying a German-style shingle house, Café Rossbach is the best dining experience in a town with few moderately priced and accessible eating options. Decor creates a barn-like atmosphere. The kuchen pastries are the star items on the menu, but the salmon is also memorable and the coffee served here is worth sampling.

Key to Price Guide *see p294* **Key to Symbols** *see back cover flap*

SOUTHERN PATAGONIA AND TIERRA DEL FUEGO

CUEVA DEL MILODÓN Caverna del Milodón $$$

Fronting Cueva de Milodón, 15 miles (24 km) NW of Puerto Natales **Tel** *(061) 411484* **Road Map** *E6*

A contemporary restaurant, Caverna del Milodón serves traditional regional cuisine that includes a hearty *parrillada*, a heaped platter of meats on a table-side barbecue. Open daily for breakfast, lunch, and dinner, this restaurant offers panoramic vistas of the serene Seno Última Esperanza.

PORVENIR Hotel Rosas $$

Hostel Rosas, Phillipi 296 **Tel** *(061) 580088* **Road Map** *E6*

Porvenir's most popular restaurant is usually packed with travelers and businessmen. This airy eatery is open daily for lunch and dinner. On offer are Chilean dishes such as *plateada* (stewed beef and potatoes). Good value for money, especially on weekdays when a three-course fixed-price menu is available. À la carte menu in the evenings.

PORVENIR Club Social Croata $$$

Señoret 542 **Tel** *(061) 580053* **Road Map** *E6*

Descendents of Croatian immigrants patronize this joint for its great seafood dishes and relaxed ambience. Club Social Croata passes for an upscale restaurant in a town with few dining options and serves lunch and dinner from Tuesday to Sunday. The restaurant's decor features sports trophies and Croatian curios.

PUERTO NATALES El Living $$

Arturo Prat 156 **Tel** *(061) 411140* **Road Map** *E6*

British-run and featuring an outdoor beer garden, this vegetarian café serves delicious sandwiches, burgers, and bruschettas. Enjoy coffee and homemade cake, and read from the café's copious stacks of English and Spanish magazines. Open for lunch and dinner from Monday to Saturday, and only for lunch on Sundays.

PUERTO NATALES Hotel Rubens $$

Km183, 5 Ruta 9 Norte **Tel** *(09) 2547943* **Road Map** *E6*

This historic, 1930s hotel operated as a pit stop for travelers when the road to Puerto Natales required 2 days, travel. Today, the charming inn still provides a break for those heading to Parque Nacional Torres del Paine. Open daily for lunch and dinner, it serves giant sandwiches made of homemade bread, and delicious, greasy fries.

PUERTO NATALES Afrigonia $$$

Eberhard 343 **Tel** *(061) 412232* **Road Map** *E6*

The incongruous Patagonian-African concept of Afrigonia is due to the restaurant's Zambian-Chilean ownership. Superbly crafted dishes pair regional ingredients such as lamb and hake with spices and sauces not normally used in Patagonia, including mint, coconut milk, and curry. Open lunch and dinner from Monday to Saturday.

PUERTO NATALES Asador Patagonico $$$

Arturo Prat 158 **Tel** *(061) 413553* **Road Map** *E6*

A high-quality *parrilla* (steakhouse) serving fresh king crab and outstanding cuts of grilled meats, including lamb barbecued on a traditional spit. Snug, rustic, and well appointed. Located in what was once an antique pharmacy, Asador Patagonico is open for lunch and dinner daily. A great bet for those who have worked up an appetite.

PUERTO NATALES Hotel Costa Australis $$$

Hotel Costa Australis, Pedro Montt 262 **Tel** *(061) 412000* **Road Map** *E6*

Puerto Natales's most elegant eatery, with light and airy whitewashed walls, a driftwood-heavy decor, and linen tablecloths. The restaurant serves beautifully executed cuisine and specializes in regional seafood. Offers a lengthy wine list that features premium vintages. Open for breakfast, lunch, and dinner.

PUERTO NATALES Mama Rosa V $$$

Hotel Indigo, Ladrilleros 105 **Tel** *(061) 413609* **Road Map** *E6*

Popular for both its food and views, Mama Rosa is one of the few restaurants in the region that offer gourmet cuisine using local ingredients such as hake. Hip ambience and a second-story lounge that serves 15 kinds of pisco sours and appetizers. Mama Rosa is open for lunch and dinner; snacks served throughout the day.

PUERTO NATALES Mesita Grande V $$$

Arturo Prat 196 **Tel** *(061) 411571* **Road Map** *E6*

Warm and lively, the Mesita Grande is composed of one long table that seats all diners. It is a concept that works well, given the pleasing vibe and the opportunity to mix with travelers from everywhere. Lunch and dinner features thin-crust pizzas baked in a stone oven, and fresh pastas and salads. Closed from June to August.

PUNTA ARENAS Dino's Pizza $$

Bories 557 **Tel** *(061) 247434* **Road Map** *E6*

This informal eatery is extremely popular for its mouthwatering sandwiches. The *barros luca*, a beef and cheese sandwich, is a must-try. Pizzas come with a range of toppings, and the star attraction is the calzone-like folded Empapizza. Offers a variety of fresh juices, including a delectable rhubarb juice. Open daily for lunch and dinner.

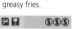

PUNTA ARENAS Lomit's $$

José Menendez 722 ***Tel*** *(061) 243399* ***Road Map*** *E6*

Locals flock to Lomit's for its sandwiches made with freshly roasted chicken and pork, and tasty *completos* – hot dogs topped with globs of condiments. A 1970s diner ambience with chefs in stiff white hats and waitresses in old-school frocks and aprons. Good draft beer on offer. Open daily for lunch and dinner.

PUNTA ARENAS Damiana Elena $$$

Magallanes 341 ***Tel*** *(061) 222818* ***Road Map*** *E6*

Set in a charming old home, this eatery is open only for dinner. Owners Julian and Martin serve regional cuisine influenced by the meals they ate growing up. Highlights include cannellonis with sea snails and spinach, and salmon with avocado sauce. The food is authentic and reasonably priced. Reservations recommended.

PUNTA ARENAS El Mercado $$$

Mejicana 617, second floor ***Tel*** *(061) 242746* ***Road Map*** *E6*

A local favorite for nearly 30 years, this diner-like restaurant draws crowds for its simply prepared, traditional Chilean meals. The specialty *curanto* is a heaped platter of meat and fish served with a tasty broth. The ambience is animated with the chatter of diners seated in comfortable leatherette booths. Serves lunch and dinner daily.

PUNTA ARENAS La Pergola $$$

Hotel Nogueira, Bories 959 ***Tel*** *(061) 711000* ***Road Map*** *E6*

Occupies a glass-enclosed space draped with grapevines, in the former home of one of Punta Arenas's wealthiest residents. Antique ambience. A photo-illustrated menu offers regional specialties and international dishes such as fresh king crab, roasted lamb, salmon, and conger eel. Service can be slow. Serves lunch and dinner daily.

PUNTA ARENAS Puerto Viejo $$$

O'Higgins 1166 ***Tel*** *(061) 225103* ***Road Map*** *E6*

Popular with cruise ship passengers due to its proximity to the pier, Puerto Viejo is tastefully festooned with thematic decor including a mock ship and fish nets. Specializes in regional cuisine and offers a spit-roasted lamb barbecue. Friendly staff who speak decent English. Open for lunch and dinner from Monday to Saturday.

PUNTA ARENAS Santino $$$

Avenida Colón 657 ***Tel*** *(061) 710882* ***Road Map*** *E6*

Located in downtown Punta Arenas, the casual Santino is popular as both a restaurant and a bar in the evenings. The menu features classic Chilean and Italian fare such as pizzas and pastas, fried conger eel, and *lomo a lo pobre* – steak with ham and fried eggs. Lively ambience with loud music. Open daily for dinner.

PUNTA ARENAS Atama $$$$

Dreams Hotel, O'Higgins 1235 ***Tel*** *(061) 204541* ***Road Map*** *E6*

Sophisticated eatery with lofty ceilings and a huge swath of glass that offers views of the Strait of Magellan. Smart decor and furnishings paired with the fusion-style menu, which leans on meats but gives king crab its due. Top-notch wine list, created by well-known Chilean sommelier Alejandro Farias. Open daily for lunch and dinner.

PUNTA ARENAS Remezón $$$$

21 de Mayo 1469 ***Tel*** *(061) 241029* ***Road Map*** *E6*

A hidden gem, Remezón celebrates the variety of meats and regional products in Patagonia, including game such as rhea, guanaco, and beaver. The king crab raviolis, the beer-stewed lamb, and delicate hake are to die for. The calafate sour cocktail is a must-try. Open for lunch and dinner from Monday to Saturday.

PUNTA ARENAS Sotito's $$$$

O'Higgins 1138 ***Tel*** *(061) 243565* ***Road Map*** *E6*

Serves hearty Chilean cuisine that focuses heavily on king crab and seafood. The king crab cannellonis are mouthwatering. Hidden behind a simple façade are cavernous dining areas that are slick and semi-formal, with linen tablecloths and waiters in bow ties delivering meals on metal carts. Open daily for lunch and dinner.

PUNTA ARENAS Hostería Faro San Isidro $$$$$

Hostería Faro San Isidro, near Cabo Froward ***Tel*** *(09) 93493862* ***Road Map*** *E6*

Lunch is served as part of a kayaking or trekking day tour, as well as to those who come to simply savor the magnificent views from this charming lodge. Food includes fresh and homemade green salads, meats, and fish dishes served buffet-style in a dining room overlooking the Strait of Magellan. Reservations necessary.

TORRES DEL PAINE Hostería Grey $$$

Hostería Grey, Lago Grey sector ***Tel*** *(061) 410172* ***Road Map*** *D6*

Convenient for travelers exploring Lago Grey, Hostería Grey's spacious dining room offers splendid views of icebergs floating toward the lakeshore. Guests can order from a fixed-price meal that includes an appetizer and dessert. An excellent selection of drinks on offer. Lunch and dinner served daily.

TORRES DEL PAINE Hostería Pehoé $$$

Hostería Pehoé, Lago Pehoé ***Tel*** *(02) 2350252* ***Road Map*** *D6*

Set in a gingerbread-style hotel that faces the Paine massif and reached via a long boardwalk across Lago Pehoé. The principal reason for dining at this *hostería* is the breathtaking view from its cozy dining room. The cuisine is decent, mainly grilled meats and fish served with with potatoes and rice. Open for lunch and dinner daily.

Key to Price Guide *see p294* **Key to Symbols** *see back cover flap*

TORRES DEL PAINE Las Torres $$$$$

Las Torres sector ***Tel*** *(061) 360360* ***Road Map*** *D6*

Hikers fresh from the challenging trek up to Torres del Paine relish a cold "victory" beer in this hotel's bar, which offers delicious sandwiches. The main restaurant serves lunch and dinner daily, with a more expensive buffet in the evenings. All the ingredients are locally grown and organic, but service and quality of food can vary.

EASTER ISLAND AND ROBINSON CRUSOE ISLAND

HANGA ROA Avareipua $$

Policarpo Toro s/n ***Tel*** *(032) 2551158*

German-owned Avareipua has no pretensions but turns out fresh fish and seafood at a fraction of the price of its neighbors. On offer are delicious preparations of *toremo*, a sea fish. More elaborate dishes include lobster. What the eatery lacks in atmosphere, it compensates for with attention. Serves lunch and dinner daily.

HANGA ROA Kopa Kavana $$

Avareipua s/n ***Tel*** *(032) 2100447*

The lunch and dinner menus at Kopa Kavana lean heavily on Polynesian cuisine, featuring main dishes such as the fish-based *remo remo* and side dishes such as fried sweet potatoes rather than French fries. Also on offer is a diversity of local fish-based food. The food is well prepared and attractively presented. Open daily.

HANGA ROA Merahi Ra'a $$

Te Pito Te Henua s/n ***Tel*** *(032) 2551125*

Located opposite Hanga Roa's soccer field, Merahi Ra'a has bigger lunch and dinner menus than most other restaurants in the vicinity. The specialty is seafood, including great seviche, but diners can also choose standard Chilean dishes. Moderate prices mean good value for money. Friendly and quick service, even when busy.

HANGA ROA Te Moana $$

Atamu Tekena s/n ***Tel*** *(032) 2551578*

This bar-cum-restaurant serves excellent food and strong, well-prepared mixed drinks. Guests can try dishes such as Asian-style curries. The service is generally good, but tends to get inconsistent when the eatery gets crowded. Popularity can make it hard to get a table at times. Serves lunch and dinner daily.

HANGA ROA Café Ra'a V $$$

Atamu Tekena s/n ***Tel*** *(032)2551530*

A casual sidewalk café-and-restaurant with Polynesian decor, Café Ra'a serves sandwiches, snacks, juices and espresso, and a variety of European-style desserts. Open for both lunch and dinner daily, but with a better choice for lunch. Smoking is permitted at the tree-shaded outdoor tables. The establishment has a book exchange.

HANGA ROA Playa Pea $$$

Policarpo Toro s/n ***Tel*** *(032) 2551575*

The location of Playa Pea near Hanga Roa's waterfront is a highlight. Diners watch the rolling waves and the setting sun from a pleasant terrace. Serves simple but tasty fish dishes such as the *albacora papillón*, prepared with red wine. The chicken and shrimp preparations are also good. Indifferent service. Lunch and dinner daily.

HANGA ROA Au Bout du Monde V $$$$

Policarpo Toro s/n ***Tel*** *(032) 2552060*

The Franco-Belgian Au Bout du Monde is one of Hanga Roa's best restaurants. The lunch and dinner menu features dishes such as prawn pesto salad and tuna in white-wine sauce. Desserts including Belgian chocolate mousse and delicious crepes. Gracious service in a simple structure. Good beers and wine offered. Open daily.

HANGA ROA La Taverne du Pecheur V $$$$

Policarpo Toro s/n ***Tel*** *(032) 2100619*

Lunch and dinner at La Taverne du Pecheur is prepared and served by its French owner-chef, who uses fresh and high-quality ingredients to create scrumptious dishes. Seafood, which includes lobster, sea urchin, and a variety of fish, is the specialty. Excellent selection of wine. Service can be inconsistent. Open daily.

SAN JUAN BAUTISTA Residencial Mirador de Selkirk $

Residencial Mirador de Selkirk, El Castillo 251 ***Tel*** *(032) 2751028*

The eatery here is part of a family-run bed-and-breakfast that offers half-board and full-board options, but is open to non-guests who give advance notice. The range of standard seafood fare includes crab and lobster dishes, simply but skillfully prepared and using ingredients that are invariably fresh off the boat. Open daily.

SAN JUAN BAUTISTA Barón de Rodt $$

La Pólvora s/n ***Tel*** *(032) 2751109*

Having survived the tsunami of 2010, the Barón de Rodt continues to overlook Bahía Cumberland from its hillside perch, and to offer fresh fish and lobster, plus a smattering of other dishes. Part of the hotel of the same name, the restaurant prefers that diners give advance notice, but is accommodating. Serves lunch and dinner daily.

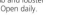

SHOPPING IN CHILE AND EASTER ISLAND

Mapuche basket

Chile is not among the world's shopping meccas, but there are several items that are worth taking home. The open economy has meant a massive influx of foreign goods, but typical Chilean products remain popular with shoppers. Visitors will find alpaca and sheep woolens from the Andean north and Patagonia, *huaso* riding gear from the Central Valley, and Mapuche basketry, silver jewelry, and weavings from the Lake District. The country's lapiz lazuli jewelry is greatly prized by experienced buyers. Wine is a favorite purchase, as is the lesser-known but equally noteworthy drink, *pisco*. Among the most eye-catching artifacts in Chile are the wooden or stone replicas of the massive *moai* statues of Easter Island. Handcrafted by skilled Rapa Nui artisans, these can be found across the country.

Row of souvenir shops reached by the Ascensor Artillería, Valparaíso

OPENING HOURS

Shops and shopping malls usually open after 10am and stay open until 9 or 10pm. Many stores are open on Saturday mornings but close around 1pm, except in tourist destinations, such as Santiago's Barrio Bellavista, where shops, particularly those in Patio Bellavista *(see p88)*, also open on Sundays. In smaller cities and towns, shops tend to close for lunch and a siesta that lasts from around 1 to 5pm.

PAYMENT, TAXES, AND BARGAINING

Payment in cash, preferably Chilean pesos, is the default option, especially in rural areas, street stalls, and artisans' markets. However, most large shops in major cities accept credit cards. Visa and MasterCard are most widely accepted, although American Express is not uncommon either. No surcharge is added to credit card purchases, but credit card agencies at home may deduct an amount on overseas purchases *(see p328)*. Most tourism-oriented businesses welcome US dollars, but euros are a relative novelty in Chile. A Value Added Tax (VAT or IVA) of 18 percent is customarily added to the purchase of most goods and services.

In Chile, bargaining is not the usual custom as in other South American countries. Haggling may be expected in crafts markets, but is considered inappropriate if the vendor has a fixed address.

CRAFTS AND SOUVENIRS

Popular handicrafts such as ceramics, ornaments, basketry, woodcarvings, and alpaca woolens are available in crafts markets and stalls across Chile. Los Andes in Central Valley is known for its decorative ceramics. **CALA**, one of the many ceramic workshops here, is open for tours and offers a range of handcrafted pottery items. **La Mano Arte** in northern Chile is an interesting crafts shop that specializes in regionally themed ceramic sculptures.

MUSEUM SHOPS

A couple of Chile's museums have shops that are worth visiting. Santiago's Museo Chileno de Arte Precolombino *(see pp60–61)* sells books, videos, and replicas of its own pieces, particularly of Andean pottery and textiles.

Operated by the **Fundación Neruda**, Pablo Neruda's three houses, located in Santiago,

Browsing through craft stalls along a cobbled street in Pucón

Valparaíso, and Isla Negra, have ceramics, crafts, and books by and about the poet.

Almacruz in Santa Cruz's Museo de Colchagua *(see p146)* has an abundant selection of regional souvenirs and wines from the area.

Located on the outskirts of the northern city of Arica, Museo Arqueológico San Miguel de Azapa *(see p161)* – home to the world-famous Chinchorro mummies – offers alpaca woolens and bags produced in the region, as well as reproductions of historic ceramics.

ARTISANS' MARKETS

The quality of Chile's local arts and crafts has greatly improved since the end of the 20th century, partly due to the development of non-profit associations such as the Artesanías de Chile *(see p97)*, who work with artisans to manufacture fine products and provide a network for the sale of wares.

The Centro de Exposición de Arte Indígena *(see p97)* is Santiago's most accessible crafts market, while Pueblo Los Dominicos *(see p91)* is the capital's biggest artisans' market. It is open daily and gets especially lively on Sundays. Located in the heart of Mapuche territory, Temuco's Mercado Municipal *(see p190)* offers finely crafted ornaments, basketry, and woodcarvings made by ethnic groups across Chile, as well as by indigenous peoples from the bordering countries of Peru and Ecuador.

Held in Puerto Montt, in the Lake District, **Feria Artesanal de Angelmó** is one of the country's largest crafts fairs featuring rows of well-stocked stalls displaying locally made textiles, pottery, woolens, and jewelry.

On the Chiloé archipelago *(see pp214–21)*, artisans' markets in Ancud and Castro, as well as in the smaller settlements of Dalcahue, Achao, and Chonchi, are well worth a visit. On Easter Island, Hanga Roa's Mercado Artesanal *(see p258)* offers custom-made *moai* and *rongorongo* tablets.

Cabernet sauvignon and carménère wines from the Colchagua Valley

FOOD AND WINE

During the summer months, visitors to Chile will find highly prized temperate fruits such as blueberries, raspberries, cherries, grapes, and olives.

Puerto Varas, in southern Chile, is the place to buy chocolates. Based in town, **Vicki Johnson** creates a range of delicious homemade chocolates and other mouthwatering treats such as smoked salmon, flavored sugar and honey, liqueurs, jams, and marmalades. Organic honey and fruit preserves can be purchased from the Parque Pumalín *(see p226)* project's retail outlet Puma Verde, which also sells books and local crafts.

Chile produces prodigious amounts of wine, and though the 2010 earthquake destroyed part of what was in storage and may affect availability over the next few years, there are still many outlets for purchasing the beverage. The best wine can be found at specialist wine shops or at the wineries themselves. Two of the best specialty shops in Santiago are La Vinoteca and El Mundo del Vino *(see p97)*, both located in Las Condes.

The majority of Chile's best vineyards are found in the fertile Central Valley. These include the excellent Viña Cousiño-Macul and Viña Concha y Toro *(see p140)*, both open for tours and tastings. In the Casablanca Valley *(see pp138–9)* located northwest of the capital, the best choice is Viña Veramonte.

Many Colchagua Valley wineries *(see pp148–9)*, such as Viña Montes and Viña Casa Silva, sell their premium vintages. The information center of Colchagua's Ruta del Vino, in Santa Cruz, also provides a wide selection of wines from the region's various vineyards.

A popular beverage across South America, *pisco* is one of Chile's favorite drinks. Good *pisco* is readily available throughout the country, and it is advisable to buy at least the 40° (80 proof) *reservado* (with 40 percent alcohol) in order to make the well-known cocktail, pisco sour. Major brands such as Planta Capel *(see p182)* and **Cooperative Agricola Control** are sold almost everywhere, but small producers such as **Fundo Los Nichos** are also worth seeking out. However, this may require a visit to remote distilleries, in this case, to the Valle del Elqui *(see pp182–3)*.

Market stalls at Temuco's covered Mercado Municipal

BOOKS AND MUSIC

Most large bookstores in Chile's urban centers stock titles in Spanish and English. The popular Feria del Libro *(see p97)* has branches across the capital. Also in Santiago, Librería Chile Ilustrado specializes in material for collectors and antiquarians.

In Punta Arenas, **Southern Patagonia Souvenirs & Books** has books on the region's wildlife, history, and culture.

Featuring a wide selection of music from across Chile and the world, Feria del Disco *(see p97)* has several outlets around Santiago. Smaller music stores across Chile offer popular international music, Chilean classical recordings, and folkloric rythms. Hotel Santa Cruz *(see p279)* in the Colchagua Valley has a small store that specializes in books and music on Chilean themes.

ANTIQUES

In the 19th century, Chile's elite and middle class could afford furniture and other items imported from Europe. Many of these, along with a range of local pre-Hispanic artifacts have made their way to antique shops in Santiago and Valparaíso. In Santiago, Antiguedades Bucharest and Antiguedades Balmaceda *(see p97)* are warehouses where several vendors display their goods. The capital also has a fine Sunday antique market on Plaza Perú, in Las Condes. Valparaíso's Plaza O'Higgins market is open on weekends and holidays. Other than archaeological items, visitors are allowed to carry most antiques out of the country.

DEPARTMENT STORES

Chain department stores across Chile sell everything from clothing to electronics and furniture. The biggest name is **Falabella**, but **Almacenes París** and **Ripley** stores are also found in most major cities.

SHOPPING MALLS

Most malls and shopping centers are massive constructions in suburban Santiago. Mall Apumanque and Alto Los Condes *(see p97)* are among the largest malls in the capital.

Cities such as Antofagasta, Iquique, Puerto Montt, and Temuco also have modern shopping malls. Great bargains are available at the duty-free Zona Franca de Iquique *(see p167)* and at Punta Arenas's **ZonAustral**. Most malls include a food court, multiplex cinemas, and play areas for children. Temuco's mall on Avenida Alemania also has a casino.

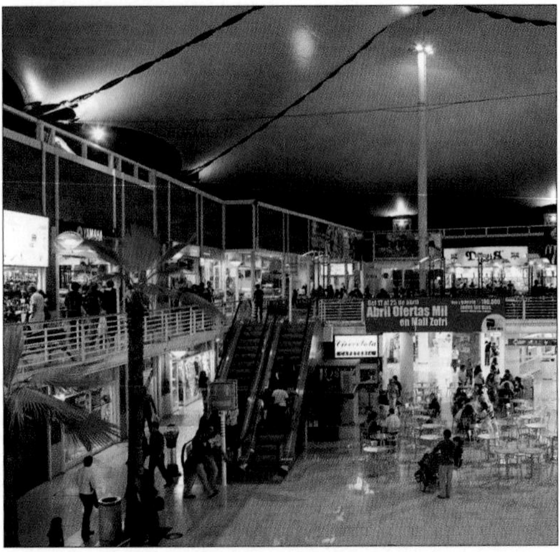

A shopping mall in the duty-free Zona Franca de Iquique

DIRECTORY

CRAFTS AND SOUVENIRS

CALA
Las Heras 150, Los Andes.
Tel *(034) 406487.*

La Mano Arte
Caracoles 450-A, San Pedro de Atacama. ***Tel*** *(055) 851312.*
www.ceramicalamano.cl

MUSEUM SHOPS

Almacruz
Avenida Errázuriz 145, Santa Cruz.
Tel *(072) 821050.*
www.museocolchagua.cl

Fundación Neruda
www.fundacionneruda.org

ARTISANS' MARKETS

Feria Artesanal de Angelmó
Avenida Angelmó, Puerto Montt.
www.angelmo.cl

FOOD AND WINE

Cooperative Agricola Control
Rengifo 240, Coquimbo.
Tel *(056) 51553800.*

Fundo Los Nichos
Pisco Elqui. ***Tel*** *(051) 451085.*
www.losnichos.cl

Vicki Johnson
Santa Rosa 318, Puerto Varas.
Tel *(065) 232240.*
www.vicki-johnson.com

BOOKS AND MUSIC

Southern Patagonia Souvenirs & Books
Avenida Bulnes Km3.5, Punta Arenas. ***Tel*** *(061) 216759.*
www.albers.cl

DEPARTMENT STORES

Almacenes París
www.paris.cl

Falabella
www.falabella.com

Ripley
www.ripley.cl

SHOPPING MALLS

ZonAustral
Avenida Bulnes Km3.5, Punta Arenas. ***Tel*** *(061) 216666.*
www.zonaustral.cl

Lapis Lazuli

A semiprecious gemstone, the intensely blue lapis lazuli has been valued since ancient times. The early Egyptians utilized it in decorative art and as a cosmetic – Cleopatra is said to have used powdered lapis as eyeshadow. The Romans considered it an aphrodisiac, and in pre-Columbian Chile, the stone formed part of ornaments and objects of functional and ritualistic use. Today, the only sizable deposits of lapis are found in Afghanistan and in the high Andes of Chile's Norte Grande and Norte Chico. Specialty stores, mostly in Santiago, offer intricate lapis lazuli jewelry, figurines, and decorative boxes.

A kingfisher-shaped brooch

FROM WORKSHOP TO SHOP

Once lapis lazuli is mined and brought to workshops, it is cut with a diamond disk and carved with abrasive emery for shape. Subsequently, sandpaper is used to remove any roughness and the gem is polished for shine. The stone is then combined with precious metals, especially gold and silver, to create prized ornaments and artifacts. These are sold at specialty stores such as the Lapis Lazuli House *(see p97)*.

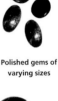

An uncut, unpolished block of lapis lazuli

Polished gems of varying sizes

Heavy necklaces, earrings, and bracelet

Sterling silver brooches fashioned to resemble an elephant and a woman

Bangle designs in lapis lazuli

Flower pendant

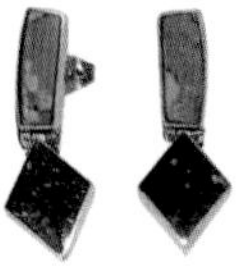

Earrings in shades of blue

Gold and silver *is inlaid with lapis lazuli to make valuable and attractive accessories. The price of each piece depends on the amount of the metal used, uniqueness of the design, and the size and number of gems inlaid. Popular items include necklaces, bracelets, earrings, cuff links, and brooches.*

Ornamental and utilitarian articles *made of lapis lazuli include finely handcrafted vases, small figurines, paper weights, ashtrays, cutlery, and key rings. Lapis lazuli is often combined with crystal and metal, as well as with other gems to create unique items.*

Carved candlesticks

A silver amphora

Turquoise and lapis lazuli mask

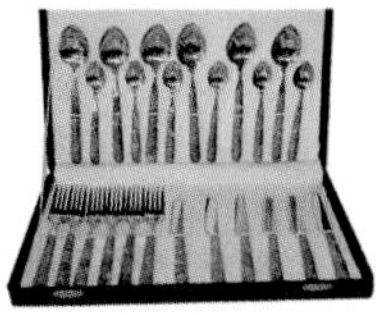

A cutlery set decorated with lapis lazuli

Blue-and-white patterened chess set

A house-shaped table clock

Replica of a classic car in metal and stone

ENTERTAINMENT IN CHILE

The range of entertainment in Chile is a reflection of its rich culture and the spirit of its people. Spectator sports form an integral part of life here. Soccer, in particular, fills stadiums all over the nation despite the difficulty of reaching the World Cup in a continent dominated by soccer powerhouses Argentina and Brazil. Equestrian sports are also popular, as racetracks across the country draw enthusiastic fans. Chile comes alive during the night and there are numerous bars and nighclubs that cater to its genial crowds. The vivid world of music and dance runs the gamut from folkloric music to contemporary rock and reggae, classical music and dance, with many artists of international fame. Chile also has an active theater scene, most notably in Santiago, and Chilean films have begun to generate worldwide interest.

Logo of the Colo Colo club

PRACTICAL INFORMATION

Local newspapers such as El Mercurio's *Wikén* and the online *Revolver Magazine* (in English) are good sources of information in Santiago. Hotel receptions and tourist offices also offer guidance and events calendars. **Punto Ticket** is an online ticket broker that also sells through Ripley department stores in Santiago, La Serena, Antofagasta, and Concepción. **Feria Ticket** sells online and through Feria del Disco and Almacenes París.

SPECTATOR SPORTS

Chilean soccer lacks the high international profile of neighboring Argentina; despite this, Santiago hosted the 1962 World Cup at its Estadio Nacional. Real First Division *clásicos* (classics) between **Universidad de Chile** and **Colo Colo** take place in this venue, but there are many other stadiums in the city. A number of regional teams also play in the First Division. Tickets are arranged through individual soccer clubs. Racetrack enthusiasts in Santiago watch horses compete at Club Hípico *(see p81)* and Hipódromo Chile *(see p101)*. The **Valparaíso Sporting Club** also hosts prestigious races, notably the Chilean Derby Stakes. Tennis is popular thanks to many high-profile players *(see p30)*. The biggest tournament, Movistar Open, is held in February in Viña del Mar.

BARS AND NIGHTCLUBS

Chilean cities, in particular Santiago and the coastal resort of Viña del Mar, are notable for a nightlife that starts early in the afternoon but gets into full swing only after midnight. Discos and dance clubs stay open until dawn, especially in the capital city's Barrio Bellavista, which also has an active gay scene. Lake District resorts, such as Pucón and Puerto Varas, also attract partygoers.

Horse racing on the track at Club Hípico, Santiago

Interior of Bar La Playa on Calle Cochrane, Valparaíso

FOLK MUSIC

Thanks to politically conscious musicians such as Violeta Parra and Víctor Jara *(see p25)*, Chilean folkloric music has gained many fans throughout Latin America and beyond. Performing in *peñas*, small informal clubs, these artistes modernized folk tradition that originated among the poor and dispossessed. Groups such as Quilapayún and Inti-Illimani absorbed Andean highland traditions from Peru and Bolivia, including characteristic instruments such as the *charango* and *zampoña* in their music. The political content of their work is obvious in albums such as *Cantata Popular Santa María de Iquique*, which features songs about the army's slaughter of nitrate miners and their families in the Atacama desert city.

Throughout Chile, there are clubs that focus on conventional folkloric entertainment

Spirited performance of Chile's national dance, the *cueca*

such as the *cueca*, a music and dance form that mimics the courtship of the rooster and hen. Particularly popular during the mid-September patriotic holidays *(see pp32–3)*, the *cueca* is the traditional face of Chilean folkloric music, and may have African as well as Spanish influences.

Despite its Argentine origins, tango has earned a niche in many urban areas, and is particularly popular in Santiago, Valparaíso, and Coquimbo. The country's best-known tango venue in the Confitería Torres *(see p80)*, a gastronomic and cultural center in Santiago.

CLASSICAL MUSIC

Having produced musical prodigies such as the pianist Claudio Arrau and the opera tenor Tito Beltrán, Chile has a small but significant classical music and dance community, centered mainly on the capital. Opera and classical music concerts take place at Santiago's Teatro Municipal and Teatro Universidad de Chile *(see p101)*. Many touring companies from Europe and North America play at these venues.

CONTEMPORARY MUSIC

Chile's pop and rock scene has a lower international profile than its folk tradition, but rock bands such as Los Tres, La Ley, and Lucybell have gained some attention in Latin America. The best place for live music is Santiago *(see pp98–9)*. Chile has one singular pop music event that makes headlines in the Spanish-speaking world – Viña del Mar's **Festival de la Canción** in February brings together international acts such as Carlos Santana, Ricky Martin, Marc Anthony, and Tom Jones.

THEATER AND FILM

Chile has an active theater community, with many major venues and dozens of small theater companies. Among the contemporary playwrights of note are Ariel Dorfman, who writes in both English and Spanish, and Marco Antonio de la Parra. Roberto Parra's *La Negra Ester*, about a prostitute in San Antonio, is the nation's most frequently produced contemporary play.

Tango at a club in Santiago

Major venues include the **Teatro Nacional de Chileno** and Universidad de Chile's **Sala Agustín Sire**, but these, and more intimate locales such as the Teatro La Comedia *(see p101)*, are for Spanish speakers.

Film directors have made an impact beyond national borders in recent years, but most cinema halls show foreign films, primarily Hollywood fare. Most of these flicks are subtitled, but animated films are invariably dubbed. Chain multiplexes include **Cine Hoyts** and **Cinemark**, but there are also repertory houses such as the **Cine Arte Biógrafo** and the **Cine Arte Normandie**.

DIRECTORY

PRACTICAL INFORMATION

Feria Ticket
Tel *(02) 5928500.*
www.feriaticket.cl

Punto Ticket
Avenida Marathon 5300, Macul, Santiago. ***Tel*** *(02) 4645557.*
www.puntoticket.com

SPECTATOR SPORTS

Colo Colo
Avenida Marathon 5300, Macul, Santiago. ***Tel*** *(02) 4602600.*
www.colocolo.cl

Universidad de Chile
Tel *(02) 8999949.*
www.udechile.cl

Valparaíso Sporting Club
Avenida Los Castaños 404, Viña del Mar. ***Tel*** *(032) 2655600.*
www.sporting.cl

CONTEMPORARY MUSIC

Festival de la Canción
www.canal13.cl

THEATER AND FILM

Cine Arte Biógrafo
Lastarria 181, Santiago.
Tel *(02) 6334435.*

Cine Arte Normandie
Tarapacá 1181, Santiago.
Tel *(02) 6972979.*
www.normandie.cl

Cine Hoyts
Huérfanos 735, Santiago.
Tel *(02) 6322539.*
www.cinehoyts.cl

Cinemark
Avenida Kennedy 9001, Local 3092, Las Condes, Santiago.
Tel *(02) 5801420.*
www.cinemark.cl

Sala Agustín Sire
Morandé 750, Santiago.
Tel *(02) 6965142.*
www.agustinsire.uchile.cl

Teatro Nacional de Chileno
Morandé 25, Santiago.
Tel *(02) 6961200.*
www.tnch.uchile.cl

OUTDOOR ACTIVITIES AND SPECIALIZED HOLIDAYS

With a splendid geographical diversity, ranging from the tropics to sub-Antarctica and from the Pacific shoreline to the highest Andean summits, Chile has outdoor activities to cater to every interest. The numerous national parks offer hiking, climbing, nature-watching, and horse riding, and, in winter, the southern hemisphere's top skiing. Watersports are also popular, with rafting and kayaking on some of the world's wildest rivers, trout fishing in the gentler streams, and year-round surfing along the coastline. For the less sporty, the Atacama desert boasts some of the continent's best-preserved archaeological sites, and its clear skies offer glimpses of constellations and planets that are invisible elsewhere on Earth. Finally, there are a number of hot springs and spas, and tours of world-class vineyards which offer great wines and gourmet cuisines.

Horse and rider, Club Hipíco

Hikers in the Torres del Paine National Park, Southern Patagonia

HIKING

Fine wild hiking can be had along the length of the Andes and the coastal mountain range, while Torres del Paine National Park in Southern Patagonia is regarded by many to be the international gold standard for this pursuit. In most areas, good hiking trails are no more than half an hour away, and the Sendero de Chile will, upon its completion in 2040, be a pedestrian, bicycle, and horseback trail that runs the length of the country.

Apart from Torres del Paine, the most popular bases for hiking are the towns of Pucón and Puerto Varas in the Lake District. There is also plenty of good hiking an hour from downtown Santiago, in the Cajón del Maipo. Also south of Santiago, the mountains east of the city of Talca offer lesser-known, but excellent trekking opportunities. The backcountry of Reserva Nacional Cerro Castillo, south of the Northern Patagonian city of Coyhaique, is gaining popularity among distance trekkers, but still gets just a fraction of those going to Torres del Paine.

Talca-based **Trekking Chile** not only provides accommodations and information on its immediate surroundings, but also covers destinations throughout the country. Santiago's **Cascada Expediciones** operates an eco-camp as the base for its multi-night treks in and around Torres del Paine. Based outside the city of Cochrane in Northern Patagonia, the US-operated **Patagonia Adventure Expeditions** specializes in the Aisén Glacier Trail, to which it has exclusive rights.

CLIMBING

Chile offers climbing for both novice and experienced climbers. Casual visitors might undertake recreational climbing along with several other outdoor activities. The ascent of Volcán Villarrica, just outside of Pucón in the Lake District, is a day trip that almost anybody in good physical condition can handle, although usually with a guide. Recreational climbing is also possible on Volcán Osorno outside Puerto Varas, but can require an overnight stay. Usually with these excursions, the view is the prime purpose of the climb. Among the tour operators who can help recreational

Climbing the snowbound Volcán Villarrica

climbers are **Sol y Nieve Expediciones**, based in Pucón, and **Alsur Expeditions**, based in Puerto Varas.

For technical climbers, there are more difficult routes up peaks such as Osorno and Villarrica, but there are also other climbs that are challenging in terms of sheer altitude, such as the 22,609-ft (6,893-m) high Volcán Ojos del Salado in the desert north. Among climbs rated for their technical difficulties are the steep granite faces of Torres del Paine in Southern Patagonia. **Antares Patagonia Adventure** in Puerto Natales and **Azimut 360** in Santiago can arrange more challenging climbs and provide logistic support.

BIRD-WATCHING

Chile's diverse ecosystems are home to a variety of birdlife and, for first-time visitors, almost everything is a novelty. Guides are provided by professional enterprises such as the **Birding Alto Andino**, based in Putre, which covers the whole northern region but specializes in bird-rich Parque Nacional Lauca. **Hualamo Birding and Natural History Tours** provide packages for central Chile, from the ocean to the Andes, and the Lake District. In Punta Arenas, **Natura Patagonia** operates in the Strait of Magellan, Tierra del Fuego, and the Patagonian steppe.

HORSE RIDING

The riding tradition is strong throughout Chile, and two comfortable lodges, both founded by Germans but with substantial Chilean input, specialize in providing backcountry trips. In the high desert, east of Ovalle city, Hacienda Los Andes *(see p184)* is a Colonial-style lodge that offers guided horse-riding trips across the Andes. East of Puerto Varas, **Campo Aventura** provides rides into rugged terrain surrounded by dense Valdivian rain forest. The Mapuche-Austrian operator **Kila Leufú** organizes day trips and longer rides near Pucón in the Lake District.

Cyclists on the Carretera Austral, stretching across Patagonia

CYCLING AND MOUNTAIN-BIKING

Chile is suitable for both local and long-distance cycling and mountain-biking. Most cities and resorts, from the Atacama to the Lake District and beyond, offer rental bikes at reasonable rates. The best destinations are San Pedro de Atacama, Pucón, and Puerto Varas, but given the progress of the Sendero de Chile, the path that is due to cover the length of the country, cycling is possible almost everywhere.

Long-distance cyclists often use the famous Pan-American Highway or Ruta 5 to travel from Alaska to Tierra del Fuego, but in the Lake District, there are many loop rides that avoid the busy highway. The Carretera Austral is another iconic route for travelers through Patagonia. For those who prefer logistic support, California-based **Backroads** organizes cycling trips through this part of Chile and certain areas of Argentina.

DRIVING HOLIDAYS

As most seasoned visitors to Chile know, the Carretera Austral is best enjoyed on a driving tour. Spectacularly scenic, this highway is a discontinuous route that starts in Puerto Montt and, with numerous ferry connections, ends just beyond Villa O'Higgins. The segment from Chaitén north to Parque Pumalín has been closed since the eruption of Volcán Chaitén, and is currently under renovation. The easiest way to explore Carretera Austral is to rent a car in Coyhaique and travel either north or south. The road is mostly gravel, but there are paved segments in both directions from Coyhaique and in the vicinity of Chaitén; 4WDs are rarely necessary.

Also ideal for automobile touring is the Lake District, from Temuco south to Puerto Montt and Chiloé, especially on trunk roads away from the four-lane Pan-American Highway. The bulk of these roads are paved, but there is the occasional gravel route.

While driving in the Atacama desert allows visitors access to remote areas, it can mean great distances and, when moving off the main roads, slow speeds. Operating out of Santiago, **Pachamama by Bus** offers van services north to San Pedro de Atacama and south to Puerto Varas and Puerto Montt. These hop-on, hop-off services operate with a minimum of just one passenger, stop at notable sights en route, and allow travelers to re-board at their convenience, with no time limit.

Horse riding over the slopes near Playa El Faro, La Serena

SKIING AND SNOWBOARDING

Chile is one of the few places where skiers and snowboarders can hit the slopes between July and September. The traditional choice for most is Ski Portillo *(see p134)*, near the Argentine border, but there is splendid skiing near Santiago, at resorts such as El Colorado and Valle Nevado *(see p140)*. Farther south, Nevados de Chillán *(see p152)* is the best choice, but there are good opportunities at Volcán Villarrica *(see p198)*, Volcán Osorno *(see p210)*, and Parque Nacional Puyehue's Centro de Ski Antillanca *(see p204)*. Santiago's **Skitotal** arranges day trips to resorts near the capital. The US-run **PowderQuest Ski Tours** offers tours to the top areas in both Chile and Argentina.

WHITE-WATER RAFTING

The steep-gradient transverse rivers of Chile offer runnable white-water barely an hour from downtown Santiago and well into Patagonia. The most popular destinations for river running are Río Trancura near Pucón, Río Petrohué near Puerto Varas, and the rivers of Cajón del Maipo. However, the gold standard is northern Patagonia's Río Futaleufú, one of the world's top-ten white-water experiences.

Day trips are organized by operators such as Santiago's Cascada Expediciones, which is also ideal for hikes, Pucón's **Politur**, and Puerto Varas' **KoKayak**. Some agents, such as **Expediciones Chile**, **Bío Bío Expeditions**, and **Earth River Expeditions** have comfortable camps along the Futaleufú for week-long programs, but they also do day trips.

White-water rafting on Río Futaleufu

FISHING

Chile attracts trout fishermen from around the world to its placid lakes and clear rivers, from south of Temuco to Aisén and Tierra del Fuego. **Southern Chile Expeditions** operates fly-fishing lodges such as Yan Kee Way near Puerto Varas and El Patagón in the more remote Aisén region. It is also possible to make arrangements with local operators and guides in towns including Coyhaique in Northern Patagonia and Pucón in the Lake District.

SURFING

With a coastline that runs for thousands of miles and hundreds of long sandy beaches, some of which are hidden in coves among dramatic headlands, Chile has almost limitless surfing potential, except in Patagonia. The most popular stretches for surfers are found along the coast of central Chile, in locales such as Viña del Mar and its suburbs, the vicinity of Pichilemu, and also in and around the northern Chilean cities of Iquique and Arica. While surfing is a year-round activity, the most challenging waves occur in winter, when large swells hit the Pacific coast. The cold Humboldt current makes a wet suit essential for avoiding hypothermia, and some beaches have dangerous rip currents.

A number of local lodges specialize in surfing, including the **Pichilemu Surf Hostal** and **Posada Punta de Lobos**, which offer classes and rental gear. In most areas where surfing is possible, windsurfing is also an alternative.

Underwater exploration off Playa Anakena, Easter Island

SEA KAYAKING

Predictably, given the region's extensive coastline, Chile is a delight for sea kayakers. However, areas facing the open Pacific may be less appealing than the coves and inland sea around the Chiloé archipelago. On the mainland, Northern Patagonia boasts some truly remote coves, access to which may require major logistic support. Santiago's **Altué Sea Kayaking**, based in the Chiloé town of Dalcahue in summer, is the major operator, but another option in the region is Alsur Expeditions, which also offers climbing expeditions.

DIVING

In the cool eastern Pacific Ocean, diving is not the pastime it is in tropical waters such as the Caribbean. However, Easter Island has two diving companies, **Mike Rapu Diving Center** and **Orca Diving Center**.

Cruise ship moored off Punta Arenas in Southern Patagonia

CRUISES

Many large cruise ships round Cape Horn on journeys between Santiago and the Argentine capital, Buenos Aires. Smaller, locally run cruise ships permit frequent, and more interesting, land excursions into remote areas on itineraries of 3 to 5 days. Among the better companies are **Cruceros Australis**, which shuttles back and forth between Punta Arenas and Ushuaia, in Argentine Tierra del Fuego. **Cruceros Marítimos Skorpios** covers some spectacular territory from Puerto Montt and Puerto Chacabuco to Laguna San Rafael, and from Puerto Natales to the fjords of the Campo de Hielo Sur, but the level of service does not compare with that of Cruceros Australis.

WHALE-WATCHING

In Chile, whale-watching is in its infancy and the logistics can be difficult. Nevertheless, there are blue whales in the Golfo de Corcovado, off Chiloé, and, more notably, accessible humpback feeding grounds in the Strait of Magellan. On Isla Carlos III, near the feeding grounds, **Whalesound** operates an island eco-camp, with accommodation in dome tents.

PARAGLIDING

Behind Iquique, the coastal range rises almost vertically, and the offshore westerlies are ideal to carry paragliders off the escarpment. Here, the local government has dedicated a takeoff site to encourage paragliding. Local operators take visitors on tandem flights that offer bird's-eye views of the city and its astounding dunes, before landing on sandy beaches. Experienced paragliders can occasionally ride the breezes as far as Tocopilla, 162 miles (260 km) to the south. The **Escuela de Parapente Altazor** helps paragliders get started and also provides accommodation for its clientele.

GOLF

Golf is not the phenomenon it is in neighboring Argentina, and Chilean courses are invariably private and clubby – it usually takes a member's invitation to get in. However, some hotels arrange passes for their guests and the coastal **Marbella Resort**, at Maitencillo north of Viña del Mar, has its own course open to guests.

ASTRONOMY

The skies of the southern hemisphere so differ from those of the north that several major international observatories have placed state-of-the-art astronomical facilities in Chile, such as the advanced Cerro Paranal Observatory *(see p177)*. The easiest to visit are **Cerro Tololo Inter-American Observatory**, near La Serena, and **La Silla Paranal Observatory**, near Santiago. Smaller municipal observatories include the Cerro Mamalluca Observatory *(see p182)*. Near San Pedro de Atacama, Frenchman Alain Maury's private **San Pedro de Atacama Celestial Explorations** is very informative.

Cerro Mamalluca Observatory in the arid Valle de Elqui, Vicuña

View from Casa Lapostolles at the Clos Apalta winery, Lake District

ARCHAEOLOGY

The nearly perfect aridity of the Atacama desert, preserving ruins and artifacts over millennia, has made northern Chile a mecca for archaeological research. The most priceless and conspicous relics of the region are the enormous hillside geoglyphs, linked geographically and historically to the Andean highlands. In addition, pre-Columbian fortresses and villages still survive throughout the desert, and Arica's Chinchorro mummies *(see p161)* are a landmark discovery. Evidence of historical archaeology, which is concerned with ancient societies that used writing, can be seen in ghost towns of the Atacama, such as Santa Laura and Humberstone *(see p168)*.

Far Horizons Archaeological and Cultural Trips, based in California, offers excursions to the Atacama, but its specialty is in trips to Easter Island; its guides are globally known scholars on the island's enigmatic past.

The country's most notable archaeological site is Monte Verde, located near Puerto Montt in Lake District. Dating from 13,000 BC, this site offers evidence of the earliest human settlement in the Americas. Around 12 miles (18 km) south of downtown Santiago, in the basin of the Río Maipo, is the location of the Cerro Chena site, where ruins of an Incan fortress have been excavated.

SPAS AND HOT SPRINGS

As part of the Pacific Ring of Fire, Chile's numerous active volcanoes also mean abundant geysers and hot springs, especially, but not solely, southward of Santiago. Many of the sites are open for day trips, notably Termas Geométricas near Pucón, but others are full-scale hotels with spa facilities. The best known are the all-inclusive Termas de Puyehue *(see p205)* and Northern Patagonia's Puyuhuapi Lodge & Spa *(see p228)*. Both offer day passes as well.

WINE AND FOOD

Chile has numerous wine routes, significantly through the Colchagua and Casablanca valleys, that offer not just wine but also fine cuisine and, in some cases, accommodation. The Ruta del Vino *(see p148)* offers the most complete services, and individual members such as **Viña Casa Silva** and the Casablanca valley's **Viña Matetic** combine wine and gourmet food with elite lodging. **Santiago Adventures** arranges trips to these wineries and to the scenic but lesser-known Aconcagua valley.

TOUR OPERATORS

Many international operators offer tours focusing on different kinds of outdoor activities and specialist interests. **LAN Vacations** is the tour branch of Chile's flagship airline, while US-based **Wildland Adventures** is highly regarded for its Patagonian trips. In the UK, **Journey Latin America** specializes in the region, while **Muir's Tours** is a reliable fair-trade operator for Torres del Paine.

The hot-spring resort Termas de Puyehue, near Parque Nacional Puyehue

DIRECTORY

HIKING

Cascada Expediciones
Las Condes, Santiago.
Tel (02) 2329878.
www.cascada.travel

Patagonia Adventure Expeditions
Cochrane.
Tel (067) 411330.
www.adventure patagonia.com

Trekking Chile
Talca. *Tel (071) 1970096.*
www.trekkingchile.com

CLIMBING

Alsur Expeditions
Puerto Varas. *Tel (065) 232300.* **www**. alsurexpeditions.com

Antares Patagonia Adventure
Puerto Natales.
Tel (061) 414611.
www.antarespatagonia. travel

Azimut 360
General Salvo 159, Providencia, Santiago.
Tel (02) 2351519.
www.azimut360.com

Sol y Nieve Expediciones
Lincoyan 361, Pucón.
Tel (045) 444761. **www**. solynievepucon.com

BIRD-WATCHING

Birding Alto Andino
Putre. *Tel (09) 98907291.*
www.birdingaltoandino. com

Hualamo Birding and Natural History Tours
www.hualamo.cl

Natura Patagonia
www.naturapatagonia.cl

HORSE RIDING

Campo Aventura
San Bernardo 318, Puerto Varas.
Tel (065) 232910. **www**. campo-aventura.com

Kila Leufú
Tel (09) 8764576.
www.kilaleufu.cl

CYCLING AND MOUNTAIN-BIKING

Backroads
Tel (800) 4622848 (USA).
www.backroads.com

DRIVING HOLIDAYS

Pachamama by Bus
Agustinas 2113, Santiago.
Tel (02) 6888018. **www**. pachamamabybus.com

SKIING AND SNOWBOARDING

PowderQuest Ski Tours
Tel (888) 5657158 (USA).
www.powderquest.com

Skitotal
Las Condes. *Tel (02) 246 0156.* **www**.skitotal.cl

WHITE-WATER RAFTING

Bío Bío Expeditions
Tel (800) 2467238 (USA).
www.bbxrafting.com

Earth River Expeditions
Tel (800) 6432784 (USA).
www.earthriver.com

Expediciones Chile
Tel (888) 4889082 (USA).
www.exchile.com

KoKayak
Puerto Varas.
Tel (09) 93105272.
www.kokayak.com

Politur
Pucón. *Tel (045) 441373.*
www.politur.com

FISHING

Southern Chile Expeditions
Tel (866) 8819215 (USA).
www.southernchilexp. com

SURFING

Pichilemu Surf Hostal
Tel (072) 842350. **www**. pichilemusurfhostal.com

Posada Punta de Lobos
Tel (09) 76092846.
www.posadapunta delobos.cl

SEA KAYAKING

Altué Sea Kayaking
Dalcahue. *Tel (09) 9419 6809.* **www**.seakayak chile.com

DIVING

Mike Rapu Diving Center
Hanga Roa. *Tel (032) 255 1055.* **www**.mikerapu.cl

Orca Diving Center
Hanga Roa. *Tel (032) 255 0375.* **www**.seemorca.cl

CRUISES

Cruceros Australis
Santiago. *Tel (02) 4423 115.* **www**.australis.com

Cruceros Marítimos Skorpios
Santiago. *Tel (02) 4771 900.* **www**.skorpios.cl

WHALE-WATCHING

Whalesound
Punta Arenas.
Tel (061) 710511.
www.whalesound.com

PARAGLIDING

Escuela de Parapente Altazor
Iquique. *Tel (057) 380110.* **www**.altazor.cl

GOLF

Marbella Resort
Km 35, Camino Concón Zapallar. *Tel (032) 2772 020.* **www**.marbella.cl

ASTRONOMY

Cerro Tololo Inter-American Observatory
La Serena. *Tel (051) 205 200.* **www**.ctio.noao.edu

La Silla Paranal Observatory
Ave. Alonso de Córdova 3107, Vitacura, Santiago.
Tel (055) 435001.
www.eso.org/paranal

San Pedro de Atacama Celestial Explorations
San Pedro de Atacama.
Tel (055) 851935.
www.spaceobs.com

ARCHAEOLOGY

Far Horizons Archaeological and Cultural Trips
Tel (800) 5524575 (USA).
www.farhorizons.com

WINE AND FOOD

Santiago Adventures
Guardia Vieja 255, Oficina 406, Providencia, Santiago. *Tel (02) 244 2750; (802) 9046798* (USA). **www**.santiago adventures.com

Viña Casa Silva
Hijuela Norte s/n, San Fernando. *Tel (072) 710 180.* **www**.casasilva.cl

Viña Matetic
Fundo Rosario, Lagunillas, Casablanca. *Tel (02) 232 3134.* **www**.matetic.cl

TOURS OPERATORS

Journey Latin America
12/13 Heathfield Terrace, London W4 2JU. *Tel (020) 87473108* (UK). **www**. journeylatinamerica.co.uk

LAN Vacations
Tel (877) 2190345 (USA).
www.lanvacations.com

Muir's Tours
97-A Swansea Road, Reading RG1 8HA.
Tel (0119) 9502281 (UK).
www.nkf-mt.org.uk

Wildland Adventures
3516 NE 155th Street, Seattle, WA 98155.
Tel (800) 3454453 (USA).
www.journeylatin america.co.uk

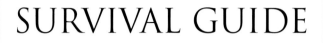

SURVIVAL GUIDE

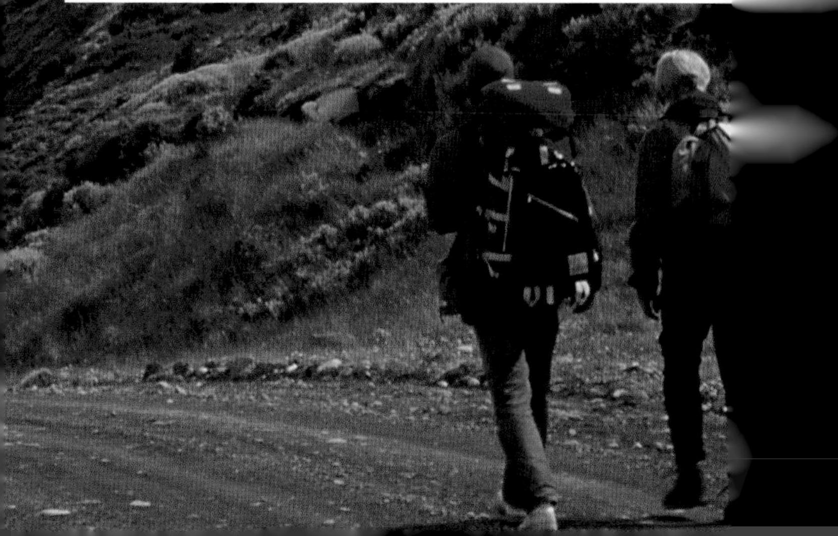

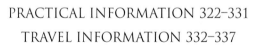

PRACTICAL INFORMATION

Logo of Sernatur

Chile's modern infrastructure is one of the best among Latin American countries, and compares well with that of most developed nations. Santiago, for instance, boasts hi-tech highways and an immaculate metro system. Telephone services, for both landlines and mobile phones, are excellent, and Internet connections are abundant. All the important tourist destinations are well equipped to receive international visitors, however facilities may be limited in remote rural areas. Chileans in general are polite and helpful, and the police are professional – to be consulted and trusted rather than feared or bribed. National tourist offices, usually with English-speaking personnel, are found in every regional capital and many other cities and towns, sometimes complemented by municipal offices. Off the main roads, however, it can be hard to find an English speaker, except in popular tourist destinations.

Skiing, a popular winter activity at the Andean resorts in Chile

WHEN TO GO

Since Chile extends from the subtropical deserts of Atacama to the sub-Antarctic icefields of Patagonia, the country offers recreation for every season. Spring and autumn *(see pp34–7)* are usually pleasant, with prices and crowds reaching their peak in January–February.

VISAS AND PASSPORTS

Citizens of most countries, including Australia, Canada, the USA, and members of the EU do not need visas to enter Chile. However, citizens of countries that require Chileans to obtain visas must pay "reciprocity fees" equivalent to the cost of those visas – Mexicans pay US$23, Australians US$90, Canadians US$159, and US citizens US$131. These fees, valid for the life of the passport, are collected only at Santiago's international airport. Passports should be valid for at least six months. On arrival, visitors receive a tourist card, valid for 90 days, which can be extended for another 90 days for roughly US$100.

CUSTOMS INFORMATION

Visitors may bring personal effects such as clothing, jewelry, and medicine, as well as personal computers and cameras, without paying duty. They may also bring 17 oz (500 g) of tobacco, 6 pints (3 liters) of spirits (for adults over 18), and small amounts of perfume. However, import of fresh fruit or other agricultural products is not allowed. The northernmost desert cities of Iquique and Arica, along with the southernmost region of Magallanes, have duty-free zones; travelers from these regions may experience internal customs checks.

EMBASSIES

Consulates of most nations, including **Canada**, the **USA**, and the **UK** are located in Santiago. Queries about visas and other formalities can be addressed to these centers, although much of this information is available on their official websites.

TOURIST INFORMATION

Sernatur, the national tourism service, has offices at international airports, in Santiago and every regional capital, and in most tourist cities. Most towns have municipal tourist offices. Hostels and hotels also provide good information.

CONAF is the governing body for all national parks, reserves, and other sanctuaries in Chile, and offers information about them.

Tourist information center in Castro's Plaza de Armas, Chiloé

◁ **Backpackers in Torres del Paine National Park, Southern Patagonia**

Travelers aboard a tour boat to the Glaciar Gray in Southern Patagonia

WHAT TO WEAR

Chile is mostly a temperate mid-latitude country, and seasonally appropriate clothing – light summer clothes, with a raincoat for the wetter areas, and warm clothes for winter – should be suitable for most purposes. Nights at high altitudes in the Atacama and the Andes can turn very cold, so winter clothing becomes necessary in all seasons.

OPENING HOURS AND ADMISSION CHARGES

Museums can charge upto US$30 for entry, but many public museums have one free day per week – usually Wednesday. Private facilities, however, can be expensive. Museum hours vary daily and seasonally, but many are closed on Mondays.

National parks are open year-round, but a few limit access to daylight hours. Most charge upto US$8 for admission, and the most popular charge differential admission for foreigners.

LANGUAGE

Spanish is Chile's official language, but the local variant, which omits final and even some internal consonants can cause problems for those who have learned the language elsewhere. Many Chileans in the tourism industry speak English, but in areas off the main highways, a working knowledge of Spanish is useful. The indigenous groups, mainly Mapuche but also Aymara and some smaller groups, have their own languages, but almost all of them speak Spanish as well.

STREET NAMES AND ADDRESSES

As in most Latin American countries, street names and addresses differ from those in English-speaking nations. The main difference is that the street name goes before the number. Most Chilean street names are not abbreviated, and while Calle is usually omitted from street addresses, Avenida and others are not.

The Chilean custom of double surname, in which an individual's father's name comes first and the mother's name second, is also applicable to road names. In Santiago, for example, Avenida Vicuña Mackenna is not the same as Mackenna (another street), and this can be problematic when asking for directions.

RELIGION AND SOCIAL ETIQUETTE

Historically, Chile is a Roman Catholic country and the Church is still influential here. However, its inability to attract priests has created a vacuum in which evangelical Protestantism is growing. The indigenous peoples, especially the Mapuche and Aymara, have their own religious traditions, but many are Catholic or evangelicals. Although Chilean society is not particularly conservative about dressing, visitors are advised to dress modestly when visiting religious venues.

Chileans value courtesy and are polite in their public behavior. When addressing a stranger, the formal titles *señor* (sir or mister), *señora* (madam), or *señorita* (miss) are used. The correct greetings are *buenos días* (good morning), *buenas tardes* (good afternoon), or *buenas noches* (good evening). Nudist beaches, though not rare, are restricted to a few areas along the central coast.

WOMEN TRAVELERS

Despite electing a female president in 2006, Chile is not entirely free of sexism. The likeliest hassle is the verbal *piropo* (unsolicited comments), which can range from the relatively innocuous to the truly vulgar – even for those who do not understand the language, the tone is usually clear. The best tactic is to ignore the offender or seek refuge in a public place such as a hotel or a café. It is best to avoid walking alone at night; if it becomes necessary, or if stranded, it is advisable to call for a radio taxi.

TRAVELING WITH CHILDREN

Chile is a child-friendly nation. Parents traveling with small children are not required to pay their bus fares unless the children occupy a separate seat. Nor do they pay for their children's stay in hotels. However, families of four or more persons should look at *cabaña* accommodations, which can be cheaper than hotels on a per person basis.

Locals and visitors thronging the Plaza José Francisco Vergara, Viña del Mar

SENIOR CITIZENS

In Chile, senior citizens can anticipate a great deal of respect and, when they need it, assistance. However, reduced admission charges enjoyed by Chilean seniors do not apply to foreign visitors.

GAY AND LESBIAN TRAVELERS

Historically, Chile is a socially conservative country and public homosexuality is frowned upon. Since the end of the Pinochet dictatorship, however, many Chilean gays have come out of the closet, and Santiago celebrates a gay pride parade in late September. There is an active gay nightlife scene in the capital's Barrio Bellavista, and in beach resorts such as Viña del Mar.

DISABLED TRAVELERS

Chile can be challenging for wheelchair-bound travelers, as narrow sidewalks, rough surfaces, and the lack of ramps can make most cities difficult to negotiate. However, many newer hotels have constructed rooms with wheelchairs in mind and others have retrofitted them. In the countryside, especially in the backcountry, wheelchair access is limited.

STUDENT INFORMATION

Many North American and European students spend a semester abroad in Chile through their home universities, with the main destinations being Santiago, Valparaíso, and Concepción. A student visa, obtained through a Chilean consulate in the home country, is required for such trips. Many visitors also take advantage of their stay to study Spanish. Santiago has a great number of quality language schools, although Valparaíso and resort-towns such as Pucón also offer courses. Courses are usually on a weekly or monthly basis, and may include homestays with Chilean families. No special visa is required for this.

Waiter attending to guests at Valparaíso's Café Turri

TIPPING

In formal restaurants – that is, those with table service and a printed menu – a 10 percent tip is usual, but many Chileans fail to observe the custom. When paying by credit card, guests can choose to either pay the tip in cash or fill in the appropriate amount in the tip box on the card statement. Taxi drivers do not expect tips unless they have provided some extra service, such as hauling luggage. A small tip is proper for a gas station attendant who cleans the windshield.

SMOKING

Many Chileans are heavy smokers, but they almost always observe the prohibition on smoking in public transportation, the workplace, and other restricted areas. The government has placed some of the grisliest possible health warnings on tobacco packaging. Nevertheless, the nationwide tobacco law is mild: while it prohibits smoking in any place frequented by minors (under 18 years of age), it does not require restaurants and bars to set aside non-smoking areas. Despite this, many restaurants have chosen to be completely tobacco-free and others have set up smoke-free sections.

Universidad de Chile, one of many centers in Santiago offering Spanish classes to overseas students

PUBLIC TOILETS

Sanitation standards are higher in Chile than in tropical Latin American countries and, in general, public toilets are safe to use. At bus stations and service stations, for instance, there is almost always a caretaker who keeps the facilities clean. However, travelers will need to pay a small charge for their use and to purchase toilet paper. Many service stations also offer shower facilities, which are used primarily by truckers, but are also open to the public at large.

MEASUREMENTS

The metric system is official and universal in Chile except for a few vernacular measures and oddities such as tire pressure, which is measured in pounds per sq inch, and airport elevation, which is measured in feet. To convert degrees Celsius to degrees Farenheit, multiply by 1.8 and add 32.

Imperial to Metric
1 inch = 2.5 centimeters
1 foot = 30 centimeters
1 mile = 1.6 kilometers
1 ounce = 28 grams
1 pound = 454 grams
1 US pint = 0.473 liter
1 US quart = 0.947 liter
1 US gallon = 3.78 liters

Metric to Imperial
1 centimeter = 0.4 inch
1 meter = 3 feet 3 inches
1 kilometer = 0.6 mile
1 gram = 0.04 ounce
1 kilogram = 2.2 pounds
1 liter = 2.1 US pints
1°C = 33.8°F

ELECTRICITY

Chile's electric system operates on 220 volts, 50 cycles, similar to the European and UK systems, but travelers from North America may need converters. However, appliances such as laptop computers and cell phones operate on both 220- and 100-volt systems. Most plugs take two rounded prongs, and adapters are necessary. A surge protector is a wise investment.

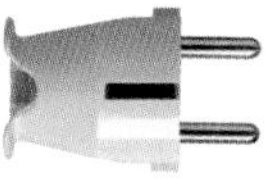

Twin-pronged electric plug

TIME

Chile is four hours behind Greenwich Mean Time (GMT) and one hour ahead of New York's Eastern Standard Time (EST). In summer, however, daylight savings sets the clock ahead another hour – the date for this varies from year to year, but it usually runs from December to March. This means that in the northernmost tropical latitudes, near the Peruvian border, sunrise does not come until after 8am for much of the summer. Easter Island is two hours behind the continent.

RESPONSIBLE TOURISM

Although some of Chile's valuable forest trees have received official protection for many decades, public awareness of broad environmental issues has developed only relatively recently. Chile lacks major energy resources except for hydroelectricity, which makes its wild and scenic areas vulnerable to massive dam projects. From Santiago north, the country has serious water deficits, in spite of which some Atacama hotels have multiple water-guzzling swimming pools. Owing to Chile's fossil fuel shortage, many cost-conscious operators have made efforts to reduce their energy consumption, and the newer hotels in particular have state-of-the-art facilities that help reduce their carbon footprint *(see p337)*.

Developments in locally based ethnotourism have been slower to catch on, but the Kunza communities of San Pedro de Atacama are gaining control over access to Geisers de Tatio, and the Aymara residents of Parque Nacional Lauca now operate accommodations and serve as guides within the park. In the south, Mapuche-run tourism businesses include farmstays. In the desert north and Patagonia, distances are great and, in some areas, public transport is limited. Here, many mountain lodges operate their own excursions, which can be a more efficient option to private car rentals.

While Chile's marine resources are diverse and delectable, certain species such as Chilean sea bass and locos have suffered overexploitation. In particular, the farming of salmon in Lake District and Patagonia, has drawn criticism for overuse of chemicals that contaminate the waterways and oceans.

The eco-lodge Casona Distante in Valle del Elqui, Norte Chico

DIRECTORY

EMBASSIES

Canada
Nueva Tajamar 481, 12th floor, Las Condes, Santiago.
Tel *(02) 3629660.*
www.canadainternational.gc.ca

UK
Avenida El Bosque Norte 0125, 3rd floor, Las Condes, Santiago.
Tel *(02) 3704100.*
www.britemb.cl

USA
Avenida Andrés Bello 2800, Las Condes, Santiago.
Tel *(02) 2322600.*
http://chile.usembassy.gov

TOURIST INFORMATION

CONAF
Avenida Bulnes 285, Santiago.
Tel *(02) 6630000.*
www.conaf.cl

Sernatur
Avenida Providencia 1550, Providencia, Santiago. ***Tel*** *(02) 7318300.* **www**.sernatur.cl

Personal Security and Health

Tsunami evacuation route sign in Chile

By international standards, Chile is a safe country for visitors who take routine precautions. Incidents of crime directed at tourists are few, but in any event, it is best to avoid displaying conspicuous valuables. Chilean medical care is among the continent's best, especially in Santiago, and there are few serious health hazards – Chile has no poisonous snakes or malaria, and no vaccinations are needed for entering Chile. Altitude sickness can be an issue, and, in the far south, polar ozone depletion makes sunburn a serious matter requiring protective measures.

A green-and-white police car at the coastal resort of Viña del Mar

POLICE

Latin American police have a reputation for corruption, and often for much worse, but the **Carabineros de Chile** – identified by their sharp khaki- and-green uniforms and pentagonal badges – are the exception to the rule. Generally considered firm but fair, the carabineros are rarely implicated in any sort of misdeed, and travelers should never attempt to bribe them. Their behavior toward foreign visitors borders on the deferential and tourists need feel no hesitation in approaching the carabineros for directions or other form of assistance. That said, few street patrolmen speak English, especially outside the larger cities, and they may need to call in someone from the precinct office in case of an emergency.

GENERAL PRECAUTIONS

Crimes directed at tourists are few, and most of those are crimes of opportunity such as pickpocketing and purse snatchings. Visitors must therefore be aware of their surroundings and, in urban areas, avoid poorly lighted areas where people are few.

Armed assaults on anyone, and particularly on foreign visitors, are unusual. As a general precaution, however, it is best to avoid traveling with or displaying expensive personal items that might attract unwanted attention. Valuables can be secured in the electronic safes provided at most mid-range and upscale hotels; any cash that needs to be carried on a journey is best kept in a money belt or leg pouch. Those who are traveling by car need to park in secure lots at night, and avoid leaving visible valuables in their vehicles.

Carabinero in khaki uniform

LOST AND STOLEN PROPERTY

While the odds of recovering lost or stolen property are low unless it is reported immediately, the carabineros will generally do their best to provide assistance. They should be asked to take a *denuncia* (a report necessary for insurance claims) that includes a *narración de los hechos* (account of the incident) and a *declaración jurada de pre-existencia de especies sustraídas* (declaration of losses). Visitors must report lost passports to their embassy or consulate *(see p325)*, which will issue a replacement. Lost credit cards shold be reported to the issuing bank *(see p328)*.

HEALTH PRECAUTIONS

Chile is a country with high public health standards. Tap water is potable almost everywhere and, other than common diseases such as cold and flu, there is little to fear. Even the 2009 swine flu breakout has had little impact. There have been cases of Chagas' disease, dengue, and hantavirus, but instances of tourists developing these infections are few. Chile requires no vaccinations for entry, though visitors from the tropics may be asked for a yellow fever certificate.

ALTITUDE SICKNESS

Chile's northern and central Andes encompass some of the highest altitudes in the western hemisphere, with areas such as the altiplano in Parque Nacional Lauca

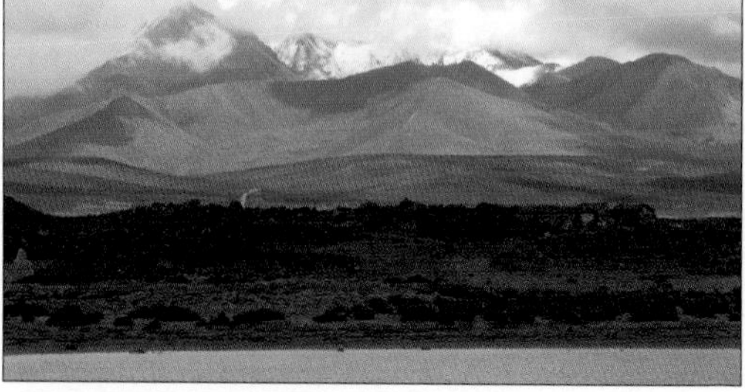

High-altitude tablelands of Parque Nacional Lauca

Ambulance with phone number emblazoned on the side

reaching elevations of over 14,440 ft (4,400 m). Even the young and healhy are affected in such oxygen-poor environments, and more than one tourist has suffered fatally from acute mountain sickness. When traveling to altitudes above 8,000 ft (2,440 m), it is advisable to spend a night at an intermediate altitude for acclimatization. Symptoms of altitude sickness include headaches, nausea, fatigue, dizziness, and dehydration, and it is best to turn back at the first manifestation of these signs.

NATURAL DISASTERS

Chile is one of the world's most seismically active countries, with frequent earthquakes and many active volcanoes. Hotels across the nation have evacuation plans that guests need to be familiar with. Chilean cities and towns such as Pucón and Curacautín maintain volcano warning systems, and most coastal towns have signs indicating evacuation routes in case of tsunamis. Fires can be a hazard in the woodlands of the Central Valley, especially in summer and autumn. There is a nationwide phone number for the **Fire Department**, and another number, monitored by **CONAF**, for forest fires.

EMERGENCIES

In Santiago, in the capitals of every administrative province, and in many smaller cities, public hospitals and clinics are prepared to deal with almost any emergency. There is also a national phone line for **Ambulance** services. Most doctors speak at least some English, but the waiting time can be substantial except for critical cases. Even the smallest villages have emergency clinics that, while they may not have doctors, can deal with intensive care until it is possible to arrange a transfer to a more complete facility.

MEDICAL TREATMENT

In Santiago, the medical care available meets the highest international standards, especially at private hospitals such as **Clinica Las Condes** and **Clinica Alemana de Santiago**. Regional hospitals are also good, but in sparsely populated areas, they can be few and far between. **Hospital Mutual de Seguridad** has branches in several cities.

Public hospitals provide competent basic care, but can be overburdened with patients from the state health system. Health insurance, including a policy for emergency evacuation, is not obligatory, but advisable as Chilean hospital care is not cheap. Most hospitals accept credit card payments, and provide bills for reimbursement.

PHARMACIES

Compared to Europe and the US, Chile has fairly liberal pharmacy laws. A number of medications that would be obtained by prescription elsewhere are available over the counter here, and pharmacists may dispense some of these based on the symptoms described to them. However, medicines are not cheap.

Pharmacies do not have fixed timings. Big pharmacy chains such as Cruz Verde, Ahumada, and Salco Brand keep open for long hours in the cities, but in smaller towns, there may only be a modest public pharmacy for emergencies.

DIRECTORY

POLICE

Carabineros de Chile
Tel 133.

NATURAL DISASTERS

CONAF
Tel 130.

Fire Department
Tel 132.

EMERGENCIES

Ambulance
Tel 131.

MEDICAL TREATMENT

Clinica Alemana de Santiago
Avenida Vitacura 5951, Santiago. ***Tel*** *(02) 2101111.*

Clinica Las Condes
Lo Fontecilla 441, Santiago. ***Tel*** *(02) 2104000.*

Hospital Mutual de Seguridad
www.mutualseg.cl

Outlet of the Cruz Verde pharmacy chain

Banking and Currency

Logo of Chile's BancoEstado

Chile's unit of currency is the peso, but US dollars are accepted in tourist destinations, in hotels, restaurants, and shops. Traveler's checks get a lower rate of exchange than dollars and can be time-consuming to change. Exchange rates are higher in Santiago than elsewhere in Chile. Credit cards are widely accepted, except at very small businesses. In rural Chile, small denomination pesos become necessary. In border areas, merchants may accept Argentine pesos, but the rate of exchange can be unfavorable. There are no restrictions on the import or export of Chilean or foreign currency, but amounts greater than US$10,000 must be declared to Chilean customs.

An armored car with an ATM for public use

BANKS

There are numerous banks in Chilean cities and even in many small towns, where the state-run **BancoEstado** usually has a branch. Opening hours are generally 9am to 2pm, from Monday to Friday only. Bank processes can be slow and bureaucratic, and it is best to visit in the mornings. *Casas de cambio* (foreign exchange bureaus) are more efficient and stay open until 6pm, but may close for lunch. Some also open on Saturday mornings. *Casas de cambio* are abundant in Santiago, but far fewer in other parts of Chile. They will change euros and most other currencies, but the exchange rates will be lower than for US dollars.

ATMS

Chile has perhaps the greatest availability of ATMs, known locally as *cajeros automáticos*, in any Latin American country. They are found at banks, supermarkets, service stations, and many other locales. There are also exchange counters at Santiago's international airport, but better rates are available from ATMs in the lobby. Mobile ATMs are found at summer resorts that may not have their own banks. Visitors with ATM cards from their home country can withdraw up to the peso equivalent of US$300 per day, but cannot withdraw any foreign currencies.

ATMs usually dispense large bills of $10,000, with a couple of $5,000 notes, so obtaining small change can be troublesome. Most Chilean banks, apart from BancoEstado and CorpBanca charge US$3–4 per transaction. Visitors using foreign ATM cards need to check what charges are imposed – some banks collect substantial fees for foreign transactions even at their own overseas ATMs. Others, such as Wells Fargo, are even more expensive. The most inexpensive cards come from credit unions.

CREDIT CARDS AND TRAVELER'S CHECKS

Credit cards are widely used in Chile, in hotels, restaurants, and shops, although the less expensive accommodations and eateries often take only cash. Credit card companies usually deduct a commission on overseas purchases, and it is advisable to check what this is to avoid any surprises. The most widely used cards are **MasterCard**, **Visa**, and **American Express**; other cards are almost unheard of. If a credit card is lost or stolen, the home company or a Chilean affiliate should be contacted, with the card number.

Traveler's checks in US dollars are among the safest ways of carrying money, as they are refundable. When changing traveler's checks, both banks and *casas de cambio* will request identification, preferably a passport. Visitors need to keep the receipt and a record of the serial numbers, in case the checks are lost or stolen.

ELECTRONIC TRANSFER

Western Union arranges electronic transfers to Chile through *casas de cambio*, and through the domestic courier service **Chilexpress**, which has nearly 200 locations throughout the country.

In addition to the usual exchange commission, Western Union collects a substantial charge per transaction. **Thomas Cook** also arranges wire transfers.

TAXES

All price tags include the 19 percent *impuesto de valor agregado* (IVA or VAT), but at most mid-range and upscale hotels, tourists are exempt from this tax if they pay in

DIRECTORY

BANKS

BancoEstado
www.bancoestado.cl

CREDIT CARDS AND TRAVELER'S CHECKS

American Express
Tel (02) 6722156.

MasterCard
Tel (02) 6982465.

VISA
Tel (02) 6982465.

ELECTRONIC TRANSFER

Chilexpress
www.chilexpress.cl

Thomas Cook
www.thomascook.com

US dollars or with a foreign credit card. However, not all hotels participate in this government rebate program, and even otherwise it is not automatic: in some cases, guests must request the hotel to complete a *factura de exportación*, for which they must show their tourist card *(see p322)*. In some cases, restaurant and excursions charges are exempt from IVA for guests who pay through their hotel bills. To avoid confusion, it is best to ask whether hotel rates are *con IVA* (with taxes) or *sin IVA* (without).

CURRENCY

The Chilean peso, the nation's official currency, has a symbol ($) similar to that of the US dollar (US$). There should be no confusion between the two, however, as a single Chilean peso is worth very little. This unit was further divided into 100 centavos, but, since 1984, inflation has rendered the centavo obsolete and these coins are no longer in circulation. For Chile's bicentennial year of 2010, the government plans to introduce $20 and $200 coins, in part to reduce the number of coins needed in transactions and to reduce minting costs.

It is best to carry some small bank notes and coins for minor purchases, particularly for services such as city buses and taxis. This becomes necessary in rural areas, where many businesses do not have large amounts of cash on hand. The custom at most shops is to round up prices to the nearest $10. A thousand pesos is known as one *luca*, a slang term that helps make large amounts of cash more comprehensible.

Coins
Peso coins occur in denominations of $500, $100, $50, $10 and $5. While $1 coins still exist, they are uncommon and almost worthless.

5 pesos

10 pesos

50 pesos

100 pesos

500 pesos

1000 pesos

Bank Notes
Issued in denominations of $1,000; $2,000; $5,000; $10,000; and $20,000, bank notes usually bear portraits of national heroes. In commemoration of the bicentennial of the Republic, new notes will be released between 2009 and 2012, with a different look and dimesions.

2000 pesos

5000 pesos

10,000 pesos

20,000 pesos

Communications and Media

El Mercurio, Chile's popular daily

In Chile, media and communications services are well developed and modern. The telephone is the most versatile means of communication. While public telephones, operated by coins and cards, are still common, mobile phones have become increasingly popular. Internet services are readily available throughout the country, even in remote areas. The mail delivery network is reasonably efficient, but private courier services are a quicker alternative. Chile has innumerable television networks and radio stations. Santiago and other major cities have multiple dailies; however, English-language newspapers and magazines are conspicuous by their absence.

Callers at one of Santiago's public phone booths

TELEPHONES

There is no single national telecommunications agency in Chile. Instead there are several competing companies known as *portadores* or carriers. Of these service providers, **Telefónica CTC** and **Entel** are the largest. Each individual agency has its own public and private telephones, phone cards, and a specific three-digit access code. To make a call from a phone owned by a particular company, you can use the phone card of any other carrier service by dialing its access code. However, no access code needs to be dialed if the card belongs to the same company as the phone. Instructions, in Spanish, are written on each phone card. While an increasing number of public phones accept only fixed-value or rechargeable phone cards, many also accept pesos. The basic rate for a local call is 100 pesos for 5 minutes. Phone cards can be purchased from news kiosks, pharmacies, and most stores, and can be used for local mobile phones as well.

It is easy to make national and international calls from *centros de llamados*, or call centers, found throughout the country. In most cases, users can enter the booth and dial directly, but in some centers, an on-site operator is available to connect the call.

While many hotels have telephones, the cost of making calls through their switchboards can be high. It is possible to make *cobro revertido* (collect or reverse charge) and *tarjeta de crédito* (credit card) calls from public and private telephones, but these can be substantially more expensive than using the *centros de llamados*. It is especially expensive to make overseas collect and credit card calls from the conspicuous bright blue telephones found across the country.

MOBILE PHONES

Cell phones are the most popular means of communication in Chile and have, in fact, exceeded the number of landlines. Cell phone coverage, however, can be weak in thinly populated areas such as the Atacama desert and Patagonia, and in areas of rugged terrain. While most international cellular services also work in Chile, overseas visitors should first check whether their service providers offer coverage in this country. A majority of network operators offer roaming facilities, but this often entails higher outgoing and incoming rates, as well as paying a substantial premium. While quad-band phones (supporting four frequency bands) from abroad continue to work in Chile, tri-band phones (supporting three frequency bands) may have limited coverage. Visitors are advised to keep their network operator's helpline number handy for emergencies and carry the insurance papers of their phone in case of loss or theft. Local SIM cards are easily available and many travelers prefer to either hire or buy a

DIALING CODES

- In Chile, telephone numbers have one- or two-digit area codes and six- or seven-digit local numbers.
- To call Chile from abroad, dial the international access code, followed by Chile's country code (56), the area code, and the local number.
- Cell phone numbers have a prefix of 07, 08, or 09, followed by eight digits. Local calls between cell phones, as well as between landlines within the same area code, do not require dialing a prefix.
- To make a long-distance call, dial the three-digit carrier code (where necessary), followed by the area code and the local number.
- To make an international call, dial the carrier code (where necessary), followed by 0, then the country code, area code, and number.
- For directory inquiries, dial 103.

mobile phone. Cell phones for hire can be found at kiosks of the different telecommunications companies, including the Telefónica CTC and Entel stands at Santiago's Arturo Merino Benítez international airport.

INTERNET, EMAIL, AND FAX FACILITIES

Cybercafés can be found across Chile, and many establishments also offer *banda ancha* (broadband) and wireless Internet access. Santiago's international airport has several Internet kiosks that charge by the minute. Most hotels and hostels include Wi-Fi in their rates. High-end international chain hotels may charge extra for Internet access, but their Chilean counterparts generally do not. A number of *centros de llamados* offer internet access at reasonable rates, usually by the hour. Fax services are available across Chile via the various telephone agencies and can be found at many call centers.

NEWSPAPERS AND MAGAZINES

There are 27 national and 206 regional newspapers in Chile. While *El Mercurio* *(see p122)* is the country's major daily newspaper, it offers limited coverage of international news. *La Tercera*, a tabloid daily, provides some competition, but the publishing

Magazines for sale at a kiosk in Valparaíso

Entrance to a *centro de llamados* in Valparaíso

phenomenon of the new millennium is *The Clinic*, a satirical weekly. *Estrategia* is the voice of Chile's business and financial community. Santiago lacks an English-language newspaper, but the online *Santiago Times* provides translations from the Chilean press and does some limited original reporting, especially on environmental issues and opinion pieces. A wide selection of non-Chilean magazines and papers is available at Santiago's airport.

TELEVISION AND RADIO

Chile has several television stations, most notably Televisión Nacional, owned by the government, and Canal 13, operated by the Universidad Católica. Cable television is found in most Chilean households and at restaurants, bars, and cafés. Most hotels also have cable TV installed in the rooms. However, an English-speaking station is rare.

Radio is quite popular in Chile. However, reception outside of towns and cities can be weak. There are over 20 FM stations broadcasting a variety of popular music and classical tunes. **Santiago Radio** is Chile's only all-English radio station.

POSTAL AND COURIER SERVICES

Correos de Chile, the country's privatized postal service, has offices in every city and town, and is reasonably reliable. Foreign visitors can receive mail at any of their post offices via the *lista de correos* or by general delivery to their address. There are ample courier services in Chile. Along with the international **DHL** and **Federal Express**, the local **Chilexpress** has hundreds of offices and affiliates throughout the country. Courier services are a faster, although more expensive, alternative to Chile's postal system.

DIRECTORY

TELEPHONES

Entel
www.telefónica.com

Telefónica CTC
www.entel.cl

TELEVISION AND RADIO

Santiago Radio
www.santiagoradio.cl

POSTAL AND COURIER SERVICES

Chilexpress
Avenida José Joaquín Pérez 1376, Pudahuel, Santiago.
Tel *(02) 3824800.*
www.chilexpress.cl

Correos de Chile
www.correos.cl

DHL
San Francisco 301, Santiago.
Tel *(02) 802000.*
www.dhl.cl

Federal Express
Avenida Providencia 1951, Providencia, Santiago.
Tel *(02) 315250.*
www.fedex.cl

TRAVEL INFORMATION

While most travelers arrive in Chile by air, overland crossings from neighboring Argentina – and to a lesser degree from Bolivia and Peru – are also fairly common. The airport at Santiago is served by major international airlines from across the world. Cruise ships connect ports such as Valparaíso with Buenos Aires in Argentina. Within the country, there are reliable air services right from the Peruvian border in the north to the tip of Patagonia and to Easter Island, but it is often necessary to change planes in Santiago. Passenger trains, however, are few and slow. Most main roads are paved and fairly good. High-quality bus services are frequent and car rentals are often useful. Traveling by ferry is most convenient in southern Chile.

The logo of Qantas airlines

ARRIVING BY AIR

Most overseas visitors arrive at **Aeropuerto Internacional Arturo Merino Benítez**, located 10 miles (17 km) northwest of Santiago. The airport is a state-of-the art facility, with flights that connect to other Chilean cities as well as to international destinations. Airports elsewhere in Chile only receive flights from neighboring countries, except Easter Island's Aeropuerto Mataveri, which is also accessible by flights from Tahiti and Australia.

The main international carrier is **LAN Airlines**, which links Chile with Europe, North America, and the Pacific Islands. **Air France**, **Lufthansa**, **Swiss International**, **British Airways**, and **Iberia** are popular European carriers, while important North American airlines include **Taca**, **American Airlines**, **United Airlines**, **Delta Airlines**, and **Air Canada**. Continental Airlines partners with Panama's airline **Copa**, while **Qantas** flies from Australia and New Zealand.

AIR FARES AND PASSES

In general, air fares to Chile are expensive, but prices vary seasonally and depend on how early tickets are booked. Fares are highest from mid-December to February and lowest during the winter months. Special packages and promotional fares may be available on airline and travel websites such as **Travelocity**, **Expedia**, and **Orbitz**. Apex tickets, booked well in advance, are cheaper than unrestricted tickets, but incur penalties for changes.

LAN Airlines is part of the alliance of airlines called **One World** that offers a Visit South America pass. This can be used for a trip to Chile alone or to other countries in the continent as well.

Passengers arriving in Chile should have an onward ticket, but this regultion is rarely enforced. Combined airline and hotel packages are ideal for shorter trips.

Shuttle van at Santiago's intenational airport

SHUTTLE SERVICES

Santiago-based operators such as **Turtransfer** and **Transvip** provide on-demand shuttle services from the capital's international airport. These vans accommodate between 10 and 12 passengers. Trips to the eastern boroughs of Providencia and Las Condes cost slightly more than those to downtown Santiago. A number of other cities also have airport shuttles, but most travelers rely on taxi service.

The departure terminal at Aeropuerto Internacional Arturo Merino Benítez

Luxury cruise ship anchored at Arica's port

ARRIVING BY LAND

Chile has numerous Andean crossings from Argentina, some of which are connected by comfortable buses. Of these crossings, the Los Libertadores pass, between Santiago and Mendoza, Argentina, has most of the traffic, but winter snow can close it for days at a time. Another busy route connects Osorno in the Lake District to the Argentine city of San Carlos de Bariloche via the Paso Cardenal Samoré, whose lower altitude keeps it open year round. Other overland crossings include the Paso de Jama from Chile's San Pedro de Atacama to Jujuy and Salta in Argentina; and the road from Punta Arenas to Río Gallegos in Argentina. During summer, the roads from Puerto Natales and Torres del Paine to El Calafate in Argentina experience heavy traffic.

The main routes to Bolivia are paved highways from the cities of Arica and Iquique to La Paz and Oruro, respectively, while the route from San Pedro de Atacama across the Bolivian salt flat Salar de Uyuni is a favorite with adventurous backpackers. Arica has convenient coastal highway crossings to and from the Peruvian city of Tacna.

Rented cars can be taken from Chile into Argentina and vice versa, but this requires additional paperwork and insurance coverage. It is even more difficult to rent a car from Bolivia or Peru into Chile, and vice versa.

ARRIVING BY SEA

While there is no regular, scheduled maritime service to Chile, cruise ships sail down the Pacific coast from Peru, around Cape Horn to Argentina, Brazil, and back. Possible Chilean ports of call en route include Iquique, Arica, Antofagasta, Valparaíso, Puerto Montt, Coquimbo, Puerto Chacabuco, Puerto Natales, and Punta Arenas. It is possible to leave a cruise at any of these ports and continue overland.

ORGANIZED TOURS

Many companies in North America, Europe, and UK offer organized tours to Chile. The UK-based Journey Latin America *(see p319)*, and the US-based **Pan American Travel Services** provide many custom-made packages across Chile. In addition, several reputed Chilean operators arrange a variety of deals. Organized tours generally comprise flight transfers, local transportation, accommodations, and guides.

Activity-oriented packages are the most common, with adventure tour agencies organizing everything from skiing, snowboarding, mountain-biking, hiking, surfing, white-water rafting, and wildlife-watching. Operators also arrange vineyard accommodations in Chile's fertile Central Valley, informative trips to Easter Island's archaeological resources, and stargazing excursions in San Pedro de Atacama.

DIRECTORY

ARRIVING BY AIR

Aeropuerto Internacional Arturo Merino Benítez
Casilla 79, Santiago.
Tel *(02) 6901900.*
www.aeropuertosantiago.cl

Air Canada
Tel *1888 247 2262* (Canada). **www**.aircanada.com

Air France
Tel *(33) 0820 320 820* (France).
www.airfrance.com

American Airlines
Tel *1800 433 7300* (US).
www.aa.com

British Airways
Tel *0844 493 0787* (UK).
www.britishairways.com

Copa
Tel *1800 359 2672* (US).
www.copaair.com

Delta Airlines
Tel *1800 221 1212* (US).
www.delta.com

Iberia
Tel *(34) 902400500* (Spain).
www.iberia.com

LAN Airlines
Tel *1866 4359 526* (US).
www.lan.com

Lufthansa
Tel *0180 583 8426* (UK).
www.lufthansa.com

Qantas
www.qantas.com.au

Swiss International
Ave. El Bosque n.500, Las Condes. **www**.swiss.com

Taca
Tel *1800 400 8222* (US).
www.taca.com

United Airlines
Tel *1800 538 2929* (US).
www.united.com

AIR FARES AND PASSES

Expedia
www.expedia.com

One World
www.oneworld.com

Orbitz
www.orbitz.com

Travelocity
www.travelocity.com

SHUTTLE SERVICES

Transvip
Aeropuerto Internacional Arturo Merino Benítez, Santiago. ***Tel*** *(02) 677 3000.* **www**.transvip.cl

Turtransfer
Aeropuerto Internacional Arturo Merino Benítez, Santiago. ***Tel*** *(02) 677 3600.* **www**.turtransfer.cl

ORGANIZED TOURS

Pan American Travel Services
Tel *1800 364 4359* (US).
www.panam-tours.com

Domestic Flights

Chile's boundaries, stretching from the tropics to the sub-Antartic, but nowhere wider than 186 miles (300 km), make air travel the preferred mode of transportation. Flying between the northern and southern parts of the country usually requires changing flights in Santiago. The more isolated destinations in southern Chile can be reached on smaller planes run by regional airlines. Bargain fares can be found on most airline websites, which, in some instances, are updated on a weekly basis. In-flight services vary depending on the airline, with the national carrier providing amenities that live up to the highest international standards.

Passengers waiting for their flights at the airport in Arica

DOMESTIC AIRLINES

There are three primary domestic airlines in Chile. At the forefront is LAN Airlines *(see p333)*, dominating at least 85 percent of the domestic market. LAN offers the widest selection of flights and is also the only scheduled airline to Easter Island. **Sky Airline** has also managed to carve a niche for itself over the years, but has fewer flights and services. **Principal Airlines** is a relatively new venture, serving only the northern cities of Iquique and Antofagasta.

Based in Santiago, **Lassa** and **Aerolíneas ATA** connect the city to Robinson Crusoe Island. Carriers such as **Aerocord**, **Aerotaxis del Sur**, and **Cielomaraustral** operate air taxis from Puerto Montt to Chaitén. However, these flights have been diverted to Palena since the 2008 eruption of Volcán Chaitén. Air taxi companies, including **Transporte Aéreo Don Carlos** and **Transportes Aéreos San Rafael**, offer services from Coyhaique in Northern Patagonia to lesser-known destinations such as the island settlement of Melinka, Parque Nacional Laguna San Rafael, Villa O'Higgins, and Cochrane. Small planes from Puerto Montt depart for the Chiloé archipelago farther south. Based in Punta Arenas **Aerovías DAP** offers flights to Porvenir, in Tierra del Fuego, and to Puerto Navarino and Chile's Antartic base at Isla Rey Jorge, where they connect with smaller cruise ships sailing around the Antarctic peninsula.

DOMESTIC AIRPORTS

The main airport is Santiago's busy Aeropuerto Internacional Arturo Merino Benítez *(see p333)*. Other major mainland airports are located in **Arica**, **Iquique**, **La Serena**, **Calama**, and **Antofagasta** in Norte Grande and Norte Chico; **Temuco** and **Puerto Montt** in the Lake District; and **Punta Arenas** and **Coyhaique** in Patagonia.

RESERVATIONS

At both LAN Airlines and Sky Airline it is easy to make reservations online. Electronic tickets are valid, but travelers need to carry a printout of the reservation or a copy of the confirming email. Websites of these two major airlines also offer bargain fares, but some of these deals may only be available for purchase in Chile. Most of the smaller airline companies also take bookings via phone or email, but reservations made in person or through a travel agent are the most reliable.

A LAN Airlines plane on the runway of Easter Island's Aeropuerto Mataveri

FLIGHT DURATION CHART

1:15 = Duration in hours: minutes

SANTIAGO					
2:45	*ARICA*				
2:30	**0:45**	*IQUIQUE*			
2:00	**4:35**	**0:55**	*ANTOFAGASTA*		
1:40	**4:35**	**4:40**	**4:25**	*PUERTO MONTT*	
4:00	**8:05**	**6:10**	**2:20**	**5:45**	*PUNTA ARENAS*

GETTING AROUND

Air travel across the length of the country entails flight transfers in certain cities. The chart reflects minimum flight times. Flying may take longer depending on available flight connections.

Family with children disembarking at Puerto Montt's airport

CHECKING IN

The process of checking in at Chile's modern airports is similar to that at European or North American airports. Travelers need to carry their paper ticket or flight number and their passport in hand. It is advisable to arrive at least 60 minutes prior to departure at Santiago's large Aeropuerto Internacional Arturo Merino Benítez. This may not be required in the extremely efficient airports in other cities and at the informal aerodromes that are served by the smaller airlines.

CONCESSIONARY FARES

Children up to the age of two travel free, but are not entitled to a separate baggage allowance or own seat. Those between two and eleven years pay around two-thirds of the fare and are entitled to full baggage allowance.

Advance purchase can lower fares substantially, and LAN Airlines offers a 3 percent discount for online purchases as well. There are no direct discounts for students or senior citizens, but the Santiago-based **Student Flight Center** can arrange cheaper tickets for students and young adults.

BAGGAGE RESTRICTIONS

On domestic flights, LAN Airlines passengers can check in up to 50 lbs (23 kg) per person, plus one handbag and a personal item such as a laptop. Business class passengers on LAN can check in up to three bags of 51 lbs (23 kg) each, plus one carry bag of up to 35 lbs (16 kg). Sky Airline passengers can check up to 45 lbs (20 kg) per person, plus one handbag weighing up to 11 lbs (5 kg). There is no business class seating on Sky Airline.

Smaller airlines, especially air taxis, have lower baggage weight limits. Airlines may charge extra for recreational equipment such as bicycles, surfboards, and skis in addition to penalties for exceeding weight limit.

DIRECTORY

DOMESTIC AIRLINES

Aerocord
Aerodromo La Paloma, Puerto Montt.
Tel *(065) 262300.*
www.aerocord.cl

Aerolíneas ATA
Avenida Larraín 7941, Santiago.
Tel *(02) 2750363.*
www.aerolineasata.cl

Aerotaxis del Sur
Antonio Varas 70-A, Puerto Montt.
Tel *(065) 252523.*
www.aerotaxisdelsur.cl

Aerovías DAP
O'Higgins 891, Punta Arenas. ***Tel*** *(061) 616100.*
www.aeroviasdap.cl

Cielomaraustral
Quillota 254, Puerto Montt.
Tel *(065) 266666.*

Lassa
Avenida Larraín 7941, La Reina, Santiago.
Tel *(02) 2735209.*

Principal Airlines
Huérfanos 811, Santiago.
Tel *(02) 6510600.*
www.aerolinea principal.com

Sky Airline
Huerfanos 815, Santiago.
Tel *(02) 6329449.*
www.skyairline.cl

Transporte Aéreo Don Carlos
Subteniente Cruz 63, Coyhaique.
Tel *(067) 231981.*
www.doncarlos.cl

Transportes Aéreos San Rafael
18 de Septiembre 469, Coyhaique.
Tel *(067) 233408.*

DOMESTIC AIRPORTS

Antofagasta
Tel *(055) 269077.*

Arica
Tel *(058) 211116.*

Calama
Tel *(055) 363004.*

Coyhaique
Tel *(067) 272126.*

Iquique
Tel *(057) 426350.*

La Serena
Tel *(051) 271877.*

Puerto Montt
Tel *(065) 294161.*

Punta Arenas
Tel *(061) 219131.*

Temuco
Tel *(045) 554801.*

CONCESSIONARY FARES

Student Flight Center
Hernando de Aguirre 201, Santiago. ***Tel*** *(02) 411 2000.* **www**.sertur.cl

Traveling Around Chile

While flying is an important mode of transportation in Chile, overland travel is also worth consideration, especially in the country's heartland. Overnight buses are comfortable and cost a fraction of flight prices. The best of them are air-conditioned and have onboard meal service and entertainment. Long-distance trains, which are few, are a slower option. An abundance of city buses known as *micros*, taxis, and *colectivos* or shared taxis make getting around cities and towns cheap and efficient. In the Lake District and archipelagic south, ferries are an indispensable part of the transportation system.

A brightly painted and spacious overnight bus

BUSES

Long-distance coaches have several categories of service. The most basic have reclining seats and are adequate for 3-or 4-hour trips. With seats that recline almost horizontally and greater leg room, *semi-cama*, (semi-bed) and *salón cama* (full-bed) buses are ideal for overnight travel. Longer trips can be a little tiring, but include meals, snacks, and drinks on board; the buses may also stop en route for meals. Shorter trips, particularly in some rural areas, may require taking buses that are smaller and cramped. Private buses also take visitors to specific destinations. For instance, **Expediciones Manzur** provides transport to various attractions in the Cajón del Maipo.

Most cities and towns have central bus terminals, but individual companies may also have their own separate departure points. In general, these terminals are safe, although they can be dreary and congested. Fortunately, it is only necessary to arrive 20 minutes before departure time.

TRAINS

The Empresa de Ferrocarriles del Estado or EFE *(see p93)* is the state-run railroad system, whose long-distance services, although inexpensive, are slower and less efficient than those offered by privately run bus systems. However, southbound commuter trains from Santiago to Rancagua and San Fernando offer good service. Operated by the EFE, TerraSur trains make the 5-hour trip, five times daily, between Santiago and Chillán in the Central Valley, with a bus link to Concepción. One of Chile's greatest rail experiences is traveling by the meter-gauge train on the short Buscarril line connecting Talca with the beach-resort of Constitución.

One of Empresa de Ferrocarriles del Estado's long-distance trains

FERRIES AND CATAMARANS

Traveling by catamarans or ferries is a crucial means of getting around in the Lake District and Patagonia, where roads and highways are interrupted by large waterbodies. In Northern Patagonia, the most useful services are **Navimag**'s overnight ferries that depart from Puerto Montt to Puerto Chacabuco, and the 3-day ferry to Puerto Natales, the gateway to Torres del Paine National Park *(see pp242–5)*. The ferry to Puerto Chacabuco sometimes also continues to Parque Nacional Laguna San Rafael *(see p233)*, as do faster catamaran services. Also starting from Puerto Montt, and sometimes from Quellón on Chiloé's Isla Grande, **Naviera Austral** serves the port of Chaitén. In January and February, it also operates a daily ferry from Hornopirén to Caleta Gonzalo, the northern access point to Parque Pumalín *(see p226)*. Shuttle ferries connect the mainland town of Pargua in the Lake District with Isla Grande and the hamlets of La Arena and Puelche, located southeast of Puerto Montt.

In Southern Patagonia, **Transbordadora Austral Broom** provides a ferry service from Punta Arenas to Porvenir, on the Chilean side of Tierra del Fuego. It also has ferries that shuttle buses, cars, and passengers across the Strait of Magellan at Primera Angostura, located northeast of Punta Arenas.

Those who wish to travel to Argentina *(see pp252–3)* can also take ferries to certain border points. At Puerto Yungay, on the southernmost part of the Carretera Austral, a free public ferry shuttles vehicles on the Mitchell fjord to Villa O'Higgins, where a seasonal catamaran carries hikers to a border post with overland connections to El Chaltén in Argentina. A ferry from Puerto Fuy crosses Lago Pirihueico to Puerto Pirihueico, the link to the Argentine city of San Martín de los Andes. **Cruce Andino** is a bus-catamaran-bus shuttle that crosses the Andes from Puerto Montt and Puerto Varas to the city of Bariloche in Argentina.

DRIVING

Stretching from the Peruvian border to Puerto Montt and Chiloé, Chile's improving highway network is ideal for driving. There is a four-lane highway from La Serena in Norte Grande and Norte Chico to Puerto Montt in Patagonia and many excellent, but sometimes narrow, secondary roads. The main highways are all toll roads and, in Santiago, they require either an electronic permit or a daily fee permit. These are available with most rental cars or can be bought up to 48 hours after entering the network. Daily passes can be bought online at **Servipag**. Chile's Gringo Trail has been a favorite with visitors, particularly backpackers, for many decades. It includes the country's popularly traveled areas from San Pedro de Atacama to Santiago, parts of the Lake District, and Torres del Paine in Patagonia. Today, this area can be explored by driving over scenic roads and highways. Much of the southerly Carretera Austral, Chile's most exciting drive through the forested Andes, is still narrow, with loose gravel and blind curves in its wildest segments. It does not require a 4WD, as long as drivers are careful. There are no SOS phones and cell phone coverage is spotty at best, but people will stop to help in case of accidents. Drivers on this highway must, by law, carry warning triangles that indicate an accident or car breakdown, a fire extinguisher, and a first-aid kit.

Driving on the Carretera Austral in Northern Patagonia

Driving is on the right, and all passengers are required to wear seat belts. There are firm laws about driving under the influence of alcohol or drugs.

RENTING CARS

International rental companies such as **Avis** and **Hertz** have affiliates in major cities. In addition, there are numerous local companies, including **Verschae** and **Seelmann**, that rent cars at cheaper rates. Unlimited mileage rates are the rule but prices are usually higher in Chile than in the US or Europe. A client must be at least 21 years old and have a driver's license, passport, and credit card. In theory, an international driving permit is required, but this is almost never enforced. The rental agency must provide the car's ownership documents, which need to be presented at police request. In general, deductibles are high on rental car insurance policies – as much as 20 percent of the vehicle's value. Cross-border rentals require a power of attorney and additional insurance.

GREEN TRAVEL

Public awareness about green travel is not widespread in Chile, but it is a practical concern for many in a country with high energy prices. While increasing prosperity has led many Chileans to buy cars, traveling by metro in Santiago, Valparaíso, and Viña del Mar is faster, cheaper, and eco-friendly. The Transantiago bus network in the capital also covers tremendous ground. Chile's rail network is not too efficient, but long-distance buses are frequent, comfortable, and quick. An overnight sleeper bus is often cheaper and more environment-friendly than a flight, and also reduces hotel costs. Nevertheless, great distances make flights essential, particularly on longer trips and over water.

Tour agents *(see p319)* are conscious of the environment. Patagonia's tour operators, for instance, are outspoken defenders of the region's rivers against mega hydroelectric projects. New hotels also have state-of-the-art insulation that lessens their carbon footprint. Some, especially in desert areas, have low-consumption toilets and showers that reduce water usage.

DIRECTORY

BUSES

Expediciones Manzur
Oficiana 507, Santiago.
Tel *(02) 7774284.*

FERRIES AND CATAMARANS

Cruce Andino
www.cruceandino.com

Navimag
Tel *(02) 4423114.*
www.navimag.com

Naviera Austral
Ave. Angelmó 2187, Puerto Montt. ***Tel*** *(065) 270430.*
www.navieraaustral.cl

Transbordadora Austral Broom
Ave. Bulnes 05075, Punta Arenas.
Tel *(061) 218100.* www.tabsa.cl

DRIVING

Servipag
www.servipag.com

RENTING CARS

Avis
www.avischile.cl

Hertz
www.hertz.cl

Seelmann
www.seelmann.cl

Verschae
www.verschae.com

General Index

Page numbers in **bold** refer to main entries

N

W

Y

Z

Acknowledgments

Dorling Kindersley would like to thank the many people whose help and assistance contributed to the preparation of this book.

Contributors
Wayne Bernhardson has been visiting Chile for more than three decades. He has written extensively for newspapers, magazines, and guidebooks including Moon Handbooks, Lonely Planet, and National Geographic Traveler. Wayne has also co-authored the DK *Eyewitness Guide to Argentina*.

Declan McGarvey is a travel writer and journalist based in Buenos Aires, where he has lived since 1999. He is the co-author of the *Eyewitness Guide to Argentina* and of the *Eyewitness Top 10 Guide to Buenos Aires*, and has also contributed to DK's *Where to Go When* series.

Kristina Schreck moved to Chile in 1998 following several years as editor of *Adventure Journal* magazine. She has since worked in every aspect of the travel industry, as a trekking guide in Patagonia, travel writer and author of the first edition of Frommer's *Chile & Easter Island*, and as the head of media relations for the Chilean tourism board.

Cartography
The maps on pages 55, 75, 83, and 102–109 are derived from © www.openstreetmap.org and contributors, licensed under CC-BY-SA; see www.creativecommons.org for further details.

Fact Checker Rodrigo Cabezas

Proofreader Janice Pariat

Indexer Hilary Bird

Design and Editorial
Publisher Douglas Amrine
List Manager Vivien Antwi
Project Art Editor Shahid Mahmood
Project Editor Michelle Crane
Senior Cartographic Editor Casper Morris
Jacket Design Tessa Bindloss, Stephen Bere
Senior DTP Designer Jason Little
Senior Picture Researcher Ellen Root
Production Controller Rebecca Short

Editorial Consultant Nick Rider

Editorial Assistance Vicki Allen, Marta Bescos, Fay Franklin, Anna Streiffert

Additional Photography Geoff Brightling, Demetrio Carrasco, Frank Greenaway, Nigel Hicks, Dave King, Greg Roden, Jerry Young, Ian O'Leary Studios

Design Assistance Janice Utton

Special Assistance Dorling Kindersley would like to thank the following for their assistance: Lawrence Lamonica at Lapis Lazuli House, Aya Nishimura from Hers Agency, and Preeti Pant.

Photography Permission
Dorling Kindersley would like to thank the following for their assistance and kind permission to photograph at their establishments:
Bar La Playa, Basilica y Museo de la Merced, Biblioteca de Santiago, Biblioteca Nacional, Bolsa de Comercio, Cancelleŕia, Casa Museo Isla Negra, Casino Espanol in Iquique, Catedral Metropolitana, Centro Cultural Estacíon Mapocho, Centro Cultural Palacio de La Moneda, Cerro Central, Iglesia de San Francisco in Chiu Chiu, Iglesia de Santo Domingo, Hotel Indigo and Spa, Isabel Aninat Galleria, Lagos in Patagonia, Mamiña Hot Springs, Mercado Central, Museo Chileno de Arte Precolombino, Museo de Colchagua in Santa Cruz, Museo de la Moda, Museo de Santiago in Casa Colorada, Museo Ferroviaria Pablo Neruda, Museo Ferroviario, Museo Muncipal Juan Pablo II, Museo Nacional de Bellas Artes, Museo Nacional de Historia Natural, Museo Naval y Maritimo, Museo Regional Braun Menendez, Palacio Cousiño, Palacio de los Tribunales de Justicia, Puyuhupai Lodge & Spa, Teatro Municipal, Termas de Socos, Hotel Zero, Zona Franca Zofri.

Picture Credits
Placement Key- t=top; tc=top centre; tr=top right; cla=centre left above; ca=centre above; cra=centre right above; cl=centre left; c=centre; cr=centre right; clb=centre left below; cb=centre below; crb=centre right below; bl=bottom left; bc=bottom centre; br=bottom right; ftl=far top left; ftr=far top right; fcla=far centre left above; fcra=far centre right above; fcl=far centre left; fcr=far centre right; fclb=far centre left below; fcrb=far centre right below; fbl=far bottom left; fbr=far bottom right.

Every effort has been made to trace the copyright holders, and we apologize in advance for any unintentional omissions. We would be pleased to insert the appropriate acknowledgments in any subsequent edition of this publication.

Works of art have been reproduced with the kind permission of the following copyright holders:
Absent Feet Airmail Painting No. 153 2002-03 tincture, photosilkscreen, sateen, and stitching on 4 sections of duck fabric 82 x 220 1/2 in/ 210 x 560 cm, courtesy of the artist and Alexander and Bonin, New York © Eugenio Dittborn 28bl; *New Nature I* and *New Nature II* © Pedro Tyler 53crb; *Fotografo II*, 2008, Ed 6 Originales Alto 165cms, Base 55 x 33cms, Height 65 x 21 x 11/16 x 13 in © Aurora Cañero 95cb; *Historia de Concepción*, Gregorio de la Fuente © Pablo de la Fuente 152 br.

The publisher would like to thank the following individuals, companies, and picture libraries for their kind permission to reproduce their photographs:

© UNESCO: CODELCO 145bc, 145cra.
4CORNERS IMAGES: Cozzi Guido 66-67; HP Huber 264-265. EDUARDO ABASOLO: 194cla, 195tl. ALAMY IMAGES: Alaska Stock LLC / John Hyde 21br; Arco Images / Stengert, N. 150bc; The Art Archive/ Gianni Dagli Orti 42clb; Roussel Bernard 16t, 126-127c; Blickwinkel/ Brehm 19br; Cephas Picture Library/ Matt Wilson 114, 149cla; Chile /Chris Howarth 90bl; Chile DesConocido 176bl, 181tl, 210tl, 214br; Dennis Cox 148tr; Creative Trails 169tr; Jan Csernoch 165bl; Danita Delimont/ Sergio Pitamitz 230-31; David R. Frazier Photolibrary, Inc. 328cl; Celso Diniz 322cl; Eagle Visions Photography/ Craig Lovell 22crb; Fabian Gonzales Editorial 21cr; FAN travelstock 179t; Eric Ghost 248-249; Chris Gomersall 18crb; Blaine Harrington III 23cra; Hemis.fr/ Hughes Hervé 187b; Jon Hicks 82; Marla Holden 259cr; Imagebroker 23cla,/Christian Handl 210clb,/Nico Stengert 28tr; Infocusphotos.com/ Malie Rich-Griffith 157b; INTERFOTO 22br, 45br,/History 9c; John Warburton-Lee Photography 31tl; Jon Arnold Images Ltd/ Walter Bibikow 208-209; Russell Kord 18tr, 332b; Frans Lemmens 251c; Yadid Levy 35tl, 35c; LOOK Die Bildagentur der Fotografen GmbH/ Michael Boyny 31cra,/ Hauke Dressler 13br; Chris Mattison 220bl; Yannis Emmanuel Mavromatakis 243cla; Megapress 92br; Randy Mehoves 293bl; Mountain Light/ Galen Rowell 14; Nifro Travel Images 199tc; North Wind Picture Archives 42bl, 135br; M. Timothy O'Keefe 8-9; Astrid Padberg 260cr; Photoshot Holdings Ltd 194bc; Picture Contact/ Jochem Wijnands 22bl, 70tl; Sergio Pitamitz 21clb, 237b; Leonid Plotkin 112tr, 115b; StockShot/ Dan Milner 31br; Top-Pics TBK 242cla; V1 37tr; Simon Vine 123cl; John G. Walter 119tl; Wide Eye Pictures 33clb; WoodyStock/ Begsteiger 37b; World History Archive 43br; Fernando Zabala 211tl. HECTOR HUGO GUTIERREZ ALVARADO: 44bc. ALEXANDER AND BONIN: Bill Orcutt 28bl. ALTOS DE LIRCAY: 151bl. ATACAMA PHOTO: Gerhard Huedepohl

4-5tc, 20cl, 20br, 20bl, 244cl, 255b, 257t, 266tl, 267c, 267br. CAROLINA ALICIA DAGACH AVILA: 98bc, 100tl. AWASI - SAN PEDRO DE ATACAMA: 273tr. BIO BIO EXPEDITIONS: 5cra, 227tl, 316tc. THE BRIDGEMAN ART LIBRARY: Naval Combat beween the Peruvian Ship 'Huascar' against the Chilean 'Blanco Encalada' and the 'Cochrane' in 1879, Monleon y Torres, Rafael (1847-1900) / Private Collection / Index 45fclb. CENTRO DE SKI ARAUCARIAS: 194clb. JOAO COLELLA: 219br. COLIBRI MUSIC: 25crb. COLO-COLO: 312tc. NIALL CORBET: 143t. CORBIS: Lucien Aigner 25tl; Bettmann 26bc, 44br, 47ctc, 47crb; Julio Donoso 220cla; Ric Ergenbright 262clb; Martin Harvey 30tr; Blaine Harrington III 18cl; Jon Hicks 77tl; Dave G. Houser 238b; NewSport/ Chris Trotman 30bc; Gregg Newton 48tl; Jonathan Selkowitz 31bl; Hubert Stadler 19cr, 206b; Sygma/Sophie Bassouls 26tr,/Carlos Carrion 47br,/Diego Goldberg 48bc,/Thierry Orban 30cr; Pablo Corral Vega 324tr; Xinhua Press/ Zhang Yuwei 30bl. DANITA DELIMONT STOCK PHOTOGRAPHY: Bill Bachmann 34tc, 36tr; Ric Ergenbright 23bl; Wendy Kaveney/ Jaynes Gallery 32bc, 292cl; John Warburton-Lee 217b; Roland and Karen Muschenetz 2-3. DAWSONLAPELICULA.CL: 251tc. MARCELA DONOSO: 215cla, 215crb, 215cb. EJECUTIVA COMERCIAL HOTELES HUILO HUILO: La Montana Magica Hotel 201br. ENDÉMICA EXPEDICIONES: 316bl. PAZ ERRAZURIZ: 61cr. CAROLINE FINK: 143bl. FOTOSCOPIO LATIN AMERICA STOCK PHOTO AGENCY: 33cra, 33bc; Horst Von Irmer 313tl. PABLO DE LA FUENTE: 152br. FUNDACIÓN ARTESANIAS DE CHILE: 10tc, 15c, 28cb, 28clb, 28fclb, 94cl, 154tr, 154cr, 154bc, 154br, 155tr, 155tc, 155cr, 155clb, 155bl, 155bc. FUNDACIÓN SEWELL: 144cla, 145crb. GERMAN DEL SOL - ARQUITECTO: 200tl. GETTY IMAGES: AFP /Staff/ Pablo Porciuncula 49bc,/Martin Bernetti 31cl, 33crb, 49cr, 49crb, 140tl,/ Maurico Lima 30cla,/Pedro Ugarte 49tl; AFP/ STF 47bl,/ STR/ Stringer 195bc; AFP/ Stringer/ Claudio Pozo 32tr, 99tr,/ Raul Bravo 292bc, 335cl/ David Lillo 32-33c,/Ronaldo Schemidt 49bl; Aurora/ Bernardo Gimenez 227cr; FoodPix/ Sheridan Stancliff 32bl; Gems/ Redferns 25tr; The Image Bank/ Frans Lemmens 314br ,/Eastcott Momatiuk 113br; Kean Collection/ Staff/ Archive Photos 43ca; LatinContent/ Max Montecinos 17ca; Lonely Planet Images/ Bethune Carmichael 112cl; National Geographic/ Stephen Alvarez 263crb,/Joel Sartore 18bl; Popperfoto 30cb; Science & Society Picture Library 51c; Time & Life Pictures/ Robert Nickelsberg 312bl; Travel Ink/ Gallo Images 133br, 175bl, 334cla. ANDREW GOULD: 126br. THE GRANGER COLLECTION, NEW YORK: 147cla. HACIENDA LOS ANDES: 315br. ISABEL ANINAT GALERIA DE ARTE: 53crb. ISTOCKPHOTO.COM: Piet Veltman 135c. FRANÇOIS JOLLY: 336br. LA SONORA PALACIOS: 25cl. LAPIS LAZULI HOUSE: 94tc, 311tc, 311cla, 311ca, 311cr, 311fcr, 311cra, 311fclb, 311cl, 311c, 311cb, 311crb, 311fcrb, 311fbl, 311bl, 311br, 311fbr. LAPOSTOLLE: 149clb; Clos Apalta Winery 147bl, 271cl, 318tl. LATIN PHOTO: Felipe Gonzalez V. 24bl, 35br; Nicolas Nadjar 154cl; Ely Negri 25cr. MARCO LILLO: 28cr, 98cla, 99b. LINDSAY SIMMONDS DESIGN: 211br. LONELY PLANET IMAGES: John Elk III 221tl. LOS HUASOS QUINCHEROS: 25bc. MAGICAL ANDES PHOTOGRAPHY: James Brunker 19cl, 186. MALL SPORT: 98tc. MARY EVANS PICTURE LIBRARY: 269c, 321c; Aisa Media 40. MASTERFILE: Graham French 84tr. DECLAN McGARVEY: 154clb. MONTGRAS PROPERTIES: 148cl. MUSEO HISTORICA NACIONAL DE CHILE: 46tl. MUSEO NACIONAL DE BELLAS ARTES, CHILE: Colección Museo Nacional de Bellas Artes de Santiago de Chile 28br. SANTIAGO RIOS PACHECO: 150tl. GREGORY PANAYOTOU: 262cla. PETER LANGER/ASSOCIATED MEDIA GROUP: 24crb, 126clb, 127crb, 144tr. PHOTOGRAPHERS DIRECT: Alimdi.net/ Thomas Muller 198bl. PHOTOLIBRARY: 136-137; age fotostock/ Wojtek Buss 262br,/Kordcom Kordcom 54,/ P Narayan 110-11; Armytage/ Anne Green 201cb; Bildagentur 268-69; Wojtek Buss 16bl; Rob Crandall 17br; Denkou Images 251b; Fresh Food Images/ Steven Morris Photography 18cr; Garden Picture Library/ J S Sira 19cb; Oliver Gerhard 245tl; Christian Handl 52cla; Paul Harris 23crb; Hemis/ Barbagallo Franco 1c; Imagebroker.net/ Oliver Gerhard 206tc,/Christian Handl 25clb,/Sepp Puchinger 24tr,/Nico Stengert 165crb, 165tl; Index Stock Imagery/ Anna Zuckerman-Vdovenko 320-321; John Warburton-Lee Photography 142tl, 254,/Paul Harris 147br, 226br,156,188tr, 210br,/ Nick Laing 270cl,/ John Warburton-Lee 242clb, 250tl,/Diego Martin 11br; Jon Arnold Travel/ Michele Falzone 11tl; Christophe Lehenaff 163tc, 177br; Lonely Planet Images/ Grant Dixon 195cr,/ Richard I'Anson 126cl,/ Paul Kennedy 146bl,/Oliver Strewe 93tl; Mary Evans Picture Library 42br, 43cb, 45tr, 61tl, 267bl; Aris Mihich 198cl; Laurence Mouton 38cla; Peter Arnold Images/ James L Amos 263cra,/Fred Bruemmer 266b, 267tr,/Alexandra Edwards 41br,/Kevin Schafer 245c,/Gunter Ziesler 19fbr; Photononstop/ Bruno Barbier 111c, 210cla,/Marc Vérin 330cl; Pixtal Images 15b, 261b, 262tr; The Print Collector 46cb; Robert Harding Travel/ Ken Gillham 216cla,/James Hager 244tl,/R Mcleod 172-73,/ Geoff Renner 92cl,/Marco Simoni 194tr, 245br, 236,/Michael Snell 53bl,/Tony Waltham 21t; Robin Smith 247tr; Tips Italia/ Wojtek Buss 259tc,/Paolo Olaco 3c; Wave 199crb; White /Medio Images 34br,/Sexto Sol 50-51; Bob Wickham 10cra. PHOTOSHOT: C2070 Rolf Haid 130bc; UPPA 87tc; World Pictures 188bl. THE PICTURE DESK: The Art Archive: Museo Nacional de Historia Lima / Dagli Orti 45clb,/ Navy Historical Service Vincennes France / Dagli Orti 41c; The Kobal Collection: Cine Experimental de La Universdad de Chile 27br. DAVID PIN: 52clb. HEINZ PLENGE: 33tl. DON PORTER: 127tl. PRIVATE COLLECTION: 41clb, 46br. QANTAS AIRWAYS LIMITED: 332tc. JAVIERA QUENAYA: 4br, 32cl. RANCHO-DE-CABALLOS: 199bl. RANDOM HOUSE MONDADORI: 26cl. ALVARO RIVAS: 193tr. SERNATUR: 322tc. SOUTH AMERICAN PICTURES: 26tl; Robert Francis 36bl; Sue Mann 34cl; Tony Morrison 22cl; Karen Ward 23tc; Rebecca Whitfield 22tr. VASILE TOMOIAGA: 23cl. TOPFOTO.CO.UK: Chilepic/ Rose Deakin 24cl. TRAVEL-IMAGES.COM: 255c; Craig Lovell 198tr, 331bl. TURTRANSFER: 332c. VINA CASAS DEL BOSQUE: 138cl, 293br. VIU MANENT: 148br, 149crb, 288tc. BERNHARDSON WAYNE: 273cr. WIKIPEDIA, THE FREE ENCYCLOPEDIA: 44t. WWW.MACONDO.CL: Clara Salina 27c.
Front Endpaper: ALAMY: Cephas Picture Library/ Matt Wilson ftl, Jon Hicks cr; MAGICAL ANDES PHOTOGRAPHY: James Brunker bl; PHOTOLIBRARY: age fotostock / Kordcom Kordcom tr, John Warburton-Lee Photography cl,/ Paul Harris tl, Robert Harding Travel/ Marco Simoni fbr.

Jacket images: Front: Photolibrary: age fotostock/Wes Walker. Back: Dorling Kindersley: Demetrio Carrasco bl, cla, tl; Photolibrary: age fotostock/Kordcom Kordcom clb. Spine: Photolibrary: age fotostock/Wes Walker t.
All other images © Dorling Kindersley
For further information see: www.dkimages.com

Phrase Book

Chileans themselves sometimes apologize for speaking bad Spanish, and anyone who has learned the language elsewhere may find it a challenge. Still, it is fairer to say that, given the country's geographical isolation, Spanish simply developed differently here. Additionally, because of Mapuche influence, there are many non-standard words, and pronunciation can also be difficult.

Chileans often omit the terminal "s," making it difficult for outsiders to distinguish singular from plural, and sometimes even the internal "s." On the tongue of a Chilean, for instance, *las escuelas* (the schools) may sound more like "la ecuela." Similarly, Anglicisms such as "show" sound more like "cho" in local speech.

In everyday informal speech, Chileans may also use non-standard verb forms. For instance, second-person familiar verbs often end in an accented "í, " as in "¿Querí?" (Do you want?) rather than the conventional "¿Quieres?".

Some Special Chilean words

aldea	*ahdayah*	hamlet
barrio	*bahreeoh*	neighborhood
carrete	*kahrehteh*	party
chupe	*choopeh*	a seafood stew
completo	*kohmplehtoh*	Chilean hotdog
copa	*kohpah*	glass (of wine)
galleria	*gahlehree-ah*	shopping mall
oficina	*ohfeeseenah*	office; in the Atacama nitrate-mining towns
parcela	*pahrsaylah*	country home or small farm
parrilla	*pahreeyah*	grill restaurant
paseo	*pahsayoh*	pedestrian mall
tasa	*tahsah*	cup (of tea or coffee)

In an Emergency

Help!	**¡Socorro!**	*sokorro*
Stop!	**¡Pare!**	*pareh*
Call a doctor!	**¡Llamen un médico!**	*yamen oon mehdeeko*
Call an ambulance	**¡Llamen a una ambulancia**	*yamen a oona amboolans-ya*
Police!	**¡Policía!**	*poleesee-a*
I've been robbed	**Me robaron**	*meh robaron*
Where is the nearest hospital?	**¿Dónde queda el hospital más cercano?**	*dondeh keda el ospeetal mas sairkano*
Could you help me?	**¿Me puede ayudar?**	*meh pwedeh a-yoodar*

Communication Essentials

Yes	**Sí**	*see*
No	**No**	*no*
Please	**Por favor**	*por fabor*
Pardon me	**Perdone**	*pairdoneh*
Excuse me	**Disculpe**	*deeskoolpeh*
I'm sorry	**Lo siento**	*lo s-yento*
Thanks	**Gracias**	*gras-yas*
Hello!	**¡Hola!**	*o-la*
Good morning	**Buenos días**	*bwenos dee-as*
Good afternoon	**Buenas tardes**	*bwenas tardes*
Good evening	**Buenas noches**	*bwenas noches*
Night	**Noche**	*nocheh*
Morning	**Mañana**	*man-yana*
Tomorrow	**Mañana**	*man-yana*
Yesterday	**Ayer**	*a-yair*
Here	**Acá**	*aka*
How?	**¿Cómo?**	*komo*
When?	**¿Cuándo?**	*kwando*
Where?	**¿Dónde?**	*dondeh*
Why?	**¿Por qué?**	*por keh*
How are you?	**¿Cómo está?**	*komo estah*
Very well, thank you	**Muy bien, gracias**	*mwee byen gras-yas*
Pleased to meet you	**Encantado/a/ mucho gusto**	*enkantad o/a/ moocho goosto*

Useful Phrases

That's great!	**¡Qué bien!**	*keh b-yen*
Do you speak English?	**¿Habla usted Ingles?**	*abla oo-sted eenglehs*
I don't understand	**No entiendo**	*no ent-yendo*
Could you speak more slowly?	**¿Puede hablar más despacio?**	*pwedeh ablar mas despas-yo*
I agree/okay	**De acuerdo/bueno**	*deh akwairdo/ bweno*
Let's go!	**¡Vámonos!**	*bamonos*
How do I get to/ which way to...?	**¿Cómo se llega a...?/¿Por dónde se va a...?**	*komo se llega a/por dondeh seh ba a*

Useful Words

large	**grande**	*grandeh*
small	**pequeño**	*peken-yo*
hot	**caliente**	*kal-yenteh*
cold	**frío**	*free-o*
good	**bueno**	*bweno*
bad	**malo**	*malo*
sufficient	**suficiente**	*soofees-yenteh*
open	**abierto**	*ab-yairto*
closed	**cerrado**	*serrah-do*
entrance	**entrada**	*entrada*
exit	**salida**	*saleeda*
full	**lleno**	*yeno*
right	**derecha**	*dairehcha*
left	**izquierda**	*eesk-yairda*
straight on	**derecho**	*dehrehcho*
above	**arriba**	*arreeba*
quickly	**rápido**	*rahpidoh*
early	**temprano**	*temprahno*
late	**tarde**	*tardeh*
now	**ahora**	*a-ora*
soon	**pronto**	*pronto*
less	**menos**	*menos*
much	**mucho**	*moocho*
in front of	**delante**	*delanteh*
opposite	**enfrente**	*enfrenteh*
behind	**detrás**	*detrahs*
second floor	**segundo piso**	*segoondo peeso*
ground floor	**primer piso**	*preemair peeso*
bar	**bar**	*bar*
discoteque	**boliche**	*bohleecheh*
lift/elevator	**ascensor**	*asensor*
bathroom	**baño**	*ban-yo*
toilet paper	**papel higiénico**	*papel eeh-yeneeko*
bribe	**coima**	*koyma*
girl/woman	**mina**	*meena*
women	**mujeres**	*moohaires*
men	**hombres**	*ombres*
child (boy/girl)	**niño/niña**	*neen-yo, neen-yah*
camera	**cámara**	*kamara*
batteries	**pilas**	*peelas*
passport	**pasaporte**	*pasaporteh*
visa	**visa**	*beesa*
tourist card	**tarjeta turística**	*tarheta tooreesteeka*
driver's license	**licencia de conducir**	*leesensyah de condooseer*
thief	**ladrón**	*lahdrohn*

cop	**paco**	*pahcoh*
money	**dinero**	*deenehroh*
lazy	**flojo**	*flohoh*
mess	**lío**	*lee-oh*
shanty town	**callampa**	*kayahmpah*
to eat	**comer**	*koh-mehr*
to nick, to steal	**robar**	*rohbahr*
to back off	**arrugar**	*ahroogahr*
to put up with	**soportar**	*sohportahr*
No way	**¡De ningun manera!**	*Day neengoonah manehra*

Health

I don't feel well	**No me siento bien**	*No meh s-yento been*
I have a stomach ache/ headache.	**Me duele el estómago/ la cabeza.**	*meh dweleh el estohmago/ la kabesa*
He/she is ill	**Está enfermo/a**	*esta enfairmo/a*
I need to rest	**Necesito decansar**	*neseseeto deskansar*

Post Offices and Banks

I'm looking for a...	**Busco una...**	*boosko oona*
bureau de change	**casa de cambio**	*kasa deh kamb-yo*
What is the dollar rate?	**¿A cuánto está el dolar?**	*a kwantoh esta el dohlar*
I want to send a	**Quiero enviar una**	*k-yairo en-vyar-oona*
letter	**carta**	*karta*
postcard	**postal**	*postal*
stamp	**estampilla**	*estampee-ya*
withdraw money	**sacar dinero**	*sakar deenairo*

Shopping

I would like...	**Me gustaría...**	*meh goostaree-a*
I want...	**Me quiero...**	*meh k-yairo*
Do you have any...?	**¿Tiene...?**	*t-yeneh*
How much is it?	**¿Cuánto cuesta?**	*kwanto kwesta*
What time do you open/close?	**¿A qué hora abre/ cierra?**	*a ke ora abreh/ s-yairra*
May I pay with a credit card?	**¿Puedo pagar con tarjeta de crédito?**	*pwedo pagar kon tarheta deh kredeeto*
expensive	**caro**	*karo*

Sightseeing

beach	**playa**	*pla-ya*
castle, fortress	**castillo**	*kastee-yo*
guide	**guía**	*gee-a*
motorway	**autopista**	*owtopeesta*
road	**carretera**	*karretaira*
street	**calle**	*ka-yeh*
tourist bureau	**oficina de turismo**	*ofeeseena deh tooreesmo*
town hall	**municipalidad**	*mooneeseepaleedad*

Getting Around

When does it leave?	**¿A qué hora sale?**	*a keh ora saleh*
When does the next train/bus leave for...?	**¿A qué hora sale el próximo tren/ autobús a...?**	*a keh ora saleh el prokseemo tren/ owtoboos a*
Could you call a taxi for me?	**¿Me puede llamar un taxi?**	*meh pwedeh yamar oon taksee*
departure gate	**puerta de embarque**	*pwairta deh embarkeh*
boarding pass	**tarjeta de embarque**	*tarheta deh e embarkeh*
customs	**aduana**	*adwana*
fare	**tarifa**	*tareefa*
insurance	**seguro**	*segooro*
car hire	**alquiler de autos**	*alkeelair deh owtos*
bicycle	**bicicleta**	*beeseekleta*
petrol station	**estación de servicio**	*estas-yon deh serveeseeoh*
garage	**garage**	*garaheh*
I have a flat tyre	**Se me pinchó un pneumático**	*seh meh peencho un nayoomahtikoh*

Staying in a Hotel

I have a reservation	**Tengo una reserva**	*Tengo oona rresairba*
Is there a room available?	**¿Hay habitación disponible?**	*I ahbbitahseeohn deesponeeble*
single/double room	**habitación single/ doble**	*abeetas-yohn senglay/dobleh*
twin room	**habitación con camas gemelas**	*abeetas-yon kon kamas hemelas*
shower	**ducha**	*doocha*
bathtub	**tina**	*teenah*
I want to be woken up at...	**Necesito que me despierten a las...**	*neseseeto keh meh desp-yairten a las*
hot water	**agua caliente**	*agwa lak-yenteh*
cold water	**agua fría**	*agwa free-yah*
soap	**jabón**	*habohn*
towel	**toalla**	*to-a-ya*
key	**llave**	*yabeh*

Eating Out

I am a vegetarian	**Soy vegetariano**	*soy behetar-yano*
fixed price	**precio fijo**	*pres-yo feeho*
glass	**vaso**	*baso*
cutlery	**cubiertos**	*koob-yairtos*
Can I see the menu, please?	**¿Puedo ver la carta, por favor?**	*pwedoh vair la carta, por fabor*
The bill, please	**la cuenta, por favor**	*la kwenta por fabor*
I would like some water	**Quiero un poco de agua.**	*k-yairo oon poko deh agwa*
breakfast	**desayuno**	*desa-yoono*
lunch	**almuerzo**	*almwairso*
dinner	**cena**	*saynah*

Menu Decoder

parrillada	*pahreeyada*	mixed grill
lomo	*lohmoh*	beefsteak
lomo a la pimienta	*lohomo ah la peemee-entah*	pepper steak
lomo vetado	*lohmoh vehtadoh*	ribeye
lomo liso	*lohmoh leesoh*	sirloin
barros luco	*bahros lookoh*	beef sandwich with melted cheese
cazuela de vacuno	*kahswaylah de vahkoonoh*	beef and vegetable stew
cazuela de ave	*kahswaylah de ahvay*	chicken and vegetable stew
centolla	*sentoyah*	king crab
pebre	*pehbray*	Chilean salsa
chorizo	*chohreezoh*	pork sausage
choripán	*choreepan*	pork sausage in a bun
churrasco	*choorrasko*	thin boneless steak on bread
cola de mono	*kohlah de mono*	aperitif of coffee, milk, and liqueur
curanto	*kooranhntoh*	stew of shellfish, meat, and potatoes
lúcuma	*lookoohmah*	eggfruit
mollejas	*moyehas*	sweetbreads
pastel de choclo	*pahstel deh chohcloh*	sweet corn pie
plateada	*plahte-ahda*	stewed beef and vegetables
terremoto	*tairehmohtoh*	cocktail of white wine, Fernet, and pineapple ice cream

humita	*oomeeta*	mashed sweet corn mixed with onion and milk
arroz	*arrohs*	rice
atún	*atoon*	tuna
azúcar	*asookar*	sugar
bacalao	*bakala-o*	cod
camarones	*kamarones*	shrimp
carne	*karneh*	beef
cebolla	*sebo-ya*	onion
chirimoya	*cheereemoyah*	custard apple
huevo	*webo*	egg
jugo	*hoogo*	fruit juice
langosta	*langosta*	lobster
leche	*lecheh*	milk
mantequilla	*mantekee-ya*	butter
marisco	*mareesko*	shellfish
pan	*pan*	bread
papas	*papas*	potatoes
pescado	*peskado*	fish
pimienta dulce	*peemee-entah doolsay*	sweet pepper
pollo	*po-yo*	chicken
postre	*postreh*	dessert
roseta	*rroseta*	bread roll
sal	*sal*	salt
salsa	*salsa*	sauce
sopa	*sopa*	soup
té	*teh*	tea
vinagre	*beenagreh*	vinegar
zapallito	*sapa-yeeto*	squash

Time

minute	**minuto**	*meenootoh*
hour	**hora**	*ora*
half an hour	**media hora**	*med-ya ora*
quarter of an hour	**un cuarto**	*oon kwarto*
Monday	**lunes**	*loones*
Tuesday	**martes**	*martes*
Wednesday	**miércoles**	*m-yairkoles*
Thursday	**jueves**	*hwebes*
Friday	**viernes**	*b-yairnes*
Saturday	**sábado**	*sabado*
Sunday	**domingo**	*domeengo*
January	**enero**	*enairo*
February	**febrero**	*febrairo*
March	**marzo**	*marso*
April	**abril**	*abreel*
May	**mayo**	*ma-yo*
June	**junio**	*hoon-yo*
July	**julio**	*hool-yo*
August	**agosto**	*agosto*
September	**septiembre**	*sept-yembreh*
October	**octubre**	*oktoobreh*
November	**noviembre**	*nob-yembreh*
December	**diciembre**	*dees-yembreh*

Numbers

0	**cero**	*sairo*
1	**uno**	*oono*
2	**dos**	*dos*
3	**tres**	*tres*
4	**cuatro**	*kwatro*
5	**cinco**	*seenko*
6	**seis**	*says*
7	**siete**	*s-yeteh*
8	**ocho**	*ocho*
9	**nueve**	*nwebeh*
10	**diez**	*d-yes*
11	**once**	*onseh*
12	**doce**	*doseh*
13	**trece**	*treseh*
14	**catorce**	*katorseh*
15	**quince**	*keenseh*
16	**dieciséis**	*d-yeseesays*
17	**diecisiete**	*d-yesees-yeteh*
18	**dieciocho**	*d-yes-yocho*
19	**diecinueve**	*d-yeseenwebeh*
20	**veinte**	*baynteh*
30	**treinta**	*traynta*
40	**cuarenta**	*kwarenta*
50	**cincuenta**	*seenkwenta*
60	**sesenta**	*sesenta*
70	**setenta**	*setenta*
80	**ochenta**	*ochenta*
90	**noventa**	*nobenta*
100	**cien**	*s-yen*
500	**quinientos**	*keen-yentos*
1000	**mil**	*meel*
first	**primero/a**	*preemairo/a*
second	**segundo/a**	*segoondo/a*
third	**tercero/a**	*tairsairo/a*
fourth	**cuarto/a**	*kwarto/a*
fifth	**quinto/a**	*keento/a*
sixth	**sexto/a**	*seksto/a*
seventh	**séptimo/a**	*septeemo/a*
eight	**octavo/a**	*oktabo/a*
ninth	**noveno/a**	*nobeno/a*
tenth	**décimo/a**	*deseemo/a*